The Augustinian Tradition

PHILOSOPHICAL TRADITIONS

General Editor

Amélie Oksenberg Rorty

The Augustinian Tradition

EDITED BY

Gareth B. Matthews

UNIVERSITY OF CALIFORNIA PRESS

Berkeley   Los Angeles   London

Alvin Plantinga's "Augustinian Christian Philosophy" is reprinted from the *Monist* 75, no. 3 (1992): 291–320, with the permission of the editor. Frederick Crosson's "Structure and Meaning in St. Augustine's *Confessions*" is reprinted with permission from *Proceedings of the American Catholic Philosophical Association*, Volume 63 (1989): 84–97. Genevieve Lloyd's "Augustine and the 'Problem' of Time" is a lightly revised version of chapter 1 of her book, *Being in Time* (London: Routledge, 1993), 14–42, and is reprinted here with the kind permission of the publisher. M. F. Burnyeat's "Augustine and Wittgenstein *De magistro*" is reprinted from the *Proceedings of the Aristotelian Society*, Supplementary Volume 61 (1987): 1–24, by courtesy of the editor of the Aristotelian Society: © 1987. Paul Weithman's "Toward an Augustinian Liberalism" is a slightly revised version of an article that appeared under the same title in *Faith and Philosophy* 8 (1991): 461–80, with permission of the editor.

University of California Press
Berkeley and Los Angeles, California

University of California Press, Ltd.
London, England

© 1999 by
The Regents of the University of California

Library of Congress Cataloging-in-Publication Data

The Augustinian tradition / edited by Gareth B. Matthews.
    p. cm.—(Philosophical traditions ; 8)
   Includes bibliographical references and index.
   ISBN 0-520-20999-0 (cloth : alk. paper).—ISBN 0-520-21001-8 (pbk. : alk. paper)
   1. Augustine, Saint, Bishop of Hippo.   I. Matthews, Gareth B., 1929–.   II. Series.
B655.Z7A95   1999
189'.2—dc21
                                                                  97-35854
                                                                  CIP

Printed in the United States of America
9 8 7 6 5 4 3 2 1

The paper used in this publication is both acid-free and totally chlorine-free (TCF). It meets the minimum requirements of American National Standards for Information Sciences—Permanence of Paper for Printed Library Materials, ANSI Z39.48-1984.

For Morton White
teacher and friend

At si [mens] novit quid quaerat,
et se ipsam quaerit,
se ipsam utique novit.

DE TRINITATE 10.4.6

CONTENTS

INTRODUCTION

Augustine was many things: a philosopher, a theologian, a writer, a bishop, a Church Father. When he is considered primarily as a philosopher, Augustine is often thought of as someone who tried to Christianize classical Greek and Roman thought. John M. Rist, in his recent book *Augustine: Ancient Thought Baptized*, develops this conception of him.

Yet Augustine's ideas are not only backward looking; they are also profoundly forward looking. Until the ascendancy of St. Thomas Aquinas at the end of the thirteenth century, Augustine was the most important Christian philosopher. Aquinas, as he himself makes quite clear, was highly indebted to Augustine, as well as to Aristotle. Moreover, the Augustinian tradition continued to flourish even after Aquinas. In the modern period Augustine's influence on Descartes, Leibniz, Rousseau, and Hegel call for special mention. But his influence is much more pervasive than any such list might suggest.

Augustine's thought is also surprisingly contemporary. Many of Augustine's most characteristic preoccupations, whether with introspective self-examination, with human motivation, with skepticism, with the workings of language, or with time and history, are also our preoccupations today.

This collection of articles is evidence of the persisting vitality of Augustine's thought. It is also evidence of a new interest in Augustine, and a new respect for him, among twentieth-century English-speaking philosophers. Remarkably, more serious work on Augustine has been done by such philosophers since the 1970s than their counterparts did in all the earlier decades of this century put together.

The papers collected in the present volume reflect something of the historical reality of the Augustinian tradition. Thus, some pieces here connect Augustine specifically with Anselm, Dante, Descartes, Locke, Jonathan Edwards, Rousseau, Kant, Wittgenstein, and even John Updike! But there is no effort here to represent all the historical strands in the Augustinian tradition. Nor is there any attempt to treat this tradition with historical detachment. To the contrary, Augustine is to be seen in these essays as a thinker who engages our own thinking today, just as he engaged and influenced thinkers all the way from his own time to ours.

This volume begins with Alvin Plantinga's apologia for an "Augustinian Christian Philosophy." As Plantinga makes clear, he does not want to resurrect or merely celebrate a historical artifact; rather, he aims to tell us how we should think about Christian philosophy today. The way of thinking he advocates, as he says, "grows out of Augustinian roots."

No doubt Augustine's most influential single work is his *Confessions,* which is arguably the first significant autobiography in Western literature. Yet despite the classic status this work has enjoyed, almost all readers have thought it poorly composed. It has proved an especially difficult problem for readers to understand how the last four books of the work could be thought to fit together with the first nine, largely autobiographical, books to make a unified whole. With uncommon imagination and insight Frederick Crosson undertakes to solve the problem of the unity of the *Confessions.*

In her paper, "Augustine and the 'Problem' of Time," Genevieve Lloyd turns specifically to book 11 of the *Confessions* and discusses the Aristotelian and Neoplatonic antecedents to the treatment of time to be found there. She then connects Augustine's subjective account of time with the self-consciousness that underlies narration and, more broadly, the literary imagination.

In her essay, "Augustine and Dante on the Ascent of Love," Martha Nussbaum draws on part of her Gifford Lectures to show how Augustine uses Neoplatonic versions of the *Symposium*'s "ladder of love" to develop a Christian idea of love's ascent. After a richly detailed survey of this motif in Augustine's vast corpus Nussbaum turns to Dante for illuminating comparisons and contrasts. At the end of her paper she offers her own assessment of the conceptions of love that emerge in Augustine and Dante.

In her "Romancing the Good: God and the Self according to St. Anselm of Canterbury" Marilyn McCord Adams discusses the ways in which St. Anselm takes up from Augustine's *De Trinitate* the Platonic images of God as paradigm, as artist, and as beloved. She goes on to find other images for God and the self in Anselm, mainly biblical ones, but again images that are also prominent in Augustine, and she ends up with an appreciation of Anselm's account of the intellectual love of God.

With Scott MacDonald's paper, "Primal Sins," we move away from Augustine's Platonic and Plotinian heritage into the realm of specifically Christian theology and moral philosophy. As MacDonald says, the idea of Adam and Eve's primal sin is "the cornerstone of Augustine's theodicy." Yet, given the unblemished moral state of Adam and Eve before the fall, how could they make evil choices? MacDonald thinks Augustine offers a plausible resolution to this problem of primal sin. In the course of making his case he discusses an important connection between practical reasoning and moral responsibility.

In his paper, "Inner-Life Ethics," William Mann first tries to give clear shape to Augustine's strongly intentionalist ethics. He then considers how this "inner-life ethics" applies to a variety of cases of lying, a variety of cases of gratuitous theft, and finally the case of committing adultery in one's dreams. These applications help us both to understand the theory and to assess its plausibility.

Ishtiyaque Haji, in his paper, "On Being Morally Responsible in a Dream," takes up the last case Mann discusses and devotes his entire discussion to it. Haji defends against a number of objections the conclusion Augustine seems to be left with—namely, that we *are* morally responsible for what we do and think in our dreams. Among Haji's conclusions is the suggestion that we need to reconceptualize the epistemic requirements for moral responsibility.

In "Avoiding Sin: Augustine against Consequentialism" Christopher Kirwan discusses Augustine's rejection of the plausible consequentialist idea "that one should aim at the best outcome." He develops Augustine's idea that one will never sin if, in preference to actually doing ill, one merely allows it to be done. He makes the fully developed form of this idea as plausible as he can. But he finds that the resulting method for "deciding what to do" founders over important cases of lying and homicide.

In his essay, "Do We Have a Will? Augustine's Way in to the Will," Simon Harrison focuses on Augustine's claim to know himself to have a will and asks what that knowledge might consist in. One reason his question is interesting and important is that Augustine is sometimes credited with "inventing" or "discovering" the modern concept of will. Through an especially thoughtful reading of an important Augustinian text, Harrison discovers that Augustine's claim to know that he has a will resembles in important respects his "cogito-like" arguments for his claim to know that he exists.

In "The Emergence of the Logic of Will in Medieval Thought" Simo Knuuttila shows how Augustine attempts to systematize his theological anthropology with the help of the notion of the will. He then shows how certain features of Augustine's account of the will influenced early medieval thought and "how this tradition gave rise to what might be called a theory of the logic of will."

In "Augustine and Descartes on Minds and Bodies" Gareth B. Matthews finds Augustine committed to the thesis that the mind of each of us knows what a mind is simply and solely by knowing itself. According to Matthews, this thesis, recently attributed to Descartes and criticized by Wittgenstein, underlies Augustine's use of the argument from analogy for other minds, as well as his argument for mind–body dualism.

In his paper, "Disputing the Augustinian Legacy: John Locke and Jonathan Edwards on Romans 5:12–19," Philip L. Quinn discusses the doctrine of original sin. He begins with an account of this doctrine as Augustine himself formulates it by appeal to chapter 5 of St. Paul's Epistle to the Romans. Noting that John Locke accepts the "Arminian assumption" that no one can be guilty for the sins of another, Quinn then discusses Locke's alternative interpretation of Romans 5. Finally, he brings out how Jonathan Edwards shows that a Lockean-type effort at reconciling the Armenian assumption with Romans 5 fails.

Picking up the theme of original sin, John E. Hare, in his essay, "Augustine, Kant, and the Moral Gap," discusses how it might be thought reasonable for us to be under the demands God makes of us, even though we are unable to meet God's demands without his own assistance. Hare notes that Kant accepted the Stoic maxim that, if we are morally good or evil, we must be responsible for becoming or being so. He then brings out how Kant translated the Christian doctrine of justification into the pure religion of reason. Yet, in the end, Hare argues, the translation project fails, and Kant fails to bridge the moral gap within the limits of reason.

Ann Hartle, in her paper, "Augustine and Rousseau: Narrative and Self-Knowledge in the Two *Confessions*," treats Rousseau's *Confessions* as a response to Augustine's work by the same name. Rousseau claims to see his interior self as God sees him. According to Hartle, it is through his creative imagination that Rousseau thinks he has gained access to his inner self. Thus, Rousseau claims a perspective on his life, she argues, that, for Augustine, is proper to God alone.

In "Wittgenstein and Augustine *De magistro*" M. F. Burnyeat traces out Augustine's reason for supposing that no person teaches another anything and finds it to rest on the Platonic assumption that knowledge requires "first-hand appreciation." He ends with a discussion of the relevance of *De magistro* to a proper understanding of the passage on language-learning from Augustine's *Confessions* with which Wittgenstein begins his *Philosophical Investigations*.

Paul J. Weithman, in his essay, "Toward an Augustinian Liberalism," takes liberalism to defend restrictions on the invocation of moral, philosophical, and religious beliefs to legitimate the exercise of public power. He argues that acts of religiously inspired political advocacy to coerce belief, purify society, or make it more Christian are often acts of pride, such as Augustine found to be rooted in original sin. The Augustinian liberalism he advocates aims at holding such pride in check, even if it cannot foster true humility.

In "St. Augustine and the Just War Theory" Robert L. Holmes explores Augustine's "interiority" in ethics and how it bears on his justification of war. His discussion leads through the elements of Augustine's theory of the just war. He concludes that the problem of war is of the first importance to Augustine's own thought. This is so because Augustine aimed to define the implications of Christianity for life in the earthly city and that definition "turns upon the understanding of war, the social and political forces that bring it into existence, and the divine purposes that allow it to endure."

In "Augustine's Philosophy of History" Rüdiger Bittner presents the Augustinian teacher of Christian doctrine as a narrator of stories rather than a "mere reasoner." Yet the fundamental conception in Augustine's philosophy of history, according to Bittner, is that God is beyond history. "History is owed to what is beyond history." Moreover, the only interesting event in the age of human history is the appearance of "what is beyond history"—namely, the incarnation of God in Christ. Bittner concludes by trying to make clear that it is largely this picture of history as represented in Augustine that most modern writers on history have been arguing against.

The volume concludes with the essay by Richard Eldridge, "Dramas of Sin and Salvation in Augustine and John Updike." Eldridge notes that Updike is well aware of his affinities with Augustine and their common preoccupations with sex, sin, and salvation. Eldridge offers a detailed and arresting comparison between Augustine, as he presents himself in his *Confessions,* and Harry Angstrom, the hero of Updike's "Rabbit" novels.

SELECT BIBLIOGRAPHY
OF RECENT BOOKS ON AUGUSTINE

Brown, Peter. *Augustine of Hippo: A Biography.* Berkeley: University of California, 1967.

Bubacz, Bruce. *St. Augustine's Theory of Knowledge: A Contemporary Analysis.* New York: Edwin Mellin, 1981.

Chadwick, Henry. *Augustine.* Oxford: Oxford University Press, 1986.

Clark, Mary T. *Augustine.* Washington, D.C.: Georgetown University Press, 1994.

Elshtain, Jean Bethke. *Augustine and the Limits of Politics.* Notre Dame, Ind.: Notre Dame University Press, 1995.

Hölscher, Ludger. *The Reality of the Mind: St Augustine's Arguments for the Human Soul as a Spiritual Substance.* London: Routledge and Kegan Paul, 1986.

Kirwan, Christopher. *Augustine.* Arguments of the Philosophers. London: Routledge, 1989.

Markus, Robert A. *Augustine: A Collection of Critical Essays.* Garden City, N.Y.: Doubleday, 1972.

Matthews, Gareth B. *Thought's Ego in Augustine and Descartes.* Ithaca: Cornell University Press, 1992.

O'Connell, Robert J. *The Origin of the Soul in St. Augustine's Later Works.* New York: Fordham University Press, 1987.

O'Daly, Gerard. *Augustine's Philosophy of Mind.* London: Duckworth, 1987.

Rist, John M. *Augustine: Ancient Thought Baptized.* Cambridge: Cambridge University Press, 1994.

Stock, Brian. *Augustine the Reader: Meditation, Self-Knowledge, and the Ethics of Interpretation.* Cambridge, Mass.: Harvard University Press, 1996.

Wetzel, James. *Augustine and the Limits of Virtue.* Cambridge: Cambridge University Press, 1992.

CHRONOLOGY OF AUGUSTINE'S LIFE

354	born Aurelius Augustinus in Thagaste, north Africa (modern Souk Ahras in eastern Algeria)
366–69	school at nearby Madauros
371	university student at Carthage
373	birth of son (Adeodatus)
375	teacher at Thagaste
376	teacher of rhetoric at Carthage
383	sailed for Rome
384	professor of rhetoric at Milan
386	converted to Christianity
387	baptized by St. Ambrose in Milan
	death of mother (Monica)
388	returned to north Africa
389	death of Adeodatus
391	ordained a priest at Hippo
395	consecrated a bishop
397–401	*Confessions*
399–419	*De Trinitate*
410	sack of Rome
413–27	*The City of God*
430	death at Hippo

The Augustinian Tradition

ONE

Augustinian Christian Philosophy*

Alvin Plantinga

How does Christianity bear on philosophy? Is there such a thing as Christian philosophy, or are there only Christians who are also philosophers? How should Christianity and philosophy be related? *Should* they be related? In "Advice to Christian Philosophers" I said that Christian philosophers should display more autonomy: they have their own fish to fry, their own projects to pursue, or their own axes to grind, as some might prefer to put it. Here I want to say more about what these projects (or fish, or axes) are like. And the right way to think about these matters, it seems to me, is broadly Augustinian. Accordingly, I want to propose a programmatic sketch (a *very* programmatic sketch) of a conception of Christian philosophy that grows out of some central Augustinian emphases. I don't claim, however, that Augustine in fact thought of Christian philosophy the way I shall suggest. The primary focus of my paper is not historical (that would in any event be beyond my competence); what I want to do is make a suggestion as to how we should think about Christian philosophy *now;* but this way of thinking of the matter grows out of Augustinian roots.[1] It's worth noting, furthermore, that what is at issue is a way of thinking not just about Christianity and philosophy but about Christianity and scholarship more generally. Augustinian Christian philosophy consists of at least four elements. The first two of these are widely recognized and relatively uncontroversial: I shall therefore be brief about them. The remaining two, however, require more by way of explanation, illustration, and defense.

---

*This paper draws heavily on my Stob Lectures, delivered at Calvin College in 1989 and entitled "The Twin Pillars of Christian Scholarship" (published in pamphlet form under the same title and available from the bookstore, Calvin College, Grand Rapids, Michigan). Here (as in those lectures) I wish to express my enduring gratitude to Henry Stob and the late William Harry Jellema; most of the ideas to be found in this paper can be traced back to what I learned from them.

PHILOSOPHICAL THEOLOGY

Clearly one thing that goes into Christian philosophy, thought of in Augustinian fashion, is philosophical theology, which is a matter of thinking about the central doctrines of the Christian faith from a philosophical perspective and employing the resources of philosophy. Philosophical theology, of course, has been part of the stock-in-trade of Christian philosophers and theologians from the very beginning. It was also practiced with distinction by Augustine; one thinks, for example, of his remarkable work on the Trinity. At present, this enterprise is faring rather well, perhaps even flourishing; the last few years have seen a remarkable flurry of activity in philosophical theology as pursued by Christian philosophers. Important work on the divine attributes has appeared: as well as the classic Stump-Kretzmann work on God's eternity, for example, there is also excellent work on omnipotence, omniscience, essential goodness, and alleged divine simplicity.[2] How God acts in the world and such central doctrines of Christianity as the atonement, original sin, and the incarnation have been the subjects of good work; and there is much else as well. Not everyone is unreservedly enthusiastic about this work; at least some theologians (especially abroad) have the impression that philosophical theology as pursued by contemporary philosophers is often unduly ahistorical and uncontextual and could profit by closer contact with what theologians know. No doubt this is correct; nevertheless, much of this work is powerful, profound, and of great interest.

APOLOGETICS

Apologetics, from an Augustinian perspective, comes in two varieties. First, negative apologetics aims to defend Christianity against attacks from its detractors. This enterprise, of course, has gone on from the very beginnings of Christianity. The attacks in question may take various forms. It was argued early on that Christianity is socially or politically subversive; Tertullian and others offered apologetic replies.[3] Some have argued, as did Nietzsche, that indulgence in Christianity promotes and encourages a weak, sniveling, inferior, hypocritical, and generally disgusting sort of person; these claims, however, seem so bizarre and far from the mark that they have called out little by way of reply. It has been argued often, during recent centuries, that the beliefs Christians typically hold are false; these arguments have typically proceeded by arguing that theism is false. For example, there are arguments for the conclusion that Christian theism or theism *simpliciter* is incoherent. Take, for example, the broadly Wittgensteinian claim that there couldn't be a person without a body; if this were so, the theistic idea of God as a person without a body would be incoherent. Responses have come from many quarters.[4] It has also been argued that the development of modern science, or certain specific teachings of modern science, or perhaps the habits of mind fostered by

modern science, at any rate something in the neighborhood, have shown that theism (or other crucial elements of the Christian faith) are mistaken. More important is the argument from evil, in both its deductive and probabilistic forms, to
which several classical and contemporary apologetic replies have been made.[5] Finally some have argued that, whatever the truth of Christian belief, such belief is
intellectually shoddy or third rate, that it is irrational or unjustified. A prime contemporary example here would be the late John Mackie's book, *The Miracle of Theism*. A second kind of argument for the irrationality or inferiority of theistic belief
has come from those who, like Freud and Marx, propose various unflattering explanations of the widespread phenomenon of religious belief.[6] Contemporary
Christian philosophers have done good work in repelling these attacks.

According to an Augustinian approach, one must keep careful track of the audience one proposes to address in working at Christian philosophy. Some elements
of Christian philosophy (see "Christian Philosophical Criticism" and "Positive
Christian Philosophy" below) are addressed primarily to the Christian community; here one can use premises and appeal to considerations that are widely
shared among Christians, even if they have little currency outside the Christian
community. Not so for apologetics. In a paradigm incarnation, anyway, the apologete addresses, not first of all the Christian community, but those outside it, those
on the edges of it, those who are considering joining it, as well as the skeptic lurking in the breast of every serious Christian.

In *positive* apologetics the intended audience is much the same as in negative
apologetics: the paradigm cases consist of those who are outside the faith, together
with those who are looking, together with the unbelieving aspect of every believer.
The efforts of the positive apologete are directed first of all toward giving theistic
proofs or arguments: proof or arguments for the existence of God. Of course this
enterprise goes back to the beginnings of Christianity;[7] it hit high water marks in
the fifth, eleventh, thirteenth, and fourteenth centuries, in Augustine, Anselm,
Aquinas, Scotus, and Ockham, and again in the seventeenth century with
Descartes, Locke, Spinoza, and (perhaps most important) Leibniz. Positive apologetics has not flourished as luxuriantly in our day, although Richard Swinburne
has done much for the enterprise.[8]

Positive apologetics has been dominated by two unfortunate assumptions. First,
much of the discussion has taken it for granted that a good theistic argument
would have to meet extremely high standards of cogency and indeed be demon-
strative. In the tradition of the high Middle Ages the idea is that a good theistic argument would provide *scientia*, scientific knowledge; one who has scientia of a
given proposition, furthermore, sees that it is true by seeing that it follows from
what one sees to be true. Such an argument would start from what is self-evident
and proceed majestically by way of self-evidently valid argument forms to its conclusion. The seventeenth-century tradition is (with the exception of Locke)
equally stringent. But why suppose a good theistic argument has to be *that* good?

After all, hardly any philosophical arguments meet conditions as stratospheric as all that. Take your favorite philosophical argument: Quine's argument for the indeterminacy of translation, or Davidson's for the claim that we can't understand anyone without assuming that most of what he thinks is true, or Wittgenstein's private language argument, or Kripke's argument that names are rigid designators: none of these arguments meets standards even remotely like the ones theistic arguments have been required to meet (in fact most of those arguments can be seen to be either unsound or dependent upon controversial premises). So why should theistic arguments be measured by such unrealistic standards?

A weaker version of the requirement is that a good theistic argument must have premises accepted by nearly everyone, or nearly everyone who thinks about the topic, or nearly everyone who thinks about it and has a view on the topic.[9] But this requirement also is much too strong. Consider, for example, theistic arguments from the existence and nature of propositions, properties, numbers, and sets. These arguments are very much worth study and development, and I myself think they are good arguments. But a crucial premise of each is that there *are* such things as propositions, properties, numbers, or sets; and not everyone believes that. Another premise of some of these arguments is that there exist many more propositions (properties, numbers, sets) than human beings have or could have thought of; and not everyone believes that either. But that doesn't mean that the argument in question is not a good theistic argument. It can be a fine argument, and a useful argument, even if not everyone accepts all its premises. If some do not accept its premises, then it won't be a good argument for them; it might nonetheless be a good argument for those who do accept its premises.

A third problem: discussion of theistic arguments has for the most part been confined to the traditional big three: in Kant's classification, the ontological, cosmological, and teleological arguments.[10] But in fact there are many more. In addition to arguments from propositions, properties, numbers, and sets there are arguments from the nature of proper function, from intentionality, from counterfactuals, and from the confluence of epistemic reliability and epistemic warrant with epistemic justification. There are arguments from reference, simplicity, intuition, and love; from colors and flavors, miracles, play and enjoyment, morality, beauty, and the meaning of life; there is even an argument from the existence of evil. The question whether these arguments are good arguments is of course controversial (just as in the case of nearly any other important philosophical argument). Many of these arguments, however, seem to me to be extremely promising and very much worth detailed attention and serious work.

Philosophical theology and apologetics are relatively uncontroversial and have been prospering. Two other important elements of Augustinian Christian philosophy, however, have not been doing as well, at least in part because their importance hasn't been sufficiently recognized. These two elements are more specifically Augustinian. I call the first of them "Christian philosophical criticism" but only because I can't think of a better name.

CHRISTIAN PHILOSOPHICAL CRITICISM

According to Augustine, human history is the arena of a great struggle, a battle or contest between two profoundly opposed forces. Augustine spoke of the City of God and the Earthly City or City of the World: the *civitas Dei* and the *civitas mundi*.[11] The former is dedicated, in principle, to God and to the fulfillment of his will and to the accomplishment of his purposes; but the latter is dedicated to something wholly different. Augustine's nineteenth-century Dutch follower Abraham Kuyper spoke of an antithesis between belief—Christian belief—and unbelief, an antithesis that in one way or another cuts across and manifests itself in every important area of human life. (I don't mean to suggest, of course, that nothing of Augustinian importance happened between the fifth century and the nineteenth.)

Kuyper and Augustine, I believe, are dead right, but I want to develop their insights in my own way. Indeed, we must do this in our own way and from our own historical perspective. The precise relationship between the civitas Dei and the civitas mundi constantly changes; the form the Earthly City itself takes constantly changes; an account of the fundamental loyalties and commitments of the civitas mundi that was correct in Augustine's day, now some fifteen centuries ago, does not directly apply at present. And even since the time of Kuyper (1837–1920), roughly a century ago, there has been substantial change, clarification, and differentiation; in some ways it is now considerably easier, I think, to see the essential contours of the ways of thinking that have emerged since the seventeenth and eighteenth centuries.

Augustine and Kuyper are right; and the contemporary Western intellectual world, like the worlds of their times, is a battleground or arena in which rages a battle for people's souls. This battle, I believe, involves three main contestants in the contemporary Western intellectual world, and I want to try to characterize them. Of course an undertaking like this is at best fraught with peril (and at worst arrogantly presumptuous); the intellectual culture of the contemporary Western world is vast, amorphous, and far-flung, including a stunning variety of ways of thinking, in an enormous variety of intellectual traditions that are never found in pure form but influence and interpenetrate one another in a thousand complex ways. We know how hard it is to get a real sense of the intellectual climate of a past era—the Enlightenment, say, or thirteenth-century Europe, or nineteenth-century America. It is clearly much more difficult to come to a solid understanding of one's own time. Real trepidation is in order. There are also special less universally applicable reasons for trepidation: wouldn't it be the historians, not the philosophers, whose job it is to figure out intellectual trends, take the intellectual pulse of the time, ferret out underlying presuppositions of the whole contemporary era? Perhaps so. I offer no defense.

As I see it, therefore, at present three main competitors vie for spiritual supremacy in the West: three fundamental perspectives or ways of thinking about what the world is like, what we ourselves are like, what is most important about the world, what our place in it is, and what we must do to live the good life. The first of these perspectives is Christianity or Christian theism; here I need say little about that. I do want to remind you, however, that, despite recent modest successes in various parts of the world, the Christian perspective has been very much on the defensive (at least in the West) ever since the Enlightenment.

In addition to the Christian perspective, then, there are fundamentally two others. Both of these have been with us since the ancient world; but each has received much more powerful expression in modern times. According to the first perspective, there is no God and nothing else beyond nature; and we human beings are insignificant parts of a vast cosmic machine that proceeds in majestic indifference to us, our hopes and aspirations, our needs and desires, our sense of fairness or fittingness. This picture goes back to Epicurus, Democritus, and others in the ancient world and finds magnificent expression in Lucretius' poem, *De rerum natura*. Suppose we call it "perennial naturalism"; an eloquent (if a bit florid) contemporary statement of this perspective is to be found in Bertrand Russell's "A Free Man's Worship." [12] According to the second perspective, on the other hand, it is we ourselves—we human beings—who are responsible for the basic structure of the world. This notion goes back to Protagoras, in the ancient world, with his claim that man is the measure of all things; it finds enormously more powerful expression in Immanuel Kant's *Critique of Pure Reason*. We could call this perspective "Enlightenment humanism" or "Enlightenment subjectivism," but perhaps a better name is "creative antirealism." Perennial naturalism and creative antirealism are very different indeed; I shall say something about each.

Perennial Naturalism

Perennial naturalism (naturalism for short), as I say, goes back to the ancient world; it is also to be found in the medieval world, perhaps among some of the Averroists, for example. It was left to modernity, however, to display the most complete and thorough manifestations of this perspective. Hobbes, the Enlightenment Encyclopedists, and Baron D'Holbach are early modern exponents of this picture; among our contemporaries and near contemporaries are Bertrand Russell, John Dewey, Willard van Orman Quine, and Wilfrid Sellars, the majority of contemporary Anglo-American philosophers, a surprising number of liberal theologians, and a host of others in and out of academia. From this perspective there is no God and human beings are properly seen as parts of nature. The fundamental way to understand what is most distinctive about us—our ability to love, to act, to think, and to use language, our humor and play acting, our art, philosophy, literature, history, our morality, our religion, our tendency to enlist in sometimes unlikely causes and devote our lives to them—the fundamental way to understand all this is in terms of our community with (nonhuman) nature. We are best seen as parts of nature and are to be understood in terms of our place in the natural world. [13]

A couple of examples: first, a trivial one. Those who endorse this view often seem to think that the way to find out how we human beings should live is to see how the other animals manage things; this is the naturalistic equivalent of the biblical "Go to the ant, thou sluggard." I recently heard a TV talk show in which a scientist was belittling traditional sexual ethics and mores—"heterosexual pair bonding," he called it—on the grounds that only 3 percent of the other animals do things this way. He didn't say anything about plants, but no doubt even more interesting conclusions could be drawn there. (In another recent talk show, the interviewee said that she had observed, on an unscientific day-to-day pragmatic and anecdotal level, that cousins are often romantically attracted to each other; she then added that she had recently discovered scientific confirmation of this observation: human beings, she said, resemble quail along romantic lines, and that is how it is with quail.)

A second, more serious example: a couple of years ago I heard a distinguished American philosopher reflecting on knowledge, belief, and the whole human cognitive enterprise. The way to understand this whole situation, he said—the way to see what is most basic and important about it—is not, of course, to see it as one of the manifestations of the image of God, a way in which we resemble the Lord, who is the prime knower, and who has created us in such a way as to be finite and limited mirrors of his infinite and unlimited perfection. This philosopher took quite a different line. Human beings, he said, hold beliefs (and so far there is little to object to); and these beliefs can cause them to act in certain ways. Put in more sophisticated if less insightful terms, a person's beliefs can be part of a causal explanation of her actions. Now how can this be? How does it happen that human beings are such that they can be caused to do certain things by what they believe? How does my believing there is a beer in the refrigerator cause or partly cause this largish lumpy physical object that is my body to heave itself out of a comfortable armchair, move over to the refrigerator, and open its door?

His answer: think of a thermostat: it too has beliefs—simple-minded beliefs, no doubt, but still beliefs. What it believes are such things as *it's too hot in here*, or *it's too cold in here*, or *it's just right in here;* and it is easy to see how its having those beliefs brings it about that the furnace or the air conditioning goes on. And now the basic idea: we should see human thinking and its connection with action as a rather more complicated case of what goes on in the thermostat. The idea was that if we think about how it goes with the thermostat, we will have the key to understanding how it goes with human beings.

This particular project is part of a much broader contemporary naturalistic project: the project of giving a naturalistic account or explanation of human cognition generally—of human perception, knowledge, and belief, of evidence, argument, discovery, and insight. And of course this is just one example of a still broader project: that of seeing *all* that is distinctive about us—literature, art, play, humor, music, morality, religion, science, scholarship, those tendencies to enlist in improbable causes in naturalistic terms. The project is to explain all of these in terms of our community with nonhuman nature.

The form this perspective takes in our own day is broadly evolutionary: we are to try to understand the above phenomena by way of their origin in random genetic mutation or some other source of variability and their perpetuation by natural selection. Consider sociobiological explanations of love, for example: love between men and women, between parents and children, for one's friends, of church, college, country—love in all its diverse manifestations and infinite variety, love is a most significant human phenomenon and an enormously powerful force in our lives. And how are we to think of love, on the sort of evolutionary account in question? Well, the basic idea is that love arose, ultimately and originally, by way of some source of variability such as random genetic mutation; it persisted via natural selection because it has or had survival value. Male and female human beings, like male and female hippopotami, get together to have children (colts) and stay together to raise them; this has survival value. Once we see that point, we understand that sort of love and see its basic significance; and the same goes for these other varieties and manifestations of love. And that, fundamentally, is what there is to say about love.

From a theistic perspective, of course, this is hopelessly inadequate as an account of the significance and place of love in the world. Love reflects the basic structure and nature of the universe; for God himself, the first being of the universe, is love, and we love because he has created us in his image. From the naturalistic perspective, furthermore, what goes for love goes for those other distinctively human phenomena: art, literature, music; play and humor; science, philosophy, and mathematics; our tendency to see the world from a religious perspective; our inclinations toward morality; the willingness on the part of some to subordinate their welfare to that of others;[14] and so on. All of these are to be seen as arising, finally, by way of the mechanisms driving evolution and are to be understood in terms of their place in evolutionary history.

Perennial naturalism has made enormous inroads into Western universities; indeed, John Lucas and others think it is the contemporary orthodoxy. In support of Lucas's claim, we might note that, oddly enough, perennial naturalism has a considerable following among allegedly Christian theologians. Thus Gordon Kaufman suggests that in this modern nuclear age we can no longer think of God as the transcendent personal creator of the heavens and the earth; we must think of him instead, says Kaufman, as "the historical evolutionary force that has brought us all into being."[15] Perhaps one may be pardoned for wondering what the nuclear age has to do with whether God is the transcendent personal creator or just a historical evolutionary force. We can imagine an earlier village skeptic making a similar remark about, say, the invention of the catapult or perhaps the long bow.

Perennial naturalism is particularly popular among those—scientists or others—who take a high view of modern science. Perennial naturalism also constantly influences and (as I see it) corrupts Christian thinking. Christians who think about science, for example, sometimes say that science can't take any account of God in giving its explanations; science is necessarily restricted, both in its subject matter and in its explanations and accounts, to the natural world. But why think a thing like that? Of course the claim might be merely verbal: "the word 'science,'" it might be said, "is to be defined as an empirical and experimental account of the natural world that is restricted, both in its subject matter and its conclusions, to the natural world." But then the question would be: should Christians engage in science? Or, more exactly, in trying to understand the world of nature should they engage *only* in science? Shouldn't they instead or in addition work out a parallel explanatory activity that takes account of all that we know, including such facts as that human beings were created by the Lord in his image?

It is hard to overestimate the dominance and influence of perennial naturalism in our universities. Yet I think Lucas errs in promoting it to the status of the contemporary orthodoxy. It is indeed orthodoxy among those who nail their banner to the mast of science; but there is another basic way of looking at the world that is, I think, nearly as influential—and just as antithetical to Christianity. Perennial naturalism gets fierce competition from creative antirealism, to which I now turn.

Creative Antirealism

Here the fundamental idea—in sharp contrast to naturalism—is that we human beings, in some deep and important way, are responsible for the structure and nature of the world; *we*, fundamentally, are the architects of the universe. This view received magnificent if obscure expression in Immanuel Kant's *Critique of Pure Reason*. Kant did not deny, of course, that there really are such things as mountains, horses, planets, and stars. Instead, his characteristic claim is that their existence and their fundamental structure have been conferred upon them by the conceptual activity of persons—not by the conceptual activity of a personal God but by our conceptual activity, the conceptual activity of human beings. According to this view, the whole phenomenal world—the world of trees and planets and dinosaurs and stars—receives its basic structure from the constituting activity of mind. Such fundamental structures of the world as those of space and time, object and property, number, truth and falsehood, possibility and necessity—these are not to be found in the world as such but are somehow constituted by our own mental or conceptual activity. They are contributions from our side; they do not constitute a grasp of what is to be found in the things in themselves. We impose them on the world; we do not discover them there. Were there no persons like ourselves engaging in conceptual, noetic activities, there would be nothing in space and time, nothing displaying object-property structure, nothing that is true or false, possible or impossible, no kinds of things coming in a certain number— nothing like this at all.

We might think it impossible that the things we know—houses, horses, cabbages, and kings—should exist but fail to be in space-time and fail to display object-property structure; indeed, we may think it impossible that there be a thing of any sort that doesn't have properties. If so, then Kant's view implies that there would be nothing at all if it weren't for the creative structuring activity of persons like us. Of course I don't say Kant clearly drew this conclusion; indeed, he may have obscurely drawn the opposite conclusion: that is part of his charm. But the fundamental thrust of Kant's self-styled Copernican revolution is that the things in the world owe their basic structure and perhaps their very existence to the noetic activity of our minds. Or perhaps I should say not minds but mind; for whether, on Kant's view, there is just one transcendental ego or several is, of course, a vexed question. Indeed, this question is more than vexed; given Kant's view that quantity, number, is a human category imposed on the world, there is presumably no number n, finite or infinite, such that the answer to the question "How many of those transcendental egos are there?" is n.

Until you feel the grip of this way of looking at things, it can seem a bit presumptuous, not to say preposterous. Did we structure or create the heavens and the earth? Some of us think there were animals—dinosaurs, let's say—roaming the earth before human beings had so much as put in an appearance; how could it be that those dinosaurs owed their structure to our noetic activity? What did we do to give them the structure they enjoyed? And what about all those stars and planets we have never even heard of: how have we managed to structure them? When did we do all this? Did we structure ourselves in this way too? And if the way things are is thus up to us and our structuring activity, why don't we improve things a bit?

Creative antirealism can seem faintly or more than faintly ridiculous; nevertheless, it is widely accepted and an extremely important force in the contemporary Western intellectual world. Vast stretches of contemporary Continental philosophy, for example, are antirealist. There is existentialism, according to which, at least in its Sartrian varieties, each of us structures or creates the world by way of her own decisions. There is also contemporary Heideggerian hermeneutical philosophy of various stripes; there is contemporary French philosophy, much of which beggars description but, insofar as anything at all is clear about it, is clearly antirealist. In Anglo-American philosophy there is the antirealism of Nelson Goodman and (one stage of) Hilary Putnam and their followers; there is the reflection of Continental antirealism in such philosophers as Richard Rorty; there is the linguistic antirealism of many followers of Ludwig Wittgenstein. All of these characteristically hold that we human beings are somehow responsible for the way the world is—by way of our linguistic or more broadly symbolic activity, or by way of our decisions, or in some other way.

Like perennial naturalism, creative antirealism is to be found *even* in theology. Indeed, it is a bit naive to say that it is found even in theology; in the sort of theology that, according to its exponents, is the most up-to-date and au courant, these notions run absolutely riot. If the publisher's blurb is to be credited, creative antirealism is expressed ("developed" would no doubt be too strong a word) in (very broadly speaking) theological fashion in Don Cupitt's book *Creation out of Nothing:* "The consequence of all this is that divine and human creativity come to be seen as coinciding in the present moment. The creation of the world happens all of the time, in and through us, as language surges up within us and pours out of us to form and reform the world of experience. Reality . . . is effected by language." This is said to be "a philosophy of religion for the future" (one hopes the very distant future) and "a genuine alternative to pietism and fundamentalism" (as well, we might add, as to any other form of Christianity). The same view has made its way into physics or at least the philosophy of physics. It is said that there is no reality until we make the requisite observations; there is no such thing as reality in itself and unobserved, or, if there is, it is nothing at all like the world we actually live in. In ethics this view takes the form of the idea that no moral law can be binding on me unless I myself (or perhaps my society) issue or set that law.

Perennial naturalism and creative antirealism are related in an interesting manner: the first vastly underestimates the place of human beings in the universe, and the second vastly overestimates it. According to the first, human beings are essentially no more than complicated machines, with no real creativity; in an important sense we can't really act at all, any more than can a spark plug, a coffee grinder, or a truck. We are not ourselves the origin of any causal chains. According to the second, by contrast, human beings, insofar as we confer the world's basic structure upon it, really take the place of God. What there is and what it is like is really up to us and a result of our activity.

Relativism

I must call attention to some complications. First, I say that on these antirealist views, it is we, the speakers of language, the users of symbols, the thinkers of categorizing thoughts, or the makers of basic decisions, who are responsible for the fundamental lineaments of reality; in the words of Protagoras, "Man is the measure of all things." But sometimes a rather different moral is drawn from some of the same considerations. Suppose you think our world is somehow created or structured by human beings. You may then note that human beings apparently do not all construct the same worlds. Your *Lebenswelt* may be quite different from mine; Jerry Falwell and Richard Rorty don't seem to inhabit the same Lebenswelt at all; which one, then (if any), represents the world as it really is, as we have really constructed it?

Here it is an easy step to another characteristically contemporary thought: that there simply is no such thing as *the* way the world is, no such thing as objective truth, no way in which the world is that is the same for all of us. Rather, there is my version of reality, the way I've somehow structured things, and your version, and many other versions: and what is true in one version need not be true in another. As Marlowe's Dr. Faustus in effect says, "Man is the measure of all things; I am a man; therefore I am the measure of all things."[16] But then there isn't any such thing as truth *simpliciter.* There is no such thing as *the* way the world is; there are instead many different versions, perhaps as many different versions as there are persons; and each at bottom is as acceptable as any other. Thus a proposition really could be true for me but false for you. (Perhaps you have always thought of this notion as a peculiarly sophomoric confusion; but in fact it fits well with this formidable and important if lamentable way of thinking.) The whole idea of an objective truth, the same for all of us, on this view, is an illusion, or a bourgeois plot, or a sexist imposition, or a silly mistake. Thus does antirealism breed relativism and nihilism.

In some ways this seems quite a comedown from the view that there is indeed a way the world is and its being that way is owing to our activity. Still, there is a deep connection: on each view whatever there is by way of truth is of our own making. The same ambiguity is to be found in Protagoras himself. "Man is the measure of all things": we can take this as the thought that there is a certain way the world is and it is that way because of what we human beings—all human beings—do; or we can take it as the idea that each of some more limited group of persons—perhaps even each individual person—is the measure of all things. Then there would be no one way everything is but only different versions for different individuals. This form of Enlightenment subjectivism, like the previous ones, suffers, I think, from deep problems with self-referential incoherence. There isn't space here to go into the matter properly, but in brief the problem, for the relativist, is that from her own perspective she can't properly disagree with anyone who holds to the strictest absolutism. For from her own perspective, she must concede that the absolutist's view is true for him even if false for her; and there is no question as to which is really true. The two views are equally really true; that is, each is true for those who accept it.

A second complication: Alasdair MacIntyre pointed out (personal communication) that my account so far leaves out a very important cadre of contemporary intellectuals. Many intellectuals think of themselves as having no firm intellectual roots or commitments at all; they float free of all commitment and intellectual allegiance. They are like people without a country, without a settled or established home or neighborhood; in Kant's figure, they are like roaming nomads, a threat to settled and civilized ways of intellectual life. They may and often do go further; they may disdain commitment as naive or ill informed, a failure to understand, a foolish failure to see something obvious and important. So, says MacIntyre, they aren't committed either to the perennial naturalism of which I spoke or to one or another form of antirealism—or, of course, to Christianity; but they are nonetheless a most important part of the contemporary picture.

This is both true and important. The attitude MacIntyre describes is indeed common among intellectuals and in academia. As a matter of fact, there is a deep connection between antirealism and relativism, on the one hand, and this intellectual nomadism on the other. Perhaps it goes as follows. The dialectic begins with some version of Kantian antirealism: the fundamental lineaments of the world are due to us and our structuring activity and are not part of the *dinge an sich*. The next step is relativism: it is noted that different people hold very different views as to what the world is like; as a consequence we get the notion that there isn't any one way things are (a way that is due somehow to our noetic activity) but a whole host of different versions (as in Goodman), perhaps as many as there are persons. On this view there isn't any such thing as a proposition's being true *simpliciter:* what there is is a proposition's being true in a version or from a perspective. (And so what is "true for me" might not be "true for you.")

To "see" this point, however, is, in a way, to see through any sort of commitment with respect to intellectual life. Commitment goes with the idea that there really is such a thing as truth; to be committed to something is to hold that it is true, not just in some version, but *simpliciter* or absolutely. To be committed to something is to think it is true, not just true relative to what you or someone believes or relative to itself. But once you see (as you think) that there isn't any such thing as truth as such, then you may also see, as you think, the futility, the foolishness, the pitiable self-deluded nature of intellectual commitment. You will then think the only path of wisdom is that of the roaming, free-floating intellectual who has seen through the pretensions or naivete of those who do make serious intellectual and moral commitments. (Indeed, you may go still further. According to Richard Rorty, those who think there is such a thing, in the words of the Westminster Confession, as a "chief end of man" must be considered not just naive but insane—in which case, presumably, they ought not be allowed to vote or take full part in the new liberal society and perhaps should be confined to its Gulags pending recovery from the seizure.) As MacIntyre observed, this lack of commitment, this seeing through the pitiful self-delusion of commitment, is rampant in academia; it is, I think, close to the beating heart (or perhaps the central mushy core) of contemporary deconstruction and its heirs.

So we have, as I said, three major perspectives, wholly different and deeply opposed: Christian theism, perennial naturalism, and creative antirealism, with its progeny of relativism and anticommitment. What we also have, as William James said in a different connection, is a blooming, buzzing confusion. The above description is only a zeroeth approximation, accurate only within an order (or two) of magnitude; much fine tuning is necessary. Each of these views calls out a sort of opposing reaction to itself; furthermore there can be a sort of dialectic or development within a given paradigm or way of thinking; and of course channels of influence flow among them. These three main perspectives or total ways of looking at man and the world can be found in every conceivable and inconceivable sort of combination and mixture. There are many crosscurrents, eddies, and halfway houses; people think and act in accordance with these basic ways of looking at the world without being at all clearly aware of them, having at best a sort of dim apprehension of them. Thus, for example, those who adopt this skeptical, ironic, detached anticommitment with respect to the great human questions don't all do so because they "see through" the committed stances. Instead, it can be or start as simple imitation of one's elders and betters: this is the cool way to think, the way the second-year grad students think, the way my teachers or the people at Harvard think. Our ways of thinking are as much arrived at by imitation of those we admire as by reasoned reflection.

As we saw above, ironically enough, both perennial naturalism and creative antirealism (with its progeny of relativism and anticommitment) find contemporary expression in allegedly Christian theology. These ways of thinking are touted as the truly up-to-date and with-it way to look at these matters. It is indeed a common human characteristic to claim that now finally we have achieved the truth (or the correct attitude to take, given that there is no truth) denied our fathers. But (another sort of irony) these positions go back, clearly enough, all the way to the ancient world; they antedate classical Christianity. What is new and with it about them is only the attempt to palm them off as developments or forms—indeed, the intellectually most viable forms—of Christianity. This is new and with it, all right, but it is also preposterous. It is about as sensible as trying to palm off, say, the Nicene Creed or the Heidelberg Catechism as the newest and most with-it way of being an atheist.

These ways of thinking are not just alternatives to Christianity; they run profoundly counter to it. From a Christian perspective the naturalist is, of course, deeply mistaken in rejecting or ignoring God. That is bad enough; but in so doing he also cuts himself off from the possibility of properly understanding ourselves and the world. And as for creative antirealism the idea that it is really we human beings who have made or structured the world is, from a Christian perspective, no more than a piece of silly foolishness, less heroically Promethean than laughably Quixotic; and the idea that there is no truth is no less absurd from a Christian perspective. These ways of thinking, then, are predominant, pervasive, and deeply ingrained in our culture; they are also deeply antagonistic to a Christian way of looking at the world.

The application to our present question—What are the essential elements of Christian philosophy?—is evident. For it is wholly clear that philosophy is not neutral with respect to the struggle between these three *Weltanschauungen*. Indeed, from one point of view, philosophy just is at bottom an effort to understand the world and ourselves from the vantage point or perspective of one or another of these ways of looking at the world. Philosophy—philosophy that is clear and deep at any rate—is fundamentally an effort to work out the implications of a world view (one of these or another) with respect to the sorts of questions philosophers ask and answer. This is what philosophers do, though with varying degrees of self-consciousness and clarity. Vast stretches of contemporary philosophy, therefore, will have spiritual or religious roots—and spiritual and religious fruits. But these fruits may be unacceptable or even noxious from the perspective of the Christian community. And one important job of the Christian philosophical community, of course, is to discern and understand these fruits, to test the spirits, to evaluate these philosophical constructions and contributions from a Christian point of view. As I argued above, vast stretches of contemporary philosophy, for example, arise out of an attempt to give a naturalistic interpretation or understanding of one or another area of thought. Thus there are efforts to understand language naturalistically, as well as mind, mathematics, modality and morality, religion, truth, and a thousand other things. What is needed is a clear view of the spiritual and religious roots and allegiances of the enterprise in question. To take an obvious example, consider once more the explanation of Mother Teresa offered by Herbert Simon (see n. 14). This arises from the perspective of a naturalistic understanding of human beings; and it is obviously inconsistent with a Christian understanding of the issues. Behaving like Mother Teresa is not at all a manifestation of "bounded rationality"—as if, if she thought about the matter with greater clarity and penetration, she would instead act so as to try to increase the number of her expected progeny. Behaving as she does is instead a manifestation of a Christlike spirit; she is reflecting in her limited human way the splendid glory of Christ's sacrificial action in the atonement. (No doubt she is also laying up treasure in heaven.) From a Christian perspective her behavior is maximally rational; there is no way to behave that is more rational; from that point of view Simon's speculations are as silly as they are ingenious.

Or consider contemporary philosophy of mind. Here an explicitly stated aim is to provide a naturalistic understanding or account of the whole range of mental phenomena: intentionality, thought, sensation, knowledge, and so on. It is clearly of crucial importance that Christian philosophers and the Christian community be aware of the spiritual roots of these research projects. It doesn't follow, of course, that Christian philosophers can't properly join in pursuing these projects; but when they do so, their position will be delicate. The Christian community can learn much from such projects even if they point in a fundamentally antithetical direction; but Christian philosophers must be aware of their orientation and must inform the rest of the Christian community, academic and otherwise, of the spiritual connections of such projects.

So I say cultural and philosophical criticism is one important aspect of the compleat Christian philosopher's job. In a way this is utterly obvious. The efforts of some of the most impressive philosophers of our times—the Quines, the Sellars, some of the followers of Wittgenstein—are explicitly directed toward developing a complete, well-rounded, and wholly antitheistic way of thinking about ourselves and the world. Christian philosophers must discern the spiritual connections of the various philosophical and quasi-philosophical currents that swirl around us and make their perceptions known to the rest of the Christian community. This job, I think, isn't being done as well as philosophical theology and apologetics.

Of course the task of criticism extends beyond the boundaries of philosophy; many other areas of culture display the same structure. Consider the role played by evolutionary theory in our intellectual world. Evolution is a modern idol of the tribe; it is a shibboleth distinguishing the ignorant fundamentalist goats from the informed and scientifically acquiescent sheep. Doubts about it may lose you your job.[17] It is loudly declared to be absolutely certain, as certain as that the earth rotates on its axis and revolves around the sun—when it is no such thing at all. And much of the reason for these exaggerations, and for the *odium theologicum* aimed at those who presume to disagree, comes not from sober consideration of the evidence but from the religious role evolution plays in contemporary intellectual society.[18] For evolution plays an essential role in naturalistic thought. According to Richard Dawkins, "although atheism might have been logically tenable before Darwin, Darwin made it possible to be an intellectually fulfilled atheist." [19] Evolution is the only answer anyone can think of to a question that would otherwise be embarrassing in the extreme to naturalistic ways of thinking: how did this enormous variety of plant and animal life get here? Naturalism requires an answer to this question; evolution is the only naturalistic answer anyone has been able to think of; and this is one reason for the quasi-religious status of evolution in contemporary society. And of course evolution is just one example, if a prominent one. There is also sociobiology, various varieties of literary theory, sociology, and psychology, and much else. In all of these areas, what the Christian community needs is a way of discerning the spirits, of testing the provenance of the bewildering variety of ideas and claims with which we are confronted. The spiritual and intellectual health of the Christian community depends upon our knowing how to think about these ideas and claims; and to know how to think about them, we need the sort of cultural criticism—both inside and outside of philosophy—of which I speak.

POSITIVE CHRISTIAN PHILOSOPHY

So the first of the two characteristically Augustinian elements of Christian philosophy is the cultural criticism of which I speak: in philosophy proper, of course, but also outside of philosophy. But there is a second like unto the first: a fourth crucial element of Christian philosophy is thinking about the sorts of questions philosophers ask and answer from an explicitly Christian point of view. For most of these questions, what is really crucial is theism—the proposition that there is an almighty, all-knowing, wholly good and loving person who has created the world and created human beings in his image—rather than specifically Christian doctrine; so we could call this fourth element theistic philosophy. Whatever we call it, the project in question is that of thinking about philosophical questions, taking for granted or starting from theism. This isn't just a matter of criticism, of examining contemporary cultural products (in philosophy and elsewhere) from a Christian perspective, although of course it will no doubt proceed hand in glove with that activity. Here there is a sort of negative/positive structure like that in the case of apologetics: cultural criticism is negative, or at any rate reactive, but this other project—call it positive Christian philosophy—is a matter of thinking about and working out answers to the whole range of questions philosophers ask and answer.[20]

For example, how shall we think about so-called abstract objects such as propositions, states of affairs, sets, properties, possible worlds, and the like?[21] A part of the current lore concerning abstract objects is that they are causally inert, incapable by their very natures of standing in causal relations. One traditional theistic view, however (Augustine's, as it happens), is that properties are really divine concepts and propositions divine thoughts. If so, are they really incapable of standing in causal relations? If Augustine is right, they stand to God in the way in which a thought stands to a thinker: this relation involves among other things their being produced by the divine thinker. But being produced by seems to be a paradigmatic causal relation. Perhaps it is part of God's very nature to think and thereby produce these objects, and perhaps God exists necessarily; in that case abstract objects would be necessary beings that are nevertheless causally dependent upon something else.[22]

Speaking of causality, how shall we understand it? Is there a kind of necessity involved in causal relations? From a theistic perspective, the paradigm cases of causal relations will involve God's productive and conservative activity. He creates us and the world, and he constantly upholds and conserves us in being. Here, clearly enough, an element of necessity is involved. In every possible world in which God wills that something happen, that thing happens. Every world in which God says "Let there be light" is a world in which there is light. So the paradigmatic cases of causality involve necessity: broadly logical necessity. But of course there are other kinds and cases of causality. Human beings have been created in the image of God. Part of this image, in us human beings, is our resembling God by way of being able to carry on intentional activity: our ability to envisage and work toward the achievement of goals. But then of course there will be some kind of causal connection between our setting out to do a given thing and that thing's happening. This connection will be of a kind different from that between God's willing something and its taking place, although it will be set in the context or arena of divine activity. How, precisely and in detail, does this go?

There are, so we are told, natural laws. From a theistic perspective, what sorts of things are these laws, if indeed there are such things? From one point of view, they constitute a sort of constant backdrop or arena for responsible human activity. God creates us as creatures capable of action, action that has a moral dimension. (Indeed, it is vast understatement to say that action has a moral dimension; actual or potential moral significance is what constitutes action.) But of course, given the kinds of creatures we are, action requires a certain regularity or constancy. So one dimension of natural law is that it is there, in part, to furnish a background or arena for responsible creaturely activity, making it possible for created persons to engage in morally significant action. Further, God establishes these laws, or puts them; he is responsible for their presence. How does that go? Could he have established other, quite different laws? What sort of necessity do these laws have, if they have any? And where does regularity or constancy associated with natural law come from; how is it to be understood? Is it a matter of the regularity of the ways in which God ordinarily treats the creatures he has made; should we follow Malebranche and Berkeley and think of natural law in a broadly occasionalistic manner? Or shall we follow Aquinas and others and think of natural law as more like the consequence of the natural activity of the kinds of creatures God has made, so that natural law has little by way of ontological priority but is instead something like a complex vector resultant of the natural activity of God's creatures?

How shall we think about knowledge from the perspective of Christian theism? One thing clearly essential is that human beings have been created, and created by God. So in an essential respect human beings, like the rest of God's creatures, resemble artifacts; they have been designed and fashioned according to a design plan. They (and their organs and parts) can function properly or improperly. This teleological notion is, I think, deeply embedded in our way of thinking about knowledge;[23] no doubt this is because theism (Christian and Jewish) has been deeply embedded in our culture for several millennia. A theistic way of thinking about warrant—what distinguishes knowledge from mere true belief—will take advantage of this fact of creation and the teleology it brings with it. There will also be a place for justification in a theistic way of thinking about knowledge and belief; justification is a matter of acting responsibly with respect to the whole cognitive endeavor, of fulfilling epistemic duty. What are these duties? From the perspective I suggest justification may not be crucial for knowledge (as far as I can see it is neither necessary nor sufficient for knowledge); but it may nonetheless be of great importance. (Perhaps, from this point of view, understanding the precise nature of knowledge is less important than understanding how cognitive faculties are responsibly used by their owners.) And just how are justification and warrant related? How shall we think about skepticism from a theistic perspective? These questions await serious effort.

A theistic understanding of warrant will draw heavily upon the notion of proper function. But how shall we think about that notion? At present a flourishing cottage industry is devoted to giving naturalistic analyses or explanations of the notions of function, proper function, purpose, and the like as they apply to human beings and other organisms. These explanations ordinarily proceed in terms of evolution; the rough idea is that an organ or system is functioning properly when it is functioning in the way that enabled its ancestors to survive and reproduce. Thus, for example, Paul Griffiths: "The proper functions of a biological trait are the functions it is ascribed in a functional analysis of the capacity to survive and reproduce which has been displayed by animals with that feature."[24] But this seems to me hopelessly inadequate. For suppose a Hitler gains control of the world. Mad as he is, he very much dislikes the way in which the human visual system works (indeed, he dislikes proper function generally). He therefore commissions his scientists to induce a mutation in the population: a mutation according to which visual acuity is vastly reduced and the use of the visual system causes great pain. Those creatures unlucky enough to be born with the mutation are able to survive, but just barely; the constant pain prevents them from doing anything more than what is required for bare survival. They can't do science or philosophy, of course, or enjoy the beauty of a fine summer day, or engage in play or sport or art or the other things that make human life worth living: their lives are a burden to them. Hitler further instructs his henchmen (over a period of years) to systematically weed out those who don't suffer from this mutation, thus encouraging it to become fixed in the population. Now consider the population after several generations: according to the above analysis of proper function, the few remaining human beings whose eyes function in the old way have a malfunctioning visual system; the visual systems functioning in the new way are the ones that are functioning properly. But this seems absurd. So proper function can't be understood in this way: how then is it to be understood?

A related area of crucial importance at the moment is the philosophy of mind. How shall we think about what it is to be or have a mind? What is it to be capable of intentional activity? How shall we understand this power we have to select an object for attention and predicate properties of it? The object need not be present; indeed, it need not be either concrete or material; how does this work? Contemporary philosophy of mind, interesting and vigorous as much of it is, will be of little help here; for the most interesting and vigorous projects, in this area, are part of an enterprise devoted to the attempt to understand mind and personhood naturalistically. This puts such severe constraints on the project that little of real value is likely to emerge; indeed, a large cadre of those engaged in the project finally deny that there is any such thing as intentionality or even belief, relegating these and other notions of "folk psychology" to the trash heap of outgrown superstitions. A theist may be able to learn a good bit from this; but fundamentally he will ask different questions and look for answers in a quite different direction. And again the first thing to remember, so it seems to me, is, that we human beings have been created in the image of God: he thinks, and so do we. One of the principal elements or aspects of this image is precisely this ability to think, to believe, to intend (in the broad sense), with all that goes with it.[25] The relation of our intentional activity to God's intentional activity and to our status as creatures capable of free and responsible activity is far more important, from a theistic perspective, than its relation to the "intentional activity" of thermostats and frogs.

These are just a few of the topics to think about from a theistic perspective. Of course there are many others: probability,[26] subjunctive conditionals,[27] the development of science, the nature of freedom, the nature of human action, the nature of language. (From a naturalistic point of view, even if you think there are such things as properties and propositions, it isn't at all easy to see how elements of our language could come to express them.) A question of quite a different sort: how shall we think of duty, on the one hand, and human flourishing, on the other, in connection with God? And how are duty and human flourishing related to each other? How shall we think about love, in all its manifestations? About our sense of beauty? Or (to take a vastly underdeveloped topic) our sense of play and humor?

These and a thousand other questions await penetrating and detailed investigation by Christian philosophers. In some instances it is crucially important to the intellectual and spiritual health of the Christian community to clearly understand the topic in question; the whole area of the relation of science to religion would be an example.

AN OBJECTION

I say Christian philosophers should address these questions and topics starting from the Christian faith, using all that they know, including Christian teachings. But here we encounter an important objection. To get a good grasp of this objection, however, we must first make a brief detour. According to historical Christianity, there are two broad sources of knowledge or true belief. First, there is reason, construed broadly so that it encompasses not just a priori knowledge but also perceptual knowledge, as well as what one learns by way of memory and induction. There is also Reid's "sympathy," by way of which one learns what others think and feel; and most Christian traditions have also embraced something like Calvin's *sensus divinitatis*.[28] There are still other sources of knowledge here, but what is central to them is that they are all part of our created cognitive heritage or epistemic endowment. For us to learn what we do learn by way of these sources, God need do nothing special: just the usual conservation of his creation, together, perhaps, with concurrence in creaturely activity. But there is also another source of knowledge or true belief, according to Christians: faith, together with its object or correlative, divine revelation. It is by way of the first sort of knowledge that we know the size of the earth, the distance to the moon, and the fact that human beings die. By way of the second, however, we know of God's plan for the redemption of humankind through the life and death and resurrection of his Son, Jesus Christ. Christians ordinarily take it that divine revelation, the Bible, is central here, although of course there are disagreements as to just how revelation works and how important tradition, for example, is in enabling us to apprehend what the Lord intends to teach in scripture. These differences won't have much if any effect on what I want to say here.

To return to the objection, then: the objector claims that if as a scholar you start from what you know by way of faith, if you employ as premises in your arguments propositions that you know by faith (rather than by way of reason), then your results will really be theology rather than philosophy, psychology, sociology, or whatever. If you start from theological convictions in a given area—in understanding love, humor, aggression, knowledge, or abstract objects, for example—then any conclusions you come to will be dependent upon theological convictions and will themselves, in consequence, be theology. Theology in, theology out, as the computer literati might say. And while a theological understanding of these phenomena may indeed be desirable or necessary, it is still theology; it isn't philosophy (or whatever). To have the latter, we must keep ourselves pure and unspotted from theology.[29]

This is a common view; it is or has been something like a semi-official position of Roman Catholic thinkers. But here we must note two quite different Christian traditions on this point: call them the Augustinian and Thomist traditions.[30] According to the latter, there is theology and there are the other sciences. The nontheological sciences are the province of reason; they contain what we can know by natural reason unaided by faith or special revelation. They concern general revelation as opposed to special revelation; and in pursuing them it is illegitimate to appeal to theology or to what one knows by way of faith. Of course the reason isn't that we don't need to know what we know by faith; theology is both important and necessary and perhaps more noble than its sister disciplines. But we also need the nontheological disciplines. According to the Augustinian tradition, by contrast, what we need and want, in studying a given area, is the best total understanding we can get, using all the resources at our command; the question whether that best understanding should be called "theology" on the one hand, or "philosophy" (or "sociology," or "psychology," or whatever) on the other is of secondary interest.

Why does the Thomist think it is important to have a philosophy or a psychology that is unspotted by theology? What is the value of such science, and why should we expend a portion of our intellectual resources on it? (After all, it is not as if the latter are unlimited.) The Thomist will answer that what we know by way of reason has for us an epistemic or epistemological or cognitive advantage over what we know by way of faith. What we grasp by faith we know by way of testimony; we take it on the authority of someone else. If that someone else is God, then the belief in question is backed up by high authority indeed; objectively speaking, furthermore, it is also maximally certain. Still, we don't really know what we take on trust, what we take someone else's word for, even if that someone else is God himself. Or, if we say that we *do* know it, we don't have the highest and best form of knowledge of it; we don't have scientia. Consider, for example, the Pythagorean theorem, or the proposition that there is no set of all sets, or Gödel's theorem on the incompleteness of arithmetic, and consider two ways of believing it. In the first way, you believe it on the authority of your favorite mathematician, who, however confused and unreliable he may be on other topics, is authoritative on ones like these. Then compare believing it by way of grasping, understanding the proof, and seeing for yourself that the theorem is not only true but couldn't possibly be false. It makes good sense to say, with the Thomist, that in the second case the knowledge you have of that truth is better, more valuable, a higher kind of knowledge than in the first case. It is more like God's knowledge—God, after all, never has to take anybody's word for anything.

This reply has a sort of appeal; but I think the appeal is limited. For in most of the sciences we don't at all have the sort of knowledge we have of the Pythagorean theorem or the fundamental theorem of the calculus; we don't have anything like the sort of certainty we have in elementary logic and mathematics. Consider physics, for example. First, most of us who know anything about physics know what we know by way of taking someone else's word for it. How do I know that the velocity of light in a vacuum is about 186,000 miles per second? I read it in a physics text, or heard it in a physics class, or saw it in an article in *Scientific American*. I certainly didn't measure the velocity of light myself and wouldn't have the faintest idea of how to do so. (I daresay the same is true for you.) How do I know that some experiments favor relativity theory over Newtonian mechanics? The same way: I learned it in a physics class. I didn't myself perform those experiments involving muon decay, the rapid transport of cesium clocks, or the measurement of parallax. Indeed, the same goes for most physicists: most of them, so far as I know, haven't performed those experiments either; most of them learned about them in class or from a physics journal. As a matter of fact, even those who performed the experiments had to take a great deal on the authority of others: that the velocity of the plane transporting the cesium clock was in fact thus and so, that the plane flew the relevant distance and the right course, and so on. Anyone who makes an advance in science obviously stands on the shoulders of others, taking an enormous amount on their say-so—for example, how the earlier experiments relevant to his project turned out. According to the Thomist, the difference in noetic value between theology and the nontheological sciences is said to be that in the former we must rely on the testimony of others (even if on such an other as God himself), while in the latter we have the level of knowledge that goes with simply seeing that some proposition is true. This difference, however, is a difference that applies very narrowly—only to elementary mathematics and logic and perhaps to such obvious perceptual beliefs as that, for example, the pointer is now between the 4 and the 5 on the dial.

My sympathies, therefore, lie with the Augustinian view; I am at best suspicious of the epistemic benefits claimed on behalf of philosophy or science untainted by theology. But perhaps there is less separation here than meets the eye. Or perhaps we can reduce the separation: I wish to make an irenic proposal. Think again about those theoretical or interpretative sciences: philosophy, anthropology, psychology, sociology, economics, and others. The best way to do these sciences, says the Augustinian, is to use all that we know, including what we know by way of faith or revelation; according to the Thomist the way to proceed is to bracket what we know by faith and appeal only to premises we know by reason. But Thomist and Augustinian agree that the Christian community badly needs that fuller understanding of these phenomena. So suppose we think of the matter as follows. There are the deliverances of faith: call them F; there is also the result of thinking about a given philosophical question or a question in one of the sciences, appealing to the deliverances of faith as well as to the deliverances of reason: call that FS. Thomist and Augustinian concur that we need FS; but the Thomist adds that FS is really theology rather than philosophy, sociology, psychology, or whatever. But now consider the conditional or hypothetical proposition *if F then FS:* the proposition that says what the implications of faith are for the particular philosophical (or scientific) question at issue. Of course there will be a very large number of such propositions (and of course there will also be one gigantic superproposition here, whose antecedent will be the conjunction of all the elements of the faith relevant to any philosophical or theological question, and whose consequent will be the conjunction of the consequents of the more particular propositions of this form). Now both parties to the discussion—both Thomist and Augustinian—agree that these bridge propositions, as we may call them, are not themselves among the deliverances of faith; we discover and learn them by reason, not by faith. It is by reason rather than by faith that we see what the bearing of the Christian faith is on psychology; it is by reason rather than by faith that we see how theism bears on ontology and how the Christian teaching of the *imago Dei* bears on epistemology or the philosophy of mind; it is by reason rather than by faith that we see how the scriptural teaching on love, or sin, or morality bears on what we study in social psychology, anthropology, or sociology.

So both sides agree—indeed, insist—that we, the Christian community, need to know how faith bears on these areas. And both agree that working at these conditionals is a matter, not of faith and theology, but of reason and philosophy or the relevant science. Further, both agree that Christians will assert the consequents of these conditionals; that is, we will assert the result of seeing how faith applies to the domain in question. The two sides differ only in this: according to the Thomist, but not the Augustinian, when you assert the consequent of such a conditional you are really doing theology rather than philosophy or the science in question. Well, why shouldn't the Augustinian peaceably concede the point, at least for present purposes? Perhaps it doesn't greatly matter whether we say that asserting those consequents is theology, on the one hand, or philosophy, psychology, economics, or whatever on the other. What is of great importance, at present, is that we work at discovering and developing our knowledge of the conditionals. And working at those conditionals is not doing theology: it clearly falls within the domain of the nontheological disciplines involved. It is not the theologian who is most appropriately trained and qualified for work on these conditionals; it is instead the psychologist, historian, biologist, economist, sociologist, literary critic— and, in the case presently in question, the philosopher. Here Augustinian and Thomist can agree. They can agree on the importance, the great importance, of this work for the spiritual and intellectual health of the Christian community, and they can agree that in working at these conditionals we are doing nontheological science rather than theology.

By way of conclusion, Christian philosophy, so I say, has at least these four major aspects or moments: philosophical theology, apologetics (both positive and negative), Christian philosophical criticism, and positive Christian philosophy. Of course all sorts of important questions remain. For just one example, how shall we think of those conditionals I was just mentioning? Presumably they aren't entailments; but then what is the connection between antecedent and consequent? Or if they are entailments, what goes into the antecedent in addition to the relevant elements apprehended by faith? Furthermore, Christians disagree to one degree or another as to precisely what the Christian faith is, precisely what is to count as the deliverances of the faith: how does that bear on the question of what goes into the antecedent of one of these conditionals? These and a thousand other questions remain. Perhaps the most important thing, however, is to work at the conditionals; and we needn't answer those questions before starting the work.

NOTES

1. To some extent here I follow Etienne Gilson in his *The Spirit of Medieval Philosophy* (Notre Dame: University of Notre Dame Press, 1991) in my way of thinking of Augustine's views on these matters.

2. Eleonore Stump and Norman Kretzmann, "Eternity," *Journal of Philosophy* 78 (1981): 429–57.

3. This sort of charge has repeatedly surfaced; in the sixteenth century the Catholic authorities in the Netherlands accused the Calvinists of sedition and political subversion; this prompted a bit of apologetics that should be eschewed rather than emulated: the notoriously censorious declaration of the otherwise warm and ecumenical Belgic Confession (1561), "we therefore detest the Anabaptists. . . . "

4. See, for example, Richard Swinburne's *The Coherence of Theism* (Oxford: Oxford University Press, 1977).

5. For contemporary replies, see, for example, John Hick's *Evil and the God of Love* (New York: Simon and Schuster, 1963) and chap. 10 of my book *The Nature of Necessity* (Oxford: Clarendon Press, 1974) along with "The Probabilistic Argument from Evil" in *Philosophical Studies* 1976; see also the pieces by William Alston and Peter van Inwagen in *Philosophical Perspectives* 5 (1991).

6. Oddly enough, some theologians seemed to have joined the throng; I think of those theologians who argue that the traditional idea of God as a transcendent person (one who knows, loves, and acts) is outmoded or inappropriate for "man come of age" or unsatisfactory in this nuclear (or global, or pluralistic) age and should itself be transcended.

7. And something like it, of course, is to be found earlier, particularly in Plato and Aristotle.

8. See his *The Existence of God* (Oxford: Oxford University Press, 1979).

9. Thus according to Swinburne a good theistic argument is one such that its premises are "known to be true by those who dispute the conclusion" (*Existence of God*, 7).

10. As is the case in my book *God and Other Minds* (Ithaca: Cornell University Press, 1967; 2d ed., 1991).

11. Augustine also (and perhaps more frequently) speaks of the *civitas homini*. Neither term is wholly felicitous: the second because the *civitas* in question includes in its ranks nonhuman persons such as Satan and his cohorts, and the first (*civitas mundi*) because the *civitas* in question must not be confused with any earthly political entity (Rome, for example). I shall use *civitas mundi*, asking you to bear in mind that caveat.

12. Bertrand Russell, "A Free Man's Worship," in *Why I Am Not a Christian and Other Essays on Religion and Related Subjects* (New York: Simon and Schuster, 1957).

13. See J. J. C. Smart, *Our Place in the Universe* (Oxford: Blackwell, 1989), for a simple and clear statement of naturalism.

14. An illustration: in "A Mechanism for Social Selection and Successful Altruism" (*Science* 250 [December 1990]: 1665ff.) Herbert Simon considers the problem, from the perspective of evolutionary naturalism, presented by altruistic behavior, such as that displayed by Mother Teresa, or the Little Sisters of the Poor. Why do these people do the sorts of things they do? The rational way to behave, says Simon, is to try to act in such a way as to increase one's personal fitness — to act so as to increase the probability that one's genes will be widely propagated, thus doing well in the evolutionary derby. Altruistic behavior, such as that of Mother Teresa and the Little Sisters, does no such thing; so what is the explanation of their behaving as they do? Simon proposes two mechanisms: "bounded rationality" and "docility": "Docile persons tend to learn and believe what they perceive others in the society want them to learn and believe. Thus the content of what is learned will not be fully screened for its contribution to personal fitness. . . . Because of bounded rationality, the docile individual will often be unable to distinguish socially prescribed behavior that contributes to fitness from altruistic behavior. In fact, docility will reduce the inclination to evaluate independently the contributions of behavior to fitness. . . . By virtue of bounded rationality, the docile person cannot acquire the personally advantageous learning that provides the increment, d, of fitness without acquiring also the altruistic behaviors that cost the decrement, c" (1666, 1667). Mother Teresa displays "bounded rationality"; she adopts those culturally transmitted altruistic behaviors without making an independent evaluation of their contribution to her personal fitness. If she *did* make such an independent evaluation (and was sufficiently rational to do it properly) she would see that this sort of behavior did not contribute to her personal fitness, would stop engaging in it, and would instead get to work on her expected number of progeny.

15. Gordon Kaufman, *Theology for a Nuclear Age* (Manchester: Manchester University Press, 1985), 43.

16. Christopher Marlowe, *Doctor Faustus*, quoted in David Lyle Jeffrey, "*Caveat lector:* Structuralism, Deconstructionism, and Ideology," *Christian Scholar's Review* 17 (1988): 436–448.

17. According to the January 1991 issue of *First Things* the *New York Times* reported recently that

> *Scientific American* denied a job to the gifted science writer, Forrest M. Mims, III. Mr. Mims had been doing a column for the magazine, titled "Amateur Scientist." But then his awful secret was discovered. According to Armaund Schwab, who was managing editor when the decision was made, Mr. Mims "was a nonbeliever in evolution.". . . . Ever vigilant against extremisms, editor Jonathan Piel determined that hiring Mims would compromise the magazine's integrity. (64)

18. See my paper "When Faith and Reason Clash: Evolution and the Bible" with replies by Ernan McMullin, Pattle Pun, and Howard Van Till, together with my response, all in *Christian Scholar's Review* 21 (1991): 8–32.

19. Richard Dawkins, *The Blind Watchmaker* (London: Norton, 1986), 6, 7.

20. Well, not the whole range; many philosophical questions and projects arise out of a particular and non-Christian perspective and can hardly be sensibly pursued outside that

perspective. Philosophers ask the question "How shall we think about mind from a natu-ralistic point of view?" or "Given that Nietzsche is right and God is dead, how shall we think about morality?" Many questions philosophers ask presuppose commitments the Christian philosopher doesn't accept; it is part of the task of Christian philosophical criti-cism to make these connections clear.

21. See Christopher Menzel and Thomas Morris, "Absolute Creation" in T. Morris, ed., *Anselmian Explorations* (Notre Dame: University of Notre Dame Press, 1987), and Christopher Menzel, "Theism, Platonism and the Metaphysics of Mathematics" in Michael Beaty, ed., *Christian Theism* (Notre Dame: University of Notre Dame Press, 1990).

22. In Aquinas's third way there is the puzzling suggestion that there cannot be an infi-nite series of necessary beings each of which gets its necessity from another. What is puz-zling here is the implicit suggestion that *some* necessary beings *do* get their necessity from an-other. Perhaps we can understand this suggestion along the above lines: perhaps, say, the proposition $7 + 5 = 12$ is both necessarily true and necessarily existent, an ingredient in every possible world. But perhaps it gets its necessary existence by virtue of the fact that God *thinks* it (thus producing it) in every possible world.

23. See my "Justification and Theism," *Faith and Philosophy* 4 (1987): 403–426, and my *Warrant and Proper Function* (New York: Oxford University Press, 1992), chaps. 1 and 2.

24. Paul Griffiths, "Functional Analysis and Proper Functions," *British Journal for the Phi-losophy of Science* 44 (1993): 409–422.

25. Thus, for example, Thomas Aquinas:

Since human beings are said to be in the image of God in virtue of their having a nature that includes an intellect, such a nature is most in the image of God in virtue of being most able to imitate God (*Summa theologiae* 1a.93.4);

and

Only in rational creatures is there found a likeness of God which counts as an image. . . . As far as a likeness of the divine nature is concerned, rational creatures seem some-how to attain a representation of [that] type in virtue of imitating God not only in this, that he is and lives, but especially in this, that he understands. (ibid., Ia q. 93 a. 6)

26. See Richard Otte, "A Theistic Conception of Probability," in Beaty, ed., *Christian Theism.*

27. See Del Ratzsch, "Nomo(theo)logical Necessity," in Beaty, ed., *Christian Theism.*

28. According to Aquinas there is a natural but confused knowledge of God (*Summa the-ologiae* 1.2.1.1).

29. Thus John Wippel: "Often enough those who reject the possibility of a Christian philosophy do so because they view philosophy only in its moment of proof—as a com-pleted set of propositions including principles, proofs and conclusions. Here, it seems to me, they conclude correctly that nothing borrowed from religious belief or theology can enter in. To admit the contributions of faith into the process of proof would be to destroy the philosophical character of the undertaking and to turn it into theology or at the least, into an extension of religious belief" ("The Possibility of a Christian Philosophy: A Thomistic Perspective," *Faith and Philosophy* 1 [1984]: 280).

30. Here again I follow the Gilson of *The Spirit of Medieval Philosophy;* and once again I am less interested in the historical accuracy of these terms than in the positions themselves.

TWO

Structure and Meaning
in St. Augustine's *Confessions*

Frederick J. Crosson

Classical philosophy's responsible and careful critique of religiousness is both summed up and embodied in the systematic treatment of Cicero's three dialogues on the philosophy of religion. The first and most important of these, *On the Nature of the Gods,* while insisting on the indispensable role of religiousness in securing the public welfare, raises questions about the consistency of the conception of the nature of the gods, which the practice of religion presupposes. The dialogue goes further than this: despite its title and the introduction of that topic as theme (i.e., the *nature* of the gods) in the dialogue itself, it raises the question of whether there is any ground, apart from the stories of the religious tradition, for affirming the existence of the gods at all.

If one brackets the stories about extraordinary events, stories that have been handed down as a warrant for religious practice and belief (and none of the dialogue's interlocutors claim firsthand experience of such hearsay prodigious events as seeing Castor and Pollux appear on the battlefield fighting for the Roman forces), then the evidence for the existence of the gods must be taken from the world around us, evidence about the nature of the whole that is available to humans from observation and inference. What would such evidence consist of? Basically, that the order of nature can be explained only by the inference that God is the origin of that order or that the gods are.

But the discovery of nature by the Greek philosophers provided an alternative to the inference that the gods were at the origin of order. The more we concede the regularity of phenomena as inhering in the natures of things and in the nature of the whole, the less we need to seek for an origin of that order in an artificer, just as, if houses grew naturally and regularly from wood and stone, we would have no need to infer architects and builders to account for their undeniable ordered character. As Cotta, the spokesman for the Academic school puts it: "the system's coherence and persistence is due to nature's forces and not to divine power: . . .

[T]he greater this [coherence and persistence of nature] is as a spontaneous power, the less it is to be supposed that it is from a divine reason." [1]

Cicero's dialogue ends with this critique of the Stoic arguments for the existence of the gods based on the order of nature. Young Cicero, the virtually silent listener to the whole discussion, comments in the last speech that in his judgment the arguments of the Stoic Balbus had more semblance of truth. But since Balbus makes no reply to the formidable criticisms of Cotta, it is hard to see the grounds for that judgment. Perhaps we can say that of the discussion's two goals mentioned in its opening sentence—namely that either one will learn about how religious practices should be properly carried out through learning about the nature of the gods or else one will learn something about the human soul—the latter goal has come closer to being realized.

Christianity's encounter with this philosophical critique of ancient religiousness ranged over several centuries. Thomas Aquinas would later say that there were two disclosures proposed by revelation: the *occultum divinitatis* and the *mysterium humanitatis Christi*.[2] The "hiddenness of God" refers to the doctrine that God stands outside the whole, sustains no real relation to the whole, does not appear within the whole. God does not belong to the nature of the whole or appear within it because he is not a kind of being—for example, one of the immortals. He does not, because he cannot, fit into the world picture. And the "mystery of the humanity of Christ" means that that hiddenness remains present in the man Jesus, in that he is not a mere appearance of a god in the likeness of men but fully present in history as a man, not a divine being peering out through a cloak of flesh, but a man. The problem of how to articulate this doctrine of the Incarnation took a long time to respond to with any adequacy, and indeed no formulation of it can ever hope to be the last word. However that may be, the Incarnation stands in a category different from the stories of divine apparitions criticized by Socrates in the *Republic*. In the course of examining the theology of the poets, Socrates argues that if God is perfect he could not subsequently surrender his perfection to assume any less-than-perfect form, and since, being perfect, he is not a deceiver, he would not appear to human beings in an illusory form, as any kind of apparition, seeming to be what he is not.

The attempt to formulate the unique status of the divinity as not within the whole, this "singularity" in the modern scientific sense of the term, already informs the thought and writing of the last and greatest thinker of Roman times, Augustine of Hippo. Both the content and the form of his greatest work, the *Confessions,* are structured by the revolutionary transformation that his meditation on the events of his life brought about. For a dozen years after his conversion he reflected on how to understand the import of that event and of what led up to it, how to regard human existence and worldly existence in its light. The words and understanding to which he won his way became, through Augustine's shaping, what has been one of the most widely read and yet least well-understood books of our tradition.

Even the distinguished historian Henri-Irénée Marrou could write that Augustine "composes badly because the ancients generally did not give to composition the attention that we do,"[3] citing the *Confessions* among a half-dozen other works. "The plan of the *Confessions* has something bizarre about it," he wrote:

> The autobiographical part . . . occupies only nine of thirteen books. With the tenth book we enter into a new phase, no longer historical, but dogmatic; St. Augustine no longer narrates his past life, he analyses the current state of his thought. . . . With the eleventh book, the exposition leaps brusquely to another terrain: the last three books are nothing else in fact but an allegorical commentary on the first chapter of Genesis . . . an independent treatise which could very well have been published separately.

And he concludes:

> Of course, it remains possible to assert that there exists between these three parts of the *Confessions* a profound and secret unity. But even those who have succeeded in showing that are the first to agree that that unity is psychological and not literary.[4]

Indeed, although thematic and psychological accounts of the unity of the *Confessions* abound, the virtually unanimous critical judgment is that it is hastily put together, moves by fits and starts, dallies here, and hurries there. For example, John J. O'Meara writes that the *Confessions* is "a badly composed book" and that it is "a commonplace of Augustinian scholarship to say that Augustine was not able to plan a book."[5]

As an "autobiography," even allowing for it being the first or among the first of the genre, it does not meet our expectations. Only in the ninth book in passing do we learn that he had a brother. In the sixth book we meet Alypius and are told that he had been a student of Augustine already in Thagaste, though no mention of him occurs there in the third book. The second book deals with his sixteenth year, the next with four or five years, the next with six or seven years. Twice he tells us that he is passing over many things because he has to hurry on to the central things.

Most attempts to deal with a structural division of the work have foundered because they begin from the most famous scene, that of the conversion in the garden of Augustine's house, and assume that the peripety of the work must occur when he is turned around from the flesh to the spirit. For example, O'Meara writes, "The central point in the *Confessions* is the conversion. The conversion itself falls into two parts or moments."[6] I shall try to show that this is not Augustine's intended structure.

DIVIDING THE TEXT

In the *Retractationes* Augustine gives us a first division of the thirteen books: ten are about him, he says, and three are about sacred scripture. Of those ten, the last stands apart from the rest by being a long meditation on memory and the soul's cognitive powers, as well as on his spiritual situation at the time he wrote the book. No one is mentioned or named, no historical events are narrated or referred to.

Now if we focus on the remaining nine (narrative) books, we can notice a number of facts that are either mere coincidences or significant. First, those nine books divide neatly in the middle of the middle (fifth) book: he leaves Carthage for Rome. The result is that the story as a whole falls into two parts, the first half in Africa and the second half in Italy. The ninth book and the narrative part of the text ends while he and Monica and the others are waiting in Ostia for a ship to return them to Africa: nothing is said about the years that have passed since then. Second, the third book ends with a discussion of Augustine's reading of the books of the Manichaeans, the fourth book ends with a chapter on his first reading of Aristotle's *Categories* (even though he tells us explicitly that he had read the book six or seven years earlier), the fifth book ends with a discussion of the Academic philosophy, the sixth book with a discussion of Epicurus, the seventh book with a discussion of the Platonists. Third, the first half of the story does not tell us the name of any of the people he encounters (with one single exception): not his mother or father or brother, not the friend whose death overshadows his life, none of his students (though Alypius is one), not his common-law wife or son, none of the Manichaeans he lives with for nine years—until Faustus, the Manichaean bishop he has waited so long to meet.[7]

Why this silence about names? No sooner have we reached Italy than the names begin to flood in on us: Ambrose, Symmachus, and Elpidius before the end of the fifth book; Alypius, Nebridius, and Romanianus in the sixth (all of whom we now learn he had known in Thagaste); Firminus and Vindicianus in the seventh; Simplicianus and Ponticianus in the eighth; and finally Adeodatus, Evodius, Patricius, and Monica in the ninth. Two principles seem to determine the naming process. One, he names only those who have been instrumental (whether knowingly or not) in the path of ascent toward God. Two, the silence about names in the first half results from the overall movement there toward his increasing estrangement from God and man. Separated by death from his boyhood friend in book 4,[8] alienated from his Manichaean friends by having ceased to believe Mani's teaching, fleeing his mother's house, his native town (*fugi de patria* [4.7.12]), he finally abandons Monica and Africa itself, sailing alone to Rome.[9] But the second half is not only an ascent toward God; it is a progressive return to community, measured by the arrival of Monica, Alypius, Nebridius, and the friends who gather together in Milan and Cassiciacum and culminating in what Augustine will call, in the very last sentence of his narrative, his "fellow citizens in that heavenly Jerusalem, which your pilgrim people sigh after from their setting forth even to their return."

The turning point of that descent into estrangement is the encounter with Faustus, who began all unknowingly "to loosen the snare" in which Augustine was caught.[10] The snare is manifold, and the liberation from it occurs in stages marked by the philosophers mentioned at the end of each book. The structural axis of the encounter with Faustus indicates that just as books 2, 3, and 4 mark stages of descent, so books 6, 7, and 8 mark successive stages of ascent. Moreover, these three stages of descent are structured according to the triad that remained central to Augustine's thought about religion over the course of his life, from the *De vera religione* to the *Enchiridion*. That triad is found in the scriptural text about the concupiscence of the flesh, the concupiscence of the eyes (i.e., of the mind), and the ambition of this world.[11]

In book 2, about his sixteenth year, he enters into the bondage of the flesh ("the madness of lust took me under its scepter" [2.2.2]). In book 3 his mind is enslaved by the images and phantasies and fables of the Manichaeans (*phantasmata* and *figmenta* [3:6]) and he wrestles for the first time with the great questions that led him to Manichaeanism: *unde est malum*, whence comes evil into the universe, and whether God is a material being (3.7.12). Book 4 commences with his description of how he "pursued the emptiness of popular glory and the applause of spectators, with competition for prize poems and strife for garlands of straw" (4.1.1). Competition for the rewards of this world leads to stressful unhappiness and deepens his isolation, and Augustine comments in retrospect on his "exile" from his "fellow citizens" in the heavenly Jerusalem (9.13.37).

But in book 6 (which begins with the image of the widow's son raised from death) he reflects increasingly on the emptiness of the worldly ambitions he now pursues with ambivalent feelings. He muses on how much happier a drunken beggar is, and he extols the model of honorable and unworldly public service, which Alypius exhibits. It is not accidental that in the last chapter of book 6, Augustine is drawn toward Epicureanism, which scorns worldly ambition.[12] In book 7 the questions of book 3 return, and he comes to see that God is incorporeal and that evil is not a substance as Mani had taught.[13] In book 8 (which begins by celebrating the truth he now possesses and is the only book to begin with the word *Deus*) he is finally emancipated from his bondage to the flesh through hearing the word of God addressing him.[14] Nor is it a coincidence that in the first chapter of book 9, immediately following his conversion in the garden, he addresses Christ directly for the first time since book 1.[15]

Without pursuing the details of this narrative structure further, let us return to the relation of the form of the *Confessions* to the understanding it embodies. The problem confronting Augustine may be posed in the following way: to tell the story of one's life in such a way that the sequence of events related is adequately accounted for and yet to tell that story in such a way that those events are not adequately accounted for. Consider why Augustine goes to Italy: he seeks to advance his career, he has heard that students are more responsible there, he wants to get out of the Manichaean community in Carthage. Yet, having said all that, Augustine adds that the reason he went to Italy was that God was leading him to Ambrose. This explanation in no sense replaces or suspends the former reasons. The divine action is not an action by a worldly agent, it does not insert itself into the sequence of motives and causes, it does not fill a gap in the account of Augustine's life. No event related in the *Confessions* is brought about by a situation inexplicable in terms of natural causes. Nature is a self-enclosed whole, not independent in its being from God but a whole whose course is adequately explainable in terms of immanent natural causes. Even the telling of the extraordinary event of hearing, in a child's voice in the garden, the overtone of a divine command never questions that the voice comes from children playing next door.[16]

The problem, then, of the literary form of the *Confessions*, as it confronted Augustine meditating through those years of its gestation, was the problem of speaking to his readers on two levels, so that the admonition of the child's voice, "Tolle, lege," could be applied to the text of his life and to the text of the *Confessions*, as well as to that of sacred scripture. For he had already learned to read the esoteric dimension of scripture:

> they were easy for everyone to read and yet safeguarded the dignity of their hidden truth within a deeper meaning, by words completely clear and by a lowly style of speech making itself accessible to all men and drawing the attention of those who are not light of heart. Thus it can receive all men into its generous bosom and by narrow passages lead on to you a small number of them. (6:5.8; cf. 3.5.9)

His aspiration was to confess his story in the same way:

> Surely I myself—and I speak this straight from my heart—if I were to write anything that would have authority, I would prefer to write in such a way that my words would utter whatever portion of truth each one could take from them, rather than put down one true meaning in such a way that it would exclude other meanings which were not false. (12.31.42)[17]

HEARING GOD SPEAK

And so we have on one level the "autobiography," which has fascinated centuries of readers, and on another level a profound reflection on the occultum divinitatis and the problem of understanding how such an utterly transcendent being can possibly appear within the whole. Does not such a conception of transcendence essentially entail nonappearance? Doesn't the question "Where does the transcendent appear in the world?" self-destruct? How do St. Paul's words that Augustine read in the garden and found meaningful differ from the *sortes Vergilianae*, which he has earlier described as popular because "If a man consults at random the pages of some poet who sings and thinks of things far different, a verse often appears that is wonderfully appropriate to the business at hand" (4.3.5)?

It is the tenth book that begins to address that problem, a problem that became more difficult for Augustine as he reflected on it. The tenth book poses the problem through a recapitulation of the theory of recollection. To know is to recognize: when one hears words, one's mind is directed either to present things, or to memories of things experienced in the past, or to things that never entered into one's memory because they were there from the beginning: "they were already in memory, but so removed and pushed back as it were in more hidden caverns that, unless they were dug up by some reminder, I would perhaps have been unable to conceive them" (10.10.17). Such are the principles and laws of numbers and geometry and the essential natures of poetry, virtue, and beauty.

Originally, as his little dialogue *On the Teacher* shows, he assimilated his Platonic conception of knowledge to his newfound Christianity without hesitation: the light of the upper portion of the divided line that reveals the forms is there identified with the logos of St. John's Gospel, the light that enlightens every man who comes into the world. At the time of writing the *Confessions*, Augustine is still willing to describe the God whom he learned to discern by reading the Platonists as a light that illuminates the soul's vision (7.10.16), but now he wrestles with how that conception of God can be assimilated to the notion of recollection. He concludes (10.26.37) that it cannot, that God was in no sense already present in his memory, hence in no way able to be recognized in the phenomena. Only by a direct noetic encounter, however obscure, can he have learned of the eternal God.

But this resolution of the problem of the transcendence and presence of the divine generates a new problem. For Augustine specifically adds that he did not find anything in the Platonists about the appearance of that divine Word within the world. What he finds missing in the eternal, immutable, transcendent One of Plotinus is *not* ubiquity or omnipresence, for he had learned that spirit is not localized as matter is; rather, what is missing in the writings of the Platonists is that "no man hears [God] *calling* to us" (7.21.27). But Augustine's experience was that "[the *man* Christ Jesus] called to me, and said 'I am the way of truth and the life'" (7.18.24).[18] So, in the eleventh book, meditating on the way in which God's timelessly spoken word enters into time and space, he says, "Thus in the Gospel, [your Word] speaks through the flesh, and this word sounded *outwardly* in the ears of men" (11.8.10).

To recognize the eternal God as the light of eternal truth above the mind is one thing; to recognize the Word made flesh, to recognize the appearance of the transcendent within the world is something else. How can we recognize that God, whose appearance in time is neither an eternal truth embedded innately in one's memory nor the utterly transcendent light above the mind? To know is to recognize, to recognize is to remember—but here the Platonic model breaks down. "If I find you apart from memory, I am unmindful of you. How then shall I find you if I do not remember you?" (10.17.26). "[H]ow do I recognize the reality if I do not remember it?" (10.16.24).

From the point of view of this problematic the comment of Etienne Gilson seems at least inadequate, if not misleading: "However different in their details, all of the Augustinian itineraries of the soul in quest of God are substantially the same: they go from the exterior to the interior, and from the inferior to the superior; ab exterioribus ad interiora, ab inferioribus ad superiora."[19] What seems to me misleading about this comment is that for Augustine, as we have seen, first, the encounter with the God of Jesus occurs in the world, not within the soul, and second, coming to Jesus is entering a community sharing in his life.

The solution to the problem of how we recognize God is integrally related to the whole conception that underlies the form and content of the *Confessions*. In the opening chapters of book 1, the puzzles concerned with the omnipresence of God are articulated with respect to space. "To what place do I call you, since I am in you?" (1.2.2). As he rids himself of the fantasies of the Manichaeans and reads the Platonists, Augustine comes to understand that God is present everywhere not by being diffused through space but by being in no place. Yet he is present always and everywhere, sustaining the whole and all of its parts in being. Augustine remarks that "the greatest and almost the sole cause" of his misunderstanding of God's omnipresence in his Manichaean days was his inability to conceive of God as other than material, spatially extended. But now he understands God not only as transcendent to the world but as acting in time. If the true conception of God utterly separates him from the world, how is it possible for us to recognize him, to confront him, in a worldly state of affairs, to literally hear the words by which he calls us?[20]

To hear God speaking is not to hear or see some paranatural event, it is to come to see the whole of nature as transfigured; it is to enter into and exist in a newly grasped meaning of the whole, illuminated by the light of faith. If an event of the world can be a disclosure of the divine, and if at the same time God cannot appear within that event, within the whole, then it can only be that the whole of the cosmos, coming to be and passing away in time, is his speaking to us. Contrary to the only way in which Cicero could conceive of it, the epiphany of the divine is not just an event within the whole, it is the whole itself as epiphany. The vehicle of God's presence is the created world, the world experienced as telling of God.[21] The illumination of the moment of epiphany, occurring in a particular locus of space and time, radiates outward, suffusing and transmuting the meaning of the whole of finite beings.

No wonder that Augustine goes on to describe that encounter in the language of sensory presence:

> You have called to me, and have cried out, and have shattered my deafness. You have blazed forth with light, and have shone upon me, and you have put my blindness to flight. You have sent forth fragrance, and I have drawn in my breath, and I pant after you, and I hunger and thirst after you. You have touched me, and I have burned for your peace. (10.27.38)[22]

Cicero's problem of how the divine agent could be understood to act within the course of nature has thus been transformed. If the riddle has been responded to, however, it is not in the manner anticipated. The question of nature and its explanation of the whole remains intact. Rather, that question has been sublated, taken up into a context unsuspected by the earlier form in which it was posed.

Hence the course of Augustine's meditation turns in the last three books to the topic of the relation of time and created nature. Clearly, this topic is not arbitrarily related to the narrative of his life. On the contrary, as mediated by the reflections of book 10, it places that story in the widest of all possible horizons for understanding it, namely the *arche* of the whole and of time itself. Just as God is not within my mind, so he is not within the whole universe. But Genesis gives an account of how the temporal universe is related to God's action, so Augustine turns to it to reflect on how, in the ultimate origin of all things, temporality and finitude are interfaced with eternity.

Self-knowledge, knowledge of humanity and of his place in the whole, was for Socrates and for classical thought a function of *nous*, which discerned the eternal natures of things within which the coming to be and passing away of terrestrial things took their natural course. But for Augustine, *memoria* signifies, for the first time in our tradition, not only a faculty of intellectual memory, of an anamnesis turned toward the Forms, but a faculty that recovers the meaning obscured by the diaspora of time.[23] The time of one's own life and the time of history reveal a dimension of meaning that falls outside the soul's vision directed only upward toward the timeless Forms. The temporality of the whole is the horizon within which the most fundamental meaning of existence is disclosed. Only the conception of creation allows hearsay to become hearing, allows the transcendent God to call to us through creatures. If faith comes through hearing, it is because utterances acquire their meaning by coming to be and passing away in time.

Let me recapitulate the second part of my argument. Book 1 begins by setting out the philosophical problem of the first half of the *Confessions* (books 1–7), namely of how God is to be understood as everywhere and yet as not in the world. For if he is everywhere by pervading all places, then there will be more of him in this large place than in that small place. Yet it is this conception of omnipresence that Augustine absorbed with his Manichaeanism.

It is only with his reading of the Platonists in book 7 that he acquires an understanding of God as immaterial spirit, transcendent to the whole, and hence as omnipresent by not being in any place. It was, as he says, his previous inability to conceive of an immaterial being that prevented him from understanding rightly God's infinite ubiquity. But this resolution creates the philosophical problem of the second half of the *Confessions* (books 7–13), namely of how such a transcendent God who cannot appear in the world can act within the world, can speak audibly to us, can call us to himself.

The second problem can be adumbrated by asking the following question. If God is everywhere, why does Augustine have to enter within himself ("intravi in intima mea" [7.10.16]) in order to find him? Why can't he encounter the omnipresent God all around him? The answer to that question is that God is not *in* the world and so cannot be encountered anywhere in space. Only in the noetic realm can he be found, as the light above the mind, but so incommensurably above our mind that we remain "in regione dissimilitudinis" (7.10.16) and can discern him only "as in a glass, darkly."

The second problem can be sharpened by reflecting on the mode of apprehension that resolves the first problem. God is discovered, is "first known," in book

7 as true being: I am Who Am. He is seen, in a timeless moment, as that which exists immutably, eternally, timelessly. Being is given in vision, in a present that never changes. Not only is he not in space, he is not in time.

But now at the end of book 8 Augustine has the experience of hearing God speak to him in the garden, an experience prepared only by the story of Anthony, an experience it seems fair to say would have been absurd for Plotinus or for any "Platonist." For hearing is an essentially temporal mode of apprehension. The unity of meaning of what we hear comes into being and passes away sequentially, necessarily, in contrast to the meaningful wholes of vision, which are given simultaneously. For hearing (as for human life) only as the one part ceases to be can the next part come into being. That mode of apprehension would seem to be absolutely antithetical to the way in which God exists (11.6.8). How can I be addressed by God in words that come to be and pass away, how can he speak such words, how can his word exist in time? [24]

Yet so it is: Augustine is addressed by God, is spoken to by God, first in the words of a child, then in those of St. Paul. Faith comes through hearing—not hearing words God spoke long ago, not hearing about God, but hearing God speak now. The scene in the garden is not a "religious experience" in the sense of William James or of Eastern religions: it is by its very nature a linguistic, temporal experience. And so the problem of the second half of the *Confessions* fits the model of Augustine's conception of the pursuit of wisdom: faith seeking understanding. What he now wants to know is how what he has experienced in faith is to be understood; and that means to understand what the relation of God to the temporal world is.

And that is why the second half of the *Confessions* is dominated by his reflections, first on the problem of memory (book 10) and then on the problem of the relation between God and the temporal world. And where else should one look, if faith seeks understanding, but in the divine revelation of how this world of temporality came to be, namely in Genesis? In those human, temporalized words of scripture, the timeless Word speaks to us and tells us how the world is related to God.

While the center of the narrative, "autobiographical" books is in book 5, in the encounter with Faustus, the center of the whole of the thirteen books is book 7, which neatly demarcates the two philosophical problems of God's transcendence and his acting in time, his Word becoming flesh.

If we return from these dizzying heights to the questions with which we began, it seems fair to say that the Christian understanding of the relation of the world, of the whole, to the divine is a rejection of the classical problematic. It is not accidental that Cicero's critique of ancient religiousness could be taken over by Christian writers and used in the struggle with that form of religiousness. Only much later, in the modern period, when religiousness becomes thought of as the "religious hypothesis," [25] when faith is conceived of (and conceives of itself) as an opinion about the existence of a divine entity, and when myth and superstition become the constituents of "positive" as opposed to natural religion (Lessing), do the classical criticisms of Plato, Aristotle, and Cicero become again as powerful as they once were.

But it is a measure of the inadequacy of the understanding of the modern period that Augustine's great work should have become the "autobiography" of a sinful, guilt-ridden soul.

NOTES

1. Cicero, *De natura deorum* 3.28, quoted from the Loeb translation (Cambridge, Mass.: Harvard University Press, 1979).

2. St. Thomas Aquinas, *Summa theologiae* 2.2.1.8.

3. Henri-Irénée Marrou, *Saint Augustin et la fin de la culture antique* (Paris: Boccard, 1938), 75. Twenty years later he retracted that global judgment, conceding that the *City of God* and the *De Trinitate* were constructed with some care.

4. Ibid., 63, 64. Cf. Gerald Bonner, *St. Augustine of Hippo* (Philadelphia: Westminster Press, 1963), 49: "What gives unity to the apparently unrelated elements of the book . . . [is that] all these are written to the greater glory of God." Bonner describes the tenth book as dealing with "the writer's spiritual and psychological condition at the time of composition" (47). Although this is commonly said, it ignores the first two-thirds of that book, which deals with the philosophical problem of memory.

5. John J. O'Meara, *The Young Augustine* (New York: Alba House, 1965), 13, 44.

6. Ibid., 11. Ann Hartle, *The Modern Self in Rousseau's "Confessions": A Reply to St. Augustine* (Notre Dame: Notre Dame University Press, 1983), 136: "the structural parallel between Rousseau's *Confessions* and Augustine's *Confessions* has at its center the 'conversions' recounted in Book 8 of each work. The conversion marks a radical turning point for both Augustine and Rousseau" (cf. 26, 27). These are, of course, hardly isolated instances. It suffices to mention the magisterial work of Pierre Courcelles on the garden scene (*Recherche sur les "Confessions" de Saint Augustin* [Paris: Boccard, 1968]).

7. St. Augustine, *Confessions* 4.3.6. This is one case where the English sense of "the exception proves the rule" is correct.

8. The friend has previously repudiated Augustine because of the latter's scorn of his friend's baptism; that is why the death was especially painful to Augustine. Toward the end of book 4 (4.15.26) he notes that he was unaware of his "exile" from his "fellow citizens."

9. So far as he tells us here, no one accompanies him to Rome.

10. Augustine carefully marks the significance of this turning point by speaking for the first time of God's acting on him, turning him about, so to speak. Chapter 8 of book 5 begins: "It was by your action upon me that I was moved to go to Rome" (Egisti ergo mecum, ut mihi persuaderetur Romanum pergere). His ascent begins from this point.

11. "Concupiscentia carnis et concupiscentia oculorum et ambitione saeculi" (*Confessions* 10.30.41). Cf. St. Augustine, *De vera religione* 38.69ff.

12. This is not the only reason; also involved are the roles of friendship in happiness (cf. Cicero, *De finibus* 1 and 2) and of pleasure (Augustine has just taken a concubine to replace his departed "common-law wife").

13. Cf. "Unde malum" in 7.7.11, 7.7.18, and—for the last time—7.16.22. For God as incorporeal truth, cf. 7.10.16 and 7.20.26.

14. Cf. "dirrupisti vincula mea" (8.1.1) and "de vinculo . . . concubitus . . . exemeris" (8.6.13).

15. *Confessions* 1.11.17 and 9.1.1. There are eighteen references to Christ in books 2–8, but no direct address. There are no mentions of Christ in the section covering his Manichaean years (i.e., 3.6–5.11).

16. Cf. 11.6.8, where Augustine asserts that God's voice from the clouds at Jesus' baptism must have been the voice of a creature.

17. Augustine is quite conscious of the fact that his story will be read on different levels by different kind of readers: cf. 1.6.10, 5.5.9, 10.12.19, 11.31.41. This rhetoric of discreteness in expression has multiple motives. For example, Demetrius (citing Theophrastus): "not all possible points should be punctiliously and tediously elaborated, but some should be left to the comprehension and inference of the hearer, who when he perceives what you have left unsaid becomes not only your hearer but your witness. . . . For he thinks himself intelligent because you have afforded him the means of showing his intelligence. It seems like a slur on your hearer to tell him everything as though he were a simpleton" (*On Style* 4.222, Loeb translation [Cambridge, Mass.: Harvard University Press, 1982]).

18. Augustine misquotes (deliberately, I think) the Johannine text: "ego sum via veritatis et vita." Msgr. John Ryan's translation, which I have generally followed, is one of the very few that do not translate this back into what it "ought" to be.

19. Etienne Gilson, *History of Christian Philosophy in the Middle Ages* (New York: Random House, 1955), 77.

20. This is why the passage to what is "Unborn, Unbecome, Uncreated, Unformed" (Buddha) or to Brahman is an escape from the illusion of time. Temporality is not, for Buddhism or Hinduism, the medium of the presence of the Abiding.

21. "To all the things that stand around the doors of my flesh I said, 'Tell me of my God. Although you are not he, tell me something of him.' With a mighty voice they cried out, 'He made us'" (10.6.9).

22. Note that Augustine here places hearing before vision.

23. Gilson says, "The fact that memory transcends time explains its importance in the doctrine of Augustine" (*History of Philosophy*, 593). But memory in the sense used here (as distinguished from the Platonic) does not transcend time but rather the *nunc* and thereby temporalizes human existence.

24. As he says in book 7 he did not yet understand the meaning of "the Word made flesh" (7.19.25).

25. David Hume, *Dialogues concerning Natural Religion* 12. Cf. ibid., 1: "Locke seems to have been the first Christian who ventured openly to assert that *faith* was nothing but a species of *reason;* that religion was only a branch of philosophy." In sharp contrast is that far more perceptive critic, Nietzsche: "To reduce being a Christian, Christianess, to a holding something to be true, to a mere phenomenality of consciousness, means to negate Christianess" (*The Anti-Christ* 39, in Friedrich Nietzsche, *Twilight of the Idols/The Anti-Christ* [Harmondsworth: Penguin, 1986], 151).

THREE

Augustine and the "Problem" of Time

Genevieve Lloyd

The connection between the idea of narrative and philosophical reflection on time and consciousness goes back as far as Augustine's *Confessions*—that remarkable venture into autobiography written by the bishop of Hippo around AD 396. What philosophers most often quote from Augustine's discussion of time in book II of the *Confessions* is his famous remark that he knows well enough what time is, as long as no one asks him, but is reduced to bewilderment if asked to define it.[1] His positive account of time is usually regarded as something of an oddity—a curiously implausible reduction of the reality of time to the workings of the human psyche. Time, he argues, rather than being an "objective" feature of the world, is a "distension" of the soul. The mind stretches itself out, as it were, embracing past and future in a mental act of attention and regulating the flow of future into past. Taken in isolation from the autobiographical reflections that frame it in the *Confessions,* such claims about time do seem implausible. As a theory of the nature of time, such a radical psychologizing of its reality must seem counterintuitive.

Although Augustine presents his view as a theory of time's nature, his interest in that question is framed by reflection on the experiential and emotional dimensions of being in time. Such concerns are, perhaps all too readily, now commonly regarded as extraneous to philosophical inquiry; but they are integral to Augustine's treatment of time. In the *Confessions* he attempts to take account of time as it bears on human existence—to engage with the ways in which time makes him "a problem to himself." The work tells the story of his gradual coming to understand what it is to be a consciousness in time. If we are to understand fully what he has to say about time, we must take seriously the fact that it occurs in the context of an autobiography. The philosophical content of the work is interwoven with its narrative form.

The relations between God's eternity and the temporality of the individual soul, for example, can seem extraneous to Augustine's treatment of the nature of time—a theological excursion irrelevant to philosophical content. But to ignore the theological context is also to set aside the literary structure of the work. The central significance of his religious belief is enacted in the narrative form of the work as a whole. Augustine, in the role of the narrator, is able to see each event in relation to a recounted past. Everything finds its place in relation to the crucial event—his conversion to Christianity. The narrator's complete vision here represents the human approximation to the complete knowledge of a changing reality, which knowledge Augustine attributes to God. In the position of the narrative's protagonist, Augustine sees his life only in a confused way. His past is continually reshaped by the addition of new experience and by expectations of the future that are continually revised in the light of that experience. In the position of the narrator, in contrast, he presents himself as seeing each event in a fixed relation to a past that has achieved its final form. From this Godlike perspective, the self has a completeness and stability that the protagonist cannot attain. Through the act of retrospective narration Augustine is able to achieve a view of himself as object that eludes him in the midst of the life he narrates. His narrated life takes on a unity, a wholeness.

The narrator has knowledge denied to the protagonist of how the story goes on. He is able to bestow unity and meaning on the events of a life directly experienced as fragmentation. The autobiographical form of the work can in this way be seen as an attempt to achieve an elusive goal that being in time puts out of reach. God is envisaged as having a completeness of self-knowledge in which no aspect or element of his being remains absent or opaque. The human mind, in contrast, cannot have it all at once. But the distension of the soul—epitomized for Augustine in memory and enacted in narrative—functions as a semblance, in the midst of time, of the everpresence of eternity. Past, present, and future, in Augustine's theory of time, are held together in a unifying act of attention; and this extended present of the act of attention—modeled on God's eternal self-presence—finds expression in the autobiographical form of the work as a whole.

To properly understand what Augustine has to say about time, then, one must see the interconnections between philosophical content and literary form. But the content of earlier sections of the work is also important to understanding what he is about in internalizing time to the mind. The philosophical discussion in book 11 is not an answer to a timeless philosophical question as to the nature of time. It is rather an attempt to resolve a problem posed to consciousness by the human experience of time. What exactly is Augustine's "problem," and how does it relate to the nature of time? To answer these questions we must examine both his account in earlier sections of the *Confessions* of the ways in which he has become a "problem to himself" and the philosophical picture to which he responds with his daring assertion that time is nothing more than the distension of the soul.

LIVING WITH "HALF A SOUL": AUGUSTINE ON GRIEF

Augustine describes two major episodes of grief in the *Confessions*. First, in book 4 he recounts his youthful response to the death of a friend. The description of grief is here interwoven with reflections on friendship that echo themes from the concluding books of Aristotle's *Nicomachean Ethics,* especially the idea of the friend as another self. Because he lives outside himself, pouring out his soul "like water upon sand" (4.8), the young Augustine experiences grief as a disorienting loss of self. He becomes a puzzle to himself—a stranger, tormented in his own country and finding even his own home "a grotesque abode of misery." Familiar places become unbearable in the experience of this new, strange absence, for they no longer whisper "Here he comes!" as they would have, had he only been absent a while (4.4).

In the immediate experience of grief Augustine cannot understand what is happening in his own soul. Reflecting on it now in memory, he comes to an understanding of what was lacking in his apparent possession of selfhood before his friend's death. His misery, it now seems to him, came from his soul's being directed outside himself—from its being "tethered by the love of things that cannot last," so that it is then agonized to lose them (4.6). Reflections on this past loss makes visible flaws in his early loves. He had loved something mortal as though it could never die, as something more than human. This defect of love has rendered his soul "a burden, bruised and bleeding," which he cannot set down. The loss of a friend loved as another self makes the soul a burden to itself. But this loss only makes visible a wretched state of separation from himself that was already there, fueled by the attachment to something external. "Neither the charm of the countryside nor the sweet scents of a garden could soothe it. . . . Everything that was not what he had been was dull and distasteful. Where could I go, yet leave myself behind? Was there any place where I should not be a prey to myself?" (4.7).

With self bound up with what is external, grief becomes intermingled with the fear of death. Augustine is obsessed by a "strange feeling," quite the opposite of the altruistic desire of friends ready to die for each other's sake. Sick and tired of living, he is yet afraid to die. Death, which has snatched away his friend, seems the most terrible of enemies, likely to seize all others too without warning. He wonders that other men should live when his friend is dead, having loved him as though he would never die. And still more he wonders that he himself, having been his "second self," the "half of his soul," should remain alive. "I felt that our two souls had been as one, living in two bodies, and life to me was fearful because I did not want to live with only half a soul. Perhaps this, too, is why I shrank from death, for fear that one whom I had loved so well might then be wholly dead" (4.6).

Augustine is delivered from this early grief by the passage of time and the possibilities it brings of new friendship. Time, which never stands still or passes idly without effects upon the feelings, works its wonders on the mind. As it passes, it fills Augustine with fresh hope and new thoughts to remember. Little by little it pieces him together again by means of the old pleasures he had once enjoyed. But time, by bringing new attachments, brings also new vulnerability—new captivations of the heart by the "huge fable" of friendship—"the long-drawn lie which does not die with the death of any one friend" (4.8).

Augustine's powerful evocation of the pleasures of friendship in book 4, section 8, is double edged. The mutual learning and teaching, the laughter and kindness, the shared pleasures of books, the regrets at absence, the glad welcomes of return are tokens of affection between friends. Signs read on the face and in the eyes, spoken by the tongue and displayed in countless acts of kindness, all "kindle a blaze to melt our hearts and weld them into one." But they hold the "germ of sorrow still to come." The delights of friendship, especially those centering on the spoken word, are woven into a fable—a long-drawn lie that our minds are "always itching to hear, only to be defiled by its adulterous caress" (4.8). Augustine loved this fable instead of God. The passage of time, though it may heal a specific grief, is itself now seen as a source of anguish—of separation and internal fragmentation of the self.

What the passage of time cannot deliver, however, Augustine finds in his own activity of narration. Reflection on memory—foreshadowing the later, more extended philosophical discussion of time—yields the kind of self-knowledge in which he sees his deliverance from the anguish of temporal experience. Memory, a "sort of stomach for the mind" in which grief can be reflected on without grief, allows him to recover himself (10.14). Through self-reflection he turns away from the love of changeable things—from friends conceived as other selves—to his own self. His reflections on past grief, and on the memory through which he is able to reflect thus, here prepare the way for the discovery of the distension of the soul, through which he will both understand and escape from the distress of the temporal. Time's destructive flight into nonexistence is countered by the act of memory. Having found in his own soul the act of attention that approximates in its all-encompassing presence the "standing present" of eternity, he will now be free to love changeable and mortal things in God, who is never lost. No longer clinging to the external and thus clasping sorrow to itself, his soul is freed to a new joy.

The second major episode of grief recounted in Augustine's narrative concerns the death of Monica, his mother. It is separated from the earlier grief by the crucial event that forms the pivotal point in the *Confessions*—his conversion to Christianity. He now knows of the "eternal wisdom" that creates "all things that ever have been and all that are yet to be" while yet it itself "simply is," subject to neither pastness nor futurity. Monica's death is preceded by a conversation in which Monica speaks with Augustine of his eternal wisdom. They felt their minds touch it, he tells us, for one fleeting instant, before returning to the sound of their own speech, in which each word has a beginning and an end (9.10).

Enlightened by this moment of contact with eternity, Augustine, as we might expect, presents his second grief as in marked contrast with the earlier one, although his immediate emotional response to it is, to his chagrin, not fully in accord with what he now knows of time and eternity. The "great wave of sorrow" (9.12) that surges in his heart is, he thinks, at odds with his religious beliefs; and his misery at finding himself so weak a victim of these human emotions becomes an added source of sorrow. Grieved by his own feelings, he is tormented by a "twofold agony" (9.12). He is plunged again into the restlessness and oppressiveness of grief. But little by little memory returns, bringing back to him his old feelings about his mother accompanied by the comfort of tears.

In his earlier discussion of grief Augustine reflected on why tears are sweet to those grieving and found no clear answer. Weeping now becomes the expression of a hope that eluded him at the death of his friend. "I had no hope that he would come to life again, nor was this what I begged for through my tears. I simply grieved and wept, for I was heartbroken and had lost my joy" (4.5). In that context tears are sweet only because in his heart's desire they take the place of his friend (4.4). His new grief, in contrast, is integrated into his own confession and transformed into prayer for his mother's soul. Memory is gathered up in a move forward in the hope of eternal life.

Augustine's newfound religious faith makes of this grief an experience different from his earlier hopelessness in the face of loss, even if his emotions lag behind his intellect. The two griefs express different responses to time. In the second episode the destructive passage of time is framed by the soul's journey toward eternity. Memory of what he has lost is no longer a source of misery but a delight in the life that held the seeds of transformation into contact with the eternal. Eternity is here not an empty abstract contrast with the reality of time but a fullness of presence to be attained after death—a fullness toward which the soul strains during life and of which it gets occasional glimpses. This shift in the emotional resonances of grief foreshadows the later discussion of time. The soul's stretching out in memory, though itself a source of distress at the lack of self-presence, becomes—through the narrative act, centered on the significance of his conversion—the basis for a reaching out of a different kind, from time into eternity. The reflections on grief foreshadow Augustine's discovering in the distension of the soul an image of eternity. The "problem" of time is resolved by finding unity amidst fragmentation. This unifying of the fragments of experience is epitomized in memory, articulated through metaphors drawn from the unity of speech, and acted out in the autobiographical narration.

Memory represents for Augustine the soul's inward turning, away from the delights of the world grasped through the senses, to search for the good and the eternal within itself. The search echoes the famous passages in Plato's *Symposium* describing the soul's ascent from things of sense toward the intelligible Forms known through the higher faculties of the soul. In Augustine's version of this journey memory represents a higher stage than sense, marking the crucial inward turning that will yield the desired contact with the eternal. To reach God, he thinks, he must carry self-reflection from sense, which he shares with the animals, on the extraordinary human power of memory. He compares memory to a "great field or a spacious palace," a "storehouse for countless images of all kinds which are conveyed to it by the senses" (10.8). In its "vast cloisters" are the sky, the earth, the sun, ready at his summons. But memory, as well as bringing the world into the self, also contains the self. He finds himself, along with other things, within this "vast, immeasurable sanctuary"; and yet it is a faculty of his soul (10.8).

Reflection on memory makes the self an object of wonder—an astonishment previously reserved for the contemplation of the world with its "high mountains, the huge waves of the sea, the broad reaches of rivers, the ocean that encircles the world, or the stars in their courses" (10.8). Although the soul's search takes it beyond memory to intellect, in some ways memory best represents the crucial shift to the self, encompassing in its cloisters even the supposedly higher faculty of intellect. For Augustine, memory retains a certain primacy in understanding the nature of the mind. Mind and memory, he says, are one and the same (10.14). To understand memory is to understand the self: "I am working hard in this field, and the field of my labours is my own self" (10.16). He has become a problem to himself—a problem to be resolved through the investigation of his self, his memory, his mind. Awe-inspiring though the profound power of memory is, it is identified with his mind, with himself.

> What, then, am I, my God? What is my nature? A life that is ever varying, full of change, and of immense power. The wide plains of my memory and its innumerable caverns and hollows are full beyond compute of countless things of all kinds. . . . My mind has the freedom of them all. I can glide from one to the other. I can probe deep into them and never find the end of them. This is the power of memory! This is the great force of life in living man, mortal though he is. (10.17)

Intellect may transcend that form of memory that retains sensory images, grasping rather "the facts themselves" (10.10). But even this achievement of intellect is framed by memory. The power of intellect resides just in its capacity to gather things that, although muddled and confused, are already contained in memory: "once they have been dispersed, I have to collect them again, and this is the derivation of the word *cogitare* which means *to think* or *to collect one's thoughts*" (10.11). Memory, with its capacity to make all things present, yields the clue to the idea of eternity. It is like a mental replica of the world, but it contains more—intellect, and even God himself. It thus offers possibilities of understanding and dealing with time that elude the soul in its thought about the physical world as object. Even the immutable God has deigned to be present in memory and forms there a "safe haven" for the mind. Memory provides the material for reflection that allows Augustine to find in God the "gathering-place" for his "scattered parts"; and as a "sort of stomach for the mind," retaining experience without its original "taste," it allows the reflection that is impeded by the immediacy of emotion. Memory and self-knowledge thus belong together. The turning away from world to self it epitomizes yields a self-knowledge in which Augustine will find the divine. The self becomes visible through a kind of detachment—it draws back from the mindless world to turn its gaze on consciousness. It is the incapacity of that mindless world of physical motion to reveal what is involved in being a mind, capable of understanding time and eternity, that Augustine stresses in his discussion in book II of the nature of time. Let us now look at his own account of what it is to be in time in relation to what he sees as the inadequacies of the Aristotelian treatment of the relations between time and consciousness.

THE "MEASURE OF MOTION": AUGUSTINE AND ARISTOTLE

Augustine's psychologizing of time aims both to secure the reality of time and to resolve puzzles about its measurement. On either side of the present, he reasons, lies an abyss of nonexistence. And even the present, in abstraction from the mind's attention, collapses internally into a nonexistent future and an equally nonexistent past, on either side of a durationless instant in which nothing can happen. His arguments for internalizing the reality of time to the mind center on puzzles about measurement. What, he asks, do we measure when we measure time? Not the future; for it does not yet exist. Nor do we measure the past, for it no longer exists. Do we then measure time "as it is passing"? But if so, while we are measuring it, where is it coming from, what is it passing through, and where is it going? It can, it seems, only be coming from the future, passing through the present, and going into the past. "In other words, it is coming out of what does not yet exist, passing through what has no duration, and moving into what no longer exists" (II.21).

We are left then with a paradoxical passage from nonexistence, through a fleeting, existence-bestowing "present," into nonexistence again. The present's fragile hold on reality, moreover, is itself encroached upon by the surrounding, voracious nonexistence of future and past. The measurement of time in the fleeting present, as it passes, cannot be insulated from the puzzles that beset the measurement of nonexistent past and future. The only time that can be called present is an instant—if we can conceive of such a thing—that cannot be divided even into the most minute fractions. However, a point of time as small as this passes so rapidly from the future to the past that its duration is without length; for, if its duration were prolonged, it could be divided into past and future. When it is present, then, it has no duration. But such a present can hardly be thought of as bestowing reality on that strange being or non-being that comes out of, and vanishes into, nowhere. There is for Augustine another dimension to the implication of the present in the nonexistence of past and future. The present itself participates in non-being; for if it were always present and never moved on to become past, Augustine reasons, it would be not time but eternity. If, therefore, the present is time only by reason of the fact that it moves on to become the past, how can we say that even the present "is" when the reason it is is that it is not to be? In other words, we cannot rightly say that time is, except by reason of its impending state of non-being.

From all this we might expect Augustine to adopt a skeptical attitude toward the reality of time. These puzzles indeed echo the temporal paradoxes that Aristotle discussed in the *Physics*. But Augustine's conclusion is that it must be in his own mind that he measures time. Everything that happens leaves an impression that remains after the thing itself has ceased to be. It is the impression that he measures, since it is still present when the thing itself, which makes the impression as it passes, has moved into the past. From this he moves—in a step that may well seem, from our own perspective, all too swift—to the conclusion that time itself must be something mental. "Either, then, this is what time is, or else I do not measure time at all" (11.27).

From the consideration of time's measurement, then, Augustine derives a shift in the understanding of its nature. From seeing past and future as nonexistent times, he moves to the claim that what we call past, present, and future are not really three different "times." Rather, there are three kinds of present: a present of past things—memory; a present of present things—direct perception; and a present of future things—expectations. But this distinction between three presents gives way to a transformed sense of the present that accommodates the presents of memory and expectation in an all-embracing act of attention. The mind's attention persists, and through it that which is to be passes toward the state in which it is to be no more.

Taken as an analysis of the nature of time, all this may well seem counterintuitive. Augustine presents his problem as understanding the fundamental nature of time and what power it has. But his description of the passage from expectation through perception into memory seems to demand an objective temporal sequence, in which the states can be said to precede or succeed one another. However, there is more going on here than a misguided attempt to totally absorb the reality of time into his own mind. The force of Augustine's remark "Either, then, this is what time is, or else I do not measure time at all" is that, if time is not integral to consciousness, then it is as nothing to him. What may seem a non sequitur deriving the nature of time from consideration of its measurement takes on a different aspect when seen in the context of the view of the relationship between time and measurement Augustine is rejecting—the Aristotelian definition of time as the measure of motion. From that, Augustine is suggesting, it is impossible to derive an adequate understanding of what it is for consciousness to be in time. A brief look at the discussion of time in Aristotle's *Physics* will clarify what kind of problem it is to which Augustine's talk of time as a distension of the mind is meant to offer a solution and why that problem cannot be adequately addressed within the confines of the Aristotelian definition.

In book 4 of the *Physics* Aristotle presents some considerations about time that could, he suggests, make one suspect that time does not exist at all, or "barely and in an obscure way." His formulation of the dilemma is similar to Augustine's. One part of time "has been and is not," while the other "is going to be and is not yet." Yet time is made up of these apparently nonexistent parts; and one would naturally suppose that "what is made up of things which do not exist could have no share in reality." Further, if a divisible thing is to exist, it is necessary that all or some of its parts exist. "But of time, some parts have been, while others have to be, and no part of it *is*, though it is divisible."[2]

From Aristotle's presentation of the paradoxes, it is clear that he does not intend them to be accepted as showing the unreality of time, although he does not offer any explicit solutions to them. His own treatment of time ties its reality securely to that of motion. Time is not movement, but it is also not independent of movement. Aristotle defines it somewhat cryptically as "number of motion in respect of 'before' and 'after' " (4.11.219b2). Time is "movement in so far as it admits of enumeration"—what is countable in movement. Time, then, is a kind of number, provided we understand this, he insists, not in the sense of that with which we count but rather in the sense of what is counted. The "nows" involved in this enumeration are to be understood not as parts of time but rather as boundaries of temporal intervals. Time is both made continuous by the "now" and divided at it, just as a point both connects and terminates length—the beginning of one and the end of another.

Any idea of time as made up of a succession of nows is foreign to Aristotle's way of thinking of time. The now can be thought of either as a boundary of intervals of time, similar to the point's role as spatial border, or as the number that measures motion. But the identification with number is only partial. Being a boundary, it cannot be detached from what it numbers in the way that the number ten can be detached from the horses it numbers when we refer to ten horses. Since the instants picked out as nows are for Aristotle not parts of time, he is able to sidestep the skeptical paradoxes about time's existence: "what is bounded by the 'now' is thought to be time—we may assume this" (4.11.219a29).

Having defined time in terms of movement and measurement, Aristotle goes on to offer a definition of being in time. To be in time means that movement—both it and its essence—is measured by time; and he thinks it is clear that "to be in time" has the same meaning for other things also: namely, that their being should be measured by time. To "be in time" means either "to exist when time exists" or to be "contained by time as things in place are contained by place" (4.12.221a10–20). That which is in time necessarily implies that there is time when it is; and it is necessary that all things in time should be "contained by time." Augustine's treatment of time can be read as expressing dissatisfaction with the implications of Aristotle's picture of time for the understanding of time's relations with mind or consciousness. He sees the Aristotelian definition of "being in time" as inadequate for understanding what it is to be a self in time.

Aristotle himself touches on the issue of time's relations with consciousness when he raises the possibility that if there were no consciousness there would be no time: "if nothing but soul, or in soul reason, is qualified to count, there would not be time unless there were soul, but only that of which time is an attribute" (4.14.223a25). On Aristotle's model mind is outside change, located as an external observer—a measurer of motion. Minds can, it is true, be said to change and hence to be in time; but there is no privileged position for soul in the definition of time other than that of the observer and measurer of change. With this model, to say that there would be no time without mind is just to say that without the possibility of measurement there would be not time but only the substratum of time—only whatever it is about motion that makes it measurable.

For Augustine some dimensions of the relations between mind and time cannot be captured in this Aristotelian picture. We will never understand the problem of time, he thinks, until we learn to examine our own consciousness, rather than treating it as the transparent performer of measurement of external change. What is problematic about our being in time is not resolvable through consideration of change in the physical world. But Augustine wants to go further—to account for the reality of time itself in terms of the capacity of consciousness to stretch itself out. It may seem, on the face of it, an extraordinary non sequitur. But it reflects a way of thinking of the relations between time and consciousness very different from that of Aristotle—a way that has some things in common with the Neoplatonism of Plotinus.

PLOTINUS: THE "STRETCHING OUT OF THE SOUL"

In the *Enneads* the third-century Greek Platonist Plotinus is strongly critical of the Aristotelian definition of time as the measurement of motion. Such approaches, he says, do not really get us to the nature of time. "It comes to this: we ask 'What is time?' and we are answered 'Time is the extension of Movement in Time.' "[3] There are great difficulties, he thinks, even in making the identification of time with any kind of measure. Does such a measure itself have magnitude, like a footrule? Time would then be understood as a line traversing the path of movement. But if it thus shares in movement, how can it be the measure of movement? Why should the traversing line be the measure rather than the movement itself? And why should the mere presence of a number give us time if it is not given by the fact of movement? Time must be something more than the mere number of movement.

Some of Plotinus's criticisms seem to depend on the interpretation of the idea of time as measure that Aristotle explicitly set aside—the identification of time with number in the sense of what we measure with rather than what is measurable in motion, the measurable aspect of change. Plotinus's insistence that to understand time we must think of "a combined thing," a "measured movement," seems to come close to Aristotle's own observation that time, unlike number, is not detachable from what it measures. But the more substantive aspect of Plotinus's rejection of the identification of time with measurement concerns the relationship between time and the soul. For him, it is not as measurer that soul is essential to the reality of time. "It is we that must create Time out of the concept and nature of progressive derivation, which remained latent in the Divine Beings" (3.7.11). But the "we" here does not refer to calculating, measuring intellects. Time for Plotinus depends on soul in a deeper, more metaphysical way that makes movement itself imbued with soul. Soul is manifested in movement, not just present to it as external measurer of a soulless substratum of time.

Plotinus's way of thinking of soul has its background in cosmological ideas developed in Plato's *Timaeus* and rejected by Aristotle in the *De anima*. But Plotinus develops the Platonic "world soul" in ways that Plato did not, giving it explicit connections with the nature of time and change. In the *Timaeus* time, though subject to change, is created to a pattern of the changeless. Soul interfuses and envelops the world; and this presence of soul is prior to the creation of time. The creator, the story goes, rejoicing in the moving, living world creature he has made in the image of the eternal gods, determines to make the copy still more like the original—the eternal, living being. So he seeks to make the universe eternal, so far as this is possible. The everlasting nature of the ideal being cannot be bestowed in its fullness on something created. So he resolves to make a "moving image of eternity" (37d). When he sets the heavens in order, he makes an eternal image, but one "moving according to number," while eternity itself rests in unity. And this image we call time.

The philosophical implications of the *Timaeus*'s story of time as the moving image of eternity are not entirely clear. It suggests that there is some movement and change in the world independent of time—that what time adds is ordered movement. Time and the heavens begin together—framed after the pattern of the eternal nature. The creation of time is the creation of orderly motion—predictable, law governed, and hence fit to convey something of the nature of the eternal. In this picture the presence of soul in the world is not particularly tied to the nature of time. The idea of time as the moving image of eternity is not specifically connected with that of the movement of the world soul that diffuses the whole of creation.

In Plotinus's version time and soul are much more closely connected. In the first *Ennead* he describes as "apt" the reference to time as a "mimic" of eternity (1.5.7). But his version of time as a representation of eternity suggests an active mimesis rather than a passive image made by an external creator. And what makes the idea apt for Plotinus is in some respects the opposite of its Platonic role. For Plato the associations of time as image of eternity are with order, predictability, permanence. Time, as the image of eternity, bestows something of its permanence on the disorderly change of a world lacking true temporal order. For Plotinus there is a darker side to the idea of mimicry. The emphasis is on the introduction of transience where before there was permanence. Time is aptly described as the mimic of eternity in that it "seeks to break up in its fragmentary flight the permanence of its exemplar." Whatever time "seizes and steals to itself" of the permanent in eternity is annihilated—"saved only in so far as in some degree it still belongs to eternity, but wholly destroyed if it be unreservedly absorbed into time." Time as mimic is time the destroyer. This twist to the Platonic idea becomes clearer in Plotinus's fuller discussion of time in the third *Ennead*. Time as the "representation in image" of eternity, he says there, can be clearly apprehended through understanding its exemplar, though we could also proceed in the other direction—from an understanding of time "upwards" to the awareness of eternity, the "Kind" that time images (3.7.1). Our awareness of eternity is crucial in Plotinus's account of time. Time, rather than being the measure of change, or even a feature of change as measurable, is a product of soul. It is a mimesis performed by soul in response not to the perception of change but rather to the eternal.

Soul, in the form in which it figures here, is not "we," who might—in the Aristotelian account—be said to measure change, but something closer to Plato's world soul. But the participation of individual minds in that soul is manifested by our awareness of eternity. We participate in the soul whose mimicry of eternity produces time. Eternity is for Plotinus thus not "alien" to time. "What understanding can there be failing some point of contact? And what contact could there be with the utterly alien?" (3.7.7). But if we do have some understanding of eternity, we must, he reasons, have some part or share in it. And how is this possible to us who exist in time? The whole question, he thinks, turns on the distinction between "being in time" and "being in eternity"; and this is best understood by probing the nature of time. To explore the nature of time Plotinus proceeds to devise a fiction, to tell a story of the origin of time. Something thus, he says, the story must run: time lay, though not yet as time, in the "All-Soul," the active principle that aimed at something more than its present. It stirred from its rest and the cosmos stirred with it.

> "And we (the active principle and the Cosmos), stirring to a ceaseless succession, to a next, to the discrimination of identity and the establishment of ever new difference, traversed a portion of the outgoing path and produced an image of Eternity, produced Time."
>
> For the Soul contained an unquiet faculty, always desirous of translating elsewhere what it saw in the Authentic Realm, and it could not bear to retain within itself all the dense fullness of its possession. (3.7.11)

Time is seen as originating in the unfolding of soul—the unwinding of "unity self-gathered." Soul, in "going forth from itself," fritters its unity away, advancing into a "weaker greatness." Soul lays aside its eternity and clothes itself with time.

> For the Cosmos moves only in Soul—the only Space within the range of the All open to move in—and therefore its movement has always been in the Time which inheres in Soul. . . .
>
> Time, then, is contained in differentiation of Life; the ceaseless forward movement of Life brings with it unending Time; and Life as it achieves its stages constitutes past Time. (3.7.11)

Time, Plotinus concludes, can be defined as "the life of the Soul in movement as it passes from one stage of act or experience to another." Eternity is life in repose, unchanging and self-identical, always endlessly complete. And time is the image of this eternity. On this version of the Platonic idea of time as the image of eternity, the "mimicry" is something acted out by soul—an unfolding, a stretching out. Time is not conceived as outside of soul; nor is it a "sequence or succession" to soul. It is "a thing seen upon Soul, inherent, co-eval to it." But, although time is not independent of soul, this does not mean that Plotinus regards it as merely subjective. It is a "certain expanse," a quantitative, "outgoing phase" of the life of the soul. If life could conceivably revert, he says, to the "perfect unity," time and the heavens would end at once. If soul were to cease its outgoing, if it became once more turned to the "tranquilly stable," nothing would then exist but eternity. If the soul withdrew, sinking into itself again—into its primal unity—time would disappear (3.7.12).

Movement as a feature of soul here takes precedence over physical motion in understanding the nature of time. It cannot be reasonable, Plotinus argues, to recognize succession in the case of soulless movement, and so to associate time with that, while ignoring succession and the reality of time in "the Movement from which the other takes its imitative existence" (3.7.13). It is the "self-actuated movement" of soul that provides the basis for the reality of time, creating a sequence by which each instant no sooner comes into existence than it passes into the next. Whereas for Aristotle soul entered into the definition of time only through the implicit reference to mind carried by the idea of measurement, for Plotinus the time of the cosmos imitates the movement of soul, just as the latter in turn imitates the eternal.

For Plotinus, then, time, as the life of the soul, is prior to the time of the cosmos, the time of physical motion. There is a "soul movement" that constitutes time and hence cannot strictly be said to be contained by it. Contrary to Aristotle, for Plotinus not all being in time involves being contained by time. We treat the cosmic movement as overarched by that of the soul and bring it under time, he says. Yet we do not set under time that soul movement itself with all its endless progression. The explanation of this paradox is simply that the soul movement responds not to time but to eternity, and the "descent towards Time" begins with this soul movement that "made Time and harbours Time as a concomitant to its Act" (3.7.13).

It comes easily to us to think of movement in the soul as merely metaphorical—an analog of the literal movement of bodies. But for Plotinus the movement of souls—as well as that of the "All-Soul" in which they participate—is prior to the movement of bodies. He makes it clear that this applies to movements in the individual soul no less than to the All-Soul in an interesting "supplementary observation" at the end of his discussion of time in the seventh section of the third *Ennead*. Take a man walking, he says, and observe the advance he has made. That gives us the "quantity of movement he is employing," and when we know this, represented by the ground traversed by his feet, we know also the movement that exists in the man himself before the feet move. We must relate the body, carried forward during a given period of time, to a certain quantity of movement causing the progress and to the time it takes, and that again to the movement, equal in extension, within the man's soul. He then goes on to consider the "movement within the Soul," asking to what we are to refer it. Let your choice fall where it may, he says. From this point there is nothing but the unextended primarily existent, "the container to all else, having no container, brooking none." And as it is with the human soul, so it is with "the Soul of All." "Is Time, then, within ourselves as well?" he asks, and responds: "Time is in every Soul of the order of the All-Soul, present in like form in all; for all the Souls are the one Soul" (3.7.13).

Plotinus's shift from physical motion to the movement of the soul as the paradigm for the understanding of time is an extension of the Platonic idea of physical motion as imbued with soul. But he gives a special status to meaningful bodily movements, and especially speech, as illustrative of the idea of unity and the overcoming of fragmentation. His most famous example of bodily movement as a metaphor of the unity of the universe is the image of the dancer. Every soul, he says, has its hour—"all is set stirring and advancing as by a magician's power or by some mighty traction." "Like is destined unfailingly to like, and each moves hither or thither at its fixed moment" (4.3.13). The configurations, by their varied rhythmic movements, make up "one total dance-play" in which the limbs of the dancers are adapted to the overall plan. The whole universe is to be understood in terms of this image of unified action. It "puts its entire life into act, moving its major members with its own action and unceasingly setting them in new positions," and brings the minor members under the system as in the movements of some one living being (4.4.33).

Plotinus elaborates the theme of soul's presence in the world through other analogies that are drawn from the spoken word and illustrate the unity and indivisibility of soul itself. He stresses, as Augustine will do later, the difference that form and meaning make to mere sounds. Speech is subject to measurement, but only insofar as it is sound. Its essential nature resides not in what makes it quantifiable like other sounds but in its significance. As significant sound it involves both activity and passivity—both action and experience. In addition to the motion involved in the act of speech there is also a countermotion. We can think of speech as both action upon air as substratum and as experience within that substratum (6.1.5). These shifts between activity and passivity, action and experience, make speech for Plotinus a fitting illustration of the unity in variety that characterizes the presence of soul. Whatever in the world is "apt for soul" will possess itself of it, just as an ear within range will catch and comprehend a spoken word. From the one identical presence, meaning will be derived by more than one hearer. The spoken word is entire at every point in the appropriate space, every listener catching the whole alike. Its sound is evidently not "strung along the air section to section." Why then, he asks, should we not think of soul as omnipresent, indwelling at every point in the totality of the All, rather than "extended in broken contact, part for part?" Having entered into such bodies as are apt for it, soul is like the spoken word. Present in the air, before that entering, it is like the speaker about to speak. Even when embodied, it remains at once "the speaker and the silent" (6.4.12).

These illustrations drawn from speech, imperfect though they are, carry, Plotinus thinks, a "serviceable similitude" to soul. It is equally a "self-enclosed unity"—the speaker silent—and a "principle manifested in diversity"—the speaker speaking. The analogy of the reception of the spoken word shows how soul can become present in some parts of the world and not in others, including the ambivalent presence of soul in individual human beings, just as, from a significant sound, some forms of being take sound and significance together, others only the sound, the "blank impact." The "participant newcomer," the "intruder," the "thing of beginnings in time" has made human beings become a duality, winding himself about "the Man that each of us was at first":

> Then it was as if one voice sounded, one word was uttered, and from every side an ear attended and received and there was an effective hearing, possessed through and through of what was present and active upon it: Now we have lost that first simplicity; we are become the dual thing, sometimes indeed no more than the later foisting, with the primal nature dormant and in a sense no longer present. (4.4.14)

Plotinus's picture of mind, turning back to contemplate the eternal out of which it comes, and in the process understanding its own role in the constitution of time, answers—as the Aristotelian account cannot do—to the experience of time and consciousness as intimately connected. It is this that attracts Augustine to images drawn from Plotinus. If time were what Aristotle takes it to be, he thinks, time would be as nothing to me. If the substratum of time were thus outside himself, he could not understand what is involved in his consciousness being in time. The challenge Augustine sets himself is to give an account of time's nature that will answer to his own experience of the stretching out of consciousness. Just as Plotinus retells Plato's story of time as mimic of eternity, Augustine now retells Plotinus's story. As a bald statement of the nature of time, identifying it with the distension of the soul may seem preposterous. But as a variation on a literary story, it emerges as a profound insight into what it is to be in time. The twists in Augustine's version of the tale of time allow him to extract from it a legend of recovering unity of consciousness in a journey out of time back into eternity. Having in mind that Augustine is not merely engaged in timeless reflection on time but is retelling an inherited story of its nature, origins, and power, let us now see what use he makes of the metaphors and analogies of the spoken word he took over from Plotinus.

AUGUSTINE'S ANALOGIES OF THE SPOKEN WORD

The consideration of the spoken word preoccupies Augustine throughout the *Confessions*. In the early sections of the work he pictures the phases of life as stages in acquiring the power of speech. It is through his growing awareness of this power that he knows his infancy has receded into the past. The power of speech is here a model of autonomy. Learning to speak involves acquiring a capacity for spontaneity—a self-directedness that contrasts with following a set system of instruction, as he does in learning to read. Through the spoken word he expresses his own observations and wishes. But this new autonomy brings with it new responsibilities. Speech takes him more deeply into the realm of the social—a "further step into the stormy life of human society" (1.8).

The freedom associated with the self-directedness of the spoken word has as its correlate a certain necessity. In book 3 verbal composition provides him with an analogy for the idea that things have from an inner necessity their own proper time. When he composed verses, he reflects, each verse was differently scanned. Although the act of poetry does not vary from one line to another, the location of each phrase is governed by rules. Through reflection on speech Augustine is better able to understand how self-directedness and necessity can come together in the relations between individual life and the unfolding of time. Recalling his early griefs, he reflects that things have their appointed times, rising and setting like the sun, growing until they reach perfection, then growing old and dying: "Not all reach old age, but all alike must die. When they rise, therefore, they are set upon the course of their existence, and the faster they climb towards its zenith, the more they hasten towards the point where they exist no more. This is the law they obey." The analogy of the spoken word provides the model of necessity and a unity that encompasses past, present, and future. Just as a sentence is not complete unless each word, once its syllables have been pronounced, gives way to make room for the next, so changeable, mortal things continue on their course. And if the soul loves them and wishes to be with them and "find its rest in them," it is torn by destructive desires. In these things there is no place to rest, for they do not last, passing away beyond the reach of our senses. "Indeed, none of us can lay firm hold on them even when they are with us" (4.10).

The most striking of Augustine's analogies between being in time and the spoken word comes toward the end of the discussion of time in book 11. Here we see the full significance of his reflections on the measurement of time. Suppose, he says, I am going to recite a familiar psalm. Before I begin, my faculty of expectation is engaged by the whole of it. But once I have begun, what I have "removed from the province of expectation and relegated to the past" now engages my memory. The scope of the action I am performing is divided between memory and expectation—the one looking back, the other forward to what I have still to recite. But my faculty of attention is present all the while; and what was future passes through it in the process of becoming past. The "province of memory" is extended in proportion as that of expectation is reduced until it is all absorbed into memory. Augustine goes on to extrapolate from this illustration of a mind consciously active in time to the understanding of temporal reality generally:

> What is true of the whole psalm is also true of all its parts and of each syllable. It is true of any longer action in which I may be engaged and of which the recitation of

the psalm may only be a small part. It is true of a man's whole life, of which all his actions are parts. It is true of the whole history of mankind, of which each man's life is a part. (11.28)

The illustration is preceded by another in which the reader is asked to imagine three sounds (11.27). In the first case a noise is emitted by a material body. The sound begins and we continue to hear it until it finally ceases. When is it measurable? asks Augustine. Not now that it has ceased, for it is no longer there to be measured. While it was present, then—while it was gaining some extent in time? But not in present time, for the present has no extent. This leads to the consideration of the second case, where the sound has begun but not yet ceased. It still cannot be measured; for we now lack a final point that could give us a measurable interval between beginning and end: "we measure neither the future nor the past nor the present nor time that is passing. Yet we do measure time" (11.27).

The beginnings of a resolution of the problem come when we move to consideration of not just any sound but sounds with meaning—speech. Consider, he says, the line "Deus creator omnium." He can measure the syllables as short or long, despite the fact that they are past. So what he measures is something that remains in memory. Reflection on the familiar experience of hearing significant speech shows him that the measurement of time goes on not in the physical world but in the mind. We are blinded to this by preoccupation with the idea of time as something objective—a feature of the physical world. The crucial shift that we have to perform is from the cosmological to the mental. What we measure are "impressions" that remain present despite the transition, whatever it may turn out to be, into the past. We measure the sound mentally, as though we could actually hear it. Even without opening our mouths, he points out, we can go over speech in our minds, and reflecting on this is supposed to bring about a turning away from the physical world to the mind, where we can hope to understand the true nature of time. Consideration of the spoken word helps shift attention away from the thought of physical motion in a changing world to our own being in time. Some of the points Augustine extracts from his psalm example are independent of the fact that it is a meaningful utterance rather than, say, a wordless melody. But the spoken word is for him the ultimate model of a unified temporal structure.

We will not resolve the problem of time, Augustine thinks, until we learn to examine our own consciousness rather than treat it as the transparent performer of measurement of external change. What is problematic about our being in time is not resolvable through consideration of change in the physical world. But Augustine of course wants to go further than this. Understanding the relations between the spoken word and time is supposed to reveal also the true nature of time itself. All motion—not just the self-movement involved in speech—is to be seen as measurable only in the mind; and for Augustine this means that time itself is to be understood in terms of the distension of the soul. Here his attempt to turn the mind around to its own contemplation may well be seen to have overreached itself. But it is important to see just what the shift achieves for understanding the soul's being in time. In moving from the Aristotelian external viewpoint on change to the consideration of what it is to be in the midst of understanding an act of speech we move from a passive model to an active one; and this shift gives the mind some redress against the sense of time's onslaught. Its distressing passivity in the face of time's bewildering passage—out of a nonexistent future through an extensionless present into an equally nonexistent past—is transformed into an active relegating of the future to the past. "All the while the man's attentive mind, which is present, is relegating the future to the past. The past increases in proportion as the future diminishes, until the future is entirely absorbed and the whole becomes past" (11.27).

By shifting attention away from the world of bodies that move independently of him to the world of consciousness, Augustine gains a new perspective on time. Consciousness is no longer present as a mere observer of external change but located, as it were, within movement. Change is now located in its inner life. The upshot of this shift is, in a way, to eliminate change. Future, present, and past are now accommodated into an encompassing presentness of the attending mind—a mental act that holds together a temporal reality that had previously been seen as having only the most tenuous of existences. Consciousness, rather than being located at a precarious vanishing point between the nonexistence of past and future, is now seen as encompassing the passage of future into past.

The shift that Augustine has made is from seeing consciousness as in time to seeing time as in consciousness. It is a shift we will see undone and remade throughout the subsequent philosophical tradition. In Augustine's version of this reversal of the relations between consciousness and time a crucial structural role is assigned to God. If you would understand your self in relation to time, he is saying, you will do so not by looking to the external world but rather by looking inward—to the inner world of consciousness where you can understand yourself in relation to God. If you would understand your own being in time, look not to the physical world of motion but to your own self in relation to eternity. It is through the contrast between the stretching out of consciousness and God's eternal present that you will come to understand your own being in time. For Augustine, as for Plotinus, consciousness understands itself by looking back to what it has come from—to its unfolding out from a unitary presence. The spoken word is the metaphor through which this crucial relation between time as the stretching out of consciousness and God's eternal now is to be grasped.

TIME AND ETERNITY

Augustine presents the process by which he gradually learns to turn away from the physical world to the world of consciousness as the story of his religious conversion. His turning away from the physical world to contemplate himself begins the process of turning toward God. But this is more than a tale of spiritual journeying into the ineffable. Let us look more closely at what Augustine has achieved. His way of thinking of the present is contrasted, on the one hand, with Aristotle's bounding instants—the instantaneous presents that are mere limits of motion. On the other hand it is contrasted with an "eternal present" that escapes in a different way the dilemmas of the nonexistent past and future. Aristotle's view of time, joining as it does the idea of what is measurable in motion with the idea of durationless instants by which it is measured, leaves no space for the Augustinian idea of the distension of the soul. Mind, as we have seen, enters the Aristotelian account only as the external observer and measurer of change—as the implicit presence of consciousness that is necessary to measurement. The kind of present associated with the distended soul brings time and soul together in a different way and also makes possible a point of connection with the idea of eternity that was not possible on the Aristotelian view.

The fact that our present, ever moving on to become the past, cannot be always present, as Augustine points out, prevents it from being identified with eternity. He elaborates the contrast between time and eternity—between the distension of the soul and the "eternal now" of God's knowledge—through an extension of the recitation analogy. Let us suppose, he says, a mind endowed with such great power of knowing and foreknowing that all the past and all the future were known to it as clearly as we might know a familiar psalm. Such a mind would be "awesome beyond belief" in its grasp of all that is to happen in ages yet to come. "It would know all this as surely as, when I sing the psalm, I know what I have already sung and what I have still to sing, how far I am from the beginning and how far from the end" (11.31). But such a mind would still be in time—spread, as it were, between past, present, and future. When we recite or listen to a recitation, our feelings vary and our senses are divided because we are partly anticipating words still to come and partly remembering words already sung. It is far otherwise with God, who is "eternally without change," knowing changing things without any change in his knowledge. Such a knower is not in time, and the eternal presence of his knowledge is quite different from the "present of attention" through which the future passes into the past.

The content of Augustine's eternal present is elusive. But it is clear that this lack of past and future is a very different kind of lack from that involved in the Aristotelian bounding instant, which can allow for no past or future because there can be in it no mind or soul. Here, as Ricoeur points out in his commentary on Augustine in *Time and Narrative,* there is a conceptually unbridgeable gap separating Aristotle's instants from Augustine's present.[4] The Aristotelian instant requires only that a break be made in the continuity of movement—a break that can be made anywhere. Mind functions here as an external observer of motion that does not intrinsically involve itself. The lack of past and future that characterizes Augustine's eternal present, in contrast, arises from a fullness of presence the human mind cannot achieve—not from absence of mind but from its presence in a superior form. Here again there are echoes of Plotinus. All progress of time, Plotinus says in the first *Ennead*, means the dissipation of a unity whose existence is in the present. Past and future are associated with this dissipation, which is time's essence. To think of eternity is to think of a life not made up of periods but "completely rounded, outside of all notion of time" (1.5.7). And in the third *Ennead* he associates eternity with the idea of a life ever varying, not becoming what it previously was not. Here there is no development but only actual presence—"not this now and now that other, but always all; not existing now in one mode and now in another, but a consummation without part or interval" (3.7.3). All its content is in immediate concentration "as at one point." The eternal remains identical within itself; what it is it remains forever. Nothing can make its way into this "standing present" that excludes past and future. Any imagined entrant will prove to be not alien but already integral. No ground is left for its existence but that it be what it is. So eternity, in contrast to time, involves stable existence, neither in process of change nor having changed—"pure being in eternal actuality." Here there is no future, for every then is a now. Nor is there any past, for nothing here has ever ceased to be. Here "everything has taken its stand for ever"—and "identity well pleased, we might say, to be as it is."

The idea of eternity plays not only a religious role in Augustine's thought on time but also a literary one. By projecting a construct of an alternative mode of presence, Augustine is able to sharpen his articulation of the temporal presence that characterizes human consciousness. Reflection on the idea of eternity serves to focus and intensify the experience of incompleteness and fragmentation that goes with being in time. The lack of eternity functions, as Ricoeur puts it, not simply as a limit that is thought but as a lack that is felt at the heart of temporal experience—"the sorrow proper to the negative."[5] The idea of the eternal present allows Augustine to integrate philosophical speculation on the nature of time with a more literary reflection on its power—on what is involved in the human experience of time. But it also serves to reconcile the mind by holding out an ideal of an alternative kind of consciousness with which the individual can identify. The distension of the soul that marks Augustine's separation from eternity also becomes through reflection the source of his deliverance from the distress of being in time. It becomes both the mark of the difference between human and divine consciousness and the reflection in him of the divine understanding. God's all-encompassing present becomes a model for the mind's act of attention, which overcomes the fragmentation of temporal experience. The extended present becomes the approximation in the soul of God's eternal now. It is through attempting to think of eternity that Augustine most strongly realizes the nature of time.

THE PHILOSOPHICAL AND THE LITERARY

We have seen that Augustine's ideal for self-consciousness finds expression in the literary form of the *Confessions* as well as in its content—that its literary form is by no means incidental to its explicit treatment of time. The movement of time in the direction of eternity, as Ricoeur points out, is the very movement narrated by the first nine books of the work. The narrative activity accomplishes the itinerary whose conditions of possibility are reflected on in books 10 and 11. And the narrative form, holding together disparate events in a meaningful unity, itself enacts Augustine's ideal of a consciousness that holds fragments together in a unity for which time is no longer a problem. The narrator, knowing what has been and what is to come, enacts his own life in the way the reciter goes through the psalm. The narrator has knowledge, denied to the protagonist, of how the story goes on. But the narrator of course is not simply "reciting" this life. He is also in some ways creating it—bestowing unity and meaning on fragmented events. The autobiographical form of the work can in this way be seen as the vehicle of an attempt to achieve the elusive goal of a consciousness fully present to itself—a goal that being in time puts out of reach. For Augustine, as for Plotinus, the distension of the soul is a disruption of unity. In contrast to God's fullness of presence to himself, we cannot have it all at once. But the distension of the soul, epitomized in memory, also functions, as we have seen, as a semblance in the midst of time of the standing present of eternity. Past, present, and future can be held together in a unifying act of attention that finds its clearest expression in the form of autobiography.

Augustine of course believed that his "resolution" of the problem of time was more than a literary device to give clearer philosophical articulation to the problem. What we call the present, for him as for Derrida, is implicated in the nonexistence of past and future. But Augustine tries to resolve the problem through appeal to the encompassing act of attention. The extended present offers a safe haven that solves the problem of the nonexistence of past and future by bringing them into consciousness. Derrida would see this as a false solution to a problem that arises only from the conviction of the primacy of the present, fed by preoccupations with the spoken word. For him, what we call the present is constituted out of what in fact never really was present. The alleged primacy of the present is an illusion. His deconstruction of the primacy of the present is at the same time the deconstruction of the self-presence of consciousness. *Différance* is Derrida's version of "taking account of time" without the false reassurance of the limiting idea of eternity. Whatever is distressing in being in time cannot be allayed by aspiring to the self-presence of the eternal word. The distension of the soul, the extended notion of the present, and the idea of eternity can provide no resolution of Augustine's dilemma. But that dilemma is of his own making, generated by the pivotal role he gives the supposed primacy of the present—in his suggestion that "wherever the past and future are, they are there not as past or future but as present" (*Confessions* 11.18); in the idea of the act of attending that makes past and future present to the mind; in the complementary idea of the distended soul; and, finally, in the crucial idea of the standing present of God's eternity.

Because the idea of God and his eternal present clearly carry the force of theological belief in the *Confessions*, it is easy to overlook their literary role in the work—their function as "fictions" that allow a clearer articulation of the experiential and emotional dimensions of being in time. Augustine's version of the interconnections between time and consciousness is at first sight outrageous. But he is attempting to answer a serious and important question: how is time to be understood by a consciousness that is itself immersed in time? His answer—that if time were not integral to consciousness it would be as nothing to consciousness—is in some ways not so very different from Kant's definition of time as "the form of inner sense." But Kant is able to give much more sophisticated expression to the interdependence of time and human consciousness, and the alternative idealized form of consciousness he uses to clarify it lacks Augustine's explicit theological commitments.

Whatever may be its deficiencies, the eleventh book of the *Confessions* remains a work of great insight into the experience of time, its connections with speech, and its expression in narrative—a profound attempt to "take account of time" and to engage philosophically with the ways in which it makes us a "problem to ourselves."

NOTES

1. St. Augustine, *Confessions* 11.14. Quotations are from R. S. Pine-Coffin's translation (Harmondsworth: Penguin, 1961).

2. Aristotle, *Physics* 4.10.218a. Quotations are from the translation by W. D. Ross, vol. 11 in *The Works of Aristotle*, ed. Richard McKeon (Oxford: Clarendon Press, 1930).

3. Plotinus, *Enneads* 3.7.8. Quotations are from the translation by Stephen McKenna, 3d ed., rev. (London: Faber and Faber, 1962).

4. Paul Ricoeur, *Time and Narrative*, 3 vols., trans. Kathleen McLaughlin and David Pellauer (Chicago: University of Chicago Press, 1984), 3:19.

5. Ibid., 1:26.

FOUR

Augustine and Dante on the Ascent of Love*

Martha Nussbaum

We hear sighs of longing and groans of profound desolation. We hear love songs composed in anguish, as the singer's heart strains upward in desire. We hear of a hunger that cannot be satisfied, of a thirst that torments, of the taste of a lover's body that kindles inexpressible longing. We hear of an opening that longs for penetration, of a burning fire that ignites the body and the heart. All of these are images of profound erotic passion. And all of these are images of Christian love. Christian love both ascends and descends, both purifying the will and recovering a receptivity that the Platonist ascent claimed to surmount. In the process, the emotions are restored to a place of value in the good human life. For while it is good to ascend, removing sin from the heart, it is also good to descend, acknowledging one's deep need for sources of good outside oneself. I shall investigate this double movement of ascent and descent, focusing on two thinkers who use and transform the traditional Platonic image of love's ascent: Augustine and Dante.

Throughout his career, Augustine repeatedly contrasts two types of love: human or earthly love, and Christian love or love of God.[1] He repudiates the one and urges us, disdaining it, to cultivate the other. Repeatedly he speaks of the progress of the soul as an ascent of love and desire from the earthly to the heavenly, an ascent that strips away and leaves behind the merely human in love. This rejection of ordinary human passion is nowhere more vividly expressed than in the *Confessions*, where Augustine movingly recalls his own intense delight in earthly

*This article derives from my Gifford Lectures of 1993, forthcoming from Cambridge University Press under the title *Upheavals of Thought: A Theory of the Emotions;* it is one in a series of investigations of philosophical accounts of the ascent or reform of love. For a related account of Dante, see my contribution ("Beatrice's 'Dante': Loving the Individual") to *Virtue, Love, and Form: Essays in Memory of Gregory Vlastos, Apeiron* 1993, number 3. I am grateful to Richard Sorabji, Myles Burnyeat, John Procope, Ronald De Sousa, David Halperin, Terence Irwin, Richard Kraut, Bernard Williams, Richard Posner, and Cass Sunstein for helpful comments.

love, portraying this delight, with contrition, as a deviation from the true love and the true passion. Thus he repudiates the example of Dido and her consuming love for Aeneas:

> I was forced to memorize the wanderings of some person called Aeneas, while I was unaware of my own wanderings, and to weep for the death of Dido, who killed herself for love, when meanwhile, in my most wretched condition, I endured with dry eyes the fact that I myself, in these matters, was dying from you, God, my life. For what is more wretched than a wretch who does not pity his own self, and weeps for the death of Dido, which was caused by love of Aeneas, but does not weep for his own death, which was caused by not loving you, God?[2]

Augustine's identification with pagan *eros* was no mere schoolboy exercise; it was a paradigm that shaped his sense of his identity as a desiring subject. That paradigm is here dismissed with scorn, as a form of both sin and self-avoidance.

And yet, as even this passage of denial suggests, the *Confessions* is itself a deeply erotic work, a work filled with expressions of erotic tension and longing. God is addressed throughout in language that Dido might well have used to Aeneas: "my beauty," "most beautiful one," "my life," "my light," "my sweetness." The central metaphors of the work express passionate longing and receptivity: images of hunger, of thirst, of an emptiness that desires to be filled. We encounter passages like this one: "You blew fragrantly upon me, and I drew in the breath; and I pant for you. I tasted you and I hunger and thirst for you. You touched me, and I burned for your peace" (10.27). And this one: "Let me leave them outside, breathing into the dust and filling their eyes with earth, and let me enter into my chamber and sing love-songs to you, groaning inexpressible groans in my long wandering, and remembering Jerusalem with my heart stretching upward in longing" (12.16). This is not language that the Stoic wise man would use, extirpating the passions. Nor is it the language of the Platonic tradition of the contemplative ascent. For while the ascending lover in that tradition is still a desiring subject, she lacks this lover's deep vulnerability to external influence, a vulnerability that paints the world in non-Platonic colors, locating the most urgent good things outside the self rather than within it. In short we are brought back, it seems, to the world of the old emotions. In some manner Christian love has reopened the space within which fear, anxiety, grief, intense delight, and even anger all have their full force. And correct love promises no departure from these other emotions—if anything, it requires their intensification. In short correct love is very much like love. As Dante—quoting Virgil's Dido—says of his own passionate response when Beatrice appears before him in her chariot, "I recognize the signs of the old passion" (conosco i segni dell'antica fiamma [*Purgatorio* 30.48; see below]). Something is the same here, however much is different. Something is preserved, however much is repudiated.

I shall now try to trace the "signs of the old passion" in Augustine and Dante, both of whom explicitly set themselves the task of rewriting and correcting the pagan ascent of love. For each there are deep psychological links between earthly and heavenly love; for each it is important to argue that the good Christian life is more volatile and erotic than the classical tradition has suggested. They represent different points of view within the Christian tradition, and I shall be investigating their differences, as well as their shared ideas. I cannot hope to do justice to the whole thought of either about love, since both have careers of great internal complexity. In the case of Dante I shall focus on the *Commedia*. In the case of Augustine I shall focus on several works written just after his conversion and then on a transitional period leading up to the *Confessions*. I shall allude more briefly to some later arguments in *The City of God*.

EARLY WORKS: THE PLATONIST ASCENT

Augustine is a disciple as well as a critic of the Platonist ascent. Profoundly influenced by Neoplatonic versions of the *Symposium*'s ladder of love,[3] he uses these ideas, early in his career, as positive paradigms for the Christian life that can easily be recast in Christian terms. I shall argue that in early works such as *De quantitate animae* and *De Genesi contra Manichaeos* Augustine endorses a Platonist characterization of the contrast between earthly love and perfected love, holding up the contemplative self-sufficiency of the philosopher as a goal both available to and good for the good Christian in this life. The good Christian life becomes, as it goes on, a life progressively emptied of erotic longing and tension. Later, however, Augustine comes to think this view of ascent unacceptable: the goal it promises is both unavailable and inappropriate. In the *Confessions* he advances a picture of ascent (or ascent combined with descent) that gives a more substantial and more positive role to certain ingredients of ordinary human love.[4]

In the Platonist tradition Augustine found an account of love's ascent that emphasized the self-sufficiency of the intellect, as it moves from stage to stage, and the complete self-sufficiency of the lover, when he or she reaches the final stage. At the top of the ladder the philosopher, contemplating the fine and good, is free from all neediness and dependency, both internal and external. The object of his contemplation is eternal and unchanging: it never varies in quality or relation. The person who contemplates it is therefore entirely secure—nothing that happens in the world can alter or diminish his happy activity. At the same time the philosophical lover is internally stable, minimally dependent on internal passions that might distract him from contemplation. His intellect, which contemplates the eternal forms, becomes increasingly like what it contemplates, pure and unvarying, impassive and hard. Its activities, completely transparent to the lover, yield accounts embodying truth and true excellence. He is the one lover who has gotten beyond the tension of erotic longing, since he has found an object that satisfies his longing to "be with" the beloved always.[5]

In Plotinus's version of the *Symposium* ascent even the lover's mortality, it becomes clear, is no impediment to the full perfection of his bliss. For the acts of the perfected intellect do not take place in time at all (*Enneads* 1.5); thus the lover's bliss does not depend on time for increase or completion. Longer is not better; or, rather, there really is no longer when contemplation is in question. Plotinus states unambiguously that the person who pursues a philosophical ascent correctly can achieve in this life a complete and self-sufficient state, beyond all seeking: "What then is the good for him? He is what he has, his own good. . . . The person in this state does not seek for anything else; for what could he seek? Certainly not anything worse, and he has the best with him. The person who has a life like this has all the needs in life" (1.4.4; cf. 1.6.9). Such a person, ceasing to need, ceases to be erotic.

In many ways Augustine sets himself in the Platonist ascent tradition. Repeatedly he uses the metaphor of ascent to speak of the Christian development of love and desire. He sometimes enumerates the stages of this ascent in a manner that shows the influence of the Platonist texts that moved him. Repeatedly, too, he speaks of the disdain for earthly love that is so much stressed by Plato as a product of ascent. And he seems to endorse the central structural principle used by Plato to explain how love can move upward: the fundamental kinship of all fine things. In two early works, however,[6] Augustine goes beyond these general Platonist commitments—which persist in some form throughout his career. Here he embraces a more thoroughgoing Platonism, defending the life of contemplative self-sufficiency as a valuable and available Christian ideal.

The complex philosophical dialogue *De quantitate animae* ends with an account of the ascent of the soul from vegetative and sensory life to contemplative perfection. The ascent has seven stages (secs. 70ff.). The soul progresses to each new stage by freeing itself from impediments to contemplation. Intellect and will are the propelling forces in its movement. The first three stages bring the human being to ordinary adulthood. On top of the nutritive and vegetative life with which he is born, he quickly develops the use of his perceptual faculties and, later, the arts and abilities of reason. Only at stage four does he begin to reject any of the influences and activities of earlier stages. Here, Augustine says, is where true goodness begins (73). In stages four, five, and six, the soul gradually detaches itself from the influences of the body and the senses. From the painful struggle against worldly distraction that characterizes stage four,[7] it moves, by intellectual effort and strength of will, to the purity of stage five, as the soul "holds itself most joyfully in itself" (74). At this point the soul has a conception of its own power; at this point, then, it can turn itself outward, in stage six, to contemplation of truth (75). It now may advance, in stage seven, to the perfection of contemplation.

As the soul advances, its confidence grows, soon excluding all anxiety and uncertainty. At stage four the soul still feels some fear of death, though a fear tempered by the thought of divine providence. By stage five, however, the soul advances toward contemplation "with a huge and unbelievable confidence"[8] In stage six the soul's desire for truth is described as "most perfect," "best," "most correct" (75). Nowhere after the conflict of stage four is there any serious opposition to the movement of the rational will, which has now been "freed," "purified," "cured." Indeed, by stage six we hear that intellect itself has "purified itself and freed itself from all desire and corruption of mortal things" (75).[9] At the last stage the ascent is completed in the perfection of philosophical self-sufficiency, a state that, Augustine assures us, has been attained by outstanding people in this life:

> We have now arrived at the vision and contemplation of truth, which is the seventh and final step. Nor is it a step any longer, but a kind of stopping place to which these steps lead up. What its joys are, what the full enjoyment of the highest and true good is like, what serenity and eternity is in the air—how can I describe all this? It has been described by certain great and incomparable souls, insofar as they thought it ought to be described, souls whom we believe to have seen these things, and to be seeing them still. (76)

In *De Genesi contra Manichaeos* Augustine depicts a similar process of ascent. The soul travels, again, through seven stages. The stages are now mapped onto the seven days of the creation, a procedure that produces some changes in their order and content. The nature of the final stage, however, emerges with particular clarity. After six "days" of action and motion, there is a stopping place, a "day" of rest. Purified from all sin and bodily distraction, "having spiritual fruits, that is, good reflections [*cogitationes*] by virtue of the stability of his mind," the human being can now have a rest and a peace that are truly comparable to God's peace: the peace of perfection, null disturbance, and clear sight: "After the very good works of these (so to speak) six days, let the human being hope for perpetual rest, and let him understand what it means to say, 'On the seventh day God rested from all his works'" (1.25).

In these two passages Augustine takes over all the essentials of the Platonist ascent tradition, with minor modifications, as a depiction of an available and good Christian life. As soon as the person weans himself from the influence of the temporal and the sensible, he achieves a remarkable independence. Intellect propels itself continuously upward, interested only in its own self-sufficient activity. It generates its own motion, waiting for nothing, receptive to nothing.[10] Because of this extraordinary freedom from circumstance, the soul's aim is completely fulfilled. Ascent and motion cease in consequence. The seventh step is no step at all but the quiet dwelling place (*mansio*) at the top of the steps. The seventh "day" is no "day" of action at all but a "day of rest" in which the soul exists outside of change. Breathing the air of eternity, the previously aspiring human being knows what it means that God rested from his labors.

THE REJECTION OF PLATONISM

As we can see already, the "air" of serenity and eternity is not the air that Augustine is breathing in the *Confessions*. Nor is the Platonist goal endorsed in that work as appropriate for a Christian life. From the *Confessions* itself, and from a roughly contemporary work, the *Ad Simplicianum de diversis quaestionibus* (396), we can elicit Augustine's reasons for turning from the Platonist picture. Augustine's criticisms of Platonism fall into two groups. He argues, first, that the Platonist goal is not attainable in this life; second, that it is not, in any case, a good or appropriate Christian aim.[11]

Augustine's Platonist works insisted that the perfected life has been lived by actual human beings. The ascent involves a difficult struggle, but the struggle can be won. By the time of the *Confessions,* however, Augustine is no longer sanguine about this possibility. The desires and activities of our fleshly existence, to which we are strongly bound by both habit and memory, are a heavier load than the Platonist tradition believes. The Platonist, who speaks of casting off the burdens of the body, underestimates the tightness of the link between soul and body, the extent of the pressures that drive even the most zealous soul back to its old habits. Augustine's deep grief at his mother's death, for example—which he could not assuage even by the most earnest prayer—"impressed on my memory by this one piece of evidence the strength of the chains of habit, even against a mind that is no longer fed on deceiving words" (9.12). One can never correct oneself fully enough, watch one's impulses carefully enough. The power of sexual desire, the distractions of worldly cares, so mar his efforts to contemplate that he now concludes that Platonist bliss is entirely unavailable to a human being in this life. He mourns the loss of this high hope:

> At some moments you admit me into a feeling that is very unlike my usual state. If it were perfectly accomplished in me it would be I know not what—but it never shall be in this life. The painful weights drag me down again to things here. I am reabsorbed in my habits. I am held fast, and I weep a great deal, but still I am very much held fast. Such is the power of the burden of custom. Here I am able to stay, but unwilling; there I will to be, but I am not able. I am wretched on account of both places. (10.40)

However much aspiring Christians may try to sever their connections to earthly desire and pleasure, the habits of that love will seize them unawares, impeding progress.

There is another reason that the ascent cannot take place as the Platonist depicts it: Plato has omitted a crucial causal factor, which is not in the individual's own control. In *Confessions,* book 8, Augustine tells us that the central defect of the Platonist books is their failure to mention grace and to depict the ascending soul as waiting, always, for grace. "No man says there, 'Shall not my soul wait upon God, seeing that from him cometh my salvation?'" (8.21). Augustine retrojects these criticisms to the time preceding his conversion; but, as his early postconversion works show, they did not dawn on him until somewhat later. The crucial turning point seems to have been in the account of grace he gives to Simplicianus.

Simplicianus has asked Augustine to explicate a verse from Paul's epistle to the Romans: "It is not in the power of the one who wills, nor of the one who runs, but in the power of God, who has pity" (9.16: neque volentis neque currentis sed miserentis est Dei). Interpreting the verse, Augustine argues that the human being cannot hope by his own will and effort to be adequate for his own salvation. His own activity—both external (running) and internal (willing)—always proves insufficient. Or to put it more precisely, his own effort is insufficient for the right sort of internal and external activity. Right willing itself, he now insists, depends upon desire for a good object; and desire itself is a response of delight and love that is summoned up in us by an external call and is not perfectly ours to control. Unless something "happens our way" (occurat) that delights and moves the soul's faculty of desire in the appropriate manner, the will can in no way be moved. "But that this something should happen our way, is not in the power of the human being" (*Ad Simplic.* 1.2.22). We can be moved to faith and appropriate effort only by being struck in such a way that our will is correctly set in motion. "But who embraces in his soul something that gives him no delight? And who has it in his power to determine that that which can delight him should happen his way, or to determine that it should delight him when it does happen his way?" (1.2.21). Different people are moved and touched in different ways, by different sorts of external calls (1.2.14); desire's responses are idiosyncratic, unpredictable, and not transparent to reason. God's call may come to us in such a way that it moves us, or it may not. God may choose to move us to delight and love (for he always *can* do this), or he may allow our hearts to remain cold (16). This may seem unfair; but these are the ways of God's secret justice, which we cannot hope to understand. As Paul has written, "He pities those he wishes, and he hardens those he wishes" (quem vult obdurat). And there is no reliable relationship between the character of our human efforts and the likelihood of being called in the requisite way.

Thus Augustine's Christian, ascending not through the pure and active intellect but through the complex psychology of receptivity and love, is deeply at the mercy of contingency in two ways. She must depend for ascent not on her own self-control but on aspects of her personality that she neither governs nor fully understands. And these responsive elements in her personality depend, in turn, for their happy activation, on the mysterious ways of God's call. She cannot count on a stable perfection. Such progress as she does make is not made primarily through her own effort. The future, as Peter Brown puts it, is "lost." Her story is one of unending longing, of bewilderment and unstable motion. God is indeed eternal, perfect, and just, whereas the objects of earthly love are inconstant, mutable, and liable to moral error. But the inscrutability of that justice and the seeming arbitrariness of that perfection make the subjective experience of a Christian lover very like the pain and longing of the old love.[12]

Does Augustine still think of the Platonist ascent as good for Christian humans yet sadly unavailable? Or does his new moral psychology lead, at the same time, to the creation of a new Christian norm? I think the second is clearly the right option: the Platonist ladder is an altogether inappropriate path for the good Christian soul.

Let us return to the difficulties for Platonism that came from the power and significance of memory. It is clearly Augustine's view that we cannot free ourselves altogether from psychological continuity with our past through memory and habit. But I believe it is just as clearly his view that we ought not to dissociate ourselves from our past in the way the Platonist urges. Certainly we can and must combat the sinful urges that are fed by a certain sort of memory. But memory is also crucial to a person's sense of identity and continuity in time. A really successful dissociation of the self from memory would be a total loss of the self—thus of all activities to which a sense of one's own identity is important. "I cannot comprehend the power of my memory," Augustine writes, "since I cannot even call me myself apart from it" (*Confessions* 10.16).

But this means that without memory, which with its links to sin makes perfection impossible, the soul cannot progress at all. The search for goodness, self-knowledge, and knowledge of God that the *Confessions* movingly records presupposes, throughout, Augustine's own sense of himself as a continuous temporal being. This temporal history may be a nonnecessary property of his soul; it is still crucial to his salvation. Self-knowledge, insofar as he achieves it, is said to be a "fruit" of confession—that is, of an activity that centrally involves the drawing forth of his past through memory. His search for God, he explicitly declares, must be carried out "in the fields and broad meadows of memory, where there are treasure-chests of innumerable images brought in from things of all sorts experienced by the senses" (10.8). Memory is a capricious faculty. It does not always obey the will, nor is its material always available for deliberate inspection. But Augustine cannot have its fruits without its difficulties and darkness. To cut it away, as the Platonist ascent urges, would be to forfeit the sense of self, therefore to cease to aspire and to love:

> I do these things within, in the vast court of my memory. For there I have at my disposal the sky, the earth, the sea, along with everything that I have been able to experience in them—and, in addition, all the things I have forgotten. There I myself happen upon myself [*mihi occurro*]. And I recollect what, when, and where I did something, and how, when I did it, I was affected. (10.8)

The Platonist, in cutting away from Enid all susceptibility to contingent occurrences, cuts away the susceptibility to an occurrence that is central to growth and knowledge: the one in which a person "happens across" himself. The use of the vocabulary of the *Ad Simplicianum* is no accident. Human development is irreformably a matter of happening. A view of moral growth must be built on this psychological reality.

The Platonist might attempt to counter this objection. Surely, he could say, we can allow ourselves to retain, in memory, enough connectedness with our past to ground the sense of self and of personal continuity without retaining the sinful memories that vex our contemplative efforts. As for these, if we can rid ourselves of them, we certainly ought to do so; and we need not fear that in so doing we will be lost to ourselves. Augustine would probably deny this as a psychological claim. For, to judge from what he sees fit to remember and record in the *Confessions,* so much of his history is taken up with sin that very little basis for his sense of continuity would survive if the memory of all that were erased. Indeed, he believes that the normal course of every human life, from infancy onward, is thoroughly steeped in sin. But even were he to concede to the opponent this point about connectedness, he has a further argument that would suffice to take him to his anti-Platonist conclusion. This argument concerns the connection between memory and responsibility.

In Augustine's view every deed one has ever committed is a deed for which one is going to be judged by God. The Christian, therefore, to be maximally prepared for this judgment and maximally able to make an adequate confession, must be not less mindful of his past than another but more mindful, not less concerned with what his bodily self has done but more concerned. He must cultivate a keen sense of his own continuity and unity. He must dredge up the past rather than sever himself from it. To use the words in which Nietzsche perceptively analyzed the operations of the Christian "bad conscience," he must, working on himself, "breed an animal with the right to make promises." [13] The work of self-recollection and self-scrutiny carried out in the *Confessions* would seem both unproductive and risky to a Platonist; to a Christian it is of the deepest importance. On the other side the Platonist curriculum of progressive dissociation from the bodily self and progressive identification with the pure intellect would seem to the Christian the creation of a fiction about the self that impedes true self-knowledge and appropriate responsibility. [14] To live with these fruits of memory, however, is to live, as well, with all of its hazards. When you explore the meaning of your past, you cannot guarantee (nor does Augustine think you can) that the power of the past will not surprise you. The Christian can only, then, take the risks and confess continually.

Furthermore, this world of chance encounters is the only world in which a Christian can live in the correct relation to God. The Platonist goal of God-like self-sufficiency is now seen by Augustine as a form of deep impiety. To pursue such a goal is to commit the sin of pride, which is based on the belief that one can live according to oneself and under one's control. The *Ad Simplicianum* made it clear that a recognition of the uncertainty of grace and of God's decisive power over our internal, as well as external, lives were essential parts of being a good Christian. Openness, waiting, longing, groaning become forms of worship and acknowledgment. If you are a human being, the sort of being who does not suffice for its own salvation, it is a deep sin to live and think as if you are sufficient. As Augustine later writes in *The City of God,* "what is pride but a craving for perverse elevation? For it is perverse elevation to forsake the ground in which the mind ought to be rooted and to become, and to be, grounded in oneself" (14.13). Love, we might say, should not ascend too high, or prop its ladder on the wrong sort of ground.

If I may now look ahead to the more systematic theoretical development Augustine gives these issues in *City of God*, the entirety of the ancient eudaimonist project is now denounced as infected by pride:

> But those who have supposed that the ultimate good and evil are to be found in the present life . . . all the persons have sought, with a surprising vanity, to be happy in this life and to get happiness by their own efforts. . . . Those philosophers . . . strive to manufacture for themselves in this life an utterly counterfeit flourishing by drawing on a virtue whose fraudulence matches its arrogance. (19.4)

But this means that the emotions come back, as forms of human excellence and appropriate rationality. For it is appropriate to acknowledge the truth; and emotions are acknowledgments of the truth of our need. The Stoics who taught the extirpation of passion are now repudiated as "interested in words more than in truth" (14.9). The city of God has a different standard of public and private rationality:

> Among us Christians, on the other hand, in accordance with the holy scriptures and their healthy doctrine, the citizens of the holy city of God, living in accordance with God in the pilgrimage of this present life, fear and passionately desire, grieve and rejoice,[15] and because their love is right, all these emotions of theirs are right. (14.9)

The difference is made by the rightness of the object of the Christian's love and fear and joy. "They fear eternal punishment, they passionately desire eternal life. They grieve because they are still groaning within themselves, waiting for the redemption of their bodies; they rejoice in hope because 'there shall come to pass the saying that is written: Death is swallowed up in victory'" (14.9).

After enumerating other proper occasions for Christian emotion—both self-regarding and on behalf of others whose salvation the Christian desires—Augustine proves his point by going carefully through the careers, first of Paul, then of Jesus, and demonstrating with ample citations the range of emotions that were exemplified in their virtuous lives. He insists that Christ's emotions were not feigned but genuine, since he was really human and really suffering in a human body.[16] When, then, we read of his anger and grief, we must not doctor the reports—we must take them to heart, as paradigms for ourselves. And we must conclude from this example that even though emotions may at times mislead us, no good life would be possible without them. As for those who exalt the *apatheia* of the Stoic wise man, they are doubly foolish. For "if *apatheia* is that condition in which no fear frightens and no grief pains, it must be avoided in this life if we wish to live rightly, that is, according to God." And, furthermore, "if apatheia is defined as that condition in which no emotion at all can touch the soul, who would not consider this stupor worse than any of the vices?" (14.9).

In short, the difference between the city of God and the earthly city lies not in the presence of strong emotions but in the emotions' choice of objects. And in a sense the diseased swollen earthly city is closer to God, because more passionate, more willing to turn outward and to search for an adequate object, than the torporous city of the Stoic wise man, wrapped in its own fatal pride. Such people, "not roused or stirred, not swayed or inclined by any emotion at all, rather lose all humanity than attain true tranquillity. For the fact that something is tough does not make it right, and the fact that something is inert does not make it healthy"[17] (14.9).

We are now prepared to understand what we find in the *Confessions:* a love of God characterized not by a neat intellectual progression toward contemplative purity but by a pervasive sense of longing, incompleteness, and passivity. This love has more in common with the Platonic picture of ordinary love than with its reformed version. The metaphor of ascent still appears, but rarely. In its place we tend to find the image of a journey that goes on and on—especially a journey deep into the inner spaces of the mind. We even find images of a *descent* of the soul into itself, with proper humility. Instead of exaltation, we find poverty and lowness, dust and ashes (e.g., 10.28; 1.6); instead of the fullness of the Platonist soul, emptiness and barrenness (e.g., 10.28; 2.10); instead of the ease with which that soul, once purified, turns to contemplation, we find toil and labor (e.g., 10.39; 10.16; 10.40); instead of safety, danger (10.35, 39); instead of light, darkness and obscurity, fog and mist (2.2; 10.5). Instead of purity and health, we find sickness, hunger, and thirst; God is invoked as "my intimate doctor" (10.3; 2.10; 10.27, 28, 43). (Here Augustine asserts himself, once again, against the pagans: for the relation of doctor to patient is not, as in Hellenistic philosophical therapies, one that is expected to lead to cure in this life; it is good to remain the patient of such a doctor.)

Augustine depicts himself as continually in danger. He stresses his openness to external happenings, comparing himself to a container (1.2, 3) that stands open to receive what God will choose to pour in (1.2, 5). Nor does he feel confident that his own internal processes are fully under his own control. In his own aspiration he exemplifies the very difficulties about grace that he described theoretically in the *Ad Simplicianum.* For he prays that God should present himself to him, happen his way, in such a manner that his soul may be moved with love and delight: "Hear, Lord, my prayer. Let my soul not fall short under your discipline . . . so that you might become sweeter to me than all enticements that I used to follow, and so that I might love you most firmly and embrace your hand with all the strength of my heart" (1.15).[18] Through prayer Augustine can make a powerful effort to become responsive to the right and only the right stimuli. But this effort does not guarantee success.

The final aim of this earthly lover, like that of his Platonist counterpart, is a complete union with the beloved object, in which all desire and emotion will at last be stilled. But this goal is now seen to be both impossible and inappropriate to this life:

> When I shall be united to you in every part of myself, there will be for me no more sorrow or toil, and my life will be alive, in every way full of you. But now . . . since I am not yet full of you, I am a burden to myself. My joys, which ought to be lamented, contend against my sorrows, concerning which I ought to rejoice. And which way the victory will go, I do not know. (10.28)

The first part of the passage points to the unattainability of the lover's aim while human life continues. The equally important second half insists that the sorrow arising from unattainability is precisely what the Christian ought to value for himself in this life, the pride of a human joy just what he should avoid.[19] What is appropriate to this life is not erotic union but erotic longing, distance, incompleteness. The wanderings of Aeneas have been rejected in favor of wanderings even more painful and laborious; and Augustine resembles Dido more than he does the somewhat Stoic Aeneas, whose journey was prompted by pietas rather than by love.

Augustine's reader may by now want to know where he has arrived, with his account of the continuity and discontinuity between human and divine love. One way to answer this question will be to tell a love story, inviting the reader to ask whose story it seems to be.

Imagine, then, that you have for many years been deeply involved in a passionate relationship that has brought you neither stable satisfaction nor a quiet conscience. You have felt yourself to be the slave of forces beyond your control, both external and internal. You feel that your entire life is out of order. For the sake of living and living well, you feel that you ought to turn away from the person whom you have loved, blinding yourself to that person's beauty and power, closing yourself to the deep influence that your response to this beauty exercises over imagination and action. You see that to succeed in this you must not merely avoid the immediate stimulus of that person's physical presence; you must also close off his access to your feelings through habit and memory, and the memory of habit, and the habit of remembering.

While you are struggling with these things, with uneven success, you are suddenly struck—briefly and obscurely, in an uncertain, momentary encounter—by another person. You feel strangely moved. You see your own responses only dimly: you cannot even begin to describe what has happened. You are exhilarated; you have a sense of motion toward something, a vague, undefinable hope. And yet you feel hopelessly far from whatever it is you want from this person, far even from being able to say what it is you want. After all, you know almost nothing about the object of this longing. You can barely give him a name. All you can do is to learn from others about who he is and what he has done. And this increases both your interest and your sense of distance. You feel convinced that this hope is the hope of a better and more fruitful life, if you could only allow yourself to be touched by it deeply enough to change. You want to respond. You also want to want to respond. But at the same time, of necessity, you continue on with the old life, since that is where your life is lived. You easily become reabsorbed in your old relationship; and when you are reabsorbed you find that you do not even want to care about anything or anyone else. The power of habit and the memory of your own previous actions and feelings stand between you and any change. You know that what must happen now is that the new person must approach you and call to you. And you must respond. But you know that you cannot guarantee your own response. He must call to you in just the right way, so that you will respond. You hope that you will be such, and that the call will be such, that your life will change; but you do not control this. You want it to happen, but you do not control happenings. What is more, you do not even see or become aware of all that is happening. You know that much of the drama is being played out in depths of memory that are not fully accessible to consciousness. You do not, however, want to sever yourself from memory and its power. For your history, as the person who has those memories and has loved that powerful love, is constitutive of whatever you are and bring to anything new in life. If the new lover does not call to and move that, it is not you that he calls and moves.

So you go about, feeling sick a great deal of the time, and powerless, and ugly;[20] feeling thirsty, and dark, and endangered. Whether you will be united with the person and life that you long to want, or whether the power of habit and the obtuseness of desire will hold you where you are—this is, to you, the most mysterious matter in the world. You feel like a child lost in a dark wood.[21] And yet it is not that you long for a life without these pains and risks, a life lived in your own power. For you obscurely judge that this contest full of bewilderment and exposure, motion and tension, is the only way to deal, humanly, with these human questions.

The drama of Christian love in Augustine is something like this human love story. It is similar both in structure and in subjective experience. But we can now take one further step, following the lead of the anti-Stoic arguments of *The City of God*. Human love and Christian love, human emotion and Christian emotion, are not merely two similar stories. They are two parts of the same story. There is only one faculty of love and desire in the human being; the only way a human being changes in its love is to redirect that same love toward a new object. It is the same love that loves Dido and loves God. The change from earthly love to heavenly love is not, then, for Augustine, simply *like* my story of the person who changes lovers. It is one *example* of that story. And whether your life story plays out that example of change or some other—this, we already know, is not fully up to you. So much depends on how you are called and how you like it when and if you are. So, we might finally say, whether your life is the human story of a change from A to B, or whether the B who happens your way and calls and moves you is in fact God—all this is a part of the drama of human love and a matter of inscrutable mystery. But to live in that mystery and that openness of expectation is (if, in God's judgment, it turns out to be so) the good life for a human being.

AUGUSTINE AND UNCONDITIONAL LOVE

Three criticisms are frequently made against the Platonist ascent as an account of human love.[22] First, reformed Platonic love is held to lack concern for the individuality of the beloved—both for agency and for qualitative uniqueness. The Platonist loves all fine or beautiful objects and thinks of them without much attention to their unique traits, loving beauty rather than the whole object;[23] and she fails utterly to conceive of the object as a separate center of choice and agency in reciprocal interaction with herself.[24] Second, Platonic love lacks unconditionality: for love is directed at beauty and goodness and is thus conditional on the presence of those features on the object. Third, Platonic love doesn't really seem like love, which seems to require receptivity toward the one loved and a willingness to put oneself at risk; it looks more like a project to make oneself impervious to love so understood.[25]

Augustine's love does not appear to be vulnerable to these criticisms. It clearly has the vulnerability and receptivity of "the old love." Both God's love for Augustine and Augustine's love for God are (for different reasons) fully unconditional: Augustine loves God without knowing anything reliable about his characteristics; God loves Augustine in the full awareness of his defective and sinful nature. And, finally, on both sides the love appears to respect both agency and qualitative particularity. God wishes Augustine to strive and confess appropriately (though agency must be qualified by a waiting for grace); Augustine is limitlessly open to the activity of God toward and in him. God is Augustine's "intimate doctor," knowing more about him than Augustine about himself and loving him in the light of that knowledge; Augustine, though unable to apprehend God's nature, knows the irreplaceable uniqueness of that nature and loves it in a way that sets it apart from everything else. We must bear in mind, however, that Augustine's idiosyncrasies are of interest in the context of his therapy. It appears that they do not play the same role in the context of salvation. As if to indicate this, the work abruptly shifts its form after Augustine's conversion, from autobiographical narrative, and the personal desires it both inspires and expresses, to scriptural commentary: to be saved would be to be without a history.[26] To this contrast I shall shortly return.

BEATRICE'S "DANTE": LOVING THE INDIVIDUAL

The Heavenly Pageant halts before Dante. Turning to the triumphal chariot, the Prophets sing the passionate words of the Song of Solomon (4:8), "Come with me from Lebanon, my bride."[27] Angels above shout the joyful cry of the Gospel, "Benedictus qui venis" (Blessed are you who come in the name of the Lord)[28]—and also, scattering flowers, Anchises' tender words of mourning for the fate of Marcellus, "Manibus o date lilia plenis" (O give lilies with full hands).[29] (The reader's recalcitrant pagan sensibilities are jolted, feeling these words of grief inappropriate to a context of joyful welcome. There will be more such jolts, as Virgil, and the pagan sensibility, depart from the poem.) I have often seen at daybreak (Dante now observes) the eastern horizon glow rose, the sky above hang limpid and serene—and the sun's face come forth veiled in mist, so that the eye can look at it without pain. Even so, from that chariot, from within a cloud of flowers, a lady appeared before me, her white veil crowned with olive, her cloak green, and, beneath it, in her gown, the color of living flame.[30] This lady is not unknown to Dante, nor he to her:

> My soul—such years had passed since last it saw
> that lady and stood trembling in her presence,
> stupefied, and overcome by awe—
>
> now, by some power that shone from her above
> the reach and witness of my mortal eyes,
> felt the full mastery of enduring love.
>
> The instant I was smitten by the force
> which had already once transfixed my soul
> before my boyhood years had run their course,
>
> I turned left with the same assured belief
> that makes a child run to its mother's arms
> when it is frightened or has come to grief,
>
> to say to Virgil: "There is not within me
> one drop of blood unstirred. I recognize
> the tokens of the ancient flame." But he,
>
> he had taken his light from us. He had gone,
> Virgil had gone. Virgil, the gentle Father
> to whom I gave my soul for its salvation!
>
> Not all that sight of Eden lost to view
> by our First Mother could hold back the tears
> that stained my cheeks so lately washed with dew.
>
> "Dante, do not weep yet, though Virgil goes.
> Do not weep yet, for soon another wound
> shall make you weep far hotter tears than those!"

> ———————
>
> "Look at me well. I am she. I am Beatrice.
> How dared you make your way to this high mountain?
> Did you not know that here man lives in bliss?"[31]

Now, at the moment when Virgil and pagan virtue have taken their departure from the poem, at the time when Dante, having completed the ascent through Purgatory, is purified of sin, he acknowledges his passionate love of Beatrice—using Virgil's own words, the words used by Dido to acknowledge her passion for Aeneas. And now, even as he weeps for the loss of Virgil's gentle guidance, he is addressed by his own name. This is the first and only time that the word "Dante" appears in the *Commedia*. The poet indicates that he records it "of necessity" (63). Its emphatic placement in the line, its isolation in the text, and the explicit reference to the anomaly of its mention all combine to give it enormous emphasis. It is as if Dante is being addressed in all his individuality for the first time. And the object of his passion, she who sees him with loving particularity of vision, she too draws attention to her own individuality. "I really am, I really am Beatrice" (Ben son, ben son Beatrice). The name is placed in close relation to its rhyme "felice" (blessed)—indicating, once again, that it is in the context of Christian salvation that individuality is most truly realized, and loved.

This passage makes, then, several claims on behalf of the Christian love that survives the ascent through Purgatory. First, it claims that this Christian love is a love of the individual. Beatrice sees and loves not some aspect or part of Dante, and not some generic notion of fallen humanity, but Dante, the very man to whom she was passionately linked in earthly life. And it is as her very self—"look closely," she challenges him (Guardaci ben)—that he sees and loves her. Second, with its unique stress on the poet's name, the scene suggests a claim that is developed in many ways throughout the *Commedia:* that it is in the context of Christian salvation that we find the truest and most adequate love of the individual, a love that most completely sees and loves the individual in all of his or her uniqueness. Individuality[32] is not only preserved in beatitude, it is heightened.

Finally, the passage seems to claim that Christian love is really love of the individual: it is not some distant contemplative appreciation but "the ancient flame," the very passion that Dante felt for Beatrice on earth, a passion linked with wonder, awe, and profound upheaval. The scene is both physically sensuous and deeply emotional. Dante's very heart melts (97–99). In the next canto, feeling "a thousand desires hotter than flame," he satisfies his ten years' thirst (31.118, 128–30; cf. 32.2).

To begin to understand Dante's idea of love's ascent, we can set over against this central paradigm two other loves with which the poem has acquainted us. For, as readers, we are invited at this point to recall the erotic passion of Paolo and Francesca, blown like birds by the winds of hell, together for all eternity, their gentle hearts once and forever seized by love, "which absolves no beloved one from loving."[33] At that stage in his journey Dante was moved to faint from pity at their fate[34]—seeing "how many sweet thoughts, how much desire, brought them to this mournful condition" (5.112–14). And now, in the narration of his encounter with Beatrice, we discover allusions to certain aspects of their doomed love—to its intensity of desire, to the uniquely strong bond its passion creates between two individuals, a bond that survives death itself. But even as Francesca used the language of Christian absolution to praise a sinful bodily desire, so Dante now uses the language of pagan desire to signify his spiritual love, purified of lust.[35] Paolo and Francesca are in Dido's company in hell.[36] Dante uses Dido's words of passion to acknowledge a love that has found salvation.

And since Beatrice's words immediately follow the departure of Virgil and the light of pagan reason from the poem, we are led, too, to consider the cases of pagan rational love with which the poem has acquainted us: above all, perhaps, the love between Dante and his teacher of Aristotelian philosophy, Brunetto Latini, a love based on mutual respect for merit and dignity, mutual well-wishing, and mutual hope of high achievement and renown.[37] Although this love is Aristotelian rather than Platonic in its emphasis on mutuality in respect,[38] it is also strongly linked with the Platonic contemplative paradigm in its emphasis on merit as the basis of love and on the self-sufficiency of personal creative achievement for a kind of immortality—also, clearly, in its connection with the homoerotic love for which Brunetto is damned. The tradition of pagan contemplative love disappears from the poem with Virgil—to be replaced by something more volatile, more mobile, more vulnerable and humble. Wonder and awe, success and victory, even respect for merit and creativity—all take on a new meaning, as Brunetto's Platonic view of the world, according to which "the human being makes himself immortal" by intellectual deeds (*Inferno* 15.85), is replaced by and acknowledgment of human neediness and insufficiency before God's grace.

CHRISTIAN LOVE AND AGENCY

What, then, makes the love of Beatrice for Dante, and of Dante for Beatrice, a love of the individual? And why is it alleged to be more truly a love of the individual than are other types of love? The two aspects of individuality are clearly distinguished in the poem, and both are given enormous emphasis, both in its overall narrative of Dante's progress and Beatrice's compassion and in its account of the love between them.

The agency component of individuality is singled out as a central feature in Christian love, and one that distinguishes this love from the erotic love of Paolo and Francesca (of Enid in her former life). Beatrice seeks Dante's salvation; but this salvation, as she knows, must be achieved by his own will, though aided by divine grace. Indeed, Dante is not ready to meet Beatrice until he has purified his will of external influences that would deform it and mar its autonomy. Excessive attachments to earthly goods are such influences; Dante must be purified of his love of material objects, of fame, and of sexual pleasure, before he is ready to be declared fully autonomous. It is only when he has passed through the fire that disciplines the lustful that he is ready to be a free agent. Virgil can now leave him to his own guidance: "Here your will is upright, free, and whole. . . . Lord of yourself I crown and mitre you" (*Purgatorio* 27.140–43).

Only in the context of Christian salvation, then, is the will fully autonomous. But this means that it is only in the context of salvation that two people can love one another with full respect for subjecthood and agency. The portrait of Paolo and Francesca bears this out. For they are passive with respect to their love. In hell they are swept along by conflicting gusts of wind—"di qua, di là, di giù, di su li mena" (*Inferno* 5.43)—because this is how desire tossed them around in life, as they subjected the freedom of their wills to the force of bodily desire. Even in the appealing and tender aspects of their love they are depicted as passive: "like doves summoned by desire,"[39] they come at Dante's call. Using the language of courtly love poetry, powerfully appealing to Dante as a leading participant in that poetic movement, Francesca depicts the very ideal of love as that of a gentle passivity, a being seized. She and Paolo are the objects of its verbs, and never subjects:

> Love, so quickly kindled in the gentle heart,
> seized my lover with passion for that sweet body
> from which I was torn unshriven to my doom.
>
> Love, who absolves no beloved one from loving,
> seized me with such a strong desire for him
> that, as you see, it has not left me yet.
>
> Love led us to one death.[40]

Seized rather than seizing, led rather than leading, they surrender their agency—not so much to one another as to a power that guides them.

The attraction of this image of gentle passivity for Dante is one of the major temptations with which he must contend during his journey, as a human being and as a poet. It therefore becomes a major task of the poem to show Dante that he can have the susceptibility of the gentle heart without its sinful passivity. Transformations in the image of the dove track his progress. In the second canto of the *Purgatorio* Dante encounters Casella, friend and fellow love-poet. Dante begs him for some of the love poetry that "used to quiet all my longing" (quetar tutte mie voglie [2.108]). Casella then begins to recite Dante's own early love poem, "Amor che ne la mente mi ragiona" (Love that discourses to me in my mind)—profoundly ambiguous words at this point in the poem, since love may "seize" the mind, removing its agency, or, on the other hand, it may become the agency of a righteous will. Dante, Virgil, and the others all listen, forgetting their higher purpose, "content as if nothing touched the mind of any . . . rapt and attentive to his notes" (fissi e attenti [117–18]).

Cato's rebuke now rouses them from their passivity: What negligence is this! "Run to the mountain, to strip off the sloth that prevents God from being manifest to you." The dove image now returns, transformed:

> As when doves collected at their feeding, picking up wheat of tares, . . . if something appears that frightens them suddenly leave their food lying, because they are assailed with a greater care [perch'assaliti son da maggior cura]; so I saw that new troop leave the song and go towards the slope, like those who go they know not where. (2.124–32)[41]

These doves have a goal, albeit one they imperfectly comprehend. They are not simply tossed about, they are agents. They are not, however, self-sufficient or, in

Platonist style, self-propelling. They are still susceptible doves. They are agents not in spite of, but in virtue of, their willingness to be susceptible to the influence of the "greater care." Quasi-erotic passivity and agency now are allies. The next time that Dante is "rapt and attentive," his object is the smile of Beatrice, a smile that quenches his thirst and draws his eyes to her "with the old net" (32.6).

Their love exemplifies the new combination of agency with receptivity. For Beatrice does not simply seize Dante in a loving embrace. Her first act, indeed, is to charge him with his faults, with the worldly ambition and material concern, the "false images of good" (30.131) that have separated him from her. Before they can be together in love, he must examine himself, confess, and repent. This confession is at once a supreme effort of will and an act of loving passivity:

> Confusion joined to terror forced a broken
> "yes" from my throat, so weak that only one
> who read my lips would know that I had spoken.
>
> As an arbalest will snap when string and bow
> are drawn too tight by the bowman, and the bolt
> will strike the target a diminished blow—
>
> so did I shatter, strengthless and unstrung,
> under her charge, pouring out floods of tears,
> while my voice died in me on the way to my tongue.[42]

As a follower of pagan philosophy Dante is an archer, his bow aiming at the target of the good human life.[43] His effort is an effort of his own agency and will. But he can be a Christian agent only by being, at the same time, the bowstring that breaks, confessing its own inadequacy.[44] To put it another way, he can have his poetic voice as a Christian love-poet only by losing his voice, in tears of humility and awe. We are on our way to the mysterious harmony of *disio* and *velle*, desire and will, with which the poem famously ends.[45] He can have that harmony only by allowing the "wheel" of his soul—desire and will both—to be "revolved" by heavenly love.

Now we can understand how the poem's conception of agency criticizes the pagan ascent of love, as well as the unreformed love from which ascent begins. For in Brunetto's way of seeing the world the human being is self-sufficient for the achievement of the highest good—opposed by Fortuna, to be sure (*Inferno* 15.93–96)—but still for the most part capable of attaining *eudaimonia* by his own efforts. He teaches Dante's "come l'uom s'etterna"—and in that reflexive verb is his damnation. In giving up susceptibility to the external the pagan philosophers abandon something crucial, Dante holds, for the attainment of the highest good. In that sense Brunetto is indeed further from salvation than are the drifting lovers: for they at least acknowledge the necessity of another's love for their good. This loving dependency can be educated so that it will eventually take an adequate object, an object that could not be attained by will alone.

So far Dante's critique of the pagan ascent is close to Augustine's. But he preserves much more than Augustine does of the pagan emphasis on reflective life

planning and choice. What Christian love requires, in effect, is a new combination
of susceptibility with the active use of reason, Aristotle's "clear distinctions" (*Paradiso* 11.27) with the lover's gentle heart. When Aquinas appears before Dante in
paradise, he supports, to some extent against the Augustinian tradition, the Aristotelian emphasis on taking charge of one's own search for the good through one's
very own reflection:

> He ranks very low among the fools, who affirms or denies without making clear distinctions . . . since often a belief, rushing ahead, inclines us to the wrong conclusion,
> and then pride binds our intellect. It is worse than vain for a person to cast off from
> the shore, if he fishes for truth without the art—for he does not return the same as
> he set out.[46]

All this is in the tradition of the pagan ascent. But Aquinas is not Aristotle, or even
Plato, with his more erotic account of the self-propelling movement of the intellect. His very first words to Dante are words of love that seem at home in courtly
love poetry:

> Since the ray of grace from which true love is kindled—
> and then by loving, in the loving heart
> grows and multiplies . . . [47]

And immediately after his praise of the philosophical art, Aquinas warns against
the false pride of the intellect and describes the unpredictable operations of grace:

> Men should not be too smug in their own reason;
> only a foolish man will walk his field
> and count his ears too early in the season;
>
> for I have seen a briar through winter's snows
> rattle its tough and menacing bare stems,
> and then, in season, open its pale rose;
>
> and I have seen a ship cross all the main
> true to its course and swift, and then go down
> just as it entered port again.[48]

Here Aquinas, in effect, accepts Augustine's reading of "neque volentis neque currentis sed miserentis est dei": will falls so far short of sufficiency for its goal that
grace can rescue a most unpropitious effort and damn one that was almost complete.

The world of Christian love, in short, is a world of sudden reversals, a world of
philosophical reason but ruled by surprising incursions of strange influence.[49] Platonism is too focused on the self-government of reason to admit a love so needy, so
open to the action of the other; Augustinian love does not retain sufficient respect
for the lover's freedom and choice. The self-propelling motion of philosophical intellect must be infused with the "intelligence of love."[50]

CHRISTIAN LOVE AND QUALITATIVE DISTINCTNESS

The love of Dante and Beatrice is, then, a love that respects subjecthood and freedom—in the singular manner in which it is mingled here with passivity, with what we might call the romance of grace. Is it also a love of the qualitatively particular? It is among the poem's most central concerns to establish that it is. In taking this stand Dante's Thomistic view argues against the Augustinian tradition, according to which the particularity of persons—their flaws and faults, their idiosyncrasies, their very bodies and their history—are all incidental accretions from the world of sin, irrelevant once redemption is achieved.[51] Accordingly, as in the scene with which I began, Dante emphasizes these components of particularity throughout the poem.

It is hardly necessary to argue that Beatrice's love for Dante embraces his faults, as well as his virtues. That, of course, would be true of Augustinian love as well. But their love is also marked by attention to idiosyncrasies that make each of them distinct from all the other souls that stand in need of salvation, both before and after salvation is achieved. Beatrice loves Dante's poetic career, his aspirations.[52] We feel that she knows well, and lovingly embraces, his entire history, even while, in her speech of denunciation, she narrates its faults. His very body is, for her, a part of his identity: she calls him by name, recognizes him, looks at him with love.

On his side the emphasis on particularity is all the more marked—as, in a sense, it needs to be, since the reader's doubt will surface most strongly here. How can this "donna beata e bella" (*Inferno* 2.53) really be Beatrice herself, as she so emphatically insists? Mysteriously, it is so. Dante recognizes her, even before he sees her face, by the power of passion that she arouses in him, the "occulta virtù che da lei mosse" (*Purgatorio* 30.38). He feels, we know, "the old love" in her presence; her whole history, and theirs, is present in her eyes, which satisfy his ten years' thirst for her. Even though strictly speaking the resurrection of the body has not taken place,[53] Dante is, without any doubt, in the presence of the bodily form of the woman whom he loves. And that body, Aquinas argues, is an essential part of the person, even in his or her redeemed condition.[54] This fact is nowhere more stressed than at the very end of the *Paradiso*, when Beatrice has ascended to her heavenly throne:

> I lifted up my eyes and saw her where she made herself a crown, reflecting from her the eternal beams. From the highest region where the thunder sounds no mortal eye is so far, were it lost in the depths of the sea, as was my sight there from Beatrice. But to me it made no difference, for her image came down to me undimmed by anything between.[55]

Her particularity transcends all barriers. In that full particularity he loves her.

The poem stresses, furthermore, that with particularity, as with agency, Christian love surpasses the forms of earthly love that are its alternatives. This is so because "the world is blind" (lo mondo è cieco [*Purgatorio* 16.66]). The lure of material goods, of fame and honor—all this creates a "fog" around the sight of the individual[56] that blocks him or her from truly perceiving the particularity of other individuals, and to some extent from being truly perceived. The sins that are purged in Purgatory are all different forms of false love (see *Purgatorio* 10, 16, 18), love in which the soul has taken excessive interest in objects that are not worthy or true objects for its love or defective interest in those that are. And this deforms the love of persons, who are worthy objects of love, in manifold ways. In pride one attends only to one's own standing. This leads to a failure to see the needs of those one loves and to a desire to lord it over them. In envy one fixes on the possessions of others and becomes competitive rather than truly loving. In anger one is filled with resentment at slights to oneself and so cannot fully attend to the particular history and needs of another. In sloth and in gluttony one is slow to go to another's need. Lust, finally, is also seen as a deformation of individual love. The suggestion is that the lustful, focusing as they do on their own pleasure and excitement, are imperfectly able to notice and respond to the needs of the persons they love or even to take in their full particularity. A person who is seen as a vessel of pleasure is not (as Aristotle already argued) seen truly for what he or she is. How do Paolo and Francesca see and respond to one another? He sees her as a "bella persona" (and she notes that this bodily form is hers no longer); she sees him as a source of "piacer" and calls him "costui," "that one." Never does she mention his name.[57]

Such insights are also Augustinian—but there is a difference. For Dante, what is seen when the "fog" is dispelled is still essentially characterized by an embodied narrative history, the sort of history souls retain in paradise. For Augustine, so long as one lives in this imperfect world, individual history must be love's preoccupation—but if the "fog" should ever be dispelled completely, love would be freed from its dependence upon narrative.

CHRISTIAN LOVE AND VULNERABILITY

But is the love of Beatrice and Dante (of the transformed Enid and her equally transformed Felix) really *love*? I have begun to answer this question by talking about the erotic character of Christian agency. Dante insists on the multifaceted character of love, the basic form, he argues, of all human desire and motivation (*Purgatorio* 14, 17). His entire poem, he tells us, is the writing of love within him (*Purgatorio* 24.52–54). In that sense any human relationship involving desire and action is bound by definition to be a relationship of love. But Dante does not stop there. He is at great pains to satisfy his reader that the love between him and Beatrice is indeed the same passion that linked them in life. And in describing those "signs" Dante carefully associates their love with paradigms of romantic, erotic love that have already been present in the poem. We find awe, trembling, being overcome ("di stupor tremando affranto" [*Purgatorio* 30.36]). We hear of a "hidden power" emanating from the loved one and binding the lover.[58] We witness tears and upheaval. We discover, in short, all the susceptibility of the "cor gentil," as Dante has both enacted and poetically represented it. We even find the image of melting (30.97–99), well known at least since Plato's Phaedrus as an image for erotic susceptibility and "madness."[59]

On the side of Beatrice we find, from the beginning of the poem, deep disturbance and concern for Dante's well-being, combined with a passionate emotionality that is never more apparent than in her first appearance before him. Commentators have frequently remarked on the fact that the solemn speech in which she denounces Dante for his sins is also a deeply personal and angry statement of betrayal.[60] She is recognizable as the Beatrice of the *Vita Nuova*.

How far do these two conceptions of love answer our criticisms of the Platonist ascent? And what new problems have they introduced in so doing? We should say, I think, that there is here a marked advance over the Platonic conception with respect to the agency and the particularity of individual love. Where agency is concerned, we find in both writers a respect for the loved one's choice and freedom that we do not find in Plato. Dante's conception stresses to a greater extent the integrity of the will; Augustine's renders the human lover more passive. But both forge conceptions of the interrelationship of agency with receptivity that are both intrinsically fascinating and unknown in the pagan tradition. Concerning particularity, we find in Augustine a commitment to embrace the history of one's sinful existence in memory and confession; in Dante we find a much stronger commitment to particularity, since the body and its history are now more profoundly, and more positively, identified with the person, not only on account of sin but for all time. This leads to a conception of love in which all the particularities of the loved one are embraced.

With unconditionality, the situation is less clear. Beatrice loves Dante; but she is perfectly prepared to see him go to hell if he proves resistant to her reprimand. And if he does go to hell, she will cease to love him. For the souls in hell have abandoned, along with "all hope," all compassion from the redeemed and heavenly world. As he goes further along in hell, Dante has to learn not to love or take pity on the sinners there[61]—even when they are there on account of accidents that seem not at all their fault. (Francesca's failure to receive absolution for her adultery is due to the fact that she was suddenly murdered by her husband.) Had Dante dropped dead in his "selva oscura," Beatrice would have been bound to treat his soul with the disdain that the damned merit from the saved. Refusing a plea to open the frozen eyes of a soul whose body still lives on earth, Dante remarks, "It was a courtesy to be rude to him" (E cortesia fu lui esser villano).[62] If this is the way Beatrice is bound to treat him, should he be damned, is her love really love? I know of no answer in Augustine to similar worries.

It would seem that we have already answered the question about the lover's receptivity and willingness to put himself at risk. Both of these conceptions have repeatedly emphasized the vulnerability of their human participants to external forces and events. But we must be cautious here. For in some ways they have not really retained the vulnerability proper to human love. The element of passivity in these lovers, their longing and sighing, their waiting upon something external—all this is a description not of their relationship to a beloved human individual but of their relationship to divine grace, therefore to the actions of a being who is both perfect and perfectly just. Augustine makes this perfectly clear. With Dante there is much room for ambiguity—for of course it is Beatrice who is the emissary and representative of divine grace. But the doves whom Cato drives onward, "assaliti da maggior cura," are not lovers of human individuals any longer. All their susceptibility points upward. And this means that once grace is assured, there is no need, really, of other human individuals and, it would seem, no continued erotic vulnerability of any sort.

Again, Augustine makes all this perfectly unambiguous, both in his explicit denunciations of earthly ties and in his description of the way eros ends in beatitude. Eros is proper to our earthly condition and is expected to end when beatitude is achieved. In Dante, once again, things are more complex. For Beatrice still feels pain at Dante's condition; and, as I pointed out, the souls in paradise still feel a hunger for the love of a new companion. But in our scene from the earthly paradise the worry begins to take shape. For, as I mentioned at the start, Virgil's tender words of grief echo oddly in this context of festivity and welcome.[63] It is the poem's intention that this should be so. For there is no room for loss or grief in salvation. Joy is assured for all eternity, and the only use for Virgil's lines—the only use for the lily, flower of death—is to celebrate. Hope, in the context of human love, is a cousin of fear. For, as the Stoics are fond of observing, the two go hand in hand, both being based on attachment to the uncertain things of the world. So defined, hope is part of the Christian pilgrimage in this world. But in paradise, hope acquires a new definition: "a sure expectation of future glory, produced by divine grace and a person's prior achievements."[64] The worst thing that can happen to a saved person is to be a bit further away from God than are other saved souls. But, as Dante sees it—encountering Piccarda Donati, who is kept low down for having been raped[65]—"Everywhere in heaven is paradise, even if the grace of the highest good does not rain there in the same measure." But is there real personal love, where there is no possibility of loss, where each lover possesses the highest good independently of the other and of the relationship between them? We must say, I think, that what there is of love's vulnerability in this world depends on the continuing relationship of heaven to the world of sin. Within heaven itself, the meanings of all emotion words have changed.

This may be a welcome development. But we must not underrate its importance. In giving the ascent a terminus of needlessness and assured bliss Augustine and Dante have radically changed the meaning of the needlessness involved in pagan eros. They have in one sense rejected the Platonic ascent paradigm in favor of "the ancient flame"; but in another sense they have not done so at all. I can make this point, in fact, by speaking about flame. In the pagan tradition, eros is at once disease and delight, destruction and birth. Flame is a persistent symbol of erotic passion—of its suddenness, its intensity, its power of both destruction and creation. (This image is frequently linked with the image of the serpent, a creature both potentially lethal and symbolic of fertility and flourishing.)[66] Such imagery is frequently used to suggest that erotic longing brings great beauty and richness to human life, a beauty that is inseparable from its danger. For Augustine, by contrast, the pain of longing—through inseparable from its value relative to the diseased condition of a sinful soul—is ultimately fully separable from what is most beautiful and most worthwhile. In bliss there is no flame, yet nothing is lacking. Dante makes this same departure unambiguously clear in his use of the image of flame itself, which he endows with a distinctly anti-Virgilian resonance. For flame, in the world of salvation, is no longer that which ignites longing in the lover. It is, instead, the purifying instrument of chastity, which burns desire away, leaving the will whole and clean. The other side of this flame lives the soul in paradise, whose life is no longer erotic. This means, however, that the "signs of the ancient flame" are not really the signs of the *ancient*, the pagan, flame, with all its ambiguity and its double splendor. What looks superficially like the same love is in that crucial respect profoundly different. Augustine and Dante restore pagan love to the self-sufficient universe of the pagan ascent tradition—but, ultimately, in the service of advancing the contrite soul toward a nonerotic life.

NOTES

1. On Augustine's doctrine of love, see Peter Brown, *Augustine of Hippo* (Berkeley: University of California Press, 1967), and Hannah Arendt, *Love and Saint Augustine*, ed. J. Scott and J. Stark (Chicago: University of Chicago Press, 1996); on the spiritual journey of Christian life in general see E. Gilson, *Introduction à l'étude de Saint Augustin*, 3d ed. (Paris: 1949); for a fine general account of his philosophy of mind see Gerard O'Daly, *Augustine's Philosophy of Mind* (Berkeley: University of California Press, 1987); on his relationship to pagan culture, see H. I. Marrou, *A History of Education in Antiquity*, trans. G. Lamb (London: Sheed and Ward, 1956).

2. St. Augustine, *Confessions* 1.13. All translations from Augustine are my own.

3. I do not take any stand on the vexed question whether Augustine actually read Plotinus or only heard of the views at second hand. This is irrelevant to my argument, since he clearly is familiar in a general way with the structure of the Platonist contemplative ascent.

4. My account of Augustine's development is close to that advanced in Brown, *Augustine, passim*, a work for which I have much admiration. In many respects I am simply giving more elaboration and philosophical structure to the picture he has laid out, though in others, as will become clear, I am critical.

5. See my account of the *Symposium* in *The Fragility of Goodness: Luck and Ethics in Greek Tragedy and Philosophy* (Cambridge: Cambridge University Press, 1987) and the revised account, "The Ascent of Love: Plato, Spinoza, Proust," *New Literary History* 25 (1993): 925–49.

6. Both works are dated to 388: they are thus among his earliest postconversion writings.

7. "Labor, et contra huius mundi molestias atque blanditias magnus acerrimusque conflictus" (73).

8. "Ingenti quadam et incredibili fiducia pergit in Deum, id est, in ipsam contemplationem veritatis" (75). One can see here how superficial the Christian modification to the Platonist conception has been: the name of God is explicated by a reference to the contemplation of truth.

9. "Ipsa cogitatio ab omni cupiditate ac faece rerum mortalium sese cohibuerit et eliquaverit." Compare the reflexive verbs of Brunetto Latini in Dante's hell—see below.

10. Even the receptivity of faith—not mentioned at all in *De quantitate animae*—figures in *De Genesi contra Manichaeos* only as the early precondition for the beginning of intellectual activity, in stage one. Once intellect takes over, it no longer plays a role.

11. Brown, *Augustine,* stresses the first group of arguments. Even his chapter title "The Lost Future" implies that some goal, still desirable, is simply being found to be unavailable. But I believe that the second group of arguments has even greater importance.

12. See Brown, *Augustine,* 155: "Augustine now moves in a world of 'love at first sight,' of chance encounters, and, just as important, of sudden, equally inexplicable patches of deadness."

13. See Friedrich Nietzsche, *Genealogy of Morals* 2. The extent of Nietzsche's sympathy with Augustine's project should not be underestimated: for Nietzsche this "bad conscience," though unfortunately linked in the Christian tradition with hatred of this world and of the body, is also the "pregnancy" out of which all great creative achievement and all philosophy must grow.

14. Here there is an especially sharp critique of Plotinus *Ennead* 1.6, where self-knowledge is equated with knowledge of the good that you are.

15. "Metuunt cupiuntque, dolent gaudentque": here Augustine succinctly lists the four well-known generic categories of passion in Stoic taxonomies, all of which the Stoic would seek to extirpate. (The taxonomy is arranged along two axes: a temporal axis [present–future] and a good–bad axis: see Martha Nussbaum, *The Therapy of Desire: Theory and Practice in Hellenistic Ethics* [Princeton: Princeton University Press, 1994], chap. 10.)

16. Augustine here seems to be arguing against opponents who had tried to assimilate Christ to Stoic portraits of the sage, insisting that he had not *pathê* (real emotions based on a high evaluation of the importance of external goods for flourishing) but only *eupatheiai,* Stoic forms of wise nonpassionate motivation that are not linked with any (to Stoics false) high evaluation of the external (see Nussbaum, *Therapy,* chap. 10). Augustine insists that this interpretation has no textual basis and is profoundly misguided.

17. "Non enim quia durum aliquid, ideo rectum, aut quia stupidum est, ideo sanum."

18. Cf. *Confessions* 10.29: "O love, you who always burn and are never extinguished, divine love, my God, set me on fire."

19. Cf. also St. Augustine, *Epistulae* 27.1: he finds delight in his very longing.

20. Cf. *Confessions* 10.27: "in ista formosa deformis inruebam."

21. Cf. *Confessions* 10.4, 35.

22. Especially in Gregory Vlastos, "The Individual as Object of Love in Plato," *Platonic Studies,* 2d ed. (Princeton: Princeton University Press, 1981); I discuss Vlastos's criticisms further in my *Apeiron* article ("Beatrice's 'Dante'").

23. In making this point Vlastos focuses above all on the flaws and defects of the individual as features omitted from the embrace of Platonic love; but one might also mention neutral idiosyncrasies and the unique spatiotemporal history of the person and the love.

24. Criticizing A. Nygren, *Agape and Eros*, Vlastos argues that the Platonic account does not exactly neglect altruism, since the lover performs many fine and creative acts; the more accurate criticism to make is that he neglects respect for subjecthood and agency.

25. This criticism is stressed not by Vlastos but by me, in *Fragility of Goodness*, chap.6, and in "Ascent of Love."

26. See John Freccero, "Autobiography and Narrative," in T. Heller et al., eds., *Reconstructing Individualism* (Stanford: Stanford University Press, 1986), 16–29; and compare the related argument in Margaret Miles, *Desire and Delight: A New Reading of Augustine's "Confessions"* (New York: Crossroads, 1991).

27. The words "with me" are not explicit in Dante's Latin version ("Veni, sponsa, de Libano"). The context is among the most intensely erotic and lyrical in the Song: "Your lips are like a scarlet thread, / and your mouth is lovely. . . . / Your two breasts are like two fawns, twins of a gazelle, that feed among the lilies. . . . / Come with me from Lebanon, my bride; come with me from Lebanon. . . . / You have ravished my heart, my sister, my bride, you have ravished my heart with a glance of your eyes. . . . / how sweet is your love, my sister, my bride! how much better is your love than wine, and the fragrance of your oils than any spice! / Your lips distill nectar, my bride; honey and milk are under your tongue; the scent of your garments is like the scent of Lebanon" (4:3–11, Revised Standard Version).

28. Matthew 21:9, the shout of the crowd greeting Jesus as he enters Jerusalem. Note that, though the Latin uses a masculine adjective, the phrase serves as a welcome to Beatrice.

29. Virgil, *Aeneid* 6.882ff.:

heu, miserande puer, si qua fata aspera rumpas
tu Marcellus eris. manibus date lilia plenis,
purpureos spargam flores animamque nepotis
his saltem accumulem donis, et fungar inani
munere.

30. "Di fiamma viva" (Dante, *Purgatorio* 30.33). The colors signify faith (white), hope (green), and Christian love (red): thus the "flame" of Christian love is introduced prior to, and prompts, Dante's acknowledgment of his own "flame."

31. *Purgatorio* 30.34–57, 73–75. I cite John Ciardi's translation (New York: New American Library, 1957), though I have rewritten 1.36, where Ciardi writes "stupefied by the power of holy awe": no word corresponding to "holy" is in the original. Some comments: in 1.39, "d'antico amor senti la gran potenza" points more vividly than does the translation to the fact that it is the *same* love, the *old* love, and it prepares for 1.48, "conosco i segni dell'antica fiamma," which links the image of flame with acknowledgment of the continuing presence of the love. Line 48 is a translation of Virgil, *Aeneid* 4.23, "agnosco veteris vestigia flammae," in which Dido, acknowledging her love for Aeneas, recognizes it as "the old" love that she once felt for her dead husband Sychaeus. (On flame as erotic image in Virgil see Bernard Knox, "The Serpent and the Flame," *American Journal of Philology* 38 [1958]: 379–400.) At 1.49 no image of "light" actually appears in the Italian, a literal rendering of which is, "But Virgil had left us bereft of him." In line 73, the emphatic and repetitious "Guardaci ben! ben son, ben son Beatrice" (Really look—I really am, I really am Beatrice)

has not been fully captured in the translation; and the significant fact that "Beatrice" is answered by the rhyming "felice" has been captured only imperfectly.

32. As will shortly become clear I am not using "individuality" as synonymous with "particularity." As in "Ascent of Love," I look separately at two components of individuality—agency and particularity—and at four different elements in particularity (flaws, idiosyncrasies, the body, the personal history) that "Ascent of Love" identified as absent from Platonic love.

33. Dante, *Inferno* 5.100–106:

> Amor, ch'ai cor gentil ratto s'apprende,
> prese costui della bella persona
> che mi fu tolta; e 'l modo ancor m'offende.

> Amor, ch'a nullo amato amar perdona,
> mi prese del costui piacer sì forte,
> che, come vedi, ancor non m'abbandona.

34. *Inferno* 5.140–41: "sì che di pietade / io venni men così com'io morisse." On the refusal of pity to the damned, see below.

35. In canto 27 Dante, gathering courage from Beatrice's name, follows the instruction of the Angel of Chastity and passes through the wall of fire that burns away lust. It is here, apparently, that the last "P" is stricken from his brow. Thus here the reference to the pagan erotic image of flame takes on a Christian and, in a sense, profoundly unerotic significance. See below.

36. *Inferno* 5.85: "uscir della schiera ov'è Dido."

37. *Inferno* 15. Dante addresses Brunetto—whose features are so scorched by the fire that he can hardly be recognized—by the reverential "Ser"; he calls Dante his "son," and Dante speaks of his paternal kindness. Brunetto urges Dante to "follow his star," and Dante recalls that Brunetto's teaching concerned "how the human being makes himself immortal." In the famous closing lines of the canto Dante compares Brunetto to a runner in the foot race at Verona and, he says, "to the winner, not the loser." Compare the account of the virtuous pagans in *Inferno* 4, where respect for merit and virtue is the central theme, and yet this respect is shown as existing in a dome shut off from the light of the sun. This, of course, is where Socrates, Plato, and Aristotle—as well as Empedocles, Democritus, Heraclitus, Diogenes, Seneca, and Cicero—are all placed, and the life of pagan philosophy with them.

38. On the relationship between Platonic *eros* and Aristotelian *philia*, see Nussbaum, *Fragility of Goodness*, chap. 12, and especially Vlastos, "Individual as the Object of Love," 3–4 and n. 4. Vlastos argues that "friendship" is inadequate as a rendering of *philia*: "'Love' is the only English word that is robust and versatile enough to cover *philein* and *philia*." The inadequacy is the more patent in Dante, where Platonic and Aristotelian paradigms are interwoven in the depiction of pagan love, and where explicit theory traces all desire and motivation to *amore*: see especially *Purgatorio* 16, 18; also 24.52–54, where Dante states that the whole poem signifies the internal dictation of love.

39. *Inferno* 5.82–84. The passage makes a subtle point: they do direct themselves toward Dante "carried by their will" (dal voler portate), but only after desire has roused them ("dal disio chiamate"). We should ask whether Augustine is more like these doves than like Dante's more will-governed Christian lover.

40. *Inferno* 5.100–106: see n. 33. In this case I have translated the lines myself, following the version I gave in "Love and the Individual" in *Love's Knowledge* (New York: Oxford University Press, 1990). I rely on Ciardi in lines 101–2 but for the rest give a more literal version.

41. I give the literal prose version of *Dante's "Purgatorio,"* trans. John D. Sinclair (New York: Oxford University Press, 1958), since Ciardi, to preserve rhyme, is forced to distort some parts of the sense that are important for my argument ("assaliti . . . da maggior cura" becomes "taken by a sudden scare," which is both weaker and lacking in the comparative dimension of the original).

42. *Purgatorio* 31.13–21, Ciardi translation.

43. Aristotle, *Nicomachean Ethics* 1094a22–4, an image also used commonly in Hellenistic ethics. It would no doubt be well known to Dante.

44. See also the use of the same image in Dante, *Paradiso* 1.120–25—where the bow is drawn by divine providence and guides receptive mortals to their goal.

45. Ibid., 33.143–45: "ma già volgeva il mio disio e 'l velle, / sì come rota ch'igualmente è mossa, / l'amor che move il sole e l'altre stelle."

46. Ibid., 12.115–23, my translation.

47. Ibid., 10.83–85, Ciardi.

48. Ibid., 13.130–38, Ciardi.

49. Notice that the souls in paradise are still susceptible lovers: they move toward Dante as fish in a fish pond move toward any external incursion, taking that to be their food; and they call out, "Behold—one who will increase our loves" (5.100–105).

50. *Purgatorio* 24.51: here Bonagiunta cites the opening line of one of Dante's own lyrics, "Donne ch'avete intelletto d'amore." It is clearly Dante's view that all forms of love involve cognitive representation; and he depicts his poetic task as that of taking down dictation from the internal speech of love (24.52–54).

51. Of course Augustine does teach the resurrection of the body; but it is an anomaly in his thought in a way that it is not in the thought of Aquinas. On Aquinas's use of Aristotle to defend the centrality of the body in the functions of the soul, see M. Nussbaum and H. Putnam, "Changing Aristotle's Mind," in M. Nussbaum and A. Rorty, eds., *Essays on Aristotle's "De anima"* (Oxford: Clarendon Press, 1993), 27–56.

52. For example, in *Inferno* 2 he is identified to her by Lucia as "he who loved you so much that for your sake he left the vulgar herd" (104–5). It is of course also important that many properties that to an Augustinian would be morally irrelevant become relevant to Dante's scheme of salvation: for in paradise souls are classified by their characteristic pursuits and ideals.

53. See *Paradiso* 14, where the souls are depicted as filled with desire for their dead bodies ("disio de' corpi morti" [l. 63])—not only their own, but those of their loved ones (ll. 61–66).

54. For discussion of this aspect of Aquinas's Aristotelianism, see Nussbaum and Putnam, "Changing Aristotle's Mind." Separated souls cannot perceive the particular things of this world without their bodily organs, Aquinas argues, and thus have only a confused and indistinct perception, before the resurrection of the body restores their faculties.

55. *Paradiso* 31.73–78, Sinclair translation, with my changes.

56. Cf. "purgando la caligine del mondo" (*Purgatorio* 11.30).

57. Dante's conception of the worldly obstacles to particular perception and love is close to the contemporary conception developed by Iris Murdoch in philosophical writings

such as *The Sovereignty of God* (London: Routledge, 1970) and *The Fire and the Sun: Why Plato Banished the Artists* (New York: Oxford University Press, 1977) but also in novels such as *The Bell, The Black Prince,* and *The Sacred and Profane Love Machine.*

58. For this motif in ancient Greek beliefs about eros, see John J. Winkler, *The Constraints of Desire* (New York: Routledge, 1990).

59. On the *Phaedrus* see Nussbaum, *Fragility of Goodness,* chap. 7, and David Halperin, "Plato and Erotic Reciprocity," *Classical Antiquity* 5 (1986): 60–80. Charles Singleton, in his classic Dante commentary (Dante Alighieri, *The Divine Comedy,* trans. Charles S. Singleton [Princeton: Princeton University Press, 1973]), ad loc., also compares Augustine, *Confessions* 7.12, the account of Augustine's misery and tears before his conversion.

60. *Purgatorio* 30.104–45: Singleton speaks of her "cutting sarcasm" (745) and writes, "[t]he Beatrice who is known to readers of the *Vita Nuova* now comes prominently to the fore—a Beatrice who in that early work is *not* an allegorical figure" (756).

61. See, for example, *Inferno* 29.98ff.: "Stay there, for you are rightly punished." At 6.106ff. Dante is given the cheerful news that at the last judgment the sufferings of sinners will be even worse and more "complete."

62. *Inferno* 33.150. This is all the more striking in that this sinner still has a chance of redemption.

63. Singleton, 734–36, explains the words as both a joyful welcome and a sad farewell to Virgil himself. This is plausible and elegant; but it does not remove my concern. The point is that it is not only Virgil who departs from the poem, it is the pagan sensibility itself, in which loss has its full weight.

64. *Paradiso* 25.67–69. Notice that Dante gives this response like a student who wants to show off how well he knows his lesson (64–66).

65. *Paradiso* 3; see canto 4 for an attempt to justify this result.

66. See Knox, "Serpent and the Flame," *passim,* on Virgil, and Nussbaum, *Therapy,* chap. 12, on Seneca.

FIVE

Romancing the Good

God and the Self according to St. Anselm of Canterbury

Marilyn McCord Adams

It is a commonplace of Christian religion that true selfhood is won by following one's vocation. Likewise evident, given our *ante mortem* condition, is our need for maps to chart the journey, models to exhibit the dynamics, for spiritual guides and skillful means. Rhetorician by trade, St. Augustine never ceased to believe that words could change lives. Most famously, he offers the *Confessions*, his own spiritual autobiography, written not for curious gossip-seekers but for readers with ears to hear and heart to feel, with the aim of effecting conversion.[1]

St. Anselm is also a consummate rhetorician[2] whose own deliberately participatory works attempt to remodel the reader. Each of his major writings is an exercise meant to stir and train up the soul to its work. Although Anselm appears to have shared personal anecdotes in teaching his brother monks, none of his principal works makes the concrete particulars of his own life the vehicle of spiritual instruction. Instead he prefers generic metaphors and models that underlie the Christian Platonist metaphysics he shares with Augustine. Nevertheless Anselm's selection is colored by his own personal situation. Anselm was a Benedictine monk who committed his whole self to the goal of seeing God's face. Philosophically, he assimilated and developed the Christian Platonism received at Augustine's hand. Culturally, he was a member of feudal society, like late antiquity still structured by the etiquette of patron–client relations and regulated by the values of honor and shame. Each of these allegiances contributed a strand of Anselm's rich and complex theory of how the human self becomes most fully itself in relation to God.

Anselm defends his first work, the *Monologion*, as thoroughly inspired by Augustine's *De Trinitate*.[3] In this chapter I separate three Platonist threads found there: God as paradigm, artist, and Beloved; creatures as mirror images, artifacts, ways of romancing the Good. I then review how Anselm uses the political patron–client analogy to structure the problem of sin and redemption in his own distinctive way. My survey will disclose how Anselm the monk-lover of God conceptually fashions the whole world in his own image (makes his fellow creatures into monk-lovers). My final section takes his *Prayers* as an illustration of how his writings attempt the same transformation of his readers, the better to enable us to become ourselves, highly focused images, knowers and lovers of God.

PARADIGM AND COPIES, MODEL AND MIRROR

Platonist that he is, Anselm believes the universe to be constituted of paradigm value, imperfectly imitated by a hierarchy of natures of descending value. Supreme Goodness (which equals Supreme Being), a being a greater than which cannot be conceived, is one and independent. It is essentially whatever it is in general better to be than not to be: immaterial, living, wise, powerful, true, just, happy, and eternal.[4] Yet, since parts are metaphysically prior to and explanatory of their wholes, the metaphysically preeminent Supreme Nature is altogether simple:[5] it is not a subject that *has* properties; rather it *is* Supreme Being, Justice, Wisdom, Truth, Goodness, Greatness, Beauty, Immortality, Immutability, Blessedness, Eternity, Power, Unity, every true good,[6] even paradigm sensory ones such as Harmony, Sweetness, and Pleasant Texture.[7] Nor is it a cluster of many paradigms, inseparably united by metaphysical glue; rather one single simple thing is at once paradigm Truth, Justice, Wisdom, Power, Beauty, Blessedness, and so forth, the "omne et unum, totum et solum bonum."[8] Nor is its being divided into many spatial or temporal parts, present or actual only successively, but is the omnipresent and eternal, "totum simul," without beginning or end.[9]

For other natures, to be is somehow imperfectly to resemble the Supreme Nature. Since the perfect can be imperfectly copied in many ways, there are many such imitations. Since similarity is a relation that comes in degrees, Anselm envisions a value-hierarchy of natures generated by varying degrees of likeness to the Supreme Nature.[10] Yet, if other natures are fundamentally imperfect likenesses of the Supreme Nature, Anselm also recognizes such a vast "ontological- or excellence-gap" between paradigm and copies as to justify claiming that the latter "scarcely exist" or "almost are not," escaping utter nonexistence only by being made something from nothing by Supreme Being.[11]

Augustinian Platonist that he is, Anselm does not understand the corollary "cognitive gap" to leave us in the "dark night" of *via negativa*. True, the Supreme Nature will ever remain partially inaccessible, "a being greater than" others "can conceive."[12] But all knowledge is through likenesses, and the dim reflection of the Supreme Nature in things here below is enough to provide significant cognitive access. If ante-mortem humans cannot see the Supreme Nature as It is in Itself, we can understand something through an image or likeness as in a mirror. The closer the likeness, the clearer the knowledge. Rational nature, with its capacity for remembering, conceiving, loving, for discerning values and willing accordingly, for broad-sense "speculation," is the best, the most fittingly regarded as an "image" of the Supreme.[13] If individuals are better beings to the extent that they more perfectly instantiate their natures, a human will be better insofar as s/he exerts her/himself to make correct value judgments and to love accordingly, indeed will be the most Godlike in imitating not only Divine activities but also their object— by bending all of its powers to the knowledge and love of God. Thus striving, the rational self is the best possible mirror of the Supreme Nature.[14]

ARTISAN AND ARTIFACT

In Plato's myth in the *Timaeus* the demiurge looks to the Forms and imposes their likenesses on preexistent, recalcitrant stuff to form moving likenesses of eternity. Following Augustine's lead, Anselm also sees God as artisan and creatures as His handiwork while insisting that the utter independence of the Supreme Nature generates systematic disanalogies. First, the Supreme Nature, as that through which all beings exist, cannot rely on any materials existing independently of itself but creates everything other than itself ex nihilo.[15] Moreover Anselm's Creator does not look outside Himself for ideas. Rather, the Supreme Nature's own nature is a single Word (thought, mental expression),[16] which is the paradigm—"forma, similitudo, regula"—of all created natures.[17]

Third, not only does the all-wise Creator have a preconceived idea of what to make, He makes natures for a purpose—an "ad-quod-factum-est" and an "ad-quod-potentiae-datae-sunt"—which He (at least partially) builds into them. Thus, if fire is made to heat, earth to seek the center, rational creatures are given reason to make value judgments (to discriminate among degrees of value) and will to love accordingly—more specifically, to love God above all and for God's own sake.[18] Moreover, as with any artisan and its artifact, the artisan's plans are normative relative to its product: any lack of correspondence signals a defect in the thing produced, not in the artisan's notion.[19] Consequently, Divine purposes are the norm or rule defining what it is to be a thing of a certain kind.[20] Fifth, from such normativity Anselm infers a correlative obligation (of uprightness or truth, even justice in the broad sense)[21] in any and every creature to be and do that for which it was made.[22] For the artisan's skill deserves to be proclaimed by the excellence of his or her works.[23] Abstracting from natural impediments, Anselm recognizes that nonrational beings fulfill their obligations, have the truth of action (e.g., fire heats and earth falls), by natural necessity, while rational beings do so or not freely and spontaneously.[24] Once again, the rational self owes it to God to spend its whole power willing to remember, understand, and love the Supreme Good[25] and qualifies as just or upright only to the extent that it complies. Sixth, by contrast, because the Creator-artisan, whose creative concepts are normative for His products (which include everything other than Himself), is not Himself an artifact; neither God's doing nor His being is governed by any external norm but Itself constitutes the universal norm just by Being what It is. Properly speaking, Anselm infers, God has no obligations to creatures.[26]

ROMANCING THE GOOD: THE DYNAMICS OF LOVE AND DESIRE

A third Platonic analogy—already assimilated and transformed by Augustine[27]—makes the universe a scene of erotic striving, a multitude of lovers romancing the Good.

The Orientation of Erotic Striving

In Anselmian romance erotic love has a double direction, is both object- and self-regarding. For, on the one hand, the Lover desires the Beloved because s/he recognizes and appreciates the Beloved's (real or apparent) value, which furnishes the Lover with his/her reason for loving. On the other, in pursuing, the Lover seeks to be appropriately related to the Beloved. In particular it desires union, or at least face-to-face intimacy with the Beloved. Erotic love differs from disinterested appreciation of value and from distinterested benevolence precisely in this element of the Lover's self-regard. Nevertheless erotic love drives the Lover to assign his/her own happiness second place after loyalty and/or relationship to the Beloved. To be sure, Love's first choice is for happy, mutually enjoyable union with the Beloved. Indeed, Love may be aroused initially by the belief that union with such a Beloved is bound to beatify! But the Lover's desire for union with the Beloved may be frustrated by the latter's temporary or permanent inaccessibility. Thus, erotic love may be ecstatic in that it drives the Lover not only toward what is outside but also to stretch for what may be out of reach. External circumstances or internal features of the two may prevent the desired union and/or the pursuit of it from being good for either. It is a distinctive feature of erotic attraction that it may be stronger than the desire for what is good for either party. Accordingly, while it is—so far as the Lover is concerned—invariably self-regarding in that it desires union with the Beloved, it is not necessarily selfish or altruistic. Rather, persistence in the face of misery and frustration may be heroic. Where no harm to the Beloved is involved, fidelity to the Beloved and/or the relationship at the cost of the Lover's temporary or permanent well-being can even be self-sacrificing; for it pays the Beloved the tribute of finding it so valuable that loyal striving after it is counted more valuable than the Lover's own being or well-being.[28]

In *propria persona* Anselm is himself a monk-lover of God whose aim is to see God's face and whose current, ante-mortem occupation is to strive into God with all his powers. Qua author, Anselm plays Cupid, endeavoring through the *Monologion*, the *Proslogion*, and the *Prayers* generally to stir up the reader into a romance with God, the Good that satisfies.

Seduction in the Monologion

Anselm begins with the assumption that his readers desire (i.e., have an appetite to enjoy) only those things that they think are good.[29] Enjoyment involves a satisfying relation to goods, and the desire for it is thus both object-oriented (the object's value is the reason that it becomes a target) and not only self-regarding but concerned with what is *good for* the agent.

Anselm assumes that this desire to enjoy what is good for the agent would motivate the agent to investigate the source of those goods because it judges them to be good.[30] Anselm's strategy is to begin with "innumerable goods" evident to the senses and reason[31] and to trace them back to a single source. He points out that among those things we think to be good there is already a certain value ordering the useful (*utilitas*) and the honorable (*honesta*), the former desired for the sake of something else and the latter prized as ends to be enjoyed in themselves, and he notes that were our value judgments true, the former being ordered to the latter would be good through it.[32]

The first four chapters argue for the being, subsequent chapters for the incommensurate excellence of the Supreme Nature. The quest for an intellectual grip on the Supreme Nature repeatedly stretches the reader beyond his/her limits (e.g., *Monologion* 15, 25–28, 36, 43, 63–65) and puts him/her in the situation of the tormented Lover: each intellectual advance confirms both how "appetizing" the Beloved is and how inaccessible. Thus the reader's persistence in the face of such frustration signals a shift in motivation, from one that prioritizes the good-for-oneself, to a loyalty to the Beloved at the expense of the reader's own temporary well-being.

Anselm's final assessment of the accessibility issue and strategy of approach to the Supreme Good comes in *Monologion*, chapters 66–67, where he explains (see above) that our best cognitive access to God is through images and that the best image is the rational mind[33] exercising its essential functions "to remember, understand, and love that which is best and greatest of all."[34] Anselm explains (see above) how rational creatures fulfill their telos by using reason to discern values and loving accordingly, in particular loving the Supreme Nature above all, loving only it and all else for its sake[35] and doing so without end.[36] Nevertheless Anselm does not characterize such telos-fulfilling pursuit as disinterested but rather as driven by the desire for enjoyment of the Good that is its object: "who so loves Justice, Truth, Happiness, Incorruptibility, that s/he does not have an appetite to enjoy them?"[37] Thus, the desire for union with the Beloved (the One True Good) leads to seeking it with the whole self, which is telos-fulfilling and has as its byproduct making the self into the best likeness of the Supreme Nature and hence the best being that it can be without further Divine aid.

In remaining chapters Anselm argues that it is only fitting that the Beloved, self-sufficient and all powerful as It is, reward such love with a satisfying relation to itself.[38] And the enjoyment will be carefree and endless.[39] Such striving into God requires one to be sustained by faith and hope,[40] which assures us that it will not ultimately be love unrequited but rather, after some time, love eternally satisfied.

"Erotic" Prayer

Anselm's prayers continue the theme of the creatures' love affair with God. Contenting ourselves for now with a sample, we may note how Anselm begins his

Prayer to Christ with desire for God and a desire to love God,[41] indeed to be in-flamed with such love.[42] As the prayer proceeds, the soul-lover protests that it thirsts, sighs, is tormented with longing for the apparently absent beloved;[43] even teases Christ-the-Beloved for denying it the intimacy of witnessing the passion;[44] refers to the bereft soul-lover as "widow-like";[45] repeatedly begs for the presence of the absent-Beloved, with all its might seeks the face[46] of its spouse.[47] Repeating much of this imagery, the third *Prayer to Mary* expresses its desire and the heart's torment at the absence of the lover;[48] sounds the theme of virginity which the soul owes, as it falls in love with its Lord and marries God.[49]

Romantic Metaphysics

The analogy of romance braids together with the others to suggest yet another "take" on the field of valuables generally. First, God is the supremely valuable One, the Good per se, not only unsurpassably but incommensurately greater than any other. Second, for everything else, to be is to be a way of striving after the Good. God is the ultimate telos of all creatures. The proximate telos—for fire, heating; for earth, reposing in the center; for rational creatures, making correct value judgments and willing accordingly—concretely defines for each the pecu-liar way of striving into God. Third, creatures are constituted by a set of powers to strive towards their concrete *teloi*. Fourth, nonrational creatures strive into God/the Good with all of their powers by the necessity of their natures, while ra-tional creatures do so spontaneously and voluntarily. Fifth, if all such lovers desire union with the Beloved, their powers are never sufficient to attain it. Imitation is the next best thing, properly, a by-product or side effect of the creature's making God its aim. In the case of nonrational creatures not even God can do anything to supplement their efforts and make them more like himself. But where humans and angels are concerned, God can confer the further grace, for which their powers alone would not suffice, of secure happiness in the intimate enjoyment of Himself. Sixth, it follows that to be is to be good, because everything other than God, the Good per se, aims at the Good and—by virtue of striving into the Good with all its powers—an imperfect copy of the GOOD. Seventh, the implicit corollary of such metaphysical optimism is the Christian Platonist doctrine that evil is a priva-tion of being.[50]

PATRON–CLIENT

Following Biblical religion, like Augustine before him, Anselm conceives of the universe by means of a political analogy according to which God is the pater fa-milias, the ultimate patron-king, whereas all creatures are His offspring and clients inasmuch as they are utterly derivative, owe their being and their well-being to God.[51] True to his Christian-Platonist leanings, Anselm would see the cosmos, governed by the Divine King as the paradigm society, of which earthly rulers and realms are pale copies, a community evaluatively structured by considerations of honor and shame.

God as Ideal Pater Familias / Patron-King

Here below, the de jure unimpeachable honor of rulers within the group is a symbolic derived from the sacred status of the group whose survival is the sine qua non objective, so that the unequivocal loyalty owed the ruler is symbolic of that owed the collective. Moreover earthly rulers secure their occupancy of that role either through power ("might makes right") with or without heredity (which is sufficient for the honor of precedence or ascribed honor, respectively) or through intrinsic virtue or excellence (which confers the honor of virtue).

In the cosmic realm normative priorities are reversed: God's honor is unimpeachable because His honor of virtue is intrinsic and unsurpassable: God is by nature a being a more worthy of honor than which cannot be conceived. God would be thus worthy of honor even if no creatures existed and hence even if there were no realm to govern. Searching for measures, Anselm declares, it would be better for countless created realms to be destroyed than for the slightest offense against God to be committed.[52] Rather, so far from GOD's deriving His worthiness of honor from the collective which He heads, the universe (almost nothing as it is)[53] derives all of its worthiness of honor from its symbolic relation to (of signifying by imperfectly resembling) God.

Again if the honor of precedence and the honor of virtue may break apart where earthly rulers are concerned, not so with God. To be sure, God is essentially Supreme Justice and Supreme Power, these are inseparable in God. Anselm further denies that might would make right in God, no matter what the content of the decree. Rather, for Anselm, Divine Justice is prior in the order of explanation: God wills whatever God wills because and only if it is just.[54] This claim finds its metaphysical ground in the doctrine that powers are "optimific"—there is no power for what is not expedient or fitting.[55] On the other hand, if Divine honor of virtue is intrinsic and inseparable, Divine honor of precedence is manifested in the fact that all creatures are subject to Him, one way or another.[56]

Sociological Metaphysics

For Anselm, the metaphysics of Divinity defines ideal patronage. Just as the survival of small villages or clans is enhanced by self-sufficiency in obtaining the necessities of life, and so self-sufficient control of primary resources a feature that makes a ruler good, so for Anselm God is metaphysically self-sufficient insofar as He is and is whatever it is in general better to be than not to be ("has" His being and His well-being) through Himself.[57] Moreover, just as a village or clan is the more secure, the more invulnerable it is to alien attack and hence the more invincible its leaders and armies; so God is metaphysically invulnerable and invincible in that God is impassible (not capable of being causally affected by anything other than Himself).[58] As Anselm says, the forces of adversity and perversity have no power over God.[59] Nor is God's hold on primary goods temporary; it is immutable and eternal.[60]

Role Expectations versus Obligations

The honor code makes honor and shame a function of performance in one's social role and recognizes that the propriety of actions of a given type is role-relative.[61] As patron-king, God's relation to creatures is governed not by any rights they might have against Him, but rather by what befits a person of His wealth and station. Earthly patrons are "expected" to share their wealth and power to benefit the poor and the powerless; failure to deliver is shameful, because it sends the message that there is not "enough to" them to do so, that they are not so wealthy as one thought. Moreover earthly rulers are expected to use their power to protect the realm from disruptive forces from within and without. Anselm insists that "God does not owe anything to anyone."[62] As altogether independent and non-derivative, He does not even owe His existence to His "parts"![63] Nevertheless Anselm's view is that God has been generous:[64] although we are almost nothing and so almost worthless, God has not only graciously conceded to rational creatures the status of clients but has destined them for eternal happy intimacy with Him[65] for the intimacy of His inner court circle, for membership in the patron's *familias*.[66] Again Anselm emphasizes how it befits God as ideal governor to maintain perfect order within the universe.[67]

Creatures are utter subjects ("belong to" God)[68] by nature, are metaphysically too minuscule in themselves to have standing either to praise or to insult God. Granted the status of clients by Divine grace, every creature owes it to God to praise Him by being that-for-which-He-made-it.[69] In the case of rational creatures this means complete and spontaneous obedience in preserving justice.[70] Moreover, since each owes its entire being and well-being to God, there is no other realm, clan, or family to which it could belong relative to which its obligation to God could be qualified. Any authority or office that one creature exercises in relation to another it does by Divine leave, and such permission can be withdrawn at any time.[71]

SIN AND SATISFACTION

The Nature of Sin, Multiply Modeled

If God is the ideal patron-king with creatures as His chosen clients, sin is a failure of the latter in their duties to the former. Anselm treats "sin" primarily as a category of (negative) symbolic value, as actions that send the lying message that God is not, after all, a being a more worthy of honor than which cannot be conceived. His reasons are not far to seek. For the Divine grip on maximal primary goods-for-Godself cannot be broken. There is no power in the universe that could have Divine harm as a side effect, much less (what would be metaphysically impossible) as its aim. Moreover God's honor of virtue is invulnerable. The only even prima facie feasible angle of attack, then, is on God's reputation (His honor of precedence), by refusing to acknowledge it, through spontaneous acts of insubordination. Whatever its content, sin is formally and fundamentally the insult delivered to God by rational creatures in refusing to obey and to praise.[72] Again sin represents the created lover's infidelity, spiritual fornication, virginity badly lost (see above), in which the creature places its own advantage ahead of loyalty to the Beloved, makes God's likeness its end rather than a mere side effect of unequivocal seeking after the Good. Again in sinning the rational creature robs the Divine artisan of the favorable advertising constituted by correctly functioning artifacts, not only by refusing itself to do/be that-for-which-it-was-made but also by diverting the other creatures it uses from their natural end (see above).[73] Accordingly, sin caricatures the image of God in the sinner, because its powers are bent in seeking a lesser good (viz., its own) than the One with which the Blessed Trinity are principally occupied (see above).[74]

Consequences of Sin

From any angle sin is ruinous for the sinner. Anselm's crisp calculations rationalize the general lines common to the varying range of Augustinian estimates. Just as seriously rebellious client/citizens deserve to be punished by the patron-king, even banished from the realm, unless they repent and make satisfaction, so sinful creatures in relation to God. Moreover, given God's unsurpassable honor, Anselm argues, the smallest sin demands satisfaction greater in value than countless worlds, while no mere creature is able to be or do anything commensurately meritorious. Second, because all rational creatures have the obligation to be just but none has the capacity to endow itself with justice if it lacks it, those who desert justice both lack and have the obligation to have it and so disable themselves for fulfilling any of their future obligations. Further, their true happiness involves a just willing of advantage and so will be impossible unless justice is restored to them by God. Third, such damage degrades. Consequently, God can vindicate His own honor by depriving sinful creatures of their honor by not renewing His gift of justice until satisfaction is made. God can restore order in the cosmic kingdom by forcibly subjecting through the punishment of happiness-deprivation those creatures who would not voluntarily submit to His will.[75] Fourth, just as in earthly realms the whole family shares in the disgrace and concrete ruin of the head-of-household, so all humans born of Adam's race participate in the multiple consequences of his fall: an obligation to have justice, which they have neither power nor entitlement to acquire; a weakened body, affected like the brutes by carnal appetites and subject to death;[76] and a soul that is weakened in being affected by carnal appetites to the point that in infancy it can't even understand or think of justice[77] and in adulthood not only lacks justice but would be unable without grace to keep justice if it were received.[78]

Divine Satisfaction

Distinctive to Anselm is the sharp focus his *Cur Deus homo* brings to the dynamics of satisfaction. Just as rebellion in a kingdom challenges the ruler's competence and hence entitlement to his role, so sin insults God by sending the lying message that creatures are rightfully insubordinate, able decisively to thwart His administrative plans. Yet God has projected an ideal society peopled by created clients, made not only angels but Adam's race for that happy company,[79] and does nothing in vain.[80] Divine Power and Wisdom must be resourceful enough to realize what Divine Generosity has purposed,[81] even though Divine Justice forbids it unless satisfaction is made by Adam's race.[82] The ingenious solution is for God to become human,[83] make the God-man the champion, to put the Devil to shame[84] and to make satisfaction for what Adam's family owes. Through His human nature, weaker, "a little lower than the angels," under greater difficulty, under duress of death Jesus Christ renders the obedience for which all rational creatures were made. Because of His Divine nature, His unjust death merits immeasurable compensation, because it is an offense against One Who is a being a more honorable than which cannot be conceived. Just as it befits the wealthy patron to compensate unjustly deprived clients even where third parties initiated the loss, so it would be appropriate for God to compensate Christ. Since as God the God-man needs nothing, it is only fitting that He apply the merits to His human family's debt![85]

RE-CREATING ADAM

Symbolically, both satisfaction and created ruin contradict sin's lie that creatures are rightfully insubordinate. But full vindication of Divine honor involves success for God's purpose, which in turn requires the full dignity of rational creatures to be restored, a way opened for them to become the selves He meant them to be. Yet not even Divine Power, Who created by fiat, can re-create instantaneously by uttering His Word. For from eternity, the Divine artisan (cf. "Artisan and Artifact," above) wanted rational creatures to be so much in His image as to mirror (cf. "Paradigm and Copies, Model and Mirror," above) His aseity, by being just somehow of themselves. To this end God created them with twin inclinations—a will for advantage, for their own happiness, and a will for justice[86]—with partial knowledge of Divine Goodness, so they could not tell whether it would be to their advantage to will an increase in happiness sooner than God willed them to will it.[87] By using their God-given power to uphold and not desert justice, angels and humans could make themselves just, improperly speaking, make themselves more like God than they originally were.[88] To restore their original dignity, God must reopen that collaborative possibility—of Divine grace taking the initiative to stir motivation, renew the gift of justice; of creatures' receiving, exercising their powers as much as they can.

Utter passivity is metaphysically impossible for creatures, for theirs to be is a striving—even for sinners, a striving into the Good (cf. "Romancing the Good: The Dynamics of Love and Desire," above). But without justice, human striving bends inward toward its own advantage, downward toward the metaphysically flimsy goods within its grasp. Narcissism and bestiality[89] become habitual, blinding, deadening sensitivity to the source from which all goods come. The deformity will be permanent unless Divine grace comes to awaken recognition of one's true condition, the vision steadied, the striving straightened through spiritual exercises. If the Benedictine monastery is a school of obedience, training the will to humility, Anselm's *Prayers and Meditations,* his written works generally, are "skillful means" for the cure of souls in their several roles and dimensions, for converting both mind and affections to God.

Restoring the Client

Satisfaction paid cannot cancel the sentence of banishment, so long as the disgraced sinner, expropriated of his power to praise and traitorous in his loves, remains unfit for the heavenly court.[90] For the soul awakened to its disqualification and abysmal need Anselm prescribes ambivalence as the appropriate approach. Prevenient mercy emboldens while fear inhibits.[91] All is hopeless unless God furnishes the means, enables the creature to conform to His wishes in thought, word, and deed; to pay the debts of piety, humility, and praise, which every client owes.[92] Surely friends of God such as Mary and John will hate God's enemies, have contempt for would-be lovers so untrue.[93] The sinner's only recourse is to acknowledge his/her own utter worthlessness and to bank everything on the mercy of God and His saints.[94] The purpose with which the All-Wise patron should be consistent is revealed in the career of the Redeemer;[95] His established policy not to hate the work of His hands.[96] Would it not be shameful for the Divine patron to let reputation outrun His actual generosity?[97] Moreover family members are supposed to "cover" for each other, and the redemptive work of Christ has forged family ties upon which the wayward client can presume.[98] Thus, Anselm's text guides its penitent to beg with importunity[99] that God give the creature something worth giving back,[100] remove the miserable evil of sin if He wants the creature to be thankful for creation;[101] to chide that God will rob Himself of a "once and future" client by abandoning the sinner to its just deserts.[102] Fresh grace empowering each request answers it in advance; the sinner using it to do as much as s/he can has already reentered Divine service.[103]

Reviving the Romance

So long curved inward and downward, the sinner's desire is deadened to the Good for which it was made to strive.[104] With motivational structure so fundamentally damaged, the soul lacks power to ascend.[105] God, the saints, must descend to meet its need.[106] God must reverse despair, rekindle the soul's desire to pray.[107] Having lost grace twice (once in Adam and again *in propria persona*), s/he is somehow worse than the devil.[108] Yet, there is this difference to tug on the Divine heart strings: s/he doesn't hate God's Goodness![109] It enters into the horror of its fornication and adultery.[110] Alive with desire, the soul is restless to love.[111] It meditates on the mighty acts of God in Christ Jesus, the better to fuel its desire, once more to fall in love with its Maker,[112] even begs miraculous restoration of violated innocence.[113] By the end of the exercise the prayer has been answered: grace has quickened the comatose soul into a heartsick lover, impatient for reunion in the chamber of Love.[114]

Reforming the Image

As Augustine taught in *De Trinitate,* so Anselm affirms that the human self made in God's image can "come to itself" only through a return to ecstasy by striving into God with all of its powers. Against apophatic spirituality Anselm insists this means loving God not only with heart and soul but also with all one's mind![115] Moreover it is not enough for each self to go its own direction; upward ascent requires the coordination of all the self's dimensions. Thus if many prayers and meditations take "affective" aim "to stir up love or fear of God,"[116] Anselm's most famous work, the *Proslogion,* stirs the mind to contemplation of God,[117] serves as a paradigm (which his other theological works covertly copy) for integrating intellectual inquiry into the dynamics of monastic prayer.[118] As a bonus, Anselm also shows us his own construal of Augustinian Divine illumination.

In the opening chapter of the *Proslogion* Anselm draws the complacent reader in with an invitation to turn aside and seek God's face,[119] only quickly to expose his/her radical ignorance of how to do it.[120] A long meditation on the consequences of Adam's fall drives home the depth of this disability;[121] anxiety mounts to climactic desperation, pours forth the soul's humble request for Divine assistance to achieve the lower aim of understanding God "a little bit."[122] Thus chastened, the soul is properly postured to approach God along intellectual avenues (in chaps. 2–13, 18–23). The *Proslogion* unveils the true nature of intellectual inquiry as a lover's exchange. First, God lures, by awakening, planting the desire, giving the ability to seek. The soul speaks to ("pros logion," "ad loquium") Truth Itself, energetically badgering with questions, puzzles, and problems. Then it pauses, awaits Divine (self-)disclosure; then tries to articulate what the Other has revealed. The process is repeated, over and over, spiraling ever more deeply into the Other's nature, understanding what seems like more than "a little bit." Now propelled by desire, Anselm suddenly takes stock, evaluates his progress in terms of his original, higher goal of seeing God's face.[123] Anxious puzzlement over how the lower goal can be reached without the higher leads to the proof[124] that God is a being greater than can be conceived. Having acknowledged this permanent limitation, Anselm renews his intellectual investigation into the Divine nature, reaching conclusions that both emphasize the ontological incommensuration between God and creatures[125] and measure God's overwhelming power to satisfy the soul.[126] Positive results, like Love's "sweet nothings," intensify desire and love yet foster hope and engender patient acceptance of the viator's vocation to go on romancing the hide-and-seek Lover, to live in the tension between faith and sight, to recognize partial understandings as tokens of intimacy,[127] as sources of interim joy and delight (chaps. 24–26)!

NOTES

1. St. Augustine, *Confessions* 11.1: "cur ergo tibi tot rerum narrationes digero? non utique per me noveris ea, sed affectum meum excito in te et eorum, qui haec legunt, ut dicamus omnes: Magnus dominus et laudabilis valde."

2. For an appreciation of this dimension of Anselm's writing see Gillian R. Evans, "The 'Secure Technician': Varieties of Paradox in the Writings of St. Anselm," *Vivarium* 13 (1975): 1–21.

3. St. Anselm, *Monologion*, "Prologus": "Quam ego saepe retractans nihil potui invenire me in ea dixisse, quod non catholicorum patrum et maxime beati AUGUSTINI scriptis cohaereat. Quapropter si cui videbitur, quod in eodem opusculo aliquid protulerim, quod aut nimis novum sit aut a veritate dissentiat: rogo, ne statim me aut praesumptorem novitatum aut falsitatis assertorem exclamet, sed prius libros praefati doctoris AUGUSTINI *De trinitate* diligenter perspiciat, deinde secundum eos opusculum meum diiudicet" (St. Anselm, *Opera omnia*, 6 vols., ed. F. Schmitt [Stuttgart: F. F. Frommann, 1968], vol. 1, p. 8, ll. 8–14; subsequent references to this work will be abbreviated in the form "S 1.8.8–14").

4. Ibid., 15; S 1.29.17–30; *Proslogion* 5; S 1.104.11–17.

5. *Monologion* 17; S 1.31.15–27.

6. Ibid., 16; S 1.31.3–8; *Proslogion* 18; S 1.114.14–16.

7. *Proslogion* 17; S 1.113.9–14.

8. Ibid., 23; S 1.117.21–22.

9. *Monologion* 22; S 1.39.3–41.18; 20; S 1.116.2–3 and 20–21.

10. Ibid., 31; S 1.47.7–11: "Sic quippe verbum summae veritatis, quod et ipsum est summa veritas, nullum augmentum vel detrimentum sentiet secundum hoc quod magis vel minus creaturis sit simile; sed potius necesse erit omne quod creatum est *tanto magis est* et *tanto esse praestantius, quanto similius est illi quod summe est et summe magnum est.*" Cf. ibid., 31; S 1.49.12–23: "Hinc etenim fortasse, immo non fortasse sed pro certo, hinc omnis intellectus iudicat naturas quolibet modo viventes praestare non-viventibus, sentientes non sentientibus, rationales, irrationalibus. . . . Quoniam vero simili ratione quaedam naturae magis minusve sint quam aliae, perspicuum est. Quemadmodum enim illud natura praestantius est, quod per naturalem essentiam *propinquius* est *praestantissimo:* ita utique *illa natura magis est, cuius essentia similior est summae essentiae.*" Cf. ibid., 31; S 1.50.12–13: "omnis essentia eo ipso

magis est et praestantior, quo similior est illi essentiae, quae summe est et summe praestat."
Cf. ibid., 4; S 1.16.31–18.3.

11. Ibid., 28; S 1.46.24–31: "Quod vero sic simpliciter et omnimoda ratione solum est
perfectum, simplex et absolutum: id nimirum *quodammodo* iure dici *potest solum esse. Et econ-*
tra, quidquid per superiorem rationem nec simpliciter nec perfecte nec absolute esse sed *vix*
esse aut fere non esse cognoscitur: id utique aliquo modo recte non esse dicitur. Secundum hanc
igitur *solus ille creator spiritus est, et omnia creata non sunt; nec tamen omnino non sunt, quia per illum,*
qui solus absolute est, de nihilo aliquid facta sunt."

12. *Proslogion* 15; S 1.112.14–17: "Ergo domine, non solum es quo maius cogitari nequit,
sed es quiddam maius quam cogitari possit. Quoniam namque valet cogitari esse aliquid
hiuiusmodi: si tu non es hoc ipsum, potest cogitari aliquid maius te; quod fieri nequit." Cf.
ibid., 16; S 1.112.18–113.4.

13. *Monologion* 66; S 1.77.7–24: "Cum igitur pateat quia nihil de hac natura possit per-
cipi per suam proprietatem sed per aliud, certum est quia per illud magis ad eius cognitionem acceditur, quod illi magis per similitudinem propinquat. Quidquid enim inter creata constat illi esse similius, id necesse est esse natura praestantius. Quapropter id et per
maiorem similitudinem plus iuvat mentem indagantem summae veritati propinquare, et
per excellentiorem creatam essentiam plus docet, quid de creante mens ipsa debeat aesti-
mare. Procul dubio itaque *tanto altius creatrix essentia cognoscitur, quanto per propinquiorem sibi crea-*
turam indagatur. Nam quod omnis essentia in quantum est, in tantum sit summae similis essentiae, ratio iam supra considerata dubitare non permittit. Patet itaque quia, sicut sola est
mens rationalis inter omnes creaturas, quae ad eius investigationem assurgere valeat, ita ni-
hilominus eadem sola est, per quam maxime ipsament ad eiusdem inventionem proficere
queat. Nam iam cognitum est, quia haec illi maxime per naturalis essentiae propinquat
similitudinem. Quid igitur apertius quam quia mens rationalis quanto studiosius ad se dis-
cendum intendit, tanto efficacius ad illius cognitionem ascendit; et quanto seipsam intueri
negligit, tanto ab eius *speculatione* descendit?" Cf. *Proslogion* 1; S 1.100.12–15: "Fateor, domine,
et gratias ago, quia creasti in me hanc imaginem tuam, ut tui memor te cogitem, te amem.
Sed sic est abolita attritione vitiorum, sic est offuscata fumo peccatorum, ut non possit
facere ad quod facta est, nisi tu renoves et reformes eam."

14. *Monologion* 67; S 1.77.27–78.11: "Aptissime igitur ipsa sibimet esse velut 'speculum'
dici potest, in quo speculetur ut ita dicam imaginem eius, quam 'facie ad faciem' videre
nequit. Nam si mens ipsa sola ex omnibus quae facta sunt, sui memor et intelligens et
amans esse potest: non video cur negetur esse in illa vera imago ilius essentiae, quae per sui
memoriam et intelligentiam et amorem in trinitate ineffabili consistit. Aut certe inde verius
esse illius se probat imaginem, quia illius potest esse memor, illam intelligere et amare. In
quo enim maior est et illi similior, in eo verior ilius esse imago cognoscitur. Omnino autem
cogitari non potest rationali creaturae naturaliter esse datum aliquid tam praecipuum
tamque simile summae sapientiae, quam hoc quia potest reminisci et intelligere et amare
id, quod optimum et maximum est omnium. Nihil igitur aliud est inditum alicui creaturae,
quod sic praeferat imaginem creatoris."

15. Ibid., 6–8; S 1.18.21–24.6.

16. Ibid., 10; S 1.24.24–25.27; cf. 29–34; S 1.47.3–54.3.

17. Ibid., 9; S 1.24.12–16; 30; S 1.48.8–12.

18. Ibid., 68; S 1.78.25–79.5; cf. 79.12–13: "Hinc itaque satis patenter videtur *omne ratio-*
nale ad hoc existere, ut sicut ratione discretionis aliquid magis vel minus bonum sive non bonum iudicat, ita

magis vel minus id amet aut respuat. Nihil igitur apertius quam rationalem creaturam *ad hoc esse factum,* ut summam essentiam amet super omnia, sicut ipsa est summum bonum; immo *ut nihil amet nisi illam aut propter illam,* quia illa est bona per se, et nihil aliud est bonum nisi per illum." Cf. *Monologion* 69; S 1.79.18: "eam esse *factum ad hoc, ut sine fine amet summam essentiam.*" Cf. *De veritate* 3; S 1.180.12–14: "*Ad hoc . . . nobis datum* est *posse cogitare* esse vel non esse aliquid, *ut* cogitemus esse quod est, et non esse quod non est." Likewise, *De veritate* 4; S 1.181.4–8: "Nam si quamdiu voluit quod debuit, *ad quod scilicet voluntatem acceperat,* in rectitudine et in veritate fuit, et cum voluit quod non debuit, rectitudinem et veritatem deseruit: non aliud ibi potest intelligi veritas quam rectitudo, quoniam sive veritas sive rectitudo, non aliud in eius voluntate fuit quam velle quod debuit." And *De veritate* 5; S 1.182.3–5: "Si ignis ab eo a quo habet esse accepit calefacere: cum calefacit, facit quod *debet.*"

19. *Monologion* 31; S 1.49.7–11: "Sic quippe verbum summae veritatis, quod et ipsum est summa veritas, nullum augmentum vel detrimentum sentiet secundum hoc quod magis vel minus creaturis sit simile; sed potius necesse erit omne quod creatum est tanto magis est et tanto esse praestantius, quanto similius est illi quod summe est et summe magnum est." Cf. ibid., 33; S 1.53.4–6; and 36; S 1.54.18–55.6: "Verbum autem quo creaturam dicit, nequaquam similiter est verbum creaturae, quia non est similitudo, sed principalis essentia."

20. *De veritate* 7; S 1.185.15: "Quidquid igitur est, *vere est,* inquantum est hoc quod ibi [in summa veritate] est."

21. Ibid., 12; S 1.191.27–192.10.

22. Ibid., 1; S 1.178.5–25: "M. *Ad quid facta est* affirmatio?/D. Ad significandum esse quod est./M. hoc ergo *debet.* . . . At cum significat quod *debet, recte* significat. . . . Cum autem *recte* significat, *recta* est significatio. . . . Item cum significat esse quod est, *vera* est significatio. . . . *Idem* igitur est *illi et rectam et veram esse,* id est significare esse quod est. . . . Ergo, non est illi aliud veritas quam rectitudo." Cf. *De veritate* 12; S 1.191.27–192.14.

23. *De concordia praescientiae et praedestinationis et gratiae dei cum libero arbitrio* 3.7; S 2.273.23–274.2. Cf. *Orationes* 7; S 3.20.64–70.

24. *De veritate* 5; S 1.182.6–10: "Unde anima adverti potest rectitudinem seu veritatem actionis aliam esse necessarium, aliam non necessarium. Ex necessitate namque ignis facit rectitudinem et veritatem, cum calefacit; et non ex necessitate facit homo rectitudinem et veritatem, cum benefacit."

25. *Monologion* 68; S 1.79.6–9: "Clarum ergo est rationalem creaturam *totum suum posse* et velle ad memorandum et intelligendum et amandum summum bonum impendere *debere* ad quod ipsum esse suum se cognoscit habere."

26. *De veritate* 10; S 1.190.1–4: "cum omnes supradictae rectitudines ideo sint rectitudines, quia illa in quibus sunt aut sunt aut faciunt quod debent: summa veritas non ideo est rectitudo quia *debet* aliquid. *Omnia enim illi debent, ipsa vero nulli quicquam debet;* nec ulla ratione est quod est, quia est."

27. In his classic work *Agape and Eros* (New York: Harper and Row, 1969), chap. 1, Anders Nygren posits a sharp divide between Platonic eros and Christian agape love. He then has considerable difficulty in grasping the motivation behind Augustine's rich and complex treatment of love (chap. 2). My own view is that Nygren gets into these problems because he misunderstands eros in the first place.

28. This analysis of romantic love contrasts with Anders Nygren's classic analysis of eros in *Agape and Eros,* chaps. 1–2. Nygren's characterization is motivated by his desire to contrast it with an allegedly New Testament notion of agape. He himself admits that his

dichotomy makes Augustine's discussions of love difficult to handle (chap. 2, pp. 471–48). I think my own analysis better fits the plots of great romances, as well as the dynamics of Anselm's own texts.

29. *Monologion* 1; S 1.13.13: "omnes *frui* solis iis appetant quae bona putant."

30. Ibid., 1; S 1.13.13–15: "*unde sunt bona ea ipsa,* quae non *appetit* nisi iudicat esse bona."

31. Ibid., 1; S 1.14.5–7: "innumerabilia bona . . . quorum tam multam diversitatem et sensibus corporeis experimur et ratione mentis discernimus."

32. Ibid., 1; S 1.15.1–3: "necesse est omne quoque *utile* vel *honestum, si vere bona* sunt, per idipsum esse bona, per quod necesse est esse cuncta bona, quidquid illud sit."

33. Ibid., 66; S 1.77.22–24; 67; S 1.77.27–78.11.

34. Ibid., 67; S 1.78.9–10.

35. Ibid., 68; S 1.78.21–79.9.

36. Ibid., 79; S 1.79.12–13 and 18.

37. Ibid., 70; S 1.80.22–24: "quis *sic amet* iustitiam, veritatem, beatitudinem, incorruptibilitatem, *ut iis frui non appetat?*"

38. Ibid., 70; S 1.80.25–31: "Quid ergo summa bonitas retribuet *amanti et desideranti* se nisi seipsam? Nam quidquid aliud tribuat, non retribuit, quia nec *compensatur amori* nec *consolatur amantem nec satiat desiderantem.* . . . Nihil ergo verius, quam quod omnis anima rationalis, si quemadmodum debet studeat amando desiderare summam beatitudinem, aliquando illam ad fruendum percipiat."

39. Ibid., 70; S 1.81.1–6: "Utrum autem ea sine fine fruatur, dubitare stultissimum est, quoniam illa fruens nec timore torqueri poterit nec fallaci securitate decipi, nec indigentiam iam experta illam poterit non amare; nec illa deseret amantem se; nec aliquid erit potentius quod eas separet invitas. Quare quaecumque anima summa beatitudine semel frui coeperit, aeterne beata erit." Cf. *Monologion* 74; S 1.82.22–83.8: "Quae vero animae incunctanter iudicandae sint sic amantes id ad quod amandum factae sunt ut illo quandoque frui, quae autem sic contemnentes ut illo semper indigere merantur, aut qualiter quove merito illae quae nec amantes nec contemnentes dici posse videntur, ad beatitudinem aeternam miseriamve distribuantur: aliquem mortalium disputando posse comprehendere, procul dubio aut difficillimum aut impossibile existimo. Quod tamen a summe iusto summeque bono creatore rerum nulla eo bono *ad quod facta est* iniuste privetur, certissime est tenendum; et *ad idem ipsum bonum est omni homini toto corde, tota anima, tota mente amando et desiderando nitendum.*"

40. Ibid., 76; S 1.83.16–20.

41. *Orationes* 2; S 3.6.10–13.

42. Ibid.; S 3.7.26–28.

43. Ibid.; S 3.7.29–33.

44. Ibid.; S 3.8.63–71.

45. Ibid.; S 3.9.85–92: "quasi vidua."

46. Ibid.; S 3.9.77–79.85–92.

47. Ibid.; S 3.9.93–97.

48. Ibid., 7; S 3.24.155–62.

49. Ibid.; S 3.19.32–35.

50. In fact Anselm qualifies this conclusion in *De casu diaboli* (26; S 1.274.8–30), where he distinguishes two types of good—justice and advantage—and two correlative kinds of evil—injustice and disadvantage. Injustice is nothing, a mere privation of justice, but disadvantage—which includes pain and suffering—is sometimes something and not merely a privation of being. He does not pause to explain how to reconcile this with the convertibil-

ity of goodness with being. Cf. my "St. Anselm on Evil: *De casu diaboli*," *Documenti e studi sulla tradizione filosofica medievale* 3, no. 2 (1994): 1–28.

51. Seminal for understanding this social system and its evaluative framework is the collection edited by J. G. Peristiany, *Honour and Shame: The Values of Mediterranean Society* (London: Weidenfeld and Nicolson, 1965), which combines contemporary anthropological studies with analyses of literature from various periods. Anselm's texts are themselves evidence of how the system worked.

52. *Cur Deus homo* 1.21; S 2.89.12–16.

53. *Monologion* 28; S 1.46.24–31.

54. *Cur Deus homo* 1.12.; S 2.70.11–30.

55. *Proslogion* 7; S 1.105.12–16: "Nam qui haec potest, quod sibi non expedit et quod non debet potest. Quae quanto magis potest, tanto magis adversitas et perversitas possunt in illum, et ipse minus contra illas. Qui ergo sic potest, non potentia potest, sed impotentia."

56. *Cur Deus homo* 1.14–15; S 2.72.8–21 and 25–74.7.

57. *Monologion* 1–3; 15–16; S 1.14.3–16.28; and 29.3–31.8. Cf. *Proslogion* 5; S 1.104.10–17.

58. *Cur Deus homo* 1.8; S 2.59.18–28. Cf. *Proslogion* 6 and 8 and 11; S 1.104.21 and 106.5–7 and 110.1.

59. *Proslogion* 7; S 1.105.13–15. Cf S 1.105.26–106.2: "quia quo plus habet hanc potentiam, eo adversitas et perversitas in illum sunt potentiores, et ille contra eas impotentior. Ergo domine/ deus, inde verius es omnipotens, quia nihil potes per impotentiam, et nihil potest contra te." Cf. *De casu diaboli* 12; S 1.253.28–31: "Hinc est quod dicimus deum non posse aliquid sibi adversum aut perversum: quoniam sic est potens in beatitudine et iustitia, immo quoniam beatitudo et iustitia non sunt in illo diverse sed unum bonum, sic est omnipotens in simplici bono, ut nulla res possit quod noceat summo bono. Ideo namque non potest corrumpi nec mentiri."

60. *Monologion* 18–22, 25, 28; S 1.32.7–41.18; 43.3–44.2; 45.24–46.31. Cf. *Proslogion* 18–21; S 1.113.18–116.12.

61. Cf. *Cur Deus homo* 1.7; S 2.57.17–28

62. Ibid., 1.19; S 2.86.7–9: "Nam deus nulli quicquam debet, sed omnis creatura illi debet; et ideo non expedit homini ut agat cum deo, quemadmodum par cum pari."

63. *Monologion* 17; S 1.31.13–19: "Quid ergo? si illa summa natura tot bona est: eritne composita tam pluribus bonis, an potius non sunt plura bona, sed unum bonum, tam pluribus nominibus significatum? Omne enim compositum ut subsistant, indiget iis ex quibus componitur, et illis *debet* quod est; quia quidquid est, per illa est, et illa quod sunt, per illud non sunt; et idcirco penitus summum non est. Si igitur illa natura composita est pluribus bonis, haec omnia quae omni composito insunt, in illam incidere necesse est."

64. *Cur Deus homo* 2.5; S 2.99.23–100.28.

65. *Proslogion* 1; *Cur Deus homo* 2.98–99.

66. Cf. *Orationes* 5; S 3.23.124–43, where the petitioner appeals to family ties as a ground for mercy.

67. *Cur Deus homo* 1.12; S 2.170.28: "non decet deum aliquid iniuste aut inordinate facere." Cf. 1.13; S 2.71.7–26. Cf. also 1.15; S 2.72.25–74.7, esp. 73.22–25: "Quasi divina sapientia, ubi perversitas rectum ordinem perturbare nititur, non adderet, fieret in ipsa universitate quem deum debet ordinare, quaedam ex violata ordinis pulchritudine deformitas, et deus in sua dispositione videretur deficere."

68. Ibid., 1.7; S 2.56.3–57.3; esp. 56.5: "diabolus aut homo non sit nisi dei."

69. *De concordia* 3.7; S 2.273.23–274.2. Cf. *Orationes* 7; S 3.20.64–70.

70. *Cur Deus homo* 1.11; S 2.68.12–18.

71. Cf. ibid., 1.7; S 2.56.2–57.13, where Boso rejects the ransom theory's assumption that the devil could secure rights against God over other creatures by persuading them to sin.

72. Ibid., 1.15; S 2.72.29–74.6; 1.11; S 2.68.12–69.2.

73. *Orationes* 7; S 3.20.64–70: "Caelum, sidera, terra, flumina, dies, nox et quaecumque humane potestati vel utilitati sunt obnoxia: in amissum decus sese gratulantur, domina, per te quodam modo resuscitata, et nova quadam ineffabili gratia donata. Quasi enim omnia mortua erant: cum amissa congenita dignitate favendi dominatui vel usibus deum laudantium, ad quod facta erant, obruebantur oppresione et decolorabantur ab usu idolis servientium, propter quos facta non erant."

74. Ibid., 8; S 3.27.29–33: "Filium irae tuae fecisti filium gratiae tuae; et ego, illa contempta, feci me filium odii tui. *Reformasti in me amabilem imaginem tuam, et ego superimpressi odibilem imaginem, heu, heu, cuius. Cuius, miser et demens homuncio, cuius imaginem superimpressisti super imaginem dei?*"

75. Cf. *Cur Deus homo* 1.14; S 2.72.8–22. where Anselm indicates that making the creature unhappy against its will is in effect Divine riposte, which demonstrates His honor of precedence: "It is impossible for God to lose His honor. Either the sinner freely repays what he owes or else God takes it from him against his will. For either a man willingly exhibits due subjection to God (be it by not sinning or be it by making payment for his sins), or else *God subjects him to Himself against his will by tormenting him and in this way demonstrates that He is his master.* In this case, we must notice that as a man by sinning seizes what is God's, so God by punishing takes what is man's . . . what God takes away conduces to His honor simply by virtue of His taking it. For by taking it away He shows that the sinner and his possessions are *subject to Him.*" Cf. *Cur Deus homo* 1.15; S 2.72.29–274.2.

76. *De conceptu virginali et de originali peccato* 2; S 2.141.12–142.5.

77. Ibid., 2; S 2.141.13–142.5; and 8; S 2.149.17–29 and 150.1–4; and 29; S 2.172.16–173.3.

78. Ibid., 8; S 2.150.1–4: "Quod illa quidem necessitas qua humana natura sola per se iustitiam recuperare nequit, et illa qua corpus quod corrumpitur aggravat animam, ut eandem iustitiam nec acceptam in aetate perfecta sine auxilio gratiae servare nec in infantibus saltem intelligere queat, ab illo simine sint alienae." Cf. ibid., 12; S 2.154.25–155.3.

79. *Cur Deus homo* 1.16–18; S 2.74.10–84.3.

80. Ibid., 2.1; S 2.97.4–98.5.

81. Ibid., 1.9; S 2.61.8–64.11. Cf. 2.4; S 2.99.3–13.

82. Ibid., 1.13; S 2.7–26; 1.19; S 2.84.6–86.15; 1.23; S 2.91.10–17.

83. Ibid., 2.6–7; S 2.101.3–102.22; 2.9; S 2.105.3–106.8.

84. Ibid., 2.11; S 2.111.8–14.

85. Ibid., 2.18–19; S 2.126.23–131.24.

86. *De casu diaboli* 12–14; S 1.255.2–259.4.

87. Ibid., 23–24; S 1.269.27–272.11.

88. Ibid., 18; S 1.263.5–32.

89. Ibid., 13; S 1.257.22–23.

90. *Orationes* 5; S 3.13.4–16.23–14.37; and ibid., 7; S 3.18.18–19.27.

91. Ibid., 10; S 3.34.33–46 and 35.50–54; ibid., 11; S 3.42.19–43.49.

92. Ibid., 1; S 3.5.4–6.17.

93. Ibid., 10; S 3.34.33–46 and 35.50–54; and ibid., 11; S 3.42.19–43.49.

94. *Orationes* 10; S 3.35.69–78 and 36.85–91. Cf. his turn to Jesus and to St. Paul (ibid., 10; S 3.36.79–84 and 39.165–72), to Mary and to Christ (ibid., 6; S 3.17.62–74).

95. Ibid., 6; S 3.17.55–61.

96. Ibid., 11; S 3.44.71–45.87.

97. Ibid., 6; S 3.16.48–17.54.

98. Ibid., 7; S 3.23.139–143.25 and 184–95.

99. Ibid., 10; S 3.39.173–76. Cf. ibid., 11; S 3.32.56–57.

100. Ibid., 7; S 3.24.163–71.

101. Ibid.; S 3.28.77–29.81.

102. Ibid.; S 3.25.174–83.

103. Ibid., 11; S 3.44.63–64.

104. *Proslogion* 1; S 1.100.4–5: "Domine, incurvatus non possum nisi deorsum aspicere, erige me ut possim sursum intendere."

105. Ibid., 9; S 3.30.12–17; ibid., 10; S 3.34.41–46.

106. Ibid., 9; S 3.30.18–20; 10; S 3.36.79–84.

107. Ibid., 2; S 3.6.10–13 and 6.15–7.28. Cf. ibid., 10; S 3.34.33–46.

108. Ibid., 8; S 3.27.34–45.

109. Ibid., 8; S 3.28.77–29.81.

110. *Meditatio* 2: Deploratio virginitatis male amissae; S 3.80.3–83.116.

111. Ibid., 7; S 3.18.4–8.

112. Ibid., 11; S 3.7.42–8.62. Cf. ibid., 7; S 3.18.9–14 and 21.76–22.107, where the exercise is used to increase desire. Cf. *Meditatio* 3: Meditatio redemptionis humanae; S 3.84.3–91.211.

113. *Orationes* 8; S 3.27.34–29.93.

114. Ibid., 7; S 3.24.155–62 and 25.196–99. Cf. ibid., 2; S 3.8.63–71 and 9.77–92. Cf. *Meditatio 3;* S 3.91.201–211.

115. *Proslogion* 25; S 1.120.17–20.

116. *Orationes,* "Prologus"; S 3.3.2–3: "*Orationes sive meditationes* quae subscriptae sunt, quoniam ad excitandam legentis mentem ad dei amorem vel timorem."

117. *Proslogion* 1: "Excitatio mentis ad contemplandum deum"; S 1.97.3. Cf. ibid., 24; S 1.117.25–26: "Excita nunc, anima mea, et erige totum intellectum tuum, et cogita quantum potes, quale et quantum sit illud bonum."

118. Cf. Benedicta Ward, "Introduction," *The Prayers and Meditations of Saint Anselm with the Proslogion* (Harmondsworth: Penguin Books, 1973), 44–51. See also Yves Cattin, "La Priere de S. Anselme dans le *Proslogion,*" *Revue des Sciences Philosophiques et Theologiques* 72 (1988): 373–96; and my "Praying the *Proslogion:* Anselm's Theological Method," in Thomas D. Senor, ed., *The Rationality of Belief* (Ithaca: Cornell University Press, 1995).

119. *Proslogion* 1; S 1.97.4–10.

120. Ibid., 1; S 1.98.1–15.

121. Ibid., 1; S 1.98.16–99.14.

122. Ibid., 1; S 1.99.15–100.19.

123. Ibid., 14; S 1.111.8–11.

124. Ibid., 15; S 1.112.14–17.

125. Ibid., 18–23; S 1.113.18–117.22.

126. Ibid., 24–26; S 1.117.25–122.2.

127. *Commendatio;* S 2.40.10–12: "inter fidem et speciem intellectum quem in hac vita capimus esse medium intelligo: quanto aliquis ad illum proficit, tanto eum propinquare speciei, ad quam omnes anhelamus, existimo."

SIX

Primal Sin*

Scott MacDonald

The central thesis of Augustine's final solution to the problem of evil and the banner under which he attacks the Manichaean dualist alternative that once attracted him is the claim that evil entered God's wholly good creation through certain free choices of God's creatures. Augustine takes the biblical stories of creaturely falls to be describing these evil-originating free choices. The fall of the angels constitutes the paradigm case since, unlike Adam's and Eve's sin in the garden, the first angelic sin is entirely unprecedented.[1] We can think of that first evil free choice as constituting primal sin.

The first sin deserves to be called primal, however, not just because it is temporally first but also because it is something radically new in creation: the first evil appears against a backdrop of utter goodness. All things created by God, including the rational creatures whose free choices are the original evils, are wholly good and without flaw. Augustine takes this to be the implication of both the creation story (in surveying *everything* that he had made during the six days of creation, God saw that it was very good [Genesis 1:31]) and the Christian conception of God as a perfect being (a perfect being is perfectly good and the source of all and *only* good things). On his account, therefore, there can be no context of defect or corruption

*The first draft of this paper was completed during a sabbatical year spent at the National Humanities Center in 1992–93. I gratefully acknowledge the support for my work provided that year by the National Humanities Center and by a University of Iowa Faculty Scholarship. I should like to thank John Boler for allowing me to see unpublished work of his on Augustine's account of the will, and George Bealer, John Boler, Evan Fales, Norman Kretzmann, Bill Mann, Gareth Matthews, Alfred Mele, and Claudia Eisen Murphy for comments on earlier drafts. I am grateful to the audiences who discussed the paper with me at public events: in Medieval Studies at Cornell University, at the Eastern Division meetings of the American Philosophical Association (in 1996), and at the State University of New York at Buffalo. Bonnie Kent provided stimulating and useful comments at the APA. I am especially grateful to Norman Kretzmann and Alfred Mele for their generosity in conversation about these issues while we were fellows together at the National Humanities Center.

into which the first sin fits. Good creatures with good wills voluntarily introduce evil into a world where there was none before. Primal sin is not only unprecedented but also seemingly unprepared for and unprompted.

Some commentators have thought that this account of primal sin as a radical voluntary initiative on the part of creatures presents us with a paradox. Critics point out, on the one hand, that it is essential to Augustine's theodicy that the first evil is voluntary and that an act's being genuinely voluntary requires that it proceed in the right sort of way from the agent whose act it is. Voluntary acts are an agent's own, and as such they must fit into a context provided by certain of the agent's internal states—for example, her desires, attitudes, beliefs, and perceptions. This context makes them intelligible as acts of a rational being. But on the other hand, Augustine insists that the first evil is a radically new occurrence in God's good creation. This seems to entail that there can be no appropriate context into which primal sin fits. For it might seem that an agent's voluntarily perpetrating evil can be made intelligible only by pointing to morally defective internal states of the agent—disordered loves or passions, vicious character traits, culpable ignorance or negligence, or something of the sort—as the source of her action. In a recent paper William Babcock has put the difficulty this way:

> The problem takes the form of a classic dilemma. *Unless* there is some recognizable continuity between agent and act, it will appear either that the evil angels' will was caused by something other than themselves (some form of compulsion) or that it was completely uncaused (a chance or random outcome). But *if* there is some recognizable continuity between agent and act, it will appear that the evil angels did not actually share the same initial moral goodness as the good angels and therefore that they were already inclined to evil even before they exercised any moral agency at all. Without continuity, then, the act—i.e., the first evil will—will not count as the agent's own; with continuity, the act will not count as the origin of evil. It was a dilemma which, in the end, Augustine could not solve.[2]

Augustine seems to be aware of the force of these considerations. Near the end of book 2 of *De libero arbitrio,* having traced the origin of evil to the act by which a created free will turns away from God toward some lesser good, he prompts Evodius with what he supposes to be the natural next question: "But perhaps you will ask: 'Since the will is moved when it turns itself away from the unchangeable good toward a changeable good, where does *that* movement, which is clearly evil even though the free will must be counted as a good . . . , come from?'"[3] But Augustine seems to have called attention to this line of inquiry only to close it off.

> Perhaps you will be disappointed if, when you question me in this way, I reply that I don't know. I will, however, have replied truly, for what is nothing cannot be known. . . . Therefore since the movement of turning away, which we agreed is sin, is a defective movement, and since every defect is from nothing [*ex nihilo*], see where it belongs and you will no doubt see that it does not belong to God. Nevertheless since this defect is voluntary, it has been put in our power. (*De libero arbitrio* 2.20.54)[4]

Once the question of the origin of evil free choices has been raised, however, Evodius takes it as his own and makes it the first and main topic of book 3. Finally, much later in that book he insists, with a hint of annoyance, that Augustine face up to it. "I still want to know, if possible, why the [good angels] did not sin, and why [the evil angels] did sin. . . . If there were no cause, there would not be this distinction among rational creatures. . . . What cause distinguishes them? . . . Don't give me the answer: 'An act of will' [*voluntas*], for I'm looking for the cause of the act of will itself" (*De libero arbitrio* 3.17.47). Augustine is unrepentant, however, and gives Evodius just the answer he says he doesn't want.

> Since an act of will is the cause of sin, and you're looking for the cause of the act of will itself, if I were to find this cause for you, wouldn't you then ask for the cause of the cause I found for you? What limit is there to the inquiry; what could bring an end to our examination and discussion? You must not look for anything beyond the root. Don't think that anything could be said more truly than that avarice—that is, wanting more than is enough—is the root of all evils [1 Timothy 6:10]. . . . Now, avarice of this sort is cupidity, and cupidity is a wicked act of will [*improba voluntas*]. Therefore a wicked act of will is the cause of all evils. . . . But if you demand a cause of this root, how will it be the *root* of all evils? (*De libero arbitrio* 3.17.48)

Augustine apparently thinks that the first evil free choices are acts for which there is no cause beyond the choices themselves and that those who look for an account that goes further search in vain.

In writing *The City of God* two decades later Augustine takes a line similar to the one we have seen him taking in *De libero arbitrio,* insisting in slightly different language that inquiry into the source of evil simply comes to a stop with evil acts of will.

> Therefore no one should look for the efficient cause of an evil act of will, for there is no efficient but [only] a deficient [cause] because [an evil act of will] is not an effect [*effectio*] but a defect [*defectio*]. For to begin to have an evil will is this: defecting from that which is highest to that which is less. To want to find the causes of these defections . . . is like wanting to see darkness or hear silence. (*City of God* 12.7)[5]

Babcock, however, assumes that Augustine's blocking inquiry into the causes of evil free choices in this way amounts to a denial that there is any recognizable continuity between primal sinners and their sin. He therefore concludes that primal sin cannot be genuinely moral action.

> If silence is the absence of sound and darkness the absence of light, deficient causality, it would seem, must be the absence of cause. . . . The notion of a "deficient cause," then, turns out to be too thin, too attenuated, to hold the fall of the evil angels within the arena of moral agency. It cannot be delineated sharply or firmly enough to distinguish the first evil exercise of will from a random outcome, an event of pure happenstance rather than the agent's own act.[6]

In short, according to Babcock, Augustine cannot deny the possibility of uncovering the causal origins of the first evil free choices while at the same time maintaining that primal sins are instances of genuine moral agency. As Babcock sees it, the appeal to so-called deficient causes is an unsuccessful attempt to have it both ways.

I think Babcock's assessment of Augustine's account is mistaken. In particular I reject the inference from Augustine's claims that primal sin can have no cause (or only a deficient cause) to the view that primal sin must be a mere "random outcome, an event of pure happenstance," and so not a manifestation of genuine moral agency. My view is that Augustine's rather abrupt refusal to undertake a search for the causes of evil free choices is misleading, in effect masking his own patient and subtle pathology of sin in general and primal sin in particular. A careful look at Augustine's moral psychology of sin will, I think, provide the materials for constructing a defensible account of the radical voluntary initiatives that, on his view, introduce evil into God's good creation.

I develop my argument in two stages. In the first I set out the main features of Augustine's explanation of how moral agents can fall into evil.[7] I argue that he identifies two sides or faces to morally evil choices. They are *defects*, but they are not simply defects; they are defective acts of will. Augustine thinks that explanations of morally evil choices must be correspondingly complex, accounting for the two distinct sides of sin. That is why his claim that the defect in primal sin can have no cause should not be read as the claim that primal sin is wholly unmotivated by or discontinuous with the primal sinner's practical reasoning. The psychological continuity between primal sinner and primal sin is provided by the other part of the explanation of the sin: insofar as sin is an act of will it is motivated in a perfectly ordinary way by the agent's beliefs and desires. The defect in the act of will must be explained differently, not by any sort of motivation but by a kind of negligence on the agent's part. This identification of the fundamental significance for moral agency of the possibility of negligence in practical reasoning is, I think, the deep and neglected insight in Augustine's account of primal sin.

In the second stage of my argument I develop and defend this Augustinian insight, showing its power to account for important phenomena in the lives of moral agents and to illuminate essential connections among practical reason, voluntary action, and moral responsibility. Although I find the materials for this part of my project in Augustine's writings, particularly *De libero arbitrio* and *City of God*, I extend Augustinian ideas beyond what I can claim to have found explicitly in the texts. For this reason I am not able (and am not particularly concerned) to distinguish clearly this constructive enterprise from the more strictly reconstructive first part of the paper. If my constructive arguments are successful, Augustine's account of primal sin ought to be seen as having important applications beyond theodicy and philosophical theology. In the paper's last section I point some of these out and argue that they constitute an Augustinian legacy in moral psychology that is worth reclaiming.

Following Augustine, I'll take the primal angelic sin as my paradigm, but I'll help myself to Augustine's account of primal human sin where that is useful for my purposes. There are, of course, two respects in which the first human and angelic sins are not alike. First, unlike primal angelic sin, primal human sin is preceded (by angelic sin) and prompted (by angelic malevolence).[8] But for reasons that will emerge Augustine nevertheless takes primal human sin to mirror in corporeal rational nature the precise structure of the incipient misuse of will found in incorporeal rational creatures. Second, Adam's and Eve's sin assumes unique significance in Augustine's theology, for the human fall is not only primal but also original sin. It is the origin of a moral corruption that debilitates all members of the human race, a moral defect transmitted to them by virtue of their descent from the first, sinful human beings. The concepts of primal sin and original sin, however, can be kept apart and, despite the fact that Augustine takes one and the same act—Adam's and Eve's sin in the garden—to instantiate both, his interest in and analysis of each are largely independent. I will have nothing at all to say about original sin.[9]

PRIMAL SIN AND THE ORIGIN OF EVIL

Augustine designed his account of primal sin for purposes of theodicy, and so we need to begin our investigation by placing it in context. Augustine's understanding of original evil is shaped by two features of that context: by general philosophical constraints imposed by the problem of evil and by the dialectical requirements of his debate with the Manichaeans. He holds that God is the perfect, highest good and that, as such, God is the source of all and only what is good. Evil, then, cannot have been directly perpetrated by God.[10] Augustine shares this much with the Manichaeanism he rejects. But since he maintains, contrary to the Manichaeans, that God is both omnipotent and absolutely sovereign, he denies the Manichaean theological dualism that identifies an ultimate cosmic principle distinct from God, to whose activity all the evils in creation can be traced. According to Augustine, every reality other than God owes its existence to the perfectly good creator who is the source of all being. He recognizes, of course, that these two claims—that everything that comes from God is good and that all reality other than God comes from God—have the seemingly paradoxical implication that all reality, everything that exists, is good.[11]

Augustine's account of the origin of evil, then, faces what we might think of as the logical problem of showing that it is not inconsistent to hold both that there is evil in the world and that everything that exists is good. His general solution to this difficulty is his doctrine that evil is no substance or nature but only a corruption or privation. Insofar as evils are corruptions or privations in creatures they are not themselves created natures. A creature's being evil does not consist in its possessing some reality additional to its nature but, rather, in its having a defective nature, lacking being to some extent. Conceiving of evil in this way allows Augustine to hold both that there is evil and that all creatures—that is, all created substances or natures—are good insofar as they have being. He can acknowledge that evil infects creation without thereby committing himself to the claim that evil is one of God's creatures.

Augustine's understanding of the particular evil that is primal sin conforms to this general account: the first evils are defective free choices that constitute a corruption in rational nature. Primal sin occurs when, by an act of free will, rational creatures irrationally turn away or defect from the highest good. With his Manichaean opponents in mind Augustine is careful to emphasize that it is the turning away, the defection itself, and not the faculty of will or the object to which it turns that constitutes the evil in primal sin: "Thus it happens that neither the goods that are sought after by sinners nor the free will itself . . . are in any way evil. What is evil is its turning away from the unchangeable good and its turning toward changeable goods" (*De libero arbitrio* 2.19.53).[12] Primal sin, then, as Augustine understands it, is a corruption of rational nature that gives evil its first foothold in God's creation.

The thornier problem Augustine's theodicy must deal with is moral: if evil cannot arise from sources outside God's creative and providential control, and if God cannot himself directly perpetrate it, then it seems that evil must originate from within creation. But if evil originates within God's own creation, it seems that God as creator must be at least indirectly responsible and thus culpable for it. Augustine's solution to this problem has two parts. First, if he is to deny that God is culpable for the evil in creation, he needs to show that someone else, some creature, is. The creaturely source of evil, then, must be not just its direct cause but a direct cause of a particular sort, namely, an agent whose activity is a locus for moral responsibility. But on his view moral responsibility attaches only to voluntary acts— that is, to agents insofar as they act voluntarily. As Augustine never tires of pointing out, sinners are justly punished for their sins only insofar as their sins are voluntary. An act of wrongdoing that is necessitated in any way—by some necessity associated with the agent's nature or any kind of coercion, whether internal or external to the agent—is not voluntary, and the agent whose act it is is for that reason free of any guilt. Hence, if the moral culpability for evil is to be located within creation itself, it must attach to creatures with wills—rational natures—by virtue of their voluntary acts. The original evils, then, must be voluntary evils—that is, sins.[13]

Second, Augustine is aware that blaming rational creatures for the evil their sin introduces into creation is not enough to show that God is not also to blame, at least indirectly. In general the discovery that a certain agent is culpable for a given evil does not rule out the possibility that other agents are culpable as well. Hence, Augustine needs to establish the stronger claim that rational creatures and rational creatures *alone* are to blame for the corruption of creation. He needs to show that the lineage of moral culpability can be traced back as far as but no farther than the primal sinner.[14]

The charge that God is indirectly culpable for the moral evil in creation might arise from either of two sides. On the one hand it might seem that God is indirectly to blame for evil by virtue of certain of his commissions—that is, by virtue of perpetrating actions that, though not themselves evil, make its occurrence in some sense likely. To defend against this charge, Augustine needs to deny that creation was designed negligently, that some sort of nisus for evil was built into God's creatures. On the other hand it might seem that God is indirectly responsible for evil by virtue of certain of his omissions or permissions—that is, by virtue of permitting or failing to prevent evil that he can prevent. To block this line of attack, Augustine must argue that God has morally sufficient reason for permitting the actual occurrence of evil that he could have prevented.

Augustine thinks that conceiving of original evils as acts of free will is the key to defending God's goodness against both these charges. Against the latter Augustine develops the main line of his famous free-will defense: God has morally sufficient reason for endowing creatures with the dangerous capacity for originating evil and permitting them to exercise it. This is because free will is itself a good and its goodness, together with the goodness of the wider economy of the postfall creation in which God weaves evil into a beautifully ordered whole (which essentially includes the just punishment of sin), outweighs the evil to which it gives rise. Making good on this line of defense may be the biggest challenge facing an Augustinian-style free-will theodicy, and it is a task I do not take up here.[15] It is Augustine's reply to the first of these two charges that brings the problem of primal sin into focus.

Augustine sees that arguing that the trail of moral culpability stops at created rational beings requires him to maintain that the first sinners are not created defective in any morally relevant way—that is, that the moral defects constituted by their primal sin are not preceded by any other morally relevant flaw in creation. With Manichaean dualism once again in view he emphasizes that, as creatures of a perfectly good God, both the evil angels and the first human beings were created without moral defect; like the rest of God's creation, they were very good.[16] In originating evil, then, the rational creatures who are the first sinners bring into creation something entirely new. On Augustine's view, their ability to do this lay in their possession of free will. Their having the power of free choice opens to them the possibility of choosing and acting de novo, of their becoming genuine originators. Hence, creatures with free will are not only loci of responsibility but also capable of radical initiatives for which they alone are responsible.

On Augustine's account, then, evil enters creation with primal sin, which is a defective act of a creaturely will. The first sins, both angelic and human, are free choices of creatures with rational natures, namely, the free acts of will by which the evil angels and the first human beings turn away from God, the highest and immutable good, toward some lesser, corruptible good. The sin, the moral evil, is the voluntary turning away itself, which, insofar as it consists in the loving of a lesser good in place of a greater good, constitutes disorder in the soul and a perversion of rational nature.

In presenting this summary account I have introduced a kind of terminological precision that is important for our purposes but that Augustine's Latin does not strictly observe. It's clear that Augustine holds that primal sin is a certain kind of act of will or choice—the act or movement of turning away or defecting from God. But he typically refers to this sort of act by means of the same term he uses to cover various other things and phenomena, namely, *voluntas* (will).[17] As Augustine uses it, *voluntas* can designate any one of at least four related phenomena: (1) a faculty or power of the soul—the will, (2) a particular act of that power such as a voluntary choice or volition, (3) any kind of passing or enduring state or disposition of that power such as an intention, attitude, want, or desire, and (4) a person's overarching or dominant bent, directedness, or volitional commitment, what we might think of as the single desire or end that is unifying and architectonic in a person's life. Thus, in order to identify and isolate the phenomena essential to primal sin, I use the terms "act of will" and "choice" where Augustine typically uses only "voluntas" (intending the second of these senses).[18] Nevertheless there is a clear and close connection between the evil choice constitutive of primal sin and the evil states, dispositions, and characters that take root in fallen creatures. Augustine's characterizing this evil choice as a turning away (*aversio*) from God and a turning toward (*conversio*) some created good suggests that he has in mind the sort of act of will that initiates or gives rise to an enduring state or disposition of will, in the way that formulating an intention (which is an act) typically initiates or gives rise to the having of the relevant intention (which is a state or disposition). In this context, then, "turning away" and "turning toward" should be thought of as "setting one's mind" in one direction rather than another, "committing oneself" to something or some course, in a decisive and lasting way. Augustine's use of the word "loving" is to be understood in the same way in these contexts. When he says that primal sin consists in loving a creature in place of God, he is referring primarily to the sort of choice whereby one commits oneself to a certain course in a certain way. But "loving" can also refer to an enduring state and to the overarching bent of a one's will that results from a commitment of that sort. Augustine can therefore hold that, after the occurrence of primal sin, sinners are in a state of loving some lesser good in place of God.[19] On his account, then, the evil *voluntas* that constitutes primal sin is a particular sort of act of will, the sort of choice or volition that initiates or causes the corresponding sort of evil *voluntas*, the enduring evil state of the will that constitutes the primal sinner's lasting corruption and self-inflicted punishment.

DE NOVO SINS AND DEFICIENT CAUSATION

Understanding the central theoretical roles played by the notion of free will in Augustine's theodicy puts us in a position to see his reasons for rejecting the possibility of finding a cause of the sort of free choice that constitutes primal sin. In the passages we've looked at, his primary purpose in rejecting that possibility is simply to rule out what later medieval philosophers will call violent causes of sin—causes that coerce or compel an agent to act as she does.[20] As we have seen, he holds that rational creatures must be responsible for evil and that they can be responsible for evil only if they bring it about voluntarily. But as he points out, an act's being co-erced is incompatible with its being voluntary. Primal sin, then, cannot be the re-sult of coercion by an external agent or a consequence of any sort of necessity of nature or irresistible internal compulsion arising from overwhelming desire or in-vincible ignorance or deception.[21] Primal sins are voluntary and primal sinners culpable only if their sin can be resisted. But if sin is resistible, then whether or not an agent sins is ultimately within that agent's own power, and no putative cause of sin outside the agent's own will can be sufficient to bring it about. Augustine con-cludes that the sinning must be up to the agent herself—that is, it must be due ul-timately to the agent's own will.

> Whatever is the cause of an act of will, if it cannot be resisted, one yields to it with-out sin; but if it can be resisted, then if one does not yield to it, one will not sin. Or perhaps one falls out of carelessness [*incautum*]? Then one should take care that one does not fall. Is the deception so great that it is altogether impossible for one to guard against it? In that case there are no sins, for who sins in connection with something that cannot be guarded against in any way? If one sins, then it can be guarded against. (*De libero arbitrio* 3.18.50)

So Augustine's view that primal sin is voluntary, and for that reason culpable, gives him good reason for rejecting any proposal that he undertake a search for violent causes of the first evil choices.

Eliminating the possibility of these sorts of causes for primal sin is clearly not the same as denying the possibility of there being reasons or motives that in some way explain or make intelligible primal sinners' evil choices. Hence, these passages seem clearly not to commit Augustine to the claim that there can be no connec-tion of the sort necessary for moral agency between primal sinners and their sins. Moreover, it's clear that Augustine does not intend to close off the search, in the case of primal or any other sort of sin, for certain kinds of reasons or motives for the sinner's action. On his view voluntary actions are necessarily motivated—that is, it is a necessary condition of an agent's acting voluntarily that there be a per-ceived object for the sake of which the agent acts: "Nothing draws the will into ac-tion [*ad faciendum*] except some object that has been perceived" (*De libero arbitrio* 3.25.74). It follows from this that since primal sin is voluntary, there must be a per-ception of some object by the primal sinner that draws the will into action.[22]

Augustine holds that sin is essentially a disordered act of will, the turning away from the highest good toward a lesser good. As he sees it, then, the sinner's act of will—the choosing of the lesser good—is motivated by the fact that the sinner perceives the goodness of the object he comes to choose. As we have seen, Augus-tine insists against the Manichaeans that the objects that move the first evil wills are goods. So on his view, there is a straightforward sense in which something moves a primal sinner's will: the object toward which the disordered act of will is directed; and a straightforward sense in which that act of will is intelligible: it is directed toward an object that is worth choosing. Augustine's denial that there is any cause of sin other than the will itself is clearly not meant to suggest that sins are bare, utterly unmotivated acts of will. On his own account events of that sort would be nothing more than unintelligible eruptions in the lives of sinners and not voluntary acts at all.

But while this account provides a motive for the sinner's choosing the object toward which the disordered choice is directed, it of course leaves unexplained the disorder in that choice. Even if the object of evil free choices is a recognizable good, and so something that can intelligibly be desired, we still need an explanation of sinners' preferring it to another, higher good. We will want to know not just why sinners turn toward some created good but also why, in doing so, they turn away from the eternal and supreme good. Strictly speaking, since it is the disorder in the act of will—the turning away from the greater good—that constitutes the sin, a motive explaining the sinner's choosing of some created good will not fully explain the sin in that act of will. We need, then, to think of the single act of will constitutive of sin as having two faces; it is at once a turning-toward and a turning-away, an embracing and an abandoning.[23] Augustine's clever and sometimes inventive rhetoric marks this distinction: an evil act of will is both a *conversio* and an *aversio*, an *effectio* and a *defectio*.[24] A sinner's perception of the goodness of the object toward which he turns makes his *conversio* toward that object intelligible, but perception of its good will not by itself explain his *aversio* from a greater good.

Primal sinners' defection from God, then, cannot be explained simply by the fact that they perceive some created thing as good and so reasonably desire it. Moreover, it is no help simply to add that they desire some created thing more than they desire God, for that irrational preference is just what needs explaining. Their loving a lesser good in place of a greater good is what constitutes their disordered choice. How can we make sense of primal sinners' voluntarily choosing something that is less good than some alternative that is equally open to them?

The difficulty in explaining irrational choices in general is exacerbated in the case of primal sin because, in that case, we cannot appeal to the kinds of factors that mitigate the unintelligibility of irrationality in other cases. The appearance of naked irrationality is dispelled, for example, if it can be shown that a putatively irrational agent was unaware of certain important facts relevant to his choice so that, although he preferred what is in fact the lesser good, he himself was unaware that it was less good than some alternative or mistakenly supposed it to be better. For two reasons, however, it is not open to Augustine to appeal to cognitive deficiencies of this sort here: first, because the primal sinner's knowledge of the relevant facts is built into the case—angels and the first human beings know God directly and know that God is the highest good—and second, because ignorance of or cognitive error with respect to the relevant facts would undermine the primal sinner's responsibility for failing to love God in the appropriate way. Insofar as ignorance and cognitive error mitigate irrationality, they also excuse it, provided that the agent is not culpable for the cognitive deficiencies themselves. And if the deficiencies are culpable, then since the voluntary acts by which the agent acquired those deficiencies must precede the act explained in part by appeal to them, the latter cannot be truly primal sin.

In other cases the absurdity in irrational choice is mitigated if it can be shown that the agent is weak willed in some way, that he fails to choose in accordance with his reasoned assessment of the relative values of the alternatives before him because of some strong conflicting motivation. But it seems impossible that primal sinners should suffer this sort of weakness—that is, that, while believing and being aware of the fact that God is the highest good, they should nevertheless voluntarily choose what they believe to be a lesser good. If clear-eyed irrationality of this sort is possible at all, it seems that it can occur only because of an internal conflict in motivation, a conflict between one's considered practical judgments and motivation arising from a source independent of one's reason. That, however, would require that a primal sinner's soul is disordered prior to the primal sin, that the primal sinner is subject to passions or desires that are out of line with right reason. This sort of antecedent defect is precisely what is ruled out in the case of truly primal sin. It must be that either primal sinners are culpable for the corruption in their souls that leads to a given instance of weakness of the will, in which case the sin resulting from that instance of weakness is not primal but derivative sin, or they are not culpable for that corruption, in which case their sins do not emerge de novo but are the acts of creatures that are antecedently defective. It might seem, then, that primal sin is a manifestation of naked irrationality and is, as such, essentially unintelligible.

To see whether Augustine can consistently hold that primal sin is an irrational free choice while at the same time denying, as his theodicy constrains him to do, that the primal sinner is relevantly ignorant or weak willed, we need to look closely at the sort of irrationality his account identifies. In a passage I've already quoted he suggests that the will falls when it fails to guard against sin.[25] It follows from primal sin's being a *sin* that it could have been guarded against. Its actual occurrence shows that primal sinners failed to guard against it. Augustine points us to a kind of failure, but in what does that failure consist? What could primal sinners have done to guard against sinning? I think the answer must be that they failed to pay attention to the reason they had for loving God above all things, namely, their knowledge that God is the highest good. Primal sinners could have resisted loving some created good in place of God—they could have avoided making an irrational choice of this sort—simply by calling to mind the reasons for choosing otherwise that were in their possession. Had they attended to the reasons they possessed, they would have seen that rationality required them to love God above all things. Moreover, since they were not weak willed, they would have chosen rationally had they seen what rationality required of them. Primal sinners, then, must have made their evil choices in some sense without thinking, without deliberating sufficiently, without taking account of relevant information that was nevertheless in their possession. The irrationality in primal sins must consist in a kind of carelessness in practical reasoning.

On this account, primal sinners are not guilty of naked irrationality, of looking the greater good squarely in the face and at the same time voluntarily and with full knowledge preferring a lesser good. In their case that sort of naked irrationality would be inexplicable because it is impossible. Primal sinners were in a position to restrain their love for themselves or other created goods within the bounds set by reasons they possessed, but by failing to consider those reasons they were able to love created goods to a degree incommensurate with their actual value. We can imagine how this failure might have occurred. Primal sinners, whose direct knowledge of God makes it impossible for them (let's suppose) to leave God entirely out of account, might nevertheless have failed to consider that God is the highest good while at the same time incorporating into their practical reasoning other facts about God. They could have attended to the fact that God is powerful, for example, or that he demands obedience to his will, without thereby attending to his perfect goodness. Since giving attention to certain truths can sometimes distract one's attention from others, this sort of selective attention to what they knew about God may provide the most reasonable explanation of primal sinners' inattention to the reasons they had for loving God above all things. The path to primal sin may have lain through primal sinners' taking God into account in their practical reasoning but not qua highest good.[26]

The story of the serpent's tempting of Eve might be read as illustrating the point.[27] We might suppose that the serpent's wiles are aimed at focusing Eve's attention on certain of her beliefs about God: "Did God say, 'You shall not eat of any tree of the garden'?" At the serpent's prompting Eve calls vividly to mind the fact that God is an issuer of prohibitions who has the power to punish offenders with death: "God said, 'You shall not eat of the tree which is in the midst of the garden, neither shall you touch it, lest you die.'" We might suppose that Eve's vividly attending to these facts about God in effect draws her attention away from other crucial facts that she nevertheless knows, among them perhaps that God, who has forbidden her to eat of the tree in the midst of the garden, is the highest good. With her attention selectively focused in this way it becomes easier for her as she deliberates about what to do to neglect the latter facts altogether. As she deliberates she needs to be careful to attend to all the reasons she has, not just the ones that are foremost in her mind. But as it happens, Eve's neglect of the overriding reasons she has for refusing to eat of the tree leaves unrestrained her desire to eat of it—a desire that, given that "she saw that the tree was good for food, and that it was a delight to the eyes, and that the tree was to be desired to make one wise," is altogether reasonable considered just in itself. Unrestrained by her countervailing reasons, "she took of its fruit and ate," thereby acting irrationally.[28]

As I read it, then, Augustine's explanation of primal sin goes as follows. Primal sinners' perception of certain created goods provides motivation for their loving and thereby turning toward them. But primal sinners have no direct motivation for preferring created goods to the highest good. They turn away from the highest good when their love for other things becomes inordinate, when it exceeds the rational order or measure, becoming incommensurate with the values of the objects loved. Love's becoming inordinate is due, in turn, to a failure on the primal sinner's part, namely, the failure to hold love to the bounds dictated by reason. But they can fail to love in accordance with their reasons only when they fail to attend to what they know. Primal sin, then, is motivated insofar as it consists in an act of will directed toward what the sinner perceives as good, but, insofar as it is an irrational choice, it is not and cannot be directly motivated.[29] The fundamental irrationality in primal sin consists in primal sinners' failure to attend to the reasons they have for choosing otherwise. That is the failure to guard against sin.

Hence, the claim that primal sin has only a deficient cause should not be read as an attempt on Augustine's part to throw rhetorical sand in our eyes, for it is genuinely illuminating in two respects. On the one hand it highlights the fact that, insofar as it consists in an irrational choice, primal sin can have only indirect motivation, for a primal sinner cannot voluntarily choose something while at the same time recognizing that choice to be irrational. The act of will that constitutes primal sin is motivated only insofar as it is a choice of something good. On the other hand claiming that primal sin has only a deficient cause highlights the fact that these irrational choices are possible because a cause that could and should have been operative—a certain sort of practical reasoning—was inoperative. An evil free choice of the appropriate kind occurs only because of something else's failing to occur.

FAILURES OF PRACTICAL REASONING

I have claimed that Augustine's pathology of sin locates sin's root in a particular kind of failure of practical reasoning, a failure to base one's choices adequately on one's reasons. To defend this part of the account of primal sin, I need to do three things. First, I need to provide a fuller account of the nature of this failure, explaining in particular what it is to fail fully to inform one's choices with one's reasons. Second, I need to show that an account that appeals essentially to failures of this sort satisfies the two constraints Augustine himself places on primal sin, namely, that it is voluntary and that it does not presuppose any prior moral defect. Finally, I need to argue that by appealing ultimately to this kind of failure in practical reasoning, Augustine's account offers a satisfactory explanation of primal sin, an explanation that shows it to be, despite its irrationality, an intelligible act of a rational creature.

My account of primal sin appeals to the notion of one's choosing or acting in a certain way without fully attending to the relevant reasons one has, and my explication of that notion must begin by identifying the sense of "having reasons" for (or against) choosing in a certain way that is at work in the account. As I use the notion, one can be said to have a reason for choosing in a certain way just in case one has, either occurrently or merely dispositionally, mental states that constitute reasons for choosing in that way (roughly, certain combinations of belief and desire).[30] This is a slightly restrictive sense of "having a reason," for ordinary usage sometimes allows us to say that a person has a reason for choosing something even in cases in which the person lacks the relevant mental states. A farmer, for example, might be said to have a reason to reduce his use of pesticides (because pesticides are slowly poisoning the well water that his family drinks) even if he himself is wholly unaware that his use of pesticides is having this effect. For present purposes, however, I will stipulate that only agents who have the relevant mental states have a reason for choosing in a certain way and that, in cases such as that of the farmer in my example, there is a reason for choosing in a certain way though the agent himself does not have that reason.[31] It is in this sense of "having a reason" that primal sinners choose without fully attending to the reasons they have: they believe that God is the highest good while choosing without attending to that belief.

Choosing without fully attending to relevant reasons one has is a common phenomenon. It is possible because, on some occasions when an agent chooses in a certain way, the reasons that inform her choice are only a subset of the reasons she has for or against choosing in that way. Imagine a simple case of practical reasoning that gives rise to a choice. Suppose that, on Friday afternoon as I am leaving the office on my way home, I meet a colleague who invites me to go for a cup of coffee. Having a desire to promote collegiality in my department and a belief that going for coffee with my colleague on this occasion will do that, I have a reason for accepting the invitation. Suppose, moreover, that I am leaving the office at just that time because I want to get home ahead of the rush-hour traffic. Recognizing that going for coffee would mean driving home in the rush hour, I have a reason against accepting my colleague's invitation. I quickly weigh these two competing reasons (taking no other reasons into account) and decide that, on this occasion, the more important consideration is the one having to do with collegiality. I therefore choose to accept the invitation.

Now, it seems that on this Friday afternoon I might well have many other reasons both for and against going for coffee, reasons that I don't take into account in my brief deliberation. I may want to follow my doctor's advice of drinking a cup of coffee daily (to elevate my low blood pressure) and believe that going for coffee with my colleague would be a way of following that advice (a reason in favor of going); it may be that I promised to take my children to the park on Friday afternoon and want to keep my promise (a reason against); and so on. In the case as I've described it I'm supposing that these reasons play no role in my choosing as I do.

It's not that I consider them in my deliberations and set them aside or judge them to be unimportant or outweighed by other reasons. On the contrary they do not occur to me at the time and do not enter into my practical reasoning in any way at all.

It seems clear, however, that, despite the fact that these reasons play no role in my choosing as I do on this occasion, they are nevertheless reasons that I actually have—these beliefs and desires are in fact dispositional mental states of mine at the time. It is evidence of this that, with very little effort, I can call them to mind and include them in my deliberations about whether to go for coffee; and if you ask me whether I have these desires and beliefs, I will without hesitation reply that I'm sure that I do. The kind of case I have in mind is to be distinguished, therefore, from cases in which one simply forgets one's reasons. When one forgets one's reasons, one ceases to have them (whether temporarily or permanently), so that if one pauses at that moment to inventory one's reasons—that is, to call them deliberately and consciously to mind—any reasons one has forgotten will not appear in one's list. When one forgets, the forgotten reasons are inoperative due to a failure of memory. By contrast, the case I have in mind is one in which a deliberate and careful roll call of one's reasons would bring the relevant reasons to mind; one has them and one has only to look to see them. It's possible, however, not to look, to make choices without attending to reasons one nevertheless has.[32] So on this Friday afternoon I do not suffer a failure of memory. I simply choose as a result of practical reasoning that is less than fully informed by my reasons.[33]

Let's say that reasons that actually inform a person's choice at a given time, reasons that enter into and play a role in the practical reasoning underlying the choice, are *operative* with respect to that choice, whereas other reasons the person has are inoperative with respect to it. In the case I've described, only my reasons having to do with departmental collegiality and rush-hour driving are operative; those having to do with remedies for low blood pressure and my promises to my children are, for whatever reason, inoperative. Let me make clear, however, that I don't mean to suggest that our operative reasons or the processes of practical reasoning in which they play a role always, or even typically, occur at the level of full consciousness. In fact I think it's quite clear that reasons need not be called consciously to mind to become operative. Sometimes, of course, we do consciously search our beliefs and desires for reasons that might be relevant to the case at hand and consciously and carefully weigh the reasons we find.[34] But these processes very often occur without our being fully conscious of them and, indeed, sometimes occur without our being conscious of them at all (at the time). That they occur (and that these processes are indeed ours) is clear from the fact that we typically know perfectly well what reasons motivate our choices and can easily report them, even in those cases in which we haven't consciously entertained them prior to or at the time of making the relevant choices. We should not suppose, therefore, that our failure to bring a reason into full consciousness is sufficient for its being inoperative in our practical reasoning.[35]

So it is possible to have reasons that are relevant to one's choices but that remain inoperative with respect to them. It is not only possible; it is also quite common. This is because many of our choices are made under the pressure of time (so that we don't have time for exhaustive practical reasoning), in more or less trivial circumstances (so that we don't feel the need to make our practical reasoning complete), or more or less spontaneously (so that we choose, for better or worse, on the basis of the first reasons that happen to occur to us). My choosing to go for coffee with my colleague falls into the last of these categories.[36]

Now for our purposes the interesting cases of one's failing fully to attend to the reasons one has are those in which reasons one fails to take into account would, if included in one's deliberations at the time, lead one to a different choice. We might say that these are cases in which reasons one has but fails to attend to would defeat the reasons on the basis of which one actually chose as one did. If we leave aside complications arising from the possibility of weakness of the will, we could describe these as cases in which one has reasons that would lead one to choose differently, were one to consider them. Suppose I have promised to take my children to the park on Friday afternoon and have a strong desire to keep my promise. My having made the promise together with my desire to keep it gives me a very strong (perhaps overriding) reason to take my children to the park then. But if, as I'm leaving the office on Friday afternoon, my colleague invites me to join her for coffee, and I decide to accept her invitation, considering only my desire to promote departmental collegiality and my aversion to rush-hour driving, my choice not only fails to be fully informed by my reasons but also fails to accord with what I have most reason to choose. In this case, if I had taken into account my promise to my children, my practical reasoning would have had a different result, for the balance of my reasons favors my taking my children to the park. Insofar as practical rationality requires that one choose what one has most reason to choose, my choosing to go for coffee with my colleague on this occasion constitutes an irrational choice, and its irrationality can be traced to my failure fully to attend to relevant reasons that I nevertheless possess.

One's choices can be irrational, then, when they are not fully informed by one's reasons. Primal sins are irrational choices of this sort.

CARELESSNESS IN PRACTICAL REASONING

By their very nature irrational choices of the sort I have just identified fail to be fully informed by relevant reasons in one's possession. But one's choices can fail to be fully informed by one's reasons without thereby being irrational. That is to say, choices based on less than complete practical reasoning can accord with what one has most reason to choose, although, because the practical reasoning on which they are based is incomplete, the conformity will be to some extent accidental. So it might happen that, despite the fact that the practical reasoning on the basis of which one chooses does not take account of all one's reasons, the reasons on the basis of which one chooses dictate the same choice as that dictated by the balance of all one's relevant reasons.[37]

Moreover, one's failure, on some particular occasion, fully to attend to one's reasons need not be culpable, even if it gives rise to an irrational choice. The failure to attend to reasons one has will be blameworthy only when it represents a kind of carelessness—a failure one could and should have avoided. For example, if the circumstances in which one finds oneself require that one choose immediately, one cannot be held responsible for failing fully to assess one's reasons when a full assessment would require more time than one has. So, too, if the choice one faces concerns something quite trivial, one may be under no obligation to deliberate carefully.

It seems clear, however, that in many cases we are culpable for irrational choices that result from failing fully to attend to our reasons. These are cases in which we are careless, in which we could and should have considered reasons we had, reasons that, had we considered them, would have changed the outcome of our practical reasoning. I could have called to mind my promise to take my children to the park, and I ought to have. When it occurs to me that my going for coffee has prevented me from keeping the promise, I not only regret my action but also justifiedly blame myself for my careless inattention to my obligations. I would have made the rational choice had I only been more careful in my practical reasoning.

Choosing without fully attending to the reasons one has, then, can be morally culpable. But I need to say more if I am to show that the culpability in such cases can *originate* with the careless practical reasoning itself and need not trace back to prior states and choices of the agent. As I read him Augustine intends the appeal to this kind of failure in practical reasoning on the part of primal sinners to put an end to the search for culpable defects in creation; culpability for evil traces back to choices resulting from these failures and no farther.

Clearly, in many cases failure in practical reasoning of the sort I have identified is due to a standing moral flaw in the agent himself. My failure to call to mind my promise to take my children to the park may be attributable to a blameworthy tendency on my part to put my career ahead of my family. Or it may be that a blameworthy weakness for coffee explains my terminating my deliberations before any serious objection to my going for coffee can arise. It could be that I am in general impulsive and prone to act on whatever reasons first pop into my mind, without pausing long enough to consider whether they are particularly good reasons. On all these scenarios my going for coffee might be culpable, my failure to consider the reasons I have for not going for coffee might be essential to explaining my choice, and my failure to consider those reasons might be explained, in turn, by antecedent moral flaws for which I am responsible.

But culpable failures in practical reasoning of the sort at issue need not always be preceded and explained by other moral flaws. It is just as easy to imagine that my failure to consider my promise to take my children to the park is not due to any antecedent moral flaw in me. It may be that I am simply careless on this occasion. I could and should have attended to this reason against accepting my colleague's invitation, but I fail to do so. I make a moral mistake when I accept the invitation, and the root of my mistake is neglectful practical reasoning. In this case and in cases like it it is reasonable to suppose that the agent's blameworthiness originates with the carelessness itself. This seems to me true to the phenomenology of the case.

To deny that failures of rationality of the sort I have identified require antecedent moral defect is not, however, to deny that agents who fall victim to this sort of irrationality are subject to certain kinds of limitation. In fact, if agents are to be capable of failing fully to consider the reasons they have, they must be creatures whose beliefs and desires are to some extent distant from them. One can fail to consider reasons one nevertheless has only if one has need, on occasion, to put oneself in touch (as it were) with one's beliefs and desires. And one would not have this need if all one's beliefs and desires were immediately present to one at all times. The cognitive limitations of angels and especially of human beings, whose flow of conscious experience cannot help but make certain of their reasons more and others less immediate at any given moment, make possible carelessness of this crucial sort and open the door to their choosing in ways that are contrary to what they have most reason to choose. Hence, primal sinners must labor under cognitive limitations.

This is in part Augustine's point when he claims that rational creatures can sin because they were created ex nihilo.[38] As he understands it creatures owe their contingency and mutability to their having been created ex nihilo, to their absolute dependence on the will and power of God. Of course, their being mutable is a necessary condition of their being corruptible, but their lacking the radical metaphysical simplicity of a being who is utterly self-sufficient and immutable is also a necessary condition of their being capable of corruption by the sort of irrationality that is sin.[39] A being all of whose beliefs and desires are always immediately present to it can never choose without attending to the relevant reasons it has. Rational creatures must have a little bit of nonbeing in them if they are to be capable of falling victim to irrationality.

But, as Augustine rightly points out, to be limited is not to be defective, and even if the cognitive limitations that characterize created rational natures are a necessary condition of sin, they themselves constitute no moral flaw in these creatures. Hence, from the fact that the kind of failure of rationality that lies at the root of primal sin depends on creatures' being limited in certain ways, it does not follow that primal sin does not arise utterly de novo or that it does not consist in something for which the primal sinner is culpable.

AN OBJECTION: CARELESS MISTAKES AND MERE PECCADILLOES

I have argued that primal sin can arise utterly de novo and nevertheless manifest genuine moral agency provided it is the kind of irrationality exemplified in certain cases in which one chooses without thinking, without taking proper care to attend to the relevant reasons in one's possession. It might be objected at this point, however, that, even if we can sometimes be morally responsible for irrational choices of the sort I have described, these kinds of mistakes typically do not in themselves constitute deep or lasting moral corruption. When it comes to my attention that my carelessness has caused me to fail to keep my promise to take my children to the park, I slap myself on the forehead in dismay, apologize, and vow to make it up to them. I acknowledge my guilt, but I don't consider myself to have manifested or initiated any deep moral corruption. My failure on this occasion does not constitute or signal any profound or lasting turning of my will. But if primal sin consists in this same kind of failure, why shouldn't the natural reaction of the primal sinner be just the same? Why shouldn't a hitherto good rational creature react to this unprecedented lapse of rationality with immediate and sincere contrition and repentance? How could simple carelessness in practical reasoning drive the evil angels to become bitter enemies of God or merit for human beings the devastating consequences of Adam's and Eve's disobedience? It might seem, then, that on my account primal sin ought to be thought of as a mere peccadillo, not as the profound moral fall that the Christian tradition has taken it to be.

I have two replies to the objection. The first is to acknowledge that, although many failures of rationality of the sort in question are momentary and relatively insignificant, there is no reason that failures of just this sort should not occur in cases of great importance and in cases that will have enduring consequences for the structure of one's will. It seems that one can be careless in attending to one's reasons regardless of the magnitude and scope of the choice at hand, and so it seems that a primal sinner can carelessly fail to attend to the reasons he has for loving God above all things.

The second and, I think, better reply is that, despite Augustine's and the Christian tradition's treating the very first moral evil as a single, distinct act that introduces utterly devastating moral corruption into creation, there seems to me no reason to preclude our thinking of the really significant, creation-altering turning away from God that constitutes angelic and human moral fall as the culmination of a gradual process.[40] Perhaps primal sin—the very first evil in creation—is not by itself constitutive of creation's deep and permanent corruption. Primal sin might be a mere peccadillo and only the beginning of a process the later stages of which introduce profound moral corruption. We might distinguish, then, between primal sin and what we might think of as moral fall. In fact our experience confirms that great moral wickedness often has humble origins and that small moral mistakes sometimes precipitate further mistakes, giving rise in the right circumstances and over time to a cascade of moral evil.

Careless choices can sometimes set one on a path from which it can be difficult to extricate oneself. Imagine a case not of great but of ordinary moral corruption—a possible continuation of the story we've been focusing on. Failing to attend to my promise to take my children to the park, I make a de novo culpably irrational choice to go for coffee, for the reason that doing so will help build my department. Suppose that the time I spend with my colleague that Friday afternoon is in fact very productive and clearly promotes just the goals I had intended. Moreover, suppose that my children are understanding and accept my sincere apology. And finally, suppose that as time passes, other similar occasions arise that to one degree or another set the needs of my department and my commitment to its flourishing in conflict with the needs of my family and my obligations to my spouse and children. It's not difficult to imagine a series of events, perhaps extending over a period of years, in which my devotion to my job gradually grows out of all proportion, eventually and wrongly displacing my devotion to my family as the primary love in my life. In this series of events there may be other relatively innocuous irrational choices stemming from simple carelessness, but there may also be more foreboding irrationalities. The taste of my diplomatic success at the Friday afternoon coffee may linger, making my goal of building the department more vivid in my mind than it had previously been. The vividness of that goal, in turn, increases the likelihood that it will be operative (and will be assigned greater weight than it merits) in my subsequent practical reasoning. Moreover, encouraged by my children's ready forgiveness, I may find it easier to take my obligations to them less seriously or to convince myself that I will be able to "smooth things over" with them after the fact. In these kinds of ways early careless choices can establish patterns of attention, thought, and behavior that increase the probability of later instances of irrationality and of falling into corresponding enduring states of character. There may be no single choice or act in this extended series of events that of itself constitutes my fall—my permanently turning away from my family. My earliest peccadilloes are not it, nor should we think of them as leading inexorably to it. Nevertheless by the end of the story I have indeed fallen, and the connection between those early peccadilloes and the later vice may not be purely accidental.

Analogously, there seems to me no reason to think that the very first culpable instances of irrationality (angelic or human) must be anything more than mere peccadilloes of the sort the objection proposes. These unprecedented culpable failures in practical reasoning may have been the sort of lapse from which an easy and quick moral recovery is possible. But the possibility of recovery does not guarantee it, especially for creatures for whom culpable lapses of rationality are possible. For some of them, small sins may have grown large and momentary carelessness may have led, in ways we have seen, to deeply misdirected love. By a process that may have been extended and complex, it may ultimately have become true of them that they had turned away from God not just momentarily but permanently.[41]

If we think of primal sinners as growing into moral corruption in this way rather than as falling into it precipitously by virtue of a single irrational choice, then we will have to acknowledge that there are instances of culpable irrationality—peccadilloes—that precede the moral fall. But there is no difficulty in this. It will still be true that primal sin arises de novo, for the very first instances of culpable irrationality—the peccadilloes that begin the process that results in deep corruption—arise de novo. Moreover, it will still be true that primal sin is the origin of full-fledged moral evil. But the peccadilloes that precede and prepare the way for the decisive and enduring defection from God that constitutes a creature's fall do not in themselves possess grave moral significance. Creation will not have been corrupted by these mere and momentary lapses in rationality, just as my family will not have been permanently damaged by my once having failed to keep my promise to take my children to the park. The evil angels and the first human beings will have introduced genuine and deep evil into creation only when their irrationality has solidified into a decisive and enduring state of will—that is, only when they have finally and utterly turned away from God. Thus we might think of Augustine's account of primal sin as telescoping into a single act of will a process that is initiated and fueled by particular acts of will and that results in the primal sinner's having turned away from God.

AN OBJECTION: THE INEXPLICABILITY
OF CARELESS PRACTICAL REASONING

It might be objected that we have not yet made any progress on the main task of resolving the paradox of primal sin, namely, showing that irrational free choices that appear necessarily unmotivated are nevertheless intelligible as the choices of morally responsible rational creatures. As we have seen, Augustine denies that primal sins are utterly unmotivated (since primal sinners have reason for loving created goods). But, if I am right, he maintains that the irrationality in primal sins (the disorder in primal sinners' love for created goods) is due to a kind of failure in practical reasoning for which there can be no reason or motive. For this reason one might object that he has only pushed the problem one step back, from unmotivated choices to unmotivated failures in practical reasoning. If an essential element in primal sin remains at bottom unmotivated, then primal sin itself must be ultimately inexplicable and therefore unintelligible as an instance of moral agency.

This objection rests on the assumption that, if primal sin is to be an instance of genuine moral agency, it must be explicable right down to the bottom, as it were, in terms of the primal sinner's reasons and motives. The objection's point is that Augustine's account leaves something in primal sin inexplicable in those terms and for that reason leaves primal sin itself unintelligible. The assumption, however, is false. What may well be true is the principle that every *act or choice* that is an instance of genuine moral agency must be explicable by reference to the agent's reasons or motives.[42] But Augustine's analysis of the act of sin satisfies that principle. His analysis splits the act of sin into two components—an act of will and a failure to attend to relevant reasons. Only one of these components—the act of will—is a positive exercise of moral agency, a choice or action undertaken by the agent; and Augustine's account provides an appropriate explanation of that. What's left over, and what's left unexplained, is not an act of the agent's at all—it's an inaction, a failure to act (a failure to attend). Strictly speaking, then, Augustine's account leaves no act of the primal sinner unmotivated or unintelligible.

Moreover, it is surely false that, in general, an agent's inactions must be explicable in the same sort of way her choices and acts must be. My not doing somersaults across the floor now is an inaction of mine, and, if that inaction requires any explanation at all, it will typically not require one that appeals to reasons and motives I have for not somersaulting.[43] It would be a mistake, therefore, to insist that the inaction that is essential to primal sin be explained directly in terms of reasons and motives the primal sinner has for being inactive in that way. Augustine is surely right to claim that he need not provide for the *defect* in primal sin an explanation of the same sort as that which he provides for the primal sinner's *effect*—the sinner's positive act of will. Hence it is not the case that primal sin will be unintelligible just because one of its components lacks an explanation in terms of the sinner's reasons and motives.

But even if it is granted that an agent's inactions need not be explained directly by the agent's reasons and motives, an objector might nevertheless insist that some sort of explanation is required for primal sinners' failure to attend to their reasons for loving God above all things. Don't we need to explain why certain angels failed to attend to reasons they possessed for loving God (and thereby sinned) whereas others did not? What distinguishes the two kinds of angels?

The answer, I think, is that nothing distinguishes them (apart from the fact that the one kind manifests a culpable failure in practical reasoning that the other does not). The Augustinian insight behind this answer is the following. Rational creatures possess a fundamental capacity for engaging in practical reasoning—a capacity that is the very bedrock of voluntary choice and action. That we *have* reasons and that *certain* reasons spontaneously occur to us on any given occasion is not typically up to us. Insofar as we are limited rational creatures subject to the flow of experience, we cannot avoid minimal practical reasoning of this sort. But our capacity for practical reasoning also endows us with the ability to extend our practical reasoning beyond this minimal level, to take account of reasons we have that may not be spontaneously immediate to us, to bring it about that our choices and actions are fully informed by our reasons. It is that ability that makes us agents in the fullest sense and our practical reasoning more than a mechanism of mere passive reaction to our experiences and desires. For that reason the exercise of that ability or the failure to exercise it is the primary (indeed primal) instance of moral agency. On certain occasions our exercising or failing to exercise that ability is simply and entirely up to us and so something for which we bear ultimate moral responsibility. In failing to attend to reasons that they could and should have attended to, primal sinners are not strictly speaking acting but are nonetheless manifesting primal moral agency. In attending to their reasons and choosing rationally the good angels are also, but differently, manifesting primal moral agency.

As I have tried to suggest, the clearest evidence for the view that these sorts of failures are rock-bottom instances of moral agency comes from reflection on cases that involve oneself. There seems to me to be no doubt, for example, that, when making the choice to go for coffee with my colleague on Friday afternoon, my failing to consider the promise I'd made to my children is simply a morally culpable de novo failure on my part—I was just careless, and there's no more by way of explanation to be said about the matter. Moreover, there is nothing peculiar, uncommon, or unintelligible about my failing to attend to reasons that I nevertheless had. I could have undertaken or extended my practical reasoning in ways that would have resulted in my choice's being fully informed by my reasons—but I simply did not. There is no further explanation of my failure, and intuitively we don't need one.

It is important to see that, in claiming that the phenomenology of the case requires one to acknowledge that there is simply no more by way of explanation to be said about one's failure, one is not expressing any kind of deep puzzlement about the sources of one's carelessness or despair in the face of any putative absurdity in these events. We have merely come up against an altogether clear and familiar but nevertheless brute instance of our own agency. The claim "I was just careless, that's all" expresses the fact that I am responsible for the failure but not by virtue of being moved to it by any reasons or motives. That these failures can be unmotivated but nevertheless entirely intelligible instances of culpable moral agency is, therefore, true to our experience as moral agents.

Let me emphasize, furthermore, that, although failures in practical reasoning of the sort we have been focusing on are brute instances of agency, they are not brute choices or acts on the part of agents. Moreover, nothing in the Augustinian account I've developed requires primal sinners or any other moral agents to be capable of brute, unmotivated acts of will. With respect to primal sins in particular my Augustinian account requires only that, all other things being held constant, primal sinners could have extended their practical reasoning with the result that they would have chosen what they in fact had most reason to choose. Thus, although Augustine holds, in general, that an agent is morally culpable for an action only if she could have chosen otherwise, the account of primal sin suggests that the ability to choose otherwise is grounded in the ability to reason otherwise. Primal sinners are able to refrain from sinning by virtue of their ability to attend to the reasons they have for refraining. Had they exercised their ability to extend their practical reasoning in certain ways, their reasoning would have had a different result, and they would have chosen otherwise, in conformity with that result.

Because my Augustinian account does not appeal to brute, unmotivated acts of will, it avoids a serious difficulty commonly raised for indeterministic accounts of free will. Notoriously, an agent's possessing what has been called the liberty of indifference with respect to certain choices requires that she be able, in those cases, to choose to do otherwise regardless of her reasons and motives—that is, utterly without reason or motivation (if she has none supporting her choosing otherwise) or even contrary to her reasons and motivation (if her reasons and motives count against her choosing otherwise). A person's liberty of indifference will therefore consist in her being capable of brute acts of will. Critics have quite rightly objected that a liberty of this sort that entirely severs free acts of will from the agent's reasons and motives is incompatible with moral agency. The Augustinian account of primal sin, however, presupposes neither that primal sinners are capable of brute acts of will nor that they possess this sort of liberty of indifference.

As I read him, then, Augustine slips neatly between the horns of Babcock's dilemma. Babcock is right to suppose that brute, unmotivated choices and acts cannot be instances of moral agency, and he is right to see that there is something in Augustine's account of primal sin that remains (and must remain) brute and unmotivated. But, as Augustine explains, the act in primal sin is neither brute nor unmotivated, and what is brute and unmotivated in primal sin is not an act. Moreover, the element in primal sin that remains inexplicable in terms of the primal sinner's reasons and motives is not only compatible with the primal sinner's moral agency but a recognizable primal instance of it.

BROADENING THE ACCOUNT

The notion of primal sin is essential to Augustine's theodicy, but it should be clear at this point that it is also interesting for reasons that have nothing in particular to do with philosophical theology (or with angels or first human beings). Primal sin is a kind of laboratory specimen of morally culpable wrongdoing perfectly designed for focusing our attention on the fundamental mechanisms of rational agency and moral responsibility. Primal sin presents us with an instance of morally evil choice with all the usual complicating, diverting, and potentially exculpatory accretions stripped away. When we examine an ordinary instance of moral wrongdoing, it is often unclear, for example, to what extent and in what ways the agent's ignorance, character, and prior moral and nonmoral choices affect the action's badness and the agent's culpability. We must be careful to distinguish between those things that are in an agent's control and those that are not and between those things that the agent is directly responsible for and those she is responsible for only because they result from things she is directly responsible for. By contrast in primal sin there can be no relevant ignorance, weakness of will, lurking evil dispositions or states of character, or prior evil choices. In primal sin we have pure morally culpable wrongdoing laid open to view.

If primal sin gives us the opportunity to examine the mechanisms of culpable wrongdoing in their pristine state, we should expect the results of that examination to give us insight not only into the nature of primal sin but into culpable wrongdoing generally. And I think this is how Augustine sees it. Like their primal ancestors, ordinary instances of culpable wrongdoing are defective or disordered acts of will. As acts of will, they must be (1) voluntary, which entails that they are both (2) motivated by the sinner's reasons and (3) avoidable. Their defect consists in their being (4) less than fully informed by the sinner's reasons. Finally, the mechanism by which sin is avoidable for both primal and ordinary sinners is the same as the mechanism that accounts for the defect in their sin, namely, their fundamental ability to attend to the practical reasons in their possession. Appropriate exercise of that ability constitutes avoiding or guarding against sin; negligent failure to exercise it on certain occasions permits their falling into sin. Given this framework for understanding culpable wrongdoing in general, the features of primal sin that distinguish it from all other sin, namely, its being first and its perpetrator's being wholly good, turn out to be inessential differences.[44]

Part of this account of sin covers familiar territory. Augustine's insistence on the connection between sin's culpability and its avoidability, for example, is something for which he is justly famous. But part of the Augustinian account I've developed has been given sufficient attention neither by Augustine's commentators nor by philosophers interested generally in moral psychology. That part of the account is its explanation of what we might think of as the mechanism of avoidability. On this view moral culpability rests on avoidability, and avoidability is to be understood in terms of deep features of sinners' practical rationality. A particular kind of failure in practical reasoning is essential not just to the satisfactory explanation of certain kinds of culpable irrationality but to culpable wrongdoing generally. The identification of this particular sort of failure in practical reasoning also uncovers and displays for us an ability that is at the very foundation of rational life. Creatures like us are capable of choosing and acting rationally or irrationally not just by virtue of our having or acting on the basis of practical reasons but by virtue of our ability to attend or fail to attend to the reasons we have. Insofar as we are rational beings we have the ability to choose in accordance with what we have most reason to choose; but insofar as we live under certain cognitive limitations we often need, if we are to be fully rational, to take care to attend to our reasons—we need to guard against practical irrationality. Cognitively limited creatures could not exemplify full practical rationality if they did not possess this fundamental capacity.[45]

The basic idea here is clear and, I think, compelling. What is important to our having the ability to choose otherwise is our having the ability to choose in accordance with practical reasoning that it is in our power to make complete. What we want is the ability to guide our choices by our reasons—not just the reasons that happen to occur to us but all the reasons we possess. We want the ability to make choices that are fully rational, given the limitations we face. The ability to undertake or extend practical reasoning is, in this way, the bedrock of our ordinary choices and a necessary condition of both our choosing freely and our bearing moral responsibility for our choices. By exercising this fundamental ability and bringing our reasons to bear on our choices we are able sometimes to save ourselves from irrationality and moral evil.

NOTES

1. Augustine takes passages such as Isaiah 14:12ff., Ezekiel 28:13ff., John 8:44, and 1 John 3:8 as describing or alluding to the angelic fall; see *De Genesi ad litteram* 11.24–5 and *The City of God* 11.16. He supposes that the angelic fall precedes the first human sin, recorded in the story of Adam's and Eve's fall (Genesis 3). He identifies the serpent in that story as an instrument of the devil, himself a fallen angel; see *De Genesi ad litteram* 11.2–3 and *City of God* 14.11.

2. William Babcock, "Augustine on Sin and Moral Agency," *Journal of Religious Ethics* 16 (1988): 45 (the emphasis is Babcock's). Babcock sees the same dilemma facing the account of the first human sin: "Precisely because Augustine emphasized the uprightness of the affective and volitional life of the first human beings, however, he made their withdrawal from God and turn to themselves utterly inexplicable, an action so thoroughly out of character that we can hardly connect it with the agent at all" (44).

3. St. Augustine, *De libero arbitrio* 2.20.54. Translations are my own except where noted. I have used the following Latin editions of Augustine's texts: *City of God*, in *Corpus Christianorum: Series Latina* (*CCL*), vols. 47–48, ed. B. Dombart and A. Kalb (Turnhout: Brepols, 1955); *De libero arbitrio*, in *CCL*, vol. 29, ed. W. M. Green (Turnhout: Brepols, 1970). Subsequent references to *De libero arbitrio* and to *City of God* will appear in the text.

4. Augustine repeats his disavowal of knowledge of what cannot be known at *City of God* 12.7.

5. "There is [nothing] that makes the will to be [evil] other than the defection by which God is deserted; a cause of this defection, too, is entirely lacking" (*City of God* 12.9).

6. Babcock, "Augustine on Sin and Moral Agency," 47.

7. I draw primarily on book 3 of *De libero arbitrio* and the roughly parallel ideas and arguments in *City of God* 11.9–22, 12.1–9, and 14.11–15, but the elements of the account are omnipresent themes in Augustine and can be found throughout his works. Although Augustine's views develop in many ways in the years separating these two works, he seems to me not to have changed his mind about the positions and arguments on which I focus. For an account of some of the developments see James Wetzel, *Augustine and the Limits of Virtue* (Cambridge: Cambridge University Press, 1992).

8. Strictly speaking, Augustine does not think that the serpent's temptings prompt the first human sin but only that they provide the occasion for an already corrupted human will to manifest itself in overt action. He holds that an inward sin (of the same sort as the evil angels' first sin) both precedes and explains Adam's and Eve's succumbing to temptation. See *City of God* 14.13.

9. I will also not be concerned with the special problems the doctrine of original sin raises for an account of postfall human freedom. Since primal sins are free choices of prefall rational creatures, we can leave aside the complex and controversial discussions of postfall humanity's bondage to sin and the implications of divine grace for human freedom that are the focus of Augustine's anti-Pelagian writings.

10. Augustine allows, however, that God can directly perpetrate the evil that is suffered by sinners as just punishment for their sins. But since he holds that God acts justly and in

accordance with his providence in perpetrating this sort of evil, it is instrumentally good despite its being evil to those who suffer it. See *De libero arbitrio* 1.1.1.

11. For discussion of this claim and its role in Augustine's rejection of Manichaean dualism, see my "Augustine's Christian-Platonist Account of Goodness," *New Scholasticism* 63 (1989): 485–509.

12. See also *De libero arbitrio* 1.16.35; 3.24.72; *City of God* 12.8; 14.11; *De Genesi ad litteram* 11.13.

13. "In fact sin is so much a voluntary evil that it is not sin at all unless it is voluntary" (*De vera religione* 14.27, trans. John S. Burleigh in *Augustine: Earlier Writings* [Philadelphia: Westminster Press, 1953]). See also *De libero arbitrio* 1.1.1; 2.20.54; 3.1.1–2; 17.49; 18.50; *City of God* 12.3, 8.

14. In reflecting on *De libero arbitrio* in his *Retractationes* Augustine says, "after a thorough examination and discussion, we agreed that the *sole* source of evil is in the free choice of the will" (1.8.1, trans. Sister Mary Inez Bogan in St. Augustine, *The Retractations*, The Fathers of the Church, vol. 60 [Washington, D.C.: Catholic University of America Press, 1968], emphasis added).

15. Eleonore Stump presents an interesting reformulation of a fundamentally Augustinian line that tries to meet this challenge in "The Problem of Evil," *Faith and Philosophy* 2 (1985): 392–423.

16. For the angels see *City of God* 11.17; 12.1, 9; *De Genesi ad litteram* 11.20–21. For human beings see *De libero arbitrio* 3.24.71–73; *City of God* 14.11; *De Genesi ad litteram* 11.9.

17. He occasionally says that sins are due to "liberum arbitrium voluntatis" (the will's free choice); see *De libero arbitrio* 1.11.75, 14.117, and 2.1.1. Augustine has no precise, technical vocabulary worked out. For background see Albrecht Dihle, *The Theory of Will in Classical Antiquity* (Berkeley: University of California Press, 1982); Charles H. Kahn, "Discovering the Will: From Aristotle to Augustine" in John M. Dillon and A. A. Long, eds., *The Question of Eclecticism: Studies in Later Greek Philosophy* (Berkeley: University of California Press, 1988), 234–60; and Neal W. Gilbert, "The Concept of the Will in Early Latin Philosophy," *Journal of the History of Philosophy* 1 (1963): 17–35.

18. In my translations of Augustine I consistently render "voluntas" (when it has this sense) as "act of will," though in my discussion of his views I often prefer "choice."

19. If we think of love as a passion—something that happens to us or that we fall into—Augustine's thinking of loving as an act of will, something we can be morally responsible for, might seem odd. But loving has clearly active, volitional elements that make Augustine's use of that concept here understandable. We can see these elements in acts of commitment such as the undertaking of a marriage vow or the decision to have or adopt a child, both of which are reasonably thought of as acts of loving (or undertakings to love). Of course Augustine also has other reasons for using the notion of loving in this context, among them that it suggests the importance to sinners of the object of their evil choices and desires since what one loves is in some way architectonic among one's goals and ends.

20. See *De libero arbitrio* 3.17.49–18.50 (part of which is quoted just below). For another argument turning on the same sort of point see *De libero arbitrio* 1.10.20–11.21 (recalled at 3.1.2) and *City of God* 12.6. Augustine's explicit identification, in *City of God* 12.6–8, of the sort of causation at issue as *efficient* causation may be intended to emphasize this.

21. Augustine's mention of irresistible deception in this connection is perhaps an allusion to the story of Adam and Eve's temptation in the garden: if the serpent's deceptions

were irresistible, then the first human beings did not act voluntarily and so did not sin; if they were resistible, then the first human beings are culpable for failing to resist them.

22. Consistent with his view that voluntary action cannot be necessitated, he insists that perceived goods that draw the will into action do not necessitate the will's action: "For there are two sources of sins: one is by way of spontaneous thought, the other by way of someone else's persuasion . . . and both of these are voluntary" (*De libero arbitrio* 3.10.29); "What one accepts or rejects is in one's power, but one has no power over what perceived objects one is touched by; therefore it must be acknowledged that the mind is touched by both superior and inferior things in such a way that a rational substance accepts what it wills from each" (*De libero arbitrio* 3.25.74; this is the continuation of the passage quoted in the text).

23. Since evil in general requires a good nature in which to reside, a rational creature's defection from the highest good must likewise reside in a positive act, namely, the love for some created good.

24. *De libero arbitrio* 2.19.53; *City of God* 12.7.

25. See *De libero arbitrio* 3.18.50, quoted above.

26. For discussion of these kinds of possibilities and their significance for primal sins, see my "Christian Faith" in Eleonore Stump, ed., *Reasoned Faith* (Ithaca: Cornell University Press, 1993), 134–73.

27. Genesis 3:1–6. The quotations below are from the Revised Standard Version.

28. My telling of the story is compatible with Augustine's insistence that the first human sin is not the overt act of eating the forbidden fruit but the inner act of will by which the first human beings turn away from God (see n. 8 above). But if he holds, as is at least suggested by *City of God* 14.13, that the serpent's wiles could have had no effect on the first human beings if they had not previously fallen inwardly, then Augustine would not endorse my use of the story.

29. This is what Augustine means, I think, when he says that "there is no efficient, natural, *or (one might say) essential* cause of an evil act of will" (*City of God* 12.9).

30. I hold that a reason for choosing in a certain way is constituted by a desire for some end together with a belief that choosing in that way is a way of attaining that end. For example, my desire to take some exercise this afternoon and my belief that playing tennis would constitute taking exercise then together constitute a reason for my choosing to play tennis this afternoon. The account of what it is to have a reason against choosing in a certain way will have the same kind of structure: a reason against choosing in a certain way is constituted by an opposing desire (either contrary or contradictory) together with a belief that choosing in the way in question would frustrate that desire. For example, my desire to avoid taking exercise this afternoon (or to spend the afternoon in the library) and my belief that playing tennis this afternoon is a way of taking exercise then (or is incompatible with my spending the afternoon in the library) together constitute a reason against my choosing to play tennis this afternoon.

31. We might distinguish between two kinds of cases in which there is a reason that the agent herself does not have: (1) cases in which it is practically possible (in some sense) for the agent to acquire the relevant mental states (viz., acquire the relevant belief or desire) and (2) cases in which that is not practically possible. We might say that in the first kind of case there is a reason that is accessible to the agent.

32. There is a corresponding distinction between remembering what one has forgotten and calling to mind what one isn't now thinking of. Remembering what one has forgotten

is something that happens to one (although one can actively try to cause its occurrence) whereas calling something to mind is something one does. The word "remember" is itself ambiguous between "remember what one has forgotten" (as in "I just remembered where I left my car keys!") and "call to mind what one isn't now thinking of" (as in "Remember the Alamo!").

33. There are, of course, ways other than forgetting in which one's reasons can fail to be operative, including, for example, ways that manifest pathologies of the sort Freud describes. The case I'm describing is not meant to exemplify any of these.

34. On occasions of particular importance we are careful not only to take account of relevant reasons that we have but also to see whether there are relevant reasons accessible to us that ought to be taken into consideration.

35. Nevertheless when we want to be sure that certain of our reasons inform our practical reasoning, we deliberately call them to mind and incorporate them into that reasoning. See my "Ultimate Ends in Practical Reasoning: Aquinas's Aristotelian Moral Psychology and Anscombe's Fallacy," *Philosophical Review* 100 (1991): 31–66.

36. I argue elsewhere that a good deal more of our choices fall into the third of these three categories than one might have thought; see "Practical Reasoning as Grounding Reasons-Explanations: Aquinas's Account of Reason's Role in Action" (in Scott MacDonald and Eleonore Stump, eds., *Aquinas's Moral Theory* [Ithaca: Cornell University Press, 1998]).

37. In a case of this sort we might want to say that the *agent* is irrational (because she failed to base her choice adequately on her reasons) although her *choice* (or action) is not irrational (because it is the choice her reasons dictate).

38. *City of God* 12.1, 6, 8; 14.13.

39. See ibid., 11.10.

40. So long as there is some point in the process at which the primal sinner can be said to have turned away from God in the relevant sense, it seems to me to make no difference whether there is also some particular, identifiable act of will that culminates the process of turning away.

41. It might be objected that these descriptions of how sinners might gradually come to have an inordinate desire presuppose that the relevant morally culpable choices are explainable by a prior moral flaw. In my turning away from my family, for example, my failure to deliberate sufficiently, my losing sight of goals and desires other than those connected with my job, is a consequence of my wanting to achieve some particular goal too much. But this is a mistake. The claim that I have come to have an inordinate desire need not imply that the inordinate desire is the cause of my failure to consider the reasons I have for choosing otherwise than I in fact did. To describe me as coming to have an inordinate desire can simply be one way of describing the failure itself. The failure just consists in choosing on the basis of a given desire when one has reasons for choosing otherwise that one nevertheless does not attend to. In certain circumstances this sort of failure is itself constitutive of the having of or the coming to have an inordinate desire. We should understand Augustine's various claims that avarice or pride is the root of sin in this same way (*De libero arbitrio* 3.17.48, 24.72, 25.76; *City of God* 12.6; 14.11, 13; *De Genesi ad litteram* 11.5, 13–15). He does not mean that pride is an antecedent state of the prospective sinner that causes sin to occur. Instead "pride" is a description of the state that constitutes the sin itself. The sinner loves himself (a particular created good) above God; that particular sort of inordinate loving is pride,

and in the case of primal sin it is what constitutes, not what causes, the sin. See William M. Green, "*Initium omnis peccati superbia*": *Augustine on Pride as the First Sin*, University of California Publications in Classical Philology, vol. 13, no. 13 (Berkeley: University of California Press, 1949), 407–31.

42. For a modest defense of this principle see my "Ultimate Ends in Practical Reasoning."

43. Of course I might have made a positive choice not to somersault, in which case explanation of my inaction in terms of my reasons and motives against somersaulting may be required. But I'm here supposing the more likely case in which I have not positively chosen not to somersault.

44. This is why Augustine is willing to think of the first human sin as relevantly primal. The fact that it is preceded by angelic sin and prompted by angelic malevolence does not affect its satisfying conditions (1)–(4). If the angels' previous sin or the serpent's temptings had made the first human sin in any sense unavoidable or irresistible, the first human sin would not have been voluntary or culpable. But if the first human sin is avoidable, it must be explained by negligent practical reasoning on the sinner's part, practical reasoning that it was in the sinner's power to conduct differently (and better). So the first human beings must themselves give rise to sin de novo as it were. The same considerations show that all sin must arise through the same mechanism and by the sinner's failure to exercise the same fundamental ability for extending practical reasoning. Each and every sin, it seems, is primal in this sense.

45. The motivations for Susan Wolf's so-called asymmetrical account of moral responsibility are similar to the ones I appeal to here, though I have restricted my discussion here to the case of culpability and so made no claims about the sort of asymmetry characteristic of Wolf's account of responsibility. See Wolf's *Freedom within Reason* (New York: Oxford University Press, 1990).

SEVEN

Inner-Life Ethics*

William E. Mann

You have heard that it was said, "You shall not commit adultery." But I say to you that every one who looks at a woman lustfully has already committed adultery with her in his heart.

(MATTHEW 5:27–28, RSV)

When Jimmy Carter acknowledged that he had on occasion lusted in his heart, his candor prompted public reactions closer to uncomprehending derision than to shock or sympathy. Perhaps the scoffers did not catch the allusion to the Sermon on the Mount. Perhaps they thought that worrying about one's impure thoughts is symptomatic of a fretfully repressed, neurotic personality. One presumes that if the scoffers had turned their attention to Jesus' identification of lustfulness with adultery *accompli*, they would have regarded it most charitably as a robust specimen of hyperbole, useful, perhaps, for proselytizing purposes but quite literally false. Even as authoritative a source *as The New Jerome Biblical Commentary* offers this deflationary account of Jesus' pronouncement:

> Since adultery is a serious matter, a wrong of injustice as well as of unchastity, acts that lead to it can also be morally seriously wrong, e.g., alienation of affection. Jesus' words here are to be taken strictly in connection with adultery. They do not condemn any thinking about sexual matters such as would be involved in the study of medicine or simple velleities. [As for the passage] *has already committed adultery with her in his heart:* This teaches the truth of experience that when a person has seriously decided to commit a wrong the moral evil is already present, even though it can be increased by further action.[1]

Consider some male, married ogler. The commentary extracts the following points from Matthew 5:27–28 as applicable to his case. (1) What makes his lustful looking wrong is that it is a symptom or an instantiation or an amplification of some other state, such as alienation of affection, that really is wrong. But (2) mere wishful thinking on his part is no more morally objectionable than the sort of clin-

---

*I thank David Christensen, Christopher Kirwan, Scott MacDonald, and Gareth B. Matthews for helpful comments on earlier versions of this essay. I also thank the University of Vermont for furthering this essay with a 1993 Summer Research Grant.

ical scrutiny that takes place in an anatomy course. (3) Should he decide to (try to) commit adultery, the decision is evil, but the evil exemplified by the decision is not identical to the wrongness that would be realized by the action. Finally, (4) should the wrongful action be attempted or actually committed, that would increase the evil of the decision.

The first thing to be said about points 1–4 is that their ordinariness makes it hard to see how Jesus could ever have impressed anyone as a great moral reformer. The second thing to be said is that, in spite of their ordinariness, each one of the four points is arguably false. If that is so, then the attribution of points 1–4 to Jesus does Christian ethics a double disservice. One authority for whom points 1–4 are false is St. Augustine. Augustine discerned a revolutionary moral outlook in the Gospels and sought to give philosophical articulation to that outlook. Although he wrote no systematic treatise in ethics, nothing that could compare in ambition to Aristotle's *Nicomachean Ethics* or in systematic unification to Kant's *Grundlegung* or Mill's *Utilitarianism,* he cast an enormous shadow over subsequent Christian ethical theorizing, both through and beyond the Middle Ages. What he bequeathed to his successors was not a tidy set of normative principles but rather a provocative framework of concepts and vivid examples from which distinctive normative judgments might issue. Augustine's posterity was thus left with some freedom to speculate about the ways in which the framework might be fleshed out; perhaps, with some caution, even about how the bones of the framework might be differently reconstructed. I will present one arrangement of them, hoping to forge connections between the components without giving the appearance of forging the connections. I will then examine three of Augustine's most distinctive discussions of moral cases, attempting to show how the cases fit into the Augustinian framework. Virtually all the important components of the framework can be found scattered throughout works written by the year 401. Although I shall have occasion to refer to later works, the fact remains that, had Augustine lived no longer than John F. Kennedy, his contribution to normative ethical theory would have been largely the same.

THEORY

Body and Soul

Augustine has no doubt that soul and body are two categorically different things. Human bodies are three-dimensional objects composed of the four elements whereas human souls have no spatial dimensions (*De quantitate animae* 1.2; 5.9). His opinion in *De quantitate animae* 13.22 is that the soul is "substantia quaedam rationis particeps, regendo corpori accommodata," a kind of substance, participating in reason, fit for ruling the body. Humans are composed of both body and soul (*De quantitate animae* 1.2; the opinion is sustained in *City of God* 13.24). Although he is clearly a dualist, Augustine is not preoccupied, as Plato and Descartes are, with explication of the metaphysics of the mind–body problem. Augustine thinks that it suffices for his purposes as Christian apologist and ethicist that soul and body are metaphysically distinct, that to be a human is to be a composite of soul and body, and that the soul is superior to the body.

The superiority of soul to body is grounded in Augustine's hierarchical classification of things into those that merely exist, those that exist and live, and those that exist, live, and have intelligence or reason (*De libero arbitrio* 2.3.7–6.13). Bodies by themselves merely exist. An animal is animate in virtue of possessing an anima, or soul, the kind of soul that confers on the animal the abilities to take on nourishment, to grow, to reproduce, and to perceive (*De libero arbitrio* 1.8.18). But animals do not possess reason (*De libero arbitrio* 1.7.16). In addition to having the same life functions as animals, humans possess reason. Augustine seems not to be content to rest the superiority of human reason over animal functioning simply on the claim that humans have what animals have plus something else (*De libero arbitrio* 2.3.7), for immediately after making the claim he offers a different argument for the superiority of reason. Perhaps he saw that his initial argument is less than persuasive. If *x* has properties *P* and *Q* while *y* has properties *P, Q*, and *R*, it does not follow either that *y* is superior to *x* or that the constellation of properties *P, Q*, and *R* is superior to the ensemble of *P* and *Q*. Augustine needs to find something intrinsic to reason that confers superiority on it over both mere existence and the functions of the soul that humans share with animals. It is true that reason enables humans to know that they are perceiving, to analyze perception into its proper and common sensibles (*De libero arbitrio* 2.3.8–9), to discern the existence of an "interior sense" (*De libero arbitrio* 2.3.8; 4.10),[2] and to distinguish (1) what is sensed, (2) the act of sensing, and (3) the capacity to sense (*De libero arbitrio* 2.3.9). But Augustine does not allow these discriminative abilities to clinch the case for the superiority of reason. For he must disallow the principle to which one would most likely appeal if one cited the ability to discriminate:

> If *x* is cognizant or is capable of being cognizant of *y*, then *x* is superior to *y*.

Human reason can become cognizant of wisdom, which we can construe as the eternal truths lodged in the divine mind, but human reason is not superior to wisdom. The principle to which Augustine in fact does appeal is different:

> If *x* judges or is capable of judging *y*, then *x* is superior to *y*.[3]

Human reason is fit to judge whether corporeal objects, the bodily senses, and the interior sense are defective or functioning correctly and in virtue of that fact is superior to them (*De libero arbitrio* 2.6.13). At the same time the judge of whether human reason itself is functioning properly is wisdom. To the extent to which human minds discover the immutable truths contained in wisdom, they function properly. Error and mental vacillation are the result of imperfect minds failing to grasp or retain wisdom (*De libero arbitrio* 2.12.34).

The relative judgmental superiority of the rational soul over physical objects and nonrational organic functions is partly an epistemological superiority, but one that is grounded in a thesis about the soul's metaphysical superiority over physical objects. If we weave together various doctrines from *De immortalitate animae* and *De quantitate animae*,[4] we can produce the following Augustinian fabric. Whatever is indivisible is superior to whatever is divisible (*De quantitate animae* 11.17); any parcel of matter, no matter how small, is divisible ad infinitum (*De immortalitate animae* 7.12); therefore, whatever is indivisible is superior to any parcel of matter. The soul is capable of comprehending incorporeal things (*De quantitate animae* 13.22); only incorporeal things are capable of comprehending incorporeal things (*De quantitate animae* 13.22–14.23); therefore the soul is an incorporeal thing. Moreover, the soul's incorporeality gives it epistemological access to other incorporeal things. If we suppose further that Augustine would accept the thesis that every incorporeal thing is spatially indivisible, then it follows that the soul, qua spatially indivisible, is metaphysically superior to any body.[5]

At times Augustine depicts the relation between soul and body as one of instrument user to instrument used (*De quantitate animae* 23.41; *De moribus ecclesiae catholicae* 27.52; *De musica* 6.5.9), at other times as one of artisan to the material on which the artisan works (*De immortalitate animae* 16.25; *De musica* 6.5.8), at still other times as master to servant (*De moribus ecclesiae catholicae* 5.8; *De musica* 6.5.13). Augustine would be the first to insist that these analogies are deficient in some respects. A pianist can trade pianos, a potter can start afresh with a new mound of clay, a master can fire a servant, but we cannot put aside our bodies. Nor does Augustine express the contempt for or disgust with the body that was characteristic of the Pythagoreans and Plato. Mindful of Paul's remarks on the Resurrection (1 Cor. 15:35–58), Augustine believes that we exist most completely as embodied souls (*De moribus ecclesiae catholicae* 4.6; *De Trinitate* 15.7.11 appears to endorse the stronger claim that we are essentially embodied souls). After all, one cannot be a flourishing pianist without any piano whatsoever. One can love and depend on one's piano even if it needs constant tuning and maintenance. And surely one might hope that in the keyboard afterlife, one's battered spinet will become transformed into a celestial Bösendorfer. Nevertheless the analogies do reflect Augustine's belief that the soul is superior to the body. If it were true that there is some appropriate sense according to which instruments cannot bring about effects in their users, worked-on matter cannot affect artisans, and servants cannot affect masters, then the analogies would be apt expressions of Augustine's metaphysical doctrine that the body cannot affect the soul. Augustine appears to regard this doctrine as a straightforward consequence of the soul's superiority over the body. He thus maintains, for example, that, with regard to sense perception, physical modifications to the body's sense receptors do not cause the soul to have sensory experiences. If the body could affect the soul in these ways, then in that respect the soul would be passive to and dependent upon the body, and in that respect the soul would not be superior to the body.[6] It is rather that the soul, in the process of monitoring the body, is able actively to take notice of the physical modifications and produce in itself the appropriate sensations.[7] It is then also capable of making judgments about the sensations that have thereby been produced.

Perhaps it has occurred to you that Augustine's hierarchical soul–body dualism, with its one-way-only causation, has normative implications. We are not inclined to blame the piano for the wrong notes plunked by the pianist. If we find ourselves praising the piano for its beautiful tone, we may on reflection come to think that the praise is more accurately directed to its maker. The legal doctrine of *respondeat superior* reflects our belief that in many cases what a servant does while in the employ of a master can and should be imputed to the master. Even if we have reservations about Augustine's dualism, we can recognize something plausible about these features of Augustine's analogies in matters of morality. It may be that an agent's bodily motions are always relevant for our assessing the agent's moral responsibility, but they surely are not always dispositive. There are cases in which the resolutions of the soul and the motions of the body come apart. It can happen that the gyrations of the body are simply the product of brute physical forces that do not have any authorization from the soul. As I tumble down the stairs my body may assume the posture of an arabesque. But I have not performed an arabesque; neither (relevant) skill nor will were lodged in my soul. Or it can happen that what the soul does competently authorize does not issue in the right bodily motions. You might decide to arise, only to discover that Lilliputians have tied you down while you slept. Because we are all susceptible to these sorts of dislocations between the soul's commands and the body's executions, we think it important to know, in morally serious cases, whether another person's behavior is an example of such a dislocation. In morally serious cases the condition and activity of the soul can make the moral difference, say, between culpable negligence and innocent mistake, murder and accidental homicide.

If the only application to ethical theory of Augustine's dualism were merely to point out the importance of mental states in assessing moral responsibility, then we would be justified in paying scant attention to it. For virtually any materialistic account of the relation between mind and body, short of ham-fisted versions of eliminative materialism or behaviorism, also allows for the existence and moral relevance of beliefs, desires, intentions, and motives. Augustine's distinctive dualism leads him, I suggest, to a more radical view about the locus of moral assessment. It is relatively noncontroversial to claim that the moral appraisal of an agent's performance should sometimes consider the agent's mental states in order to assess the agent's physical deeds. It is much more controversial to claim that moral appraisal should focus primarily—perhaps exclusively—on the agent's mental states themselves, attending to the bodily behavior only insofar as that behavior might be evidence for the state of the agent's soul. Such a claim is essential to what we might call inner-life ethics.[8] Augustine's views constitute a fairly extreme version of inner-life ethics. Thus, for example, in *De continentia* 2.3–5 Augustine puts forward three theses intended to apply to all sins, and in particular to the sins cited in Matthew 15:19: "For out of the heart come evil thoughts, murder, adultery, fornication, theft, false witness, slander."

> The necessity-of-consent thesis: No specimen of bodily behavior counts as an example of sin unless it is preceded or accompanied by the soul's consent to the sin.[9]
>
> The sufficiency-of-consent thesis: To consent to sin is itself to commit a sin, even though the consent may never result in any outward, bodily behavior.[10]
>
> The guilt thesis: According to the laws of God, consent is sufficient to establish moral guilt for the very sin to which consent is given.[11]

The necessity-of-consent thesis maintains that there are no strict liability sins, that is, no sins that one commits merely by moving one's body in a certain way, irrespective of the state of one's soul. The sufficiency-of-consent thesis alleges that a certain state of the soul, consent to commit a sin, is all that is needed for one to have committed a sin. From the point of view of the sufficiency-of-consent thesis it is irrelevant to the fact that a sin has been committed (as opposed to our coming to know that a sin has been committed) that the sin was never translated into bodily action, for lack of opportunity. What the guilt thesis contributes is the contention that the moral guilt that attaches to the inner sin is guilt for having committed the same sin as the one to which one has consented. If Jones intends to kill Smith, then the guilt thesis attributes to Jones moral guilt for murder, not attempted murder or conspiring to commit a felony or any other substitute sin, even if Jones never carries out the intention. To put it provocatively, the sufficiency-of-consent thesis and the guilt thesis entail that Jones can be morally guilty of murder without killing anyone or without even trying to kill anyone.

The remarkable nature of Augustine's views can be brought out by contrasting them with the four points extracted from the *New Jerome* commentary. (1) Lustful looking is wrong, not merely because of its connection to alienation of affection or any other state extrinsic to the looking itself. It is wrong precisely for the reason Jesus said it was wrong: it is a genuine commission of adultery *in corde*. (3) As a consequence of the response to (1), the evil exemplified by the decision to commit adultery is the same as the evil realized by the overt action. (4) As a consequence of the response to (3), the commission of the action does not increase the evil of the decision.[12] If there were any common ground between Augustine and the *New Jerome* interpretation, it would have to reside in point (2), which alleges that there is nothing especially wrong with wishful thinking. I shall give reason to believe that Augustine would deny point (2) also. The Augustinian theses make it clear that consent is an important concept for Augustine's inner-life ethics. To see how Augustine might have arrived at these theses, we need to understand the fundamentals of his normative theory, including the notion of consent.

Happiness, Love, and Goods

Augustine takes it as axiomatic that everyone wishes to be happy (*De beata vita* 2.10; *De moribus ecclesiae catholicae* 3.4). Genuine happiness requires love for and possession of a good that is supreme, eternal, steadfast, and inalienable from the lover (*De beata vita* 2.11; *De moribus ecclesiae catholicae* 3.5, 6.10). Only God can fill this bill. Thus Augustine connects the quest for human happiness to the divine commandment to love God with all one's heart, soul, and mind (Matthew 22:37, Deuteronomy 6:5; see *De moribus ecclesiae catholicae* 8.13). Following in Plato's footsteps, the Stoics had attempted to unify the virtues by identifying them with prudence or ways of being prudent. As if in reply, Augustine redefines the virtues of self-control, courage, justice, and prudence as ways of loving God: self-control is keeping one's love of God unblemished, courage is maintaining love of God in the face of adversity, justice is loving God undividedly, prudence is loving God in such a way that one chooses to further that love and avoids hindering it (*De moribus ecclesiae catholicae* 15.25, 25.46). In fairly swift order, then, Augustine attempts to incorporate the attractive pagan ethical notions of *eudaimonia* and the *aretai* into a Christian ethical framework.

God commands us not only to love him but also to love our neighbors as ourselves (Matthew 22:38). Augustine links the two commandments of love in the following way. We love ourselves properly only when we love God more than we love ourselves. When we love God more than ourselves, we want to attain the supreme good that only God can bestow. Although the following step is not explicitly taken by Augustine, it appears to be well-nigh irresistible and connects love of God to neighborly love: when we love God more than ourselves, we want to attain the ends that he seeks to attain by following the commands that he gives us, including the command to love our neighbors as ourselves. When we do love our neighbors as ourselves, we want them also to attain the supreme good as much as we want ourselves to attain it (*De moribus ecclesiae catholicae* 26.48–49; see also *De doctrina Christiana* 1.26.27). Recognizing that they, like us, are embodied souls, we will endeavor to care for their physical well-being, which is the function of human mercy, and their spiritual well-being, which is the function of moral education (*De moribus ecclesiae catholicae* 27.52–28.55). We should note that, if this portrayal of Augustine's analysis is correct, then the analysis has the consequence that, since fulfillment of the second commandment essentially includes wanting our neighbors to love God as we do, fulfillment of the second commandment depends logically on fulfillment of the first, even though both commandments could be temporally fulfilled simultaneously (*De moribus ecclesiae catholicae* 26.51). Although nothing of importance in this essay hangs on it, I shall assume that Augustine believes that genuine neighborly love can only flow from love of God.

Because God is the creator of all things, everything that exists is good. This thesis lies at the heart of Augustine's rejection of Manichaeanism (see, e.g., *Confessions* 7.12.18–13.19; *De natura boni contra Manichaeos* 1). Nevertheless some things are better than others: the soul, for example, is superior to the body. Augustine offers a threefold hierarchy of created goods in *De libero arbitrio* 2.18.47–19.51. The highest goods are those goods without which we cannot live rightly and which we cannot use evilly (if we possess them at all): Augustine's examples are the virtues. The intermediate goods are goods without which we cannot live rightly but which we can use evilly (or well). Augustine describes these goods as "powers of the mind" (potentiae animi). The only example overtly identified by Augustine is the power of making free decisions, or free will, although it is reasonable to assume that he also meant to include reason and memory as intermediate goods (see *De libero arbitrio* 2.19.51).[13] The lowest goods are goods without which we can live rightly and which can be used either well or badly. The lowest goods thus include things that are neither virtues nor powers of the mind. Augustine's examples include bodily health, strength, and beauty, the bodily senses, political freedom, friends and family relations, political institutions, honor, praise and popularity, and worldly possessions (*De libero arbitrio* 1.15.32; 2.18.49).

Enjoyment and Use

Augustine's distinction between enjoyment (*frui*) and use (*uti*) helps to connect his soul–body metaphysics and his ontology of goods to his inner-life ethics. To enjoy a thing is to love it for its own sake. "Use" is a term of art for Augustine. To use a thing is to employ it as a means for obtaining something loved, subject, we shall see momentarily, to two limitations. In *De diversis quaestionibus* Augustine had characterized vice as the desire to use what should be enjoyed and to enjoy what should be used (*De diversis quaestionibus* 30). In the somewhat later book 1 of *De doctrina Christiana*, however, he drops mention of a desire to use what should be enjoyed, singling out only the desire to enjoy things that should be used as comprising a sort of slavish, inferior love (*De doctrina Christiana* 1.3.3). Notice, then, that, if the omission is significant, Augustine depicts vice as a kind of second-order desire, a desire to love for its own sake what should be used. The omission is significant and can be explained on the reductive hypothesis that Augustine came to think that a desire to use what should be enjoyed is an incoherent desire and that he added to that thought the further thought that, although incoherence is a cognitive failing, it is not a vice. The type of incoherence exhibited by such a desire does not preclude people from having the desire. It will, however, deter a suitably informed, rational person, who has made the relevant, obvious inferences from his correct beliefs, from forming or maintaining such a desire. To see how the desire is incoherent in this sense, we must investigate Augustine's concept of use more fully.

One limitation Augustine places on the concept of use is that one cannot properly be said to use something, *x*, to obtain something else, *y*, that one loves, if *y* is not worthy of being loved; such a "use" is really a case of abuse (*De doctrina Christiana* 1.4.4). Augustine offers the following argument for the limitation. If a person uses *x* badly, then *x* benefits no one. If *x* benefits no one, then *x* is not useful. But if *x* is useful, then *x* is useful by being used. Thus, if *x* is used, then *x* is useful. Thus, if *x* is not useful, then *x* is not used. Therefore, according to Augustine:

> If a person uses *x* badly, then that person does not use *x*. (*De diversis quaestionibus* 30)

Setting aside objections to the soundness of the argument, we can note that Augustine is urging, in effect, that we take *uti*, or at least his use of it, to function as a success verb.[14] The following principle,

> If a person who loves *y* uses *x* to obtain *y*, but *y* is not worthy of being loved, then that person uses *x* badly,

along with the conclusion of the *De diversis quaestionibus* 30 argument, yields the limitation put forward in *De doctrina Christiana* 1.4.4.

If everything that exists is good, we might think that everything has a claim to being loved, and so we may wonder how it is that an object can be unworthy of a person's love. Recall the hierarchy of goods sketched in *De libero arbitrio* 2. Although everything that exists is good, some things are better than others. It is natural to infer not only that everything that exists is worthy of being loved *simpliciter* but also that the strength of our love should be proportionate to the worthiness of the beloved object. Proportionality fails, according to Augustine, when a person attempts to use a superior good merely as a means to obtaining an inferior good: such an attempt inverts the order of goods and invests in the inferior end a love that is disproportionately high compared to the love one has for the superior means (*De diversis quaestionibus* 30). Augustine appears to subscribe to this version of the principle cited above:

> If a person who loves *y* uses *x* to obtain y, but *y* is less worthy of being loved than *x* is, then that person uses *x* badly.

The second limitation Augustine imposes on the concept of use is that it must presuppose a capacity for reasoning in the user. To use a thing requires having knowledge, both about the end to which the thing being used is a means and about the thing as a means to that end (*De diversis quaestionibus* 30). It is important to note that Augustine specifies knowledge, not belief. If one acted on the basis of false or unjustified beliefs about means or end, then one would be using a thing badly, which, given the first limitation, would really not be using the thing at all. Knowledge about means and ends depends on a rational soul. Thus Augustine claims that if we speak strictly we cannot say that animals use anything.

The only thing that should be enjoyed is God, the Trinity of Father, Son, and Holy Ghost (*De doctrina Christiana* 1.5.5; 33.37).[15] All created things, including one's own rational soul and the souls of others, should be used, in a way that exemplifies the two commandments of love, in order to achieve enjoyment of God (*De diversis quaestionibus* 30; *De doctrina Christiana* 1.22.20–21; 35.39). We are now in a position to explain why Augustine would have thought that a desire to use what should be enjoyed is an incoherent desire. It is not that no one has such a desire. It is rather that, once one traces out the implications of the desire, one will see it to be unintelligible. Since God is the only being who should be enjoyed, such a desire would be a desire to use God.[16] But it is impossible to use God, for at least two reasons. First, recall that, for Augustine, use entails knowledge. To use God, then, entails that one possess knowledge about God sufficient to establish that God is a suitable means to some superior end. There can be no such knowledge. Virtually any knowledge about God entails knowing that God is not the sort of being who can be used. So a desire to use God is incoherent because it entails having adequate knowledge of God when adequate knowledge of God entails knowing that God cannot be used. Second, to use anything for whatever purpose entails taking it as inferior means to obtain a superior end. Because nothing can be superior or even equal to God, so to "use" God is to use God badly, which is in turn not to use God at all. Once again, a desire to use God, the only being who should be enjoyed, is incoherent.

If the reductive hypothesis is correct, then it is Augustine's considered opinion that every human vice can be explicated as a desire to enjoy what should be used. It does not follow that whenever one enjoys a created good one is thereby expressing a vice. Even though God is the only being who should be enjoyed, and even though God cannot be used, Augustine maintains that there are things that should be enjoyed and used (*De doctrina Christiana* 1.3.3). There is no incompatibility here, as long as Augustine is interpreted as saying that God is the only being who should be enjoyed without any eye to use whereas created goods should not be enjoyed without also using them licitly as means to achieve enjoyment of God. There is nothing wrong with finding oneself enjoying what one is using, or with enjoyment supervening on use, but there is something wrong with one's seeking to enjoy a good instead of seeking to use it. Augustine illustrates the distinction repeatedly: here are two examples. Pleasure generally accompanies the nourishment necessary to sustain one's body, but desiring to eat and drink solely for gustatory relish rather than sustenance is sinful (*Confessions* 10.31.44). When it brings us closer to God, we use sacred music properly; when we delight more in the singing than in what is being sung about, we do not (*Confessions* 10.33.49–50).[17]

Two Trichotomies

Augustine discerns a crucial difference, then, between enjoying something and desiring to enjoy it. The sketchy delineation of vice as a kind of second-order desire in book 1 of *De doctrina Christiana* is not accidental. The picture on which the sketch is based is displayed more fully in *De sermone Domini in monte*. In commenting on

Jesus' pronouncement on adultery in Matthew 5:27–28 Augustine says that any sinful action is the product of three events or processes in the soul: suggestion, pleasure (or delight), and consent (*De sermone Domini in monte* 1.12.34). Memory and the bodily senses are the sources of suggestion. It is not clear whether Augustine thinks that a suggestion always has propositional content, but if it does the proposition will typically be expressed in the subjunctive rather than the optative mood. We may suppose that a nascent adulterer begins by musing about what it would be like to sleep with some person. The next three sentences describe a generic process that splits, as we shall see in the next section, into two species. Pleasure can ensue from the suggestion, although there is nothing in Augustine's description that precludes the possibility of pleasure arising simultaneously with the suggestion. If, as in the present case, the content of the suggestion is something sinful, the person should repress taking pleasure in the enjoyment of the suggestion. If the person consents to the suggestion, then a sin has been committed: the sufficiency-of-consent thesis has been fulfilled.

Before we examine more closely Augustine's notion of consent we should look at another trichotomy that follows on the heels of the suggestion–pleasure–consent trichotomy. A person can sin in the heart, in deed, or in habit (in consuetudine; *De sermone Domini in monte* 1.12.35).[18] Augustine's contrast between sinning inwardly (in the heart) and sinning outwardly (in deed) is familiar enough by now. Habitual sinning is a less familiar notion, about which Augustine makes the following claims. Habitual sinning arises from the repeated commission (in deed) of illicit acts. Subsequent suggestions to commit the same type of sin are accompanied by a more intense level of pleasure. The habitual sinner thus derives greater pleasure in the commission of the sinful act than does the casual sinner. It is the latter fact that explains why evil habits are hard to break (*De sermone Domini in monte* 1.12.34). The habitual sinner has acquired a vice. If we unite the *De sermone Domini in monte* theory of habit with the *De doctrina Christiana* thesis about vice, we can say that it is Augustine's view that the desire for the heightened pleasure that supervenes on repeatedly enjoying what should be used is what makes the vice a vice and also makes it difficult to extirpate.

The Grammar of Consent

What is it to take pleasure in a suggestion? Is it that one derives pleasure from mentally entertaining the content of the suggestion? Or does the content of the suggestion lead one to think that acting to fulfill the suggestion would bring pleasure? In similar fashion, what is it to consent to a suggestion? Is it merely to continue to entertain the content of the suggestion? Or is it to take steps to act on the suggestion, preparing to bring about what it suggests? Augustine's version of inner-life ethics allows for positive answers to all four alternatives, although not necessarily regarding the same case. At *De sermone Domini in monte* 1.12.33 Augustine provides a counterfactual analysis of consent: if one consents to a pleasant suggestion, then one would realize the suggestion if the opportunity were to arise. So construed, this conception of consent is tantamount to intention. The intention is to perform a certain action, given the opportunity, namely, the very action specified by the content of the suggestion. If φ is a variable ranging over types of action, then we can depict what might be called action-consent in this way:

A person action-consents to the suggestion that she φ only if she intends to perform the action φ given the opportunity.

But Augustine's discussion of the suggestion–pleasure–consent trichotomy also alludes to another notion of consent. While entertaining the suggestion of an adulterous liaison, a person might never come to formulate an intention to commit adultery yet continue to fantasize nevertheless about the suggestion. The person consents to the suggestion in this case by failing to repress it, by giving it full play in the imagination. We could call this notion fantasy-consent:

A person fantasy-consents to the suggestion that s/he φ only if s/he does not repress the suggestion but takes continued pleasure from the contemplation of φing.

It need not follow that the person who fantasy-consents believes that acting to fulfill the fantasy would bring pleasure. The two notions of taking pleasure in a suggestion can thus come apart, as fantasy-consent itself can occur apart from action-consent, even though in many other cases they (the two ways of taking pleasure and the two kinds of consent) will tend to be conjoined.

Let us return to the three theses extracted from *De continentia*. It seems clear that action-consent applies to the necessity-of-consent thesis:

The necessity-of-action–consent thesis: no specimen of bodily behavior counts as an example of sin unless it is preceded or accompanied by the soul's intention to perform the sin given the opportunity.

Fantasy-consent need never eventuate in overt action; when it does, the vehicle of translation, as the necessity-of-action–consent thesis maintains, is not fantasy-consent but rather action-consent or intention.

In contrast, the sufficiency-of-consent thesis and the guilt thesis appear to accommodate both notions of consent:

The sufficiency-of-action–consent thesis: to intend to commit a sin given the opportunity is itself to commit a sin, even though the intention may never result in any outward, bodily behavior.

The sufficiency-of-fantasy–consent thesis: to take continued pleasure from the contemplation of sinning is itself to commit a sin, even though the contemplation may never result in any outward, bodily behavior.

The intentional-guilt thesis: according to the laws of God, intention is sufficient to establish moral guilt for the very sin intended.

The fantasy-guilt thesis: according to the laws of God, continued pleasure taken
from the contemplation of sinning is sufficient to establish moral guilt for the
very sin contemplated.

Note that the sufficiency-of-fantasy–consent thesis contradicts point (2) extracted
from the *New Jerome* interpretation; there can indeed be something wrong with
mere wishful thinking. We will discuss these theses more fully below.

Taking Stock

Augustine's inner-life ethics occupies a territory distinctive in normative ethical
theory. To get some sense of its uniqueness, we should see how it contrasts with
other, perhaps more familiar, positions.

One feature that is not unfamiliar is the foundation in love of God and one's
neighbor. Because he holds that every created thing is good, Augustine cannot
consistently say that it is wrong per se to desire or love any particular created thing.
A desire for a created thing could be wrong only if the desire is inconsistent with
one's loving God or one's loving one's neighbor as oneself. At this point it is natural to confront Augustine with a version of the problem of weakness of will: if a
desire for a finite good conflicts with love for the infinite goodness that is God, how
is it possible to come to have such a desire? How can what is worse come to be as
attractive or more attractive than what is better, especially when what is better is
infinitely better? Once the question is put that way, one might expect Augustine to
avail himself of the Platonic reply that such a desire is due to some sort of cognitive shortcoming. It could be that we desire something in a way that is inconsistent
with loving God because there is something we do not know. We might not yet
know that God is the supreme good. Or we might know that God is the supreme
good and fail to realize that a particular desire we have for some created good is
inconsistent with love for God, just as I might desire bodily health and fail to realize that my craving to smoke is detrimental to it. Perhaps all wrongful desires,
then, are the result of ignorance?

Augustine does not deny that there are such cases. It is rather that they do not
interest him when he discusses wrongful desires. The cases that do capture his attention are ones in which a person desires something, knowing that to have the desire is wrong. The latter cases more than the former dramatize for him the sheer
willfulness of evil. If rationalism is the thesis that knowledge of the good is sufficient to gain mastery over the promptings of the will, and if voluntarism is the denial of that thesis, then Augustine is a voluntarist, not a rationalist.[19]

Because Augustine lays so much moral emphasis on the state of the soul and so
little on bodily execution, it may be tempting to infer that he is an anticonsequen-
tialist. But in fact no such inference follows. It is important to distinguish between
two anticonsequentialistic theses. One maintains that the consequences of an action or a state of affairs are not always relevant to the moral appraisal of the action or state of affairs: the other maintains that they are never relevant. Augustine

has reason to accept the first thesis but reject the second. Even though bodily states can never affect the soul, and even if, by some sort of soul-in-a-vat thought-experiment, the soul were never to bring about any bodily states, the fact would remain that one state of the soul can bring about another state of the soul. If the second soul-state is morally significant, then it is open to Augustine to appraise the first soul-state in terms not only of its intrinsic value or disvalue but of its instrumental value or disvalue. For example, unrepressed musings about adultery are evil in themselves, by the sufficiency-of-fantasy–consent thesis, but also evil insofar as they are just the sorts of states that tend to lead to the formation of intentions to commit adultery (by the sufficiency-of-action–consent thesis).

There is a long tale about the influence of Stoic thought on Augustine, a tale that I am not able to tell.[20] Any adequate telling of it, however, must include the following points of divergence. Stoicism provides an ethical theory that is perfectionistic yet that also claims that its practitioners are naturally self-sufficient. It is Stoicism's contention that each of us innately has the wherewithal to lead the ideal life, a life in conformity with the rational necessity exhibited by nature, given only our natural endowment, including the capacity to reason. Augustine must reject the Stoic conception for at least two reasons. First, it fails to recognize that, as a consequence of the Fall, humans are no longer naturally capable of living the life they should live: from Augustine's point of view, Stoicism commits the same kind of error that would soon be committed by the Pelagians. The second reason lies behind the first. Natural reason, unaided by divine revelation, cannot give us the central content of Augustinian ethics, that we should love God and love our neighbors as we love ourselves.

APPLICATIONS

Lying

Augustine wrote two works devoted to moral issues raised by lying, the early *De mendacio* and the late *Contra mendacium*. In both of them he argues that one must never lie, not even in an attempt to secure someone else's salvation (*De mendacio* 8.11), nor in order to disguise one's religious convictions in a hostile society (*Contra mendacium* 2.2), nor in order to trap heretics (*C. mend.* 3.4). I shall concentrate on the early work, connecting it to inner-life ethics.

Augustine recognizes that uttering a falsehood, even with the intention of uttering a falsehood, does not count as lying, lest jokes be labeled lies (*De mendacio* 2.2). Nor does uttering a falsehood count as lying when one believes that what one is uttering is true (although one might be culpable for being misinformed; *De mendacio* 3.3). Consider the following non-Augustinian defense of this Augustinian claim. It may be that Jones mendaciously tells a falsehood to Smith but that Smith has good reason to trust Jones's veracity. If Smith then passes on the falsehood to you, then whatever Smith has done, Smith has not thereby lied to you. It is more surprising to see Augustine claim that one can be lying while saying what is true. In an attempt to get you to fail your geography examination, I tell you that the capital of North Dakota is Bismarck, believing that the capital is Fargo. In fact North Dakota's capital is Bismarck. Then I have lied to you while telling you the truth (*De mendacio* 3.3). Thus it is Augustine's opinion that uttering a falsehood is neither sufficient nor necessary for telling a lie.[21]

Whether one has succeeded in uttering a truth or a falsehood depends in part on the way the world is.[22] It should come as little surprise to find out that, according to Augustine, whether one has lied or not depends not on the way the world is but on the desires and motives one has. Here are two cases, modeled closely on Augustinian examples (*De mendacio* 4.4). You must choose between two paths. Fiends await you on path A; path B leads to warmth and safety. You do not know which path is which, and time is of the essence. Both Jones and Smith know which path is which, but they also know that you distrust them deeply. Unbeknownst to you, Jones wants you to avoid the fiends, while Smith wants the fiends to fasten upon you.[23] Jones tells you that there are no fiends on path A, hoping that your distrust of him will lead you to believe that there are fiends on path A and thus to choose the safe path B. Smith tells you that there are fiends on path A, counting on your distrust in her to lead you to believe that path A is fiend-free. Augustine makes the following claims about these cases.

(1) If lying entails saying something with the desire to say something false, then Jones lies and Smith does not lie.

(2) If lying entails saying something with the desire to deceive, then Smith lies and Jones does not lie.[24]

(3) If lying entails saying something with a desire for some element of falsity ("cum voluntate alicujus falsitatis"), then both Jones and Smith lie; Jones because he desires that what he says be false, Smith because she desires that you believe something false based on her true statement.

(4) If lying entails saying something with the desire to say something false in order to deceive, then neither Jones nor Smith lies; not Jones, because he desires to convince you of the truth by saying what is false, not Smith, because she desires to speak the truth in order to convince you of something false.

Augustine concludes that a person who willingly makes a false statement from a desire to deceive is clearly one kind of liar (*De mendacio* 4.5). Given his claim that one can lie by telling the truth, he must believe that there are other kinds.

It will help to set this fourfold inventory in its proper perspective if one distinguishes three questions. What is lying? What makes lying wrong? When has one lied? In Augustine's hands the questions receive different sorts of answers. Lying is wrong, for example, because it contravenes the commandment against bearing false witness, a commandment justified in turn by the commandment to love God and one's neighbor. The sufficiency-of-action–consent thesis and the intentional-guilt thesis give a distinctive answer to the question about when one has lied—perhaps earlier than one might otherwise have thought. (Thus the "when" in "When has one lied?" is at least partly a request for temporal conditions.) In the early chapters of *De mendacio* Augustine is engaged in examining the first question by exploring for a definition of lying. The options offered in the fourfold inventory are significant both for what they contain and what they do not contain. Inasmuch as he presents the inventory immediately after he has severed (to his satisfaction) any necessary connection between lying and saying what is false, the inventory seems to present what he takes to be the serious remaining candidates available for defining the notion of lying. Notice, however, that the options offered in the inventory are couched solely in terms of desires—that is, states wholly internal to the agent's soul. It appears that when he wrote *De mendacio*, Augustine thought that one could come closest to answering the question what lying is not just by knowing only what goes on in a person's soul but even more narrowly, by knowing only what goes on in a person's will.

To appreciate the radical nature of Augustine's view about what lying is, contrast it with the following attempt to specify the notion:

A person lies if and only if the person (a) says what is in fact false, (b) believing that it is false, (c) in a communication context governed by a convention requiring truth-telling.[25]

Condition (c) makes explicit why jokes, lines uttered in plays, the use of rhetorical figures, and the like should not count as lies. Condition (b) rules out the case of the sincere but misinformed person and makes explicit something to which Augustine assented in *De mendacio* 3.3: moreover, Augustine's "clear" case of a liar, a person who willingly makes a false statement from a desire to deceive, is not a clear case unless we suppose additionally that the person believes of the false statement that it is false. Condition (a) classifies my attempt to mislead you about the capital of North Dakota and Smith's attempt to get you to choose the path frequented by fiends as non-lies, whatever else might be said by way of moral criticism of our performances. Recall that Augustine rejects condition (a). Note also that in contrast to the emphasis that Augustine places on them, desires play no role in the characterization.

While Augustine flirted with the idea of giving a purely internalistic answer to the question of what a lie is—an answer framed, that is, entirely in terms of a person's desires—it may not be obvious what role inner-life ethics plays in *De mendacio*. Augustine thinks that some lies are less serious than others. In *De mendacio* 14.25 and 21.42 he gives the following list of types of lies, graded from most to least sinful:

Lie 1: A person lies in the teaching of religious doctrine.
Lie 2: A person lies, causing harm to someone without helping anyone.
Lie 3: A person lies, causing harm to someone while helping someone else.

Lie 4: A person lies solely for the pleasure of lying.

Lie 5: A person lies solely from the desire to please his comrades.

Lie 6: A person lies, causing harm to no one while saving someone's possessions.

Lie 7: A person lies, causing harm to no one while saving someone's life.

Lie 8: A person lies, causing harm to no one while saving someone from bodily defilement.[26]

Even if one waives questions about whether Augustine has got the order right, one cannot help but note that external consequences seem to contribute in large measure to the construction of the order. It would take only a slightly quirky utilitarianism to produce the same order.

To see how Augustine's list squares with his inner-life ethics, let us begin by distinguishing an act's being wrong from its being harmful, allowing the latter to include harms done to the body and harms done to the soul. Consider now an unsophisticated variety of consequentialism that maintains that no action is wrong unless it produces harm. On this version of consequentialism harm is necessary for wrongfulness but not sufficient: an agent may be insulated from a charge of wrongdoing if the agent's harmful act results in the avoidance of greater harm or in the production of greater good, or if the act is unavoidable. A defender of our imagined consequentialism will have no quarrel with the concept of wrongfulness but will claim nevertheless that it can be assimilated to the notion of unjustifiable, avoidable harm. When the consequentialist compares lie 2, for example, with lie 6, he will protest that the cases are insufficiently specified. If it is made explicit that both lies are avoidable and have no further relevant long-range consequences, then the reason lie 2 is worse than lie 6 is simply that it is more harmful.

Without denying the existence of harm, inner-life ethics denies it the dispositive moral role that it plays for consequentialism. In particular, even though lie 2 is more harmful than lie 6, the inner-life ethicist must maintain that that fact does not explain why lie 2 is more sinful than lie 6. Like the consequentialist, the inner-life ethicist will insist that the two lies are insufficiently specified. But further specification should proceed, not outward, in the direction of consequences and avoidability, but inward, to the state of the liar's soul. Consider variations of lies 2 and 6:

Intentional lie 2: A person lies, intentionally causing harm to someone without helping anyone.

Inadvertent lie 2: A person lies, inadvertently causing harm to someone without helping anyone.

Intentional lie 6: A person lies, intentionally causing harm to no one while saving someone's possessions.

Inadvertent lie 6: A person lies, inadvertently causing harm to no one while saving someone's possessions.

Augustine can agree that inadvertent lie 2 is more harmful than inadvertent lie 6 while regarding them as morally equal; ceteris paribus, neither is more sinful than the other. I suggest that when Augustine wrote *De mendacio* he had in mind a comparison between intentional lie 2 and intentional lie 6. Intentional lie 2 is more sinful than intentional lie 6, not for the reason that it is more harmful but rather for the reason that to harm someone intentionally is to be further removed from fulfilling God's commandment to love him and one's neighbors. When one considers similar variations on all but one of the other kinds of lies on Augustine's list, one can easily see how the order fits in with inner-life ethics. The problem case is lie 4. I shall defer discussing it until another section.

The Theft of the Pears

Augustine's well-known account, in *Confessions*, book 2, of his teenage theft of pears is calculated, I submit, to dramatize his inner-life ethics. Immediately after proclaiming the sexual lust attendant upon his attaining puberty, and telling of his striding the streets of Thagaste as if he were wallowing in the mire of Babylon (*Confessions* 2.3.6–8), Augustine devotes the remaining seven chapters to a meditation upon the theft. The following points emerge from the meditation. Appearances to the contrary notwithstanding, the theft is a case of an especially serious misdeed. And appearances are to the contrary. Augustine makes no claim to the effect that the theft brought financial hardship to the tree's owner: it is compatible with everything he says about the case that the owner never even noticed the loss. Augustine suggests that he would not have stolen the pears had he not had companions (*Confessions* 2.8.16–9.17), but the necessity of confederates does nothing to explain why the theft is so seriously wrong. The core of his explanation is contained in chapters 4–6, which comprise a sequence of observations alternating between rejections, as inapplicable to his case, of various hypotheses typically used to explain many sinful deeds, and the repeated assertion of what must be the correct account of the theft, an account that underscores its sinfulness from the point of view of inner-life ethics.

Let us consider the rejected explanatory hypotheses. First, there are cases in which people steal out of need. Augustine, however, did not need the pears he stole; he in fact had plenty of better pears of his own (*Confessions* 2.4.9). Second, there are cases in general in which people sin because they are unduly attracted by worldly goods, such as gold and silver, honor, political power, and friendship (*Confessions* 2.5.10). The cases recall the third and lowest class of created goods from *De libero arbitrio* 2. In the terminology of *De doctrina Christiana*, book 1, they are cases of seeking to enjoy what should only be used. But Augustine did not seek to enjoy the pears he stole: he threw them to the pigs. Third, there are cases in which a person sins simply as a means to attain some desired good. Although Catiline sometimes committed crimes just to keep in practice, Augustine points out that even those crimes at least had instrumental value for Catiline (*Confessions* 2.5.11). In contrast, Augustine's theft was not undertaken as a means to any extrinsic end. Fourth, there are cases in which sinful acts are best explained as the expressions of vicious habits or culpable mental conditions. Much evil doing flows from such character flaws as pride, the craving for honor and glory, cruelty, lasciviousness, idle curiosity, culpable ignorance, folly, sloth, licentiousness, prodigality, avarice, envy, anger, timorousness, and moroseness (*Confessions* 2.6.13). As Augustine's account of his sin makes clear, it might have been that he had some of these vicious character traits, but if so, they were not salient factors in his commission of the theft.

Augustine maintains that he stole the pears solely for the sake of doing something that was sinful (*Confessions* 2.4.9, 6.12, 6.14). It is worth the effort to dwell on the case a bit more than Augustine does. The necessity-of-action–consent thesis entails that no episode of bodily behavior counts as an instance of theft unless it is accompanied by the intention to steal. Every theft is thus intentional. The sufficiency-of-action–consent thesis and the intentional-guilt thesis yield the result that it is the intention to steal that makes the theft wrong. (If pressed further, Augustine would have to ground the wrongness of the intention to steal ultimately in its contravention of love of God and of one's neighbors.) So far, however, we have not uncovered any reason that would set apart his theft of the pears from his other sinful deeds or, for that matter—given the two versions of the sufficiency-of-consent thesis—that would set apart his theft from other unperformed but intended or contemplated deeds. To take but one example, why did he not choose to expatiate in *Confessions*, book 3, on his sexual misconduct while in Carthage?

In reporting on the notorious Stoic thesis that all sins are equal, Cicero had pointed out that the Stoics, in an effort to explain the intuition that some actions are more seriously wrongful than others, had maintained that one and the same action might instantiate several sins.[27] Perhaps, then, Augustine's theft was a number of sins wrapped up in one action. He intended to steal and he intended to do something wrong. If Augustine were to suppose that the second intention is logically independent of the first—that is, that one could intend to steal without thereby intending to do something wrong—he could eke out two sins in this case by dint of the sufficiency-of-action–consent thesis. Still, the census is not very impressive, certainly not enough to justify the space that Augustine devotes to considering the theft. More important, to proceed in this quantitative fashion is to concede too much to the Stoics. As the hierarchy of lies demonstrates, not all sins are equal: some single sins are worse than others.

The purpose of the theft of the pears was not to acquire any created good but rather simply to perform some action, an action not taken as means to some further end but an action done for its own sake. Now an action done solely for its own sake seems already to be morally suspect by virtue of the use–enjoyment distinction. Suppose, for example, that I while away a portion of my time solving crossword puzzles, not for any purpose extrinsic to the activity—such as a desire to win a prize or even just to refresh my soul—but simply because I enjoy doing them. Recall that for Augustine, time itself is a part of God's creation (more accurately put, it is the mode of created existence; *Confessions* 11.13.15–14.17). As such, time is a good that can be misused. It is possible to deploy the use–enjoyment distinction to subject my activity to the following criticism: in dedicating a portion of my time to mere enjoyment, when the object of enjoyment is not what should be merely enjoyed, I am using my time badly. Now even if time-wasting action done solely for its own sake does not pass over the threshold into the realm of moral disapprobation, surely action done solely for the sake of the intrinsic wrongness of the action itself does. If God is the only being whom one ought to desire to enjoy, then to desire to enjoy the sheer activity of theft, when theft is known even by unbelievers to be intrinsically bad (*Confessions* 2.4.9), is a desire to enjoy something virtually as far removed from God's goodness as is possible.[28] It is that desire that Augustine comes to recognize later in life as morally monstrous.

Let us imagine the youthful Augustine in different sorts of circumstances—in different possible worlds, if you will—in Thagaste. In each circumstance the theft occurs and appears exactly as it actually appeared: hidden-camera recordings of the individual thefts would all be visually and acoustically indistinguishable. The first circumstance is the actual one; seven others track lies 2–8:

Theft 1: Augustine steals from the desire to enjoy doing something wrong.
Theft 2: Augustine steals, causing harm to someone without helping anyone.
Theft 3: Augustine steals, causing harm to someone while helping someone else.
Theft 4: Augustine steals solely for the pleasure of stealing.
Theft 5: Augustine steals solely from the desire to please his comrades.
Theft 6: Augustine steals, causing harm to no one while saving someone's possessions.
Theft 7: Augustine steals, causing harm to no one while saving someone's life.
Theft 8: Augustine steals, causing harm to no one while saving someone from bodily defilement.

What is the difference between theft 1 and theft 4? Is theft 1 like lie 1 in being more sinful than all its confreres?

Let us take on the first question while revisiting lie 4. The type-4 liar or thief is, I suggest, a person whose relevant behavior is the expression of a sinful habit, according to the account given in *De sermone Domini in monte* 1.12.34–35. That is, such a person derives augmented pleasure from repeated acts of lying or theft.[29] The person's behavior is thus vicious, in the original sense of the term but—unlike the intentional behavior of type-2 and type-3 sinners—not necessarily malicious: the habitual sinner need not intend harm to anyone. In contrast, if we assume that lies 5–8 and thefts 5–8 are not themselves expressions of habitual behavior, we are entitled to say that they are less sinful than lie 4 and theft 4, respectively.

If Augustine's theft had been theft 4, he would have acted under the influence of a habit but not necessarily with malice. It is clear that he does not take his behavior to be explicable as habitual. If theft 1, Augustine's actual theft, is more sinful than thefts 2 and 3, then it is reasonable to suppose that theft 1 is malicious. Yet the target of the malice is not explicitly identified. I suggest that Augustine's retrospective opinion is that the target was God, even though the youthful Augustine had no clear conception of God's nature. Had the youthful Augustine had a clearer conception, he would have realized that his malice could not be realized by harming God. Nonetheless the older Augustine can recognize that, whether his younger persona realized it or not, the theft, motivated as it was, constituted an attempt to offend God by flouting God's commandment against theft. At one point Augustine characterizes his theft as an effort to arrogate omnipotence to himself by doing something that is but a shadowy imitation of God's omnipotence (*Confessions* 2.6.14).

There are differences between lie 1 and theft 1, but I believe that Augustine thinks they are both affronts to God, attempts to subvert God's sovereignty either by intentionally misrepresenting the nature of that sovereignty or by defying it sheerly for the sake of defying it. It is this feature of theft 1 that makes it more sinful than the other types of theft and thus explains Augustine's choice of it to illustrate his youthful perversity.

Sinful Dreams

If inner-life ethics bases its moral appraisal of an agent upon what goes on in the agent's soul, what difference does it make whether what goes on occurs while the agent is awake or asleep? Is there any moral difference between one's consenting to the suggestion that one commit adultery and one's dreaming of committing adultery? Writing about the issue twice (*Confessions* 10.30.41–42 and *De Genesi ad litteram* 12.15.31), Augustine finds it hard to locate a significant difference.[30] It would never have occurred to him to deny that dreams involve mental activity, nor to deny that the same kinds of mental activity occur in dreams and waking experiences: to dream of consenting to the pleasure taken in an adulterous suggestion is to consent to the suggestion. He considers the possibility that he is not the agent acting in his dreams but rejects it, claiming that God's grace is necessary to cleanse his soul so that it will not continue to do in dreams what it would not do while awake (*Confessions* 10.30.42). That God's grace is necessary underscores Augustine's belief that it is not an excuse merely to plead lack of control over our dreams. The *Confessions'* discussion of sinful dreams follows immediately after the famous plea, "You command continence: give what you command and command what you will" (*Confessions* 10.29.40). The core of Augustine's anti-Pelagianism is that not all sinful action can be avoided without God's grace. So even if we cannot avoid sinful dreams without God's grace, Augustine worries that that fact by itself does not provide sufficient grounds for claiming that the dreams are not really sinful.

When Augustine returns to the issue of sinful dreams in *De Genesi ad litteram*, he has in mind dreams culminating in nocturnal emissions. He appeals to the following exculpatory analogy. Just as there is nothing sinful in the thoughts of a person awake discussing the phenomena of nocturnal emissions, so there is nothing sinful in the dreamt thoughts leading to an emission. The analogy is reminiscent of point (2) of the *New Jerome* commentary on Matthew 5:27–28. But the analogy is faulty and inconsistent with Augustine's inner-life ethics. Faulty, because the person awake may be discussing nocturnal emissions not for clinical but for lecherous purposes. Inconsistent with inner-life ethics, because, as Matthews puts it, "what Augustine exonerates—the nocturnal emission following a lewd dream image—is different from what, in his own terms, would incriminate him, namely, a suggestion within the dream of the possibility of having intercourse." [31] The locus of sin is not in the bodily behavior. Nor does it lie in the possession of the concepts necessary for dreaming the relevant dream or carrying on the relevant discussion. Augustine confounds the issue by picking a type of dream that has overt physiological consequences. Think instead of a dream with no relevant external consequences. You dream of strangling the mindless lout who abruptly cut into your lane as you drove along the freeway earlier in the day, only to wake up to find your hands resting at your sides. If the same sorts of activities go on in your soul when asleep as when awake, are you guilty of homicide, according to the sufficiency-of-action–consent and the intentional-guilt theses?

Here is the inner-life ethicist attorney for your defense. "I agree with Augustine and against the Pelagians that unavoidability is in general no excuse. But I assert that it is an excuse in the special case of dreamt misdeeds. Consider the cases in which we discount unavoidability. Some behavior, such as behavior while intoxicated, may be unavoidable because of the agent's now-impaired faculties, but we hold the agent culpable because the agent got into that impaired state voluntarily and avoidably. Other behavior, such as behavior that results from beliefs and attitudes instilled in a person while very young, may have been unavoidably instilled; they are culpable nonetheless if the agent can avoid the circumstances that elicit the behavior and take steps to extinguish the offensive beliefs and attitudes. Dreaming, however, is not like either of these situations. We cannot voluntarily avoid sleep. As Augustine himself points out, our dreams have us do what we would never do when awake. Why not then think of our dream episodes as entertaining, for an instant, what we firmly reject when we awaken? Where is the sin in that? Surely it cannot be a sin to overcome the momentary temptation to sin."

And here is the inner-life ethicist attorney for the prosecution. "I can agree with much of what my opponent has just said, because he defends where I do not choose to attack. He has not succeeded in exculpating his client, for reasons that Augustine would have appreciated. Dreams are like plays, in which the dreamer is sometimes a member of the cast, sometimes a member of the audience, but of which the dreamer is always the author. The *De Genesi ad litteram* discussion of sinful dreams falls fast on the heels of a discussion of diabolical deception (*De Genesi ad litteram* 12.14.30; see also *De Genesi ad litteram* 12.18.39–21.44), yet Augustine never even hints that dreams are produced in the dreamer by any agency other than the dreamer. Authors bear the onus of moral responsibility for the works they produce. If we think that there is something morally reprehensible about the very depiction of scenes of unjustified and unpunished violence or wanton depravity, then we should worry about our depiction of such scenes in our dreams. Our sinful dreams indicate that we are closer to the portrayer of sadism or the pornographer than we would like to admit. Augustine is aware of this fact. In *Confessions* 10.30.42 he says that God's grace will enable him not only not to commit sinful deeds in dreams but also not even to consent to them. The notion of consent in this context cannot be action-consent, because action-consent is what is involved in committing the deeds in dreams. To pursue the play analogy a bit further, we can say that one indulges in action-consent in those dreams in which one is a member of the cast. But in those dreams in which one is merely a member of the audience, one still engages in fantasy-consent. Not only is one the dream's author, but one fails to storm out of the theater when confronted with the depravity that one concocts. What God's grace can enable one ultimately to do is to cease having both sorts of dreams altogether, to cleanse one's soul so thoroughly that one will not even entertain sinful dreams. Augustine claims that Solomon's soul was in this state (*De Genesi ad litteram,* 12.15.31; see 1 Kings 3:5–15). But until our souls are in this state, we are responsible for our sinful dreams."

What verdict should the jury deliver?

Conclusion

Think of our plight as an exercise in moral progress. Our first task is to gain control over our external behavior. But that is not enough. We must also put our internal house in order; our behavior must issue from the right motives and intentions. But that is still not enough. The Sermon on the Mount enjoins us to be perfect. We must strive to purge the wrong motives and desires from our souls, even were they never to gain the upper hand. There is nothing wrong with overcoming temptation, but, pace the attorney for the defense, there is something wrong with being tempted. Sinful dreams bear the unwelcome tidings that we have not yet succeeded in the third task: dreams provide the stage on which desires we are able to overcome while awake can still strut their stuff. It takes a Solomon to walk—and dream—in the ways of the Lord. It is Augustine's belief that no one can do that without divine assistance. It may be fortunate that other humans cannot eavesdrop on our dreams. For that reason I believe that Augustine would tell us that the present case can only be adequately tried before a judge who is both supremely just and supremely merciful.

NOTES

1. Raymond E. Brown, Joseph A. Fitzmyer, and Roland E. Murphy, eds., *The New Jerome Biblical Commentary* (Englewood Cliffs, N.J.: Prentice Hall, 1990), 642.

2. The interior sense is reminiscent of Aristotle's "sensus communis."

3. See also St. Augustine, *De musica* 6.4.6.

4. *De quantitate animae* was written no later than a year after *De immortalitate animae* was (387–88).

5. It does not follow that the soul, qua immortal, is superior to the body. Augustine argues for the immortality of the soul in St. Augustine, *Soliloquia* 2.19.33, and idem, *De immortalitate animae, passim,* but does not claim that the soul's immortality in itself makes it superior to matter. He takes the natural indestructibility of matter as evidence that the soul too must be naturally everlasting, since the soul is superior to matter (*De immortalitate animae* 7.12). To avoid circularity, Augustine must then base the soul's superiority on grounds independent of its immortality, grounds such as its indivisibility and causal activity (see below). It is consistent with this position to hold, nevertheless, that any particular physical object is an ephemeral combination of indestructible matter.

6. I am indebted to Scott MacDonald for reminding me of the importance of this point.

7. See, for example, *De immortalitate animae* 16.25; *De musica* 6.5.9–15; St. Augustine, *De Genesi ad litteram* 12.16.32–33. Note that it would be hard to square Augustine's account with a Humean theory of causation as constant conjunction between events.

8. I am indebted to Arthur Kuflik for this term.

9. "They do nothing through the agency of the body that they had not first spoken in the heart," but "He has not yet spoken who has not consented by an inclination of the heart to the suggestions occurring in the heart from whatever sensory impressions" (St. Augustine, *De continentia* 2.3; reemphasized several times throughout *De continentia* 2.3–5). Thus, for example, genital arousal is not a transgression of continence if the arousal is involuntary (*De continentia* 2.5).

10. "So also the other evil deeds of men, which no bodily movement brings about, and of which every bodily sense is unaware, have their secret guilty agents; even consent in thought alone—that is, an evil word of the interior mouth—defiles them" (*De continentia* 2.4). Immediately preceding this passage, Augustine had rung the changes on the list given in Matthew 15:19 with a series of rhetorical questions, all of the form, "Even if the agent is not successful in carrying out the sin in question, is he not guilty of that very sin nevertheless?"

11. "Even if he has not acted by means of his hand or some other part of the body, he has acted nevertheless because he has now decided in thought that the act itself is to be done; he is guilty of the act according to the divine laws, even though it is hidden from the human senses" (*De continentia* 2.3).

12. For a dissenting opinion, see Christopher Kirwan, *Augustine* (London: Routledge, 1989), 75–76.

13. Augustine constructs an analogy between the three intermediate goods of will (as love), memory, and understanding and the three persons of the Trinity; see St. Augustine, *De Trinitate* 15.20.38–23.43.

14. Augustine could consistently maintain that there are other uses of *uti* according to which it does not function as a success verb. Think of an analogous situation in English. A: "He answered the question incorrectly." B: "Then he didn't answer the question at all." C: "Of course he *answered* the question: he didn't simply leave that part of the examination blank." I am inclined to think that there are circumstances in which B's response is appropriate and circumstances in which C's response is appropriate.

15. In St. Augustine, *De diversis quaestionibus* 30, Augustine suggests that some invisible, incorporeal things, such as beauty, are fit to be enjoyed. In *De diversis quaestionibus* 46.2 he argues that the Platonic Ideas are eternal but depend for their existence on God's mind. In enjoying beauty, then, we are enjoying what is, from our point of view, an aspect of God.

16. Of course desire contexts are opaque. I may want to be the discoverer of the Pharaoh's tomb while not wanting to be the first victim of the Pharaoh's curse, even though the two definite descriptions have (or will have) the same reference. If we are seeking to show that a particular desire is genuinely incoherent, however, it is fair to treat the desire context as if it were transparent.

17. For other examples, see William E. Mann, "The Theft of the Pears," *Apeiron* 12 (1978): 52–53. Note that many if not all of the ingredients of the doctrine of double effect are nascent in Augustine's discussion of use and enjoyment.

18. For further discussion of this passage see Christopher Kirwan's "Avoiding Sin: Augustine against Consequentialism," in this volume.

19. I believe that his voluntarism on this score fits hand-in-glove with Augustine's views about the calamitousness of the fall; see, for example, his discussion of the nature and effects of original sin in St. Augustine, *City of God* 14.11–15. His voluntarism is also bolstered by a plausible reading of Romans 7:22–23.

20. See, for example, James Wetzel, *Augustine and the Limits of Virtue* (Cambridge: Cambridge University Press, 1992), and the references cited therein.

21. In St. Augustine, *Contra mendacium* 12.26, a lie is characterized as a false signification with the desire to deceive. The characterization appears in the context of a discussion of figurative biblical language. It looks as though a false signification need not be anything more than a misleading interpretation and that I could provide a false signification by uttering nothing but true propositions.

22. "The world" includes the states of my soul, for I can dissemble about them as well as I can about the capital of North Dakota.

23. Augustine points out that Jones's wanting you to avoid the fiends is compatible with Jones's not wishing well for you; Jones may want himself to be the agent of your destruction. Although the example Augustine gives spoils the point, he also thinks that Smith's wanting the fiends to fasten upon you is compatible with Smith's wishing well for you: it may be that your fate is so dismal otherwise that encountering the fiends is the best that can happen to you (St. Augustine, *De mendacio* 4.4).

24. One may certainly dissent from Augustine's assessment of Jones's case. Although Jones may wish you well, it does not follow that he does not try to deceive you. The success of Jones's strategy depends on your correctly taking his action to be deceptive: Jones counts on his deception, coupled with your mistrust, being the vehicle that will deliver you safely from the fiends. Note that Jones has not deceived you about what path the fiends are on; he has deceived you instead about what his beliefs are about the two paths.

25. This characterization was suggested by David Christensen.

26. By bodily defilement Augustine has heterosexual and homosexual rape in mind. Since lie 8 is less evil than lie 7, it seems to follow that bodily defilement is worse than death. In *De mendacio* 7.10 Augustine maintains, in effect, that, if one is sexually assaulted, one retains bodily chastity if and only if one retains spiritual integrity (by not consenting). Left-to-right, because if one consents, one ipso facto loses bodily chastity (even if the assailant then never carries out the deed). Right-to-left, because one's retaining spiritual integrity is

sufficient for one's retaining bodily chastity. Augustine thus thinks that it is possible for a sexual assault to be physically committed without its affecting the victim's bodily chastity.

The eightfold classification of lies exerted great influence; see, e.g., St. Thomas Aquinas, *Summa theologiae* 2a2ae.110.2.

27. Cicero, *Paradoxa Stoicorum* 3.2.25.

28. Virtually; the desire to enjoy blasphemy would be further removed. Augustine's anti-Manichaeanism entails that the further a thing is removed from God's goodness, the closer it is to being nonexistent (*Confessions* 7.12.18; St. Augustine, *De natura boni contra Manichaeos* 6). Thus at one point Augustine asks rhetorically whether his theft can be a thing that exists at all (*Confessions* 2.6.12). Note that Augustine's retrospective assessment does not maintain that he knew at the time of his theft how monstrous it was.

29. Aquinas understands Augustine's type-4 liar in this way; see *Summa theologiae* 2a2ae.110.2.

30. These passages have been discussed recently in Gareth B. Matthews, *Thought's Ego in Augustine and Descartes* (Ithaca: Cornell University Press, 1992), chap. 8 ("The Moral Dream Problem"). See also Gareth B. Matthews, "On Being Immoral in a Dream," *Philosophy* 56 (1981): 47–54, and William E. Mann, "Dreams of Immorality," *Philosophy* 58 (1983): 378–85.

31. Matthews, *Thought's Ego in Augustine and Descartes*, 102. Strictly speaking, it would be consent to a suggestion that would incriminate him.

EIGHT

On Being Morally Responsible in a Dream*

Ishtiyaque Haji

Are we are morally responsible for what we do or think in our dreams? Right at the outset this moral dream problem reeks of philosophical misgivings. After all, it might plausibly be urged that all moral responsibility ultimately traces to responsibility for actions, and there is a stark difference between one's performing an action and one's dreaming that one performs an action.[1] It would perhaps be perfectly legitimate to inquire about whether we are morally responsible for bringing it about that we have certain sorts of dreams, just as it is philosophically unproblematic to inquire about whether we are morally responsible for bringing it about that we have certain fairly settled long-term traits that are constitutive of our characters.[2] But this sort of concern is far removed from the seemingly suspicious concern over whether one's dream self is, for instance, blameworthy for pilfering pears. Yet venerable philosophers like Plato and Augustine have seriously entertained what is presumably the minority view that we are indeed responsible for the thoughts or actions of our dream selves.[3]

In this paper I first show that what appear to be two forceful arguments against the minority view are not in fact beyond reproach. Both lose much of their attraction if we grant the Augustinian doctrine that dreaming involves mental activity in which the dreamer can experience certain sensations, undergo sundry emotional reactions, and make miscellaneous judgments. A key incentive to discussing these arguments is to explain how various principles suggested by Augustine's deliberations on the minority view are directly germane to the ongoing debate on moral responsibility for intentional behavior. In particular I think Augustine's discussion exerts pressure to reject the condition that one cannot be blameworthy for performing an action unless that action is wrong. I take an Augustinian insight to be that blameworthiness should be associated with one's

*I thank Lory Lemke and Gary Matthews for their valuable comments and suggestions on this chapter.

"inner" attitudes toward one's acts and develop the idea that one is blameworthy for performing an action only if one takes oneself to be doing wrong in performing the action. I end by sketching a line of reasoning in favor of an attenuated version of the minority view, according to which it is at least possible for one to be blameworthy (or praiseworthy) for the thoughts of one's dream self.

AN ARGUMENT FROM ALTERNATIVE POSSIBILITIES

The famous principle of alternative possibilities, which says that one is responsible for doing only what is in one's power to avoid doing, fuels a seemingly telling argument against the minority view:[4]

(A1) One is responsible for doing something only if one could have refrained from doing that thing.

(A2) What one does in one's dream is not something one could have refrained from doing.

(A3) If (A1) and (A2), then one is not morally responsible for what one does in one's dream.

(A4) Therefore, one is not morally responsible for what one does in one's dream.

One response that most readily comes to mind against this argument, and indeed against the minority view itself, is that, contrary to what (A2) presupposes, one does not intentionally or otherwise do anything in one's dreams. Passages in the *Confessions,* however, strongly suggest that Augustine would eschew this response:

> You commanded me not to commit fornication. . . . You gave me the grace and I did your bidding. . . . But in my memory . . . the images of things imprinted upon it by my former habits still linger on. When I am awake they obtrude themselves upon me, though with little strength. But when I dream, they not only give me pleasure but are very much like acquiescence in the act. The power which these illusory images have over my soul and my body is so great that what is no more than a vision can influence me in sleep in a way that the reality cannot do when I am awake. Surely it cannot be that when I am asleep I am not myself, O Lord my God? And yet the moment when I pass from wakefulness to sleep, or return again from sleep to wakefulness, marks a great difference in me. During sleep where is my reason which, when I am awake, resists such suggestions and remains firm and undismayed even in face of the realities themselves? Is it sealed off when I close my eyes? Does it fall asleep with the senses of the body? And why is it that even in sleep I often resist the attractions of these images, for I remember my chaste resolutions and abide by them and give no consent to temptations of this sort?[5]

As Gareth Matthews has commented, when Augustine speaks of remembering his chaste resolutions of not succumbing to temptations of evil in some of his dreams, the implication is clearly that in other dreams he does give real consent.[6]

So Augustine admits that both real consent and real withholding of consent is possible in our dreams. He would not then accept line (A2).

Augustine goes on after the part of the passage I have cited and adds that what he does or thinks in his dreams is something that is in his power, together with the gratuitous assistance of God, to refrain from doing or thinking:

> The power of your hand, O God almighty, is indeed great enough to cure all the diseases of my soul. By granting me more abundant grace you can even quench the fire of sensuality which provokes me in my sleep. . . . By your grace [my soul] will no longer commit in sleep these shameful, unclean acts inspired by sensual images, which lead to the pollution of the body: it will not so much as consent to them.

The passage paves the way for the suggestion that Augustine is well equipped to jettison line (A1). With the aid of God's grace, Augustine implies, he will be able to refrain from consenting to evil suggestions in his dreams. A reasonable presumption is that there are at least some cases that are such that if God exists and by his grace he ensures that some agent refrains from consenting to an evil suggestion in a dream, then that agent cannot fail to refrain from consenting. But since it is through God's grace that the agent cannot refrain, the agent is still morally responsible for refraining; intervention by God through his grace is not a responsibility-undermining factor. Some situations in which one does something with the gratuitous assistance of God can perhaps profitably be compared to a situation of the following sort. Suppose one can perform a particular action only if one does it under hypnosis. Suppose one consents to being hypnotized for the purpose of performing the action, fully knowing that, once hypnotized, one will not be able to refrain from performing the action. If one subsequently performs the action under hypnosis, one may well be morally responsible for doing so. There is then, I believe, a significant moral difference between intervention by God that results in some agent's performing an action by compulsion, or in a manner that emancipates the agent from responsibility, and intervention by God through his grace that does not subvert responsibility. It would seem, in consequence, that Augustine is justified in spurning (A1).

There is an alternative rejection of (A1) inspired by examples developed by John Locke and more recently by Harry Frankfurt.[7] Suppose Augustine freely steals some pears. Assume that had he shown any inclination of failing to steal— had he, for example, even begun to choose or decide not to steal the pears—Satan would have intervened and caused Augustine to act on an intention to steal the pears. We would then, arguably, have a case in which Augustine is morally responsible for stealing the pears (as, amongst other things, he acted just as he would have had Satan not been keeping vigil), although he could not have done otherwise.

The Augustinian and the Locke–Frankfurtian responses to the argument from alternative possibilities should prompt the adversary of the minority view to search for other grounds to dispose of that view. Before looking at other grounds, we should consider a case in support of the minority stance.

AN ARGUMENT IN FAVOR OF THE MINORITY VIEW

By relying on the view that real consent is possible in one's dreams, one might attempt to defend the minority view in this way:

(B1) One's dream self consents (on some occasion, say) to an evil suggestion.

(B2) If (B1), then one's dream self (freely and knowingly) does evil.

(B3) If one's dream self (freely and knowingly) does evil, then one's dream self is morally blameworthy for doing evil.

(B4) Therefore, one's dream self is morally blameworthy (and so morally responsible) for doing evil.

It might credibly be counseled that the argument collapses at line (B2). For surely it does not follow from the fact that one consents to do something, like committing the evil that is adultery, that one does what one consents to doing. In failing to do the evil one consents to doing one has not done that evil and hence is not blameworthy for that evil.[8]

In his lucid discussion of the moral dream problem William Mann opposes or at least thinks Augustine would oppose this rejection of (B2).[9] For Mann believes Augustine endorses the principle that consenting to wrongdoing is sufficient for having done something wrong.[10] Mann submits that to consent to a suggestion (presumably when the consent is sincere) is to form an intention to do what the suggestion suggests. He then recommends that Augustine be understood as enunciating not the fallacious doctrine that to consent to do something is to do that thing but rather: "Consent Principle: If to do A is to do something wrong, then intending to do A is also something wrong."[11]

As I understand it Mann's defense of the consent principle turns on the consideration that intentions themselves can be right or wrong.

> Judgments of right and wrong . . . take as their domain at least two distinct categories of activities, actions and intentions. The notion of a right or wrong intention is, be it granted, parasitic upon the notion of a right or wrong action: a specific intention is right (wrong) if and only if the action which would realize it is right (wrong). Central to Augustine's . . . [consent] doctrine is the proposition that a person's intentions themselves can be *right* or *wrong*, not merely *good* or *bad*.[12]

Although Mann's defense of the consent principle is engrossing, I think it has a difficulty. Suspect is Mann's proposal that a person's intention to perform an action is wrong if and only if the person's action that would realize that intention is itself wrong. Presumably Mann would concede that on the received view of subjunctive conditionals, determining the normative status of an agent's intention would require identifying the closest possible world in which that agent intends to do some action and in which that agent's intention has been realized by that action. It seems perfectly possible, though, that there could be two such worlds, equally close, but in which the agent's intention has been realized by one action with some normative status in one of the worlds but by an action with a different normative status in the other world. For example, suppose Sin has decided on his own to commit adultery and he freely acts on his decision, although he is aware that he could have refrained from doing so. We may assume that in this situation Sin's intention to commit adultery has been realized by an action that is wrong. Now suppose again that Sin has decided on his own to commit adultery and he freely acts on his decision. But this time assume that, had Sin revealed even the shadow of an inclination not to commit adultery, Satan would have intervened and would have caused Sin to act on his decision. In this "Frankfurt-type" situation, unlike in the first, Sin could not have done otherwise. In addition, in this situation, but not in the first, Sin's act of adultery is not wrong (though it may well be overall evil): the principle that "ought" implies "can," together with the principle that one has a moral obligation to perform an action if and only if it is morally wrong for one not to perform that action, entail that it is morally wrong for one to perform an action only if it is within one's power not to perform that action.[13] Since it is not within Sin's power not to commit adultery, Sin's act is not wrong (though Sin may well be morally blameworthy for committing that act).[14] Arguably, though, the world in which Sin could have done otherwise is equally close to the one in which he had no alternative possibility. A retreat to the stance that an intention is right (wrong) if and only if the action that realizes it is right (wrong) would prove detrimental as many intentions are never realized in action.

We have a standoff. The argument from alternative possibilities against the minority view is not sound; nor is the argument from consent in favor of that view. Perhaps some headway can be made by considering a second attack against the minority view.

A SECOND ARGUMENT AGAINST THE MINORITY VIEW: THE ARGUMENT FROM BLAME

One might grant that dreams are experiences involving mental activity consistent with being skeptical about the Augustinian view that one's dream self can refrain from consenting to an evil suggestion. The skepticism might be motivated by a number of different considerations. So, for instance, whereas one might concede that a dreamer can experience various sensations, one could plausibly deny that the dreamer can consent or refrain from consenting to a misdeed as, one might insist, there is a difference between real consent or real restraint and "dream consent" or "dream restraint."[15] Or whereas one might allow for the possibility that one's dream self can consent or refrain from consenting to an evil suggestion, one could deny that one's dream self could intentionally do these things; the actions of the dream self, if it really acted at all, would be akin to those "actions" of a clockwork doll. Then, banking on the principle that "ought" implies "can" and "ought not to" implies "can refrain from," one could generate an argument against an aspect of the minority view having to do with blameworthiness in this fashion:

(C1) One's dream self cannot consent nor can it refrain from consenting to evil.

(C2) If (C1), then it is false that one's dream self has a moral obligation to refrain from consenting to evil.

(C3) If it is false that one's dream self has a moral obligation to refrain from consenting to evil, then it is false that it is wrong for one's dream self to consent to evil.

(C4) If it is false that it is wrong for one's dream self to consent to evil, then one's dream self is not morally blameworthy for consenting to evil.

(C5) Therefore, one's dream self is not morally blameworthy for consenting to evil.

On the assumption that one is identical to one's dream self, one could draw the desired conclusion that one is not morally blameworthy for consenting to evil in a dream.[16] We have already canvassed possible rationales for (C1). Let's review the other premises.

Line (C2) is supported by the "ought" implies "can" principle (K): one has a moral obligation to perform (not to perform) an action only if it is within one's power to perform (not to perform) that action. If K is true, and one cannot refrain from consenting to evil, then one cannot have an obligation to refrain from consenting to evil.

Line (C3) rests on this principle (OW): it is morally obligatory for one not to do (to do) something if and only if it is morally wrong for one to do (not to do) that thing. If it is false that one has an obligation not to consent to evil, then given OW, it is false that it is wrong for one to consent to evil.

Finally (C4) is defended by appealing to the principle (call it "Blame") that one is blameworthy for doing something only if it is wrong for one to do that thing.

Even if we grant the first premise of what we can dub the "argument from blame," the argument is vulnerable at other points. So, for instance, Mann and Matthews both report that, in his stance against the heresy of Pelagianism, Augustine rejects principle (K).[17] I want to focus on another problem. An interpretation of certain Augustinian views raises the possibility that blameworthiness may not be associated with wrongness in the manner expressed by Blame. Adumbrating some features of Augustine's mind–body dualism will facilitate comprehending these views.

INNER PERSONS AND OUTER PERSONS

It appears that Augustine conceives of a person as a composite self made up of two distinct entities, the soul, or inner person, and the body, or outer person:[18]

[a] man is not a body alone, nor a soul alone, but a being composed of both. This, indeed, is true, that the soul is not the whole man, but the better part of man; the body not the whole, but the inferior part of man; and that then, when both are joined, they receive the name of man—which, however, they do not severally lose even when we speak of them singly. For who is prohibited from saying, in colloquial

usage, "That man is dead, and is now at rest or in torment," though this can be spoken only of the soul; or "He is buried in such and such a place," though this refers only to the body? Will they say that Scripture follows no such usage? On the contrary, it so thoroughly adopts it, that even while a man is alive, and body and soul are united, it calls each of them singly by the name "*man,*" speaking of the soul as the "inward man," and of the body as the "outward man," as if there were two men, though both together are indeed but one.[19]

The passage illuminates what appears to be Augustine's estimation that the body is something merely physical; no psychological or mental predicates apply to it. The soul, in contrast, is nonphysical and is separable from the body at death. Augustine maintains that the soul is superior to the body and animates it; it is the soul's activities that make the difference between merely physical endeavors and purposive behavior characteristic of living human beings.[20] Augustine, it seems, would agree that the inner acts and speeches of one's soul constitute one's true psychological life. But what about one's moral life?

Of vital import is Augustine's alluring suggestion that the inner person can perform (inner) actions. Augustine typically takes thinking, remembering, and visualizing to be inner activities. An intention to do something, furthermore, is conceived as doing that thing already in one's heart.[21] Seriously entertaining the idea of inner agency enables us to give a rationalization of Augustine's verdict that, if one intends or consents to commit adultery, one has already committed adultery in one's heart (and that one has therefore already defiled oneself), which coheres well with Augustine's inner–outer person dualism. One could read Augustine as proposing that the reason that the state of affairs *S intends to commit adultery* (or *S decides to commit adultery*) is wrong is that, in intending to commit adultery, S's inner self has performed some inner action that is wrong. Generalizing, one could construe Augustine as theorizing that what is of relevance in assessing the normative status of an outer action (or what we would generally take to be an action) is something mental or intentional—inner actions figure centrally here. More specifically, Augustine's view could be taken to be that the notion of an outer action's being right or wrong is parasitic upon the notion of an inner action's being right or wrong in this way: for any agent, S, outer action, A, and inner action, IA, if S performs A and A is "backed" by an inner action, IA, then A is right if and only if IA is right. (Call this principle "Inner Dependence.")

This reading of Augustine dovetails nicely with some of Augustine's remarks on sin. In his discussion of the Sermon on the Mount Augustine says that there are three things that go to implement sin: suggestion of an evil act arising from memory or perception, attraction to it, and consent. He explains that, if consent has taken place, "we would commit sin surely, a sin in the heart known to God, though actually it may remain unknown to man."[22] So it is an inner activity of consent, Augustine seems to insist, that constitutes the essential ingredient of sin. Whether one carries out by means of bodily activity what one has consented to in one's heart, Augustine implies, is by and large irrelevant to whether one has already sinned and so irrelevant to whether one is a rational candidate for blame.

Augustine's inner–outer person dualism raises a number of arresting questions and puzzles.[23] So does Inner Dependence. (For example, how exactly are we to understand the notion of backing ? Also, if intentions are inner actions, and inner actions are bona fide actions, then why need anything like Inner Dependence at all? Shouldn't there be a single normative ethical theory whose "domain" is all actions?) I shall for the most part ignore these enigmas and questions. I emphasize that I am ultimately not so concerned about whether in the end Augustine would subscribe wholesale to the composite-self view sketched above and whether Augustine would accede to Inner Dependence. (Part of the complication here is that as he matured as a philosopher, Augustine changed his mind on a number of issues, including those having to do with sin and voluntariness.) However, I believe that if we suppose that motives (intentions included) are "inner entities," and that an activity like believing that something or thinking that something is an "inner activity," understanding Augustine on some aspects of the composite-self view— notably, those aspects having to do with the inner self's performing inner activities—in the manner in which I have done, unearths some engaging possibilities about blameworthiness. Some of these possibilities cast perilous doubt on line (C4) of the argument from Blame.

REJECTION OF THE ARGUMENT FROM BLAME

Motivational elements (perhaps paradigm candidates of "inner elements") are intricately affiliated with the issue of whether one is blameworthy for performing an action. Luck might have it that a right action (fortuitously) results from a reprehensible intention (or cluster of motives). But if one performs such a right action in light of the belief that one is doing wrong, then arguably one is still deserving of blame: if, for example, Nero forces what he takes to be the poisoned wine down Cicero's gullet with the intention of murder, then he would be blameworthy, it appears, even if the poison has been replaced by droplets from the fountain of youth and the droplets rejuvenate frail and aged Cicero. In light of this connection between motivational elements and appraisability for actions I suggest replacing Blame with

> Blame*: An agent is blameworthy for performing an action, A, only if he has an occurrent or dispositional belief, B, that A is wrong and he performs A despite entertaining B and believes (at least dispositionally) that he is performing A. (Entertaining a belief involves accessing it in some way and not merely having it—one must in some fashion, perhaps even unconsciously, be cognizant of it.)

Whereas Blame* associates blameworthiness with belief in what is wrong, Blame associates blameworthiness with (objective) wrongness. Blame*, I believe, is superior to Blame as the second scenario involving Sin (or Nero's case) strongly suggests. In this scenario Sin freely commits adultery, although he could not have refrained from doing so. If Blame is true, then Sin cannot be blameworthy for committing adultery, for his act of committing adultery is not (objectively) wrong (though it may of course be evil). It will not do to suppose that one is not blameworthy for performing an act unless, in performing the act, one brings about a greater balance of intrinsic evil over intrinsic goodness: if we allow for at least moderate consequential considerations, it is possible that each one of one's options, if it were performed, would result in overall intrinsic evil and that one of these options—the one least overall evil—is obligatory. In many situations one would not be blameworthy for doing what is obligatory though overall intrinsically evil. Let's assume that Sin believed that he would be doing something wrong if he were to commit adultery. Then Blame*, unlike Blame, enables us to validate the intuition that, since Sin (freely) does something in light of the belief that he is doing wrong, Sin is blameworthy for his action.

Apart from calling into question principle Blame, one might take some of Augustine's remarks on inner activities to be suggestive of another normative principle, this time a principle linking motives and obligatoriness. Whatever we make of Inner Dependence, the following Inner Dependence-like principle may well be true:

> Motives: For any agent, S, action, A, and motive, M, if S does A, A is motivated by M, and S cannot do A unless S has M, then it is morally obligatory for S to do A only if it is morally obligatory for S to have M.

Motives can be defended in this way: suppose the very normative ethical theory for assessing the normative status of actions is also the theory for assessing the normative status of (the having of) motives that underlie actions. Then in order for such a theory to be acceptable, it must not be the case that the theory assign "incompatible" normative statuses to an action and to the motive that gives rise to that action. It must not, for instance, be the case that the theory entails that an action, A, is obligatory although it is wrong for A's agent to have the motive that gives rise to A. If such were not the case, then sometimes the directives of the theory would be inconsistent with one another.[24] Think of the matter in this way. It appears that the following principle is true:

> Prerequisite: If S cannot do A without doing B (for instance, out of physical necessity), and S can refrain from doing B, then if it is obligatory for S to do A, it is obligatory for S to do B.

Now suppose S ought to do an action, A, and S cannot do A unless S has a certain motive, M, that gives rise to A. Then Prerequisite (or an appropriately modified version of Prerequisite) entails that it is obligatory for S to have M. If the true (or correct) normative theory is relevant to assessing both actions and motives that underlie those actions, then the theory must be consistent with Prerequisite, which appears to be a general truth about moral obligation. Such consistency can only be guaranteed if Motives is true.

It's time to take stock. Through a somewhat circuitous route, we have been able to marshal support against line (C4) of the argument from Blame. The adversary of the minority view need not yet, however, capitulate. For she might urge that, while we may well have undermined some arguments against the minority view, we have so far advanced few, if any, positive considerations in its support. This concern is reasonable and pressing. My modest aim, in what follows, is to motivate the view that it is possible to be blameworthy for some of the thoughts of one's dream self, on the supposition that the dreamer can, amongst other things, make various judgments. I shall pursue the following strand of thought. We can be morally responsible for thinking certain thoughts. On the assumptions that (i) just as one can engage in unconscious deliberation, one can engage in unconscious thinking of certain thoughts (unconscious fantasizing about stealing pears, for instance); (ii) one can be blameworthy for an episode of one's unconscious thinking of certain thoughts; (iii) possibly, dreaming, for example, that one steals some pears is relevantly like engaging in unconscious thinking about stealing some pears, it is possible for one to be blameworthy for at least some of the thoughts of one's dream self.

BLAMEWORTHINESS FOR THOUGHTS

Appraisability (that is, blameworthiness or praiseworthiness) for thinking certain thoughts presupposes that agents are able to exercise control over thinking thoughts. A rough distinction will prove useful. One can engage in thinking about something with a view to intentionally doing something concerning that thing. For instance, one can canvass reasons for or against A-ing, form a decision to A, and then execute this decision. Alternatively, one can engage in thinking about something without a view to forming an intention or arriving at a decision to do anything about that thing. For example, a student can engage in thinking about what it would be like to slit her professor's throat without intending to form an intention or arrive at a decision to slit her mentor's throat. It is presumably this latter sort of thinking that is often involved in intentional imaginings (as in intentional "day dreaming") or intentional fantasizings (and it is this sort of thinking that will figure prominently in the discussion of appraisability for unconscious thoughts). That we are able to exercise control over both these sorts of "thinking about things" acquires partial confirmation from the following. First, thinking is an activity, much of which can be intentional, and much of which can be initiated, sustained, or stopped. I can now, for example, begin to think about a specific problem, briefly set it aside to attend to the phone, and then resume thinking about it. In addition, thinking about something and imagining something are frequently alternatives that I can contemplate and undertake on a specific occasion. After spending the day teaching, Al might consider cleaning the car, watching television, or thinking about where to invest funds. Of course, Al could perform the complex act of cleaning the car and thinking about where to invest. Being one of his alternatives, it can be legitimate to inquire into whether Al's thinking about where to invest is the alternative that Al morally ought to undertake, or the alternative he believes he ought morally to undertake. Third, just as one can acquire motivation to steal a pear, so one can acquire motivation to think about something and then act on that motivation. By reflecting on the lifestyle he wants to lead when retired, Al might acquire motivation to think about various investment strategies and then act on the motivation.

Imagine that Sid is disgruntled with his performance in a course. Although he knows that he is solely responsible for his poor showing, he blames his professor. He consoles himself by constructing an elaborate "thought scenario" in which he slowly slits the throat of his mentor. But not morally insensitive, Sid believes, let us suppose, that it is wrong for him to entertain such thoughts. Still, the pleasure he derives from thinking such thoughts is so great that he acts against his moral belief. He lowers himself into a comfortable couch, closes his eyes, and imagines what it would be like for him to perform the gruesome deed. Sid on this occasion engages in an intentional (complex act, let's suppose) of thinking certain thoughts. Call this act "ACT." It certainly seems possible for Sid to exercise the sort of control required for moral responsibility over ACT. Imagine, for example, that, having seated himself on the couch, Sid intentionally dismisses from his mind the option of constructing the elaborate thought scenario, arrives at a decision instead to think about what he can do to improve his performance in the course, and then acts on that decision. Here Sid's thought of slitting his mentor's throat appears to be under Sid's control. It is, roughly, under the control of Sid's practical reasoning; it is responsive to his reasons.

To clarify, very sketchily, the relevant notion of control, let's use "desire" broadly to refer to any factor of intentional action having inherent motivational force. I assume that each intentional action is caused in part by some proximal desire that is "the motivational precursor" of that action. I also assume that when an agent acts intentionally she relies on her evaluative scheme. Such a scheme is composed, roughly, of normative standards the agent believes ought to be invoked in reasons for action; the agent's long-term goals — her values; deliberative principles the agent uses to arrive at first-person practical judgments about what to do or how to act; and motivation to act in accordance with, or on, her normative standards and values using her deliberative principles. Now we can introduce the notion of volitional control. Action, A, performed by agent, S, is under her volitional control if and only if, holding constant the motivational precursor of A and S's evaluative scheme, there is a scenario (with the same natural laws as the actual world) in which, relying on her evaluative scheme, S decides or forms an intention to do something other than A and she successfully executes that intention or decision. For a desire in one scenario to be the same desire as a desire in another scenario, the two should have the same relative strength—they must have the same strength relative to competing desires.[25] I propose as a control condition (Control*) that an agent is morally responsible for a bit of behavior only if she has volitional control over that bit of behavior.

Sid exercises volitional control over his thought of slitting his mentor's throat: there is a scenario in which, holding constant his evaluative scheme and the motivational precursor of his mental act—the act that is Sid's thinking to slit his mentor's throat—he forms an intention to think otherwise and successfully executes that intention. It appears, then, that we have good grounds for supposing that Sid is deserving of blame for performing ACT: he intentionally performed ACT, took himself to be doing wrong in so doing, and exercised the type of control over ACT that is required for blameworthiness.

It is unproblematic that a great deal of our thinking is unconscious and that unconscious actional elements like beliefs and desires frequently give rise to actions. In exploring appraisability for engaging in unconscious thinking of thoughts one should start with some distinctions. S's desire D to A is weakly unconscious if and only if S does not know or believe that she has D; similarly, S's belief B that p is weakly unconscious if and only if S does not know or believe that she has B. S's desire D to A (belief B that p) is strongly unconscious if and only if D (B) is weakly unconscious, and apart from outside help or careful self-scrutiny, she cannot come to know or believe that she has D (B).[26] Now I think that a person can be blameworthy for performing an action that issues even from strongly unconscious beliefs and desires. Suppose, in the name of discipline, I severely criticize a student for a petty error she committed. It is only later, with the help of a discerning colleague, that I come to appreciate the true motive of my behavior: I genuinely dislike the student and was venting disguised hostility. Suppose I had no good cause for disliking the student; suppose, in addition, that I did, just prior to censuring the unfortunate student, have the ability to engage in self-control and greatly attenuate my criticism; suppose, finally, that at the time of my unfortunate outburst I held the weakly unconscious belief that it was wrong to denounce the student so harshly for the paltry error. Then it appears that I am blameworthy for the denunciation, even though at the time of the denunciation I was unaware of its motivational springs and would have remained in the dark about them in the absence of consultation with my colleague. I should add that our judgment regarding my being to blame for the invective would presumably be quite different if we were to learn that the denunciation stemmed from some strongly unconscious irresistible motivational precursor; or if I acted out of ignorance that is straightforwardly excusing (for example, I falsely believed but on very sound grounds that the student was guilty of plagiarism).

What about appraisability for engaging in unconscious thinking about certain thoughts or unconscious fantasizing? Again, beginning with some distinctions, S engages in weak unconscious thinking (imagining, fantasizing, etc.) if and only if S does not know or believe she is engaging in such thinking; and S engages in strong unconscious thinking (imagining, fantasizing, etc.) if and only if S engages in weak unconscious thinking and, apart from outside help or careful self-scrutiny, she cannot come to know or believe that she is engaging in such thinking. The student might wonder about why the sight of the blood-smeared butcher's knife so disturbs him. After a little probing on the part of a concerned friend it might surface that the student had been (strongly) unconsciously entertaining the scenario of slitting the throat of his professor, and these unconscious musings of his largely explain his agitation at the sight of the bloodied knife.

I now want to adduce considerations in support of the view that it is at least possible for an agent to be blameworthy for unconsciously entertaining certain thoughts.[27] My strategy here is to show that the requirements for blameworthiness laid down by the epistemic condition in Blame* and the control condition in Control* can be satisfied by an agent's unconsciously entertaining certain thoughts and that this should give us some reason to believe that we can be blameworthy for some of our unconscious mental doings. It appears that an agent can engage in a bit of practical reasoning without being conscious of it as reasoning.[28] Consider this case. Suppose Bea believes that Earl has the uncanny ability of accurately judging what is on her mind independently of Bea's vocalizing, or otherwise overtly exposing, what is on her mind. Perhaps partly because she has been embarrassed by some of Earl's revelations regarding her thoughts, she desires to hurt Earl. Assume that this desire (DB) is strongly unconscious; Bea has repressed it partially on the basis of having a standing dispositional belief that it is wrong to hurt a good friend. Given the tug of her repressed desire, she begins, unintentionally, to notice ways of hurting Earl. Bea is bent on starting up a periodical. She is looking for partners. She discovers that sensitive Earl would be extremely hurt were he to learn that Bea had so little as toyed with the thought of dismissing him as a possible associate in her promising venture. On the basis of this discovery she forms the belief (BB) that Earl will be hurt if she merely entertains the thought of not having him as an associate and he discerns this thought. Suppose her venture is steaming along, matters have to be finalized, and Bea must select her associates. Over coffee with Earl, looking directly at him (so that he can "read" her thoughts), she forms the judgment to entertain the thought of excluding Earl and (nondeviantly) acts on the judgment—she imagines excluding Earl.

In the case sketched thus far it is only Bea's desire to hurt Earl that is strongly unconscious. We can, to modify the case a bit, suppose that her relevant belief (BB) is strongly unconscious, given Bea's considerable powers of rationalization. (She might, for instance, rationalize that Earl does not really enjoy "desk jobs," that working too closely with him might wreck a good friendship, etc.) So far, I believe, there is nothing incoherent about the case. I submit that no incoherence results on the additional supposition that her repressed desire (DB) to hurt Earl, in conjunction with her now assumed unconscious belief (BB), issues in an intention, of which Bea is unaware, to entertain the thought of excluding Earl, which in turn leads to Bea's entertaining the thought; and this bit of mental activity—Bea's entertaining the thought—is itself veiled from Bea's consciousness. Perhaps Bea's "directing her mind" to this thought would be exceedingly painful to her.

Is it reasonable to suppose that Bea is blameworthy for her unconscious mental act of entertaining the thought of excluding Earl? At least one feature of the case supports an affirmative reply: Bea has the dispositional belief that it is wrong to hurt Earl, and she unconsciously entertains the thought of excluding Earl—she performs this mental act—in spite of having this belief. So it seems that the epistemic condition of blameworthiness captured by Blame* is satisfied by Bea's mental act. But what about control? Does Bea exercise the sort of control required for blameworthiness over her unconscious mental act of entertaining the thought of excluding Earl? Notice, first, that Bea's unconsciously entertaining the thought of excluding Earl is not simply something that happens to Bea; rather, it is something that is generated by a desire (DB) and a belief (BB) of Bea's. Notice, second, that the motivating unconscious desire (DB) to hurt Earl is not irresistible; indeed, there is nothing in the description of the (modified) case that suggests that Bea lacks the ability to refrain from acting on it. Nor is it one such that Bea could refrain from acting on it only at the cost of suffering considerable psychological damage. The desire, in short, does not seem to be one that undermines control. Notice, third, that there do not appear to be other responsibility-undermining factors such as coercion or wayward causation in the sequence of events leading from the acquisition of desire (DB) and belief (BB) to execution of the unconscious mental act generated on the basis of these actional elements. Notice, finally, there does seem to be a scenario (having the same natural laws as the actual world) in which, given Bea's evaluative scheme and the motivational precursor of the unconscious mental act, Bea forms an intention to do something other than entertain the thought of excluding Earl, and she successfully executes this intention. Here's one: imagine that Bea has a standing dispositional desire (DE) not to hurt Earl along with her repressed desire (DB) to hurt Earl. Assume that (DB) has the same relative strength in this scenario as it does in the actual. However, in the counterfactual scenario, Bea focuses her attention on the attractive aspects of acting in accordance with her desire (DE) not to hurt Earl; she does not wish to jeopardize the friendship, and she wishes to avoid the guilt she would later feel if she were to hurt Earl. Furthermore, Bea refuses to entertain second thoughts about the unconscious judgment not to hurt Earl that she makes. So in this (counterfactual) scenario Bea forms the intention not to hurt Earl and she translates this intention into action. We have, then, reasonable grounds to believe that Bea's unconsciously entertaining the thought of excluding Earl is something over which she has the sort of control required for blameworthiness.

Reverting to the minority view, suppose we grant the Augustinian doctrine that dreaming involves mental activity in which the dreamer can experience certain sensations, undergo sundry emotional reactions, and make miscellaneous judgments. Imagine that Bea, with her repressed desire (DB) to hurt Earl and her (unconscious) belief (BB) that she can hurt Earl merely by entertaining the thought of excluding him as an associate, a belief veiled from her consciousness by rationalization, retires for the day. She tucks herself in bed and falls into a slumber. If dreaming involves mental activity in which the dreamer can make judgments, it seems possible that Bea's desire (DB) and belief (BB) can give rise to a judgment on Bea's part to entertain the thought of excluding Earl, and Bea now (in her slumbers) entertains this thought. (Of course, Bea in her sleep is not aware that she is entertaining this thought—so this during-sleep-mental-activity of hers qualifies as unconscious.) In turn, if entertainment of this thought in her sleep is constitutive of a dream, or part of a dream episode, then it seems that Bea can be blameworthy for it: such entertainment—a mental act—is generated by a desire (DB) and belief (BB) of Bea's, and the other considerations discussed above that lend credibility to the view that Bea (while awake) can be blameworthy for an unconscious entertaining of a certain thought are the very same ones that should lead us to believe that Bea can be blameworthy for entertaining a certain thought while asleep.

In conclusion, Augustine's meditations on the minority view persuasively suggest that the view should not be dismissed as a mere philosophical oddity. I have attempted to defend the view against a number of objections. I have also submitted that Augustine's reflections can be taken to point to some fruitful possibilities that bear directly on central issues concerning moral responsibility. I have recommended, for instance, that some of his thoughts on the moral dream problem motivate reconceptualizing the epistemic requirements of moral responsibility. Further, I have proposed that, if the idea that we can be morally responsible for some of our unconscious thoughts can be defended, then there may well be a way to provide positive support for the view that it is at least possible for us to be deserving of blame for some of the thoughts of our dream selves.

NOTES

1. The view that all moral responsibility traces to moral responsibility for actions has recently been advocated by Robert Audi, "Responsible Action and Virtuous Character," *Ethics* 101 (1991): 304–21. For an opposing view see James Montmarquet's "Epistemic Virtue and Doxastic Responsibility," *American Philosophical Quarterly* 29 (1992): 331–40.

2. The venerable champion of the view that we are morally responsible for our characters is, of course, Aristotle.

3. Some of Plato's discussion on dreams can be found in the *Republic* 571c–573b and the *Theaetetus* 158b–d. Augustine discusses the dream problem, among other places, in book 10 of the *Confessions* and book 12 of *De Genesi ad litteram*.

4. This principle (or principles very similar to this one) has taken center stage in recent discussions on moral responsibility. See for example, Gary Watson's introduction in Gary Watson, ed., *Free Will* (Oxford: Clarendon Press, 1982), 2–5; Peter Van Inwagen, *An Essay*

on Free Will (Oxford: Clarendon Press, 1983), chaps. 3 and 4; and Harry Frankfurt, "Alternate Possibilities and Moral Responsibility," *Journal of Philosophy* 66 (1969): 829–39.

5. St. Augustine, *Confessions* 10.30, trans. R. S. Pine-Coffin (Harmondsworth: Penguin, 1961). All quotations are from Pine-Coffin's translation, unless otherwise noted.

6. Gareth B. Matthews, *Thought's Ego in Augustine and Descartes* (Ithaca: Cornell University Press, 1992), 98; and "On Being Immoral in a Dream," *Philosophy* 56 (1981): 47–54.

7. See John Locke's *Essay concerning Human Understanding* (Oxford: Clarendon Press, 1984), bk. 2, chap. 21, secs. 8–11; and Frankfurt's "Alternate Possibilities and Moral Responsibility." For a recent thorough and insightful discussion on alternative possibilities see John Martin Fischer's *The Metaphysics of Free Will* (Cambridge, Mass.: Blackwell, 1994), chap. 7.

8. It might be objected that consenting to do evil is itself wrong even though one does not later do what one consented to do. This objection, however, is indecisive. There are cases in which consenting to do evil may be wrong, cases, for instance, in which consenting (to do evil) itself harms oneself or another. (Dream cases are presumably not cases of this sort.) But in other cases consenting to do evil may not be wrong. A possible case here is this: one consents to inflict harm on an innocent party but then fails to carry through, as one realizes that one would be doing wrong if one were to carry through.

9. William E. Mann, "Dreams of Immorality," *Philosophy* 58 (1983): 378–85.

10. Ibid., 378.

11. Ibid., 380.

12. Ibid., 381. I take it that Mann's position is not that in *forming* an intention to commit adultery one does something wrong, and that the wrongness of forming an intention to commit adultery is inherited by the intention (to commit adultery) itself.

13. It should be stressed that Mann rejects principle (K), the "ought" implies "can" principle. (I don't think his rejection is conclusive.) It should also be noted that rejection of the principle of alternative possibilities is consistent with the retention of (K). Frankfurt in *The Importance of What We Care About* (Cambridge: Cambridge University Press, 1988), 96, goes so far as to say that "the Kantian view [that "ought" implies "can"] leaves open the possibility that a person for whom only one course of action is available fulfills an obligation when he pursues that course of action."

14. It can be true that Sin's act is not wrong consistent with Sin's being morally blameworthy for performing this act. See below.

15. In *Contra academicos* (3.11.26) Augustine seems to reject the supposed distinction between the apparent pleasure of a dream and the real pleasure of waking life. Perhaps he would do the same with respect to the alleged distinction between dream consent and waking consent.

16. Augustine, it appears, identifies one's dream self with one's self. St. Paul, it would seem, would take a strikingly different view. St. Paul seems to suggest that he is not identical to his evil self, or at least that he is not morally responsible for the doings of his evil self:

> I do not understand my own actions. For I do not do what I want, but I do the very thing I hate. Now if I do what I do not want, I agree that the law is good. So then it is no longer I that do it, but sin which dwells within me. For I know that nothing good dwells within me, that is, in my flesh. I can will what is right, but I cannot do it. For I do not do the good I want, but the evil I do not want is what I do. Now if I do what I do not want, it is no longer I that do it, but sin which dwells within me.

So I find it to be a law that when I want to do right, evil lies close at hand. For I delight in the law of God, in my inmost self, but I see in my members another law at war with the law of my mind. . . . Wretched man that I am! Who will deliver me from this body of death? (Romans 7:15–24, Revised Standard Version)

17. Matthews, *Thought's Ego*, 99; and Mann, "Dreams of Immorality," 379–80.

18. An excellent discussion of Augustine's inner man–outer man dualism can be found in Gareth B. Matthews, "The Inner Man," *American Philosophical Quarterly* 4 (1967): 166–72.

19. St. Augustine, *The City of God* 13.24.2, trans. Marcus Dods, D.D. (New York: Random House, Inc., 1950).

20. Matthews, "Inner Man," 171.

21. For textual evidence of these points and discussion on them see ibid.

22. St. Augustine, *The Lord's Sermon on the Mount* 1.12.34, trans. J. J. Jepson, Ancient Christian Writers, no. 5 (Westminster, Md.: Newman Press, 1948).

23. See Matthews, "Inner Man," and Gareth B. Matthews, "Ritual and the Religious Feelings," in Steven M. Cahn and David Shatz, eds., *Contemporary Philosophy of Religion* (New York: Oxford University Press, 1982), 154–66.

24. I am assuming that we have control over at least some of our motives that give rise to actions: we are free to acquire or form such motives just as we are free to acquire or form (some) intentions. Robert Adams ("Motive Utilitarianism," *Journal of Philosophy* 73 [1976]: 467–81) has argued that the directives of traditional varieties of act utilitarianism are inconsistent in this way. The directives of Fred Feldman's nontraditional variety of utilitarianism are not inconsistent in this way. See Feldman's "On the Consistency of Act- and Motive-Utilitarianism: A Reply to Adams," *Philosophical Studies* 70 (1993): 201–12.

25. Further development of the account of volitional control appears in my *Moral Appraisability: Puzzles, Proposals, and Perplexities* (New York: Oxford University Press, 1998). My account has been influenced by John Martin Fischer's discussion of reason's responsive mechanisms in his "Responsiveness and Moral Responsibility," in Ferdinand Schoeman, ed., *Responsibility, Character, and the Emotions* (Cambridge: Cambridge University Press, 1987), 81–106.

26. For discussion on unconscious belief see Robert Audi's "Self-Deception, Action, and Will," *Erkenntnis* 18 (1982): 137–38. In this paper Audi also defends the views that one can be morally responsible for actions deriving from unconscious beliefs and that unconscious beliefs and desires can play a substantial role in practical reasoning.

27. If S strongly unconsciously entertains a thought, then S entertains that thought, and, apart from outside help or special self-scrutiny, she cannot come to know or believe that she is entertaining that thought.

28. For more on unconscious deliberation see, for example, Robert Audi, *Practical Reasoning* (London: Routledge, 1991), chap. 5, sec. 4.

NINE

Avoiding Sin:
Augustine against Consequentialism*

Christopher Kirwan

Augustine accepted the Greek commonplace that the goal of human life—both the proper and the actual goal for normal adults—is to be happy. A book on the requirements of a happy life, *De beata vita,* was one product of the brief period when Augustine was free to live as a philosopher, between giving up the rat race at his conversion in 386 and the onset of pastoral business with his ordination in 391. After that there was no more time for moral philosophy. But a pastor is asked for advice, and Augustine's intellectual bent led him sometimes to advise his correspondents (and doubtless many others of his flock) not just what to do but how to decide what to do. The decision problem, in the sense of a search for a method or procedure, had not been prominent in Greco-Roman ethics; if "Do as the wise man does" appeared to be the most helpful rule of life that philosophy could find, that fact did not generally make philosophers uneasy. Rules obtruded on Christians, of course, from Judaism and its law, perhaps also from other cults the philosophers had hitherto held at arm's length. But even those rules tended to be, like human laws, not so much methods for solving practical problems as constraints on acceptable solutions to them. Augustine, paradigm witness of his century's unsettled moral climate—the Bible superimposed on attenuated Stoicism—shows us the beginning of an interest in methods (but for an anticipation see the "formula" at Cicero, *De officiis* 3.19).

Utilitarianism is standardly presented as a test of the rightness of actions rather than a method of deciding what to do. But there is also what might be called a utilitarian decision method, as follows: judge what attainable outcome embodies the

*This paper has evolved in reaction to good, sometimes devastating, comments on earlier versions from audiences in many places: Prague, Rice University, where a version was delivered as the 1992 Tsanoff Lecture, the University of Arizona at Tucson, the University of Texas at Austin, Calvin College, Grand Valley State University, the University of Houston, and the Scottish Association for Classical Philosophy at Edinburgh. I am grateful for the invitations, and the criticisms.

most happiness, and act so as to produce that.[1] Here an outcome is a state of affairs produced by action and is attainable by someone when some action that will produce it is in that person's power. The method, like utilitarianism itself, puts together two things: the consequentialist idea that one should aim at the best outcome and the eudaemonistic idea that happiness is the sole measure of an outcome's goodness or value. Augustine does not deal with the latter aspect of the utilitarian method, which presumably had some appeal for him, though presumably not in its classical modern form in which the happiness that ultimately measures value is summed or averaged over everyone (I shall not consider his treatment of the Golden Rule, which he commends at *De doctrina Christiana* 3.14.22, near-quoting Tobith 4:16; cf. Matthew 7:12, Luke 6:31). What particularly caught Augustine's eye was the consequentialist aspect of the method; and that aspect he rejected. In its place he did not put anything very general, so that his philosophical contribution is mainly negative, though interesting.

Before introducing Augustine's text, I shall begin with an imaginary story of my own. Ferelith is a woman student at an Oxford college. Like all Oxford colleges hers has a junior common room, a society of students providing services and charging a subscription, to which every student is required to belong. Ferelith adheres to a religious group that objects to membership in any secular organization, and although the college itself is, in origin, a religious foundation the rules of her group forbid association with its common room. Ferelith holds these rules in high respect. Furthermore the common room does nothing to repress, and even seems to encourage, habits of drunkenness and sexual freedom, which she finds wicked and repulsive. The president of the common room is male and the very embodiment of these vices. Soon after her arrival in the college he summons her to his room and reminds her that membership is compulsory. But, he says, there is an alternative. He will release her from conformity and take the consequences on himself if she will consent to his taking photographs of her naked.

What should Ferelith do? A friend advising her would need to ask many questions—to know more facts, to appraise her feelings, perhaps even to change her feelings—and might still be at a loss when the facts were in; for after all there might be no correct answer to the question what she should do. At any rate it seems clear that the story I have told does not provide us with enough information to find the correct answer, if there is one (whatever course she takes, we can easily imagine the story being developed in such a way that she remains its heroine). However, the point of the story was not to exercise our moral imaginations in finding solutions to practical problems but to test the consequentialist method of finding solutions, and for that purpose our shortage of information about Ferelith's situation does not matter—indeed will be an advantage to the extent that it leaves her case typical of a wider range of cases.

Schematically, the consequentialist method applies to Ferelith's case in the following simple way. It instructs her to compare two outcomes, in one of which she is photographed but keeps free of membership of the junior common room, while in the other she joins the common room unphotographed. She must judge which of these outcomes is (to put the point in its broad consequentialist terms) better. If then she also judges that both outcomes are attainable by her—that is, the actions that will produce them are in her power—and that no other outcomes are attainable by her, she must act so as to produce whichever of the two she has judged better.

When the goodness of outcomes is measured by happiness, classical utilitarianism goes for the greatest total or average, ignoring distribution; it is indifferent between objects (at least human objects) of good or ill deeds, beneficence and maleficence. Although other forms of consequentialism might avoid that implication, no form can escape being impersonal in a second way, as between agents of beneficence and maleficence: as Bernard Williams has pointed out, they leave no room for a "difference which consists just in my bringing about a certain outcome rather than someone else's producing it."[2] Ferelith faces a situation in which, so far as she can see, every attainable outcome involves somebody doing ill, and her task is to balance the ills in those ill doings and their consequences. But in striking the balance she must not, according to the consequentialist method, give any weight to the fact that if she makes one of the available choices, to join the common room, it will be herself who does the ill, whereas if she makes the other choice, to submit to the photograph, the ill doer will be somebody else, the president. Consequentialists require that Ferelith should minimize bad outcomes. Since the fact of ill having been done is a bad outcome, they therefore require that, other things being equal, she should minimize ill doing. But it makes no difference who is the ill doer. For the purposes of deciding what to do she may as well think that she would herself be an ill doer in both cases, because in both cases there will be ill that she chooses not to avert.

Augustine rejected this indifference between agents, the second form of impersonality. In 396, the year of his entering full office as bishop of Hippo, he wrote the first of what would eventually become a pair of treatises about lying, this one called *De mendacio*. In the course of it he acknowledged that a lie may be the only means of averting some greater evil. He recognized also that there is a method of decision, the consequentialist method, that would in such cases commend the decision to tell a lie. Augustine devises his own story to illustrate the method:

> We must listen with care to those people who say that nothing is such an ill deed [malum factum] that it ought not to be done in avoidance of worse, and furthermore that to men's deeds pertain not only what they do but also what is done to them with their consent. Hence if a Christian had cause to choose to burn incense to idols, in order not to consent to sexual abuse which his persecutor threatened him with unless he did so, they think they have a right to ask why he should not also lie in order to avoid

such an outrage. For the consent itself—to suffer sexual abuse in preference to burning incense to idols—would be, they say, not something that is done to him but something that he does: it was in order not to *do* it that he chose to burn incense. (*De mendacio* 9.12)

This story, though coming from a less gentle era than our own, is like Ferelith's in concerning a persecutor and in being fictional. But there are differences too: Augustine's fiction is founded on history—history almost within his contemporaries' memory, of the Christian persecutions that had ended about forty years before his birth; also, it more clearly excludes any third course of action, since Augustine's Christian cannot escape the jurisdiction that oppresses him, unlike Ferelith, who could resign from her college.

Augustine's story has been accompanied by an argument in favor of the consequentialist method of deciding what to do ("the consent itself . . . would be . . . something that he does"), and his response to the argument will be twofold. First, he will contend that consent is not a deed, from which it follows that consent to ill doing need not amount to ill doing. Then he will add that, anyhow, the choice of acquiescing in ill in preference to doing it does not amount to consent. Accordingly, his reply to the consequentialist argument he has presented is going to be that it fails doubly: the Christian who consents to ill being done does not thereby do ill himself; and in any case, the Christian who submits to being abused does not thereby consent to ill being done. Let us consider the two parts of the reply in turn.

In the first part of it (*De mendacio* 9.13) Augustine works with a different example. He now imagines that the persecutor's demand is not only to burn incense but also to give "false witness" by denying Christ's name. At this stage, therefore, we are dealing with the problem of lying itself, on which Augustine thinks that "it is not easy to reach a verdict" (9.12). There is also a change in the threats facing the Christian who refuses these demands: not abuse now, but death, either his own or his innocent father's. The persecutors point out that, if he chooses one of these deaths, he chooses that they should do something that they would not have done if he had acted otherwise. In that way, they say, he cooperates in their killing: "How can [you] fail to be doing it *with* [us], when [we] would not be doing it if [you] did the other thing?" (9.14).

The imputation is that I do something if it would not have happened but for my choosing not to do something else. Augustine rightly rejects this analysis. He scorns its implication that we ought to call the steadfast Christian a suicide or a parricide (*De mendacio* 9.13). "At that rate," he complains, "we break the door *with* the housebreakers, because if we did not lock it, they would not break it; and we kill *with* the robbers, if we know their plans, because if we got in first and killed them, they would not kill others" (9.14). Yet although Augustine is right to reject the analysis that extends what a person does to everything that would not happen if he did otherwise, this part of his response fails to meet the point at issue. To say that the Christian martyr is a suicide, or that Ferelith photographs herself, would indeed be false; but how does the argument of Augustine's opponents imply those falsehoods? Two assertions in the opponents' argument are relevant, the first of which says merely that "to men's deeds pertain . . . what is done to them with their consent." That is unspecific. If we ask for specification—if, for example, we ask what deed is done by Ferelith when she is photographed with her consent—we are not forced to understand the opponents as answering that the deed she does is to photograph herself, so that she cooperates with the president in the sense that both of them photograph her. A more reasonable interpretation of the opponents' meaning is provided by their second assertion, that "the consent itself . . . is . . . something that [they] do." On that interpretation Ferelith's alleged deed is not to photograph herself but to consent to being photographed, and, if so, nothing in Augustine's response prevents our regarding her consent as a deed.

Accordingly the first part of the reply fails. Nevertheless Augustine will have destroyed the consequentialist argument if he can show, in the second part, that the Christian who submits to abuse when he could prevent it does not necessarily consent to being abused. He proceeds to argue for this conclusion as follows: (i) there is no consent without approbation; but (ii) a preference for one outcome rather than another need not amount to approbation of it.

The argument begins with advice how the Christian should defend his choice of submitting to the abuse—that is, forbearing to prevent it. He should say: "My own will was that neither ill should be done, but the only one I was able to guard against being done was the one in my power. The other was someone else's, and since I was not able to dispose of it by persuasion, I was not obliged to prevent it by my own ill doing" (*De mendacio* 9.14). Augustine proceeds to comment, in his stylish, elaborate Latin:

> Accordingly, if one refrains from sinning in someone's place, one does not thereby approve of his sinning, and neither thing is acceptable to someone whose will is that neither should be agreed to. But as regards what pertains to such a person himself, since he also has the power, he does not perform it; as regards what pertains to someone else, since he has only the will, he condemns it. (9.14)

By condemning what is allegedly not in his power the Christian does all that is necessary for avoiding approbation and therefore for avoiding consent. He does not, Augustine ends, even choose the course he prefers but can truly say: "For my part I choose neither, I hate them both. You have my consent to none of these things" (9.14). In this way Augustine seeks to vindicate the distinction between what a person does—his deeds—and what is done to him. What is done to him will not be his deed unless, at least, he consents to it; and by "hating" it he may avoid consent. Such is the second part of the reply to the consequentialist.

Yet there are evident flaws in this part too, as we can see by returning to the example of Ferelith. First, it is false to say that Ferelith can "guard against" only one of the perils facing her, membership in the common room, and that as regards the other, being photographed, she "does not have the power" but "has only the will." To be sure there is a difference between the two outcomes, in that she can guard against joining by not joining, whereas she cannot guard against being photographed *by not taking any photograph. That* method will not work because the president, not she, will take it; in Augustine's words, the photography "pertains to someone else." Nonetheless she can guard against being photographed by other means, for she can guard against it by joining the common room. So there is no reason to deny that the deed of photograph taking, though someone else's, is in Ferelith's power. And that makes it dubious, second, whether as Augustine claims Ferelith can truly say that she "chooses" neither outcome.

All the same, and admitting that there are these errors in Augustine's development of the reply, it remains reasonable to agree with him that being photographed does not have Ferelith's consent: even if she cannot truly say "I choose neither," Augustine is right that she can truly say "you have my consent to none of these things." So in the end he is successful in rebutting the argument he has ascribed to his consequentialist opponents.

The upshot is not, of course, to confound the consequentialist method, for which other and better support is available than Augustine has marshaled. What Augustine's reply does achieve is to vindicate the everyday distinction between what you do and what is done to you and thereby to keep space open for methods of deciding what to do that are not impersonal in the way I have described, methods that, even if they take into account the value of outcomes, take into account who produces the outcomes as well. The consequentialist argument has failed to squeeze such methods out of existence, and therefore they remain possible alternatives to the consequentialist decision method and possibly better alternatives.

At the same time Augustine's strategy may well suggest to us that he thinks the consequentialist method would have been right had there been no difference between what a person does and what she acquiesces in having done to her, even without her consent. It would not be surprising if his own preferred decision method were consequentialism somehow modified: for example, "Promote the best outcome, provided that you never do ill yourself." In fact, however, we shall find that he does not aim at any complete decision method in the passages still to be examined; and if there are others where he does, I have not spotted them. At any rate in *De mendacio* he modifies consequentialism without telling us whether the result of the modification remains in other ways unsatisfactory.

The modification is presented in section 14, where we return to the example of the Christian threatened with sexual abuse:

> "Was he obliged [debuit] then," someone may say, "to go through with the abuse rather than burn incense?" If you are asking which [course] he was obliged [to follow], he was obliged [to follow] neither; for if I say he was obliged [to follow] one of them, I shall approve of one of them, whereas I disapprove of both. But if the question is which of them he was *more* obliged to *avoid*, when he could not avoid both but

could avoid either one, I shall answer, "His own sin more than someone else's, and a slighter sin of his own more than a graver sin of someone else's." (*De mendacio* 9.14)

Two things are implicit here: a method for deciding what to do and a principle from which the method is derived. The method prescribes only how you should act when there is a choice between doing ill yourself and having ill done to you, and its prescription is: always prefer the latter. The principle from which that prescription derives is that, in choosing to have ill done to you in preference to doing it, you will never sin; the sin, if there is one, will be someone else's. The derivation presupposes that doing ill is a sin and that sins should always if possible be avoided—we shall touch on the presuppositions eventually. Meanwhile let us consider Augustine's principle about sin.

It is a bold one, and it becomes all the bolder when we see that he must intend to generalize it. In itself it states that you never sin when, in preference to doing ill, you submit to ill being done to you. But Augustine has already considered a different kind of case, where the penalty for refusing to burn incense was that ill would be done not to you but to your father (similarly, we might imagine that Ferelith was to acquiesce in a third party being photographed). No one reading these chapters of *De mendacio* is likely to doubt that Augustine would give the same verdict when the sufferer is going to be somebody other than the person making the decision.

Can we generalize still further? In all of Augustine's examples the price of avoiding ill doing is that some *person,* oneself or another, will suffer ill and that the suffering will be the *deed* of some third person. But perhaps neither of those features is essential to his principle. Perhaps if an example had been put to him in which the price was some bad outcome other than personal harm, or in which the bad outcome was the result of a natural process, he would have extended his principle to cover such cases. Suppose, for example, that you are working underwater in the construction of a beautiful bridge. You are running out of air. I control the hoist that will bring you to the surface. There is a fault in the hoist so that, if I raise it, a fire will start that will destroy the bridge; but you will escape. This example differs from Augustine's in both the above ways: now the price of rescuing you is that ill will happen to the bridge, not to a person, and now it will happen by natural processes, not by the deed of any third party. Perhaps Augustine would hold that even in such a case acquiescence in the bridge's destruction is not a sin.

A passage from his treatise on the Sermon on the Mount, *De sermone Domini in monte,* written in 394, about two years before *De mendacio,* confirms Augustine's commitment to this double extension of the principle about sin. Discussing Jesus' remarks about adultery (Matthew 5:27–28), he distinguishes "three varieties of sin itself, in heart, in deed, and in habit, like three deaths" (*De sermone Domini in monte* 1.12.35). You sin in the heart when you consent to do ill (1.12.34), in deed when you do it, in habit when you are disposed or habituated to ill doing. Augustine holds that even sins in the heart are "full" sins: "But if consent has been given, there will be a full sin, known to God in our heart even if it is not made known to men in deed" (1.12.34).[3] In this passage consent reveals itself as something that does not necessarily involve two people but rather two (Platonic) parts of the soul, reason and appetite. Consent to lust, Augustine goes on, is present when someone "turns to a woman with the aim and the mind to desire her" (1.12.33) and when we do not "confine our pleasure to the rule of governing reason" (1.12.34); the consent lies in the reason ("in ratione . . . consensio"; 1.12.34). So in consent to lust the mind and reason concur with appetite; the consent is, so to speak, a conspiracy between these two parts (echoes are audible here of the Stoic *sunkatathesis,* even though Cicero had translated that word as "*ad*sensio," assent).

As we have seen, acquiescence in ill that happens by somebody else's agency or by natural processes does not in Augustine's opinion imply consent; and without consent acquiescence is not a sin in the heart. In view of his robust rejection of the consequentialist case for counting what is done to you as part of what you do it must also be Augustine's view that acquiescence without consent is not a sin in deed either, for it is not a deed at all. Even less is it a habit of ill doing. So acquiesence in ill that happens is not, without consent, a sin at all.

It is worth emphasizing, though, that even this broader principle about sin does not generate for Augustine a complete decision procedure. One kind of case for which the extended principle still provides no guidance is how to decide between prevention of different ills: for example, should Ferelith submit herself to be photographed if the alternative is that her friend in the group, not herself, will be forced to join the common room? On the other hand the extended principle does offer a sure recipe for avoiding sin, for you will avoid sin in deed if you do nothing, and you will avoid sin in the heart if you withhold consent from any ill happening that occurs as a result. So whenever it is in your power (i) to do nothing, (ii) to recognize sin in consequent ill happenings, and (iii) to withhold consent from those happenings, you are equipped with an effective procedure for avoiding sin. (Augustine himself, of course, believed that it is not in your power to do those things unaided, since you have need of God's grace, prevenient and cooperative.)

According to the account in Matthew's gospel this procedure was used by Pontius Pilate, who

> when [he] saw that he could prevail nothing, but that rather a tumult was made, . . . took water, and washed his hands before the multitude, saying, I am innocent of the blood of this just person: see ye to it. Then answered all the people, and said, His blood be on us, and on our children. (Matthew 27:24–25, Authorized Version)

Of course we need not believe the historicity of this account, with its impossible implication that Jesus was crucified without Roman authority, and its terrible assumption by the crowd of guilt on their "children"; and neither of those features is clearly present in the other three evangelists (Mark 15:15, Luke 23:23–25, John 19:15–16). Augustine himself, commenting on the episode in a sermon, used elements from John, Matthew, and Luke to derive the judgment that Pilate, despite saying that he would not act in the matter, "nevertheless acted" and so shares blame with the Jews ("fecit tamen"; *Enarrationes in Psalmos* 63.4). However, if for the sake of argument we allow ourselves to rely on the report in Matthew, then application to it of Augustine's doctrine of sin in *De sermone Domini in monte* will vindicate Pilate's claim of innocence. Washing your hands works.

At this point things look bad for the fragment of a decision method that Augustine has put in place of consequentialism, because it appears to exonerate Pilate; but in fact, as I shall end by trying to show, the real objection to his method lies elsewhere. He can escape the charge of exonerating Pilate by modifying the doctrine of sin in *De sermone Domini in monte,* and *De mendacio*'s decision method survives the modification. Despite this the method will turn out to be indefensible, either leading to absurd decisions or generating no definite decisions at all, and so failing to be a method.

The reason Augustine can escape the charge of exonerating Pilate is that more than two courses of action were open to Pilate. As between crucifying Jesus and handing him over to the Jews to crucify, Augustine's method does indeed prescribe that it was better for Pilate to do the latter; that way he would avoid his own sin, an unjust execution, at the price of acquiescing in the sin of others. But Matthew's account does nothing to exclude a third possibility, that Pilate should veto the Jewish death sentence and accept the resulting "tumult." Since on Augustine's own principles such a course of action would have been better still, we are free to blame Pilate, even on the Matthew story, without challenging Augustine's doctrine of sin.

In fact, however, Matthew's story does challenge the doctrine in another way, because it challenges the implication of *De sermone Domini in monte* that doing nothing is never sinful: didn't Pilate, we want to ask, sin by *omission?* There is evidence—not surprisingly—that Augustine himself recognized sins of omission. In his defense of Catholic morals against the Manichaeans, written about 389, some five years before the treatise on the Sermon on the Mount, he had commented on the Pauline text "Love does no ill to a neighbor" (Romans 13:10): "There are two ways in which one may sin against a man, by harming him, or by refusing help that one is able to give" (*De moribus ecclesiae catholicae* 26.50). Paul's reference to neighbors (he was commenting on Leviticus 19:18 and Luke 10:27) will have reminded Augustine of the parable of the Good Samaritan, which Augustine read as teaching that *everyone* is my neighbor (*De doctrina Christiana* 1.30.31–33, on Luke 10:29–37). But it will need no such bold maxim as universal love to persuade us that Pilate the governor had a duty of care toward all those lawfully within his territory, the duty at least of protecting them against known threats of injustice, even when those threats came (as to some extent they may have done) from the exercise of reserved Jewish powers. Augustine's treatise on Catholic morals therefore makes Pilate—the Pilate of Matthew's account—a sinner after all and not sinless as the formula in *De sermone Domini in monte* was later to imply.

From the contradiction in which Augustine is thereby caught there are in principle four possible ways of rescuing him; but only one of the four is really attractive. The first way would be to discount the evidence that Augustine believed in sins of omission. However, we shall surely not wish to discount even the one piece of evidence I have cited; and there are doubtless others. Second, omissions might be included among deeds, at any rate when they are sinful. But that would relax the robust attitude we have found Augustine adopting in *De mendacio* to sustaining the everyday distinction between what you do and what you acquiesce in somebody else doing, either to yourself or to a third party such as your father or, in Pilate's case, Jesus. A third possibility is to insist that all sins of omission have the sinner's consent, so that, although they are not sins in deed, they fall under the classification of *De sermone Domini in monte* as sins in the heart. That too would be a strange solution,[4] since, although Augustine always maintained that sin is voluntary, he took consent, as we have seen, to require the concurrence of the mind and reason and to require approbation, which is more than voluntariness; yet he is unlikely to have reckoned failure in a duty of care as sinful only when the sinner approves of the outcome he forbears to prevent. Only one more possibility remains: the list of varieties of sin in *De sermone Domini in monte* must be judged incomplete, and sins of omission must be added as a fourth variety.

The effect of this solution is to prevent Augustine from deriving his method of deciding what to do from the doctrine of sin in *De sermone Domini in monte,* since the starting point of the derivation, "It is never sinful to do nothing, provided that you do not consent to what happens as a result," now turns out not to be part of Augustine's morality. Hence failure to prevent the sin of another may be, for all we have shown so far, one's own sin too; and when Ferelith submits to being photographed, she may after all be guilty of complicity with the president, even though she does not cooperate with him in the sense of photographing herself, and even though she "hates" the outcome.

But the principle about sin in *De mendacio* still remains, and that principle suffices for deriving Augustine's method. It remains because it did not claim that you will always avoid sin if you do nothing and hate what ensues but only that you will always avoid sin if you take such a course *in preference to* your own ill doing; forbearing to prevent ill happening, it contended, is not sinful if the sole alternative is your own ill deed and hence is always preferable to your own ill deed. Accordingly Ferelith will be preserved from complicity in sin if she submits to being photographed in preference to (sinfully) joining the common room, even though she might—Augustine's method being silent at this point—be guilty of sin were she to submit when the alternative is her friend's being forced to join; and similarly Pilate's hand washing would be sinless were the only alternative a (sinful) Roman execution, even though it might not be sinless in preference to setting Jesus free or punishing him in some other way (supposing Pilate had jurisdiction to do those things).

Accordingly the Augustinian method survives our examination of the case of Pilate. But there is a different objection, a dilemma that will prove decisive against it: either the method leads to absurd decisions or it fails to be a method. This will emerge if we put side by side two parts of Augustine's moral teaching, on lying and on homicide.

In a handbook on morals and religion addressed to one Laurentius in 421 he wrote, "But here lurks an extraordinarily difficult and intricate question: . . . whether it is ever required of a just person to lie" (*Enchiridion* 18.6). The question is difficult because, as we have seen, Augustine is conscious of the advantages that telling a lie may bring, to the liar or others; as the U.S. senator said, a lie is an abomination unto the Lord and an ever-present help in time of need.[5] Nevertheless he concluded in both his treatises on the subject, *De mendacio* (42) and the later *Contra mendacium*, written in 422, that lying is a sin and therefore should never be preferred when there is an option of keeping silent.[6] Yet surely that is a doctrine of senseless rigor, a doctrine that scarcely anyone will live by all the time and scarcely anyone will think it right to live by in all possible situations.[7]

By contrast Augustine did not agonize for long over homicide. In the first book of *De libero arbitrio* (1.4.9), written in 386, he questioned but quite soon approved the opinion that "a soldier [killing] an enemy, and a judge or his agent [killing] a criminal . . . do not seem to me to sin when they kill a man." Killing people usually transgresses God's law, but not always: it is permitted to those who take up arms "with the command or permission of a legitimate superior power" (*Contra Faustum* 22.70), and it is enjoined against victims "whom God commands to be killed either by an enacted law or by express command referring to some person at some time [e.g., the sacrifice of Isaac—Genesis 22:1–19]" (*City of God* 1.21).

Augustine's concept of sin has two roots, in the Bible and, through Cicero, in Stoicism; a Stoic sin (*hamartēma, peccatum*) is a lapse from what virtue requires, a Christian sin (*hamartia, peccatum*) is a transgression of God's law. Both these conceptions ensure that, on Augustine's moral view, homicide is not always a sin. It then follows by one of the presuppositions of his method that homicide is not always an ill deed either and hence that—even when not expressly commanded by God—it can sometimes rightly be committed in preference to doing nothing. In this way Augustine avoids the rigors of pacifism, rigors that, incidentally, many people will regard as far short of senseless, unlike those of abjuring every lie. But what happens now to the doctrinal value of Augustine's method of deciding what to do? It begins to look as if the method will no longer provide guidance over practical questions that are neither trivial nor fanciful, questions such as "Should I kill him?"; and if the method no longer provides general guidance (within its admittedly incomplete range of application), it is not a method at all.[8]

The problem now is that we need a test for ill deeds. Anybody who comes to decision theory with a prereflective respect for consequentialism, as Augustine appears to do, will be tempted to propose the value of outcomes—utility—as this test. Indeed Augustine's own imaginary opponents would have done their case good by pressing such a proposal. We have seen how, in defense of their view that "nothing is such an ill deed that it ought not to be done in avoidance of worse" (*De mendacio* 9.12), those opponents were presented by Augustine as arguing that any worse happening you might avoid by your own ill deed would itself be your own ill deed. A better argument would have been that such a worse happening ensures that your own averting deed is not ill.[9]

That way, Augustine's method could avoid senseless rigor but at the cost of slipping back toward consequentialism, and very likely right into it. Of course there may be strategies for heading off such an upshot; but when we face the problem of discriminating among homicides, it is unclear to me what alternative strategy Augustine himself would wish us to adopt.

NOTES

1. I call this method utilitarian without implying that utilitarians in general are committed to recommending it; on the contrary, as is well known, there might be utilitarian reasons for not recommending it.

2. Bernard Williams, "A Critique of Utilitarianism," in J. J. C. Smart and B. A. O. Williams, eds., *Utilitarianism, for and Against* (Cambridge, Cambridge University Press, 1973), 96.

3. Cf. *De continentia* 2.3–5, discussed in W. E. Mann, "Inner-Life Ethics," this volume, pp. 140–65, and St. Augustine, *De duabus animabus contra Manichaeos* 10.12: "Justice holds guilty those sinning only by an evil will, even though they were unable to accomplish what they willed."

4. As I now think, contradicting *Augustine* (London: Routledge, 1989), 202.

5. Senator John Tyler Morgan of Alabama, according to D. McCullough, *The Path between the Seas: The Creation of the Panama Canal, 1870–1914* (New York: Simon and Schuster, 1977), 260.

6. See Kirwan, *Augustine*, 196–204.

7. For a curious theological defense of the rigor see P. T. Geach, *God and the Soul* (London: Routledge and Kegan Paul, 1969), chap. 9.

8. The same difficulty notoriously infects Paul's repudiation of "those people who claim we say 'Let us do ill that good may come' " (Romans 3:8).

9. This is not to deny that there is also a problem about the boundary between killing and doing something else that has death as an outcome. Augustine himself was willing to say in a sermon that the Jews killed Jesus, even though Pilate gave the order: they killed him "with the sword of their tongue" when they shouted "Crucify, crucify" (*Enarrationes in Psalmos* 63.4).

TEN

Do We Have a Will?

Augustine's Way in to the Will

Simon Harrison

In the *Confessions* we read the following narrative:

> (1) I directed my mind to understand [cernerem] what I was being told [quod audiebam], namely that (2) the free choice of the will is the reason why we do wrong (3) and suffer your just judgement; (4) but I could not get a clear grasp of it. (5) I made an effort to lift my mind's eye out of the abyss, but again plunged back. I tried several times, but again and again sank back. (6) I was brought up into your light by the fact that (7) I knew myself to have a will *in the same way and as much as I knew myself* to be alive [tam sciebam me habere voluntatem quam me vivere]. (8) Therefore [itaque] when I willed or did not will something, I was utterly certain that none other than myself was willing or not willing. (9) That there lay the cause of my sin I was now *gradually beginning* [iam iamque] to recognize. (10) I saw that when I acted against my wishes [invitus facerem], I was passive rather than active [pati me potius quam facere videbam]; (11) and this condition I judged to be not guilt but a punishment [non culpam sed poenam]. (12) It was an effortless step to grant that, (13) since I conceived you to be just, (14) it was not unjust that I was chastised.[1]

In this narrative Augustine claims that he knows himself "to have a will" (7). He sets this claim within a story of intellectual progress and at the beginning of an argument ("therefore. . . . " [8]). In this essay I want to show that what gives this claim philosophical importance is the way that Augustine goes about making it, what I here call Augustine's "way in to the will." It is true that Augustine plays a pivotal role in the history of "will," making it a central concept in philosophy.[2] Quite what the nature and significance of his role is, however, is a difficult question.

Perhaps the best place to begin is by asking the simple question, Do we really have such a thing as will? Do we know what a will is? Can we take it for granted that we understand what Augustine means by "voluntas"? What, after all, is or ought a will to be? Can we say that Augustine "discovered" something that was really out there waiting to be identified, as Dihle seems to suggest, or should we characterize Augustine's contribution as the "invention" of one of the great false trails of philosophy's history (rather like, to take Ryle's example, phlogiston)?[3] We should, I suggest, begin thinking a concept as difficult as the will with some modest skepticism.

But this question, Do we have a will? is already asked by Augustine in his dialogue *De libero arbitrio.* There the reply is "nescio" (I do not know).[4] This reply we do well to take seriously. First because it is a perfectly sensible initial response to such a difficult question, and second because it is Augustine's response. Augustine's question and answer in *De libero arbitrio* form the beginning of what I want to call "Augustine's way in to the will." In *De libero arbitrio* 1.12.25 and *Confessions* 7.3.5 Augustine sets up and adopts a certain procedure for thinking about will. In *De libero arbitrio* this takes the form of an investigation of the consequences of saying "nescio"; in *Confessions* this procedure is characterized as a particular way of attaining knowledge. Moreover this procedure is explicitly and significantly related to arguments found in various places in Augustine's work, arguments that have, ever since 1637, been discussed in relation to Descartes' "I think therefore I am." Augustine's "way in" to the will here is thus the meeting point of his two most celebrated and discussed contributions to the history of philosophy: his "invention" of the will and his adumbration of Descartes' *cogito.* Augustine, in short, approaches and gives philosophical content to the concept of will by means of a "cogitolike" argument.

In *Confessions* 7.3.5 clause (7) is the turning point of the narrative. Not only is it presented as a moment of breakthrough—before (7) Augustine is in perplexity, and after it he presents a coherent argument ("itaque" [8])—but it is clearly marked as a particular kind of Augustinian thought, a cogitolike argument. To appreciate the significance of both these features we must return to the beginning of the passage. At this stage in the story Augustine has rejected Manichaeanism and with it its attempted dualist solution to the problem of evil (*Confessions* 7.2.3; cf. 3.7.12; 5.10.20; 7.1.1–3.4). Now, Augustine does have another, nondualist solution already available to him—the Catholic (represented here by clauses [2] and [3]). It is one thing, however, to have the answer staring oneself in the face and another to recognize and understand that it really is the answer. And it is the transition from the former to the latter that Augustine undertakes here. Much effort has been expended in trying to work out precisely where Augustine heard the propositions here labeled (2) and (3) and to locate them in Ambrose's sermons.[5] It is, however, much more important to notice that Augustine does not tell us their provenance. "Audiebam" need not imply that Augustine literally heard (2) and (3); rather Augustine uses the word, contrasted with "seeing" (cernerem), to emphasize the fact that they came to him from a source external to himself. The contrast in the vocabulary between the two senses, hearing and seeing, picks up the distinction, so important in Augustine's theory of knowledge, between knowledge at first hand (by direct vision) and knowledge at second hand (from testimony). Only the first is "knowledge" properly so called, which is conceived in terms of "understanding," the second is merely "belief." This, Platonic, theory of knowledge is explored in Augustine's dialogue *De magistro*.[6] Augustine here is attempting to turn the second into the first.

I suggest, then, that it is not Ambrose's sermons that are significant for this passage but Augustine's silence as to his sources. Indeed I would suggest further that we might speak here of Ambrose's silence. To illustrate what I mean by this I would like to show the reader two related narrative figures that recur throughout the *Confessions*. The first I call "episcopal silence," the second "reading as if."

EPISCOPAL SILENCE

At *Confessions* 3.12.21 Monica asks a bishop (who is moreover a former Manichaean) to talk to her Manichaean son (and future bishop) and talk him out of the heresy ("for he used to do this for those whom perhaps he found suitably disposed"). The bishop, to Monica's distress, refuses. Again, in a much discussed passage, Ambrose, bishop of Milan, reads a book silently, and Augustine is again left to work his problems out for himself (*Confessions* 6.3.3). In both cases the two bishops seem to be doing the opposite of the Augustine of *De libero arbitrio* 1.2.4.[7] The reasoning behind all three cases is, however, the same. The unnamed bishop finds the young Augustine "unready to learn, because I was conceited about the novel excitements of that heresy." He also finds that Augustine is capable of working things out for himself: "by his reading he will discover what an error and how vast an impiety it all is" (*Confessions* 3.12.21).

Ambrose, in contrast, does not give his reasons; rather his silent reading invites the visitors (and Augustine's readers) to make their own suggestions for his reasons. Augustine lists a few and asserts that "whatever motive he had for his habit, this man had a good reason for what he did" (*Confessions* 6.3.3). The dullest of modern explanations is the use of this passage as evidence that ancients usually read aloud when they read.[8] I suggest that Ambrose's good reason (in terms of the narrative at least) is to invite his audience (and hence readers of the *Confessions*) to work things out for themselves. As with the unnamed bishop's silence in book 3, so here the burden is thrust upon Augustine. In this way Augustine presents, in narrative form, what is the philosophical conclusion of his dialogue *De magistro:* no one can teach another person anything. You cannot do the work of understanding for someone else (since then it would be you, not the other, that had understood). Understanding, moving from *audiebam* to *cernere*, is something one can, in the last analysis, do only for oneself.

READING AS IF

In the story from book 3 Augustine's conceit is cited as a reason the bishop did not bother to argue with him. Augustine is simply not in a position to make sense of anything the bishop might say to him. Likewise in *De libero arbitrio* 1.12.25 Augustine says to his interlocutor, "I oughtn't to give you an answer to your questions unless you want to know the answer." However, the anonymous bishop says something to Monica, to which she responds in an interesting way. He says, rather testily, to her, "It cannot be that the son of these tears should perish." These words provide the climax of the third book; or, rather, these words and the final sentence: "In her conversations with me she often used to recall that she had taken these words as if they had sounded from heaven [accepisse . . . ac si de caelo sonuisset]."

Part of what is required to understand an answer to a question is to grasp that it is the answer. Monica's response to the bishop's words gives us an idea of what this might look like. This is the figure "reading as if." In the *Confessions* it is particularly associated with conversion. There are a large number of times when, quite apart from the intention of the speaker, a listener takes something to heart and a change is effected. One such example is Alypius being cured of his addiction to the circus (*Confessions* 6.7.12). There are other examples (such as Monica's rebuke at *Confessions* 9.8.18), but the most significant is Augustine's own conversion in book 8. There, in the garden scene, the moment of conversion is marked as the moment of "reading as if" (8.12.29). There the one reason given for Augustine's decision is, "For I had heard how Antony happened to be present at the gospel reading, and took it as an admonition addressed to himself when the words were read [tamquam sibi diceretur quod legebatur]." Augustine takes the command "Tolle, lege" as if it were addressed to him, and he takes the words of St. Paul as a command addressed directly to himself. The removal, however, of all other possible intentional external agency in the garden scene shows how the conversion is entirely "up to" Augustine (and at the same time fully the work of God).[9] At *Confessions* 7.3.5 Augustine deploys these narrative figures to illustrate the argumentative process to which they are related, to illustrate what is "up to us."

We are now in a position to begin to see the significance of the breakthrough at clause (7). Augustine is attempting to understand clauses (2) and (3). He takes it on trust that they are the true solution to the problem of evil but is attempting to understand how they are the solution, and he is attempting to do so by and for himself. What is it about clause (7) that allows Augustine to succeed? The clause gives us three pieces of information:

(a) Augustine knows that he has will.
(b) He also knows that he is alive.
(c) There is a connection between these two items of knowledge, expressed by the words "tam . . . quam."

The burden of my claim here is this. It is not simply knowing that he has will that allows Augustine to construct this argument. It is the way in which he knows it. Item (c), the connection between (a) and (b), is the crucial realization that frees Augustine from his intellectual "abyss." It has long been recognized that there is something special about the way Augustine knows himself to be alive (item [b]).

This knowledge is attained by means of what are generally known as Augustine's cogitolike arguments, which are usually discussed in relation to Descartes.[10] I am not going to deal with the similarities and dissimilarities between the Augustinian and Cartesian cogitos.[11] What I want to do here is to bring out Augustine's knowledge that he has a will and its relation to this family of arguments. Augustine's breakthrough is precisely to see the resemblance between the way of knowing that I am alive and the way of knowing that I have a will. It is this resemblance that enables him to use the tam–quam relationship. My emendation of Chadwick's translation deliberately overtranslates the "tam . . . quam" to make my point. I suggest that it here means both "in the same way" and "as much as." That is to say both that Augustine has a method of getting to know that he is alive and that this method produces firm, certain, and irrefutable knowledge. This method can be applied to the knowledge that one has a will, with the same resulting strength.[12]

Our next word is "therefore" (itaque) in clause (8). With clause (7) Augustine does indeed begin to present an argument for the truth of propositions (2) and (3). Proposition (2) is comprehended from clauses (8) and (9) and proposition (3) from clauses (10)–(14). Clauses (8) and (9) perform what I would like to call "the exclusion of external agency" and clauses (10)–(14) the "redefinition of action and passion" (or "of active and passive"). Both of these achievements, exclusion and redefinition, are related to the two narrative figures, episcopal silence and reading as if.

Clauses (8) and (9) argue that, from clause (7), we can be absolutely certain that no one else can do our willing for us. Or, rather, I should rephrase that in the first-person singular: I am certain that no one else can do my willing for me.[13] This means that, when I will (or indeed do not will), then it really is I that am doing the willing and not, say, something other than me, something from which I can disassociate myself. My willing is thus entirely my responsibility. It is entirely, to paraphrase the Greek philosophical expression, "up to me" (ἐφ᾽ ἡμῖν).[14] This corresponds to the principle behind episcopal silence and reading as if: no one else can do the work of learning and understanding for me, my learning, what I understand is mine alone.

But this is not all. Because of (7) I am now in a position fully to comprehend the relationship between my volition and my action, between what I want and what I actually do. Notice the two occurrences of the verb "facere" in (10). This appears at first sight a puzzling sentence. "I saw that when I acted . . . I was passive rather than active." It seems that by qualifying the verb "facio" with "invitus" (against my will) I can redefine my action (the first "facere") as *patior*, as something that happens to (is done to) me. Some things that would at first sight appear to be "actions" of mine now turn out to be things that are "done to" me. If I don't like what I am doing, we might say, then *I* am not really doing it. Rather my wish not to be a party to what is happening reveals that I am not the action's "author." (For more on the distinction between what we might call the "active" and "passive" voices in Augustine's grammar of action see *De libero arbitrio* 1.1.1.)

Now it is the case that things do happen to me that I do not think of as good, things that I do not particularly want. But I cannot be blamed, I cannot be guilty for what I do not do (11). If we add the extra premise, here labeled (13), that God is just, and the unexpressed premise that God exercises total and providential control over everything that happens, then it becomes clear that even the bad things that happen to me are controlled by God. They must, therefore, be punishment, and just punishment, punishment for something I have already done. (This just punishment, to go beyond our passage here, implies an early voluntary evil action and hence implies that we need some sort of theory of "original sin." This theory is, however, not my concern here. I note only that it comes some way further down the line of thought initiated by clause [7].) What I want to stress is that neither of these achievements, the exclusion of external agency or the redefinition of action and passion, can be understood unless clause (7) is understood. What is it about clause (7) that allows me to assert the rest of the argument with such certainty?

The answer to this question lies in the cogitolike argument it refers to. Let me sketch an answer, under two other headings, "self-evidence" and "stripping away,"that correspond, roughly, to my two narrative figures, episcopal silence and reading as if.

Like my knowledge of my being alive, my knowledge that I will is self-evident. By this I do not mean it is obvious; I mean it is known per se. Nothing else makes it known. It is not, say, the conclusion of a syllogism. Remember the principle behind episcopal silence: no one else can teach me. Just so here: nothing else (no premise) can ground the proposition "I have a will." Self-evidence, however, is not necessarily obvious. Augustine, as we see here, has had to struggle hard to attain it. He has to "strip away" all that gets between him and his knowledge in order to arrive at his direct vision of what is self-evident.

This process of stripping away is best illustrated in Augustine's work *De Trinitate*. In book 10 we find Augustine trying to understand what the mind is. Part of the process Augustine undergoes involves "stripping away," eliminating from the inquiry, what the mind is not, or rather stripping away all the false opinions about what it is. Here this stripping away takes the form of doubt. I can doubt that my mind is simply, say, air, but there are some things about my mind I cannot doubt. This process of doubt, of "calling into question," thus reveals something that cannot be called into question about the one who doubts. One of these things revealed is that the doubter is alive; another is that the doubter wills.

> But we are concerned now with the nature of mind; so let us put aside all consideration of things we know outwardly through the senses of the body, and concentrate our attention on what we have stated that all minds know for certain about themselves. Whether the power of living, remembering, understanding, willing, thinking, knowing, judging comes from air, or fire, or brain, or blood, or atoms, or heaven knows what fifth kind of body besides the four common elements; or whether the very structure or organization of our flesh can produce these things; people have hesitated about all this, and some have tried to establish one answer, others another.

Nobody surely doubts, however, that he lives and remembers and understands and wills and thinks and knows and judges. At least, even if he doubts, he lives; if he doubts, he remembers why he is doubting; if he doubts, he understands he is doubting; if he doubts he has a will to be certain; if he doubts, he thinks; if he doubts, he knows he does not know; if he doubts, he judges he ought not to give a hasty assent. You may have your doubts about anything else, but you should have no doubts about these; if they were not certain, you would not be able to doubt anything.[15]

Again, the knowledge that I live is explicitly linked to the knowledge that I will. It is linked, again, through a process of thought that aims to reveal the self-evident. This process of thought is that employed in Augustine's other, more explicitly cogitolike arguments. The most developed are those found at *De libero arbitrio* 2.3.7 and *City of God* 11.26. At *City of God* 11.26 Augustine argues that he can be certain he exists because "si fallor, sum" (if I am deceived I am):

I am quite certain that I am, that I know that I am, and that I love this being and this knowing. Where these truths are concerned I need not quail before the Academicians [Skeptics] when they say: "What if you should be mistaken?" Well, if I am mistaken, I exist. For a man who does not exist can surely not be mistaken either, and if I am mistaken, therefore I exist. So, since I am if I am mistaken, how can I be mistaken in believing that I am when it is certain that if I am mistaken I am.[16]

Therefore in order to take the most evident things as our starting point, I ask you whether you yourself exist. Are you perhaps afraid of being mistaken in this question, although if you did not exist you could not be mistaken at all? (*De libero arbitrio* 2.3.7)

To deny that I exist would be self-refuting, in the sense that for me to be wrong (in thinking that I exist) itself implies my existence. Augustine's cogito works by revealing the self-evidence of the existence of one who might be deceived. My existence is shown, when I think about it, to be a brute, inescapable fact staring me in the face. Likewise for Augustine living and willing can be revealed to be self-evident to the mind because they are implied and involved in the activity of the mind itself. This implication and involvement is revealed by the process of taking seriously the possibility of doubt.

I began by quoting a question from *De libero arbitrio* 1.12.25. Like the *Confessions De libero arbitrio* is presented as autobiography (1.2.4), and like the *Confessions* it contains a presentation of Augustine's "way in" to the will. This time, however, the way in is presented in the form of a dialogue, and what is doubted is the will. The exchange quoted above continues:

A.: Do you want to know?

E.: I do not know this either.

A.: Then ask me nothing more.

E.: Why not?

A.: Because I oughtn't to give you an answer to your question unless you want to know the answer. And secondly because, if you don't want to attain to wisdom, I ought not to discuss such things with you. And finally because we cannot be friends unless you want things to go well for me. But look to yourself and see whether you, as regards yourself, do not want to be happy.

E.: I admit that it cannot be denied that we have a will. Go on, let us now see what follows from this. (1.12.25) [17]

This argument, like clause (7), forms something of a starting point in the sequence of the dialogue's argument. As such it is parallel to and shares some resemblances with two other such starting points in *De libero arbitrio,* both of which are clearly cogitolike arguments, at 1.7.17 and 2.3.7.[18] As with *Confessions* 7.3.5, note the epistemological context: what is at stake is knowledge. The argument turns on what we could describe as a condition for knowledge ("unless you want to know").

The first-person perspective is, again, very important: the argument does not generalize beyond the claim that I know that I have a will. As at *City of God* 11.26 and *De Trinitate* 10.10.14 it must be "appropriated"[19] in the first-person singular. Evodius is invited to see for himself.[20] As in *Confessions* 7.3.5 Augustine uses "voluntas" to reveal and mark the individual's responsibility and freedom. It is up to Evodius to look to himself and see whether he has a will; and the willing itself is up to Evodius. Augustine can do neither for him.[21] According to Augustine's argument at *De libero arbitrio* 1.12.25 I can come to see that there is a choice, an option inalienably mine that no one can make for me. This forms the basis of the move in *Confessions* 7.3.5 that I labeled the exclusion of external agency. Again the argument is one of exposing a self-defeating claim. My denying that I have a will is, we might say, self-defeating, in the sense that it does away with a condition for my further participation in the conversation and for my learning: *my* will to know. Thus Augustine evokes a notion of what is inalienably up to me alone, a notion of responsibility.

On the other hand Evodius *could* (that is, it is open to him to) persist in denying knowledge of the will. It is open to him simply to keep saying "nescio." This, however, would entail his giving up on knowledge, on the search for knowledge, and indeed on the dialogue. Evodius is not constrained to choose knowledge over continued denial, but continued denial would get him nowhere. The mistaken thinker of *City of God* 11.26 is already thinking and existing. The doubter of *De Trinitate* 10.10.14 is already engaged in the act of doubting and as such is already "wanting to be certain." The shape of the argument in *De libero arbitrio* 1.12.25 does not of itself guarantee that Evodius in fact wants to know. His wanting is a necessary condition of his knowing, but it is not thereby shown to exist. What is inescapable is Evodius' choice, the choice between the desire to know and giving up on the search for knowledge. Augustine, I suggest, creates a sense of vertigo: we could simply give up.[22] In this way Augustine evokes a concept of freedom.

In *De libero arbitrio* 1.12.25 and *Confessions* 7.3.5 Augustine comes to realize that the knowledge that he has a will is self-evident and immediate. Because of the way Augustine has come to see this self-evidence he now has a secure grasp of the will as a concept on which he can build an informative argument to (2) and (3). It appears there is nothing that can be known with more certainty, with more immediacy, by me than that I have will. This is because will is here discovered as a condition for knowledge. No one, according to Augustine's account of knowledge, is going to know anything unless they already want to know it. Nothing, therefore, is going to be able to take away this knowledge. What knowledge will there be, then, what theory of determinism, of habit or emotion, that can possibly be used to impugn the clear and certain knowledge that I do indeed have a will? Similarly, what theory could one think up that could impugn one's knowledge that one is alive? The priority of my knowledge of my will is what enables me to go on to perform both the exclusion of external agency and the redefinition of active and passive.

Now I do not say, nor do I need to say, that Augustine has said everything he has to say about will and free will already in *Confessions* 7.3.5 or *De libero arbitrio* 1.12.25—notice my emphatic translation of Augustine's "iam iamque" (gradually beginning), and consider the paragraphs immediately following my quotation from *Confessions* 7.3.5. Another two books follow upon the "way in" of *De libero arbitrio* 1.12.25, and the rest of *Confessions* 7.3.5 states the problem from which *De libero arbitrio* 2 begins. Indeed book 7 of the *Confessions* and *De libero arbitrio* both cover the same territory. But I do say that at *Confessions* 7.3.5 and *De libero arbitrio* 1.12.25 Augustine has hit upon the starting point, the way in, from which to find the answers to all his other problems about the will.

A way in to thinking about freedom and responsibility and their place in a systematic understanding of the universe—all this Augustine has achieved by taking the ordinary term "voluntas" and calling it into question. He has taken the possibility of doubting that I have a will seriously and shown it to be self-defeating. This is precisely the cogitolike argument adopted at *City of God* 11.26 and elsewhere to argue the security of my knowledge of my existence, and my being alive, and to use this knowledge as a starting point for further reflection.[23] As is so often the case with Augustine the significance, the interest, and the thinking lie in asking questions, even of what seems obvious. And, as so often, "nescio" (I do not know) turns out to be not such a bad answer to begin with after all.

NOTES

1. St. Augustine, *Confessions* 7.3.5. The translation is adapted from *Saint Augustine: Confessions*, trans. H. Chadwick (Oxford: Oxford University Press, 1991). My alterations are given in italics. I have divided and numbered the text for ease of reference.

2. On this much discussed topic see A. Dihle, *The Theory of Will in Classical Antiquity* (Berkeley: University of California Press, 1982); Charles H. Kahn, "Discovering the Will: From Aristotle to Augustine," in J. Dillon and A. A. Long, eds., *The Question of Eclecticism: Studies in Later Greek Philosophy* (Berkeley: University of California Press, 1988); and T. Irwin, "Who Discovered the Will?" *Philosophical Perspectives* 6 (1992): 453–73.

3. Dihle, *Theory of Will in Classical Antiquity*, 143–44; G. Ryle, *The Concept of Mind* (London: Hutchinson, 1949), 62.

4. St. Augustine, *De libero arbitrio* 1.12.25; translations are my own. I have relied on the edition in vol. 6 of *Oeuvres de saint Augustin*, ed. G. Madec, 3d ed. (Paris: Bibliothèque Augustinienne, 1976).

5. Cf. J. J. O'Donnell, ed., *Augustine: Confessions,* 3 vols. (Oxford: Oxford University Press, 1992), 400–401.

6. The theory is clearly elucidated by M. F. Burnyeat, "Wittgenstein and Augustine *De magistro,*" in this volume.

7. "You raise precisely that question which, when I was a young man, worked me so very hard wore me out, and cast me down among heretics. And I was so wounded by this fall, and so suffocated under heaps of empty myths, that had love of finding out the truth not obtained divine assistance for me, I would not have been able to get out of there into that first freedom to seek, and to breathe again. And since my case was so carefully proceeded with that I was delivered from that inquiry, I will proceed with you following the same order as that which I followed and so escaped."

8. See A. K. Gavrilov, "Techniques of Reading in Classical Antiquity" *Classical Quarterly* 47 (1997): 56–73.

9. Augustine's is not the only conversion recorded in *Confessions* 8 involving this narrative figure: there is also, of course, that of Alypius (8.12.30). And there are more. There are six other conversions recorded: those of Marius Victorinus (8.2.4—reading Luke 12:9), of the two friends of Ponticianus and their fiancées (8.6.15), as well as that of St. Antony himself. All are linked by this common act of reading something *tamquam sibi diceretur.*

10. Again a vast literature on the subject exists. See, for example, G. B. Matthews, *Thought's Ego in Augustine and Descartes* (Ithaca: Cornell University Press, 1992).

11. I might, however, simply point out that Descartes insists as much as Augustine on the importance of thinking things through for and by oneself. "I shall not waste time here by thanking my distinguished critic for bringing in the authority of St Augustine to support me, and for setting out my arguments so vigorously that he seems to fear that their strength may not be sufficiently apparent to anyone else" (René Descartes, *Fourth Set of Replies,* in *The Philosophical Writings of Descartes,* vol. 2, trans. J. Cottingham, R. Stoothoff, and D. Murdoch [Cambridge: Cambridge University Press, 1984], 154). Cf. his letter to Mersenne, 21 January 1641: "But, to follow the passage from St Augustine which you sent me, I cannot open the eyes of my readers or force them to attend to the things which must be examined to ensure a clear knowledge of the truth; all I can do is, as it were, to point my finger and show where the truth lies" (ibid., 3:168–69).

12. This is, first of all, a point about the meaning of the Latin phrase and open to refutation as such. I hope that my reading of the progress of Augustine's argument, and of St. Augustine, *De libero arbitrio* 1.12.25, supports this point of translation. The nearest equivalent I can find is in St. Augustine, *De duabus animabus* 10.13, where Augustine again relates these two items of knowledge with a "tam . . . quam."

13. On the significance of the first person for such arguments see G. E. M. Anscombe, "The First Person," in S. Guttenplan, ed., *Mind and Language* (Oxford: Clarendon Press, 1975), and Matthews, *Thought's Ego in Augustine and Descartes.*

14. Cf., for example, Kahn, "Discovering the Will," 240.

15. St. Augustine, *De Trinitate* 10.10.14, trans. E. Hill (New York: New City Press, 1991). Cf. 15.12.21, which also links the knowledge of being alive with will; and Descartes, *Second Meditation,* in *Philosophical Writings of Descartes,* 2:19.

16. St. Augustine, *The City of God* 11.26, trans. D. S. Wiesen (Cambridge, Mass: Harvard University Press, 1988).

17. This exchange is not easy to translate into English without losing the coherence of the vocabulary. Where I have translated "will," to "want," and to "wish," the Latin has the

noun "voluntas" and its verb, "volo." In particular I have taken the liberty of translating the antepenultimate sentence with a verb ("want") where Augustine speaks of a "will to be happy" ("voluntas . . . beatae uitae").

18. Resemblances between 1.12.25, 1.7.17, and 2.37: All three (1) are points at which the sequence of argumentation begins afresh; (2) involve a "calling into question" of a fundamental idea, which is thereby shown to be "undeniable": I am alive, I know that I am alive (1.7.17), I have will (1.12.25), I exist, I live, I understand (2.3.7); (3) involve an analysis of what it is to know and understand; and (4) involve an idea of value: "which . . . seems to you superior?" (1.7.17 and 2.3.7), "what value do you set on this will?" (1.12.25).

19. I take the term "appropriation" from Anscombe, "First Person," 45.

20. Evodius is the name that is printed as that of the "minor" interlocutor of the dialogue and has been ever since the great Maurist edition of 1679. The attribution is, however, inaccurate and misleading. None of the manuscripts gives it—although all of them offer a variety of other names (see the critical apparatus of W. M. Green, ed., *Corpus scriptorum ecclesiastorum Latinorum*, vol. 74 [Vienna: Hölder, Pichler, Tempsky, 1956]). Indeed the giving of the names of characters in either literary or dramatic dialogues is a practice more modern than ancient (see J. Andrieu, *Le Dialogue antique* [Paris: Les Belles Lettres, 1954], and N. G. Wilson, "Indications of Speaker in Greek Dialogue Texts," *Classical Quarterly* 20 [1970]: 305). Augustine does not give any indication of the identity of his speakers in the text of the dialogue, and, from what we know of ancient practice and the manuscript evidence, it seems highly unlikely that he indicated any names in the margin. What, after all, would Evodius' name have meant to a contemporary reader? Rather, what the modern "Evodius" conceals is the fact that Augustine here uses the dialogue form to illustrate and instantiate his form of argument. In a discussion about human responsibility Augustine deliberately leaves it "up to" the reader to work out who its speakers are and what the relationship between them is.

21. I give a couple of quotations from the *De magistro*, italicizing in the first case the verb "volo" and in the second the noun "voluntatem" (translations are my own):

This much can words do, to attribute to them as much as possible. They merely prompt us to look for things. They do not show them to us so that we know them. He teaches me who puts before my eyes, or any bodily sense, or even my mind itself, those things which I *want* to know. (11.36)

But as for all the things that we understand, we do not consult someone speaking externally but inwardly the truth that presides over the mind, prompted, perhaps, by the words. And it is he who is consulted that teaches, that is, Christ who is said to dwell inside a man, who is the immutable and eternal wisdom of God. It is wisdom that every rational soul consults, but wisdom is available to each soul only as much as each soul is able—on account of its own good or bad *will*—to receive. (11.38)

22. It is, I suggest, helpful to think of this passage as significant in the history of boredom and hence related to the theological tradition of acedia, or sloth.

23. The cogitolike arguments of *The City of God* 11.26 and *De libero arbitrio* 2.3.7 are not ends in themselves; rather they are, like *De libero arbitrio* 1.12.25 and *Confessions* 7.3.5, the secure starting points for, "ways in" to, larger discussions. *City of God* 11 is not simply a refutation of skepticism but a discussion of our place in creation; *De libero arbitrio* 2.3.7 provides an exordium, a "beginning," from *manifestissimis*, "most evident things" for sorting out the problems of theodicy in books 2 and 3 of *De libero arbitrio*.

ELEVEN

The Emergence of the Logic of Will in Medieval Thought

Simo Knuuttila

AUGUSTINE: CREATOR OF THE MODERN CONCEPT OF WILL?

In his book *The Theory of Will in Classical Antiquity,* Albrecht Dihle argues, contrary to what the title might lead one to expect, that there is no explicit conception of will in ancient philosophy.[1] According to Dihle, will and intention were always dealt with together with their sources in thinking or instinct, but never "in their own right." Although there were different philosophical conceptions of reality, there was no disagreement about the principle that only rational understanding of reality leads to a good life. Adequate intellectual evaluation of things was considered the basic impetus for morally good practice, and the rational part of the soul was provided with the task of ruling over all spontaneous motions of the soul. In the case of acratic behavior this control had broken down and action was generated by inadequate and restricted evaluations. Dihle says that emotions or instincts provided the only psychological alternative to reasoning with regard to the ensuing impulse toward action. Correspondingly, volition was treated merely as an implication of the act of intellectual cognition or of emotional desire.

Some quotations from Dihle's book may shed light on the question of what kind of theory of will the author has in mind in arguing that one does not find it in ancient thought. "Our term 'will' denotes only the resulting intention, leaving out any special reference to thought, instinct, or emotion as possible sources of that intention. . . . Kant's remark about good will as the only factor in human life which is unconditionally praiseworthy makes no sense whatever in Greek ethical thought. . . . So volition did not gain, in the context of ethical speculation, the independence that could have enabled it to become the psychological point of reference in ethical evaluation of man's actions."[2] Dihle is interested in the conception of will as a psychological faculty that functions as an ultimate and free arbitrator between possible modes of behavior. He calls this conception the modern notion of will, and his main thesis is that it was fully formulated for the first time by Augustine.[3] In Augustine's thought it mainly resulted from self-examination and was supported by "the indistinct but persistent voluntarism that permeates the Biblical tradition." This view is neither new nor radical; according to Dihle, it is generally accepted that the notion of will, as it is used as a tool of philosophical analysis from early Scholasticism to Schopenhauer and Nietzsche, was introduced by Augustine.[4]

There are many philologically and historically valuable results in Dihle's learned book. A critical reader might ask whether "the modern notion of will" is a convenient interpretative tool in a historical study. I think that this notion is not as clear as Dihle assumes, but I do not find the general approach problematic as such. It is trivially true that ancient and medieval ideas and positions are investigated by comparing them with our ways of thinking. To avoid anachronism is to be aware of one's interpretative starting points, and one manages better the more one is acquainted with contemporary systematic thought. Studies in historical semantics are often led by an interest in similarities and analogies between historical and contemporary ways of thinking, but it is also part of the task to analyze conceptual differences and dissimilarities between them and the historical background of different modes of thinking. These disparities are often philosophically the most stimulating results of historical studies, because analyzing and evaluating views that deviate from ours can raise our consciousness about the conceptual presuppositions of our own modes of thinking. The chapter about Augustine's view in Dihle's book remains in this respect unsatisfactory, because it is thought to be sufficient to demonstrate that, as distinct from his predecessors, Augustine developed a theory of autonomous will that shows similarities to our conception of will. Even if this is in some sense true, a closer comparison between the philosophical analysis of action, evaluation, and motivation in Augustine and in other ancient thinkers might have shown how far Augustine's new ideas were connected with assumptions shared by his predecessors. A more detailed analysis of these connections could have shown that Augustinian "voluntarism" is embedded in a conceptual context that is certainly different from the rudiments of various modern approaches.

Arthur O. Lovejoy in his famous book *The Great Chain of Being* thought that there are certain basic unit ideas that have survived through the centuries and that individual authors have applied to their thought in different ways. The task of a historian of ideas is to isolate those unit ideas and to trace their occurrences in different combinations. Dihle and some others who have written about Augustine's theory of will seem to assume that there is an idea of will invented by Augustine and that it can be studied in the way suggested by Lovejoy.

Rather than accept Lovejoy's view, I think that it is often better to speak about historical analogies instead of unit ideas. In the history of philosophy one can find prima facie identical conceptions as the origins or consequences of quite different lines of thinking. The conceptual context of a conception is part of its meaning in an individual author. Augustine's conception of will is connected with a Platonist theory of the division of the human soul and with a special theological theory of corruption and grace. This fact is sufficient to make one hesitant to call him the inventor of our modern notion of will. My purpose in this paper is not to investigate how some features that are similar to the "modern" ones figure in Augustine's theory of will. What I shall do is pay attention to certain features of Augustine's theory and show how they influenced early medieval thought and how this tradition gave rise to what might be called a theory of the logic of will. That such a theory was invented is a remarkable historical fact—it may be regarded as an aftermath of Augustine's somewhat reductionistic attempt to systematize a great part of his theological anthropology with the help of the notion of will.

THE BASIC USES OF THE TERM "WILL" IN AUGUSTINE

Some aspects of Augustine's conception of will can be seen from his comments on ancient theories of emotions. Augustine's most extensive discussions of the philosophical theories of emotions are to be found in books 9 and 14 of *The City of God*. They are greatly influenced by Cicero's *Tusculan Disputations* and by Cicero's work *On the Ends of Good and Evil*. Following Cicero, Augustine states that all philosophical schools considered passions as spontaneous motions of the soul and that the dominating part of the soul should impose laws on the passions and keep them within strict bounds. According to Augustine, passions are generally thought to include an evaluation that affects the subject and a suggestion to act in a certain way (*City of God* 9.4). Even though the spontaneous affective evaluations are not wholly under the control of the higher soul, accepting or refuting the suggestion to behave in a certain way is voluntary (14.19). Referring to the story about a Stoic philosopher in the *Attic Nights* of Aulus Gellius (*City of God* 19.1), Augustine tries to show that the Stoic doctrine of the extirpation of passions is misleading, because the Stoics give to the words some meanings that deviate from the common usage: "What does it matter whether things are more properly called 'goods' or 'advantageous,' seeing that Stoic, no less than Peripatetic, turns pale with dread at the prospect of their loss? They use different words for them, but put the same value on them" (9.4).

It is not necessary to enter into details of some obvious shortcomings in Augustine's description of the philosophical theories.[5] He assimilates them to a popular Platonic model, which, in addition to the standard Stoic classification, he often employed also in the *Confessions* while describing his own emotional development. In this approach passions are motions of the lower parts of the soul. The evaluations included in them are particular judgments formed by the lower cognitive capacities of the sensitive soul and as such may differ from the considered view of the superior part of the soul. Because of the corruption of the soul, the suggestions of emotions are often bad and should be continuously controlled by the superior part.[6]

It is interesting for our purposes to notice that Augustine sometimes called all occurrent passions volitions (*City of God* 14.6–7). One might ask how they can be acts of will if the will as a special faculty belongs to the superior part of the soul, as Augustine often states (e.g., 13.11.12) and passions are motions of the lower parts. It seems that Augustine had both a broad notion of volition that refers to all kinds of dynamic acts of the soul and a more restricted notion of volition that refers to the acts of the dynamic and controlling power in the superior part. These notions are linked together by the fact that the motions of the soul can be controlled by the superior part. Even if passions in their initial state are spontaneous, the superior will can control the actualized affective states and in particular can either consent to emotional suggestions or refuse them. Independently of what the superior will does, the emotional motions are voluntary as soon as they can in principle be defeated or consented to (cf. *De Trinitate* 12.12; *City of God* 14.19). Actual passions can also be called voluntary in the indirect sense that their quality and strength are influenced by the voluntarily formed habits of treating them (*Confessions* 8.5.11; *De sermone Domini in monte* 1.12.34).

Many authors could have made remarks of this kind by combining some elements from popular Platonist and Stoic works. What is new in Augustine's approach is his attempt to relate all impulses and inclinations of the soul to will as a dynamic center of personality, which, as Dihle stresses, is a capacity relatively independent with respect to theoretical intellect and lower desires.[7] The tasks of the will are not, however, very different from those given to the dominant part of the soul by later Platonists. The controlling will is either rightly or wrongly directed and its orientation determines its activities.

In Augustine's theory things are said to be willed in at least four different ways. (1) The faculty of seeing is said to be joined with the object of perception by the will, and similarly all acts of human beings and animals that can be regarded as intended in some way can be said to be willed.[8] (2) All external actions and omissions that are not externally compelled and all perceptions, cognitions, and emotional motions (except their incipient activations) are counted as willed by the superior part of the soul. This claim is based on the view that will is the controlling faculty that even when not initiating things with a particular act can be regarded as letting all those things happen that it does not prevent (*De spiritu et littera* 31.53). (3) All acts of the superior will are willed; they have no efficient cause other than the will itself (*De libero arbitrio* 1.16, 3.3). (4) Some preferential evaluations are willed only in an optative sense. To will things in this way is to wish that they will take place. The acts of will are either effective or ineffective. Effective acts may correspond with preferential evaluations, but it is also possible that the actual acts of will differ from what a person optatively regards as the best alternative. Augustine described ineffective wishful inclinations as incomplete acts of will. (See, e.g., *Confessions* 8.5.11, 8.9.21; and see below.)

According to Augustine the corrupted human will is not able to resist the improper lower impulses effectively. It yields to them and begins to seek satisfaction in the external world of changeable pleasures instead of clinging to better inclinations. As people cannot repair the fragmented will by themselves, they are not able to begin to will right things wholeheartedly. Only divine grace can restore the right orientation and help the will to preserve it in the struggle against evil impulses.[9] This theological setting strongly determined Augustine's discussion of the questions pertaining to will. Against this background the only effective "voluntarist" decision between different ends seems to be the choice through which a Christian can abandon the right orientation of will restored by grace.

THE WILL AND THE FIRST MOTIONS

The passage from Aulus Gellius I mentioned above was connected with a certain development in the Stoic theory of emotions. According to Chrysippus passions are wrong judgments accompanied by psychophysical affections, of which Stoic therapy can completely cure people. This theory was heavily criticized, and one popular counterexample was that the Stoic philosophers themselves were not as calm as they should have been. The later theory, described in the works of Seneca and Epictetus and reported by Aulus Gellius, was meant to explain this phenomenon. It was said that extraordinary appearances may affect the soul to some extent, but this affection is not a passion, because no emotional judgment is made. Passions were taken to be judgments that some external thing is personally significant to the subject. According to the Stoic theory, rational beings should understand themselves as instances of the well-organized rational whole, and when they have this right view of reality they understand that affections are based on mistaken beliefs about one's position in the world.[10]

Augustine's reading of the passage from Aulus Gellius shows that he probably misunderstood the point of the Stoic doctrine of propassions, although the idea of involuntary first motions greatly influenced his own view of emotions. Let us have a closer look at the Stoic theory. At the beginning of the second book of his treatise *On Anger* Seneca describes the birth of anger as follows. An appearance of injustice induces a mental agitation that is accompanied by bodily changes. This first motion of mind is involuntary. Seneca calls it a preparation for passion, because it suggests an emotional interpretation of the situation ("I am harmed and I should exact retribution"). The presence of this proposition in the mind is not a passion, however; the mind's assent to it is still needed. As distinct from the first motion, the assent is voluntary. Seneca thinks that there are differences between preparatory passions depending on whether people accept the evaluation and are ready to act in accordance with it "at all costs" or whether they think that the evaluation can be qualified by further thoughts.[11] In the quotation from Epictetus in Aulus Gellius it is similarly said that a wise man may be disturbed by terrible appearances but he neither consents to them nor sees in them anything that ought to excite fear.

Augustine comments on this passage that the agitation of the wise man quite clearly shows that he feels fear. Augustine thought the Stoics did not want to call

first motions passions, because passions in their opinion include erroneous judgments about good and evil and as such could not befall philosophers. In his reply
Augustine was content to refer to his view of passions as spontaneous motions of
the lower parts of the soul. As already mentioned, he took them to include an evaluative awareness of something that affects the subject in a pleasant or unpleasant
way and an inclination to behave in a certain way. The higher rational judgment
can agree or disagree with them, and, correspondingly, the will can consent to
them or dissent from them. The Stoics would not have accepted Augustine's correction of their terminology, because they did not accept the Platonic view of the
parts of the soul, and, furthermore, their point was that the first motions do not involve any evaluative commitments.[12]

Augustine thought like the Platonists that people should not trust their spontaneous emotional reactions, because they are usually harmful rather than useful.
The basic attitude of morally good persons should be introspective, and they
should be ready to react to inner motions immediately when they take the wrong
direction. The main points in Augustine's analysis of sinful passions are as follows.
The corruption of the soul causes spontaneous evil desires to arise. These are signs
of original sin, but they are not counted as fresh additional sins if they are immediately defeated by the controlling will. They become sins through the consent of
will, which can take place in two ways. A person may keep a pleasant sinful
thought actual without any intention to behave in the way suggested by it. This
may take place directly by willing the cogitation or indirectly by not trying to
damp it down. This sin is less significant than the decision to act in accordance
with the suggestion. When Augustine says that desire leads to action through suggestion, pleasure, and consent (*suggestio, delectatio, consentio*), suggestion refers to the
cause of an actual desire, pleasure to its initial state, and consent to the acceptance
of thinking about the deed with pleasure or of the inclination to act (*De Trinitate*
12.12; *De sermone Domini in monte* 12.34–35).

Augustine's analysis of the sinful motions of the soul became one of the dominant models for treating emotions and will in early medieval literature. The inner
logic of the development of this tradition is easily explained. In the monastic culture
people found all wrongly directed motions of the soul particularly harmful. Developing effective tools against them was considered an important task, and a detailed
analysis of the first motions and the ability of will to defeat them was part of this
project. The introspective monastic culture induced authors to develop finer and
finer distinctions between the stages of the motions of the heart and between the
degrees of their sinfulness. It is typical that the mental events that were in the scope
of interest were usually assumed to take place long before a fully formed intention
to act was created. Many twelfth-century authors referred in this connection to the
Platonic distinction between the irascible part and the concupiscible parts of the
soul. Their spontaneous activations were called first motions and also propassions.[13]

By way of example, let us have a look at a quotation from a mid-twelfth-
century collection of questions attributed to Odo of Soisson:

> Evil will is sometimes so strong that reason accepts it, and then it is a criminal sin, but when reason does not consent to it, it is a venial sin and it is called a propassion, for the first motions are not within our power. Reason consents to will, when one decides to fulfil it as soon as one gets an opportunity. . . . Propassion, titillation and first motion mean the same. Adam sinned through a propassion; however, his sin was not venial, but criminal, because it was within his power to refrain from the first motions. This is beyond our power. . . . It is our sensual part which first consents to evil will, and this consent is a venial sin; then reason consents to it, and this consent is a criminal sin.[14]

Distinguishing between the first stage of an occurrent emotion and the consent to a corresponding action was only a rough first orientation for those authors interested in developing the finer distinctions of the scale of sins. Peter of Capua summarized some basic teachings as follows:

> Sometimes a motion of the sensual part toward forbidden things—for example, anger or fornication—arises without a thought or decision to realize or not to realize it, and this is always a sin, though a venial one. Some people draw a distinction here. They say that some of these motions are primarily first motions, namely those to which we do not offer any opportunity and which occur involuntarily, and they think that these are not sinful. Motions to which we offer an opportunity are secondarily first motions—for example when someone goes to a party for recreation and something seen there gives rise to a first motion without cogitation—and these are venial sins. We call both venial sins, but the latter ones are more serious. . . . It may happen that somebody cogitates upon a motion toward forbidden things and upon the pleasure connected with them without deciding to realize them even if there were an opportunity; if this cogitation is of short duration only, it is a venial sin, but if it lasts for a longer time, it is a mortal sin even though there is no decision to realize it, since man should immediately repel woman in order to be not involved in a lengthy pleasure, and if it is not repressed, it is in a sense consented to. If a decision to act is made, one can say that man also consents. The mortal sin then becomes deeper.[15]

Here the degrees of sinful motions before consent to action are presented in an ascending order as follows: (1) an accidental emotional activation without any cogitative involvement; (2) the same in a situation in that the person could have avoided as probably stimulating in this way; (3) an emotional activation that leads to a short-term cogitation upon the realization of the emotive suggestion without a decision; (4) the same with a long-term cogitation that is counted as consent to the motion even when there is no consent to action. (There are a great number of other similar twelfth-century examples in the chapter about first motions in Lottin's work.) The sentence about man and woman refers to the tradition of using Adam and Eve as symbols for different parts of reason or soul.[16]

The idea that a longer cogitation upon a pleasure means consent to it was mentioned by Peter of Lombard (*Sentences* 2.24.12) and was based on Augustine's remark that one should immediately expel an improper thought ("statim ut attigerunt animum respui debuerunt"; *De Trinitate* 12.12). Peter Lombard and the authors of the above texts were representatives of the view that the first motions toward illicit things are sins even at their initial stage. Augustine preferred to think that "we don't sin when having an evil desire, but when giving our consent to it." [17] The view that certain motions of the soul are sins in themselves was particularly enforced by the interpretation Gregory the Great gave to Augustine's psychology of sin. [18] According to him an emotional activation in a forbidden direction is immediately a sin. Gregory wrote to Augustine, bishop of the church of Canterbury:

> The seed of sin is in suggestion, its nourishment in pleasure, and its completion in consent. . . . And although the body cannot experience pleasure without the mind, yet the mind, in contending against the desires of the body, is to some extent unwillingly chained to them, so that through reason it refuses to give its consent, and yet it is bound by bodily pleasure but strongly regrets its bondage. It was for this reason that the great soldier in God's army confessed with sorrow: "I see another law in my members." [19]

This view became more dominant in the second half of the twelfth century; many of the earlier twelfth-century theologians preferred to call the first motions temptations or something other than sins, reserving the latter term to chosen acts or to acts that in principle can be chosen. [20] Abelard's discussion of the subject is based on Augustine's view of sin as consent with the exception that he did not distinguish between the notions of consent to cogitation and consent to action, apparently thinking that, morally speaking, it would not make any difference. Michael Lapidge has recently argued that Abelard's distinction between lust and consenting to lust is precisely the Stoic doctrine of "natural impulse" on the one hand and "assent to the impulse" on the other hand and that "it is Abelard's original contribution to apply the notion of assent to that of sin in a Christian context." [21] I think that the views of Augustine and Abelard show the same similarities and dissimilarities with the Stoic doctrine in this connection.

A central theme in the Augustinian tradition described above was the question of the relation between will and passions as spontaneous first motions, and it was treated by trying to show how an illicit affection becomes more sinful step by step. The reason for this discussion was the attempt to avoid sins at their initial stages, and correspondingly the analysis was concentrated on the question of the relationship between spontaneous evaluations, feelings, acceptance, and intention. Although the treatment of passions tended to be schematic in the literature influenced by the Augustinian psychology, it greatly contributed to the fact that the concepts of will and intention became dominant in medieval ethics and theory of action.

A profound change in the medieval discussion of emotions took place in the thirteenth century, mainly caused by the increasing influence of Aristotle's works. As distinct from other ancient philosophers, Aristotle thought that a complicated system of natural and socially learned emotions is an essential part of the human form of life in general and that the aim of education is to improve the emotional evaluations and reactions instead of eliminating them or making the rational part some kind of citadel against them.[22] One can see from Aquinas's doctrine of emotions (*Summa theologiae* 2.1.22–48) how the reappearance of the Aristotelian theory changed the former approaches to emotions and how the medieval view of will affected the Aristotelian theory. Due to the Aristotelian influence, emotions began to be treated from a more extrovert point of view. The scope of theoretical interest was enlarged and emotional dispositions as constituents of virtues were given a more autonomous and constructive role than they had in early medieval thought.[23] But Aquinas's attempt to clarify the basic types of actual emotions with the help of distinctions pertaining to the stages of motion (2.1.23.2–4) is very similar to Augustine's theory of emotions as volitions (*City of God* 14.7), and the Augustinian idea of the controlling will occurs also in his conception of akrasia as a bad choice and "transitory vice."[24] An interesting example of later medieval discussions of the relations between the cognitive and dynamic aspects of actual volitions and emotions is Adam of Wodeham's critical survey of the views of his English contemporaries in the 1320s.[25] It offers a picture of a controversy that shows many similarities to recent philosophical debates about the components of an occurrent emotion.

TOWARD THE LOGIC OF WILL

Augustine often discussed reluctant (*invitus*) actions, and some of his remarks about this matter were dealt with in the twelfth century and later in the Middle Ages. The basic type of reluctant action in Augustine is similar to what Aristotle called a mixed voluntary action at the beginning of the third book of the *Nicomachean Ethics*. Mixed acts are such that no one chooses them as such, though they can be chosen as necessary means to an end in certain circumstances. Aristotle mentions as an example the act of throwing goods from a ship floundering on a stormy sea. Augustine says that acts of this kind are said to be done reluctantly or unwillingly, because people do not like to do such things and they wish they did not have to do them. They are done contrary to what is willed, when "what is willed" refers to what is wished. But Augustine thought that the decisive will of a person is seen from behavior, provided that there is no external compulsion, and therefore all reluctantly chosen acts can be said to be willed (*De spiritu et littera* 31.53).

One of the best-known aspects of Augustine's theory of will is the idea that not just means to an end are sometimes reluctantly chosen. The basic orientation of the will itself can be reluctant. In book 8 of his *Confessions* Augustine describes his conversion as an example of such a gap between evaluation and effective motivation. He was sure that it would be better to improve his way of living radically, but he continued to follow his settled habits. He did it willingly in the sense that will as the decisive power let it happen. He willed that he would will to live otherwise, but his will to will it was ineffective and, as he said, partial and imperfect.

As for the effective will, Augustine thought that if S wills that p, S also wills that S wills that p. If S wills that p and says that S wills that S does not will that p, this second-order will may correspond to S's evaluation, but it is a wish and imperfect will as long as it remains ineffective. As for the effective will, Augustine accepts the form

(1) $$Wp - WWp.$$

If the first-order will operator refers to effective will in

(2) $$Wp \ \& \ W\text{-}Wp,$$

the second-order will operator is not taken in the same sense as the first-order operator, if (2) is possible. It refers to wish. The Augustinian doctrine of reluctant acts was widely discussed in the twelfth century. In his *Ethics*, Peter Abelard says that when acts that are necessary conditions for achieving a willed end are of such a nature that they would not be separately willed, it is more natural to say that they are tolerated than that they are willed. Reluctant acts of this kind are voluntary, however, because they are a concomitant of the chosen attempt to achieve something.[26] Abelard's remarks are based on some similar formulations in Augustine, but Abelard associated the notion of what is willed with what is wished or desired more systematically than Augustine. When he referred to effective acts, he used the Augustinian term "consent" rather than "will." In later discussions it became more usual to refer to all practical decisions as acts of will. The problem of calling reluctant acts willed was then solved simply by saying that things may be willed as such or they may be willed because of something else (*propter aliud*) only.[27]

In his influential *Summa aurea* (c. 1225) William of Auxerre said that in the case of reluctant actions the means are willed together with the end (*coniunctim*) but not separately (*divisim*) and that the in-itself preferred but unrealized alternative can be called an object of conditional will (*voluntas conditionalis* or *velleitas*). The notion of conditional will was introduced in the late twelfth century, as can be seen from Stephen Langton's distinction between *voluntas absoluta* and *voluntas conditionalis* in question 96 of his *Questiones theologiae*.[28] In the thirteenth century the notion of conditional will was understood in two different ways. Some authors accepted William of Auxerre's view that conditional will is a nonrealized readiness to will something instead of the reluctantly accepted alternative when conditions different from the actual ones prevail (*promptitudo volendi sub conditione*). This is how Thomas Aquinas spoke about conditional will.[29] Some others called the reluctant act of willing the means-to-an-end conditional will, because it was necessitated by the end as its condition. In this approach the conditional will was also separated from the latent wish (*velleitas*).[30]

Augustine thought that willing the end effectively implies that what is thought to be a means to the end is also willed, even if it may be willed reluctantly. This principle, which Kant called an analytic truth about will, was commonly accepted in the Middle Ages, though there were some terminological differences. William

Ockham formulated the idea by saying that when S has chosen a goal X, S is required to will the means to X, although S can liberate himself or herself from this necessity by ceasing to will the goal.[31]

If a means is treated as a necessary condition of an end, one might think that in this case willing the antecedent implies willing the consequent. It is historically remarkable that the general validity of the principle expressed in this way began to be discussed in the twelfth century.

In his *Ethics* Abelard deals with examples that could be formulated as follows: if p implies q and S wills that p, does it follow that S wills that q?[32] Abelard's treatment of the question remains ambiguous, however, because his term "will" seems to refer to wish in this connection. Nobody would be inclined to believe that this logical principle would hold of wishing. After Abelard, however, there were other twelfth-century masters who asked just this question and applied it to efficient will, as Peter of Poitiers mentions in his *Sententiae*, written around 1170.

These remarks on the logic of will are early examples of what became a much-used tool of analysis in medieval logic. In this approach the basic rules for modal sentences de dicto were taken as a starting point, namely

(3)
$$\frac{L(p \to q)}{Lp \to Lq}$$

and

(4)
$$\frac{L(p \to q)}{Mp \to Mq}.$$

It was then thought that we can begin the investigation of the logical properties of many other concepts which show prima facie similarities with purely modal terms by substituting them for necessity (L) or possibility (M) under the inference line in (3) or (4). This was how the discussions of the concepts of knowledge and belief (epistemic logic) and the normative concepts of obligation, permission, and prohibition (deontic logic) were introduced as branches of applied modal logic. It is typical of later medieval epistemic and deontic logic to notice that even though the mutual relationships between the epistemic notions of knowledge and belief or between the normative notions of obligation and permission are to some extent analogous to the mutual relationships between the modal notions of necessity and possibility, their logical behavior differs from that of purely modal terms. It was also commonly thought that one of the differences is that neither (3) nor (4) hold for epistemic or deontic terms without qualification. The first steps toward this kind of analysis for the notions of knowledge, obligation, and will were taken in the twelfth century.[33]

Some twelfth-century authors noticed that, even though willing an end effectively implies that a necessary means to it is also willed, (3) cannot be applied without restriction to efficient will in the form that, if S wills the antecedent of a valid consequence and knows it to be such, *S* also wills the consequent. The principle holds about the end–means relationship, but the necessary means are not the only consequents of what is willed. Peter of Poitiers formulated a counterexample as follows: if *S* repents of a sin, *S* is guilty of a sin, and *S* wills to repent of a sin, but *S* does not will to be guilty of a sin.[34] Stephen Langton's counterexample is of the same type: if a man visits his sick father, the father is sick. This man wills to visit his sick father, but it does not follow that he wills that the father is sick.[35]

When it was realized that one cannot apply (3) to effective will without qualifications, medieval authors found it interesting to ask in which cases a rational agent does not will the consequents of what he or she wills. (i) The twelfth century examples just mentioned specify the case in which to will something in certain circumstances implies that those circumstances prevail, though this is something the agent does not will. This case was found philosophically interesting and was also used in later medieval deontic logic (see below). (ii) Another relevant but more problematic idea was that a separately unwanted side effect of what is willed is willed more indirectly than a separately unwanted means to an end. This line of thought forms the background to Thomas Aquinas's distinctions between directly and indirectly voluntary acts and between states of affairs willed per se and *per accidens*.[36]

One can follow the discussion of the question of how (3) should be qualified with respect to will by tracing the comments on the example of a man who "wills to be in the mud and have 100 marks" (*in luto esse cum 100 marchis*). The example was found ambiguous, and it was possible to interpret it (i) as a case of willing reluctantly to become dirty as a means of receiving 100 marks, (ii) as a case of willing to become dirty as a side effect, or (iii) as willing something in a situation in which one will become dirty in any case.[37]

MEDIEVAL DEONTIC LOGIC

Many fourteenth-century authors were interested in the question of whether (3) and (4) can be applied to the normative notions of obligation and permission respectively. The most extensive treatment of these rules and other principles of deontic logic is included in the second article of the opening question of the *Commentary on the Sentences* by Roger Roseth, an English Franciscan who lectured on the *Sentences* in the period between 1332 and 1337. Roger Roseth first defines some rules of consistency of the system of norms. The rest of the second article consists of discussions of possible objections to those rules, and in this part Roseth developed the basic principles of his theory of norms. He separated different kinds of permission, commented on acts of supererogation, and discussed the problem later called the paradox of the good Samaritan. Using examples such as "If one repents of a sin, one is guilty of a sin," Roseth wanted to demonstrate that (3) and (4) cannot be used in deontic logic without qualification. Some norms, such as the obligation to repent of one's sins, regulate one's behavior only after one has violated other norms. Similarly there are norms that regulate conduct in situations in which a moral agent has not violated any rules but in which one cannot will to find oneself without violating some rules. This is how one is obliged to help the victims of accidents. According to Roseth conditional obligations of this kind are indispensable in factual normative systems, and consequently (3) is not an acceptable deontic rule of inference as such. Similar remarks can be made on the notion of permission and rule (4).

Roseth's detailed discussion of the question concerning how conditional obligations should be understood contains some of the themes that have occurred in the contemporary debate about contrary-to-duty imperatives. To avoid various difficulties, Roseth finally formulated conditional obligation as follows:

$$(5) \qquad\qquad p{\rightarrow}Oq \ \& \ -L(p{\rightarrow}q) \ \& \ M(p \ \& \ q).$$

This form comes close to some suggestions in contemporary deontic logic.[38]

The detailed examinations of deontic inferences and conditional norms in Roseth's treatise entitle one to characterize it as the first systematic study on deontic logic; but, as already mentioned, there were shorter remarks on deontic inferences in other works of the same period as well. Roger Roseth's attempt to treat the basic questions of ethics with the help of the principles of deontic logic was anticipated by the deontological theory of ethics developed by William Ockham.[39] Because the notions of will and intention were fundamental to Ockham's ethics, it was natural that the question of the conceptual properties of the notion of will became closely connected with the question of the logical behavior of normative notions. An example of how the logic of will was assimilated to deontic logic is Roger Roseth's theory of two types of conditional obligations mentioned above. They correspond to the examples of willing to repent of one's sins and willing to visit one's sick father, which were formulated in the twelfth century as examples of the cases in which willing the antecedent does not imply willing the consequent.

One historically interesting source of Roseth's theory of conditional obligations is medieval obligations logic. Medieval logical treatises on obligations (*De obligationibus*) contain rules for disputations between an opponent and a respondent and discussions of various problems connected with them. Some general tenets of this branch of logic can be illustrated by having a look at the disputation called *positio*. The opponent puts forward an initial proposition (*positum*) that is usually contingent and false. The respondent is obliged to treat the *positum* as he treats propositions he knows to be true. After the *positum* the opponent puts forward new propositions and the respondent must react by saying "I grant it," "I deny it," or "I doubt it." The opponent tries to trap the respondent into conceding something contradictory to the *positum*, to propositions that are correctly granted or are opposites of propositions correctly denied, or to propositions that follow from these. The respondent's task is to answer in a logically consistent way while the opponent tries to break this consistency. Obligational disputations were practiced as parts of logic courses, and obligational treatises can be characterized as investigations of questions that arise in such exercises. The general interest in obligations logic and the attempts to apply it in different areas show, however, that there was a tendency to regard it as a general theoretical frame for discussing the basic logical questions of rational discourse.[40]

The obligations rules as such have nothing in particular to do with morality or ethics. However, some medieval authors located obligational disputations in a wider context of what may be called the general ethics of disputation. They stated that in a disputation in which one party puts forward assertions, the other party must grant, deny, or doubt them, according to whether he or she knows or does not know them to be true or false. These rules specify certain duties of truthfulness or honesty; one could call them prima facie duties of the respondent in a disputation or, more generally, the duties of a person answering yes–no questions. The respondent is partially freed from the honesty rules in a *positio* disputation; those rules are overridden by the obligational consistency rule.

One example of the interest in normative notions in obligations treatises is the discussion of disputations in which the expression "must be granted" (*concedendum*) is included in the initial *positum*. It was realized that a *positum* of the type "That you are in Rome must be granted" can be read prescriptively as a norm or descriptively as a proposition expressing the existence of an obligation. The initial proposition including "concedendum" is read descriptively in a *positio* disputation, but it is read normatively in the species of disputations called *petitio*.

In his *De obligationibus* (1302), Walter Burley discusses some problems of formulating conditional norms in connection with the disputations called *positio dependens, positio cadens,* and *positio renascens*. What they have in common is that a proposition begins or ceases to be the *positum* when a condition is fulfilled. The condition is a disputational act. Burley distinguishes between the cases in which the obligation to treat something as the *positum* comes into force only after the disputational act that fulfills the condition and in which obligation comes into force at the same time when the condition is fulfilled. One should not accept a conditional obligation the condition of which is fulfilled by a disputational act that violates the obligation.[41] Questions of this kind were known to Roger Roseth when he put forward the carefully considered formulation (5) of conditional obligation.

NOTES

1. Albrecht Dihle, *The Theory of Will in Classical Antiquity* (Berkeley: University of California Press, 1982), 20–67.

2. Ibid., 24, 37, 53–54.

3. Ibid., 45, 144.

4. Ibid., 127, 123.

5. For the theories of emotions in Hellenistic philosophy, see Martha Nussbaum, *The Therapy of Desire: Theory and Practice in Hellenistic Ethics* (Princeton: Princeton University Press, 1994).

6. St. Augustine, *The City of God* 14.19; for Augustine's theory of emotions and its sources see also G. O'Daly, *Augustine's Philosophy of Mind* (London: Duckworth, 1987), 40–54.

7. Dihle, *Theory of Will in Classical Antiquity*, 127–29.

8. St. Augustine, *De Trinitate* 11.2; Dihle, *Theory of Will in Classical Antiquity*, 125–26.

9. See, e.g., *Expositio quarumdam propositionum ex epistola ad Romanos* (in J. P. Migne, *Patrologiae cursus completus, series Latina*, 35:2065–66).

10. For the Stoic theory of emotions see B. Inwood, *Ethics and Human Action in Early Stoicism* (Oxford: Oxford University Press, 1985); T. Engberg-Pedersen, *The Stoic Theory of Oikeiosis* (Aarhus: Aarhus University Press, 1990); J. Annas, *Hellenistic Philosophy of Mind* (Berkeley: University of California Press, 1992); and Nussbaum, *Therapy of Desire;* for the spontaneous motions that were called *propatheiai* see K. Abel, "Das Propatheia-theorem: Ein Beitrag zur stoischen Affektenlehre," *Hermes* 111 (1983): 78–97.

11. Seneca, *De ira* 2.3–4.

12. For the failure to understand the Stoic theory in the Platonist tradition see also J. Dillon, "Metriopatheia and Apatheia: Some Reflections on a Controversy in Later Greek Ethics," in J. J. Anton and A. Preus, eds., *Essays in Ancient Greek Philosophy*, vol. 2 (Albany: State University of New York Press, 1983).

13. This Stoic term became known through Jerome's commentary on Matthew. See Migne, *Patrologiae Latina*, 26:38.

14. For the Latin term see O. Lottin, *Psychologie et morale aux dix-septième et dix-huitième siècles,* vol. 2 (Louvain: Abbaye de Mont César, 1948), 496–97

15. Quoted in Lottin, *Psychologie et morale,* 499; my translation.

16. Augustine, *De Trinitate* 12.12; Gregory I, *S. Gregorii Magni moralia in Job* 4.27.49, ed. M. Adrien, Corpus Christianorum, series Latina, 143 (Turnhout: Brepols, 1979).

17. *Expositio quarumdam propositionum ex epistola ad Romanos,* in Migne, *Patrologiae Latina,* 35:2066.

18. Cf. C. Straw, *Gregory the Great: Perfection in Imperfection* (Berkeley: University of California Press, 1988), chaps. 5–6.

19. Bede, *Ecclesiastical History of the English People* 1.27.9, ed. and trans. B. Colgrave and R. A. B. Mynors (Oxford: Oxford University Press, 1972); my translation. Also translated by L. Sherley-Price, revised R. E. Latham (Harmondsworth: Penguin, 1968).

20. See the examples in Peter Abelard, *Ethics,* ed. and trans. E. Luscombe (Oxford: Clarendon Press, 1971), 14–15.

21. Michael Lapidge, "The Stoic Inheritance," in P. Dronke, ed., *A History of Twelfth-Century Western Philosophy* (Cambridge: Cambridge University Press, 1988), 98.

22. For Aristotle's view on emotions see, e.g., Nussbaum, *Therapy of Desire.*

23. For recent discussions of Aquinas's theory of emotions see M. Jordan, "Aquinas's Construction of a Moral Account of the Passions," *Freiburger Zeitschrift für Philosophie und Theologie* 33 (1986): 71–97, and C. Marmo, "Hoc autem et si potest tollerari: Egidio Romano e Tommaso d'Aquino sulle passioni dell'anima," *Documenti e studi sulla tradizione filosofica medievale* 2 (1991): 281–315.

24. See R. Saarinen, *Weakness of the Will in Medieval Thought* (Leiden: Brill, 1994), for the confrontation of the Augustinian view of the will with the Aristotelian theory of choice in the medieval discussions of *akrasia*.

25. Adam de Wodeham, *Lectura secunda in librum primum Sententiarum*, ed. R. Wood, vol. 1 (St. Bonaventure, N.Y.: St. Bonaventure University Press, 1990), 272–93.

26. Abelard, *Ethics* 10.2–6, 16.24–32.

27. For some twelfth-century examples see Saarinen, *Weakness of the Will in Medieval Thought*, 60–63.

28. See the edition in R. Quinto, "Die Quaestiones des Stephan Langton über die Gottesfurcht," *Cahiers de l'Institut du Moyen-Age Grec et Latin, Université de Copenhague* 62 (1992): 140.

29. See, e.g., Aquinas, *Summa theologiae* 2.1.6.6., 3.21.4, and *De malo* 16.3.9.

30. This analysis is found in the so-called *Summa Halensis*, partially written by Alexander of Hales (c. 1185–1245), and in some other texts; see Saarinen, *Weakness of the Will in Medieval Thought*, 77–81.

31. William Ockham, *Quaestiones variae*, ed. G. I. Etzkorn et al. (St. Bonaventure, N.Y.: St. Bonaventure University Press, 1984), *q.* 6, *a.* 9.

32. See, e.g., Abelard, *Ethics* 16.11–18.

33. For further details see S. Knuuttila, *Modalities in Medieval Philosophy* (London: Routledge, 1993).

34. Peter of Poitiers, *Sententiae* 4.16, in Migne, *Patrologiae Latina*, 211:1199.

35. Langton, *Questiones theologiae*, in Quinto "Die Quaestiones des Stephan Langton über die Gottesfurcht," 129–30.

36. See, e.g., *Summa theologiae* 2.2.64.7–8; *De malo* 2.1.

37. See S. Knuuttila and T. Holopainen, "Conditional Will and Conditional Norms in Medieval Thought," *Synthese* 96 (1993): 121–25.

38. See Knuuttila, *Modalities in Medieval Philosophy*, 190–96. The relevant texts of Roseth are translated in S. Knuuttila and O. Hallamaa, "Roger Roseth and Medieval Deontic Logic," *Logique et analyse* 149 (1995): 75–87.

39. See Knuuttila and Holopainen, "Conditional Will and Conditional Norms in Medieval Thought," 118–21.

40. For medieval obligations logic see M. Yrjönsuuri, *Obligationes: Fourteenth-Century Logic of Disputational Duties*, Acta Philosophica Fennica 55 (Helsinki: Philosophical Society of Finland, 1994).

41. See Knuuttila, *Modalities in Medieval Philosophy*, 189–90.

TWELVE

Augustine and Descartes on Minds and Bodies

Gareth B. Matthews

No doubt the most striking anticipation of Descartes's famous reasoning, "I think, therefore I am" (cogito, ergo sum),[1] is to be found in this passage from Augustine's *City of God:*

> For we are, and we know that we are, and we love to be and to know that we are. Moreover, in the three things I have [just] said there is no falsity resembling truth to trouble us. For we do not take hold of these things with any bodily sense, as we do what is outside us. Thus we perceive colors by seeing, sounds by hearing, odors by smelling, flavors by tasting, hard and soft things by touching; and in thought we turn over incorporeal images that resemble these sensible things and we hold them in the memory and by their means we are aroused to desire the sensible things themselves. But without any teasing imagination of appearances or illusions, it is most certain to me that I am, that I know it, and that I love it.
>
> Concerning these truths I fear no arguments of the Academicians in which they say, "What if you should be mistaken?" For if I am mistaken, I am [si fallor, sum]. For one who does not exist cannot be mistaken either. And so I am, if I am mistaken. Because therefore I am, if I am mistaken, how am I mistaken about my existence when it is certain that I am if I am mistaken? Because therefore I, who would be the one mistaken, would have to exist to be mistaken, there is no doubt I am not mistaken in knowing that I am.
>
> Moreover, it follows that I should not be mistaken even in knowing that I know. For just as I know that I am, so also I know that I know it. And when I love these two things, I also add to the things I know a third and no less valuable something, this very love.[2]

Among Descartes's own contemporaries, Mersenne, Colvius, and Arnauld all pointed to a similarity between Descartes's cogito and reasoning, such as in the passage above, that can be found in Augustine. Other commentators have tried to bring out the differences, as well as the similarities, between Augustine's "si fallor,

222

sum" and Augustine's cogito. Since Descartes seems to have been less than fully candid about his debt to Augustine, commentators have naturally taken on the task of setting the record straight.[3]

In the 350-year-long discussion of what Descartes owes to Augustine, however, there has not been much attention directed to the relation between (1) cogito-type reasoning in these two thinkers and (2) their respective versions of mind–body dualism. As I shall try to show in this paper Augustine offers reasoning about what each mind can know concerning itself to support the dualist thesis that the mind is an incorporeal substance. This reasoning, usually identified with Descartes, rather than with Augustine, has been the subject of heated philosophical debate in the twentieth century, especially among the followers and critics of Wittgenstein.

THE PROBLEM OF OTHER MINDS

Before I turn to what Augustine thinks each mind can know concerning itself I want to discuss briefly the "other-minds problem," the problem about how each of us can know there are other minds. It is commonly assumed that, having assured himself of his own existence as a mind, or thinking thing, Descartes needs to have a good reason to suppose there exist minds in addition to his own. Some readers even assume that the following passage, from near the end of the second meditation, offers such a reason:

> [I]f I look out of the window and see men crossing the square, as I just happen to have done, I normally say that I see the men themselves, just as I say that I see the wax. Yet do I see any more than hats and coats which could conceal automatons? I *judge* that they are men. And so something which I thought I was seeing with my eyes is in fact grasped solely by the faculty of judgement which is my mind.[4]

First of all, there is, of course, no *argument* here, not even an argument for the existence of "men" rather than mere automata. And, second, there is no explicit concern about how we can know there are *minds* to go with certain clothed and moving bodies. So the problem of other *minds* is not even stated here, let alone solved, or resolved.

The other place in Descartes's writings where one might think to find an argument for other minds is in part 5 of the *Discourse on Method*. There Descartes argues that whereas

(i) if any . . . machines had the organs and outward shape of a monkey or . . . other animal that lacks reason, we should have no means of knowing that they did not possess entirely the same nature as these animals.

(ii) if any such machines bore a resemblance to our bodies and imitated our actions as closely as possible for all practical purposes, we should still have two very certain means of recognizing that they were not real men.[5]

The two tests Descartes offers for telling machines from "real men" are these:

The first is that they could never use words, or put together other signs, as we do in order to declare our thoughts to others. . . . Secondly, even though such machines might do some things as well as we do them, or perhaps even better, they would inevitably fail in others, which would reveal that they were acting not through understanding but only from the disposition of their organs.[6]

As Descartes goes on to add, these two tests—the ability to use language and the possession of general, rather than merely task-specific, intelligence—also mark off beasts from human beings.

Is this a solution to the problem of other minds? No. The issue here is not how I can know whether there is some other mind in addition to my own. Descartes assumes throughout this discussion that all (living) human beings have minds. Thus he assumes there are other minds—that is, minds in addition to one's own. His question is how we can tell whether, among the various beings with minds, machines or beasts, and not just human beings, have minds.

There is, in fact, no discussion of the problem of other minds anywhere in Descartes; but there ought to be. Given Descartes's radical skepticism at the beginning of part 4 of the *Discourse* and throughout the first meditation, and given the assurance that he finds, through the cogito, that at least one mind exists, namely his own, he does need to confront and deal with the question, How can I know that there are minds in addition to my own?

By contrast, Augustine both raises the question of other minds and tries to solve it. In fact he tries to solve it by presenting a version of what has come to be called "the argument from analogy." Here is the passage:

For we also recognize, from a likeness to us, the motions of bodies by which we perceive that others besides us live. Just as we move [our] body in living, so, we notice, those bodies are moved. For when a living body is moved there is no way open to our eyes to see the mind [*animus*], a thing which cannot be seen by the eyes. But we perceive something present in that mass such as is present in us to move our mass in a similar way; it is life and soul [*anima*]. Nor is such perception something peculiar to, as it were, human prudence and reason. For indeed beasts perceive as living, not only themselves, but also each other and one another, and us as well. Nor do they see our soul [*animas*], except from the motions of the body, and they do that immediately and very simply by a sort of natural agreement. Therefore we know the mind of anyone at all from our own; and from our own case we believe in that which we do not know [ex nostro credimus quem non novimus]. For not only do we perceive a mind, but we even know what one is, by considering our own; for we have a mind.[7]

It may be useful at this point to make some remarks about Augustine's use of words for mind and soul. Augustine uses both the feminine word in Latin, *anima*, and the masculine word, *animus*, for "soul." These Latin words are, of course, cognate to the English word "animate," as they are also cognate to the Latin verb *animare*, which means both "ensoul" and "make alive." It is therefore natural for Augustine, as a Latin speaker and writer, to think of the soul, the *anima/animus*, as what makes a certain kind of body alive.

Augustine tends to use *anima* more generically for any soul, including a human one, and *animus* more specifically for the human or rational soul. Thus an *animus* is a rational *anima*.

In addition to *anima* and *animus* Augustine also uses the feminine word *mens* for a mind or rational soul. By the time we get to book 10 of *De Trinitate* Augustine focuses especially on the *mens*, or mind. But I take it that, having presented his argument in book 8 for other rational souls (*animi*), he has, equivalently, presented an argument for other minds (*mentes*).

KNOWING FROM ONE'S OWN CASE

It is, of course, essential to the argument from analogy for other minds that one begin with the assumption that one knows what a mind is from one's own case. Since this assumption is at the heart of the discussion to follow, I shall single out a very strong form of it and call it "thesis T":

Thesis T: The mind of each of us knows what a mind is simply and solely by knowing itself.

One should be reluctant to try to identify *anything* in the history of philosophy as totally original, lest someone come along and find an anticipation of that very thing in the writings of some earlier thinker. Nevertheless, in defiance of reasonable caution, I want to say that thesis T is original with Augustine. It is expressed, clearly and eloquently, in this passage from the paragraph immediately preceding the argument from analogy for other minds quoted above:

as regards the soul, we not unfittingly say that we, therefore, know what a soul is because we also have a soul. We have never seen it with our eyes, nor formed a general or special idea of it from any similarity with other souls that we have seen, but rather, as I said, because we also have a soul. For what is so intimately known, and what knows itself to be itself, than that through which all other things are likewise known, that is, the soul [*animus*] itself?[8]

Implicit in this passage is the suggestion that we might form a generic idea of a tree or a specific idea of, say, a palm tree by somehow noting similarities among the various trees we have seen. But however exactly that story might go, and Augustine is certainly aware of the problems in understanding how we can learn what an F is by being shown examples of F's,[9] he makes clear that, in his view, such a procedure is not available for learning what a mind is. And the reason is that one's own mind is the only "case" one can know in the relevant way.

Here are two more formulations of thesis T from the very next book of the *De Trinitate*:

When the mind [*mens*], therefore, knows itself fully and nothing else with itself, then its knowledge is equal to it, because its knowledge is not from another nature when it knows itself. And when it perceives itself fully and nothing more, then its knowledge is neither less nor greater than itself.[10]

When the mind [*mens*], therefore, knows itself, it alone is the parent of its own knowledge, for it is itself both the object known and the one that knows. . . . Hence, when it knows itself, it begets a knowledge of itself that is equal to itself. For it does not know itself as less than it is, nor is its knowledge that of another essence, not only because it is itself that which knows, but also because it knows itself. (9.12.18)

When Augustine talks in these passages about the mind knowing what it itself is, he means to include in that knowledge knowing what a mind is, or, as we might put it, knowing what is essential to being a mind. Here, in the next book of the *De Trinitate*, Augustine inquires into the nature of mind:

But since our inquiry concerns the nature of the mind [*mens*], let us remove from consideration all knowledge obtained externally through the senses of the body, and attend more diligently to that which we have set down: that every mind [*mens*] knows and is certain concerning itself. (10.10.14)

Three chapters earlier Augustine had canvased various philosophical theories as to the nature of the mind:

some thought it to be the blood, others the brain, others the heart. . . . Others believe that it consisted of very minute and indivisible bodies called atoms which meet and cling together. Others said that its substance was air, others fire. Others could not think of any substance except as a body, and since they found that the soul was not a body, they said that it was not a substance at all, but the harmony itself of our body, or the combining of the primary substances by which that flesh is as it were joined together. And, consequently, all of these have regarded the soul as mortal; for whether it was a body or some combination of the body, in either case it would certainly not live forever.

But some have declared that its substance was a kind of life, altogether different from corporeal life. For they have found it to be a life that vivifies and animates every living body, and have attempted to prove, as each one could, that it must logically be also immortal, since life cannot be without life. Some add a fifth body—I do not know what it is—to the well-known four elements of this world and from it, so they say, mind comes. (10.7.9)

In this survey of views about the nature of mind and soul we can recognize the doctrines of Empedocles, who seems to have thought consciousness resides in the blood; the ancient atomists, who thought that the mind, or soul, is a collection of subtle atoms; and Plato, who thought of the soul as an animator, or vivifier. At the end of the *Phaedo* Plato has Socrates argue for the immortality of the soul on the ground that the soul, which always brings life with it, cannot admit of its opposite, death.[11] Earlier in the same dialogue Plato had let his character, Simmias, present the view that the soul is a harmony,[12] which also figures in Augustine's survey.

AN ARGUMENT FOR DUALISM

Augustine now has in place all the elements he needs for an internalist argument for mind–body dualism. Thus he has already claimed that "every mind [*mens*] knows and is certain concerning itself" (*De Trinitate* 10.10.14), by which he means that each mind knows and is certain

- (a) what it itself is (namely, a mind);
- (b) what it is to be a mind;
- (c) that is, what is essential to being a mind.

What, according to Augustine, is essential to being a mind, and how does he arrive at his answer? Those of us who know our Descartes may be struck by a similarity between Augustine's way of arriving at the essence of mind and Descartes's "method of doubt":

> Let this remain to it, which not even they have doubted who regarded the mind [*mens*] as this or that kind of a body. For not every mind [*mens*] regards itself as air, but, as I mentioned above, some regard it as fire, others as a brain, and others as this or that kind of a body. All know, however, that they understand and live; they refer what they understand to the understanding, but refer being and life to themselves. And no one doubts that no one understands who does not live, and no one lives who is not [i.e., who does not exist]. (10.10.13)

As Augustine makes clear in the next section the point is not just that no philosopher has happened to doubt that one who understands also lives and also exists. The rhetorical questions in the following quotation are meant to bring out the idea that no one *could* doubt these things, even though each of us can doubt whether the mind is blood, atoms, harmony, or whatever.

> For men have doubted whether the power to live, to remember, to understand, to will, to think, to know, and to judge is due to air, to fire, or to the brain, or to the blood, or to atoms, or to a fifth body . . . or whether the combining or the orderly arrangement of the flesh is capable of producing these effects. . . .
> On the other hand who would doubt that he lives, remembers, understands, wills, thinks, knows, and judges? For even if he doubts, he lives; if he doubts, he remembers why he doubts; if he doubts, he understands that he doubts; if he doubts, he wishes to be certain; if he doubts, he thinks; if he doubts, he knows that he does not know; if he doubts, he judges that he ought not to consent rashly. Whoever then doubts about anything else ought never to doubt about all of these; for if they were not, he would be unable to doubt about anything at all (*De Trinitate* 10.10.14).

As we can see, Augustine is moving in this section to the same conception of mind, *mens*, as what Descartes later calls "a thinking thing" (res cogitans). The oddity of this discussion, from a Cartesian point of view, is the inclusion of life, or living, as a mental function. In other respects Augustine's idea that the mind is that whereby one "remembers, understands, wills, thinks, knows, and judges" is thoroughly Cartesian.

Part of what Augustine has in mind when he takes living to be a mental function is preserved in the question we might ask today: "Is there life after death?" When we ask that question we mean to be asking whether we will survive our deaths—that is, whether we will *exist* after bodily death. We don't mean to be asking specifically whether we will be alive in a biological sense of "alive."

Having said that, I must add that Augustine also thinks of the human *mens* as an *animus,* an animator of our bodies in this life, whereas Descartes does not. So there is a respect in which Augustine's inclusion of living among the functions of mind is certainly un-Cartesian, even though there is a respect in which it is not.

According to Augustine, then, a mind is something that lives, remembers, understands, wills, thinks, knows, and judges. Augustine thinks further that a mind knows what a mind is, not from observing other minds and developing an idea of what a mind is from them but simply from knowing itself.

Could these powers or functions of mind be the powers or functions of some corporeal thing? "Those who regard the mind [*mens*] either as a body, or as the combination or harmony of the body," he writes:

> wish all these things to be seen in a subject. Thus the air, the fire, or some other body would be the substance which they call the mind [*mens*], while the understanding would be in this body as its quality. . . . And even those who do not regard the mind as a body, but as the combination or harmony of the body, are pretty nearly of the same opinion. For they differ in this respect: the former say that the mind itself is a substance, wherein the understanding is present as in a subject; but the latter declare that the mind itself is in a subject, that is, in a body of which it is the combination or harmony. (*De Trinitate* 10.10.15)

On Augustine's view, then, those who suppose that mind is something corporeal agree that the mind is something that understands, wills, and so forth. They just think that the thing that performs these functions is a body, or something bodily, such as a bodily harmony.

Augustine now returns to what he thinks he has established in the previous two books, that is:

(1) The mind knows and is certain concerning itself.

What (1) means includes the idea that:

(2) The mind knows and is certain that it is a mind.

The mind does not, according to Augustine, manage this feat by examining a number of instances of minds and figuring out what they have in common that makes them minds. Rather, he insists, the mind recognizes in itself what a mind is. This is part of thesis T.

Augustine continues his reasoning this way:

(3) If (a) the mind is something corporeal that understands,
    wills, thinks (etc.), then,
      if (b) the mind knows and is certain of its essence, then (c) the mind knows and is
certain that it is something corporeal.

Here is where Augustine's review of the various, and contradictory, theories of the corporealists comes into play. The divergences between their various theories, as well as the failure of any of them to command even general, let alone, universal consent, shows, he thinks, that

(4) The mind is not certain that it is anything corporeal.

So (c) above is false. Yet (b) is true. That is,

(5) The mind knows and is certain of its essence.

Thus the conditional in (3), if (b) then (c), is false. And so, by *modus tollens*, (a) is false. That is,

(6) The mind is not something corporeal that understands, wills, thinks (etc.).

Yet

(7) The mind is something that understands, wills, thinks (etc.).

What must be rejected is therefore the claim of corporeality. Thus,

(8) The mind is not a body, or anything bodily.

Here is the passage in which the core of this reasoning, (1) through (8), occurs:

All of these people overlook the fact that the mind [*mens*] knows itself, even when it seeks itself, as we have already shown. But we can in no way rightly say that anything is known while its essence [*substantia*] is unknown. Wherefore, as long as the mind knows itself, it knows its own essence [*substantia*]. And when it is certain of itself, it is certain of its essence [*substantia*]. But it is certain about itself, as what we have already said clearly demonstrates. But it is by no means certain whether it is air, or fire, or a body, or anything of a body. It is, therefore, none of these things. (*De Trinitate* 10.10.16)

The key word in this passage is "substantia," which, in the admirable translation by Stephen McKenna I have been using here, is rendered "substance." In the case of this passage, however, I have changed McKenna's "substance" to "essence." That alternative is licensed, I think, by Augustine's remark in book 5 of the same work that "the usage of our language has already decided that the same thing is to be understood when we say *essentia* as when we say *substantia*" (*De Trinitate* 5.9.10). It is underwritten, I think, by the realization that, according to Augustine, the mind couldn't just *happen* to be something corporeal. His idea seems to be that, if it is something corporeal, it is essentially corporeal.

In this argument Augustine rejects the possibility that, although the mind is indeed something that thinks, understands, wills, and so forth, and although the mind recognizes itself to be something that thinks (etc.), it does not know, or is somehow not certain, whether it is a *corporeal* thing that thinks (etc.). If the mind were something corporeal that thinks (etc.), he reasons, it would have to be essentially something corporeal. And if it failed to realize this, it would be unknown to itself in its essence. But, he asks, rhetorically, "What is so present to the mind as the mind itself" (*De Trinitate* 10.7.10). In being immediately and directly known to itself, Augustine reasons, the mind knows its own essence.

Augustine does not, however, rule out the possibility that some bodily condition must be satisfied for there to be a mind. Having read Descartes, we expect him to try to prove that I could exist, and therefore a mind exist, even though there were no bodies. Although there is one passage, in his *Against the Academicians*, in which Augustine entertains, briefly, the solipsist hypothesis,[13] he seems never to return to it again. He seems to take it for granted that, in this life anyway, he is a soul in a body.

As for the afterlife, Augustine has little to say about the environment of the soul in the period after bodily death and before the resurrection. This passage from his *Literal Commentary on Genesis* is as interesting for what it leaves out as for what it includes:

> But why must the spirits of the departed be reunited with their bodies in the resurrection, if they can be admitted to the supreme beatitude without their bodies? This is a problem that may trouble some, but it is too difficult to be answered with complete satisfaction in this essay. There should, however, be no doubt that a man's mind, when it is carried out of the senses of the flesh in ecstasy, or when after death it has departed from the flesh, is unable to see the immutable essence of God just as the holy angels see it, even though it has passed beyond the likenesses of corporeal things. This may be because of some mysterious reason or simply because of the fact that it possesses a kind of natural appetite for managing the body.[14]

So far as I can see, it is open to Augustine to say, somewhat in the fashion of Aquinas, that the mind is not really a complete thing without the body it, as he puts it in the passage above, "possesses a natural appetite for managing." I hasten to add that I know of no passage in which Augustine actually puts forward a positive claim along those lines.

In any case Augustine obviously thinks it is at least appropriate for us to have bodies in the resurrection, even if he remains somewhat puzzled about why we need them. The puzzlement is perhaps offset somewhat by Augustine's belief that the resurrection bodies will be much superior to the rather crude bodies we have had in this life. With the "pneumatic body" (soma pneumatikon) of the resurrection, he says, the soul "will have the perfect measure of its being, obeying and commanding, vivified and vivifying with such a wonderful ease that what was once [the soul's] burden will be its glory."[15]

THE WITTGENSTEINIAN CRITIQUE

The idea that one could come to know from one's own case what a mind is, or what thinking or feeling or having a pain is, has come in for a great deal of discussion in twentieth-century philosophy. "If one has to imagine someone else's pain on the model of one's own," writes Wittgenstein, "this is none too easy a thing to do: for I have to imagine pain which I *do not feel* on the model of the pain which I *do feel*." [16] Here is a passage from Norman Malcolm's essay, "Knowledge of Other Minds," in which Malcolm argues that the idea of such analogical reasoning is all a mistake:

> [T]he most fundamental error of the argument from analogy . . . is the mistaken assumption that *one learns from one's own case* what thinking, feeling, sensation are. . . .
>
> A philosopher who believes that one must learn what thinking, fear, or pain is "from one's own case," does not believe that the thing to be observed is one's behavior, but rather something "inward." He considers behavior to be related to the inward states and occurrences merely as an accompaniment or possibly an effect. He cannot regard behavior as a *criterion* of psychological phenomena: for if he did he would have no use for the analogical argument . . . and also the priority given to "one's own case" would be pointless. He believes that he notes something in himself that he calls "thinking" or "fear" or "pain," and then he tries to infer the presence of the *same* in others. He should then deal with the question of what his criterion of the *same* in others is. This he cannot do because it is of the essence of his viewpoint to reject circumstances and behavior as a criterion of mental phenomena in others. [17]

This is not the place to evaluate such criticism of the argument from analogy for other minds. I mention it only because it has occupied such a prominent place in recent philosophy and because its target is thesis T, as well as, of course, the internalist argument for mind–body dualism and the argument from analogy it inspires. Many people assume that it is Descartes who provides Wittgenstein and Malcolm with their target. But the thinking they criticize is not only present in Augustine but is more clearly present in him than it is in Descartes, who is often taken to be its progenitor.

In fact, as I have already pointed out, there is no statement of the argument from analogy for other minds in Descartes. Rather, Descartes assumes, without argument—indeed, without thinking that he needs an argument for this assumption—that other human beings have minds. Thus there is in him no extrapolation from one's own, singular, case; there is only a question about whether one can extrapolate from the general, human, case to any nonhuman cases. Although arguing from the general, human, case to the case of, say, nonhuman higher primates, or computers, does raise interesting and difficult philosophical issues, they are not the same issues as those discussed by, for example, Norman Malcolm in the quotation above.

Not surprisingly, there is in Descartes no clear statement of thesis T, either. Since it doesn't strike Descartes that there is a problem about how he knows that there are minds to go with other human bodies, he is not led to maintain, explicitly at least, that one comes to know, from one's own case, what a mind is. Of course, he conducts his philosophical investigation from his own, first-personal, point of view. But, since he doesn't see that there is a problem about how he knows that there are minds to go with other human bodies, he isn't led to formulate the Augustinian thesis that each mind knows what a mind is simply and solely by knowing itself.

NOTES

1. René Descartes, *Discourse on the Method*, pt. 4.
2. St. Augustine, *City of God* 11.26, my translation.
3. For my own attempt to accomplish this, see chaps. 3 and 4 of my book *Thought's Ego in Augustine and Descartes* (Ithaca: Cornell University Press, 1992).
4. René Descartes, *The Philosophical Writings of Descartes*, vol. 2, trans. J. Cottingham, R. Stoothoff, and D. Murdoch (Cambridge: Cambridge University Press, 1984), 21.
5. Ibid., 139–40.
6. Ibid., 140.
7. St. Augustine, *De Trinitate* 8.6.9, my translation.
8. Ibid.
9. As is shown in this passage:

AUGUSTINE: Come now, tell me; if I, knowing absolutely nothing of the meaning of the word [for walking], should ask you while you are in the act of walking what walking is, how would you teach me?

ADEODATUS: I should walk somewhat more quickly . . .

AUGUSTINE: Do you know that walking is one thing and hurrying another? (St. Augustine, *De magistro* 3.6)

10. *De Trinitate* 9.4.4. With one exception, yet to come, this and all later quotations from the *De Trinitate* will follow Stephen McKenna's fine translation (St. Augustine, *The Trinity* [Washington, D.C.: Catholic University of America Press, 1963]). Subsequent citations will appear in the text.
11. Plato, *Phaedo* 105d ff.
12. Ibid., 85e ff.
13. "And so I call this entire thing, whatever it is, which surrounds us and nourishes us, this object, I say, which appears before my eyes and which I perceive is made up of earth and sky, *or what appears to be earth and sky* [emphasis added], the world. If you say nothing is seen by me, I shall never err. . . . If you are asleep, you will say, is that also the world, which you see? I have already said I call that the world, which appears to me to be such" (St. Augustine, *Contra academicos* 3.11.24–25).
14. St. Augustine, *De Genesi ad litteram* 12.35.68.
15. Ibid.
16. Ludwig Wittgenstein, *Philosophical Investigations*, vol. 1 (Oxford: Basil Blackwell, 1967), 302.
17. Norman Malcolm, *Knowledge and Certainty* (Ithaca: Cornell University Press, 1963), 136–37.

THIRTEEN

Disputing the Augustinian Legacy*

John Locke and Jonathan Edwards on Romans 5:12–19

Philip L. Quinn

If St. Augustine were to appear today and enjoy as little authority as his modern defenders he would not accomplish anything. God has ruled his Church well by sending him earlier, and endowed with authority.

PASCAL, PENSÉES 517

One of Augustine's most impressive accomplishments was his complete triumph over his Pelagian opponents. As a result Augustinian accounts of major Christian doctrines and their scriptural bases came to dominate Western Christianity. But, though Augustine's achievement endured for over a millennium, it came under sustained attack in the modern disputes between Arminians and Calvinists. Arminians challenged both Augustinian understandings of doctrine and Augustinian scriptural exegesis. Calvinists responded by defending them both. This paper is about one such controversy that involved two great modern philosophers. It is a story of philosophers as biblical exegetes and also a case study from which I propose to draw a philosophical moral.

The Christian doctrine to be considered is the doctrine of original sin. The scriptural crux, both theologically and exegetically, is the difficult series of verses at Romans 5:12–19. The great philosophers who wrestled with interpreting them are the Arminian, John Locke, and the Calvinist, Jonathan Edwards. The paper has three parts. In the first I provide background information about the Augustinian account of original sin, its influence, and the problems of scriptural exegesis it involves. In the second I present Locke's interpretation of crucial aspects of Romans 5:12–19. And in the third I discuss the powerful critique Edwards directed against the Lockean interpretation of those verses he found in the work of John Taylor. In a brief conclusion I set forth my own evaluation of the Locke–Edwards controversy and speculate a bit about what contemporary philosophers might learn from it.

"IN QUO OMNES PECCAVERUNT"

Richard Swinburne devotes a chapter of his book on responsibility and atonement to the topic of original sin. According to Swinburne, a full doctrine of original sin

*I am grateful to Paul Weithman for comments on an earlier version of this chapter.

has three distinguishable components. The first, which he accepts, is the claim that there is a proneness to sin, an original sinfulness, in all humans (except perhaps for Jesus and his mother, Mary). The second, which he rejects, is the claim that it was the sin of the first sinner that caused in other humans original sinfulness, the proneness to sin, through their descent from Adam. And the third, which he also rejects, is the doctrine of original guilt, the claim that all of Adam's descendants, with the two possible exceptions already noted, are guilty for Adam's original sin. Swinburne rejects the doctrine of original guilt because he concludes that "no one can be guilty in a literal sense for the sins of another, unless he had some obligation to deter that person and did not do so. Since none of us today could have had the obligation to deter the first sinner from sinning, we cannot be guilty for his sins." [1]

Because it plays a crucial role in the debate between Arminians and Calvinists, let us think of the principle that no one can be guilty of the sins of another, appropriately qualified if necessary, as the Arminian assumption. Swinburne appeals to the prophets Jeremiah and Ezekiel for scriptural support of the Arminian assumption. They both quote the proverb, "The fathers have eaten sour grapes, and the children's teeth are set on edge." According to Ezekiel God's response is this: "For all lives are mine; the life of the father is like the life of the son, both are mine; only the one who sins shall die" (Ezekiel 18:4). And it continues thus: "Only the one who sins shall die. The son shall not be charged with the guilt of his father, nor shall the father be charged with the guilt of his son. The virtuous man's virtue shall be his own, as the wicked man's wickedness shall be his" (Ezekiel 18:20). Swinburne blames Augustine for fastening the doctrine of original guilt on the Western church for centuries. He notes that in the *Enchiridion* Augustine thinks of Adam's descendants as already contained seminally in him and for that reason guilty for his sin.

Why did Augustine subscribe to this harsh doctrine of original sin? No doubt he had several reasons. George Vandervelde summarizes one line of argument in this way:

> As proof of the culpable subjection of infants to original sin, Augustine adduces the practice of baptizing them in the remission of sins and the exorcism of the devil. From this liturgical practice Augustine concludes that, since he has not yet committed any personal sin, the infant is cleansed of original sin and thus liberated from the power of satan. Moreover, Augustine did not shrink back from affirming the corollary of this function of baptism: an infant dying without baptism suffers the punishment of hell. [2]

But it is clear that one of Augustine's reasons was that he thought Romans 5:12–19 stated the doctrine. For the sake of convenience, I reproduce the version of this passage Locke uses as his text:

V.12. Wherefore as by one man sin entered into the world, and death by sin; and so death passed upon all men; for that all have sinned.

13. For until the law sin was in the world, but sin is not imputed when there is no law.

14. Nevertheless, death reigned from Adam to Moses, even over them that had not sinned after the similitude of Adam's transgression, who is the figure of him that was to come:

15. But not as the offence, so also is the free gift. For if through the offence of one many be dead, much more the grace of God, and the gift by grace, which is by one man, Jesus Christ, hath abounded unto many.

16. And not as it was by one that sinned, so is the gift: for the judgment was by one to condemnation; but the free gift is of many offences unto justification.

17. For if by one mans offence, death reigned by one; much more they which receive abundance of grace, and of the gift of righteousness, shall reign in life by one, Jesus Christ.

18. Therefore as by the offence of one, judgment came upon all men to condemnation: even so by the righteousness of one, the free gift came upon all men unto justification of life.

19. For as by one mans disobedience many were made sinners: so by the obedience of one shall many be made righteous.[3]

How is this difficult text to be interpreted as support for Augustine's harsh doctrine? Elaine Pagels has recently popularized the notion that Augustine rests his case entirely on Romans 5:12, which he interprets idiosyncratically. She says:

> The Greek text reads, "Through one man [or "because of one man," $\delta\iota$' $\dot{\epsilon}\nu\grave{o}\varsigma$ $\dot{\alpha}\nu\theta\rho\dot{\omega}\pi o\upsilon$] sin entered the world, and through sin, death; and thus death came upon all men, *in that* [$\dot{\epsilon}\phi$' $\tilde{\dot{\omega}}$] all sinned." John Chrysostom, like most Christians, took this to mean that Adam's sin brought death into the world, and death came upon all because "*all* sinned." But Augustine read the passage in Latin, and so either ignored or was unaware of the connotations of the Greek original; thus he misread the last phrase as referring to Adam. Augustine insisted that it meant that "death came upon all men, *in whom* all sinned"—that the sin of that "one man," Adam, brought upon humanity not only universal death, but also universal, and inevitable, sin.[4]

And Pagels herself is rather harsh in judging Augustine for this misinterpretation. Her view is stated thus:

> Augustine attempts to rest his case concerning original sin, for example, upon the evidence of one prepositional phrase in Romans 5:12, insisting that Paul said that death came upon all humanity because of Adam, "*in whom* all sinned." But Augustine misreads and mistranslates this phrase (which others translate "in that [i.e., because] all sinned") and then proceeds to defend his errors *ad infinitum*, presumably because his own version makes intuitive sense of his own experience.[5]

The mistranslation about which Pagels complains does not appear in the text of Romans 5:12 to which Locke appeals, which is the Authorized (King James) Version. In that text the verse ends with the phrase "for that all have sinned," and this is close to the rendering Pagels favors, "in that [i.e., because] all sinned." Augustine's Latin phrase, "in quo omnes peccaverunt," translates nicely into the English phrase "in whom all have sinned." Thus understood, Romans 5:12 teaches that all have sinned in one man, Adam. This understanding has been very influential. For example, canon 2 of the Council of Trent's decree on original sin appeals directly to it:

> If anyone asserts that Adam's sin was injurious only to Adam and not to his descendants, and that it was for himself alone that he lost the holiness and justice which he had received from God, and not for us also; or that after his defilement by the sin of disobedience, he "transmitted to the whole human race only death" and punishment "of the body but not sin also, which is the death of the soul": let him be anathema. "For he contradicts the words of the Apostle: 'Through one man sin entered into the world, and through sin death, and so death passed upon all men; in whom all have sinned.'"[6]

But if "in quo" is a mistranslation of "ἐφ᾽ ᾧ," it is far from clear that one would contradict what the Apostle says in this verse if one were to deny that Adam transmitted sin, which is the death of the soul, to the whole human race.

Pagels is certainly correct in claiming that Augustine often appeals to Romans 5:12 to provide a scriptural basis for his doctrine of original sin. In a famous passage in the *Enchiridion* the connection is particularly direct:

> Having sinned, he [Adam] was banished from that place, and by his sin he laid upon all his descendants, whom he had vitiated in himself as their source, the penalty of death and condemnation. As a result all the children born of him and his spouse who had led him into sin and was condemned together with him—children born through carnal lust as a retribution in kind for the act of disobedience—contracted original sin. Because of this sin they were drawn through a variety of aberrations and sufferings to that final unending punishment together with the rebel angels, their corrupters and masters and companions. Thus, *by one man sin entered into the world, and by sin death; and so death passed upon all men, in whom all have sinned* [in quo omnes peccaverunt]. By the "world" the Apostle in that passage of course means the whole human race.[7]

By my count Augustine alludes to, paraphrases, or quotes Romans 5:12 at least fourteen times in *Contra Julianum*, a response to his Pelagian opponent Julian of Eclanum. Apparently Julian, like Swinburne, had cited Ezekiel against Augustine. Referring to the first of the two verses quoted above, Augustine's retort is that Julian has misunderstood it:

> For the last and supposedly strongest argument for your case, you refer to the prophetic testimony of Ezekiel, where we read that there will no longer be a proverb in which they say the fathers have eaten sour grapes and the teeth of the children are on edge; the son will not die in the sin of his father nor the father in the sin of his son, but the soul that sins, the same shall die. You do not understand that this is the promise of the New Testament and of the other world.[8]

According to Augustine what God communicated to Ezekiel was the New Testament's promise; only of those who have been cleansed of original sin by baptism is it true to say that only the one who sins shall die.

As the case of Aquinas shows, Swinburne's estimate of the influence of the Augustinian doctrine of original sin on the Western church is on the mark. Aquinas begins a question about original sin with an article on whether the first sin of our first parent is contracted by his descendants by way of origin. Among the objections to a positive answer he mentions the second of the two verses from Ezekiel quoted above, and he counters the objections by quoting the first half of Romans 5:12. His own answer goes as follows:

> According to the Catholic Faith we are bound to hold that the first sin of the first man is transmitted to his descendants, by way of origin. For this reason children are taken to be baptized soon after their birth, to show that they have to be washed from some uncleanness. The contrary is part of the Pelagian heresy, as is clear from Augustine in many of his books.[9]

And he has this to say in response to Ezekiel:

> The son is said not to bear the iniquity of his father, because he is not punished for his father's sin, unless he share in his guilt. It is thus in the case before us: because guilt is transmitted by the way of origin from father to son, even as actual sin is transmitted through being imitated.[10]

According to Aquinas there are exceptions to Ezekiel's rule. The son is not to be charged with the guilt of his father unless he shares that guilt, and in the case of original sin the son does share his father's guilt because guilt is transmitted by way of origin from father to son.

The third article of the same question is about whether Adam's sin is transmitted by way of origin to all his descendants. Aquinas counters the objections to a positive answer by quoting the second half of Romans 5:12: "On the contrary, The Apostle says: *Death passed upon all men in whom all have sinned* [in quo omnes peccaverunt]."[11] His own answer begins in this way: "According to the Catholic Faith we must firmly believe that, Christ alone excepted, all men descended from Adam contract original sin from him: else all would not need redemption which is through Christ; and this is erroneous."[12] And in the fifth article of that question Aquinas appeals again to Romans 5:12, this time to its assertion that sin entered the world by one man, to back his own claim that original sin is transmitted to the children not by the mother but by the father.[13]

As far as I can tell, contemporary biblical exegetes are close to a consensus in thinking that "ἐφ᾽ ᾧ" should not be translated as "in whom." In a paper first presented at a meeting of the Evangelical Theological Society, S. Lewis Johnson Jr. gives a terse summary of the difficulties under which the Augustinian reading labors. They are three in number:

(1) The normal force of ἐφ' ᾧ is opposed to *in whom;* ἐν would be much more natural. (2) The usage of ἐφ' ᾧ is opposed to his view. In the Pauline usage the phrase may mean *because* (cf. 2 Cor. 5:4), *for which* (cf. Phil. 3:12) or "for indeed" (Phil. 4:10), but never *in whom.* The same can be said for the other NT usages (cf. Luke 5:25; Acts 7:33). (3) The words ἑνὸς ἀνθρώπου are so far removed that they do not form an obvious antecedent.[14]

And he goes on to remark that translating ἐφ' ᾧ as "because" is something that now "has the overwhelming support of the commentators."[15] So it seems clear that we should agree with Pagels in thinking that Augustine misreads Romans 5:12.

But I think we should not go along with her assumption that Augustine's case rests entirely upon the evidence of one prepositional phrase in Romans 5:12. Henri Rondet, a French Jesuit, has explained why. After acknowledging that Julian of Eclanum, who knew Greek, understood that ἐφ' ᾧ should be translated as "quia (because)" and not as "in quo (in whom)," Rondet goes on to insist: "Augustine, unreliable exegete as he was with regard to detail, had nevertheless better understood the chapter as a whole and the force of verse 19: 'as by the disobedience of one man many were made sinners, so by the obedience of one man many will be made righteous.'"[16] So even if Romans 5:12 is not telling us that all sinned in Adam, it seems that Romans 5:19 is telling us that many were made sinners by Adam's first sin of disobedience. And this seems to support the Augustinian doctrine of original guilt according to which many, if not all, are guilty for Adam's original sin. Hence convicting Augustine of a misreading of Romans 5:12 does not by itself suffice to show that his doctrine of original sin lacks a scriptural basis in Romans 5. If one wants to undercut the harsh Augustinian doctrine by deconstructing its scriptural support, one will have to do more exegetical work than Pagels has done.

Can the extra work be done? John Locke tries to do it. So we next turn our attention to his attempt to grapple with the perplexities of Romans 5:12–19.

THE METONYMY GAMBIT

In Locke's day Calvinists accounted for original sin in terms of the so-called federal theology.[17] According to federalism Adam was, by covenant with God, the federal head or representative of the whole human race. All Adam's posterity stood their probation in him, and so his sin is imputed to them in consequence of his having fallen while acting as their covenant head. As the Puritan theologian John Preston puts it there was "a compact and covenant between God and him, that if *Adam* stood, all his seed should stand with him; but if he fell, then that all that were borne of him should by virtue of that covenant, compact or agreement have his sinne imputed to them, and so should be corrupted, as he was, and die the death."[18] Federal theologians do not deny that Adam's descendants were seminally present in him or that a sinful disposition is biologically transmitted from

Adam to his posterity. But they do insist that these biological facts, this natural solidarity of Adam's descendants with him, is insufficient to explain why the guilt of Adam's sin is imputed to his posterity. Thus, as one recent commentator remarks:

> The representative view insists that by divine appointment, in addition to being the *natural* head of the species, Adam was constituted the *covenant* head of his posterity. Therefore, the ground on which the guilt of the first sin is imputed to the species is that divinely ordained representative principle on the basis of which the species is reckoned to have stood its probation in Adam.[19]

So, on this view, although original sinfulness, the proneness to sinning, is biologically transmitted to Adam's descendants, the guilt of his transgression is imputed to them because he represented them when he first sinned by disobedience.

Many Calvinists distinguish between imputed sin and inherent sin, or between original sin as guilt and original sin as corruption. According to the theory of immediate imputation the guilt of Adam's first sin is directly imputed to his posterity, and so in them guilt logically precedes and is the ground of inherent sin or corruption. Adam's descendants are corrupt because they are guilty. According to the theory of mediate imputation, which originated with Josua Placaeus, the order is reversed; corruption in Adam's descendants logically precedes and is the ground of imputed sin or guilt. They are guilty because they are corrupt. C. Samuel Storms nicely captures the contrast between the two doctrines: "Thus whereas the former doctrine insists that the imputation of Adam's sin precedes corruption of nature and is reckoned to be its cause, the latter doctrine maintains that the imputation of Adam's sin follows hereditary depravity and is its effect."[20] And, naturally enough, there are disputes about whether scripture as a whole and Romans 5:12–19 in particular teach immediate imputation or mediate imputation.

Locke regards the federal theology as a pernicious extreme. In section 1 of *The Reasonableness of Christianity* he tells us we ought to conduct a diligent and unbiased inquiry in order to discover what scripture shows we lost by Adam because extreme views on this topic either shake the foundation of all religion or reduce Christianity to almost nothing. He then describes the extremes this way:

> For whilst some men would have all Adam's posterity doomed to eternal infinite punishment, for the transgression of Adam, whom millions had never heard of, and no one had authorized to transact for him, or be his representative; this seemed to others so little consistent with the justice or goodness of the great and infinite God, that they thought there was no redemption necessary, and consequently that there was none, rather than admit of it upon a supposition so derogatory to the honor and attributes of that infinite being; and so made Jesus Christ nothing but the restorer and preacher of pure natural religion; thereby doing violence to the whole tenor of the New Testament.[21]

According to Locke the federal theology seems inconsistent with the goodness of God because it condemns all of Adam's posterity to eternal punishment for his first sin, even though none of them had authorized him to act as a representative and many of them had never heard of him. So rather than deny the goodness of God, those who reject the federal theology go to the opposite extreme, deism, and reduce Jesus Christ to a mere preacher of natural religion. The federal theology is thus to be faulted for driving the morally sensitive into the arms of the deists.

In section 2 Locke ventures his own opinion about what scripture shows we lost by Adam. It was immortality. After Adam disobeyed the divine command "death then entered, and shewed his face, which before was shut out, and not known, so St. Paul, Rom. V. 12, 'By one man sin entered into the world, and death by sin'; i.e. a state of death and mortality: and I Cor. XV. 22, 'In Adam all die'; i.e. by reason of his transgression, all men are mortal, and come to die." [22] Of course, as Locke acknowledges in section 3, there is disagreement about how to interpret the doctrine that death came on all his posterity by Adam's sin:

> for some will have it to be a state of guilt, wherein not only he, but all his posterity was so involved, that every one descended of him deserved endless torment, in hell-fire. I shall say nothing more here, how far, in the apprehensions of men, this consists with the justice and goodness of God, having mentioned it above.[23]

But Locke does not need to say anything more to make it plain that in his apprehension at least such a state of guilt or imputed sin in Adam's posterity is not consistent with God's justice and goodness. Nor does he have kind words to say about inherent sin or corruption. In section 4 he observes:

> If by death threatened to Adam, were meant the corruption of human nature in his posterity, 'tis strange that the New Testament should not anywhere take notice of it, and tell us, that corruption seized on all because of Adam's transgression, as well as it tells us so of death. But, as I remember, every one's sin is charged upon himself only.[24]

Locke, then, accepts the Arminian assumption that no one can be guilty for the sins of another. He must therefore hold that death in Adam's posterity is not a punishment for Adam's first sin imputed to his descendants. In section 6 he claims precisely this, arguing that the state of immortality is not due to the posterity of Adam or to any creature. If God gives Adam's descendants temporary, mortal lives, they are gifts of God's bounty, and Adam's posterity cannot claim them as theirs by right. A fortiori, Adam's descendants have no right to immortality, and so God does not punish them by not giving them this gift. "And therefore," Locke concludes, "though all die in Adam, yet none are truly punished, but for their own deeds." [25] It is immortality, and only immortality, that we lost by Adam; death, and only death, came upon Adam's posterity by his first sin.

So Locke rejects the claim that Adam's first sin is imputed to his posterity either in the form of guilt or in the form of corruption. How is this to be reconciled with the teaching of Romans 5:12–19, particularly the claim of verse 19 that by one man's disobedience many were made sinners? To see how Locke answers this question, we must turn from *The Reasonableness of Christianity* to *A Paraphrase and*

Notes on the Epistles of St Paul. In this work, Locke begins by quoting the text of Romans 5:12–19 from the Authorized Version as I have reproduced it above. He then offers his own paraphrase of the text, and he defends or explains the paraphrase in a series of notes. Thus the paraphrase of verse 12, for example, goes as follows:

> Wherefore to give you a state of the whole matter from the beginning. You must know, that as by the act of one man Adam the father of us all, sin entered into the world, and death, which was the punishment annexed to the offence of eating the forbidden fruit entered by that sin for that Adams posterity thereby became mortal.[26]

In going from text to paraphrase Locke has made what appears to be a major change in the troublesome final phrase. He has replaced "for that all have sinned" with "for that Adams posterity thereby became mortal." What, for Locke, justifies making this change? The note to verse 12 explains:

> *Have sinned* I have rendered *became mortal* following the rule I think very necessary for the understanding St Pauls Epistles (viz) the making him as much as is possible his own interpreter. I Cor. XV. 22 cannot be denyed to be parallel to this place; this and the following verses here being, as one may say, a comment on that verse in the Cor: St Paul treating here of the same matter but more at large. There he says *As in Adam all die* which words can not be taken literally, but thus, that in Adam all became mortal. The same he says here but in other words, putting, by a noe very unusual metonymie the cause for the effect (viz) the sin of eating the forbidden fruit for the effect of it on Adam viz Mortality, and in him on all his posterity: A mortal father, infected now with death, being able to produce noe better than a mortal race. Why St Paul differs in his phrase here from that which we find he used to the Corinthians, and prefers here that which is harder and more figurative, may perhaps be easily accounted for if we consider his stile and usual way of writing, wherein is shewn a great likeing of the beauty and force of antitheses as serving much to illustration and impression. In the XV. Cor: he is speaking of *life* restored by Jesus Christ, and to illustrate and fix that in their minds, the *death* of mankind best served: Here to the Romans he is discoursing of *righteousness* restored to men by Christ, and therefore here the terme *sin* is the most natural, and properest to set that off. But that neither actual nor imputed sin is meant here or ver. 19 where the same way of expression is used he that has need of it may see proved in Dr Whitby upon the place: If there can be any need of any other proof when it is evidently contrary to St Pauls designe here which is to shew that all men from Adam to Moses died solely in consequence of Adams transgression: see ver. 17.[27]

But the supposedly not unusual metonymy, which involves putting the cause, Adam's sin, for the effect, his mortality, is nonetheless no small thing. As a recent book about Locke on depravity points out it committed him to reading verse 12 "in what was an unquestionably Pelagian sense."[28] On this interpretation not only does that verse not teach that all have sinned in Adam, it does not even teach that all have sinned. If Locke is right, it speaks neither of Adam's sin being imputed to his posterity nor of the universality of actual, personal sins among Adam's descendants. Let us think of this clever hermeneutical ploy as the metonymy gambit.

It is, of course, easy to extend the metonymy gambit to verse 19, and this is just what Locke does. His paraphrase of that verse goes as follows: "For as by one mans disobedience many were brought into a state of mortality which is the state of sinners soe by the obedience of one shall many be made righteous, i e be restord to life again as if they were not sinners." [29] The note to this verse is terse: "*Sinners.* Here St Paul uses the same metonymie as above ver. 12 putting *sinners* for *mortal* whereby the Antithesis to righteous is the more lively." [30] On this reading verse 19 does not tell us that many were made sinners by Adam's disobedience; instead it merely informs us that many were made mortal by that act. To be sure, Locke does not deny that these mortals, or at least those among them who outlive infancy, are sinners. For Locke sin was "very unPelagian in its universality, in the sorry fact that each and every individual had opted for the way of sin at some point in his life, thus making necessary Christ's sacrifice." [31] This is why mortality is, in fact, the state of sinners. But their sins are their own doing; Adam's sin and its guilt are neither transmitted nor imputed to them.

But does the metonymy gambit work? Does it really allow us to read Romans 5:12–19 in a way that renders it consistent with the Arminian assumption? Jonathan Edwards argues that it does not. So now we turn to his attempt to defend an old-fashioned Calvinistic interpretation of those verses. It is part of a heroic effort to defend an account of original sin that was increasingly under attack in the eighteenth century.

THE GREAT CHRISTIAN DOCTRINE OF ORIGINAL SIN DEFENDED

It would make a nice story if Edwards had responded directly to Locke's reading of Romans 5:12–19. Unfortunately, history is not this tidy, and the connection is indirect. Locke's *A Paraphrase and Notes on the Epistles of St Paul* was published in installments in the period 1705–7. It contributed to a rising tide of Arminianism in both Great Britain and America. Another contribution worth mentioning is *A Free Inquiry into the Nature and Origin of Evil* by Soame Jenyns, published in 1757 in London. Clyde A. Holbrook summarizes Jenyns' views about original sin in this way:

> The term "original sin," Jenyns explained, was a contradiction in terms, since "original" meant "innate," and "sin" referred to the "act of an accountable being." Original sin therefore cannot mean original or innate guilt "for that is absolute nonsense," but it can only mean "original depravity or an innate disposition to sin." [32]

Yet another is Samuel Webster's *A Winter Evening's Conversation upon the Doctrine of Original Sin,* published in New Haven in the same year. According to Webster, "sin and guilt (so far as I can see) are personal matters, as much as knowledge, and I can as easily conceive of one man's knowledge being imputed to another as of his sins being so." [33] But the most influential contribution was made by John Taylor of Norwich in the form of *The Scripture-Doctrine of Original Sin, Proposed to Free and Candid Examination* (1738) and *A Supplement to the Scripture-Doctrine of Original Sin* (1741).

The first of these is a substantial treatise. In a later work Taylor boasts by telling the story of a Calvinist pastor in northern Ireland who "warned his flock against its pernicious teachings, calling it a 'bad book and a dangerous book and an heretical book,' but woefully conceding that it was unanswerable."[34] In *The Great Christian Doctrine of Original Sin Defended* (1758) Jonathan Edwards answered Taylor. And, according to a tale told by Sereno Dwight, his reply "was so devastating that Taylor's days were shortened by mortification!"[35]

Taylor acknowledged the influence of Locke. In his *A Paraphrase with Notes on the Epistle to the Romans* (1745) he says this: "But to Mr. *Locke* I am so much indebted, for the sense of the Epistle, that I question whether I could have wrote my Paraphrase and Notes, had he not first written his."[36] He shares many of Locke's views about original sin. Like Locke, and for similar reasons but with greater indignation, he rejects the federal theology's account of Adam's covenantal headship or representation of the whole human race. In the *Scripture-Doctrine* he says this:

> But that any man, without my knowledge or consent, should so represent me, that when he is guilty I am to be reputed guilty, and when he transgresses I shall be accountable and punishable for his transgression, and thereby subjected to the wrath and curse of God, nay further that his wickedness shall give me a sinful nature, and all this before I am born and consequently while I am in no capacity of knowing, helping, or hindering what he doth; surely anyone who dares use his understanding, must clearly see this is unreasonable, and altogether inconsistent with the truth and goodness of God.[37]

Not only is this unreasonable, it is, for Taylor, downright wicked. In the *Supplement* he makes the point with even greater vehemence: "A representative of moral action is what I can by no means digest. A representative, the guilt of whose conduct shall be imputed to us, and whose sins shall corrupt and debauch our nature, is one of the greatest absurdities in all the system of corrupt religion."[38] Moreover, like Locke, Jenyns, and Webster, Taylor denies the doctrine of original guilt because he accepts the Arminian assumption. In language that is echoed by Webster he observes of the sin of the progenitors of the human race that

> as the evil action they committed was personal, done only by them; so also must the real Guilt be personal, and belong only to themselves; that is, no other could, in the Eye of Justice and Equity, be blameable and punishable for that Transgression, which was their own Act and Deed, and not the Act and Deed of any other Man or Woman in the World.[39]

According to Taylor, then, guilt is not imputed to Adam's posterity on account of his disobedience; nor does corruption come down to Adam's descendants from him. So it is not unfair to suppose that, when Edwards attacks Taylor, he is attacking a Lockean position on these matters.

Nor is this the end of the similarities between Locke and Taylor. Like Locke, Taylor applies the metonymy gambit to Romans 5:12 and 5:19; unlike Locke, he tackles the latter verse first and then deals with the former quite briefly. According to Taylor, in verse 19 Paul means "neither more nor less, than that by one Man's Disobedience, *the many*, that is, Mankind, were made subject to Death, by the judicial Act of God." [40] In support of this reading he cites the Hebraic use of metonymy in several Old Testament texts. And, in the following passage, he makes it clear that he interprets Paul as he does in order to avoid the doctrine of original guilt by imputation:

> Now any one may see, there is a vast Difference between a Man's making *himself* a Sinner by his *own* wicked Act, and his being made a Sinner, by the wicked Act of *another*, of which he is altogether guiltless. They who are *made Sinners* by the Disobedience of *another*, without their own Knowledge or Consent, surely *can* be *Sinners* in no other sense, but as they are *Sufferers*. *They* are *Sinners* by sharing in the Calamities of those that have sinned; which may be, without any Wrong to them, by the just Appointment of God, not as a Punishment, but for other good Reasons. [41]

So, for Taylor, those who are said to be made sinners by Adam's disobedience share in the sufferings, but not in the guilt, consequent upon it. Hence the death they suffer is no punishment. And the transfer of this line of thought to verse 12 is accomplished by means of a single rhetorical question:

> Seeing then the Phrase (*all are made sinners*, ver. 19.) hath been demonstrated to signify; *all are subjected to Death by the judicial Act of God;* and seeing the Apostle's whole Argument turns upon this Point, that all Men die, not thro' their *own* Sins, but thro' the one Offence of *Adam*, who can doubt but the Words, *for that all have sinned*, must be understood in a like sense to those, *all are made Sinners*, however the particular manner of Expression be accounted for? [42]

Thus, if Taylor is right, the final phrase of verse 12, "for that all have sinned," actually means "for that all have become subject to death." In this respect, too, Taylor is a good Lockean.

Jonathan Edwards argues at great length that Taylor is not right on these exegetical points. He concedes that in some places in the Old Testament, such as Jeremiah 51, Genesis 20:9 and 31:39, and 2 Kings 7:9, "Hebrew words, which signify sin, iniquity, and wickedness, are sometimes put for the effect or punishment of iniquity, by a metonomy of the cause for the effect." [43] But he denies that these uses of metonymy support Taylor's rejection of the doctrine of original guilt because

> it does not appear, that these words are ever used for enduring suffering, where the suffering is not spoken of under any notion of a punishment of sin, or a fruit of God's anger for sin, or of any imputation of guilt, or under any notion of sin's being at all laid to the charge of the sufferer, or the suffering's being at all of the nature of any recompense, compensation, or satisfaction for sin. [44]

According to Edwards the suffering referred to in all these instances is punishment for sin, and so they actually undermine Taylor's view that the many, who are subjected to death by Adam's disobedience, do not suffer it as a punishment for the guilt of sin. He goes on to suggest, by means of a series of rhetorical questions, that Taylor's interpretation is quite alien to the usage of the New Testament in general and of Paul in particular. With reference to Paul, Edwards asks:

> He abundantly uses the words "sin" and "sinner"; his writings are full of such terms: but where else does he use them in such a sense? He has much occasion in his epistles to speak of death, temporal and eternal; he has much occasion to speak of suffering, of all kinds, in this world, and the world to come: but where does he call these things "sin," and denominate innocent men "sinners" or say, "they have sinned," meaning that they are brought into a state of suffering?[45]

And if Paul does not speak in such ways elsewhere, one cannot help suspecting that applying the metonymy gambit to Romans 5:12 and 19 is an ad hoc device being used solely to evade the doctrine of original guilt.

Edwards also argues that Taylor's reading of verse 12 labors under the inconvenience of assigning to the word "sinned" a meaning very different at the end of the verse from that assigned to "sin" earlier in the same verse and in the next verse, as well as from that assigned to "sinned" in verse 14. He says:

> Here, by "sin," implied in the word, "sinned," in the end of the sentence, our author understands something perfectly and altogether diverse from what is meant by the word "sin," not only in the same discourse, on the same subject, but twice in the former part of the very same sentence, of which this latter part is not only the conclusion, but the explication: and also entirely different from the use of the word twice in the next sentence, wherein the Apostle is still most plainly discoursing on the same subject, as is not denied: and in the next sentence to that (v. 14) the Apostle uses the very same verb, "sinned," and as signifying the committing of moral evil, as our author himself understands it.[46]

This is more evidence that reading "for that all have sinned" at the end of verse 12 as "for that all have become subject to death" is completely ad hoc, if not clearly mistaken. And, not content with merely criticizing Taylor's interpretation of this verse, Edwards proceeds to offer his own paraphrase of it. It goes as follows:

> The things which I have largely insisted on, viz. the evil that is in the world, the general wickedness, guilt and ruin of mankind, and the opposite good, even justification and life, as only in Christ, lead me to observe the *likeness* of the manner, in which they are each of them *introduced*. For it was by one man, that the general corruption and guilt which I have spoken of, came into the world, and condemnation and death by sin: and this dreadful punishment and ruin came upon all mankind, by the great *law of works*, originally established with mankind in their first father, and by his *one offense*, or breach of that law; *all* thereby becoming sinners in God's sight, and exposed to final destruction.[47]

This is, of course, no theologically neutral paraphrase of Romans 5:12. It contains a capsule summary of the federal theology's account of Adam's covenantal headship of the whole human race. What is more, Edwards also thinks this verse teaches a doctrine of the imputation of Adam's sin to his posterity. In the last paragraph of the long chapter he devotes to interpreting Romans 5:12–19 Edwards says this:

> As this place in general is very plain and full, so the doctrine of the corruption of nature, as derived from Adam, and also the imputation of his first sin, are both clearly taught in it. The imputation of Adam's one transgression, is indeed most directly and frequently asserted. We are here assured, that "by one man's sin, death passed on all"; all being adjudged to this punishment, as having sinned (so it is implied) in that one man's sin.[48]

Thus Edwards concludes his case for the scriptural rootedness of the doctrine of original guilt.

What are we to make of this case? I myself find his arguments against Taylor's interpretation of Romans 5:12–19 persuasive, and so I conclude that the Locke–Taylor metonymy gambit fails. Moreover, though I lack the expertise in biblical scholarship to be confident in this judgment, I am inclined to think that the Edwardsian interpretation of Romans 5:12, or something much like it, remains defensible, though not coercive, at present. After giving reasons for rejecting several alternatives, Johnson, in the paper cited above, presents six arguments combining exegetical and theological considerations for the conclusion that this verse is best interpreted in the light of the theory of immediate imputation. He summarizes his conclusion as follows:

> the connection between Adam's sin and universal human sinfulness and death is most lucidly explicated by the doctrine of immediate imputation. Adam, our federal representative, failed his probation and plunged his posterity into sin, wrath, and judgment, imputed to them directly. As a result of his fall, all men enter life "constituted sinners" before God—their only hope being the imputation of righteousness provided by God through the saving work of the last Adam, the federal head of the company of the elect.[49]

I think Johnson has made a fairly strong but not conclusive cumulative case for thinking that Romans 5:12–19 is best interpreted as supporting this conclusion. And, of course, this conclusion appears to be inconsistent with the Arminian assumption.

In an excellent recent discussion of Edwards on original sin William J. Wainwright discusses five models of the moral or legal relation that might be involved in Adam's being the covenantal head or representative of his posterity. Having found philosophical reasons to reject them all, Wainwright comes down squarely on the side of the Arminian assumption: He says: "One must have committed an act to be guilty of it, and one cannot commit another's act. Thus, even though liability can be transferred from one person to another, guilt cannot. Adam's posterity cannot be guilty of Adam's fault unless Adam's act is somehow *literally* their own."[50] Unfortunately, he does not devote much attention to what Edwards has to say about scripture since his concern is not the scriptural warrant of the doctrine of original guilt but the arguments Edwards gives for its rationality. However, in a note appended to his claim that the texts Edwards cites do not clearly show that Adam's guilt is ours, Wainwright does say this:

> It is important to distinguish the following claims: (1) Because of Adam's sin, we are subject to death. (2) Because of Adam's sin, our nature has been vitiated, i.e., our mind has been darkened, our concupiscence awakened, our will weakened, etc. (3) Because of Adam's sin, we are guilty. The first is clearly taught by scripture; 2, and possibly 3, might be inferred from (e.g.) Romans 5. Nevertheless, it is worth remembering that 3 was not widely held before Augustine.[51]

But the fact that it was not widely held before Augustine that we are guilty because of Adam's sin might be explained by the sort of assumption that Rondet makes when he says that Augustine had a better understanding of Romans 5 as a whole than did Julian of Eclanum. It may well be that Augustine had a better understanding of that chapter than did his predecessors. And it is far from being a matter of universal agreement among the relevant contemporary experts that the doctrine of original guilt is merely a possible inference from Romans 5. If scholars such as Johnson who attend to both exegetical and theological considerations are right, a fairly strong cumulative case can be made for the conclusion that the doctrine of original guilt is part and parcel of the best available interpretation of that chapter.

I think friends of the Arminian assumption who also want to take this Pauline text seriously still have work to do if they are to succeed in rebutting this case. As far as I can tell, the interpretation that Edwards favors has not been shown to be, at least in its broad outlines, mistaken or rationally indefensible.

CONCLUSIONS

Like Locke, Jenyns, Webster, and Taylor among our intellectual ancestors, and like Swinburne and Wainwright among our contemporaries, I am powerfully attracted to the Arminian assumption on moral grounds independent of my theological beliefs. So I hope there is a solution to the problem of reconciling the teaching of Romans 5:12–19 with that assumption. It is greatly to their credit that people like Locke and Taylor recognized the problem, took it seriously, and proposed a solution. But, as I see it, the Locke–Taylor metonymy gambit does not solve the problem; this is what Edwards succeeded in showing. Can an adequate solution to the reconciliation problem be found? I do not know.

As long as such a solution is not forthcoming Augustine's legacy remains a problem for those who would like to accept both the Arminian assumption and the teaching of Romans 5:12–19, properly understood. This is a group to which many contemporary Christian philosophers, myself included, belong. It may be that we cannot have our cake and eat it too. If that is so, we will confront an unhappy choice. Christians ought to be reluctant to reject the teaching of this Pauline text. Of course it is possible to take the teaching of a scriptural text seriously and yet dissent from it for weighty reasons, and there is no doubt that the intuitions that support the Arminian assumption are weighty in the minds of many Christians. They ought also to be reluctant to fly in the face of such intuitions. So if the choice is forced by the absence of a solution to the reconciliation problem, it will not be and, indeed, should not be an easy one.

We Christian philosophers who remain stuck in this predicament on account of the continuing vitality of the Augustinian tradition have a stake in the outcome of the contemporary continuation of the Locke–Edwards controversy over how to read such texts as Romans 5:12–19. Since we have a stake in its outcome, we should get involved in the debate, and we will have to engage more closely with biblical exegesis than has been customary for philosophers in the recent past in order to do so. It has been nearly two-and-a-half centuries since Edwards wrote to defend Calvinism's federal theology of original sin against the Arminians, and biblical scholarship has undergone large changes in the intervening period. But I think both Locke and Edwards as biblical exegetes continue to be exemplary in at least three ways. One is the depth of their engagement with Augustine's legacy. Another is the seriousness of their concern with scriptural exegesis and the time they were willing to devote to exegetical work. The third is the intelligence, learning, energy, and passion they brought to the formidable task of interpreting such theologically and exegetically tangled knots as Romans 5:12–19. I suggest that they are models today's Christian philosophers ought to admire and strive to emulate.

NOTES

1. Richard Swinburne, *Responsibility and Atonement* (Oxford: Clarendon Press, 1989), 144–45.

2. George Vandervelde, *Original Sin* (Washington, D.C.: University Press of America, 1981), 19.

3. John Locke, *A Paraphrase and Notes on the Epistles of St. Paul*, vol. 2 (Oxford: Clarendon Press, 1987), 523.

4. Elaine Pagels, *Adam, Eve, and the Serpent* (New York: Random House, 1988), 109.

5. Ibid., 143. Incidentally, the point Pagels makes here was made by Erasmus almost five centuries ago. In his *Paraphrase on Romans* (1517) Erasmus takes a Pelagian line on Romans 5. His paraphrase of Romans 5:12 goes as follows: "Accordingly, through Adam alone, who first transgressed the law of God, sin crept into the world, and sin dragged along death as its companion inasmuch as sin is the poison of the soul. And so it happened that the evil originated by the first of the race spread through all posterity, since no one fails to imitate the example of the first parent" (*Collected Works of Erasmus*, vol. 42 [Toronto: University of Toronto Press, 1984], 34). In their note to the second of these sentences John B. Payne, Albert Rabil Jr., and Warren S. Smith Jr. credit Erasmus with being "the first in the history of Western exegesis to understand the ἐπί here as having a causal sense ('because all have sinned')" (147). But Erasmus can hardly have been the first, since Augustine attacks Julian of

Eclanum, his Pelagian opponent, for doing so at *Contra Julianum* 6.75. Erasmus's paraphrase of the first half of verse 19 repeats the Pelagian point about imitation: "one man, Adam, by his failure to submit to the precept of God, dragged very many into sin as imitators of the transgression of their ancestor" (*Collected Works of Erasmus*, 42:35–36).

6. Heinrich Denzinger, *Enchiridion symbolorum*, quoted in Vandervelde, *Original Sin*, 35.

7. St. Augustine, *Enchiridion* 26.

8. St. Augustine, *Contra Julianum* 6.82.

9. St. Thomas Aquinas, *Summa theologiae* 1a2ae.81.1.

10. Ibid., 1a2ae.81.1.1.

11. Ibid., 1a2ae.81.3.

12. Ibid.

13. Ibid., 1a2ae.81.5.

14. S. Lewis Johnson Jr., "Romans 5:12: An Exercise in Exegesis and Theology," in Richard N. Longenecker and Merrill C. Tenney, eds., *New Dimensions in New Testament Study* (Grand Rapids, Mich.: Zondervan, 1974), 304–5.

15. Ibid., 305.

16. Henri Rondet, *Original Sin: The Patristic and Theological Background*, trans. Cajetan Finegan (Shannon, Ireland: Ecclesia Press, 1972), 129.

17. For a recent, prize-winning study of this aspect of Calvinist thought, see D. A. Weir, *The Origins of the Federal Theology in Sixteenth-Century Reformation Thought* (Oxford: Clarendon Press, 1990).

18. John Preston, quoted in William J. Wainwright, "Original Sin," in Thomas V. Morris, ed., *Philosophy and the Christian Faith* (Notre Dame: University of Notre Dame Press, 1988), 42.

19. C. Samuel Storms, *Tragedy in Eden: Original Sin in the Theology of Jonathan Edwards* (Lanham, Md.: University Press of America, 1985), 227.

20. Ibid., 228.

21. John Locke, *The Reasonableness of Christianity*, ed. I. T. Ramsey (Stanford: Stanford University Press, 1958), 25.

22. Ibid., 26.

23. Ibid.

24. Ibid., 27.

25. Ibid., 28.

26. Locke, *Paraphrase*, 2:523.

27. Ibid., 523–24. Dr. Whitby is Daniel Whitby of Salisbury, who was the author of *A Paraphrase and Commentary on all the Epistles of the New Testament* (1700), which later formed part of *A Paraphrase and Commentary on the New Testament* (1703). For a brief discussion of his relations to Locke see Arthur W. Wainwright, "Introduction," in Locke, *Paraphrase*, 1:12.

28. W. M. Spellman, *John Locke and the Problem of Depravity* (Oxford: Clarendon Press, 1988), 150.

29. Locke, *Paraphrase*, 2:527.

30. Ibid.

31. Spellman, *John Locke and the Problem of Depravity*, 151.

32. Clyde A. Holbrook, "Original Sin and the Enlightenment," in Robert E. Cushman and Egil Grislis, eds., *The Heritage of Christian Thought* (New York: Harper and Row, 1965), 149.

33. Samuel Webster, *A Winter Evening's Conversation upon the Doctrine of Original Sin,* quoted in Clyde A. Holbrook, "Editor's Introduction," in Jonathan Edwards, *Original Sin* (New Haven: Yale University Press, 1970), 12.

34. John Taylor, *History of the Octagon Church, Norwich* (1848), quoted in Holbrook, "Editor's Introduction," 3.

35. *The Works of President Edwards* (1829–30), 1:613.

36. John Taylor, *A Paraphrase with Notes on the Epistle to the Romans* (1745), quoted in Wainwright, "Introduction," 67.

37. John Taylor, *The Scripture-Doctrine of Original Sin, Proposed to Free and Candid Examination* (1738), quoted in Storms, *Tragedy in Eden,* 225.

38. John Taylor, *A Supplement to the Scripture-Doctrine of Original Sin* (1741), quoted in Storms, *Tragedy in Eden.*

39. Taylor, *Scripture-Doctrine,* quoted in Storms, *Tragedy in Eden.*

40. Taylor, *Scripture-Doctrine,* quoted in Storms, *Tragedy in Eden,* 42.

41. Taylor, *Scripture-Doctrine,* quoted in Storms, *Tragedy in Eden.*

42. Taylor, *Scripture-Doctrine,* quoted in Storms, *Tragedy in Eden,* 43.

43. Edwards, *Original Sin,* ed. Holbrook, 326–27.

44. Ibid., 327.

45. Ibid., 329.

46. Ibid., 331.

47. Ibid., 344.

48. Ibid., 348.

49. Johnson, "Romans 5:12: An Exercise in Exegesis and Theology," 313.

50. Wainwright, "Original Sin," 47.

51. Ibid., 58.

FOURTEEN

Augustine, Kant, and the Moral Gap

John E. Hare

AUGUSTINE AND LUTHER ON THE MORAL GAP

This essay is about an Augustinian theme that emerges in Kant, especially in his later works in the philosophy of religion. The theme is the gap between what God demands of us and our natural capacities after the fall to meet that demand. Augustine lays out a series of doctrines about God's assistance to human beings, and these doctrines explain how it is reasonable, even given our natural incapacity, to think of ourselves as under the demand; it is not that we are unable to meet God's demand but that we are unable to do so without his assistance, and the demand has the function of causing us to see the need to ask for his help. This structure comes to Kant through Luther and the Reformation. But Kant undertakes the project of translating these doctrines within the limits of the pure religion of reason. This essay is about what the doctrines look like after the translation.

It is not my concern to engage in a detailed exegesis of Augustinian texts. I will start, however, by locating in some familiar places the theme of the moral gap. In the tenth book of *Confessions* (10.29.40) Augustine prays to God, "And my whole hope is only in Thy exceeding great mercy. Give what Thou commandest, and command what Thou wilt." In support Augustine quotes a passage from the Wisdom of Solomon that he quotes about twenty times in his works.[1] Whether the reference of this passage is to continence, as Augustine supposed, or to wisdom, the point is that God's command is met only by God's gift. The view is that, in what matters most to our lives, the relationship with God, we are unable by our natural devices to provide the means to repair the damage that has been produced by our own sin. "Can men do anything by the free determination of their own will?" Augustine asks; and the answer is, "Far be it, for it was by the evil use of his free will that man destroyed both it and himself" (*Enchiridion* 30). God demands of us, then, what we cannot by our own devices supply; but he offers to us the means to supply it. "God bids us do what we cannot, that we may know what we ought to seek from him" (*De libero arbitrio* 16.32). It might be thought that we can at least ask on our own for his assistance. But Augustine denies this. "This is also of the divine gift," he says, "that we pray; that is, that we ask, seek, and knock" (*De dono persever- antiae* 23.64).

This combination of doctrines was recovered as one of the main theological in- spirations of the Reformation. Luther and Calvin quote Augustine more often than any other theologian and see themselves as recapturing his emphases and his spirit for the condition of the church at their time. Again, it is not my purpose to discuss the use the Reformers made of Augustine. I want to go past them to Kant. But I will make a few references to Luther on the way. Kant grew up in a pietist Lutheran home and went to pietist Lutheran school. We should expect to hear Luther in his work, mediated through the pietists such as August Hermann Francke and Philipp Jakob Spener.[2] I will try to show that Kant remains closer to his upbringing than is usually supposed. Before I do this, however, I want to locate in Luther the theological theme of human helplessness in sin and divine sover- eignty in grace. Like Augustine, Luther holds that the commands of God are given not because we can meet them on our own but because we can thereby see our need for his assistance. "Reason thinks that man is mocked by an impossible commandment, whereas I maintain that by this means man is admonished and awakened to see his own impotence."[3] Luther compares the image of parents teaching their children to walk. "How often do parents thus play with their chil- dren, bidding them come to them, or do this or that, only in order that it may ap- pear how impotent they are, and that they may be compelled to call for the help of the parent's hand?"[4] We start off, in this doctrine, as slaves to sin, despising God. "And doubtless that ignorance and contempt are not seated in the flesh, in the sense of the lower and grosser affections, but in the highest and most excellent powers of man, in which righteousness, godliness, and knowledge and reverence of God should reign—that is, in reason and will, and so in the very power of 'free- will,' in the very seed of uprightness, the most excellent thing in man." He con- tinues, "Where reason is in error and the will turned away, what good can man at- tempt or perform?"[5]

KANT'S USE OF SCRIPTURE

In Kant's later work this theme is emphasized. He gives it, moreover, scriptural warrant, as both Luther and Augustine regard themselves as bound to do. Before describing Kant's treatment of the theme, therefore, I wish to discuss briefly his use of scripture. This is one place where the secondary literature has put him fur- ther from traditional Christianity than he belongs. It is said, for example, that Kant is a deist about special revelation, allowing only for God's revelation to human reason, which is universal in all human rational agents. Or it is said that Kant made concessions to traditional Christianity to appease his faithful manservant or the Prussian censors.[6] But Kant himself is fiercely attached to sincerity both in the content and the form of what he writes, and we should not interpret him as disguising the truth about his views unless we have to.[7] We would have to do this if there were no other responsible interpretation of the texts in which he talks about his relation to scripture, but there is in fact a perfectly good interpretation of him that uses a label he himself invented, namely "pure rationalist." To be a pure rationalist in his sense is to accept special revelation but not to regard this acceptance as necessary for every rational agent.[8] The pure rationalist is thus unlike both the naturalist, who does not accept special revelation at all, and the pure supernaturalist, who thinks acceptance is necessary for all rational agents. For Kant the Christian scriptures are a vehicle of what he calls pure rational religion, or the religion of pure reason. This latter is all that is necessary for saving faith; but there may be many people (including Kant himself) who have been introduced to this pure rational religion by the Bible. For such people the Bible was necessary in their personal history and may continue to be necessary in order to "strengthen [the moral precepts of reason] within their souls."[9]

In the preface to the second edition of *Religion within the Limits of Reason Alone* Kant suggests that we try the experiment of thinking of revelation as like two concentric circles. In the inner circle is the religion revealed to pure reason and in the outer circle (the region of the larger circle not covered by the smaller) the revelation to historical faith. The experiment will be successful if we can show that the contents of the two areas are not only consistent with each other but have the sort of unity that means that a person who follows the prescriptions of the one will also be following those of the other. To demonstrate this kind of consistency and unity, he proposes to translate the central items of the historical faith into language available to the philosopher in the inner circle. This translation will use the moral concepts, which operate (as reason always does) without the use of singular terms.[10] Thus the categorical imperative requires the agent to will the maxim of her action as a universal law.[11] The interpretation of this formula is complex and controversial. I will say here, dogmatically, that the formula requires the agent to continue subscribing to the prescription that calls for the action even when all singular terms have been eliminated from the maxim. The agent is thus not allowed to mention herself and has to prescribe for the situation as if she did not know which role in it she was going to play. Suppose that we now try to understand the central doctrines of the historical faith, namely creation, fall, redemption, and second coming, "in the light of the moral concepts." This would mean that they have to be understood without reference to the Garden of Eden or Sinai or Calvary. Kant accomplishes this translation, as we shall see in more detail later, by reading language about the Trinity in terms of moral demand, moral disposition, and humanity in its moral perfection. In this way the Christian doctrines can be stated without making reference to the three persons: God the Father, God the Holy Spirit, and God the Son.

SPENER'S PROBLEM

This is the project; and we can now look at how Augustine's theme is repeated and changed in carrying this project out. The first point to make is that Kant recognizes what he calls "Spener's problem," after the famous pietist Philipp Jakob Spener. The problem is, how can we become *other* men and not merely better men (as if we were already good but only negligent about the degree of our goodness)?[12] The problem is one that Kant elsewhere expresses in terms of "ought" and "can," just as Luther and Augustine had done before him. If the morally good life is one that we cannot live, because of the corruption of our initial dispositions, then it seems it is not a life that we ought to live. But this conclusion is, to Kant, intolerable. One way out of the difficulty is to deny the initial premise about the corruption of our dispositions. But Kant is not willing to do this either. In this matter *Religion* represents an advance over the *Groundwork*. The fundamental moral battle, as it is presented in *Religion*, is not between respect for the moral law and respect for the inclinations. Rather it is between the good maxim, which subordinates the inclinations to duty, and the evil maxim, which reverses this order of incentives. The good maxim tells us to pursue our own happiness only in as far as this is consistent with our duty. The evil maxim makes our happiness a condition of following the moral law. *Both* of these maxims reside in the will, and a fundamental choice has to be made between them. Here Kant is like Luther, who says that the ignorance and contempt (of God) are not located in the flesh, in the sense of the lower and grosser affections, but in the highest and most excellent powers of men (the reason and the will).[13] The choice for the evil maxim is a choice of our wills and is thus imputable to us. But it is also, in Kant's view, innate. We are *born* with the propensity to evil, even though it is also true that we are born with the predisposition to good (what Luther calls "the seed of uprightness"). Kant here recapitulates the structure of creation and fall. The predisposition to good is overlaid with the innate (but imputable) propensity to evil and survives only as a seed of goodness that cannot develop (as it otherwise would) into a good disposition. Here, then, is Spener's problem. If we are initially under the evil maxim, how can we accomplish the revolution of the will that is necessary to take us into submission to the good maxim? How can a person, as Kant also says, become "a new man"? He is clear that, since the propensity to evil is radical, it is inextirpable by human powers, "since extirpation could occur only through good maxims, and cannot take place when the ultimate subjective ground of all maxims is postulated as corrupt."[14] What we have here is an antinomy, an apparent contradiction within practical reason. Kant solves it by appeal to a "higher, and for us inscrutable, assistance."[15]

We have to distinguish, however, between his appeal to divine grace in the outer of his two circles and his appeal as translated within the inner circle. It is the translation process that accounts for Kant sounding both Augustinian, when he is talking about the outer circle, and hyper-Pelagian, when he is talking within the inner circle, the religion of pure reason. This strange transformation is what I want to focus on for the rest of this essay.

THE STOIC MAXIM

To see what the Christian doctrines look like after translation, we will start with what I shall call (following Nicholas Wolterstorff) "the Stoic maxim," that a person herself must make or have made herself into whatever, in a moral sense, whether good or evil, she is to become.[16] Kant is talking here about our making ourselves good, in contrast with ascribing this making us good to God. He is not talking about an individual making herself good as opposed to ascribing the creation of her goodness to other human beings.[17] He puts this constraint negatively as follows: "the calling to assistance of works of grace cannot be adopted into the maxims of reason, if she is to remain within her limits."[18] Note that Kant here is not saying that we ought not to believe in works of divine grace. On the contrary his view is that we are required to believe in them. What he says is that reason cannot adopt divine grace into its maxims (at least, not without translation). In expanding on this constraint we can distinguish between reason in its theoretical and its practical employments and see how Kant cannot allow the appeal to divine assistance in the maxims of either one.[19] Theoretical reason is constrained by the categories of the understanding, so that we cannot talk about knowing what we could not experience with the senses. In particular the categories of cause and effect are constrained in this way, so that reason in its theoretical employment has to forgo appeal to causes (like divine grace) that we could not possibly experience. Reason in its practical employment operates with maxims governing the actions of the agent. We cannot reason practically, Kant says, about what some other agent (for example, a divine agent) would have to do. We cannot, therefore, make use of divine grace in the maxims of either theoretical or practical reason. We may, nonetheless, have to make room (*einräumen*) for divine grace in our *belief*. The reason we may have to do so is that we are faced otherwise with the antinomy of practical reason, or with Spener's problem.

The Stoic maxim seems, on its face, to deny God's assistance in making us good. But it does not in fact do so, as is clear in the context in which Kant introduces it. After stating the maxim he first gives the reason for us to believe it. "Otherwise," he says, "man could not be held responsible for [being or becoming good or evil] and could therefore be *morally* neither good nor evil." The argument here is that, if we are morally good or evil, we must be responsible for becoming or being so, and therefore we must produce or have produced this character in ourselves. When we say, therefore, that we were created good, or that our initial predisposition is good, we do not mean, Kant says, that we are already actually good; rather, we bring it about that we become good or evil depending on whether we choose to put ourselves under the good or evil maxim. Then he goes on, "Granted that some supernatural cooperation may be necessary to [man's] becoming good, or to his becoming better, yet, whether this cooperation consists merely in the abatement of hindrances or indeed in positive assistance, man must first make himself worthy to receive it, and must *lay hold* of this aid (which is no small matter)—that is, he must adopt this positive increase of power into his maxim, for only thus can good be imputed to him and he be known as a good man." The need for supernatural cooperation is granted here in response to Spener's problem. As elsewhere in *Religion* we are told that this cooperation may take a positive or negative form, either the removal of hindrances or a positive increase of power.[20] This passage adds, however, some instruction about what attitude to take within the inner circle, the pure religion of reason, to this divine assistance. We should say that we have to think of ourselves as making two contributions: first making ourselves worthy of the assistance and, second, laying hold of it, or choosing in our maxims to receive it. This passage tells us that we must do so *if* we are to be or to become morally good. But the hypothetical is removable. It is Kant's doctrine that we *are* under the moral law. This is what he calls in the second critique the fact of reason.[21] If we are, then we are responsible, and therefore we have to regard ourselves as making these two contributions. Within the inner circle, then, Kant sounds like Pelagius. Pelagius held that we retain after the fall our freedom of choice, at least in the sense of "the capacity of abstaining from sin." [22] As reported by Augustine he said "that what is good is more easily [facilius] fulfilled if grace assists" (*Contra duas epistolas Pelagianorum* 2.8.17). As in Kant's inner circle we have the responsibility of asking on our own for grace, even though grace may be necessary for doing what is good. But then we are faced immediately with the antinomy produced by the admission we have already made that these contributions are impossible for us. This is what Kant immediately confronts. "How it is possible for a naturally evil man to make himself a good man wholly surpasses our comprehension; for how can a bad tree bring forth good fruit?" I will return to this difficulty in a moment, but first I want to describe what the doctrine of God's assistance looks like when translated within the inner circle, the pure religion of reason.

KANT'S TRANSLATION OF JUSTIFICATION AND ATONEMENT

I suggested earlier that in translating "in the light of the moral concepts" Kant operates with the rule that the categorical imperative also prescribes, namely the elimination of singular reference. I will try now to describe briefly how the work of God is translated under this constraint. I will take as a paradigmatic example Kant's treatment of justification and atonement.

Justification is the Christian doctrine according to which God sees us as just by imputing to us his Son's righteousness. According to the Lutheran *Formula of Concord* "He bestows and imputes to us the righteousness of the obedience of Christ; for the sake of that righteousness we are received by God into favor and accounted righteous."[23] Kant puts this doctrine by saying that God judges us as a completed whole "through a purely intellectual intuition."[24] Intellectual intuition is, in Kant's vocabulary, productive. That is, God makes what he sees in this way; he does not merely receive it. So justification, in this view of the doctrine, is constitutive, not merely negative.[25] The heart, as it is seen by God after justification, is "essentially well-pleasing to him," even though all we experience in our lives is a gradual process of reformation or improvement, not a revolution of the will. But what does this doctrine mean within the pure religion of reason, after translation? It means that a human being comes to have a morally good disposition when the idea of holiness countenances the disposition as instantiating humanity in its moral perfection.

The doctrine of the atonement is translated by taking Christ as the "new man" after the revolution of the will that takes a person from a life under the evil maxim to a life under the good. There is, Kant points out, considerable sacrifice involved in this revolution. There is the pain of discipline, the remorse, and the reparation. The new man, we can say, takes these sacrifices vicariously as a punishment on behalf of the old man, who properly deserves them. As in the traditional Christian account it is the innocent who suffers on behalf of the guilty.

We have in these translations a reading of the three persons of the Trinity. Christ is understood as humanity in its moral perfection. This premise means that man, so conceived, is not created but begotten (through eternity), that all things are made for him, and that he is the brightness of God's glory. Kant ends this list with studied nonchalance: "Only through him (that is, mankind in his moral perfection) and through the adoption of his disposition can we hope 'to become the sons of God,' etc."[26] Kant is here suggesting that we do the same kind of translation with all the rest of traditional Christian doctrine about the Son of God. God the Spirit is translated as the good disposition, which exists within us, is seen as our "Comforter," and provides us with assurance (through our actions, which are its fruits) of its own presence within us. God the Father is translated as the idea of holiness. This is an idea that humans will never realize, because holiness of the will requires the absence of independent inclinations. Humans do, however, have in them the Idea of holiness, even though they do not have holiness of the will.

It is easy for traditional Christians to feel offended by the translation project itself, but I think this is a mistake. Hauerwas and Willimon, for example, say "by the very act of our modern theological attempts at translation, we have unconsciously distorted the gospel."[27] It is a different complaint, which I shall make myself, that Kant's actual translation *fails.* I shall claim that his translation of historical faith within the pure religion of reason fails to do the work he needs it to do in answer to Spener's problem. But there is nothing in itself damaging to traditional Christianity in the project of seeing how much of the traditional doctrine can be understood in terms of general revelation or the revelation to reason. It *would* be distorting the gospel if we were to go on to say that we should believe only in the doctrines as translated. But Kant does not say this. Indeed, as I have argued, he denies it.

The translation of the doctrines of justification and atonement can be connected with the Stoic maxim as follows. We know by the translation of these doctrines that humanity has to provide its own salvation. In Christian doctrine salvation is in Christ alone. Once we translate Christ as "humanity in its moral perfection," salvation will lie in humanity alone. We can understand this in terms of happiness and virtue. What we need, if we are to believe that Providence will give us eternal happiness, is a belief that we can become worthy of such happiness (that we can become virtuous). But with the translation of the Christian doctrine of justification within the pure religion of reason this means that we can rely only upon humanity to give us this virtue. And this is the Stoic maxim. "Man himself must make or have made himself into whatever, in a moral sense, whether good or evil, he is to become."

THE FAILURE OF THE TRANSLATION

I claimed that Kant's translation failed to do the work he needed it to do in answer to Spener's problem. He is faced with a dilemma. Either he is going to allow himself within the pure religion of reason to make use of the appeal to extrahuman assistance, or he is not. If he does not, and this is the first horn of the dilemma, he is left with Spener's problem and the antinomy of practical reason. The problem is not that he has an obligation to show us *how* extrahuman assistance might save us. Kant can legitimately say that speculation about this matter is out of bounds to human reason, going beyond the limits of human understanding. The problem is that he has to show us *that* he can appeal to extrahuman assistance. If he cannot show us this, we will be left inside the inner circle with the violation of the principle that "ought implies can," since the overcoming of our adherence to the evil maxim, which reverses the proper order of incentives, "could occur only through good maxims, and cannot take place when the ultimate subjective ground of all maxims is postulated as corrupt." [28] This reversal is *both* a condition for any moral improvement *and* something we cannot accomplish on our own. What the translations make clear is that Kant does take this horn of the dilemma. This is true whether he is translating the doctrine of God's call, or election, or atonement, or justification, or sanctification. I have not given the details of most of these translations in this essay, but they all follow the same paradigm as do the translations of the doctrines of justification and atonement, which I briefly described. He does not rule out the possibility of extrahuman assistance, but he cannot *use* this assistance within the maxims of theoretical or practical reason, and therefore he cannot use it within the pure religion of reason.

On the other hand Kant might take the second horn of the dilemma and admit works of grace within the pure religion of reason. He might admit that they are necessary at the very beginning, necessary for the revolution of the will, and necessary, as Augustine says, even for the asking of assistance. Now Kant can solve Spener's problem. But he has not solved the antinomy, because he is now faced with an impossibility on the other side. It is impossible on his principles for reason to admit works of grace, since reason cannot admit the irreducibly particular. This difficulty can be stated in two ways. First, there is the difficulty that God's choosing some people for salvation and not others, without making this choice on the basis of differential merit, is arbitrary when considered morally. This is why Kant calls the doctrine of election in its Augustinian form the "*salto mortale* of human reason."[29] He is happy to attribute belief in this kind of work of grace, the election of a special people, to the Jews. But it is this very belief that disqualifies Judaism, on his view, from setting up the universal church. He does not think the Jews had a *moral* relation to God at all.

There is a second and more basic way to state the difficulty. Inside the religion of pure reason we are operating only with maxims that allow the elimination of singular reference. This is the way I described, dogmatically, the operation of the categorical imperative in its first formula, the formula of universal law. I am not allowed by morality to make special reference to myself or any other particular person or place or time. Of special relevance in the present context is that I am not allowed to make reference to God, except as this reference is translated in some of the ways we have been considering. This view of reason is not confined to practical reason. Science also is seeking for universal laws. The scientist is not interested in whether some particular copper sulphate crystal changed color at a certain temperature but in the law governing what any substance of this kind does in this kind of circumstance. In the same way Kant sees the moral agent as looking for the universal law governing what any agent should do in situations of a certain kind, where (I have argued) the agent does not know which *role* in the situation he or she is going to play.

PRACTICAL REASON AND PARTICULARITY

Though I cannot argue for this here, it seems to me a mistake to think that practical reason requires universalizability of this kind. Much recent work in ethical theory casts doubt on this assumption, some but not all of it in feminist ethics. I have given elsewhere a defense of the thesis, which I call "particularism," the view that moral judgments do not have to be universalizable in all their term positions.[30] Though some of morality requires universalizability in all term positions, not all morality does so. I distinguish between various positions in a moral judgment about a proposed action. There is the position of the agent, of the addressee, of the recipient, and of the action to be done by the agent to the recipient. It is possible for moral judgments to be universalizable in the action position, but not in the other three. The Ten Commandments, for example, as initially addressed to the people of Israel, told them never anywhere to commit adultery. But these commandments were part of the covenant between a particular people and their God, even though traditional Christianity has taken them to apply eventually to all people. For a universalist, they are *moral* in character only if they so apply. But this is a restriction that is comparatively recent in the history of philosophy. In Aristotle, for example, our moral relations are always to this family, or this *polis*. It is possible to be related to another person, for example a friend, in such a way that one treats him as an end in himself and therefore, as Kant says, shares his ends as far as the moral law allows; but one may not be committed in one's moral judgments that have him in the recipient position to treating anyone else, even any other friend, in the same way one thinks one ought to treat him. These "particular" moral judgments are like fully universalizable moral judgments in two ways; they treat another person as an end in herself, and they give reasons for action. They do this because they prescribe that, whenever my friend Tom is in some kind of circumstance, I should act in a certain way. But they do not prescribe such action toward anyone else, even anyone else in Tom's sort of position.

We need a distinction, then, like the one Augustine makes between two forms of rational activity and two forms of excellence, namely wisdom and knowledge (*sapientia* and *scientia; De Trinitate* 12.15). He says that the intellectual cognizance of eternal things belongs to wisdom but the rational cognizance of temporal things to knowledge. He therefore puts action, by which we use temporal things well, in the domain of knowledge and contemplation of eternal things in the domain of wisdom. Augustine has a particular view of the hierarchy between these two, which orders *scientia* teleologically to *sapientia*. But we do not need to follow him here, and in particular we do not need to suppose (like Kant) that *God's* moral thinking has to be of the universalizing sort. Even if we grant that God is to be seen as rational, there is nothing in the formal conditions of practical reason to prevent him choosing a particular people for salvation. There is also nothing in the formal conditions of practical reason to prevent our including reference to God in the maxims of our actions.

This particularist view will probably not be persuasive without further argument. If it is right, however, we can see a basic mistake in Kant. He wants to restrict practical reason too narrowly and therefore to restrict theology within the limits of reason alone too narrowly. If I am right that practical reason allows singular reference, it can allow singular reference to God. It may be that there are doctrines, such as the ones Kant attempts to translate, that *can* help with Spener's problem, even though (as I have argued) they cannot help as translated. If Kant is wrong about the demands of reason, then reason could use these doctrines to escape the antinomy, produced by the moral gap, within its practical sphere. It is not the purpose of this essay, however, to explore further whether this is so. Another possibility is that these doctrines, in the form in which Kant inherited them from Luther and eventually from Augustine, are liable to insuperable objections. All I have done is to show how Kant can start from doctrines about radical evil that are very close to Augustine and then, because of his views about reason and the constraints it imposes, end up with a translation that is very far from him. I have also urged that these doctrines after translation cannot do the work in Kant's moral philosophy that he shows he needs them to do.

NOTES

1. See Harry Wolfson, "Philosophical Implications of the Pelagian Controversy," *Proceedings of the American Philosophical Society* 103 (1959): 558, who argues that Augustine has misunderstood the Greek text, which refers to wisdom and means "And as I knew that I could not otherwise obtain it, except God gave it."

2. Francke and Spener are credited with shifting the religious emphasis of the entire age "from 'true' doctrine to right action, from theological speculation to devotional earnestness, from ontological to psychological interest, from an intellectualized to an experiential approach to the Christian faith, from systematic theology to biblical exposition, from that which God has done in history to that which he wants to do in every human being now, from passive reliance on God's initiative to human responsibility" (F. Ernest Stoeffler, *German Pietism during the Eighteenth Century* [Leiden: E. J. Brill, 1973], 23). It is easy to trace most of these emphases in Kant.

3. Martin Luther, *The Bondage of the Will*, trans. J. I. Packer and O. R. Johnston (Old Tappan, N.J.: Revell, 1957), 158.

4. Ibid., 152.

5. Ibid., 280–81.

6. I am replying here to Allen Wood, "Kant's Deism," in Phillip Rossi and Michael Wreen, eds., *Kant's Philosophy of Religion Reconsidered* (Bloomington: Indiana University Press, 1991), who attributes deism of this kind to Kant and describes Kant as "cushioning his evident denial of supernaturalism" (11). See also Heinrich Heine, *History of Philosophy and Religion in Germany*, trans. John Snodgrass (Boston: Beacon Press, 1959), 119, "Old Lampe must have a God, otherwise the poor fellow can't be happy," put into the mouth of Kant. See also Yirmiahu Yovel, *Kant and the Philosophy of History* (Princeton: Princeton University Press, 1980), 114: "cover techniques."

7. Immanuel Kant, *The Conflict of the Faculties*, trans. Mary J. Gregor (New York: Abaris Books, 1979), 19 (10). Here, as in all references to works by Kant, the second page number (in parentheses) is from the Prussian Academy edition.

8. Here I am paraphrasing Kant, *Religion within the Limits of Reason Alone*, trans. Theodore M. Greene and Hoyt H. Hudson (New York: Harper and Row), 142 (156). I give a fuller defense of the claim that Kant is a pure rationalist in *The Moral Gap* (Oxford: Clarendon Press, 1996), 41–45.

9. Kant, *Conflict of the Faculties*, 77 (44).

10. Kant does not actually put his principle this way, since this way of putting it relies on developments in logical theory after his death. See R. M. Hare, "Could Kant Have Been a Utilitarian?" *Utilitas* 5 (1993): 1–16, for a defense of this understanding of Kant's view.

11. Kant's formulation is "Act only on that maxim through which you can at the same time will that it should become a universal law" (*Groundwork of the Metaphysics of Morals*, trans. H. J. Paton [New York: Harper and Row, 1964], 88 [421]).

12. Kant, *Conflict of the Faculties*, 97 (54).

13. In the *Groundwork,* by contrast, Kant tends to locate the source of evil in the inclinations. Kant was reading Plato's *Phaedo* as he wrote the *Groundwork,* and there is the same tendency in the *Phaedo.*

14. Kant, *Religion with the Limits of Reason Alone,* 32 (37).

15. Ibid., 41 (45).

16. Ibid., 40 (45). See Nicholas Wolterstorff, "Conundrums in Kant's Rational Religion," in Rossi and Wreen, eds., *Kant's Philosophy of Religion Reconsidered,* 48.

17. Kant does have a view, however, about the assistance of other human beings. He denies that we can suppose that associating with other human beings will produce our goodness. Human morality has particular difficulties to encounter that are specific to human beings and not, for example, angels. See Steven Smith, "Worthiness to Be Happy and Kant's Concept of the Highest Good," *Kant-Studien* 75, no. 2 (1984): 172. Kant says, "Envy, the lust for power, greed, and the malignant inclinations bound up with these, besiege his nature, contented with itself, *as soon as he is among men.*" He sounds here like Rousseau. It is what we are to each other that brings on the evil inclinations. This is consistent with saying that we have an innate propensity to evil, for it is the association with others that is the occasion for the propensity to produce its evil fruit.

18. Kant, *Religion within the Limits of Reason Alone,* 48 (53).

19. I am paraphrasing Kant's argument, ibid., 48 (53).

20. Francke has this same dichotomy, illustrated vividly in his account of his own conversion. See Peter C. Erb, *Pietists: Selected Writings* (New York: Paulist Press, 1983), 105.

21. See Louis White Beck, *A Commentary on Kant's Critique of Practical Reason* (Chicago: University of Chicago Press, 1960), 166ff., and Henry E. Allison, *Kant's Theory of Freedom* (Cambridge: Cambridge University Press, 1990), 231–39.

22. Pelagius, *Contra Julianum opus imperfectum* 1.78.

23. *The Formula of Concord,* pt. 1, chap. 3, aff. 2.

24. Kant, *Religion within the Limits of Reason Alone,* 60–61 (67).

25. For a treatment of different theologies of justification and their connection with Kant see Hare, *Moral Gap,* 259–63.

26. Kant, *Religion within the Limits of Reason Alone,* 54 (62).

27. Stanley Hauerwas and William H. Willimon, *Resident Aliens* (Nashville: Abingdon Press, 1989), 21.

28. Kant, *Religion within the Limits of Reason Alone,* 32 (37).

29. Ibid., 111 (121).

30. See Hare, *Moral Gap,* chap. 6.

FIFTEEN

Augustine and Rousseau

Narrative and Self-Knowledge in the Two *Confessions*

Ann Hartle

In his profound and illuminating essay "St. Augustine and the Modern World" Erich Przywara writes that "the modern world is indeed the advent of Augustine, but an advent to overcome it from within."[1] The truth of Przywara's claim is manifest in the presentation of the self in Rousseau's *Confessions*. I believe that a case can be made that Rousseau deliberately wrote his *Confessions* as a response to the *Confessions* of St. Augustine. But even if this were not so, a comparison of the two works reveals the extent to which "the transition to modernity required the repudiation of characteristically Augustinian modes of thought, feeling and action."[2] This paper will explore one aspect of the search for self-knowledge as it is conducted in very different ways in the two *Confessions*.

INTRODUCTION

In books 1–9 of his *Confessions* Augustine presents a kind of narrative of his life, himself, as it were, spread out over time. This narrative presentation of himself is necessary but not sufficient for the task he has set himself.

While Augustine is "in time" his self-knowledge and happiness are radically imperfect. It is only in union with God that he will see and be what he truly is. Augustine tells us this in the same passage in which he expresses the problem of time and self-knowledge:

> But because *Thy loving kindness is better than all lives*, see, my life is a kind of distraction and dispersal. And *Thy right hand upheld me* in my Lord, the *Son of Man, the Mediator betwixt Thee*, the One, and us, the many (many also in our many distractions over so many things), so that *through Him I may apprehend in whom I have been apprehended* and that I may be gathered up from my former days to follow your Oneness, *forgetting what is behind*, not wasted and scattered on things which are to come and things which will pass away, but intent and *stretching forth to those which are above*—no longer distracted

but concentrated *as I follow on for the prize of my heavenly calling,* where *I may hear the voice of Thy praise,* and contemplate Thy delight which is neither coming nor passing. But now *are my years spent in mourning,* and you, my comfort, my Lord, my Father, are eternal. But I have been divided up in time whose order I do not know; my thoughts, the innermost bowels of my soul, are torn apart with the crowding tumults of variety, and so it will be until all together I can flow into you, purified and molten by the fire of your love.[3]

Augustine cannot now grasp all that he is. He will see himself, see what he is, only when he "stands" in God, in his "own true form" (11.30). Only when he no longer moves through time, only when he is gathered up, will he know what he is, see his life for what it is. It is God who knows Augustine, and Augustine does not have access to God's knowledge: he does not see as God sees.

When Augustine recognizes his dissipation, his distraction over many things, he returns to his own self. "I entered into the innermost part of myself, and I was able to do this because you were my helper. I entered, and I saw with my soul's eye (such as it was) an unchangeable light shining above this eye of my soul and above my mind" (7.10). Entering into the innermost part of oneself (the mind) is not sufficient to know oneself. What is revealed to the soul's eyes is not the self into which one has entered but something *above* the mind. The unchangeable light above the mind points up the radical deficiency of the mind to see itself. Augustine can see the light above the mind only because God is his helper. What this light enables him to see is that his mind (his self) is to be understood only in terms of what is other than (above) his mind and what must be shown to him.

The self, then, is seen only when it has been transcended. Augustine permits us a glimpse of this transcendence in his recounting of the incident that takes place shortly before his mother's death. Augustine and his mother are alone, looking out a window over the garden. They are talking about what the eternal life of the saints could be like. They agree that the greatest possible delights of the bodily senses do not even deserve mention when compared with the joys of eternal life.

Then, with our affections burning still more strongly toward the Selfsame, we raised ourselves higher and step by step passed over all material things, even the heaven itself from which sun and moon and stars shine down upon the earth. And still we went upward, meditating and speaking and looking with wonder at your works, and we came to our own souls, and we went beyond our souls. (9.10)

Beyond their souls is eternal wisdom, in whom there is no place for "to have been" or "to be going to be." And Augustine and his mother "just lightly came into touch with her." Before death one might have only this briefest glimpse, this moment of understanding, of what eternal life will be. This moment takes one beyond the self, beyond or above what has been and what is going to be. If one seeks wisdom, one cannot stop in the soul, in the innermost self. The self can be seen only for what it truly is from above the self and thus from outside the self. This perspective on the self, on one's own life, is proper to God alone.

Rousseau, however, claims a "divine" perspective on his life: he sees man from the standpoint of the divinity.[4] He claims the perspective that, for Augustine, is proper only to God. That is, Rousseau claims to know himself in a way in which Augustine cannot claim to know himself, for Rousseau claims a perspective outside of time. This becomes apparent from the very opening paragraphs of *The Confessions.* What Rousseau says of himself in *The Confessions* is what he would say of himself on the day of the last judgment. He says to the "Eternal Being," "I have unveiled my interior as you yourself have seen it" (17). Rousseau sees himself as God himself would see him: he sees himself precisely as he *is.* The standpoint of the Eternal Being is a standpoint outside of time. For God there is no past and future; for God there is only the eternal now. Rousseau, then, does not claim the standpoint of the Eternal Being because of any knowledge of the future. He speaks of "contingent futures." And even his knowledge of his past is incomplete and inaccurate. In spite of his poor memory and his inability to see the future, he can reveal himself as God himself, the Eternal Being, would see him.

What Rousseau claims to see and reveal, then, is not the story of his life insofar as his life is the details of his life. The reader can "finish knowing a man" by finishing his *Confessions.* It is not necessary to know all the details of Rousseau's life to know him. Yet *The Confessions* takes the form of a chronicle of the details of his life, a chronicle that is halted almost eight years before his death. If a man is not simply the sum of what happens to him, then why present the portrait of a man as he is according to nature in the form of a story of a life, of what he did and what happened to him?

The form of Rousseau's presentation seems even more puzzling when one considers certain passages in which he comments on his enterprise. In book 2 he pauses to justify his recording of the minute details of certain incidents. His enterprise is that of showing himself "entirely." To accomplish this, Rousseau must make sure that nothing remain obscure or hidden; the reader must not lose sight of him for a single instant. There must be no voids, no gaps, no occasion for asking "What has he done during that time?" In book 4 he claims that, to render his soul transparent to the eyes of the reader, no movement of his soul must pass unperceived. He is simply "saying all," detailing all that happened to him, all that he did, thought, and felt.

Augustine, on the other hand, does not even attempt a detailing of all that happened to him. He chooses certain incidents in which he sees most clearly the action of God in his life.[5] The gaps in his story are obvious. The form of Augustine's *Confessions* is a prayer. Within the context of this prayer of praise he recounts certain incidents in which God's providence is most manifest to him. Augustine makes no attempt at a coherent tale, an uninterrupted history. The unity of Augustine's story is in terms of God's providence.

The gaps in Rousseau's story are hidden: *The Confessions* has the appearance of a coherent tale. But Rousseau *has* selected certain incidents and omitted others. And he admits to voids by referring to gaps that are caused by his poor memory.

Yet those gaps do not affect the completeness of his story. Rousseau is revealing his *interior,* what he truly is. He is not the sum of all that he does and all that happens to him. When Rousseau seeks to reveal himself, seeks to grasp and show what he is, he reenters himself. "The single object of my confessions is to make known exactly my interior in all the situations of my life. It is the history of my soul that I have promised, and in order to write it faithfully I do not need other memoirs: it is sufficient for me, as I have done until now, to re-enter inside myself." The perspective of the divinity is not above him, outside him, but precisely within him. Rousseau is not "divided up in time," whose order he does not know. His memory is poor, he cannot see the future, and his present is in darkness. Yet he sees himself as the Eternal Being would see him. Rousseau is "always the same at all times" (257).

The problem of time and self-consciousness is the problem of grasping the self that seems to be "dissipated" in a past that is no longer, a present that one cannot get hold of, and a future that is not yet. Augustine claims he will know himself only when he "stands" in God, only when he is no longer "in time," and Rousseau claims to see himself from a perspective outside of time. What is to be considered here is the question of the grounds for the making of these claims. That is, why does Augustine claim that he cannot fully grasp what he is and why does Rousseau claim that he sees himself as he is? The problem of time and self-consciousness gives way to a discussion of memory and imagination as instruments in the achievement of self-awareness, for these faculties would seem to be our only access to the past that is no longer and the future that is not yet.

AUGUSTINE ON "RECOLLECTION"

Augustine's account of his conversion is presented at the very end of book 8 of his *Confessions.* In book 9, chapter 1, he asks the question, "Who am I and what am I?" But Augustine asks this question about himself after he asks, "O Lord, who is like unto Thee?" and he asks the question about himself not of himself but of God. The question "Who am I and what am I?" is followed by Augustine's account of his baptism, his "rebirth," and of his mother's death. The concluding paragraph of book 9 contains Augustine's plea to God that his parents be "remembered" by those "who are my brethren under you, Our Father, in our Catholic mother [the church] and my fellow citizens in the eternal Jerusalem for which your people in their pilgrimage sigh from the beginning of their journey until their return home" (9.13). Augustine sees himself as a child of God and of the church and thus as a pilgrim. His life, like that of his mother Monica, is a pilgrimage, a journey toward God. The life of the pilgrim is continuous movement from birth (baptism) to death.

Augustine *must* ask the question "Who am I and what am I?" of God, for while he is a pilgrim, while he is "on the way," he cannot grasp who he is. But Augustine shows us his attempt to grasp himself and in doing so reveals the futility of that attempt. The futility of the attempt sheds light on what he is.

It might be said that the subject of book 10 of Augustine's *Confessions* is memory. In some sense this is obvious, for most of the book is devoted to a discussion of memory. Yet the very obviousness of the concern with memory may work to conceal the context in which the question about memory is raised. If this context is overlooked, the question about memory cannot be seen for what it is.

Augustine begins book 10 with the prayer "Let me know You, my knower; *let me know Thee even as I am known.*" Augustine asks that he may know God even as God knows Augustine. Augustine's first request is that he may know *God;* he does not first ask that he may know himself.[6] He asks that he may know as he is known. It is only then that he takes up, raises again, the question about himself. "Who am I and what am I?" is first the question about God's knowledge of Augustine and not Augustine's knowledge of himself. "For *Thou, Lord, dost judge me;* because, although *no man knoweth the things of a man, but the spirit of a man which is in him,* yet there is still something of man which even the spirit of man that is in him does not know. But you, Lord, know all of him, you who made him" (10.5). God the Creator knows perfectly what he has made; man, the creature, does not know himself perfectly. And while he is "in time," man is faced with the radical imperfection of his knowledge of God and of himself.

> *Certainly now we see through a glass darkly,* and not yet *face to face,* and so as long as I am on pilgrimage away from You, I am more present to myself than to you; . . . So I will confess what I know of myself, and I will also confess what I do not know of myself; because what I know of myself I know by means of your light shining upon me, and what I do not know remains unknown to me until *my darkness be made as the noonday* in your countenance. (10.5)

It is because he is more present to himself than to God that Augustine's knowledge of himself becomes the subject of inquiry.

But why does Augustine make this *public* inquiry about himself? He tells us that he does so at the command of God for the sake of his "fellow pilgrims" (10.4). He confesses what he has been and what he is, what he once was and what he is at the very moment of writing his confessions, so that the sharers in his mortality may be glad for his good deeds, which are the work of God, and sad for his evil deeds, which are Augustine's faults and God's punishments. Augustine has shown what he was, and in book 10 he will show what he is *now* and what he *continues to be.* He will confess what he knows of himself and what he does not know of himself. That he knows and does not know is due to what he is.

What Augustine does know about himself is that he loves God. There is no doubt in his mind about this: he feels it with certainty. He loves God because God has struck his heart with his word; his love for God is God's work. But what is God? Augustine addresses this question to all the things that stand about the gates of his senses, and all of them reply that they are not God. Then Augustine asks them to tell him something about God, and they answer, "He made us." Their answer is in their beauty. Augustine proceeds in his search for God. "And I turned my attention on myself and said to myself: 'And you, who are you?' And I replied: 'A man'" (10.6). Augustine finds in himself a body and a soul, the one exterior and the other interior. The interior part is the better part, for it is ministered to by the outer part. Here, Augustine identifies the "I" with the "inner man," with the soul. Man is body and soul; the "I" is soul. The soul is the life of the body, and God is the life of the soul. It seems, then, that God is to be sought in the soul. The soul gives not only life to the body but also perception to the flesh and "through these senses, with all their diverse functions, I act, retaining my identity as one soul." But life and perception are not proper to man, as he is different from the other animals. One must seek God "above the summit of [the] soul," and so one must go beyond the forces of life and perception in order to "ascend" to God (10.7). When one passes beyond these forces, one comes to memory.

Now, "memory itself is mind" (10.14), and "it is I myself who remember, I, the mind" (10.16). The "I" is the mind and the mind is memory: "this thing [memory] is the mind, and this thing is I myself" (10.17). Augustine seeks to encounter God in his mind, and he both finds him and does not find him. "And I went into the seat of the mind itself (which the mind has in memory, since the mind remembers itself), and you were not there. . . . You are not the mind itself. . . . Certainly you do dwell in my memory, because I remember you from the time I first learned of you and I find you there when I call you to mind" (10.25). God is above the mind, not the mind, but there is nowhere else to look for him.

It is on the way to God, on the way to what is above himself and what is not himself, that Augustine encounters himself. He encounters himself inside himself in the huge court of his memory.

> There too I encounter myself; I recall [recollect] myself—what I have done, when and where I did it, and in what state of mind I was at the time. These are all the things I remember to have experienced myself or to have heard from others. From the same store too I can take out pictures of things which have either happened to me or are believed on the basis of experience; I can myself weave them into the context of the past, and from them I can infer future actions, events, hopes, and then I can contemplate all these as though they were in the present. (10.8)

The self is recalled, recollected, in the memory. It encounters itself in the act of "remembering" itself. And the memory gives access not only to the past but also, in some sense, to the future. Future actions, events, and hopes are *inferred* by means of the "pictures" or images stored up in memory. The memory enables one to recollect oneself from the past and future and to make oneself *present* for oneself.

But when he encounters himself in his memory, Augustine is forced to exclaim: "How great, my God, is this force of memory, how exceedingly great! It is like a vast and boundless subterranean shrine. Who has ever reached the bottom of it? Yet this is a faculty of my mind and belongs to my nature; *nor can I myself grasp all that I am.* Therefore, the mind is not large enough to contain itself" (10.8; emphasis added). Memory is a help to self-discovery, but it is also a bottomless descent. One finds and does not find oneself in the memory. That is, one cannot fully grasp all that one is. It seems that the self is somehow outside the self. Yet where else is one to look for the self but within the self?

The incompleteness of the self-awareness afforded by the memory is manifested in the manner in which Augustine writes the story of his life. The gaps in Augustine's "autobiography" are obvious and numerous. He does not attempt to write a coherent tale and does not attempt to tell us all that he remembers. He recounts those incidents that he *now* sees most clearly as the providential action of God. Surely God has "provided" for him, cared for him, at *every* moment of his life. Even the moments that Augustine cannot remember, cannot recollect, are seen by God. Augustine is not entirely "there" for himself as he is for God.

It is only when Augustine is united with God, only when he sees God "face to face," that he will see himself and be at one with himself. Of his attempt to recollect himself he must say: "Great indeed is the power of memory! It is something terrifying, my God, a profound and infinite multiplicity: and this thing is the mind, and this thing is I myself. What then am I, my God? What is my nature? A life various, manifold, and quite immeasurable" (10.17). Augustine's life is a "puzzle" to him; he is a problem to himself, for "what can be nearer to me than my own self? Yet this force of my memory is incomprehensible to me, even though, without it, I should not be able to call myself myself" (10.16). Both God and the self are seen only "through a glass darkly." It is God who is sought first; God is the subject of Augustine's inquiry. Augustine's way to God (his "pilgrimage") is through his own mind, his own self. In seeking God he finds that he cannot even find himself. This is why Augustine must tell us those things he does know about himself and those things he does not know about himself to reveal what he is. The mind cannot contain itself, and certainly it cannot contain God, who is above the mind. Yet the mind is the only "place" where one can look for God and for oneself. "Place there is none; we go *backward and forward,* and there is no place." How, then, does one find God so as to have him at all in the memory? "I could only have found you in yourself, above me" (10.26). It is God who effects Augustine's finding of God. And it is only in God that Augustine will find himself, will grasp all that he is. "I find no secure place for my soul except in you, and in you I pray that what is scattered in me may be brought together so that nothing of me may depart from you" (10.40). It is only God who can recollect Augustine out of the temporal things in which he is scattered and out of the moments in which he is divided up. Augustine will be together with himself and will see himself only when he "stands" in God, in his "own true form." When he sees God face to face, he will be and will see what it is that he truly is.

Augustine's question about himself, "Who am I and what am I?" cannot now be fully answered. Augustine is a problem to himself. The memory is the only means to self-awareness and the memory is bottomless. What Augustine shows us is the radical finitude of man, the radical dependence of the creature on the Creator. Man does not make himself and thus he does not know himself. He is understandable only in terms of God's providential intention, and this he sees only through a glass darkly. One's recollection of oneself is radically and essentially incomplete.

ROUSSEAU ON "IMAGINATION"

Rousseau's *Confessions*, on the face of it, seems to be the work of Rousseau's memory. That is, it has the appearance of a sequence of recollections and reflections on those recollections. *The Confessions* seems to provide us with the story of Rousseau's past. Yet it turns out that memory plays only a secondary and perhaps even minor role in Rousseau's *Confessions*. The imagination shows itself to be of much greater importance. Indeed, there is a sense in which remembering is, for Rousseau, a function of the imagination. The imagination is the principle in terms of which *The Confessions* is constructed and is thus central to Rousseau's account of how man understands himself.

When Rousseau seeks to encounter himself, he reenters inside himself. "The single object of my confessions is to make known exactly my interior in all the situations of my life. It is the history of my soul that I have promised, and in order to write it faithfully I do not need other memoirs: it is sufficient for me, as I have done until now, to re-enter inside myself" (262). When he enters inside himself, Rousseau finds himself; he does not encounter his self in his memory. His memory gives him access to his past, to some of "the situations of his life," but it does not give him access to his interior (self).[7]

What gives Rousseau access to the interior history of his soul is his imagination. It allows him to connect the discrete situations of his life into a unitary self that has gone through these situations. Rousseau says of himself that he is "always the same at all times."

Rousseau's uses of the term "imagination" suggest that the meaning of the term is varied. On the one hand images are more or less spatial or bodily events (in contrast to "concepts") located in a faculty classically contrasted with the more spiritual "intellect." This use of the term involves the understanding of images as inseparable from sense perception.[8] Imagination is the faculty by means of which we "make pictures" and have on hand such perceptions as odors and sounds. Imagination, in this sense, is essential to remembering: as Augustine put it, "the images of things perceived are there ready to hand for thought to recall" (*Confessions* 10.8). Rousseau makes considerable use of this sense of the term: he tells us that his heart was full of the "image" of Mme. de Warens (107), that all his ideas are in "images" (169).

But Rousseau goes well beyond this use of the term. "Image" does not simply refer to "images of things perceived" that are somehow present for thought. In his account of his development of the *Second Discourse* Rousseau recalls his visit to St. Germain. He goes into the forest there and finds the "image" of the first times of which he traces the history (362). While he is on the Ile de St. Pierre, he finds pleasure in sitting near the lake, especially when it is agitated. He "makes the image" of the tumult of the world and the peace of his habitation, and this "idea" is so sweet as to sometimes make him weep (596). "Image" in this sense seems to refer to a kind of *connection* between what he perceives and something he does not perceive. What he perceives, the "picture" of what he sees, is an "image" of something other than what he sees. The imagination is far more, for Rousseau, than the picture-making faculty at the service of memory. It is not simply the faculty that receives "copies" of perceptions. The image, in this case, is less closely connected with perception as such. Rousseau's characterizations of the forest as an image of the first times and the agitated lake as an image of the tumult of the world suggest a more active intellectual role for the imagination. The connection between the forest and the first times, between the agitated lake and the tumult of the world, is imaginary. The "images" are the connections between what is perceived and what is not perceived: the ideas are connected by means of the imagination. And *all* his ideas are in images. For Rousseau the imagination is that faculty that constructs, that weaves feelings and possibilities; the imagination is the peculiarly *creative* faculty in man.

Rousseau makes specific reference to the creative imagination three times in his *Confessions.* He speaks about his "imagination créatrice," the imaginary objects he creates and embellishes, and the objects created or embellished by his imagination. In each case he is referring to his delightful reveries, chimeras, fictions. These imaginary objects are understood as distinguished from real, actual objects. When he finds himself disappointed in his situation, Rousseau turns to the world of chimeras. "The impossibility of reaching real beings threw me into the land of chimeras and, seeing nothing existent which was worthy of my delirium, I nourished it in an ideal world which my creative imagination had soon peopled with beings after my own heart" (398). In this land of chimeras he spends hours and days without counting, and he loses the memory of all other things. The beings he creates are not found "here below": his perfect "creatures" are "celestial."

Most of the imaginative creations Rousseau describes occur during journeys he makes alone and on foot. "Never have I thought so much, existed so much, lived so much, been so much myself, if I dare say so, than on those [journeys] I made alone and on foot." Far from everything that reminds him of his dependence, he experiences a greater audacity of thinking. He finds himself thrown into the immensity of beings in order to combine them, choose them, and appropriate them to his taste without constraint and without fear. "I dispose of the whole of nature as its master; my heart, wandering from object to object, unites itself, identifies itself with those that delight it, surrounds itself with charming images, intoxicates itself with delicious feelings" (157–58). In his imagination Rousseau is like God. He is alone and he is master of the universe.[9] He has never been so much *himself.* Augustine is on a journey toward God; Rousseau, on his journeys, is like God. And when he is most like God, he is most himself.

There is, however, a difference between what he experiences while making a journey for the sake of the journey and what he experiences when he is "on the way" to some specific destination. In these cases he is often "limited" by the real object that awaits him. When he leaves Lyon, he sees before him only an agreeable future with Mama; he is content but does not experience any delightful reveries. "Occupied with the expectation of seeing my Mama so soon again, I gave my chimeras a little truce and the real happiness that awaited me relieved me from looking for it in my visions" (166). When he leaves M. Le Maître, he travels back to Mama at Annecy as quickly as possible. His return is so prompt and his mind so distracted that he does not have the least memory of his journey. The tenderness and truth of his attachment for Mama had uprooted from his heart all imaginary projects and all the follies of ambition (128). The real, the actual situation, curbs his imagination, provided that the real situation is agreeable. Anticipation of pleasure makes one want to cover the distance to fulfillment as quickly as possible.

But these journeys to Mama are "returns"; he has already experienced what he anticipates. The journey to Turin and the journey to Paris are somewhat different. On the journey to Turin he experiences a kind of sweet inquietude that has Mama as its object, and this object fixes his imagination. He looks upon himself as almost her lover, and his reveries are delightful. No fears, no doubts about his fate trouble his reveries. He is young, vigorous, healthy, confident in himself and others. And there is vanity in his dreams: to follow Hannibal across the Alps seems to him a glory beyond his years (64). The journey to Paris is recalled as one of the happiest of his life. He is on his way to become a cadet; he is young, has enough money, and much hope. Alone and on foot, "my sweet chimeras kept me company and never had the heat of my imagination given birth to more magnificent chimeras." As he walks he builds the edifice of his fortune. He sees himself in an officer's uniform with a beautiful white plume; he is inflamed with this noble idea. He believes himself to be le Maréchal Rousseau. "I became so inflamed over these follies that I saw nothing but troops, ramparts, gabions, batteries, and myself, in the midst of the fire and smoke, calmly giving my orders with my field-glass in my hand" (154). But in the midst of his glory he comes upon a peaceful country scene and renounces forever the works of Mars. The two journeys are similar, for they are both undertaken with a new destination, a destination he has never before reached, in view, and they are both occasions for dreams of glory. The new, the unexperienced, inflames his imagination. And at the end of each journey he finds disaster, terrible disappointment.

On two occasions he undertakes journeys because of "chimeras." He abandons a secure and promising career to go off like a vagabond with Bâcle and his heron-fountain. He imagines that the fountain will provide his subsistence for the rest of his life. The heron-fountain is the principle on which he and Bâcle build the edifice of their fortune (102). He goes off to Paris with his system of musical notation. "Full of the magnificent ideas which had inspired me, and always the same at all times, I left Savoy with my musical system as before I had left Turin with my

heron-fountain" (257). Again, his expectations are not met; his journeys end in dis-
illusionment, for they were begun from illusions. Rousseau's glorious visions of
himself are invariably shattered. He creates for himself a world of future glory
and great fortune, and each time he is disillusioned. The reveries in which he indulges *because* of his disappointment with real situations result in his glory: *Julie* is
the product of his "escape" from real beings.

The imagined is not the ordinary. The distance between the real and the imaginary is the place of misery. "The real world has its bounds, the imaginary world
is infinite; as we cannot enlarge the one, let us shrink the other; for all the sufferings which really make us miserable arise from the difference between the two." [10]
One's "vision" of oneself and one's happiness are somehow related in terms of
the imagination.

It is not the imaginary that is the source of misery but the *difference between* the
real and the imaginary. The imaginary is both more pleasant and more painful
than the real. Through the imagination one sees oneself in situations where one
would wish to be and in situations where one would not wish to be. When
Rousseau suffers an attack of his malady, M. de Luxembourg brings him a doctor
who tells him that he will live a long time. His imagination is repressed, and he no
longer fears a cruel death. He is delivered from imaginary evils that are more cruel
than real evils and he suffers less (528). Rousseau tells us that the night he spent
with the Princesse de Ferrare, one of the characters in his opera, was a hundred
times more delightful than he would have had in the arms of the princess herself
(277). In the first incident the imaginary is more painful than the real, and in the
second incident the imaginary is more delightful than the real. The difference between the two incidents is that in the case of his illness the imaginary may become
real, and in the case of the princess the imaginary is seen for what it is. Rousseau
sees his cruel death as if it were real and beyond his power to prevent. But he has
the princess as he wants her: he can do with her as he likes precisely because she
is not real.

What the imaginative creations show is the powerfulness of man. In his imagination he is master of the universe. He is anything he wants to be: Hannibal, Maréchal
Rousseau, God. But in the "real world" he is far from all-powerful: it is rare that he
can bring about what he wishes and prevent what he does not wish. It is the attempt
to make the delightful imaginary world the real world and the attempt to prevent
imaginary evils as if they were real that are at the source of misery. The imaginary
creation is in the mind and *only* in the mind. God creates what *is;* man creates what
is not. The creative imagination works in the realm of the possible, not the actual.

CREATIVE IMAGINATION

Thus the creative imagination has to do with what is not. Man creates what is not,
and his creation acts upon him. He sees himself as what he is not and thus "becomes" what he is not. Rousseau describes the role played by his imagination.

This was [the decision] to nourish itself on situations which had interested me in my reading, recalling them, varying them, combining them, appropriating them to myself so much that I became one of the characters I imagined and saw myself always in positions most agreeable to my taste; and that, finally, the fictive state in which I succeeded in putting myself made me forget my real state with which I was so discontent. This love for imaginary objects and this facility for occupying myself with them ended by disgusting me with everything around me and determining this taste for solitude which has always since remained with me. (48)

He *becomes* the person he imagines. And as this person he moves in an imaginary world doing whatever he pleases. This requires solitude: he must be removed from the real world, the world of other men. The imaginary world is precisely private. To be Hannibal, Maréchal Rousseau, or God in public is to be mad. One can be whatever one wants to be within the confines of one's skull. That is, one can see oneself in any situation one chooses, one can make any *connections* one wishes between oneself and what is not oneself.

In one's imagination, then, one can be in a different "present": what is not is present to one not as what is no longer or what is not yet, but as *now*. Rousseau shows us this presence in his account of the kind of life he would have had if he had fallen into the hands of a better master. As an engraver his ambition would have been limited. "Having an imagination rich enough to embellish all states with its chimeras, powerful enough to transport me, so to speak, at will from one to the other, it was of little importance in which state I was in fact" (50). It is not ambition at the root of his transporting himself, not some hope for the future. Through his imagination he can be in another state, another place, in the present. This is how he enjoys women without possessing them, without having them actually present (28). This is why he leaves Mama, when she has visitors, in order to have her as he wants her (176). Through the imagination fulfillment can follow immediately upon desire. The time between desire and fulfillment is eliminated: the "future" is eliminated.

But the realm of the possible as opposed to the actual is the future. The faculty that gives one access to the future is the imagination. The future is entirely imagined: one can imagine countless possibilities. One imagines what might happen and therefore what is not and may never be. The imagination creates futures for us. It goes out in advance and places us in possible situations. We are and feel ourselves in these situations as if they were actual. And these created futures cause us to act in order to prevent them or bring them about. The future that is not is made present within the imagination and brings about, actualizes, what occurs in the space between the present and the imagined future. This is what we call prudence or foresight, and this is how we make mistakes. The prudent man is the man who anticipates correctly, who imagines the right future. Rousseau shows us his imprudence in the story of his conversion to papism and in the story of his causing Mama expense in his effort to save her from ruin.

The imagination has us always living in the future, in what is not and may never be. It dissipates us in the countless possibilities that are its own creation. It has us wrenching ourselves apart between desire and fear. This is Rousseau's "history." "My cruel imagination, which always runs to meet misfortunes, ceaselessly showed me this one [Mama's ruin] in all its excess and in all its consequences. I saw myself in advance [ahead of himself].... That is how my soul was always agitated. Desires and fears devoured me alternately" (210). The future reaches back to the present and destroys it: the making present of the future destroys the present as present.[11] The past is not nearly so powerful. "My cruel imagination, which torments itself without ceasing in foreseeing evils which are not yet, distracts my memory and prevents me from recalling those which are no longer." This is because "against what is done there are no more precautions to take and it is useless to occupy oneself with it" (540). The past is a source of concern for him only insofar as it might cause some future harm. Rousseau's memory, which retraces for him only agreeable objects, is the fortunate counterweight of his frightened imagination, which makes him foresee only cruel futures (261). The very disagreeable objects he retraces in his *Confessions,* especially in part 2, occupy him because they are part of the "chain of events" that stretches ahead of him into the cruel future.

The imagination is that faculty by means of which one "pictures" oneself in "future" situations. In fact, one can picture an entire future for oneself: one sees oneself stretched out ahead of oneself. The imagination does not simply present us with situations that are not yet and may never be: it presents us with *ourselves* in those situations. And it is possible for us to imagine a whole lifetime for ourselves in an instant. Rousseau describes one of the walks he took outside the city while he was living with Mama. His heart is full of her image and of the desire to spend his life with her.

I saw myself as in ecstasy transported to that happy time and that happy place.... I do not remember ever having leapt into the future with more force and illusion than I did then; and what struck me most in the memory of this reverie when it became actual was having found objects again exactly as I had imagined them. If ever the dream of a man awake had the air of a prophetic vision surely this one did. I was disappointed only in its imaginary duration; for the days and the years and an entire life took place there in an inalterable tranquility, whereas in fact all this lasted only a moment. (108)

Desire has us imagining no end to its fulfillment. It encourages us to deceive ourselves by ignoring the passing character of things human. Rousseau's reverie does not admit the possibility of a change in his happy situation. The contrast between this reverie and what actually occurs when he is supplanted by Wintzenried is revealing. "In a moment I saw evaporate forever the entire blissful future I had painted for myself.... This moment was frightful.... I saw before me only the sad remains of an insipid life" (249). When he is happy, he desires that his happiness be without end and imagines it without an end. When he is sad, he sees only sadness before him. This failure or reluctance to imagine an end is also clear from his account of his contentment with Thérèse. "The future no longer touched me or touched me only as the prolonged present: I desired nothing but to assure its duration" (311). But as we see in his account of himself on the Isle of St. Pierre Rousseau learns of the passing character of human things. He desires the continuation of his stay on the island but fears being forced to leave; this fear of a possible future event destroys his happiness.

Now the most complete and irreversible of all "passings" is death. And death is that future event that is certain: it is not simply one among many possibilities. It is not yet but it surely will be. Just as we tend to imagine present happiness and present sadness to extend before us indefinitely, so we tend to imagine ourselves before an indeterminate future. Perhaps it is precisely because it is certain that death can be "imagined away": it does not haunt us as a possibility. Rousseau is familiar with the "image" of death; he has looked death in the face. He has been "near enough" to death to familiarize himself with its image.

Rousseau "sees himself" as a dead man. There is a sense, then, in which Rousseau has his entire future present to him. It is not that he knows the details, the events, of the rest of his life. It is that, no matter what the events, it *will be* himself who will go through the events. It is not the future but *himself* that he sees in advance, stretched out before him. This seeing is the work of the creative imagination. But what of Rousseau's seeing of himself in the past, in what is no longer? Is this not the work of the memory? Surely, *The Confessions* is Rousseau's "memoirs."

ROUSSEAU ON MEMORY

Rousseau often speaks of memory as his means of access to the past. The memory is concerned with that which is no longer. It makes that which is no longer somehow present. When Venture visits him many years after their close association, the years of Rousseau's youth are brought back to him. "I had felt [bewitching ecstasies] then in all their force and I believed their time past forever" (372). But the times past are not simply reproduced, repeated in the mind. Remembering is not simply running the film again or playing back the recording. One sees the past only from the perspective of the present. After recounting his abandonment of Le Maître, Rousseau writes, "That is how I saw the thing then; I see it differently today" (130). This is Augustine's experience when he looks back upon his past sins; he sees them differently now and he sees them for what they are. Augustine's memories of his sinful pleasures are painful, bitter. Rousseau consoled himself easily over his abandonment of Le Maître immediately after he did it. Now, as he writes about it, he feels remorse.

But, for Rousseau, it is not just that his feelings about the events change with the perspective provided by the distance of time. He can, if he wishes, "go through" the events again, relive them. The reliving is not simply a repeating. "Moments precious and so regretted, ah, begin again for me your delightful course;

flow more slowly through my memory, if it is possible, than you really did in your fugitive succession" (215). The rememberer can make a longer time; he does not simply recall but somehow reproduces as the painter re-creates. Of certain memories Rousseau can say, "This coming together of objects vividly retraced has delighted my memory a hundred times, as much and more than in reality" (121). The past *is* not and cannot be what it *was*. Rousseau's "objectivity" is not at issue here. Rousseau does not claim to have access to himself through his memory. It does not matter whether or not he can "remember": the frankness and accuracy he promises us are not about the situations of his life. At the beginning of part 2, after having "remembered" the years of his youth, he writes: "The single object of my confessions is to make known exactly my interior in all the situations of my life. It is the history of my soul that I have promised and in order to write it faithfully I do not need other memoirs: it is sufficient for me, as I have done until now, to re-enter inside myself." Rousseau's memory gives him access to some of the situations of his life, situations that are no longer but that can be recalled. He, his self, is not those situations. Throughout part 1 he has not been remembering but entering inside himself.

What Rousseau means by "entering inside himself" is understood in terms of what all of this seeming "remembering" really is. Of the time he spent at Les Charmettes Rousseau writes:

> Nothing of all that happened to me during that precious epoch, nothing of what I did, said and thought all the time it lasted has escaped from my memory. The times that precede and that follow come back to me at intervals. I recall them unequally and confusedly; but I recall that one entirely as if it still lasted. *My imagination, which in my youth always went in advance and now goes backward,* compensates by these sweet memories for the hope that I have lost forever. (215–16; emphasis added)

Rousseau recalls, remembers, some of the situations of his life. He *imagines* himself in those situations. The movement from birth to death is the growth of the past and the diminishing of the future. As one moves from birth to death the imagination goes less and less in advance and more and more backward. Rousseau's access to the past is through memory; his access to the history of his soul is through imagination. It is his imagination that allows him to connect the discrete situations of his life into a unitary self that has gone through these situations. Rousseau says of himself that he is "always the same at all times." He is not divided up in time, whose order he does not know; he is not lost in the bottomless, boundless subterranean shrine of memory. Through what is no longer and what is not yet there extends the imagined and always imaginable Rousseau.

During the course of his narrative Rousseau pauses several times to consider what might have been the case had circumstances been different. He tells us what his life, the events of his life, would have been. Had he fallen into the hands of a better master, he would have been an engraver, a good Christian, citizen, father, friend, worker. After having spent an obscure and simple but equal and sweet life he would have died peacefully and been soon forgotten (51). Had he married Merceret, he would have lost great pleasures, but he would have lived in peace until his last hour (142). Rousseau constructs "possible" lives for himself.[12] He takes us through these entire lives right up until the death that would end them. One might argue, then, that since he is able to distinguish between what might have been (the possible) and what did in fact happen, his account of what did happen corresponds to something real, a real life, a real self.

But at the very beginning of book 1 Rousseau tells us that "I have been able to suppose true what I know to have been possible." He has filled up the voids, the gaps in his story that are occasioned by the failure of his memory. He has filled these gaps with accounts of events that might have happened, that could possibly have happened. And he does not even tell us when he does this. He does not show us which parts of his *Confessions* are "fables." How, then, is this supposedly real life different from the possible lives he constructs for himself? The mistakes he makes because of his poor memory and the fables he uses to fill in the gaps occasioned by his poor memory do not interfere with the "truth." Thus it is not his memory but something very like a creative imagination that appears to guarantee the truth of what is said. His "true life" seems to be just as surely a construct of his imagination as the possible lives he constructs for himself.

Rousseau, then, is *not* the sum of the details of his life. The truth about himself is not revealed in an accurate chronicle of what he did and what happened to him. This is why he can, at the very end of his *Confessions,* make his declaration: "I have told the truth. If anyone knows things contradictory to what I have just exposed, were they proven a thousand times, he knows lies and impostures." The truth is that *no matter* what the details of one's life, one is "always the same at all times." One is always the same self. And this self is accessible through the creative imagination. The self that is spread out in the past that is no longer and the future that is not yet is at any moment imagined to be the same self.

THE FEVERS OF IMAGINATION

Yet to claim that it is the imagination that gives one access to one's true being is to raise many serious difficulties. The imagination, as Rousseau represents it, is the creative faculty that constructs, weaves possibilities, connects the discrete situations of his life. The creative imagination makes one life out of the many moments of his life. His life is a coherent whole, a unity, because the imagination allows him to connect all of the parts with each other, to "systematize" the details of his life. Now in book 7 of his *Confessions* Rousseau tells the story of his friend Mussard, who has retired from public life to find rest and enjoyment before he dies. Mussard is described as a true "philosophe de pratique" who lives in a house he has built himself and a garden he has planted with his own hands. The story continues:

While digging deeply in the terraces of this garden, he found some fossil shells, and he found them in such great quantity that his lively imagination saw only shells in nature and, finally, he sincerely believed that the universe was only shells and remains of shells and that the entire earth was nothing but shell deposits. Always occupied with this object and with his singular discoveries, he became so excited with these ideas that they would have finally turned into a system in his head, that is to say, into madness, had not death—fortunately for his reason but unfortunately for his friends who were very attached to him and found at his house a most agreeable refuge—removed him from them by a most strange and cruel disease. (348)

Mussard's imagination would have constructed a system in which everything would be explained in terms of the principles of shells. And the system would have been an expression of madness. Rousseau calls Mussard's preoccupation with his shells "conchyliomanie." Just as Mussard, the true "philosophe de pratique," has built his house himself, so he builds in his head an entire universe of shells. Although this is a mania, a madness, Rousseau tells us that he worked in Mussard's study with as much pleasure as Mussard.

"Conchyliomanie" is the result of the imagination, the creative imagination gone wild. On the basis of a few shells in his garden Mussard creates a system that accounts for all that is. Everything is *connected* with everything else. But these connections, or rather this connection, is imaginary, just as the connection between the agitated lake and the tumult of the world is imaginary. The question that arises here is that of the truth or falsity of the "system." Are the connections *merely* imaginary? Is the imagined unity an illusion having no relation to reality? Or does the creative imagination give us access to the truth, to what is in fact the case? It is true of man that he constructs, creates, a unity he calls his life. But is the self, which is the unifying principle of this life, a mere figment of the imagination having no relation to what is real?

The problem of the constructive creative imagination as the means of access to the self is revealed most strikingly in the apparent contrast between parts 1 and 2 of *The Confessions*. Rousseau's division of his *Confessions* into parts 1 and 2 marks a division in the work itself rather than a division in the life of which *The Confessions* is the story. There is a space of two years of silence between the writing of part 1 and the writing of part 2, and Rousseau calls attention to this space in the very opening sentence of the second part. Part 1 is the story of a not terribly extraordinary life, a life marked by joys and sorrows, good fortune and bad fortune, of a rather common character. Part 2, however, is dominated by Rousseau's preoccupation with the Great Plot; he seems to believe that a conspiracy of enormous proportions is being mounted against him, and we are never quite sure of what its "real" character is. But within the wider context of the Great Plot of part 2 Rousseau discusses a lesser conspiracy—the brief Jesuit plot of book 11—which he ultimately comes to see for what it is, a figment of his imagination.

The publication of the *Émile* had been suspended, and he had not been told the reason. "Here now is my imagination, kindled by this long silence, busy conjuring up phantoms for me." He torments himself in looking for the cause of this delay and, as usual, imagines the worst; in the delay in printing he sees the suppression of the book. But he cannot imagine the cause of this suppression. Then he learns that a certain Jesuit, P. Griffet, has been speaking about the *Émile* and has given an account of certain passages from it. "At that instant my imagination went off like lightning and unveiled for me the whole iniquitous mystery: I saw its progress as clearly, as surely as if it had been revealed to me." He figures out that the Jesuits are furious over the disdain with which he has spoken of their colleges and are trying to have the printing delayed until after Rousseau's death. Then they would be able to alter the work and attribute to Rousseau their own views. The mystery is solved. "It is astonishing what a crowd of facts and circumstances came into my mind and traced themselves on this madness and gave it an air of probability, even going so far as to show me evidence and to demonstrate it." Guérin is the instrument of the Jesuits; his friendly advances have been prompted by the Jesuits. "I saw nothing but Jesuits everywhere." He considers Malesherbes' objections to his "vision," yet his vision persists (523). But the *Émile* is published. The Jesuit plot is the work, he finally realizes, of his perfervid imagination. He refers to this construct as a phantom, a madness. There is no plot: he had connected numerous events and circumstances and formed them into a coherent system to which nothing "real" corresponds.

The Great Plot of part 2 is of a different order of magnitude. Immediately after, indeed in the same paragraph as his reference to the "mad" Jesuit plot, Rousseau refers to "today" when he "sees proceed without obstacle to its execution the blackest, most frightful plot that has ever been woven against the memory of a man" (525). He sees himself surrounded by enemies: as he takes up his pen to begin writing his second part, he tells us that the roof above him has eyes, the walls surrounding him have ears, and spies are all around him (263). Everything that happens to him is fitted into the scheme of those who are seeking to destroy him. Apparently innocent and even kind acts are really intended to work toward his ruin: visitors come to spy on him, "friends" are kind to him so that he will confide in them. The enormity of the plot is even more fully spelled out in the *Dialogues:* an invisible hand directs *all of Europe,* from the great and powerful to shopkeepers and children playing in the street, in a conspiracy for the destruction of Jean-Jacques Rousseau. He sees clearly that "all the events related to him which seem accidental and chance are only successive developments concerted in advance and so ordered that all that is to happen to him subsequently already has its place in the picture and will have its effect only at the appointed moment." [13] This account of the plot takes place within a discussion concerning the various portraits (paintings) of Jean-Jacques.

ROUSSEAU AS "ICONOGRAPHER"

In *The Confessions* Rousseau does not tell us who it is who directs the conspiracy. He is in darkness, lost in the underground tunnels of the present: he feels the blows and perceives the immediate instrument of his suffering, but he does not see the hand by which the variety of intermediary causes are combined to work the strange events of his life (544). The reader must recognize the importance of even the least details of the events (e.g., the time at which the decree against him is issued) if he is to discover the secret causes by induction, if he is to follow the thread of the plot (543). It is clear from *The Confessions* who the "author" of the plot is. The hand that directs a successful conspiracy of such enormous proportions must be that of an all-knowing, all-powerful being. And this is confirmed in the *Dialogues*. "The bringing together of all these causes is too inferior to the effect in order not to have some other more powerful cause [than man], a cause that it is impossible for me to imagine."[14]

The Great Plot that dominates part 2 of *The Confessions* is of much greater magnitude than the Jesuit plot, but is it different in kind? In the same passage Rousseau speaks about the Jesuit plot, which was "demonstrated" for him and which he finally sees as a mere figment of his imagination, and the Great Plot, which he seems to regard as real. He must have been aware of the similarity between the two.[15] The characterization of his construction of the Jesuit plot as "mad" points to the character of the Great Plot as a figment of his imagination. Both are clear examples of paranoiac invention that Rousseau places before us so that we may see their madness.[16] Both are the work of the creative imagination.

Clearly, the Great Plot of part 2 is presented as a negative image of providence, the working of an evil genius. Everything that happens to him is fitted by Rousseau into the scheme for his destruction. Even the smallest details of every event are important within the plan, and all are connected by the invisible hand that directs the conspiracy. Part 2 of *The Confessions* is a representation of the belief in providence. Rousseau is consciously intending and deliberately seeking to expose the "madness" of Augustine's interpretation of the events of his life as a whole, as the working out of God's design for him.

Support for this understanding of Rousseau's response to Augustine is found in the "History of the Preceding Document," which follows his *Dialogues*. Here Rousseau tells us the "history" of the *Dialogues*. He decides to place the manuscript on the altar of Notre Dame, but when he enters the church he finds his way to the altar barred by a grille he had never seen there before. At first he is terrified, for he interprets the barring of his way as a sign that God, too, is against him. On reflection, however, he realizes the foolishness of his plan and thanks heaven for preventing him from carrying it out. Then he learns of the presence in Paris of an old acquaintance and regards the news as "a direction of providence" that indicates to whom he should entrust the manuscript. He gives the manuscript to this man but is disappointed in his response. Next, he is visited by a young Englishman who had been his neighbor at Wootton. Rousseau believes he sees the finger of God in this occasion and decides to entrust the manuscript to the young visitor. But now he has doubts on the wisdom of this choice. And so the story goes on. Rousseau sums up the "history" of this example of the workings of providence. "I did what all unfortunates do who believe they see in all that happens to them an express direction of destiny. I said to myself: here is the depositary that providence has chosen for me; [providence] has sent him to me. It has rejected my choice only to lead me to its choice." [17] "Providence" really explains nothing: each failure is really the result of a "bad choice." [18] Providence admits of bad intentions but not of bad choices, not of mistakes, for God does not make his intentions accessible to man's mind. The principle of providence, which seems to account for everything, really accounts for nothing, just as the "Jesuit" principle and Great Plot really account for nothing. These all-inclusive explanations are the work of the creative imagination and correspond to nothing real.

Now behind Augustine's account of God's providential action toward him stands the account of God's providential action toward all men, the Bible. As already noted the most striking example of God's care for men is found in the story of Jesus Christ. Jesus' life is entirely preordained from all eternity. Everything that he does and everything that happens to him is the result of divine design. Twice in his *Confessions* Rousseau tells us that he has been called the Anti-Christ (579, 586). The incident of the stoning of his house recalls the attempted stoning of Christ reported in the Gospels. And Rousseau even goes so far as to put in his own mouth a close paraphrase of the words of Jesus to the Pharisees. When he is secretary to the ambassador in Venice, a dispute arises between them over the secretary's customary stipend for the issuance of passports. Rousseau says to the ambassador, "Let your Excellency keep what is his and leave me what is mine" (281). Indeed, from the very opening pages of his *Confessions,* Rousseau ascribes to himself a uniqueness that the Christian could only ascribe to Christ. "I am not made like any of those I have seen; I dare to believe that I am not made like any of those who exist." Nature has broken the mold, the form, in which she has cast him (17). The attack on Augustine's understanding of his life as the work of providence must come to grips with the basis of that understanding, the revelation in Christ of God's loving care for men. [19]

There is a sense, then, in which Rousseau compares himself not only with Augustine but also with Augustine's God. Rousseau claims a perspective on his life that for Augustine would be proper to God alone. "I have unveiled my interior such as you yourself have seen it [Eternal Being]." God, the Creator, holds the moments of Augustine's life together in one eternal "glance." And God is somehow creating Augustine at every moment. For Rousseau it is the creative imagination that holds the moments of his life together. Rousseau's "life" is his own construct.

NOTES

1. Erich Przywara, "St. Augustine and the Modern World," in *St. Augustine* (Cleveland: World Publishing, 1957), 252.

2. Alasdair MacIntyre, foreword to Ann Hartle, *The Modern Self in Rousseau's Confessions: A Reply to St. Augustine* (Notre Dame: University of Notre Dame Press, 1983), xi.

3. St. Augustine, *Confessions* 11.29. Quotations from Augustine's *Confessions* are from the translation by Rex Warner (New York: New American Library, 1963), with emendations.

4. Jean-Jacques Rousseau, *Confessions*, trans. J. M. Cohen (Harmondsworth: Penguin, 1953), 362. Subsequent references will appear in the text.

5. With respect to Augustine's selection of incidents Robert J. O'Connell has argued in both his *St. Augustine's Early Theory of Man* (Cambridge, Mass.: Harvard University Press, 1968) and his *St. Augustine's "Confessions": The Odyssey of Soul* (Cambridge, Mass.: Harvard University Press, 1969) that Augustine wrote the *Confessions* in light of a theory of man derived from Plotinus' notions of the fall and return of the soul. Augustine would, then, have chosen the incidents that support this theory. "The meanings we have progressively imposed upon experience place certain landmarks in the limelight, leaving others cloaked in shadow" (O'Connell, *St. Augustine's Early Theory*, 281). But for O'Connell "the metaphysical underpinning of the *Confessions* represents a twilight struggle between an emanationism in which the soul can be thought of as 'fallen' and 'distant' from God and a fundamentally different view in which nothing can be 'distant' from the Omnipresent" (284). Ultimately, then, O'Connell is critical of Augustine for not being clear about the problem of reconciling providence and free will. In *St. Augustine's "Confessions"* (181) he concludes that "creaturely activity, including man's free action, has in the end been swallowed up in God's unique activity." And this happens without Augustine's realizing it. "Augustine would hardly have wanted this to happen, would very likely have been most uncomfortable on realizing that his metaphysics had brought him to such an impasse. It could only have occurred, then, contrary to his daylight intentions." O'Connell "wonders if there is any genuine place in such a scheme of thought for that autonomy of human will whereby its actions are, in a true sense, its own" (180). My own discussion of the *Confessions* does not deal specifically with the problem of reconciling providence and free will, and, for purposes of contrast with Rousseau, I have emphasized the role of providence. I would not argue that Augustine selected the incidents related in the *Confessions* simply and solely on the basis of their revealing God's action in his life: his sins are always acknowledged to be his own.

Further, the question of the unity of the *Confessions* and the place of individual incidents within that whole is beyond the scope of this study. But I would maintain that Augustine himself was not confused about the problem of providence and free will, whether or not he resolved it. In book 7, for example, he says within a few pages both that God governs the whole world even to the fluttering of the leaves of the trees (chap. 6) and that he is certain that, when he wills, it is he and no other who wills (chap. 3). The incidents that Augustine relates do not betray any lack of lucidity with respect to this difficulty. Indeed, they place the difficulty constantly before us.

6. B. Groethuysen, *J. J. Rousseau*, 8th ed. (Paris: Gallimard, 1949), 238. Groethuysen claims that, for Rousseau, the question about man precedes the question about God and that the question about man is a question about nature.

7. Compare Jean Starobinski, *Jean-Jacques Rousseau: La Transparence et l'obstacle, suivi de sept essais sur Rousseau* (Paris: Gallimard, 1971), 235–39; Pierre Burgelin, *La Philosophie de l'existence de J.-J. Rousseau*, Bibliothèque de Philosophie Contemporaine (Paris: Presses Universitaires de France, 1952), 148; Marcel Raymond, *Jean-Jacques Rousseau: La Quête de soi et la rêverie* (Paris: Librairie Jose Corti, 1962), 74–75, 78; Georges Poulet, *Studies in Human Time*, trans. Elliott Coleman (Baltimore: Johns Hopkins University Press, 1956), 24–25, 174–79; Bernard Gagnebin and Marcel Raymond, "Introduction" and "Notes et variantes," in *Les*

Confessions, vol. 1 of *Jean-Jacques Rousseau: Oeuvres complètes,* ed. Bernard Gagnebin and Marcel Raymond (Paris: Gallimard, 1969), xxxv–xxxviii. Starobinski attempts to resolve the problems of accuracy and completeness by references to Rousseau's total reliance on the "affective memory." According to Burgelin, the unity of the self is, for Rousseau, the work of the affective memory. Gagnebin and Raymond claim that the affective memory is the principle of continuity of Rousseau's being. Poulet maintains that, for Rousseau, the veracity of the memory of feelings is absolute; it is the affective memory that gives Rousseau "a deeper consciousness of a self which, properly speaking, belongs neither to the past, nor to the present, nor even to duration" (178).

8. Aristotle, *De anima* 3.3, trans. J. A. Smith, in *The Basic Works of Aristotle,* ed. Richard McKeon (New York: Random House, 1941).

9. In connection with Rousseau's chimeras Burgelin, in his *La Philosophie de l'existence,* 169, writes, "The imagination assures us the domination of the world."

10. Jean-Jacques Rousseau, *Émile ou de l'éducation,* in *Émile; Éducation; Morale; Botanique,* vol. 4 of *Jean-Jacques Rousseau: Oeuvres complètes,* bk. 2, 305.

11. On the question of the anticipatory imagination and its relation to unhappiness see Poulet, *Studies in Human Time,* 163–65; and Burgelin, *La Philosophie de l'existence,* 132.

12. See Jacques Voisine, introduction to *Jean-Jacques Rousseau: "Les Confessions"* (Paris: Éditions Garnier Frères, 1964), lxxxiii, cvi.

13. Jean-Jacques Rousseau, *Rousseau Juge de Jean-Jacques: Dialogues,* vol. 1 in *Jean-Jacques Rousseau: Oeuvres complètes,* 781.

14. Rousseau, *Dialogues,* 914

15. Compare Jean Starobinski, *La Transparence et l'obstacle,* 192–93. Starobinski's account of the relationship between the two plots is that there is "a strange demarcation" which "separates a 'zone' of consciousness where Rousseau is still capable of recognizing that his imagination interprets the signs in a delirious manner, and a zone where anxiety, ceasing to be conscious of its interpretive work, accepts the delirious idea as massive and indisputable evidence." According to Starobinski, Rousseau's "self-criticism" is limited to the single incident of the *Émile;* Rousseau revokes his first interpretation of this lesser plot in order to give greater weight to his interpretation of other complaints.

16. Compare this understanding of Rousseau's deliberateness with Starobinski, *La Transparence et l'obstacle,* 65; Jean Guéhenno, *Jean-Jacques Rousseau,* 2 vols., trans. John Weightman and Doreen Weightman (New York: Columbia University Press, 1966), 1:430; Raymond, *La quête de soi,* 126. It is noteworthy in this context that Guéhenno, 2:187–89, cites the fact that the "happy" books of part 1 of *The Confessions* are written during the period of Rousseau's quarrel with Hume. Hermine de Saussure, *Rousseau et les manuscrits des "Confessions"* (Paris: Éditions E. de Boccard, 1958), 269–71, maintains that, from the first crisis (the *Émile* incident) until Rousseau's last years, one can follow a marvelous struggle between understanding and madness. Part 2 of *The Confessions,* according to Saussure, marks a change in the purpose of Rousseau's writing—that is, his defense; however, "it is remarkable that, in spite of this change of orientation of *The Confessions,* the style is hardly affected." Also compare Christopher Kelly, *Rousseau's Exemplary Life: "The Confessions" as Political Philosophy* (Ithaca: Cornell University Press, 1987), especially 210–14.

17. Jean-Jacques Rousseau, "Histoire du précédent écrit," in *Les Confessions,* vol. 1 of *Jean-Jacques Rousseau: Oeuvres complètes,* 983.

18. Rousseau, *Dialogues,* 952.

19. With reference to Rousseau's usurpation of the place of Christ, see Burgelin, *La Philosophie de l'existence,* 328. Burgelin refers to *The Confessions* as the "new Gospel": Rousseau finds an eternal model in himself and holds out his *Confessions,* saying "Tolle, lege." It is noteworthy that Burgelin, whether deliberately or not, has Rousseau repeat the command that Augustine claims to have heard on the occasion of his conversion.

SIXTEEN

Wittgenstein and Augustine *De magistro**

M. F. Burnyeat

Augustine, in describing his learning of language, says that he was taught to speak by learning the names of things. It is clear that whoever says this has in mind the way in which a child learns such words as "man," "sugar," "table," etc. He does not primarily think of such words as "today," "not," "but," "perhaps."

WITTGENSTEIN, *BLUE AND BROWN BOOKS*

Everyone in this audience will know that Wittgenstein is referring to the passage from Augustine's *Confessions* (1.8.13) that he borrows for the opening words of the *Philosophical Investigations*. Not everyone will know that, immediately before the passage that Wittgenstein quotes, Augustine claims that his elders did not teach him to speak. He taught himself. Fewer still, I imagine, will be aware that on this point the adult Augustine's account of his childhood derives from a quite general philosophical thesis to the effect that no man ever does or can teach another anything.

It is the general thesis, as elaborated and defended in Augustine's *De magistro*, that I aim to discuss here. I started with Wittgenstein not from any desire to complain at Wittgenstein's "creative misprision" of Augustine but because some of Wittgenstein's reasons for denying that language is taught in the way his Augustine depicts are strikingly similar to some of the historical Augustine's reasons for denying that language, or anything else, is taught.

One recent critic of Wittgenstein, offering *homo viator* the blessings of modern cognitive psychology, has said that Augustine has it precisely and demonstrably right when Wittgenstein protests that he "describes the learning of human language as if the child came into a strange country and did not understand the language of the country; that is, as if it already had a language, only not this one."[1] Others see in *Confessions* 1.8.13 an *Urbild*: a primitive, prephilosophical picture of language, antecedent to argument, from which grow all the evil theories which it is the calling of expositors of the *Philosophical Investigations* to combat.[2] I shall exhibit the passage Wittgenstein has made famous as the precipitate of some 800

---

*I am grateful for assistance from Thomas Ebert and Brian McGuinness; for comment on an earlier draft by Julia Annas, Robert Brandom, C. A. J. Coady, Gareth B. Matthews, John Procopé, and Richard Sorabji; for a published critique by Alexander Nehamas ("Meno's Paradox and Socrates as Teacher," *Oxford Studies in Ancient Philosophy* 3 [1985]: 26–29); and above all for a penetrating commentary prepared by Norman Kretzmann for a discussion at Cornell.

years of Platonist philosophizing. This will be a historical inquiry. But I hope that it will contribute to a more nuanced sense than either Wittgenstein's critics or his expositors have achieved of his relationship to the Platonist writer he admired and opposed.

AN EXCERPT FROM *CONFESSIONS* 1.8.13

I was no longer an infant who could not speak, but already a chattering boy. This I remember, and I have since realized from what source I had learned to speak [et memini hoc, et unde loqui didiceram, post adverti]. For it wasn't that my elders had been teaching me, presenting words to me in a definite order of training as they did a bit later with my letters. Rather, I had been teaching myself [3] with the mind which you, my God, gave me, when I tried to express the feelings of my heart by cries and different sounds and all sorts of motions of my limbs (in order to get my own way) but could not manage to express everything I wished to everyone I wished. I had been taking thought with the aid of memory [pensabam memoria; here begins *PI* par. 1] when they (my elders) named some object, and accordingly moved toward something, I saw this and I grasped that the thing was called by the sound they uttered when they meant to point it out. Their intentions were shown by their bodily movements, as it were the natural language of all peoples: the expression of the face, the play of the eyes, the movement of other parts of the body, and the tone of voice which expresses our state of mind in seeking, having, rejecting, or avoiding something. Thus, as I heard words repeatedly used in their proper places in various sentences, I gradually learnt to understand what objects they signified; and after I had trained my mouth to form these signs, I used them to express my own desires.

Augustine's memory is of being already able to talk as a boy, not of how he had earlier learned to talk, and it is the first stage in his autobiographical narrative to be certified by memory. For the earlier period, going back to birth and conception, Augustine repeatedly says that he has no memory but believes the testimony of his parents and others and makes conjectural inferences from his (adult) observation of other babies. Thus the famous account of language learning is not presented as a deliverance of memory, real or apparent.

But neither does it rest on testimony or inference from observation. "Post adverti" (I have since realized) is stronger than and different from "credidi" (I believed) and "conieci" (I conjectured) in, for example, 1.7.12. Its only parallel in the preceding narrative is in 1.6.7 on the comfort of women's milk:

Neither my mother nor my nurses filled their breasts by themselves. It was you who gave me, through them, the food of infancy . . . because you, my God, are the source of all good and everywhere you preserve me. This is something I realized later [animadverti postmodum], because you proclaim it through all these things you give me, both within and without. At the time all I knew [noram] was how to suck.

That little Augustine sucked at the breast and learned to speak are two ordinary empirical facts of family history, vouched for in ordinary ways by testimony and inference from like cases. But what the autobiographer is pointing to is the divine presence that explains them both. (Compare 1.12.13 on God's good use of his parents' bad reasons for putting him through the miseries of school.) The account of language learning in 1.8.13 is neither a simple memory nor an empirical psychologist's conjectural hypothesis but a highly self-conscious contribution to theological understanding.

I conclude from this that for the author of *Confessions* 1.8.13 its central focus is on God's responsibility for the mind teaching itself. In 1.14.23 Augustine is more precise: he must have learned some words at his own prompting, "non a docentibus sed a loquentibus"—that is, in the manner described in 1.8.13 and without being taught by others. The *Confessions* does not provide argued justification for either claim. The earlier *De magistro* does.[4] To give Augustine's own account of the matter: "At the same time [389 or 390 AD] I wrote a book entitled *On the Teacher* in which after discussion and investigation it is discovered that there is no teacher who teaches man knowledge [scientia] except God, as it is in fact written in the Gospel: 'One is your Teacher, Christ' " (*Retractationes* 1.12).[5]

THE DIALOGUE *DE MAGISTRO*

At first sight the thesis that no man (homo) ever does or can teach another has nothing to recommend it but the authority of the scriptures. Moreover, if so paradoxical a thesis were true, it would apply to itself. Augustine could not have learned it from St. Matthew (23:10), nor could he have taught it to his sixteen-year-old son Adeodatus in the discussion (real or imaginary)[6] presented in the *De magistro*. But Augustine never tires of telling us to believe that we may understand. And in fact at the end of the dialogue (14.46) Adeodatus accepts that he has not been taught by his father that no man can ever teach another. Nonetheless he has learned that this is so; he knows it now, without a trace of doubt. I take this to be a deliberate indication by Augustine that his dialogue is meant to illustrate its own message—that we will understand his thesis, and maybe see that it is not so paradoxical after all, if we relate it not just to the arguments he has provided but to the whole course of the discussion in which Adeodatus learns without being taught.

Augustine, like most of us, thinks of teaching as imparting knowledge. The question whether teaching is (humanly) possible is the question whether one human being can bring another to know something. So it is worth a preliminary digression to ask about Augustine's conception of knowledge (*scientia*).

There is an important and revealingly Platonist passage in the *Retractationes*, the work in which Augustine in his old age gave his considered judgment on ninety-three of his earlier writings. Here he is supplying a clarification or qualification to an epistemological distinction drawn in the *De utilitate credendi* of 391–92 AD:

And when I said . . . "What we know, therefore, we owe to reason, what we believe, to authority" [quod scimus igitur, debemus rationi, quod credimus, auctoritati]. This is not to be taken in such a way as to make us frightened in more ordinary conversation of saying that we know what we believe on adequate testimony. It is true that when we speak properly [proprie], we say we know only that which we grasp by firm reasoning of the mind. But when we speak in language more suited to common use, as even the Holy Scripture speaks, we should not hesitate to say we know both what we perceive by our bodily senses and what we believe on the authority of trustworthy witnesses while nevertheless understanding the distance between these and that. (*Retractationes* 1.14.3)

It is tempting to read this passage as introducing two senses of the verb "to know," a strict or philosophical sense that preserves the truth of Augustine's earlier dictum, "What we know, we owe to reason," and a plain man's sense that makes it false because in this sense we also know things that we believe on good authority. But temptation should be resisted. What Augustine distinguishes here is the proper meaning of the verb "to know"[7] and the catachrestic or improper way it is used in ordinary conversation. The ordinary use is harmless; it would be pointless pedantry to object to it: but it remains true that in the proper acceptation of the term we know only what we owe to firm reasoning of the mind. Thus it is not that a change of meaning is involved when in ordinary life we claim to know what we believe on adequate testimony but that the standard meaning is loosely and improperly applied to a case that strictly speaking it does not fit.

This interpretation is confirmed by the fact that both uses of the verb "to know" seem, in modern terms, to involve justified true belief. The difference between them is drawn in terms of the mode of justification. When a true belief is justified by sense perception or trustworthy testimony, the plain man calls it knowledge, the philosopher belief. But this belief is vastly important for Augustine, since it includes the Christian's belief in the testimony of the scriptures. When he says it is not knowledge, in the proper acceptation of the term, this is not to disparage belief, or to impugn its rationality, or to deny that it is fully justified; the testimony is, after all, described as adequate and trustworthy. What is missing, by comparison with cases where a true belief is justified by the mind's firm reasoning, is something other than justification: something that justification by reasoning contributes along with and in addition to justification as such and that justification by sense perception or testimony cannot supply.

What that extra something is becomes clear, I think, when we look back to the original statement in the *De utilitate credendi*. We discover that the contrast between believing and knowing (*scire*) was presented there (11.25) as a contrast between believing and understanding (*intellegere*). The original statement was, "What we understand [intellegimus], we owe to reason." If Augustine feels that it makes no odds whether he writes "scire" or "intellegere," that implies that in his view the proper meaning of "scire" is "intellegere." And that in turn explains why he thinks it loose or improper to use "knowing" (scire) in the ordinary way of what we believe on adequate testimony. "Intellegere" would not fit here at all. Adequate testimony is excellent justification for believing something, but it does not contribute an understanding of the thing believed. Firm reasoning of the mind, on the other hand, does both: it justifies a belief in such a manner as to enlighten it with understanding.[8]

This would have been a very traditional conception of knowledge, reflecting the continuing influence of Plato and Aristotle on the philosophical climate of the times. But influences are less important than what the *De magistro* itself can tell us about Augustine's understanding of "understanding." For if it is correct to suggest that Augustine thinks of understanding rather than justification as the differentiating ingredient of knowledge, the main thesis of the *De magistro,* that no man can teach another knowledge (scientia), can now be glossed as the claim that no man can teach another to understand something. The argument will not be that information cannot be transmitted from one person to another but that the appreciation or understanding of any such information is a task that each person must work at for himself. And while this as it stands is by no means clear and lucid, it is at least a proposition one could imagine coming to appreciate and understand in the course of working through the dialogue.

De magistro begins with what looks like an exercise in the Academic procedure of arguing both sides of a question. It is first argued that all teaching is effected through words or, more generally, through signs (1.1–10.31), then that no teaching is effected through words or signs (10.32–36). But the two sides are not in fact equally weighted. The second thesis prevails and the remainder of the dialogue (11.36–14.46) explains how, given that words and signs teach nothing, we can and do learn things without them. In retrospect, therefore, the long first section is cast as an exposition of the view to be overthrown. The thesis that all teaching is effected through words and signs is the wrong answer, which has to be worked through first, before the right answer can establish itself in the mind as a satisfactory and illuminating solution. As Augustine (or Plato) would have been happy to say, "To convince someone of the truth, it is not enough to state it, but rather one must find the *path* from error to truth."[9]

It is obvious enough why it should be tempting to think that some teaching is effected through words or signs. As we ordinarily think of it, a good deal of what teachers do is "talk and chalk." Words and signs are the instruments by which knowledge is transmitted from them to us. That is the commonsense view of teaching, and it implies no great distinction between teaching and information-communicating discourse in general; or at least they come to much the same once we set aside as inessential any institutional associations that the word "teaching" may introduce. Accordingly, the dialogue begins with a perfectly general question about the intended effect, or function, of speaking, to which an answer is returned that gives to the notion of teaching an extremely general scope: "Speech is instituted for no other reason than for teaching [docere] or for reminding [commemorare]" (1.2).

Some objections to this large and implausible generalization are dealt with by deciding that a question, for example, teaches the other person what it is you want to know (cf. *PI* par. 24) and that words addressed to God in inward prayer are reminders to oneself (*De magistro* 1.1–2). But remember that Augustine is engaged in a dialectical exercise. "Play with the purpose of sharpening up the mind" is how he will characterize it later on (8.21), and the final message of the dialogue is that all through he has been using words neither to teach nor to remind but to stimulate his son to learn for himself. What matters at this stage is that both common sense and many theorists (ancient or modern) will agree that one absolutely central function of language is the transmission of information, letting people know things, teaching (*docere*). Adeodatus' first task is to get clear about the implications and ramifications of his commonsense belief that, when someone does not already know that *p*, he can be told or taught by means of words and thereby come to know what he did not know before.

If, then, some teaching is by words, how do words effect the teaching, how do they convey the information they are instituted to convey (cf. 9.25–26)? The answer given is that words are signs and teach by signifying (2.3, 10.30). Here Augustine starts a lengthy and intricate argument for the thesis that all words signify something, even connectives like "if" and prepositions like "from," and consequently all words are names. We are at once reminded of Wittgenstein's use of Augustine as a stalking horse for his attack on the idea that the words of a language are names and its sentences combinations of names. Wittgenstein suggests (*PI* par. 1, BB as quoted above) that one falls victim to the temptation to think this way when one concentrates attention on common nouns like "table" and proper names, leaving other kinds of words to take care of themselves. The historical Augustine was more thorough. Not only did he expressly argue for the namehood of words other than nouns, he was also careful to explain (*De magistro* 6.17) that of course he did not mean that a word like "from" is a noun like "table" or "Socrates" (*nomen* as one of the eight parts of speech). What he meant is neither more nor less than that "from" is a sign of or signifies something (not, of course, a physical object but, if you like, a separation of the things in question), and that the contribution made by "if" to a sentence is different from the contribution made by "because" in the same position (2.3–4, 5.16).

No doubt it is true that "When we say: 'Every word in language signifies something' we have so far said *nothing whatsoever;* unless we have explained exactly *what* distinction we wish to make" (*PI* par. 13). (Augustine could add, rightly, that the same holds when we say "All words are names.") But in the ancient context there was a distinction, indeed a dispute, between the claim (originally Stoic) that every word signifies something and a rival (Peripatetic) view that this holds for nouns and verbs only, other words being merely "co-significant," not significant in their own right, because they are essentially devices for combining and embellishing.[10] Augustine makes it clear that he is just playing with Adeodatus in *De magistro* 2.3–4 when he forces him to try to *specify* the something signified by "if," "from," and "nothing." (He accepts "for the moment" that "if" signifies a mental state of doubt, he will not stop to bring counterexamples against the "separation" account of "from," and it would be absurd if the discussion was held up by nothing.) But his remarks about "if" and "because" in 5.16 can be taken as a serious-minded illustration of what is meant by the thesis that all words are names.

If I see an object in the distance and I am uncertain what it is, I should be satisfied with saying, "If it is a man, it is an animal," but not satisfied with saying, "Because it is a man, it is an animal." This establishes that it makes a difference whether you use "if" or "because." Now consider the following sentences (remember that Augustine is writing before the age of inverted commas):

> If satisfies me [placet si].
> Because does not satisfy me [displicet quia].

If we apply the modern use–mention dichotomy, it is clear that "if" and "because" are not used as they were in the original sentences. But an earlier argument (5.13–14) confirms that Augustine would also refuse to opt for the other half of the modern dichotomy. For it is not the *sound* that satisfies or does not satisfy (as if I were trying to compose a sonorous poem). It is the meaning, or (perhaps better) the word considered along with its meaning, that Augustine elsewhere calls "dictio" in contrast to "verbum" or the word as sound (*De dialectica* 5). The thesis that "if" and "because" are names is, first, the thesis that they can be used to name (stand for, refer to) their own meanings or themselves as *dictiones*.[11] This holds for all words (7.20), and, second, any word can be used autonymously, to name itself as *verbum* (8.22–24).

Presumably it is a matter of convention to allow "if" and "because" to be used in these extra ways, just as it is a matter of modern convention to use inverted commas instead. The substantive claim—but it is not very radical—is that even connectives make a distinct, hence nameable, contribution to speech. The reason Augustine insists on this, I think, is that his topic is teaching. He wants to say that every word contributes to the information content of the sentences in which it occurs, to what is taught by them. That is the burden of the thesis that all words are names.

So interpreted, the thesis is entirely compatible with the sensible (Stoic) view that you *specify* the meaning of "if" and "because" by stating the truth-conditions of whole sentences in which they occur.[12] The fact is that, while Augustine is having fun, what he is having fun with, for Adeodatus' benefit, is dry and sensible (often Stoic) theory. He is not in the grip of an *Urbild* when he says that all words are names. Nor has he succumbed to another idea that figures centrally in Wittgenstein's picture of Augustine's picture of language, the idea that the meaning of any word just is the object for which it stands (*PI* par. 1). Or at least the historical Augustine does not succumb in a simple way. He has various remarks that distinguish between what a word signifies and the way in which it signifies. "Colored" and "visible," "name" and "word," are pairs of words that signify the same things but in different ways, in virtue of different aspects of the things signified; and on the strength of this Augustine describes them as having different meanings or significations (*De magistro* 5.12, 7.20). Nor, finally, does Augustine think that we can rely on ostension to teach the meanings of words, even with more favorable examples than "if" and "from":

> *Aug:* Supposing I had no idea of the meaning of the word "walking," and I were to ask you when you were walking what "walking" means, how would you teach me?
>
> *Adeo:* I should walk a little more quickly. The change in speed would give notice that I was replying to your question, and I should still be doing what I was asked to demonstrate.
>
> *Aug:* But you know there is a difference between walking and hastening. He who walks does not necessarily hasten and he who hastens does not necessarily walk. We speak of hastening in writing, reading and very many other things. Consequently, if, after my query, you did what you had been doing, only a little more quickly, I should conclude that walking was the same thing as hastening, for the acceleration was the new feature of your behaviour. So I should be misled. (3.6)[13]

To which Adeodatus later adds that you are no better off trying to teach someone what "walking" means by starting to walk than by speeding up your walking; for he might take you to mean not walking but walking a certain distance (10.29).

From all this Augustine gets Adeodatus to conclude that nothing whatever is taught without words or, more generally, signs (10.31). The inference is unsound and invalid. That ostension is open to a variety of interpretations is a Wittgensteinian point well taken but, as father and son will shortly acknowledge (10.32), it does not prove that ostension never succeeds in teaching someone the meaning of a word. Even if this was proven, and we accepted as true that all teaching about words requires the use of other words (or at least nonverbal signs like pointing— cf. 3.5–6, 10.34), it does not follow from

(a) Some teaching is effected through words or signs,

plus

(b) All teaching about words or signs is eVected through words or signs,

that

(c) All teaching whatsoever is through words or signs.

But Augustine knows that it does not follow. He warns his son not to be upset when an opinion held as the result of a too ready and precipitate assent is shattered by a contrary argument (10.31).

The shattering blow is this:

> Suppose someone ignorant of how birds are deceived by twigs and birdlime should meet a birdcatcher equipped with his instruments but merely travelling and not actually engaged in his work. Suppose he followed the birdcatcher step by step and

wonderingly thought and inquired what could be the purpose [meaning, significance][14] of the man's equipment. Suppose the birdcatcher, seeing him all attention, and eager to display his skills, got ready his twigs and tubes and hawk and caught a bird he spotted nearby, would he not teach the spectator what he wanted to know by the action itself and without any signs? (10.32)

Formally, this is just a counterexample to the rash generalization (c): "It is sufficient for our present purpose that some men can be taught some, not all, things without a sign" (10.32). The trouble is that it is also a counterexample to the final conclusion of the entire dialogue. For Augustine is about to argue that

(d) No teaching is effected through words or signs (10.33ff.),

and thence, by another questionable inference, that

(e) No man teaches another anything (14.46).

In the end the counterexample seems to have been a temporary dialectical concession.

This bewildering sequence of about-turns shows that Augustine, like Plato often (and Wittgenstein), is determined not to tell us how to read his writing. I think that we can understand what is going on if we distinguish between teaching by telling and teaching by showing. In the first part of the discussion showing was gradually squeezed out in favor of telling. Indeed, if teaching is restricted to telling, (a), (b), and (c) are innocuously true. What is more, the dry and sensible semantic theory invoked to prove that all words are names can stand as an innocuous account of how one does tell things with words. In the second part of the discussion, by contrast, showing is privileged over telling. If teaching is restricted to showing, (d) is innocuously true, and in arguing for (d) Augustine does so restrict it: "The utmost value I can attribute to words is this. They bid us look for things, but they do not show them to us so that we may know them. He alone teaches me anything who sets before my eyes, or one of my other bodily senses, or my mind, the things which I desire to know" (11.36). It is the example of the birdcatcher that pivots the discussion from telling to showing. And I would suggest that, if we look carefully at the example, we can see how to resolve the contradiction between the claim that the birdcatcher teaches and the final conclusion (e) that no man teaches another.

As Augustine describes the case the birdcatcher knows that he is being watched by someone who wants to know what his equipment is for and he catches a bird with the intention of satisfying the spectator's desire to know. That is all. It is not said or implied that the birdcatcher has the further (Gricean) intention that the spectator should realize that he is putting on the show for this very purpose, in order that the spectator may learn from it what he is so curious to know. In no sense is the birdcatcher trying to communicate the information that the equipment is for catching birds.[15] He is merely doing something from which he knows the spectator can gather that information for himself. No wonder Augustine proceeds to claim that God is constantly showing the sun, the moon, the stars, the earth, and the sea and the innumerable things they bear to everyone who looks at them (10.32; cf. the wall at 3.6). In that sense I could teach everybody about flowers simply by putting some on view in a vase. But most of us would agree that this is not really teaching, or even showing. It is merely providing an occasion for the spectator to learn.[16]

In sum if showing or teaching requires no more than deliberately so acting or arranging things that other people may, if they wish, learn for themselves, then nothing is easier and the birdcatcher is a perfectly good teacher. What Augustine is denying when he reaches his conclusion (e) is that anyone can do what telling is supposed to do, namely, transmit knowledge to another mind. On that common-sense understanding of "teaching" the birdcatcher does not teach.

This brings me to the central and most interesting issue of the dialogue. Why is it impossible to bring another person to know something by telling him? Augustine proceeds to tell Adeodatus (who does not speak again until the end of the dialogue) in a long discourse that starts with a sentence from the story in the book of Daniel about the three youths whose strength of belief enabled them to survive the fiery furnace of King Nebuchadnezzar:

> If we consider this a little more closely, perhaps you will find, that nothing is learned even by its appropriate sign [per sua signa]. If I am given a sign and I do not know what it is the sign of, it can teach me nothing. If I know what it is the sign of, what do I learn through the sign? When I read [Daniel 3:27: LXX Daniel 3:94]: "Their *sarabarae* were not changed," the word *sarabara* does not show me the thing it signifies. If some covering of the head is so called, I surely do not learn from being told this[17] what a head is, or a covering. Those things I knew already, and the knowledge of them came to me not when they were named by others but when I actually saw them. After all, when these two syllables first struck my ear, *ca-put*, I was as ignorant of what they meant as I was of the meaning of *sarabara* when I first heard or read it. But when the word, *caput*, was frequently repeated, observing when it was said, I discovered it was the name of a thing well known to me from my having seen it. Before I made that discovery the word was merely a sound to me. I learned that it is a sign when I found out what it is the sign of—the thing itself, as I said, I learned not from any signifying but from my own seeing. So the sign is learned from knowing the thing, rather than the thing itself being learned when the sign is given. (10.33)

The first sentence in the quotation indicates that the argument (a semantic version of Meno's paradox) concerns individual words.[18] No word shows me the thing it signifies. No word, taken singly, tells me what it signifies or anything about what it signifies. Someone may tell me that a sarabara is a certain covering for the head, but that is no help unless I already know what a covering is and what a head is. Fair enough, but suppose I do know what a covering is and what a head is. Augustine argues that I still do not know what a sarabara is.[19] It is not just that the word "sarabara" cannot teach me this. Neither can any other word or combination of words, even words I understand perfectly well. I have to look at some actual sarabarae. The most that words can do, provided I understand them, is tell me to look and see when some sarabarae are on view (10.35). Thus telling is not so unlike the birdcatcher's showing as we might have expected it to be: in their different ways neither does more than prompt people to learn for themselves, but both can be of value for so doing.

At this point it becomes obvious, I think, that already in the *De magistro* Augustine has special requirements on what it is to know something. Knowledge is not just a matter of having the information and being justified in accepting it. It is not more or better justification that I need to know what that peculiar word "sarabara" signifies but a particular kind of firsthand justification that, now that sarabarae are extinct, none of us can ever have.[20] This emphasis on firsthand justification is confirmed when Augustine moves on from the individual word "sarabara" to the whole narrative in which it occurs. When words are combined to form sentences and stories, they still cannot impart knowledge to the hearer but *tertium datur* between knowledge and ignorance, namely, belief. A story about the triumph of belief is used to illustrate the importance of belief for an epistemology that insists that knowledge requires firsthand learning:

> But you may say: granted we cannot know those head-coverings, the sound of whose name we remember, unless we see them, and that we cannot fully know the name until we know the thing. But what about those young men of whom we have heard [Dan. 3] how they vanquished King Nebuchadnezzar and his fiery furnace by faith and religion, how they sang praises to God, and won honours from their enemy? Have we learned about them otherwise than by means of words? I reply, Yes. But we already knew the meaning of all these words. I already knew the meaning of "three youths," "furnace," "fire," "king," "unhurt by fire"[21] and all the rest. But Ananias, Azarias and Misael, are as unknown to me as those *sarabarae,* and their names did not help me one bit to know them, nor could they help. I confess I believe rather than know that everything we read of in that story happened at that time, just as it was written down. And the writers whom we believe were not ignorant of the difference. For the prophet says: "Unless ye believe ye shall not know" [Isa. 7:9: LXX]. This he would not have said if he judged that there was no difference. What I understand I also believe, but I do not understand everything that I believe. All that I understand I know, but I do not know all that I believe. And I know how useful it is to believe many things which I do not know, among them this story about the three youths. Thus although there are many things I cannot know, I do know how useful it is to believe them. (10.37)

Augustine, it turns out, is a firm believer in what Jonathan Barnes has called epistemic categories.[22] He sorts all knowable truths into two classes: (1) truths such that if x knows that p, then x has perceived by sense that p, (2) truths such that if x knows that p, then x has perceived by the mind that p. If x has not yet perceived that p in either way, he can only believe that p, not know it. This is the effect of 12.39–40:

Everything we perceive we perceive either by bodily sense or by the mind. The former we call "sensible things," the latter "intelligible things"; or, to use the terminology of our Christian authors, the former we call "carnal things," the latter "spiritual things." When we are asked about the former we reply if they are present to our senses, for example, if we are looking at the new moon and someone asks what it is like or where it is. If our questioner does not believe them, but he learns nothing unless he himself sees what he is asking about. When he sees he learns not from words uttered but from the objects seen and his sense of sight. . . .

But when we have to do with things which we behold with the mind, that is, with the intellect and reason, we speak of things which we look upon directly in the inner light of truth which illumines the "inner man" and is inwardly enjoyed. There again if my hearer sees these things himself with his inward eye, he comes to know what I say, not as a result of my words but as a result of his own contemplation. Even when I speak what is true and he sees what is true, it is not I who teach him. He is taught not by my words but by the things themselves which inwardly God has made manifest to him.

It is a direct consequence of this epistemological stance that there is no such thing as historical knowledge or knowledge transmitted by the word of another person.[23] All knowledge has to come from firsthand learning, by the intellect or by my own sense perception, just as Plato maintains in the *Meno* that mathematical knowledge has to come by reasoning and knowledge of the road to Larissa by actually traveling there and in the *Theaetetus* that what happened at the scene of a crime can only be known by the eyewitness who saw it with his own eyes.[24]

You get a stronger Platonic position—more like Plato's position in dialogues other than the *Meno* and *Theaetetus*—namely, that knowledge is rational understanding, if you demote the category of truths known by sense perception and say that this is knowledge only by courtesy, by an improper manner of speaking. That is what Augustine does in the passage from the *Retractationes*, quoted earlier, and elsewhere.[25] Plato's vacillation over whether to allow knowledge of sensible things has often been discussed. The fact that it has a parallel in Augustine suggests to me that it derives from their shared stress on firsthand learning.

I suggest, in fact, that in the *De magistro* Augustine needs the analogy of sense perception precisely to enforce the point that knowledge requires firsthand appreciation and that it is for the same reason that Plato in the *Meno* and *Theaetetus* needs to be able to appeal to the knowledge of the eyewitness or of the man who has made the journey to Larissa. The need is the need of advocacy. For Augustine has no *argument* for the thesis that knowledge requires firsthand learning. There is no such argument in Plato either. What there is, in both Plato and Augustine, is the attempt to make the thesis persuasive to us by calling upon our sense of a great gap between the epistemic position of an eyewitness who watches an event with his own eyes and that of the jury later, or, in Augustine's example, the position of present-day readers of the book of Daniel.

Plato and Augustine want to persuade us that this gap is the one between knowledge and mere true belief. We may reply that the alleged gap is no more than a difference: secondhand justification is a different kind of justification from firsthand, but it is not *eo ipso* less of a justification. Suppose, then, that I am justified in believing that *p* on the strength of an eyewitness's story, and suppose further that *p* is true. I claim that I know that *p*, just as the eyewitness does, although not on his ground. But typically there will be other, connected facts of the case that I do not know because the eyewitness has not told me. The eyewitness frequently knows more than he tells. He saw the whole thing. That synoptic grasp in which the knowledge that *p* is just one element does mark a gap, a cognitive difference between him and me. And it is this that makes the eyewitness such a useful analogy for a philosopher who wants in the end to assimilate knowledge to rational understanding.[26] For I take it that the important difference between knowledge and understanding is that knowledge can be piecemeal, can grasp isolated truths one by one, whereas understanding always involves seeing connections and relations between the items known. "The only part of modern physics I understand is the formula '$E = mc^2$' " is nonsense. "The only part of modern physics I know is the formula '$E = mc^2$' " is merely sad.

There are several passages in the *De magistro* that imply that the understanding that Adeodatus is aiming for is a matter of being able to get a clear synoptic grasp of a large complex field (10.31, 12.40, 14.46). But I suspect that Augustine has a weaker conception of knowledge as understanding than Plato would recommend. For Plato, like Aristotle, makes it a condition on knowing or understanding that *p* that one grasps the explanation of *p*. This of course involves seeing the connection between *p* and a whole lot of other propositions, but it is not mere connectedness so much as explanatory connectedness that counts, and it is by way of this thought that Plato and Aristotle reach the conclusion that knowledge in the full sense— that is, understanding—requires the synoptic grasp of a whole field.[27] Augustine, however, says nothing in the *De magistro* about explanation. He may intend a more full-blooded Platonic view in the *Retractationes* when he demotes sense perception and speaks of knowledge as owed exclusively to firm reasoning of the mind. (In sense perception one may perceive a complex of elements as a coherent whole, but one does not perceive explanatory relations between one element and another.) But the important point for our purposes is that the emphasis on connecting one item with another is enough by itself to yield the conclusion that knowledge, in the sense of understanding, cannot be taught or conveyed by words from one person to another. Knowledge must be firsthand if it is essentially of connections.

I can of course be given the information that *p* is connected with *q*, *r*, and so on, just as I can be given the information that *p* is true because *q* is true. What is more, I can accept that this is so with adequate justification and thereby, in the ordinary sense, know it. But every schoolboy is familiar with the fact that it is one thing to know in that external way *that* the connection holds (e.g., that these propositions constitute a proof of that theorem) and quite another to understand the connection, to see how the elements hang together. That is something one can only do for oneself.[28] And we still describe the moment when this is achieved as a moment of illumination.

The *De magistro* was Augustine's first extended presentation of his famous doctrine of internal illumination. The doctrine has been described as a misguided transference of the idea of empirical vision into the intellectual sphere.[29] The same charge has repeatedly been leveled at the visual metaphors of which Plato is so fond. Both philosophers are represented as holding that knowledge or understanding is an immediate relation to an isolated abstract object, in much the same way as seeing a table is a relation to a single physical object. Both philosophers are in fact saying the very opposite, that knowledge or understanding is of the connections between things, of things only as parts of a whole interrelated system; that is why, like empirical vision, it involves seeing things for oneself. Both philosophers also have the ideas that there is such a thing as the complete synoptic vision that embraces all partial understandings and that any understanding that falls short of this is not in the fullest sense knowledge because it does not see all the connections. In other words the whole truth is also the light that gives understanding. All Augustine adds is that this Truth and this Light is God as present to our mind. Hence the dictum that Christ is the only Teacher, the one source of understanding.

It is eloquent testimony both to Augustine's philosophical acumen and to the coherence of the Platonic epistemology that Augustine should have been able to reconstruct it, on the basis of a quite new set of arguments, so much better than many people who have actually read Plato's dialogues.[30] Whatever is to be said about Adeodatus, of Augustine at least it is true that he learned it for himself, without being taught.

WITTGENSTEIN AND THE *CONFESSIONS*

It is inconceivable that Augustine should have forgotten the *De magistro* when he came to write the *Confessions* (397–401 AD). The dialogue was too painfully associated with the death of his son soon after its dramatic date.[31] Besides, Wittgenstein's quotation from *Confessions* 1.8.13 exactly matches what Augustine says about how he learned the word "caput" in *De magistro* 10.33. Add the preceding sentences, which Wittgenstein omitted; view the whole in the wider setting provided by the *De magistro;* and it becomes clear, I submit, that Augustine's concentration, in the now famous account of language learning, on words for objects that can be pointed out or shown (*ostendere*) is due to epistemological considerations rather than a primitive theory of meaning. Language learning starts with the interplay between visible objects and visible adults because these are things the child can see for himself, and his task is to discover for himself that certain of the sounds adults emit are connected with things he already knows. To repeat: "I learned that it is a sign when I found out what it is the sign of—the thing itself, as I said, I learned not from any signifying but from my own seeing. So the sign is learned from knowing the thing, rather than the thing itself being learned when the sign is given" (10.33). We have seen, moreover, that Augustine shares with Wittgenstein a strong sense that nothing other people may do or say, and no fact about the world around me, can determine me to respond in the right way. No one can achieve my understanding for me, not for the trivial reason that it is mine but because to internalize the requisite connections is to go beyond what is presented on any occasion of so-called teaching. Augustine does not have Wittgenstein's subtle arguments to bring out the multiplicity of ways in which I might seem (to myself and others) to understand and later turn out to have missed the point, which in turn demonstrates the multiplicity of connections involved in understanding itself. But we might read Wittgenstein as reviving the ancient understanding of the complexity of understanding. And we certainly should read *Confessions* 1.8.13 as agreeing with Wittgenstein that the description quoted in *PI* paragraph 1 is wholly inadequate to explain how little Augustine came to grasp his first words. Divine help was needed, in the form of the mind (*mens* or *memoria*), which Augustine inherited from the Platonic tradition.

My final suggestion—for obvious reasons it can be no more than a suggestion—is that Wittgenstein probably knew much better than his expositors what he was doing when he omitted the sentences preceding his quotation.[32] To leave out God and the Platonic mind for the beginning of the *Philosophical Investigations* was to accept Augustine's problem as his own and to declare that it must now be solved in naturalistic, purely human terms:

> Would it not be possible for us, however, to calculate as we actually do (all agreeing, and so on), and still at every step to have a feeling of being guided by the rules as by a spell, feeling astonishment at the fact that we agreed? (We might give thanks to the Deity for our agreement.)
>
> This merely shows what goes to make up what we call "obeying a rule" in everyday life. (*PI* pars. 234–35; cf. *Confessions* 10.40.65)

NOTES

1. Jerry A. Fodor, *The Language of Thought* (Hassocks 1976), 64. For older and more theological versions of this assessment, beginning with Augustine himself, see the classic study by Gerhart B. Ladner, "*Homo viator:* Mediaeval Ideas on Alienation and Order," *Speculum* 42 (1967): 233–59.

2. G. P. Baker and P. M. S. Hacker, *An Analytical Commentary on Wittgenstein's "Philosophical Investigations,"* vol. 1 (Oxford: Blackwell, 1983), 21–23. Hereafter, Wittgenstein's *Philosophical Investigations* will be referred to in the text as *PI*.

3. With "sed ego ipse mente" supply "me docebam" from "non docebant me," as in the translation by R. S. Pine-Coffin (Harmondsworth: Penguin, 1961), the Budé by P. de Labriolle, 2d ed. (Paris: Société d'Édition "Les Belles Lettres," 1933), and the Biblothèque Au-

gustinienne translation by E. Tréhorel and G. Boissou (Paris: Desclee de Brower, 1962). This is the only possible translation of the Knöll text (Leipzig: Teubner, 1898), which Wittgenstein possessed and read (Garth Hallett, *A Companion to Wittgenstein's "Philosophical Investigations"* [Ithaca: Cornell University Press, 1977], 761), and of any text that follows Knöll (as do both Labriolle and the most authoritative modern edition, Skutella [Leipzig: Teubner, 1934]) in ending the sentence at "to everyone I wished." The Pusey translation (London: J. M. Dent, 1929, now in the Everyman series), which Baker and Hacker, *Analytical Commentary*, p. 21, reproduce to give the immediate context of Wittgenstein's quotation, is a translation of Pusey's text (text and translation appeared as companion volumes in A Library of the Fathers of the Holy Catholic Church Anterior to the Division of the East and West [Oxford: 1838]). Pusey followed the seventeenth-century Maurist edition (Migne, *Patrologia Latina* 32) in printing "praesonabam" instead of "pensabam" and a comma instead of a full stop before it so as to make "praesonabam" the main verb after "sed ego ipse mente": "but I . . . did myself, by the understanding which thou, my God, gavest me, practise the sounds in my memory." The effect of this is to submerge, if not totally to drown, Augustine's claim to have taught himself. The Maurist comma was retained by John Gibb and William Montgomery (Cambridge: Cambridge University Press, 1908), who were also still tempted by "praesonabam," but the only disagreement among more recent editors is whether to begin the new sentence with "pensabam" (Knöll, Skutella) or with (not the weak "praesonabam" but) another variant, "prensabam" (Labriolle, Solignac in the Bibliothèque Augustinienne edition): "I had been trying to grasp [words] with my memory." *This* disagreement, unlike the Maurist comma, has no philosophical consequences.

On Wittgenstein's knowledge of Latin see Herbert Spiegelberg, "Augustine in Wittgenstein: A Case Study in Philosophical Stimulation," *Journal of the History of Philosophy* 17 (1979): 320. In any case the translation that Hallett (*Companion to "Philosophical Investigations,"* 761) reports that he owned, by O. F. Lachmann (Leipzig: Reclam, 1888), manages the right translation even with the Maurist text.

4. Contrast Hallett, *Companion to "Philosophical Investigations,"* 73, and Baker and Hacker, *Analytical Commentary*, 22, who tell students of Wittgenstein (apparently on the authority of Norman Kretzmann's article "Semantics, History of," in Paul Edwards, ed., *The Encyclopedia of Philosophy* [New York: Macmillan, 1967], cited by Hallet) that *De magistro* is critical of the primitive view expressed in *Confessions* 1.8.13.

5. In the *Retractationes* Augustine can be quite scathing about his early works. That he has nothing self-critical to say about the *De magistro* implies continuing satisfaction with its methods and conclusion.

6. According to *Confessions* 9.6.14 all the ideas ascribed to Adeodatus in the *De magistro* were genuinely his: another marvel for which God alone can be responsible. But Augustine does not claim, as some scholars have supposed, that the *De magistro* is the report of an actual historical discussion.

7. The meaning of "proprie" is well illustrated in the next paragraph: "we cannot *proprie* call little children wise or foolish."

8. This conclusion fits well with R. A. Markus's account of Augustine's conception of knowledge in *The Cambridge History of Later Greek and Early Medieval Philosophy*, ed. A. H. Armstrong (Cambridge: Cambridge University Press, 1970), 348–53, 362ff. But it must be tempered by a recognition that when Augustine has his sights trained on Academic skepticism (e.g., in *Contra academicas* and *De Trinitate* 15.12.21), he will insist in no uncertain

terms that both sense perception and testimony yield knowledge (*scire*). Further qualifications below.

9. Ludwig Wittgenstein, "Remarks on Frazer's *Golden Bough*," in C. G. Luckhardt, ed., *Wittgenstein: Sources and Perspectives* (Ithaca: Cornell University Press, 1979), 61.

10. The evidence is too complicated to set out here (it is persuasively assembled in an as yet unpublished Cambridge Ph.D. dissertation by C. Atherton), but some sense of the debate can be gathered from Plutarch's lengthy attack on the Stoic view in his *Platonic Questions* 10. At 1011c Plutarch complains that the Stoic theory makes speech an enumeration like a list of magistrates or days of the week.

11. Compare the pseudo-medieval theory of *suppositio semantica* invented by N. E. Christensen, "The Alleged Distinction between Use and Mention," *Philosophical Review* 76 (1967): 358–67, to deal with the example "You should never say 'never,' " which would require a translator to render into the foreign language *both* the two *different* occurrences of "never."

12. Diogenes Laertius 7.71–74. Stoic also, in all probability, is the thesis that any word can be used autonomously, to name itself: direct evidence is lacking, but it is the most likely explanation of Chrysippus's claim that absolutely every word is ambiguous (Aulus Gellius, *Noctes Atticae* 11.12; Augustine, *De dialectica* 8–9; cf. Cicero, *De inventione rhetorica* 2.117, Quintilian, *Institutio oratorio* 7.9.1). In a world without inverted commas Chrysippus's claim is simply true. The additional ambiguity imported by the *dicto–verbum* distinction, if I am right about it, may well be Augustine's own development.

13. This and future quotations from the *De magistro* are given in the translation of John H. S. Burleigh, *Augustine: Earlier Writings*, Library of Christian Classics, vol. 6 (Philadelphia: Westminster Press, 1953), adjusted to Daur's text (Corpus Christianorum 1970) and with a number of corrections of my own.

14. "Quidnam sibi . . . vellet" is a phrase that could equally well be used to formulate a question about the meaning of a word. No doubt that is why Augustine chose it.

15. Here, of course, I am drawing on H. P. Grice's famous article "Meaning," *Philosophical Review* 67 (1957): 377–88.

16. I do not deny it can be called teaching/showing. Ordinary usage extends "teaching" to any *x* such that I learn something from *x*, regardless of whether *x* intends to teach or intends me to learn, regardless even of whether *x* is an animate being. Examples are: "She taught/showed me what courage could be," "The mountain taught me the value of life," and Augustine's example of the wall showing itself at 3.6. But inadvertent and inanimate teaching are presumably so called only because there is deliberate teaching, and I suggest that the same holds for deliberately contrived opportunities to learn.

17. Alternatively, "from hearing this word."

18. This saves Augustine from being guilty of the view that Kretzmann, "Semantics, History of," ascribes to him, that knowing what the words mean in "Armadilloes are mammals" *eo ipso* precludes one's learning anything through hearing that sentence uttered. Augustine simply supposes, and reasonably, both here and later, that knowing what the words mean is a necessary condition for such learning. The bad argument that Augustine does not use may, however, be observed in Sextus Empiricus, *Outlines of Pyrrhonism* 3.267–69.

19. This further point, which is the vital one, is missed in the (frequently inaccurate) account of the *De magistro* given by Étienne Gilson, *The Christian Philosophy of Saint Augustine* (New York: Random House, 1960), 66ff.

20. Anyone who wants to know (and is content to be told) what "sarabara" really means may however be referred to a fascinatingly learned article by G. N. Knauer, "*Sarabara* (Dan. 3, 94 [27] bei Aug. mag. 10, 33-11,37)," *Glotta* 33 (1954): 100–118.

21. This last example shows that Augustine has not forgotten that not all words are nouns.

22. Jonathan Barnes, "Socrates and the Jury: Paradoxes in Plato's Distinction between Knowledge and True Belief," *Proceedings of the Aristotelian Society,* supplementary volume 54 (1980): 193–206.

23. Augustine accepts the consequence, so far as history is concerned, at *De diversis quaestionibus* 48 (PL 40.31) and *Epistulae* 120.2.9—in flat contradiction with *De Trinitate* 15.12.21 (n. 8 above).

24. On Plato's treatment of these issues see my "Socrates and the Jury: Paradoxes in Plato's Distinction between Knowledge and True Belief," *PASS* 54 (1980): 173–91, to which the present chapter is a sort of sequel.

25. Cf. *Soliloquia* 1.3.8 and references in Markus, *Cambridge History of Later Greek and Early Medieval Philosophy.*

26. The philosopher in question need not be a Platonist. In Locke, *An Essay concerning Human Understanding* 1.3.24, eyewitnessing, the need for firsthand learning, knowledge as understanding, and connectedness all come together for his anti-Platonic attack on innate principles.

27. See my "Aristotle on Understanding Knowledge," in E. Berti, ed., *Aristotle on Science: "The Posterior Analytics"* (Padua: Editrice Antenore, 1981), 97–139.

28. This answers an objection brought by Barnes, "Socrates and the Jury," 203, against my earlier (and more detailed) arguments on this subject.

29. R. A. Markus, "Augustine," in D. J. O'Connor, ed., *A Critical History of Western Philosophy* (New York: Free Press, 1964), 87.

30. Augustine thinks of himself as an admirer of Plato and refers to the *Meno* often enough, but *De Trinitate* 12.15.24 implies that he does not know what questions Socrates put to the slave. This would be because he read about the *Meno* in Cicero, *Tusculan Disputations* 1.57–68. See further Pierre Courcelle *Late Latin Writers and Their Greek Sources* (Cambridge, Mass.: Harvard University Press 1969), 168ff., who suggests that Augustine's firsthand knowledge of Plato was confined to the portion of the *Timaeus* translated by Cicero. What he did read, thanks to God's intervention, was "the books of the Platonists" (*Confessions* 7.9.13, 8.2.3)—Plotinus and his followers.

31. *Confessions* 9.6.14.

32. The first time he copied out (some of) his Augustine quotation, in the 1936 revision of *BB* published as *Eine philosophische Betrachtung* (vol. 5 of the *Schriften* [Frankfurt: Suhrkamp, 1970], 117), he began it, "cum . . . appellabant, etc." Not even this minimal gesture toward a larger context is to be found in, for example, Robert L. Arrington, "'*Mechanism and Calculus*': Wittgenstein on Augustine's Theory of Ostension," in Luckhardt, ed., *Wittgenstein,* 322–29; as a result I have to say that what Arrington presents as "Augustine's theory" is largely fiction.

SEVENTEEN

Toward an Augustinian Liberalism*

Paul J. Weithman

The title of this paper no doubt elicits some measure of surprise and confusion, for Augustine's name and his doctrines are no longer the common coin in political philosophy that they once were. Moreover, the term "Augustinian liberalism" will strike those familiar with Augustine's politics—as he developed them during the Donatist controversy, for example—as oxymoronic.[1] The political theories historically associated with Augustine and Augustinianism have not, after all, been notably tolerant. Finally, the qualities of character liberalism fosters—among them tolerance and self-assertion—might be thought antithetical to Augustinian Christianity. There are, however, arguments to support political liberalism that can appropriately be described as Augustinian, and the aim of this paper is to lay them out. Before turning to them, it will prove helpful to state what I mean by the term "political liberalism" and to say to whom I am offering these Augustinian arguments.

LIBERALISM AND POLITICAL ADVOCACY

"Liberalism" has been and continues to be used to denote a widely extended family of political and philosophical positions that differ in significant respects. The element common to this family is often said to be an overriding concern for the rule of law and for the personal and political liberties of conscience, speech, assembly, and of the press. The common element is sometimes said to be a commitment to rights that guarantee freedom to exercise these liberties.[2] Still others characterize liberalism by the political agenda that these philosophical positions are deemed to entail. My own working characterization, however, takes as central to political lib-

*I am twice grateful to Phil Quinn for illuminating comments on two very different drafts. Thanks also to the Center for Philosophy of Religion at the University of Notre Dame for the opportunity to work on the paper in so stimulating and congenial an environment.

eralism[3] neither rights, nor liberties, nor agenda but a criterion of the legitimate exercise of public power.[4]

It is not peculiar to liberalism to argue that power ought only be exercised legitimately. But there are distinctively liberal principles of political legitimacy, principles that restrict the reasons and values that can be appealed to when justifying the exercise of public power if that exercise is to be legitimate. Political liberalism as I shall understand it is a position characterized by fidelity to one or another of the members of this family of liberal principles of political legitimacy. An adequate characterization of political liberalism as I understand it therefore requires adequate characterization of what is common to the restrictions various liberal principles of legitimacy impose.

Jeremy Waldron has located at the foundations of liberalism the "demand that the social order should in principle be capable of explaining itself at the tribunal of each person's understanding."[5] This demand suggests that liberal principles of political legitimacy have in common their insistence that exercises of public power are legitimate only if they can be justified in terms that "explain [themselves]" to every citizen. David Lyons makes a similar suggestion, saying that the justification of public policy must be "accessible" to everyone.[6]

These broad characterizations leave ample scope for disagreement among liberals about which values and principles do and which do not legitimate the exercise of public power; the literature of recent liberalism reflects this disagreement. John Rawls inclines to the view that public power is legitimately exercised only when it can be justified by appeal to a range of values on which all could agree and which are peculiar to what he calls "the domain of the political."[7] Robert Audi's arguments suggest that he thinks exercises of power legitimate only when they can be justified by what he calls "secular reasons"; to appeal to religious values or principles is to offer reasons that not all citizens do or could accept. But Audi seems not to insist, as Rawls does, that legitimating reasons appeal only to values that are distinctively political.[8] The great Catholic liberal John Courtney Murray, on the other hand, seems to have held that *some* religious propositions and values can legitimate the use of public power in the United States because he thought that there are some religious values or propositions all Americans could come to accept.[9]

Ample room also remains for disagreement about those to whom the exercise of power must be justified or justifiable. Rawls suggests that such exercise need by judged legitimate only by those who are or are trying to be reasonable.[10] Bruce Ackerman seems to think that agreement must be reached among all contending parties whether or not they regard one another as reasonable. Still others who are liberal by Waldron's criterion—Seyla Benhabib, for example—worry that any standards of reasonableness framed prior to the process of justification tend uncritically to legitimate the status quo and so do not really legitimate at all.[11]

Fortunately, I need not adjudicate among competing liberal principles of political legitimacy. For my purposes it suffices to note that political liberalism addresses those who live in a society of moral, religious, or philosophical pluralism and attempts to narrow their disagreement about the use of public power. It attempts to do so by defending restrictions on the invocation of moral, philosophical, or religious beliefs and values to legitimate the exercise of that power. The restrictions on beliefs and values are to be restrictions on which all, or all reasonable, citizens could come to agree because liberalism is premised on the view that at least the most significant exercises of public power must be justifiable to all or to the reasonable.

In what follows I shall be concerned with the implications of political liberalism for *political advocacy*—for citizens' advocacy and defense of the use of public power. For a citizen to be a liberal requires that her political advocacy conform to one or another liberal principle of political legitimacy. The liberal citizen therefore adduces reasons for the exercise of public power that would render that exercise legitimate by the standards of one or another liberal principle of political legitimacy. A Rawlsian liberal would appeal to political values in her political advocacy, an Audian liberal would appeal to secular reasons, and a Murrayan liberal, while permitted appeal to some religious beliefs, would not appeal to narrowly sectarian propositions or to those that depend upon revelation. I shall argue that there are Augustinian reasons for imposing some liberal restrictions on one's political advocacy and defense and so to be a political liberal, provided others do likewise. Before proceeding, however, some qualifications and explanations are in order.

First, I have in mind only political advocacy that is recognizably argumentative. Verbal but nonargumentative political advocacy, as is found in drama, poetry, music, and graffiti, to take but four examples, would have to be considered in a full theory of legitimacy and political advocacy.[12] So too would the nonverbal political expression of the visual arts, dance, flag burning, and vigils of silent prayer. But, having noted their importance, I shall prove myself no exception to the unfortunate philosophical trend of ignoring nonargumentative political expression.

Second, I am concerned only with political advocacy by ordinary citizens. The role of judges whose opinions have the force of precedent, for example, no doubt imposes special requirements on those who happen to be judges, especially on religious jurists. Judicial advocacy and defense of the exercise of public power therefore requires special treatment and would exceed the scope of this paper.[13]

Third, I am not going to argue that citizens need in fact be moved by the reasons they adduce for the exercise of political power. A citizen counts as a liberal, in my view, if the argument in which her advocacy consists is liberal; this is compatible with her being moved even by highly idiosyncratic religious, philosophical, or moral views.[14]

Finally, I am not going to argue that there are overriding Augustinian reasons to a political liberal, just that there are good Augustinian reasons. I therefore leave aside the very difficult questions of whether someone whose political advocacy is illiberal thereby violates a moral obligation or fails to be a good citizen.

My arguments are intended to show that Christians have reason to accept some form of political liberalism. The arguments are premised on an Augustinian analysis of pride. I shall argue that Christians, because they have religious reasons to curb their pride, have reason to be concerned with the political manifestations of that vice and that Christians therefore have reasons to value the humility and restraint fostered by conforming their political advocacy to a liberal principle of political legitimacy if others do the same. Further, if pride is understood according to this Augustinian analysis, all and not just Christians have reasons to check their pride. All, therefore, have reasons to value the humbling and restraining effects of political liberalism.

My arguments linking liberalism and concern with pride are not intended to move those in all times and places. They are directed at those who live in what might be called maturely pluralistic democratic societies. These are societies with a democratic political culture and democratic institutions and traditions. They are characterized by what Rawls has called "the fact of pluralism": they are societies composed of those who adhere to diverse philosophical, religious, and moral conceptions of the good life. They are, finally, societies without institutional barriers that prevent adherents of minority views from learning enough about their own or the democratic tradition to engage in reasoned political argument. Augustinians in societies with histories of minority repression or without democratic institutions may have good reason to be liberals, but they do not have the reasons to which I shall appeal.

AUGUSTINE, AQUINAS, AND THE SIN OF PRIDE

Augustine's views on the origin and purposes of political society and on the legitimate uses of political authority are extremely complex. I cannot do them justice here; surely the political liberalism for which I will argue departs significantly from Augustine's political thought in some respects.[15] Even so, labeling this liberalism Augustinian is not without fidelity to Augustine's own views or to the tradition of their interpretation.

First, Augustine himself numbered the human tendency to pride among the legacies of original sin. He believed that political authority was instituted as a consequence of and a remedy for original sin, and he numbered among the primary functions of political authority the humbling of its subjects.[16] Indeed it is in part because Augustinian politics ascribes this function to political authority that some liberals—most notably Judith Shklar[17]—have tried to distance themselves from it and to supplant an Augustinian moral psychology stressing pride with an alternative psychology thought more congenial to liberalism. I want to suggest, on the contrary, that a concern with the vice of pride and with the consequent need for humility provide reasons for accepting political liberalism as it is discussed in the previous section. This stress on the humbling function of political liberalism qualifies the liberalism defended as Augustinian.

Moreover, that liberalism is Augustinian insofar as the account of pride on which it is premised is of Augustinian provenance: the essentials of that account are laid out in Augustine's works. Unfortunately, Augustine's own account is somewhat unsystematic. Its central elements were later masterfully combined and harmonized by Aquinas, and it is therefore on Aquinas's developed account of Augustinian ideas about pride that I rely.[18]

The pride that Christianity has traditionally considered the deadliest of the deadly sins is often thought of as contempt of God or as a desire to cast God down and to put oneself in his place. The paradigms of pride so conceived are Adam and Eve in their commission of original sin and Milton's Lucifer in his rebellion against divine sovereignty. Aquinas thinks that human beings do sometimes act from intentional contempt of God and his law. He is, however, committed to the view that pride is a pervasive moral phenomenon, found in a wide variety of faulty human acts.[19]

Pride, Aquinas says, is a failure to subject oneself to God and to the rules he has ordained.[20] Aquinas thinks that a failure to observe God's commands and a turning away from God toward what Aquinas calls "commutable goods" is the very nature of sin. He therefore thinks that every sin is, in effect, a failure properly to subject oneself to God; he concludes that every sin, however motivated and whatever its object, is in effect a sin of pride.

But this account is insufficient for Aquinas's purposes. While it does explain a rather weak way in which pride is present in every sinful act, Aquinas wants an account of pride that has explanatory power, one in which pride explains sinful acts and is not merely shown by them. Some of this explanatory power is provided by Aquinas's account of how pride removes impediments to immoral action. Aquinas thinks that intentional violation of moral rules requires some explanation. Here, he thinks, pride can have an explanatory role, for among the manifestations of pride is thinking oneself above such rules. Pride can thus remove the impediment to sin posed by a prima facie inclination to observe moral rules.

Even this account, however, is not enough. Aquinas thinks that pride is not only present in or explains many sinful acts; it also motivates them. Aquinas's commitment to pride's pervasiveness as a motive therefore requires a more nuanced account, one that will accommodate the Miltonian view of pride but also one that shows how wide a variety of acts pride can lead agents to perform. The key to this account is Aquinas's specification of pride's characteristic motive.

Aquinas argues that the characteristic motive of acts of pride is an undue desire for what he calls "one's own excellence." He does not have in mind an undue desire for one's own perfection or for the fulfillment of one's potential. Rather acts of pride are primarily motivated by an undue desire for *preeminence* or *superiority*. This undue desire for preeminence or superiority can, Aquinas concedes, be accompanied by a contempt for those over whom superiority is sought. This might be contempt for God and his commands; but, Aquinas insists, pride can also engender contempt for other human beings.[21] It is crucial to Aquinas's account of pride that contempt, whether for God or man, is not the motive primarily associated with pride. The primary motive remains undue desire for preeminence. To appreciate the variety of acts pride can engender, it is necessary to appreciate the variety of acts one could be led to perform by such a desire. This undue desire can show itself in two ways.

An undue desire for superiority, Aquinas would say, is sometimes a desire for undue superiority, a desire for moral, spiritual, or intellectual goods that human beings cannot attain. It is to this undue desire for superiority or preeminence that Aquinas would appeal to explain how acts of pride can be attempts to attain equality with God or to usurp his place: the goods desired are goods that properly belong only to God, and it is an essay in usurpation for a human being to desire them for herself. Most often, Aquinas believes, the usurpation of God's place is unintentional, and acts attributable to pride are not chosen under descriptions that refer to usurpation. They are instead chosen from a desire for the moral, spiritual, or intellectual good in question. What makes the consequent acts acts of pride is that the goods desired are desired as a means to superiority.

Adam and Eve's original sin therefore exemplified extraordinary pride. Adam and Eve, Aquinas says, wanted to be like God inasmuch as they wanted the undue spiritual good of being able to prescribe moral rules for themselves.[22] The extremity of their pride, he thinks, consisted in their knowingly trying to be like God. Thus does Aquinas's account enable him to accommodate the Miltonian view; thus also does it make of the Miltonian view an extreme and not a typical case of pride.

Pride of this first sort may be accompanied by a contempt for God, since the proud person implicitly denigrates him in the attempt to make herself in some respect his equal. Just as it is rare for someone knowingly to try to usurp God's place, so it is rare, Aquinas thinks, for someone consciously to hold God in contempt. Indeed his interpretation of the fall, according to which Adam and Eve wanted to make moral rules for themselves, suggests as much. If they were contemptuous at all, Aquinas's interpretation suggests, their contempt was primarily for God's commands and only secondarily for the God who commanded. And even in Adam and Eve's case, their original sin was motivated not by their contempt but by desire for their own superiority.

Aquinas also argues that there is a second sort of undue desire for superiority or preeminence, an undue desire to be superior to other human beings in some respect or for the power over others that superiority often confers.[23] A vice closely related to pride so understood, Aquinas says, is that of vainglory; the vainglorious person is moved by a desire that others praise and acknowledge her preeminence and power. Aquinas does not, however, think that the objects of vainglory and of this second sort of pride—superiority and power, praise and acknowledgment—are the intended objects of many of the acts properly described as acts of pride or vainglory. Few acts of these vices, Aquinas would say, are chosen from a desire for these objects that the agent herself recognizes. Acts of pride and vainglory often masquerade as acts of other vices—acts of seizing more money than one needs or is one's due, or foolhardy acts on the battlefield. What makes the act in question one of pride or vainglory rather than of injustice, intemperance, or rashness is that an undue desire for superiority, power, or praise is the appropriate explanation for seeking too much money or taking too many risks in battle. Because people can excel or gain the advantage over others in so many ways and by the use of so many objects from possessions to battlefield victories, pride of the second sort can, like pride of the first sort, lead the proud person to perform any of a variety of sinful acts.

Pride of the second sort, like pride of the first, can be accompanied by contempt. Attempts to secure preeminence over others can be accompanied by contempt for them, for God, or for moral rules. But Aquinas thinks that what makes an act one of pride is the role that desire for one's own superiority plays in that act's explanation.

In summary, Aquinas argues that in one sense every sin, regardless of agent or motive, is a sin of pride. He further argues that pride is needed to explain someone's knowing violation of a moral rule. And he argues that, because so many wrong acts can be means to attaining superiority, an undue desire for one's own superiority can motivate an agent to perform any of a wide variety of wrong acts. Indeed Aquinas says that pride can motivate someone to a wrong act of any kind.

Despite the fact that pride can explain so wide a variety of human failure, there are classes or "species" into which Aquinas thinks acts of pride can be sorted: imputing to oneself some good one really does not have, reputing oneself to have attained some good on one's own merits, failing to acknowledge the excellence or help of another in the attainment of some good, and seeking to excel others in some material, moral, intellectual, or spiritual good that one should have in the same way they do. Aquinas describes these classes of acts rather abstractly, but it is plausible that acts that fall into them are acts one would perform to usurp God's place, to gain preeminence over others, or to assure oneself of one's own superiority. His description of the classes of acts associated with vainglory is more concrete; he numbers hypocrisy, discord, contention, and pertinacity among what he calls the "daughters" of vainglory.

Aquinas's analysis indicates how pride motivates offenses against God and other human beings. The links he sees among contempt for rules, contempt for God and man, and desire for superiority over either or both suggest the corrosive effects of pride on the passions of the proud person. Certainly contempt for moral rules and a belief that one is above them can lead not only to their violation but also to the habit of excusing oneself for the violations. This in turn inhibits proper function of the moral sentiments of guilt and shame. Contempt for moral rules can also prevent proper responses to the good works of others that are worthy of admiration; and the habit of excusing oneself for having acted badly makes it more difficult properly to appreciate forgiveness granted by others. Contempt for others distorts the moral sentiments so that sympathy, pity, and remorse are not properly felt on the occasions that call for them. Insofar as the proper operation of the moral passions is part of a well-lived human life and contempt born of pride impedes them, pride is a fault both the religious and the nonreligious have reason to avoid.

Several features of Aquinas's account are especially worthy of mention. First, Aquinas thinks that appeal to pride is often required to complete the explanation of wrong action; in the vast majority of such cases, however, the agent believes herself motivated by interests or desires other than those associated with pride and vainglory. Indeed Aquinas might say that pride has so pernicious an effect on human character precisely because it flourishes in the dark, artfully playing a background and supporting role in the performance of wrong actions.

Second, while Aquinas recognizes that acts of pride can be acts directly against God, he also thinks that pride and vainglory engender wrongs done to other human beings—taking too much or taking credit for too much, slighting others to seem superior oneself, fighting, cleaving obstinately to one's own opinion from a desire to win an argument. This is as true of pride that contemns God as it is of pride that contemns man.

Third, this rich account of pride suggests ample reason for reckoning pride a vice. Those who do not believe in God will abhor pride because it hurts the proud and carries in its train contempt for one's fellow human beings. They will see pride as a vice of ambition and domination that impoverishes the emotional life and fathers a number of offenses against other human beings. Those who do believe in God will share these sentiments but will have distinctively religious reasons for wanting pride checked. They will believe that God takes offense at all the wrongs pride engenders and will want to avoid the contempt for God and his commands that pride sometimes entails. The religious and the nonreligious can overlap in their condemnation of pride as Aquinas explicates it, though the religious have additional reasons for curbing that vice.

What I earlier alluded to as the Miltonian picture of pride as willful attempts to usurp God's place has important implications for political theory. That pride so understood is the worst of wrongs is a claim that might seem, and has seemed to many, to stand in no need of justification. And, it might be thought, it is this claim and the Miltonian view of pride that together support Augustine's view that a primary function of political authority is the humbling of those subject to it.

Judith Shklar has argued that political liberalism must reject this Augustinian view of political authority and the claims about pride that support it.[24] It is essential to liberalism, she argues, to ignore the deadly sins identified by patristic and medieval Christianity and to deplore instead the vices that she, following Montaigne, dubs "ordinary." Cruelty, treachery, snobbery, and betrayal are, she intimates, more ordinary than the deadly sins in three senses. First, they are ubiquitous vices. Everyone can lapse into them because they do not demand the great strength of character that Satan's rebellion required, the knowing defiance of God. Second, they are vices the acts of which are directed against other creatures rather than against the Creator. Finally, the claim that the acts these vices engender are wrong requires no justification beyond pointing out that they visit harm on other creatures.

Cruelty must be reckoned the worst of the ordinary vices, Shklar argues, because pain and the fear of pain are the worst harms humans can inflict on each other. Since to be a liberal is to be concerned with the ordinary and not the deadly vices, liberals "put cruelty first," hate it most of all, and deny that political authority should be concerned with pride's restraint. Indeed the hatred of cruelty, Shklar argues, provides the most compelling reason to be a liberal, for it is definitive of liberal regimes to shun state-sponsored cruelty. On the other hand, she argues, the Christian hatred of pride gives little reason to endorse a liberal politics: history testifies that those who hate pride and not cruelty most of all often resort to "pious cruelty" to restrain offenses to God.[25]

Perhaps a novel or film in which characters exemplify pride and vainglory would better bring these vices to life than does Aquinas's discussion of them. Philip Quinn has argued that readers of Albert Camus's *The Fall*, for example, gain direct and vivid acquaintance with pride through the self-revelation of the novel's protagonist, the judge-penitent.[26] But if Aquinas's analysis lacks the vividness and impact of a great novel, his discussion of pride, vainglory, and their offspring can still do much to refine our moral categories and sharpen our moral perceptions. Certainly his discussion provides a picture of pride that is far more subtly shaded and finely grained than is the Miltonian portrait of that vice that Shklar's argument takes for granted. Indeed the picture of pride Aquinas sketches is of a subject quite "ordinary" in its potential for motivating wrongs done to others.

Pride as Augustine and Aquinas understand it is first of all ordinary in its commonness. It is a vice that motivates a wide variety of human acts in a wide variety of human beings. The knowing rebellion of Satan may have required extraordinary strength, but the ordinary pride and vainglory of everyday life do not. It is also an ordinary vice in that many acts of pride are acts directed in the first instance against other human beings and not against God. They are often motivated by contempt for other creatures or by a desire for superiority over them. Those who regard harm done to other creatures as ipso facto wrong therefore have reason to think pride a vice.

Pride's ordinariness thus far understood does not imply that concern with pride supplements the reasons those who put cruelty first have to be liberals. More important, it does not imply that those who put pride first have, in their abhorrence of pride, some reason to be political liberals. I want now to argue, therefore, that embracing political liberalism in what I have called maturely pluralistic societies helps contain or ameliorate the vice of pride. Those who are concerned with pride, whether for religious or secular reasons, have reason to accept liberal constraints on their political argument.

PRIDE AND POLITICAL ADVOCACY

Aquinas's Augustinian account of pride, vainglory, and the vices associated with each provides a helpful guide to the temptations posed by engagement in any kind of argument. Arguments can, after all, be highly competitive affairs, and the winners often enjoy a sense of their own superiority. Sometimes too they enjoy the acknowledgment of their intellectual superiority by the vanquished or their auditors. Undue attachment to these spoils of victory can lead one to argue for the wrong reasons, to endorse bad arguments, to refuse to listen to the interlocutor. This is no doubt why Aquinas numbered the argumentative vices of contention, discord, and pertinacity among the daughters of vainglory.

Temptation can be especially strong in political argument, for the winners of political argument can enjoy rewards that are especially attractive. Among the spoils that go to the victor are political power and acknowledgment of power exercised by oneself or by a group to which one gives allegiance. By moving one to intransigence and pertinacity, undue attachment to these goods can severely hinder the sort of consensus building that subsequent social cooperation requires.

The restraint demanded by political liberalism is one effective check on these manifestations of pride. Liberal principles of political legitimacy impose restrictions on the reasons that can be offered to justify or advocate the use of public power and do so precisely to foster the civility of argument threatened by unrestrained pride, contentiousness, and discord.[27] To the extent that simply barring certain reasons from political argument makes that argument more civil, consensus building is advanced and instransigence and pertinacity are curbed.

An interest in civil political argument motivated by attachment to social goods rather than individual domination provides a reason for restraining pride and endorsing liberalism that anyone, whether Christian or not, can accept. It is a reason that should have special purchase on Christians, at least on Christians sympathetic to Augustine's discussions of original sin and its effects. These Christians should, as a result of their sympathy with Augustine, already be sensitive to their own undue attraction to the prospect of dominating others and aware of their need to curb it. Aquinas's treatment of pride brings home the facts that this attraction can subvert any argument and that the goods available in political argument pose a special temptation. Liberalism, insofar as it fosters habitually restrained pursuit of victory in argument, fosters habitual restraints on the desire to dominate others. It should therefore seem especially attractive to Christians Augustinian in their view of original sin.

Moreover, recall that Aquinas's analysis warns us of hypocrisy by including it among the likely consequences of vainglory. That hypocrisy could ultimately be rooted in pride seems a plausible piece of moral psychology. The proud person, Aquinas says, is inclined to attribute to herself goods, including moral goods, that she does not have; the vainglorious person seeks a reputation for goodness of one sort or another. The hypocrite ties pride to vainglory by trying to secure a reputation for qualities pride leads her to affect or exaggerate. The religious hypocrite wants to be known for religious goods—for a sanctity, a closeness to God, or a religious uprightness—that she does not possess. Argument, including political argument, provides an occasion for religious hypocrisy by providing the opportunity for seeming to argue from religious motives that one really does not have or that are not as strong as one would like others to believe. Robert Audi's especially strong form of liberalism forbids political argument from religious motives unless one also has sufficient secular ones. Adherence to Audi's liberalism therefore has in its favor that it removes the near occasion of religious hypocrisy. Adherence even to a weaker form of liberalism, one that forbade appeal to religious reasons in political argument, would also remove the occasion of religious hypocrisy, since political argument would not afford the opportunity to show allegiance to a religious position.

The disruption of political argument may seem an obvious way in which pride poses political problems; at least it is obvious once Aquinas's association of pride with vainglory and the argumentative vices is before us. There are other areas in which Aquinas's Augustinian account of pride is an even more valuable guide, because it points out dangers we might have been prone to overlook. It is here that Christians and non-Christians part company, for in what follows I shall be especially concerned with temptations to pride that politics poses for Christians and with the helpfulness of Aquinas's discussion in showing where those temptations lie.

These dangers arise when Christians engaged in political argument appeal to the whole truth as they see it. They arise, for example, when Christians argue from religious reasons for public policy that they think is required by their Christian commitments, that they think is necessary to make their society a Christian one or one in which they think themselves best able to lead a Christian life. The danger pride poses to such arguments is not only, as in the cases discussed earlier, that it can lead one to continue the argument for the wrong reasons or that argument will break down because of the pride of those involved. Adopting and adducing religious reasons for religiously inspired political positions can themselves be acts of pride. The Christian and the non-Christian can overlap in or concur on the need to hold pride in check because of its adverse political consequences; the Christian, however, has further religious motivations to restrain her pride, since she knows that it offends God.

The first of the species of pride Aquinas distinguishes is that of imputing to oneself goods, especially moral or spiritual goods, that one does not really possess. This species includes, presumably, imputing to oneself moral or spiritual goods that one cannot or ought not have but that belong only to God. Such arrogance is clear in the advocacy of perfectionist political projects, projects in which political power would be employed to eradicate sin or to impose on human beings political institutions that their fallen nature makes it impossible to sustain.[28] Only God could make the fundamental changes in fallen human nature necessary for the maintenance of these institutions, and it would be an act of pride for human beings to suppose they could do so. Moreover many defenders of religious liberty have argued that religious faith is a gift from God and that it cannot be compelled even by political coercion or the threat of repression. It seems to follow from these claims that advocating attempts to coerce belief is an act of pride because it is an attempt—often unwitting—to do what only God can do.

But the advocacy of less radical political programs can also be an act of pride. Those who believe themselves chosen by God as his instruments to purify society or to rid it of features that seem contrary to the demands of Christianity, for example, are sometimes moved to advocate the use of public power to eliminate what they find objectionable. The belief that one has been chosen as a divine instrument tempts one to think that God has done so because of one's own spiritual worthiness for the purpose, to think that one enjoys special favor with him or a special proximity to him. It tempts one, that is, to attribute to oneself a spiritual or moral good that one cannot be sure one has and, sometimes, a good that one does not have. Insofar as beliefs and desires connected with these mistaken attributions motivate political advocacy, that advocacy is an act of pride.

A similar invitation to pride lies in the belief that the United States is a country especially favored by God or one in which the biblical prophecies concerning Israel are to be fulfilled. These beliefs enjoy some contemporary currency and have a long history in popular American political thought and culture.[29] They are beliefs that can and have in the past motivated political advocacy, for they can lead and have in the past led some to suppose that they should function as God's instruments to help America fulfill the purposes he has for it. I have already discussed how advocacy motivated by belief that one is God's instrument can be an act of pride.

Finally, determining what policies a well-functioning political society requires is obviously extremely complicated. Drawing political values, principles of justice, or specific public policies from a religiously based conception of a well-lived human life and drawing them for a society that includes those who do not share that religious view are extremely difficult. That difficulty results in part from the fact that drawing such implications requires a significant amount of political theory. Even if one's religious view straightforwardly implies the immorality of acts of a certain kind, for example, a great deal of argument is required to support the conclusion that such acts should be legally prohibited. This argument must take up some of the thorniest questions of political theory: those concerning the nature and functions of law and of political authority.

Political advocacy based solely on one's religious view can be an act of pride if accompanied by failure to acknowledge both one's own fallibility in very difficult matters of political theory and practical politics. Christians who accept a doctrine of the fall ought to be especially worried about pride of this sort. That doctrine is often taken to imply that human capacity to deliberate about moral truth is hindered or impaired and that self-interest and the desire for power often impede moral reasoning. The more difficult forms of reasoning, about practical politics and other matters far removed from the substance of revelation, might seem to be especially imperiled. In these areas Christians ought to be most sensitive to their readiness to believe that, far from being corrupted by original sin, they have special facility in political reasoning that absolves them of the need to take seriously the arguments of others. They ought, that is, to be especially sensitive to their propensity to pride in these cases.

I have adduced a number of reasons for thinking that resort to religious grounds in political argument can be an act of pride. I have thereby adduced a number of reasons Christians might have for being political liberals. How compelling those reasons are depends, of course, on whether the political benefits of religiously based argument outweigh the risk of pride such argument poses. Many Christians, perhaps, believe that the potential results of such political arguments do outweigh the attendant dangers. They deem their reliance on religious argument necessary to outlaw abortion and pornography and to achieve racial and economic justice. These results, they may think, would be so great that they will or should run the risk of pride in order to secure them.

This line of antiliberal reasoning depends on the supposition that the only arguments available to support the policies Christians favor are religious arguments. It is worth recalling, however, that the political theory of liberal democracy is over three centuries old and has been articulated in an atmosphere of intellectual and political freedom. Indeed this long history of development under reasonably favorable intellectual conditions accounts for the maturity of the pluralism I discussed earlier.

As a result liberal democratic theory is by now extremely well developed and contains ample resources for the criticism of extant regimes that purport to realize liberal and democratic ideals. Certainly the theory of liberal democracy has sufficient conceptual resources to criticize institutions and practices of racial injustice. It therefore has sufficient resources on which to base arguments for policies to implement racial equality. Perhaps Rawls's greatest contribution to the political philosophy of liberal democracy is that of drawing out its implications for the just distribution of income and wealth.[30] Rawls's work thus testifies to the availability of arguments for economic justice that are "internal" to liberal democratic theory. Susan Moller Okin argues that a commitment to liberal democracy has profound implications for the division of labor within the family.[31] John Courtney Murray argued that it required public funding of parochial schools.[32]

The diverse implications that ideals of liberal democracy have been taken to have holds out the possibility that Christians can mine those ideals for arguments supporting the public policies they favor. There may be limits to what arguments

Christians can find in liberal democratic theory; perhaps arguments for the illegality of all abortions, for example, will not be forthcoming. But given Christian abhorrence of pride, Christians would do better to look for and employ such arguments than to run the risk of pride that religiously based political argument poses.

THE LIMITS OF AUGUSTINIAN LIBERALISM

I have argued that acts of religiously inspired political advocacy—of the use of political power to coerce belief, to purify society, or make it more Christian—are often acts of pride. Liberalism requires limiting the range of values and principles to which political advocacy appeals; compliance with at least some liberal principles of political advocacy would preclude political arguments premised on the purposes God has for America or on his use of some people as instruments in doing his will. Political liberalism therefore prevents acts of pride that take the form of religiously inspired advocacy appealing to such premises.

But can liberalism do more than preclude acts of pride? Can it develop habits of mind and sentiment that contain the vice of pride itself? Liberal democracy fosters citizens' self-assertion and sense of self-worth; that it does so is often thought one of its strengths. The self-assertion and respect that liberal democracy fosters are sometimes believed to be at odds with the quality of humility. It might therefore seem that humility, the opposite of pride, is a quality of character incompatible with the habits elicited by liberal democracy.

Certainly liberalism is incompatible with habits of servility or excessive acquiescence toward other human beings.[33] Countering the pride I located in religiously inspired political advocacy does not, however, require a humility so abject. Rather such pride could be effectively contained by coming to respect other citizens as reasonable: as capable of deliberating well about what conception of a good life to pursue and as capable of participating in political argument and honoring the demands of justice.[34] This respect for others as reasonable suffices to contain the pride discussed earlier because the various forms of political advocacy I discussed were all, insofar as they were acts of pride, motivated by the belief in or desire for superiority to citizens who do not share one's religious views. Advocacy of paternalistic policies is motivated in part by the conviction that other citizens cannot determine what is for their own good; other forms of advocacy are motivated by the presumptuous supposition of nearer proximity to God than one's fellows. But there is no reason to think curbing these beliefs and desires requires abject humility before other human beings; their replacement by beliefs and desires associated with respect for other citizens as reasonable would suffice. To show that liberalism fosters the requisite respect, I borrow arguments from John Rawls.[35]

The discipline liberalism imposes on political argument requires that someone advocating the use of public power—from whatever motive, religious or otherwise—try to cast her arguments in terms that others could accept even without accepting her religious views. This requires an exercise of the moral imagination, an attempt to imagine what it would be like to lack our own religious reasons to accept the position in question. Regular exercise of the moral imagination to ascertain the reasons and motives of another, regularly putting ourselves in another's place, as it were, should over time lead us to an appreciation of others' ability to grasp and act on moral reasons and political convictions. This appreciation, in turn, engenders our respect for other citizens as moral agents capable of moral reasoning; it engenders, that is, our respect for citizens as reasonable.[36]

More important in the development of respect for other citizens is the reciprocity of liberal political argument. First, if we repeatedly observe that others also observe the strictures of political liberalism, we come to appreciate how others are restraining themselves and trying to meet us halfway. When political liberalism is long and generally adhered to, the recognition that others restrain themselves and regard us as reasonable elicits reciprocity on our part; it elicits our regard for them as reasonable. Second, the fact that others' adherence to political liberalism makes available goods we could not otherwise realize reinforces our respect and good will toward them. Civility of argument and the cooperation civility makes possible are important elements of the common good that would be very difficult to attain without the adherence of all to the restraints liberalism imposes on political advocacy. Seeing that others work to maintain the conditions of cooperation heightens our regard for them as capable of reasonable participation in political argument. Seeing that they make possible some goods of which we avail ourselves elicits or heightens our good will.

I have argued that dispositions associated with and motivating some acts of pride can be ameliorated by the cultivation of respect for one's fellow citizens as reasonable. I have further argued that the habit of respect for others develops with continued and general adherence to political liberalism. But while this respect may restrain pride, is it fittingly described as part of the humility to which Christians aspire?

Christians must conclude that Augustinian liberalism is a politics with limited ambitions. It does not claim that a liberal political regime can replace pride with truly Christian humility before God. Nor does it claim that the mutual respect liberalism engenders comes to fruition in a Christian love of neighbor. It aims only at inculcating habits that hold pride and contempt in check. Christians who want more humility than this must seek it in the revelation of divine greatness and in the practices of their churches. Thus Augustinian liberalism at best reinforces or prepares the way for the humility Christians must learn elsewhere. Its limited ambitions should not, however, be held against it, for in this Augustinian liberalism is consonant with Augustine's own views. No one was more pessimistic than Augustine about reliance on political authority to do more than hold pride in check or to foster genuine moral improvement.[37] Non-Christians and the nonreligious too will find Augustinian liberalism limited in its ambitions. I have employed Rawlsian arguments to claim that liberalism checks pride by fostering mutual respect. I have not, however, argued for Rawlsian liberalism, nor have I claimed that curbing pride requires the high level of mutual respect that would characterize Rawls's well-ordered society or Kant's realm of ends.

I have expressed disagreement with Judith Shklar on a number of points. It might now be helpful to indicate a point on which we concur. Shklar's defense of liberalism rests on her argument that the habits of liberalism best discipline our indulgence in the ordinary vices, especially cruelty. Hers is a liberalism of limited moral aspirations that focuses on the evils restrained rather than on the virtues elicited. In this I have followed her lead, arguing that political liberalism can hold pride in check even if it cannot foster true humility. It is a liberalism that should appeal to all who reckon pride a vice, but it should have special appeal to Christians who follow Augustine in abhorring it most of all.

NOTES

1. On the Donatist controversy see Peter Brown, "St. Augustine's Attitude to Religious Coercion," *Journal of Roman Studies* 54 (1964): 107–16.

2. For the primacy of these liberties see John Rawls, "The Idea of an Overlapping Consensus," *Oxford Journal of Legal Studies* 7 (1987): 18 n. 27; for liberalism as a more general commitment to the broadest scope of personal liberty see Judith Shklar, "The Liberalism of Fear," in Nancy Rosenblum, ed., *Liberalism and the Moral Life* (Cambridge, Mass.: Harvard University Press, 1989), 21–38.

3. The adjective "political" is employed in deference to John Rawls's distinction between political and comprehensive liberalism. Briefly put, political liberalism specifies ideals, values, and obligations that apply to the political domain: it specifies, for example, ideals, values, and obligations associated with good citizenship, political advocacy, and distributive justice in a liberal society. Comprehensive liberalism, by contrast, attempts to found these ideals, values, and obligations in a liberal moral theory that is more comprehensive in scope: a theory of moral obligation generally, for example. Rawls's is a theory of political liberalism; Kant's and Mill's are theories of comprehensive liberalism. See Rawls, "Idea of an Overlapping Consensus," 9. From now on I will use "liberalism" and "political liberalism," "liberal" and "political liberal," interchangeably.

4. The notion of "public power" is no doubt difficult to specify precisely, as the arguments of John Stuart Mill, *On Liberty,* chap. 3, make amply clear. For present purposes I take the notion of an exercise of public power to be exhausted by the action of the state and by its functionaries and office holders in their official capacities.

5. Jeremy Waldron, "Theoretical Foundations of Liberalism," *Philosophical Quarterly* 37 (1987): 149. The family analogy I employ also appears in Waldron's piece.

6. David Lyons, *Ethics and the Rule of Law* (Cambridge: Cambridge University Press, 1988), 190.

7. See John Rawls, "The Domain of the Political and Overlapping Consensus," *New York University Law Review* 64 (1989): 233–55, especially 242ff. Rawls is concerned primarily with exercises of power that impinge on what he calls "constitutional essentials." For a more recent statement of his views see Rawls's "The Idea of Public Reason Revisited," *University of Chicago Law Review* 64 (1997): 765–807.

8. Robert Audi, "The Separation of Church and State and the Obligations of Citizenship," *Philosophy and Public Affairs* 18 (1989): 259–96; "secular reason" is defined at p. 278. For a more recent statement of his views see Audi's "The State, the Church, and the Citizen," in Paul Weithman, ed., *Religion and Contemporary Liberalism* (Notre Dame: University of Notre Dame Press, 1997).

9. Thus Murray thought that religious diversity could be significantly narrowed and that Americans, at least, could achieve consensus on some propositions of natural theology. See John Courtney Murray, S.J., *We Hold These Truths* (New York: Sheed and Ward, 1960), 30 (for approval of Supreme Court decisions in which God's existence is affirmed), 125ff. (for the prospects of narrowing religious pluralism), and 328 (for a brief discussion of natural theology).

10. Rawls, "Domain of the Political and Overlapping Consensus."

11. Seyla Benhabib, "Liberal Dialogue versus a Critical Theory of Discursive Legitimacy," in Rosenblum, ed., *Liberalism and the Moral Life*, 143–56, especially 146–49. I rely on Benhabib's very interesting essay for my characterization of Ackerman's position.

12. Michael Walzer's perceptive remark that social criticism is naught but the educated cousin of common complaint should suffice to answer those who doubt that graffiti can be a form of political advocacy.

13. See, for example, Sanford Levinson, "The Confrontation of Religious Faith and Civil Religion: Catholics Becoming Justices," *DePaul Law Review* 39 (1990): 1047–82; also Lawrence B. Solum, "Faith and Justice," *DePaul Law Review* 39 (1990): 1083–1106.

14. See Paul J. Weithman, "The Separation of Church and State: Some Questions for Prof. Audi," *Philosophy and Public Affairs* 20 (1991): 52–65.

15. See Eugene TeSelle, "Toward an Augustinian Politics," *Journal of Religious Ethics* 14 (1986): 87–108, for a helpful but concise introduction to Augustine's political theory.

16. See St. Augustine, *City of God* 19.14 and 15; also *Enarrationes in Psalmos* 124.7–8. See also Peter Brown, "St. Augustine," in Beryl Smalley, ed., *Trends in Medieval Political Thought* (New York: Barnes and Noble, 1965), 5.

17. Judith Shklar, *Ordinary Vices* (Cambridge, Mass.: Harvard University Press, 1984).

18. Augustine's views on pride are well laid out and documented in Oliver O'Donovan, *The Problem of Self-Love in St. Augustine* (New Haven: Yale University Press, 1980), chap. 4. I have expanded the discussion of this and subsequent paragraphs in my "Thomistic Pride and Liberal Vice," *Thomist* 60 (1996): 241–74.

19. Both Aquinas and Augustine are committed to pride's ubiquity and explanatory power by their fidelity to a biblical text, "The beginning of all sin is pride" (*Ecclesiasticus* 10:15); see O'Donovan, *Problem of Self-Love*, 95.

20. The following discussion of Aquinas on pride relies most heavily on his *Quaestiones disputatae de malo*, question 8, especially articles 2 and 3. His discussion of pride in the *Summa theologiae*, at 2–2, 162, is also very instructive.

21. "Ad quartum dicendum quod superbia secundum quod importat Dei contemptum secundum affectum, non potest esse peccatum generale; immo etiam est specialius quam

superbia secundum quod significat appetitum perversae excellentiae: potest enim esse appetitus perversae excellentiae non solum si contemnatur Deus, sed etiam si contemnatur homo" (Aquinas, *De malo* 8,2 ad 4).

22. "Sed primus homo peccavit principaliter appetendo similitudinem Dei quantum ad scientiam boni et mali, sicut serpens ei suggessit: ut scilicet per virtutem propriae naturae determinaret sibi quid esset bonum et quid malum ad agendum" (Aquinas, *Summa theologiae* 2–2,163,2).

23. Thus does Aquinas accommodate the *libido dominandi* that Augustine associates with pride; see Herbert Deane, *The Political and Social Ideas of St. Augustine* (New York: Columbia University Press, 1963), 48–49.

24. My characterization of Shklar's views draws on her "Liberalism of Fear" and on her *Ordinary Vices*, 1–15 and 226–49.

25. Shklar, *Ordinary Vices*, 240.

26. Philip Quinn, "Hell in Amsterdam: Reflections on Camus's *The Fall*," *Midwest Studies in Philosophy*, vol. 16, ed. Peter French, Theodore Uehling, and Howard Wettstein (Notre Dame: University of Notre Dame Press, 1991).

27. For the importance of civility see Audi, "Separation of Church and State," 282–83; Murray, *We Hold These Truths*, 297.

28. Aquinas seems to think that commonality of property would be such a political institution, though he thinks it can be sustained as an institution of ecclesiastical communities; see *Summa theologiae* 2–2,66,2 for its impossibility as a political institution.

29. For a contemporary example see the passage quoted in Harvey Cox, *Religion in the Secular City* (New York: Simon and Schuster, 1984), 27; for historical examples and discussion see Mark Noll, *One Nation under God* (New York: Harper and Row, 1988), 7–8, and "The United States as a Biblical Nation," in Nathan Hatch and Mark Noll, eds., *The Bible in America* (Oxford: Oxford University Press, 1982), 39–58.

30. For discussion of Rawls's difference principle as a natural extension of democratic ideals see Joshua Cohen, "Democratic Equality," *Ethics* 99 (1989): 728–31.

31. Susan Moller Okin, *Justice, Gender, and the Family* (New York: Basic Books, 1989).

32. Murray, *We Hold These Truths*, 143–54.

33. See Michael Walzer, *Radical Principles* (New York: Basic Books, 1980), 14–15, for a brief but eloquent statement.

34. That is, such pride could be effectively contained by coming to respect other citizens as capable of exercising the two moral powers Rawls specifies; see his *A Theory of Justice* (Cambridge, Mass.: Harvard University Press, 1971), 12. I use "reasonable" to include both moral powers, while for Rawls it names only the latter.

35. The arguments of the next paragraphs draw heavily on Rawls, "Idea of an Overlapping Consensus," 20–21. My discussion also presupposes the principles of reasonable moral psychology at "Idea of an Overlapping Consensus," 22.

36. In this argument and that of the next paragraph the reasons for addressing my arguments to societies I called "maturely pluralistic" should be clear. Without the rights and liberties entailed by *mature* pluralism those who do not share the dominant religious view may not have the opportunity to develop their capacity sufficiently to warrant the appreciation on which my arguments rely.

37. See, for example, the arguments of *City of God* 19.17. There Augustine says that political authority aims only at what he calls "earthly peace" and that Christians can expect

authority to do no more; these claims are repeated near the end of 19.26. Suggestive but not conclusive in this connection are Augustine's remark in chapter 25 that true virtue is available only where the true God is worshiped and his claim in chapter 27 that true peace, to which true justice "is related," cannot be had in this life. Also important is Augustine's sustained attack on Cicero's claim that republican Rome depended upon and elicited the virtues from her citizens; the attack culminates in 2.21.

EIGHTEEN

St. Augustine and the Just War Theory*

Robert L. Holmes

The just war theory represents a continuing and virtually unparalled effort to bring moral considerations to bear upon one of the most pervasive, complex, and destructive of human practices, one that has played a historic role in shaping modern societies and their institutions.[1] The resurgence of interest in the theory during the last half of the twentieth century has brought a better understanding of the traditions from which it has evolved, as well as a better appreciation of its religious and secular dimensions and the parallels among Christianity, Judaism, and Islam.[2]

The prevailing view is that, at least within Christianity, the father of just war thinking is St. Augustine,[3] a view supported by the medievalists' heavy reliance upon him[4] and the deference to him by both early jurisprudentialists and just war revivalists in the twentieth century. The extent of his influence is documentable. If that is all that is meant by his being called father of the just war theory (or of the just war tradition, as some prefer to put it), the claim is certainly correct. But if one means more than that, the claim needs closer scrutiny. For although Augustine clearly seeks to justify war, what is less clear is what he offers in the way of original thinking about war, and whether his views hold together in a coherent and consistent fashion—both on their own and within the broader context of his overall thought, which is vast in scope and rich in social, psychological, and philosophical insights.

What makes this issue difficult to assess is that Augustine's discussions of war are brief, scattered, and unsystematic.[5] In fact many who deal with topics in his writings to which war would seem to be relevant either do not discuss his views on war at all or do so only in passing. At the same time metaphors of war recur in his

*I am indebted to Barry Gan for helpful comments on an earlier draft of this chapter, as well as to the faculty and students at College of the Holy Cross and St. John's Seminary, where it was presented.

writing. Perhaps most notably, Augustine, like Plato, uses the language of war to characterize what he sees as an ongoing psychological conflict within each person,[6] which suggests that whatever its role in shaping his beliefs about the actual practice of armed conflict, the idea of war has deep roots in his thinking. But whereas Plato and Aristotle understand war in the context of an impersonal teleological natural order,[7] Augustine understands it in terms of a divine order and—as do writers in Judaism, Christianity, and Islam alike—accordingly seeks war's legitimation in the relationship between God and humankind. The problem for Christianity is that Christ seems to proscribe war and violence in the commandment to love, particularly as that applies to enemies. To overcome this presumption against war is the central challenge to Augustine.[8]

It is a challenge I believe he fails to meet. Despite a complex and sophisticated attempt,[9] Augustine in fact departs radically from the pacifism of the early church,[10] wedding Christianity to a militarism that to this day is a hallmark of societies that profess it. Indeed, the most striking feature of his position is its acceptance of war, just or unjust, as an inevitable part of the human condition. Insofar as the just war theory is thought to provide moral criteria by which to judge whether to go to war (*jus ad bellum*), and how to conduct war once in it (*jus in bello*), there is, I maintain, little of such guidance in Augustine, hence little ground on that score for representing him as the father of the just war theory. Indeed, the practical import of his views puts him closer to the tradition of Hobbes and recent political realists than to either the pacifists of the early church or subsequent just war theorists.

A contrary view merits consideration at the outset, if only because it enables us to highlight one of the central problems in understanding Augustine on the issue of war. Although the prevailing view is that Augustine is progenitor of the just war theory, he has also been read as a personal pacifist, whose views are peaceful in essence, on a continuum with pacifists of the early church.[11] Augustine's thought, on this view, is distorted by later writers who obscure its essentially pacifistic character and give it an increasingly militaristic coloration.

That Augustine was almost certainly a personal pacifist may be granted. He denies that private individuals may kill even in self-defense. Short of assuming the duties of an official of the state or an agent thereof (as he understands soldiers to be), one not only need not but may not, on Augustine's view, engage in killing. It should not be surprising that as a bishop of the church, and not an official of the state, Augustine would have been unwilling personally to participate in war. In later medieval writers the prohibition of clergy from participating in war came, in any event, to be thought consistent with the Christian sanction of war. One can personally renounce war and yet believe in its justifiability as waged by others. Moreover, it is arguably true that Augustine stands on a continuum in many respects with earlier Christian writers—certainly if one counts St. Ambrose among those writers, since he expressly supports war and killing.[12] Even discounting Ambrose, and emphasizing those typically identified with the pacifistic sentiments of

the early church—like Origen, Tertullian, and Lactantius—there are many similarities. Augustine talks continually about peace and love and laments the horrors
of war. That is not in question. What is in question is whether, despite this, his
thought places Christianity on a different path from what it was in the view of
most Christian writers prior to Ambrose and prior to its de facto militarization by
Constantine.

The claim I believe needs close scrutiny is that Augustine's interiority, as it is
often called—his emphasis upon subjective inner states—renders consistent his
probable personal pacifism and denuciation of war's horrors with his justification
of war. For Augustine unquestionably turns Christianity inward. He says that
Christ's injunctions in the Sermon on the Mount do not apply to outward action
but rather to inner attitude; the "sacred seat of virtue," he says, is the heart.[13] And
this, if it can be rendered both intelligible and plausible, does indeed seem to open
the door to one's being a pacifist in his heart and yet supporting the killing of warfare. And that in turn would be a step in the direction of enabling Augustine, at
one level, to remain committed to the pacifistic testimony of the New Testament
and at the same time, at another level, to reorient Christianity to the path of militarism.

Augustine's interiority stands out in his statement that "not what the man does is
the thing to be considered; but with what mind and will he does it." Contrasting
God's giving up of his Son and Jesus's giving up of himself with Judas's giving up
of Jesus in betrayal, Augustine says, "The diverse intention therefore makes the
things done diverse." With regard to the acts of Jesus and Judas, "though the
things be one [presumably a giving], yet if we measure it by the diverse intentions,
we find the one a thing to be loved, the other to be condemned; the one we find a
thing to be glorified, the other to be detested. Such is the force of charity. See that
it alone discriminates, it alone distinguishes the doings of men."[14]

Here the thing done is presumed in some sense to be the same, but intentions determine whether it is praiseworthy or blameworthy. Then Augustine speaks of cases
where the things done in two cases are different: a father beating a boy, a boy-
snatcher caressing one. The first case represents "a man by charity made fierce," the
other, a man "by iniquity winningly made gentle." Here not only do the outward acts
differ, they differ deceptively. The beating is an act of love, the caressing an act of
evil. It is the "mind" or "will" with which they are done that makes the difference.[15]

In this latter case, however, it is not merely that the intentions differ. It is that
the motives differ as well—love in the one case, concupiscence in the other. Neither Augustine nor Aquinas after him carefully distinguishes motives and intentions. But the distinction is of the first importance for understanding his position.

At stake is the grounds for sometimes judging similar acts differently and different acts similarly, a recurring concern of Augustine's that he believes requires
looking beyond the outward act. In his letter to Marcellinus he says:

For just as in the case of different persons it may happen that, at the same moment, one man may do with impunity what another man may not, because of a difference not in the thing done but in the person who does it, so in the case of one and the same person at different times, that which was duty formerly is not duty now, not because the person is different from his former self, but because the time at which he does it is different.[16]

Augustine here appears to deny the universalizability of moral judgments,[17] intending us to understand that identical acts may be prideful or loving, hence may have different moral characters. "In the works," he says, "we see no difference."[18] Ever ready to expose hypocritical do-gooding, Augustine emphasizes that as measured by outward acts there need be no difference between pride and charity.

Although Augustine speaks in this passage as though a difference of time *simpliciter* were a morally relevant difference, a more charitable understanding of him is as holding that motives and intentions, representing as they do "mind and will" as distinguished from outward act, are morally relevant aspects of situations. They differ from outward acts, yet are transformative of the moral character of such acts. The implication is that without some difference in motives or intentions, or both, acts cannot differ morally.

Augustine emphasizes diverse intentions in the case of giving. But a specification of intentions does not suffice to reveal the "inward disposition" of the heart. One can intend good but do so from pride. One who fights the flames in a burning building may intend to save the child but do so from a desire for praise. A right intention, to be sure, is necessary for a rightly done act (Augustine sees a bad intention as sufficient to condemn Judas). But it is not sufficient. Indeed all of the acts of charity—from feeding the hungry to clothing the poor—can be done from pride. When they are, the intentions (to see the hungry fed and the poor clothed) will be the same as if they were done from charity. Not acts of charity but only the motive of charity can properly be the root of our conduct. "It alone," says Augustine, "distinguishes the doings of men."[19]

Thus while it is arguably true that evil intentions can spring only from evil motives, good intentions can spring from either good or evil motives. This makes possible the seduction of "good deeds" against which Augustine cautions. With prideful motives concealed, we seek praise through outwardly good acts. Such acts can abound. We can easily identify them. Truly good works we cannot—at least reliably—because they are done from love, and that motive is hidden from us.

If this is correct, it means that Augustine's interiority is rooted in motivation, not (merely or basically) in intention. Both motives and intentions can determine the moral character of acts (though intentions cannot do so invariably, since a well-intentioned act can yet be basely motivated). But motives are basic, because they determine the character of intentions as well as of acts.[20]

There remains, however, the question of the precise role of motivation in determining correct conduct. This is crucial to understanding the justification of war and brings us to one of the most difficult areas of Augustine's philosophy. There arises here a problem that continues to plague love-centered ethics. It is found in one of Augustine's homilies on the Epistle of St. John:

> See what we are insisting upon; that the deeds of men are only discerned by the root of charity. For many things may be done that have a good appearance, and yet proceed not from the root of charity. For thorns also have flowers: some actions truly seem rough, seem savage; howbeit they are done for discipline at the bidding of charity. Once for all, then, a short precept is given thee: *Love, and do what thou wilt:* whether thou hold thy peace, through love hold thy peace; whether thou cry out, through love cry out; whether thou correct, through love correct; whether thou spare, through love do thou spare: let the root of love be within, of this root can nothing spring but what is good.[21]

At the heart of this passage is the directive, Love, and do what you will. But the directive is ambiguous. It could mean, as it most readily suggests:

1. Love, then do whatever love moves you to do.

This would give full weight to love as a motive. If love is commanded, and to be motivated by love is to be governed by that motive (as opposed, say, to merely being inclined in the direction it points), then everything one wills when one loves would issue into right outward conduct.[22] And if (*per impossibile* for humans) love fully and completely motivated us, then all of our conduct (at least all of it that is voluntary) would be right. Where for Plato to know the good is invariably to do it, for Augustine, on this interpretation, to love perfectly would be invariably to act lovingly.

But a second interpretation is suggested by that part of the passage that says, "whether thou hold thy peace, through love hold thy peace; whether thou cry out, through love cry out; whether thou correct, through love correct; whether thou spare, through love do thou spare." Here it looks as though the directive may actually mean:

2. Do what you will, but whatever you do, do it from love.

This suggests something different. It suggests that what you do in the way of outward conduct may, in the end, be unimportant; what is important is that whatever you do, you choose to do it from love. Whereas (1) implies that love moves us to perform certain outward acts, presumably because there is something about those acts (for example, their goodness) that makes them the appropriate objects of love, (2) implies that outward acts are indifferent in themselves and that it is only when they enter into the appropriate relationship with love—being selected (or rejected), as it were, by loving persons—that they acquire their particular moral significance.[23] According to both (1) and (2) any act is right if done from love. But according to (1) that is because love reliably guides us to perform only those acts that are antecedently and independently right. According to (2) it is because any acts chosen by love thereby become right.[24]

Augustine at times inclines toward the consequentialist view suggested by (1)—that love moves us as it does because that is the direction in which the good lies (and ultimately, of course, because that is what God has ordained). At other times he inclines toward the nonconsequentialist view suggested by (2)—that whatever love produces in the way of conduct is thereby constituted good and hence right.[25] The consequentialist rendering is suggested by Augustine's saying that "there is a certain friendliness of well wishing, by which we desire at some time or other to do good to those whom we love"[26] and that, when we are not situated so as to be able to do good, benevolence—the "well wishing"—must suffice. Loving, it seems here, means doing good (acting beneficently) when we can and wishing good (being benevolently disposed) when we cannot. By extension we may presume that acting beneficently when possible (and benevolently otherwise) is to do what is right. In this spirit Augustine contends that love of enemies has an end that is an obvious good: the transforming of them so that they are no longer enemies.[27] The problem with this rendering is that it seems to reduce love to benevolence, which, though a motive, is only a motive to do good. And this would leave unexplained why God commands love rather than benevolence.[28] Yet Augustine seems to regard love and benevolence as two different things. He says, for example, that when one cannot act beneficently "the benevolence, the wishing well, of itself sufficeth him that loves."[29] If they are not two different things, love becomes vacuous, its content emptied into the notion of benevolence.

The nonconsequentialist interpretation, on the other hand, is suggested by the final thought of the above passage in which Augustine says, "let the root of love be within, of this root can nothing spring but what is good." This suggests that love cannot fail to produce good.[30] If this means only that love reliably directs us to the good, and invariably moves us to it (or promotes it), then it is consistent with interpretation (1). But if it means that love cannot in a logical or conceptual sense fail to produce good, then it supports (2). It is not that the good is out there and love simply directs us to it; it is that something's being good (and perhaps right) simply is its issuing from love. It is as though when one loves one necessarily (given how God has ordered the world) brings about good. Thus otherwise identical acts may have different moral characters depending upon whether they are done from love. Acts done from pride sometimes produce good and sometimes not. But acts done from love necessarily produce good.[31]

Let us now return to Augustine's alleged personal pacifism and the question of whether he stands more in the tradition of the church's earlier pacifism than in that of subsequent just war theorists.

A "personal pacifist" is one who is unwilling to participate in war himself but who refrains from judging that others should do so as well. Such a person might believe that wars must sometimes be fought but simply not want to be personally involved; in that case the maintenance of clean hands is paramount. On the other hand such a person might believe that war is wrong but, perhaps owing to humility, or moral tolerance, or both, simply be unwilling to legislate morally for others, leaving it to them to make up their own minds about what to believe and how to act.

If Augustine were a personal pacifist of the second sort, it would indeed put him closer to early Christian pacifists than to later just war theorists. But then we could make little sense of his determination to justify war—which after all represents an attempt to justify it for all Christians, and by implication at least, for non-Christians as well. So to render his position consistent we must view him, it seems, as a personal pacifist of the first sort: as one who believes that wars are sometimes justified but who would be unwilling, even then, personally to participate in them.

If one reads him as a personal pacifist of this first sort, there is no difficulty in reconciling his position with the justification of war, hence no ground, on this basis, for challenging the standard view of him as progenitor of the just war tradition. If that is the case, then the interpretation that would put Augustine more in the tradition of the early Christian pacifists than in that of later Christian just war theorists derives little support from Augustine's personal pacifism. Even if Augustine maintained that not only he but others as well should be pacifists, the situation would not change. His interiority would render even universal pacifism consistent with the waging of war and with doing so justifiably.[32] If the command to love is God's principal directive, and if it requires a right inner disposition rather than specific outward conduct, then there is no inconsistency between advocating pacifism and justifying war. This is true on either interpretation of the precept to love and do as you will. If that precept is understood, as in (2), to require an inner transformation that is compatible with any outward conduct (nonmorally described)—and I tend to believe this is Augustine's view—then, rather than outward conduct being changed by love, that conduct is simply given a moral coloration when motivated by love. It is what love is thought to require that is changed, refashioned to fit the exigencies of the temporal world. Turning the other cheek, loving one's enemies, and not returning evil for evil then become fully consistent with striking back, killing one's enemies, and returning suffering, death, and destruction for evil.

But even if one adopts the consequentialist rendering of the love commandment, as represented by interpretation (1), there is still no inconsistency between pacifism and the justification of war. For when one looks at what Augustine considers loving conduct (as opposed to merely motivation) one finds it repeatedly associated with notions like "severity," "discipline," "correction," and "chastisement." Love is not preserved by gentleness.[33] It can inflict terrible suffering, and often does.[34] Whereas on interpretation (2) love so transforms the moral character of conduct that otherwise indifferent acts become permitted, on interpretation (1) the pain, suffering, and death almost universally taken to be evil become good when inflicted by love.[35]

Even though interpreting Augustine as a personal pacifist of this sort lends little support to the view that he belongs in the tradition of early Christian pacifists, nothing in the preceding compels placing him in the later just war tradition either. The appeal to his interiority does not settle the question one way or the other whether he belongs more to one tradition than to the other. If we accept the sharp inner–outer dualism of his interiority, there is no inconsistency in representing him as both pacifistic and militaristic in different respects, and it becomes a matter of emphasis which side of him one takes to be most important. Where that emphasis properly belongs then becomes a matter of judgment based upon a fuller consideration of the specifics of his views on war. Moreover, as I shall suggest, nothing in the preceding precludes the possibility that Augustine has carved out a position that distinguishes him from both the pacifists of the early church and the just war theories of the later church. So let us turn now to the specifics of his views on war.

With regard to the two recognized dimensions of just war theory, *jus ad bellum* and *jus in bello,* Augustine says little about the second, beyond sanctioning ambushes, prohibiting vengeful cruelty (see below), and acknowledging the need for truthfulness in dealing with an enemy. He says more about *jus ad bellum* but even there without much elaboration.

The exception to this is with regard to wars commanded by God. Like Ambrose, Augustine looks for much of his justification of war to the Old Testament and God's directives to the Israelites to conquer, and in some cases annihilate, various peoples. What is commanded by God, for Augustine, is absolutely obligatory.[36] Thus there is a sharp dichotomy in his justification of war between his treatment of wars approved by God, which are unquestionably just, and those not so approved, which may or may not be just.[37] To be justified in waging a war not approved by God, one must have legitimate authority and a just cause. Sometimes it is thought that he requires a right intention as well. I shall maintain that this is true, but only in a trivial sense; it is not until Aquinas that right intention is fully enshrined in Christian thinking about just war.

Just cause is provided by a state's having suffered a wrong at the hands of another state, either by direct action of the other or by actions of its citizens for which it refuses to make restitution.[38] The war such a just cause warrants is punitive in nature, to avenge that wrong. It may be a war of self-defense, but it need not be. A just cause may entitle a state under a ruler with legitimate authority to initiate a war. This sets Augustine against those contemporary theorists who see self-defense as the *only* justification for war. It also sets him against the twentieth-century paradigm for a justified war, which is one fought in self-defense against an aggressor.

Legitimate authority is framed by Augustine's Christian world view. In his hierarchical ordering of things husbands dominate their families, monarchs their subjects, and God all persons, who ought to be submissive and obedient to his will.[39] As war takes place between states, only persons with the appropriate authority within states may initiate war, and only their agents may fight. When those agents do, they do so with impunity.[40] As William R. Stevenson Jr. effectively summarizes this aspect of Augustine's thinking:

> For the subjects of rulers, the fact of the *providentia voluntaria* means that they should obey, essentially without question. Whatever the content of a particular regime, it serves a purpose ultimately good and consequently should not be hindered through disobedience. God bestows power on representatives of all degrees of human perversion; nonetheless, Augustine asked rhetorically, "although the causes be hidden, are they unjust?" Consequently, subjects ought to be both passive and obedient in the face of superior human power. For them, too, power equals authority. If the subjects are soldiers, they are obliged to carry out the orders of their commanders even if those orders require fighting and killing. If they kill under military orders they are not guilty of murder; on the contrary, if they do not kill when ordered, they are guilty of treason. Soldiers ought therefore to obey even the possibly unrighteous commands of infidels, such as Julian the Apostate. Even in such a case, "the soldier is innocent, because his position makes obedience a duty."
>
> Within the framework of historical providence, then, the matter of authority is a simple one: the ruler, whoever he might be and whatever he might do, rules with God's sanction. He can do nothing without God's foreknowledge of the deed and, if the deed issues from a perverted will, without God's ultimate compensatory historical intervention. Rulers thus war at their discretion, and subjects fight in obedience to their rulers.[41]

The one part of this that is misleading is that which says that rulers war "at their discretion." As descriptive of the behavior of rulers this may well be true. But as normative of what rulers may justifiably do, it is not quite accurate. For rulers are constrained morally by the requirement of a just cause. What is left to their discretion is the determination of what constitutes such a cause. As Augustine sees the matter "it is the wrongdoing of the opposing party which compels the wise man to wage just wars."[42]

What of right intention? It is true, in a sense, that Augustine expects there to be a right intention in warfare, in that he believes that everyone who wages war—justly or unjustly—does so for the sake of peace.[43] It is just that different rulers have different conceptions of what peace is. The question is whether any particular "right intention" deserves to be realized. And that goes back to whether that intention is in the service of a just cause. It will be useful to speak here of a formally right intention, by which I mean one that aims at the perceived good of a particular peace. Augustine recognizes a right intention of this sort. But since it characterizes the unjust and the just alike, and hence can always be presumed to be present,[44] it cannot be normative of what constitutes a just resort to war.

This provides a preliminary account of the specific conditions Augustine lays down for *jus ad bellum*. But its full import can be understood only by seeing how it fits with our account of Augustine's interiority. For here the radical dualism of Augustine's metaphysics affects his ethics and social and political philosophy as well. Moreover, we have seen earlier that a right intention can issue from either a good or a bad motive and that it is the motive that ultimately determines the character of what one does; "it alone," Augustine says, "distinguishes the doings of man."[45] The possibility of a formally right intention, therefore, cannot suffice to provide a viable condition in the criteria to distinguish just from unjust wars.

Because rectitude is tied to virtue, and virtue to love, we can know whether someone acts rightly only by knowing that person's motivation. And that, according to Augustine, is hidden from us—often even in the case of our own actions. We presumably know when we are deliberately acting pridefully. But when we think we are acting lovingly, we may unwittingly be motivated by pride. In any event, as we have seen, it is difficult to know what love requires in any given case.[46] It is God, after all, who has commanded us to love. And Augustine says repeatedly that God's ways are inscrutable. So whether we read Augustine in consequentialist terms or in nonconsequentialist terms, it is evident there is no sure way to determine in specific cases what constitutes right conduct, certainly not with regard to justice in war. Even if we were able to determine accurately the consequences of our actions and their value, hence to know what beneficence calls for, we would remain unable to know whether our underlying motivation is correct.[47] And if we cannot know when we are motivated by love, we cannot know when we are acting rightly. Add to these cognitive deficiencies our motivational inadequacy even to love fully without divine grace, and the obstacles to acting rightly are formidable. They may not be insurmountable, but the obstacles to our ever knowing they have been surmounted seem insurmountable.

This means we must recognize a distinction between true virtue and temporal virtue and, in the case of war, between true justice and temporal justice. True justice is that which is actually just according to what God ordains both in broad historical terms and in particular circumstances; temporal justice is that which humans warrantably *judge* to be just according to standards accessible to them and in view of their cognitive and motivational limitations. Reliance upon temporal justice is necessitated by our inability both to know what true justice requires and to know, either in general or in any given case, whether our conduct accords with it.

The conditions of a truly just war can now be filled out in keeping with our earlier discussion. In addition to legitimate authority and just cause we may now include right intention, appropriately qualified. I have said that since rulers who go to war do so with the intention of achieving the perceived good of a peace of their choosing, both sides in a war can be presumed to have a right intention. But in addition to a formally right intention in this sense we can distinguish (though Augustine does not) a materially right intention—one that aims not only to bring about a perceived good but also to achieve a rightly chosen, just peace. Peace, for Augustine, entails order, and a given temporal order can be just or unjust (at least, can vary in degrees of injustice, since, strictly, no temporal order can be completely just). One ought only to aim for a just peace.

But if what we have said earlier is correct, even the best of intentions, if measured only by the states of affairs it is their purpose to bring about, are not enough.

For good deeds can be done from pride. It is only when intentions issue from love that they are materially right. But even that is not quite enough. We have been assuming that by "love" is intended the love commanded by God. But sometimes Augustine speaks as though love in another sense is at the root of sinful conduct—the love of things that can be taken from us against our will.[48] As with formally right intentions such temporal love (as we may call it) can always be presumed to be present when states go to war, hence cannot be normative of what constitutes true justice in war. Only love as prescribed by Christ—that is, *agape*—can provide a proper love. This "right love," as Stevenson calls it, must be the soil from which intentions spring if they are to be materially right. What forces us to rely upon the conditions of temporal justice is not that these conditions can never be met. It is that we can never know that they have been met. When the conditions of temporal justice are met, we then have a warrant for acting, if only because that is the best we can do. Such conduct is then actionably just.

The completed picture of the Augustinian view with regard to the justification of war is thus a complex one, varying both according to the relationship of the war in question to God's express will (all wars ultimately accord with God's will in the sense that he allows them to take place and turns them even when they are unjust to his purposes) and according to the dichotomy between true justice and temporal justice. These interrelations can be represented as follows:

Just Wars

	Commanded by God	Not commanded by God
	Truly just	Truly just	Temporally just

Commanded by God | *Not commanded by God*

Truly just | Truly just | Temporally just

Truly just

1. Legitimate authority   1. Legitimate authority
2. Just cause   2. Just cause
3. Materially right intention
4. Right love

Because God indisputably commands wars in the Old Testament, there can be nothing intrinsically wrong with war. For early Christians this created the dilemma of how to reconcile the Old Testament's sanction of some wars with the New Testament's implied rejection of war—a dilemma they resolved by supporting the New Testament over the Old. Augustine resolves it by reinterpreting the New Testament to accord with the Old. The result is a sharp division in his thinking between true justice and temporal justice.[49] While we can, on Augustine's view, know when God commands us to go to war and can in the absence of such commands make determinations of temporal justice with sufficient confidence to act upon them, true justice in such circumstances cannot be known, hence cannot provide an effective guide to conduct.

Despite the otherworldliness of his theological outlook, and the sharp dualism entailed by his interiority, Augustine seeks to understand and provide guidance for this world, not least of all in its social and political dimensions. Much of his work as bishop was devoted to providing such guidance, as were many of his letters, including those to men troubled by war and killing. How to provide such guidance in the face of the unknowability of true justice creates a continuing, unresolved tension in his thought.

There are, however, grounds in Augustine's thought for partially bridging the gap between true justice and temporal justice. The direction in which they point is not one that Augustine pursues, perhaps because it would almost certainly have led him back to the early church's renunciation of war. But it makes of the commandment to love something more than the "impossible ideal" that it later becomes for Niebuhr, the twentieth-century's leading Augustinian in social and political thought.[50]

The first ground is broadly epistemological and is tied to Augustine's understanding of the state and its authority. The fundamental pragmatic imperative for Augustine is to obey the state. Even an oppressive state at least serves as the agent of God's chastisement for our sins and, moreover, provides order, which is essential to peace. In its restraint of sinful conduct the state provides an opportunity for such transitory moments of happiness (or, perhaps more accurately for Augustine, relief from misery) mortal life provides. This need for obedience extends to participation in war. Even when the cause is unjust,[51] one must fight when commanded to do so by the appropriate authority. One does so, in that case, with legal immunity from the standpoint of temporal justice. Moreover this gives soldiers on both sides in a war—the just and the unjust alike—a kind of moral immunity as well. Each has an equal right to kill, establishing a moral equality among soldiers.[52]

In his early writings Augustine is troubled by this. He expresses uncertainty whether, by the eternal law, even those who kill with full legal sanction are free of sin.[53] But, as though resigned to the unfathomability of the answer to that question, he proceeds later to view the duty of obedience as very nearly absolute,[54] even when one is confronted with (temporally) unjust commands. Moral license, therefore, extends to soldiers on all sides in war, providing only they are acting as agents of a legitimate authority.

Are those who must fight if commanded to do so by a legitimate authority free of guilt no matter with what inward disposition they do so? More specifically, if right love and intention are requirements of true justice, will not their absence mean that, whatever the standards of temporal justice, those who fight do so wrongly by the standards of true justice? It is hard to see how Augustine can consistently answer this other than by an affirmative. It is just that he would contend that the unknowability of the presence of right love and intention makes temporal standards nonetheless actionable for practical purposes.

The problem with this contention is that we can know, so it seems, and so Augustine gives reason to believe, when we are willfully and self-consciously acting from motives other than love—motives like selfishness, greed, malice, and the like. Augustine reveals no skepticism on this score. It is not as though when we deliberately give rein to selfish, greedy, or lustful impulses we may be mistaken and actually be acting from love. Although when we strive to act from love we can never be certain we are in fact doing so, when we self-consciously act from these other motives we can be certain we are not acting from love. In those cases, then, we can know that our conduct does not accord with true rightness. And in the case of war we can know that temporal justice when accompanied by illicit motives does not accord with true justice. On the unproblematic assumption that when true justice and temporal justice conflict it is true justice that takes precedence, this means that in a limited way true justice then is practically as well as ideally normative for human affairs. It does not tell us in all cases what we ought to do, but it does tell us conclusively in some cases what we ought not to do.[55]

One would expect, for that reason, that it would at least be a necessary condition of the conduct of soldiers being truly just, and (assuming they are under the command of a legitimate authority) a sufficient condition of their being temporally just, that they not be acting from an identifiably evil motive. And indeed one can read at least one well-known passage in Augustine's reply to Faustus as consistent with this. He says:

> What is the evil in war? Is it the death of some who will soon die in any case, that others may live in peaceful subjection? This is merely cowardly dislike, not any religious feeling. The real evils in war are love of violence, revengeful cruelty, fierce and implacable enmity, wild resistance, and the lust of power, and such like; and it is generally to punish these things, when force is required to inflict the punishment, that, in obedience to God or some lawful authority, good men undertake wars.[56]

What this suggests is that, in the broader context of Augustine's views, what is important in war, if one is being realistic, is not that we act from love, since we cannot do that without divine grace and cannot in any event ever know for certain that we are doing it but that we be certain we not act from love of violence, revengeful cruelty, lust of power, and the like. For whatever the obstacles to minimizing the power of these motives, we can at least know when we are consciously acting from them. Thus, in addition to the two interpretations of the precept to love, we need to recognize another precept of more limited scope, applicable to the conduct of warfare:

3. Do as commanded (by a legitimate authority), but do it without cruelty, enmity, love of violence, lust for power, and so forth.

By this, to minimize the evils of war, we should purge ourselves as nearly as possible of those elements of sin that can readily be identified. Death and suffering there will be. But their infliction considered outwardly is neither right nor wrong by itself. The determinant of what they are lies in our motivation.

So I suggest that Augustine's full account of the moral equality of soldiers requires that soldiers not kill for the love of it. If one cannot be certain he is ever acting from right love, that can only be because he cannot be certain that, even when he believes he is acting from love, he is not acting from some base motive like revengeful cruelty, lust of power, and the like in disguise. Whether or not we are capable of fully removing these motives, or at least of preventing them from controlling our conduct, it makes sense to view their removal as a requirement of nonculpable participation in war, hence as a condition of the moral equality of soldiers.

As for rulers their legitimacy need have no more warrant by earthly standards than the power by which they enforce order. For that is what is necessary to avoid the even greater evils of license and disorder.[57] Since rulers have no more privileged access to what constitutes true justice than anyone else and arguably have even less if they are non-Christian, they can be guided at best by temporal justice. If they do not have sole moral discretion to do as they please, they at least have, as we have noted, sole discretion to decide what temporal justice requires of the state. Their judgments to that effect will be fallible and can always fall short of true justice. But the standards of temporal justice to which they appeal are constraints nonetheless, fragile though they may be. Given that opposing rulers in war are both seeking peace as they conceive it, and given that each may believe he acts justly, it can easily happen, and indeed may usually happen, that wars are fought by sides equally convinced of their justice. And the killing that results is done by soldiers who, whatever they think of the justice of the cause they serve, enjoy legal and (temporal) moral immunity for their actions. But there is, I suggest, contrary to what some have maintained,[58] no reason to suppose that Augustine believes that both sides in war can in fact be just, even from the standpoint of temporal justice. If not, then nothing in this aspect of Augustine's account is a bar to considering his account of the moral reality of war as fully coherent and consistent.

The second ground for bridging the gap between true justice and temporal justice in war relates to Augustine's denial of the right of self-defense. Properly understood, love can only be for that which we cannot lose against our will.[59] To cling to such things—earthly possessions, even our mortal lives—is the way of sin; it is trying to sustain ourselves other than in and through God. Because we can have no assurance of saving our own lives, we may not kill in defense of them.[60] But we can no more be assured of saving our neighbor's than our own. And thus—although Augustine does not expressly preclude defense of others in the way he precludes self-defense—it would seem we ought not to cling to their lives (or the preservation thereof) either, at least not when to do so would involve killing. Just as assailants can assault or kill us against our will but cannot thereby truly harm us (unless we allow fear or hatred to corrupt our wills as we try to cling to life or bodily integrity), they can do the same to others without thereby truly harming them either. Our intervening on their behalf does not change that. If an attacker cannot harm others by his act alone, then we cannot, by ours alone, preserve them.[61]

The only ground for love's inflicting pain, suffering, or even death upon another, as it may justifiably do for Augustine, is for the other's sake. Punishment can only be inflicted to chasten the offender. An enemy is confronted, Augustine says, always as the brother he may become, not as the enemy he now is. It is only what he does that one may hate, not the person himself. And if you truly love him, you act on his behalf, even to the point of inflicting pain or death.[62]

From all Augustine says, however, love is hardly the motive governing the conduct of most persons, including rulers and soldiers. Even if we thought it were, we could well be mistaken. But we have seen that we can have virtually conclusive evidence of the absence of that motive, namely, when we self-consciously act from sinful motives. And Augustine repeatedly speaks as though he thinks this is so in the case of war. It is greed, rapacity, desire for domination, and conquest that he finds manifest in war. Even a (temporally) just cause provides no assurance that its prosecution is from love.[63] The desire to punish for the sake of punishing, to harm for the sake of harming, to satisfy desires for revenge—and throughout to profit from the spoils of war—ensures that even a temporally just war that has these characteristics cannot be truly just and indeed can be known not to be truly just.

If, therefore, there is this bearing of true justice upon judgments of actual wars, then it may be that by a consistent Augustinian analysis (though not by Augustine's own) virtually all of the wars prior to and during Augustine's time[64] will have been unjust. This may partly explain why warfare under Christianity, particularly during the crusades, came increasingly to be justified on expressly religious grounds,[65] for such grounds would help minimize the influence of self-consciously base motives. What later Christians seem to have given insufficient attention to is the Augustinian skepticism regarding our ability to certify love as a motive in our own conduct. It may even be—if one gives credence to the more skeptical and pessimistic passages in Augustine—that no actual wars are in fact just; and that, whether or not Augustine was a personal pacifist, he should have been and, to be consistent, should have been a universal pacifist as well.

If the preceding is correct, the problem of war is of the first importance to Augustine's thought, not because he identifies it as such and not because he expressly devotes extensive attention to it. It is important because what is of concern in his thought, and of paramount concern in his later thought, namely, to define the implications of Christianity for life in the earthly city,[66] turns upon the understanding of war, the social and political forces that bring it into existence, and the divine purposes that allow it to endure. For no human practice flies more directly in the face of what seem to be the teachings of Christ than the organized, deliberate, and systematic infliction of death and destruction.

Thus there is much in Augustine's philosophy that is important to understanding war, but most of it is directly relevant to understanding the philosophy of war in general rather than the just war in particular. For insofar as the just war theory is understood as a theory in applied ethics, meant to provide practical guidance in deciding when to go to war and how to conduct war when in it, there is, as I have said, little in Augustine of such a theory; and such as there is shows limited concern with the complexities that have concerned subsequent just war theorists. There is more in the way of a theoretical account of the conditions that make for true justice in war. But even much of that is only implicit and in any event—unless developed beyond Augustine's treatment—of limited relevance to providing practical guidance to civil magistrates and individuals contemplating soldierhood.

When one looks at the practical import of Augustine's account, on the other hand, as opposed to his philosophy and theology of war, one finds an acceptance of war, with only the frailest of constraints against entering into it, constraints that even optimists regarding human nature could hardly expect not to provide rulers with a rationale to go to war practically whenever they want. And one finds virtually no constraints against individuals participating in war, provided only that they do so without otherwise forsaking God and without feelings of revenge, cruelty, and so forth. The way is then prepared for Christians to lament the horrors of war and at the same time actively to support war's perpetuation. Power on the part of rulers and submissive obedience on the part of subjects enable the state to run roughshod over the teachings of the Sermon on the Mount. In its practical import, then, as opposed to its theoretical and philosophical import, Augustine's account sets the stage more nearly for Hobbes, Machiavelli, and twentieth-century political realists (some of the most prominent of whom have been Christians) than for just war theorists.

One suspects that Augustine's desire to counteract Christianity's critics was so great that, when it brought him into conflict not only with Christ's injunctions but also with the implications of his own interpretation of those injunctions, he chose to let the latter yield. In this way the self-confessed weaknesses of one of the great thinkers of the Western world may, in the end, have influenced his thought in ways he never suspected, leading him to presume to redirect Christianity's moral course from pacifism to militarism. And this, paradoxically, may at the same time be the greatest compliment to his analysis of the unrelenting power of pride in human nature—that it found confirmation in the very account by which he warned against it.

NOTES

1. Indeed, Paul Ramsey, in *War and the Christian Conscience: How Shall Modern War Be Conducted Justly?* (Durham, N.C.: Duke University Press, 1961), xxiii, characterizes the just war theory as the "longest-continuing study of *moral decision making* known in the Western World." The nature and justification of political authority represents a longer tradition, although for the most part it deals with the justifiability of social and political systems rather

than with specific, deliberately undertaken actions of a sort common to nearly all social arrangements. Historians of ethics focus primarily upon the history of ethical theory. But some of the most important contributions to philosophical ethics, from Plato through the classical utilitarians, have been in applied ethics, and it is to applied ethics that the just war theory belongs.

2. See particularly John Kelsay and James Turner Johnson, eds., *Just War and Jihad: Historical and Theoretical Perspectives on War and Peace in Western and Islamic Traditions* (New York: Greenwood Press, 1991), 2.

3. For example, Roland Bainton writes that Augustine's view "continues to this day in all its essentials to be the ethics of the Roman Catholic church and of the major Protestant bodies" (*Christian Attitudes toward War and Peace* [New York: Abingdon Press, 1960], 99). For challenges to this interpretation see particularly David Lenihan, "The Just War Theory in the Work of Saint Augustine," *Augustinian Studies* 19 (1988): 37–70; George J. Lavere, "The Political Realism of Saint Augustine," *Augustinian Studies* 11 (1980): 135–45; and Reinhold Niebuhr, "Augustine's Political Realism," in *Christian Realism and Political Problems* (New York: Charles Scribner's Sons, 1963), 119–46. For a balanced analysis of the issue see William R. Stevenson Jr., *Christian Love and Just War: Moral Paradox and Political Life in St. Augustine and His Modern Interpreters* (Macon, Ga.: Mercer University Press, 1987).

4. On Augustine and the medievalists see Frederick H. Russell, *The Just War in the Middle Ages* (Cambridge: Cambridge University Press, 1975).

5. The principal passages in which Augustine discusses war have been usefully compiled by David Lenihan in "Just War Theory in the Work of Saint Augustine":

1) *De libero arbitrio* 1.5
2) *Contra Faustum* 22
3) *Epistulae* 138, to Marcellinus
4) *Epistulae* 189, to Boniface
5) *Epistulae* 222, to Darius
6) *Quaestiones in Heptateuchum* 6.10
7) *De sermone Domini in monte* 30
8) *City of God*

6. As Plato has Clinias say, "Why, here . . . is the field in which a man may win the primal and subtlest victory, victory over *self,* and where defeat, defeat by *self,* is most discreditable as well as most ruinous. There lies the proof that everyone of us is in a state of internal warfare with himself" (*Laws* 626, trans. A. E. Taylor, in *The Collected Dialogues of Plato,* ed. Edith Hamilton and Huntington Cairns [Princeton: Princeton University Press, 1971]). Compare Augustine: "What war, then, can be imagined more serious and more bitter than a struggle in which the will is so at odds with the feelings and the feelings with the will, that their hostility cannot be ended by the victory of either?" (*City of God* 19.28, trans. Henry Bettenson [New York: Viking Penguin Inc., 1986]). See also *City of God* 19.4.13; 21.15.16; *Contra Faustum* 22.22; *Confessions* 10.

7. Plato understood war in the broader context of the nature of the state, viewing it as an art of acquisition to facilitate expansion when expensive tastes created wants that outstripped needs. In this way he thought it sprang from the same causes as all of the evils of the state (*Republic* 2). Aristotle added that some people were meant to be dominated by others, and when they refused to submit it was "naturally just" that war be made against them

(*Politics* 1.8). There was believed to be a teleological order to nature and a natural justice to war when it conformed to this order.

8. On the moral presumption against war in recent Catholic thought see *The Challenge of Peace: God's Promise and Our Response,* A Pastoral Letter on War and Peace, May 3, 1983 (Washington, D.C.: American Catholic Conference, 1983).

9. The attempt is motivated in part by the desire to respond to Christianity's critics who charged that its teachings had weakened the Roman state and thus made it vulnerable to attacks like that of the Visigoths in 410.

10. At least partially in support of this his biographer, Peter Brown, writes: "In an atmosphere of public disaster, men want to know what to do. At least Augustine could tell them. The traditional pagans had accused the Christians of withdrawing from public affairs and of being potential pacifists. Augustine's life as a bishop had been a continual refutation of this charge. He knew what it was to wield power with the support of the Imperial administration. Far from abandoning civil society, he had maintained what he believed to be its true basis, the Catholic religion; and in his dealings with heresy, lawlessness and immorality, he had shown not a trace of pacifism" (*Augustine of Hippo* [New York: Dorset Press, 1967], 291).

11. See Lenihan, "Just War Theory in the Work of Saint Augustine."

12. In extolling fortitude Ambrose says: "Nor is the law of courage exercised in causing, but in driving away all harm. He who does not keep harm off a friend, if he can, is as much in fault as he who causes it. Wherefore holy Moses gave this as a first proof of his fortitude in war. For when he saw an Hebrew receiving hard treatment at the hands of an Egyptian, he defended him, and laid low the Egyptian and hid him in the sand" (*Duties of the Clergy* 1.36.179). And in the course of his defense of the divinity of Christ for the Emperor Gratian, who was about to go forth to help ward off the Goths in the Eastern Empire, Ambrose says: "I must no further detain your Majesty, in this season of preparation for war, and the achievement of victory over the Barbarians. Go forth, sheltered, indeed, under the shield of faith, and girt with the sword of the Spirit; go forth to the victory" (*Exposition of the Christian Faith* 2.16.136). Both quotations are from *St. Ambrose: Select Works and Letters,* in Philip Schaff, ed., *A Select Library of Nicene and Post-Nicene Fathers of the Christian Church,* 2d ser. vol. 10 (Grand Rapids, Mich.: Eerdmans, 1955). The justification of war on the grounds of its necessity to defend the innocent has repeatedly been attributed to Augustine. See, for example, Ramsey, *War and the Christian Conscience,* chap. 3; and James Turner Johnson, *Just War Tradition and the Restraint of War: A Moral and Historical Inquiry* (Princeton: Princeton University Press, 1981), 145, 350, and idem, *Can Modern War Be Just?* (New Haven: Yale University Press, 1984), introduction and 176. But this line of justification is more properly attributed to Ambrose than to Augustine, as Johnson recognizes in his more recent "Historical Roots and Sources of the Just War Tradition in Western Cultures," in Kelsay and Johnson, eds., *Just War and Jihad,* 9. For a closer analysis of the inappropriateness of attributing this justification to Augustine see my "St. Augustine on the Justification of War," in *On War and Morality* (Princeton: Princeton University Press, 1989), chap. 4.

13. "If it is supposed that God could not enjoin warfare, because in after times it was said by the Lord Jesus Christ, 'I say unto you, That ye resist not evil: but if any one strike thee on the right cheek, turn to him the left also,' the answer is, that what is here required is not a bodily action, but an inward disposition. The sacred seat of virtue is the heart" (*Contra Faustum* 22.76, in Saint Augustine, *Writings in Conection with the Manichaean Controversy,* in Philip Schaff, ed., *Select Library of the Nicene and Post-Nicene Fathers,* vol. 4.

14. St. Augustine, *Homilies on the First Epistle of John* 7.7, trans. H. Browne, in *Select Library of the Nicene and Post-Nicene Fathers,* vol. 7.

15. Ibid.

16. Letter 138.4, trans. J. G. Cunningham, in *Select Library of the Nicene and Post-Nicene Fathers,* vol. 1.

17. That is, he seems to be denying universalizability if that thesis is understood to require that similar acts be judged similarly. It is doubtful that he is denying the thesis, however, if one interprets it more broadly as requiring that relevantly similar *cases* or *situations* be judged similarly. For he does think that there are relevant dissimilarities in the cases he would have us judge differently. And he is almost certainly not denying the thesis if it is taken to mean that acts or cases must be judged similarly unless there are relevant dissimilarities between them.

18. *Homilies on the First Epistle of John* 8.9.

19. Ibid., 7.7.

20. Barry Gan has suggested to me that if good intentions were understood as those that aim at creating or maintaining a virtuous character, and if it were assumed that a virtuous character entailed good motive, then, while it would still be true that the moral character of motives determines that of intentions (or, at least, that good motives determine good intentions), this would not allow that good intentions may be produced by evil motives. It would then be difficult to explain how the road to hell can be paved with good intentions, as Augustine pretty clearly thinks it may be.

21. *Homilies on the First Epistle of John* 7.8 (emphasis added).

22. If, on the other hand, it is supposed that one can love but not always be governed by love—if, that is, love, when present, does not invariably provide a motive or at any rate a governing motive for conduct—then doing "whatever thou wilt" would authorize doing only those things actually impelled by love. This would leave open whether acts not motivated by love should be foregone or judged by some other criteria.

23. This would accord with what Augustine says in the well-known passage regarding the seat of virtue being in the heart, as well as with the Stoic doctrine that, in the classification of all things as good, bad, or indifferent, everything other than virtue (an intrinsic good) and vice (an intrinsic bad) is indifferent, including human actions. This appears to be the understanding of William R. Stevenson Jr. when he says of Augustine's view that, "So long as one truly loves, *what* one does does not really matter; any action based in and arising out of true love is by definition 'right' " (*Christian Love and Just War,* 107).

24. The difference between (1) and (2) is analogous to that involved in divine-command ethics. Whereas one can ask whether God commands what he does because it is right, or whether it is right because God commands it, here one can ask whether love motivates us to do what is right because it is right, or whether what is right is so because love motivates us to do it.

There are further possible complexities that we cannot explore fully here. It may be that love selects certain acts not because they are right but because they are good and that they are then rendered right because of the good they promise to actualize. This would make Augustine basically a divine-command deontologist, holding that we ought always and invariably to do as God commands, but at the same time a pragmatic teleologist, holding that when we do as God commands (that is, act lovingly in all that we do) we as a matter of fact do what is best, given God's ordering of things.

25. Strictly speaking, both (1) and (2) would appear to be nonconsequentialist if they are taken without elaboration and also taken to be basic principles. It is when one understands (1) (as I am) to presuppose that love impels us to do good that it becomes consequentialist and axiological, for then it requires of us that we calculate the value of the consequences of our acts in the determination of what is right.

26. *Homilies on the First Epistle of John* 8.5.

27. Ibid., 8.10. It is possible that there is something else about the character of certain acts besides their goodness or rightness that leads love to move us to do them, but it is difficult to see what that would be for Augustine.

28. On related topics see William K. Frankena, "Love and Principle in Christian Ethics," in Alvin Plantinga, ed., *Faith and Philosophy: Philosophical Studies in Religion and Ethics* (Grand Rapids, Mich.: Eerdmans, 1964), 203–25.

29. *Homilies on the First Epistle of John* 8.5.

30. And if one is troubled by the possibility that some of what one does from love may seem harmful to others (and here we should be mindful that, as Augustine conceives of love, it can lead to war and killing), Augustine counsels: "Therefore hold fast love, and set your minds at rest. Why fearest thou lest thou do evil to some men? Who does evil to the man he loves? Love thou: it is impossible to do this without doing good" (*Homilies on the First Epistle of John* 10.7).

31. To render all of this coherent, one would have to say that it is sufficient to make an act (and presumably its consequences) good that it be performed from love, but it is not necessary, since good can be done from pride as well. It may, on the other hand, be both necessary and sufficient for an act's being right that it be done from love. In that case acts and consequences would not be fully value-neutral independently of their being produced by love; but their character as right or wrong would be. This, however, takes us well beyond anything that can reliably be attributed to Augustine's actual thought.

32. That is, it would render it consistent in his own mind. Whether in fact one can render wholly consistent this combination of positions is less clear.

33. *Homilies on the First Epistle of John* 7.10.

34. Despite the death and destruction love can inflict upon enemies, it may be that Augustine thought that love of enemies is a purer form of love even than love of the poor and needy. This is speculative, it should be cautioned. He does imply that there is an ordering of the purity or perfection of love when he points out that loving the poor and needy is fraught with pitfalls because of the risk of pride creeping into one's motivation. "With a truer touch of love," he says, on the other hand, "thou lovest the happy man, to whom there is no good office thou canst do; purer will that love be, and far more unalloyed" (ibid., 8.5). When shortly later he discusses love of one's enemies, he says: "Thou lovest not in him what he is, but what thou wishest him to be. Consequently, when thou lovest an enemy, thou lovest a brother. Wherefore, perfect love is the loving an enemy: which perfect love is in brotherly love" (ibid., 10). He may mean here only that perfect love entails loving one's enemy. But the fact that he apparently recognizes an ordering of degrees of purity of love suggests that he may mean that, just as loving a happy person will likely be freer of pride than loving those for whom we can provide outward manifestations of charity, so love of an enemy is purer still, since it requires overcoming and going against the very interests of the temporal self pride cherishes.

35. A problem for this interpretation is that if the infliction of death and destruction is reckoned good for purposes of understanding the conduct of warriors and civil magis-

trates, it is hard to see (consistent with this interpretation) how such actions can fail to be good when performed by evil persons. For it is the evaluation of the outward conduct (and its effects) that is here involved, not the motivation. If one says that it matters whose conduct it is, so that what is done from loving motives is good and what is done from prideful motives evil, then interpretation (1) collapses into (2). For then, once again, it is only in *relation* to good or bad motives that conduct is good or bad.

36. See *City of God* 1.21.

37. I shall speak of "approved" here, because Augustine speaks of acts of killing—presumably intending acts of war as well—that are permitted although not specifically commanded by God, and I shall consider those to be covered by "approved." See, for example, his treatment of Moses' killing of the Egyptian as recounted in Exodus 1.2. (Cf. *Reply to Faustus the Manichean* 22.70.)

38. *Quaestiones in Heptateuchum* 6.10, in John Eppstein, *The Catholic Tradition of the Law of Nations* (London: Burns, Oates and Washbourne, 1935), 74.

39. Interestingly, the traits that are at the heart of Augustine's conception of the relationship of humans to God are the stereotypically feminine traits of submissiveness and obedience.

40. *City of God* 1.21.

41. Stevenson, *Christian Love and Just War,* 69.

42. *City of God* 19.7, trans. Marcus Dods, in *Select Library of the Nicene and Post-Nicene Fathers,* vol. 2.

43. *City of God* 19.12.

44. The American Catholic bishops, on the other hand, tie right intention specifically to just cause, saying, "Right intention is related to just cause—war can be legitimately intended only for the reasons set forth above [protecting innocents, preserving conditions of decent human existence, and securing basic human rights] as a just cause" (*Challenge of Peace,* 30).

45. *Homilies on the First Epistle of John,* 7.7.

46. This applies, strictly, only to (1), since according to (2) love does not specifically direct our outward conduct.

47. It might be argued, in defense of Augustine, that the consequentialist interpretation does not require that we be able to determine consequences. It requires only that love (so to speak) do that in moving us always to perform acts that are best, whether or not we can otherwise see them to be best. This I think is plausible. But it still leaves the problem of knowing precisely when we are motivated by love. Knowing that will be practically equivalent to knowing what acts will have best consequences. To the extent such knowledge is hiding from us, so, it seems, must be the knowledge of what would be best in conduct.

48. *De libero arbitrio* 1.

49. This dualism is probably prompted partly by Augustine's desire to reconcile the New Testament with the Old, but it is almost certainly facilitated by his Platonistic inclinations. For an account that alleges an expanded list of conditions for Augustine see Franziskus Stratmann, *The Church and War: A Catholic Study* (New York: P. J. Kennedy and Sons, 1928), chap. 3.

50. See, for example, Reinhold Niebuhr, *An Interpretation of Christian Ethics* (New York: Meridian Books, 1956).

51. And, presumably—though Augustine is not clear about this—when the cause is known to be unjust as well, at least from the standpoint of temporal injustice.

52. As Michael Walzer puts it in defending what he calls the moral equality of soldiers (*Just and Unjust Wars* [New York: Basic Books, 1977], chap. 3).

53. *De libero arbitrio* 1.15.12, trans. Carroll Mason Sparrow (Charlottesville: Dietz Press, 1947).

54. Excepting only commands that one do things disrespectful of God.

55. It does not follow from this, of course, that acting from *all* motives other than love entails acting contrary to the requirements of true justice. Whether that is so depends upon whether those requirements demand perfection of us, motivationally.

56. *Contra Faustum* 22.74.

57. It is the Pauline spirit speaking here, best represented in Paul's epistle to the Romans:

> Every person must submit to the supreme authorities. There is no authority but by act of God, and the existing authorities are instituted by him; consequently anyone who rebels against authority is resisting a divine institution, and those who so resist have themselves to thank for the punishment they will receive. . . . You wish to have no fear of the authorities? Then continue to do right and you will have their approval, for they are God's agents working for your good. (Romans 13:1–4, New English Bible)

58. See, for example, Stevenson, *Christian Love and Just War*, 44–45. Paul Ramsey contends that, to be consistent, Augustine should have denied that one side only can be just in war, in *War and Christian Conscience*, 28.

59. *De libero arbitrio* 1.

60. Not only may we not, in our capacity as private persons, kill another to save our own lives, we also may not even kill ourselves to prevent others from sinning against us, as in the case of threatened torture or rape (*City of God* 1.24–25).

61. Augustine says: "For whatever man may do to thee, he shall not straiten thee; because thou lovest that which man cannot hurt: lovest God, lovest the brotherhood, lovest the law of God, lovest the church of God. . . . If no man can take from thee that which thou lovest, secure thou sleepest" (*Homilies on the First Epistle of John* 10.6).

62. *City of God* 19.17. It is but a short step from this, of course, to justifying the thinking behind the inquisition.

63. See, for example, *City of God* 5.17.

64. Counting as wars, for this purpose, the sack of Rome by the Visigoths in 410 and the Vandal incursion into Africa that had Carthage under siege at the time of Augustine's death in 430.

65. See Frederick H. Russell, *The Just War in the Middle Ages* (Cambridge: Cambridge University Press, 1975), chap. 1.

66. As Peter Brown, puts it, "So the *City of God*, far from being a book about flight from the world, is a book whose recurrent theme is 'our business within this common mortal life'; it is a book about being otherworldly in the world" (*Augustine of Hippo*, 324).

NINETEEN

Augustine's Philosophy of History

Rüdiger Bittner

THE MEANING OF "HISTORIA"

To speak of Augustine's philosophy of history is anachronistic in more than one way. Not only was the expression "philosophy of history" coined by Voltaire in the 1760s only, and coined precisely to herald a treatment of history that has cast off the fetters of a Christian conception. What is more important, Augustine does not use the term "historia" in the modern sense of "history," which in the modern sense can refer to events rather than to reports of events and to a totality of events or even to *the* totality of events. Thus in the latter case "history" can be used absolutely: it need not be some person's or some institution's history, it can be history, period.[1] In fact it is this sense of "history" that first invites a philosophy of history. Take the standard question of a philosophy of history: whether there is meaning in history. Whatever may be meant by "meaning" here, it is clear that "history" in this question means the events rather than what people write and say about the events. And what is asked here is not whether the events, taken individually, have meaning but whether the whole of which they are parts does. Augustine's concept of historia is different. For him, historia is a narrative.[2] It is not what we call history, since we can refer by this term to events and indeed to a totality of events, which Augustine by his term cannot. Augustine's "historia" is not "history," it is "story."

"Historia," while not appearing very frequently in Augustine's writings, is a basic concept in Augustine's thought. According to *De vera religione* 7.13 the chief part to take in in Christian religion is "the narrative [historia] and prophecy of the temporal dispensations of divine providence for the salvation of mankind." Just because the dispensations of divine providence for the salvation of mankind are temporal, it takes historia, a narrative of things past, and prophecy, a narrative of things to come, to represent them. That means you cannot prove the heart of Christian doctrine by rational arguments; you have to tell a story to communicate it. Witness the Platonists: here are the best philosophers in the world, and they do get as far as to produce persuasive arguments for what is effectively the logos doctrine in John. Still, incarnation, crucifixion, and resurrection are beyond their reach, for these happened in time, and as philosophers they have knowledge only of what is timeless. To learn of what happens in time there is no way but to listen to stories.[3] For teaching Christian religion, accordingly, Augustine recommends giving the pupil "the full story" (narratio plena), running "from where it is written: 'In the beginning God made heaven and earth' up to the present times of the church" (De catechizandis rudibus 3.5). Here it is evident that the doctrine comes as a story: it is only in a story that you can continue right down to the present time. So while you can indeed reach truth by sheer rational argument and skepticism is out, you cannot reach all important truth by sheer rational argument. This is why philosophers are standardly said to suffer from pride (Confessions 7.9.13; City of God 2.7): they try to go it alone, renouncing the help that comes from things received through listening.[4] That philosophers trust their reasonings as far as they go is fine. That they trust their reasonings to give them all the truth they need is their mistake. Some truth we need is "storical."[5]

It may appear to be an invidious understatement to say that incarnation, crucifixion, and resurrection need to be represented in stories. It is not just a story to report these events, one may protest, it is an enunciation of an altogether higher dignity. This protest is justified insofar as our term "story" sometimes carries the connotation of "a mere story," something made up. Still, "story" can also be used in a neutral sense, without an implication of truth or falsity. Taken in that way, the term fits Augustine's use of "historia." It is historia to represent incarnation, crucifixion, and resurrection in speech, and it is in the same sense historia to indicate who was Roman consul in a given year.[6]

Indeed, it is historia in the same sense to tell some fable about the gods (Epistulae 17.1.3). The exposition of Christian doctrine for Augustine does not recede to a different literary genre. It is a story like the others people tell. It differs from pagan fables simply in being true. From reports on past human institutions it does not differ in truth, for these may be true, too, and in the same sense.[7] From them it differs, first, in importance: "What is contained in worldly writings, be it true or false, does not carry anything of weight whereby to live right and well."[8] It differs, second, in authority: "the wisdom of God, whereby everything was made, transfers itself into sacred souls, makes them friends of God and prophets and tells them silently in their inner self his works; . . . and one of these was he who said and wrote: 'In the beginning God created heaven and earth'" (City of God 10.4; also 11.3). Thus, if worldly books and the scripture contradict each other, the latter trumps the former by its immediate divine authority, for God himself told the writer his works. This is also why pagan fables, insofar as they are incompatible with what the scripture says, must be rejected as untrue. On the other hand, since worldly writings and the scripture are in the same field, both offering reports of things that happened, Christian doctrine can occasionally use the material provided by secular books for a clearer or more reliable chronology of the events of which it speaks (*De doctrina Christiana* 2.28.42). So to tell of Christ's incarnation, crucifixion, and resurrection is not different in kind from ordinary stories about what people did in various times and situations. It is the same sort of business, only the Christian story is better because it is more important and because it is authorized by him who is the origin of whatever any true story is about.[9] As Augustine puts it in *De libero arbitrio* (1.3.7) the Christian story (historia) excels by divine authority over other books. Yet if it excels, it must be in the same contest.

SACRED AND PROFANE HISTORY

There is a distinction in the literature between sacred and profane (or sacred and secular) history.[10] The foregoing considerations suggest that, for "historiae"—that is, stories—there is no distinction in kind between what sacred and secular books contain, only a difference in importance and a difference in reliability. Turning now and in the following from historia to history in the sense of what true stories report, what Augustine often calls "gestae" (things done),[11] the above considerations suggest that a distinction between sacred and secular history cannot be maintained at all.[12] Clearly the different degree of reliability of sacred and secular reports does not constitute a difference in kind between what these reports are about, since that is a difference that concerns only our access to events, not the events themselves. A similar point holds for the difference in importance of sacred and secular narratives. This difference derives, to be sure, from the difference in importance of the events narrated, but that difference is a difference only in what the events mean for us; it does not constitute a difference in kind among the events themselves. In itself history, the course of happenings, is homogeneous. There are not two strands,[13] the sacred and the secular, which, twisted together, form the rope of history. The whole of history is running from one spool. The fact that the Word became flesh and the fact that I had breakfast this morning do not belong to different realms of things or on different levels of events. The former fact is just more important than the latter, and better known. The reason for claiming that Augustine regards history as homogeneous is that otherwise sacred and profane narratives could not so much as contradict each other, which according to Augustine they sometimes do (see above), nor could the secular story support the chronology of the sacred one, as again according to Augustine it sometimes does (see above). You can only contradict or supplement what somebody else said if the two of you are talking about the same sort of things. Once you settle for different strands, levels, or something of the sort, the argument between the two of you is off.[14]

The teacher of Christian doctrine, then, is a "storian" as opposed to a mere reasoner: he offers a narrative. And he is a historian as opposed to a narrator of fables: he says what happened. Not all that happened, of course; no historian does that. He tells about some events. Augustine, it is true, rejected the idea of being a historian (*City of God* 3.18), and since he did consider himself a teacher of Christian doctrine there seems to be a contradiction here. In fact it is only apparent. When Augustine denies being a historian, this means only that he is not a historian whose attention is devoted to the things historians normally care about, like names of consuls, sizes of armies, results of battles. He is a historian whose concern is with other matters, namely those relevant for salvation. It may be objected that then there is a distinction between profane and sacred history after all; namely the distinction between the history ordinary historians are interested in and the history described by teachers of Christian doctrine. Indeed there is that distinction; and in this sense one can speak of sacred history as one strand of history. However, this is too weak a sense to support the use of the distinction in the literature. True, there is a strand of sacred history, but in no more interesting a sense than the one in which there is also a strand, say, of Norwegian history. That is to say, it is unexcitingly true that from all that happened in history a historian singles out one series of events and disregards the rest. So does the historian who is a teacher of Christian doctrine, and the events he singles out may well be called sacred history. This does not say anything, however, about what constitutes history; it does not say anything about history as such. It just says that there are these events in which these historians are interested, and that is boring news, since there are other events in which other historians are interested. The metaphor makes the point: though there can be said to be a strand of sacred history, there cannot really be said to be a strand of profane history, since profane history is just what remains when you subtract sacred history,[15] and that is not a strand because it lacks unity. To divide history into sacred and profane is as illuminating as to divide history into Norwegian and other. Such a distinction only serves to demarcate the field of interest of this or that historian.

GOD AND THE REASON THERE IS HISTORY

It is not my task to repeat the full story that, on Augustine's view, a teacher of Christian doctrine should tell. The task is to illuminate the basic conception of history that shapes it. This conception is what may be called Augustine's philosophy of history, in spite of the fact that he does not have such an expression.[16] The fundamental idea of this conception is that something is outside history; history is a limited field. To put the point more precisely, take a fact to be what is stated in a true statement; then the point is that history is not all the facts there are. This so far is just Platonism: conceptual and mathematical truths state facts that belong to a realm outside history. Augustine goes beyond traditional Platonism, though here perhaps not beyond Neoplatonism, in holding that what is outside history is not just the dead stuff investigated in conceptual analysis in the manner of Plato's dialogue *The Sophist* or in mathematics but a reality that is life and indeed mind. It is God who is beyond history. His is an unchangeable substance (*City of God* 11.2).

That he is good, for instance, is one of those facts outside history: it is a fact exempt from change (*City of God* 12.6).

History and what is outside history, however, are not on a par. Augustine was convinced from early to late that what is exempt from change is higher and better than what is not. This holds both metaphysically ("God is the highest being, i.e. he is most highly; and so he is unchangeable" [*City of God* 12.2; see also *Confessions* 12.28.38]) and morally ("to do evil is to neglect what is eternal and to pursue what is temporal" [*De libero arbitrio* 1.16.34; see also *Confessions* 12.11.11]). Given, then, that what is outside history is superior to history, the task is to understand what the place of history is below the eternal. We cannot leave it at saying that there is God unchangeable and then there is a changeable world. For someone convinced of the superiority of what is unchangeable it is hard to understand why there should be such a thing as history at all.

The answer is creation. There is history because God made it. There is even time because God made it. In fact they were made together, for an empty time is incomprehensible,[17] and the world, being changeable (*City of God* 11.4; *Confessions* 11.4.6), cannot be without time. God's will, then, is what makes the transition: eternal, it gives rise to the temporal. It is eternal, for it is itself God (*Confessions* 11.10.12; 12.15.18; 12.28.38): God did not change his mind in creating the world (*City of God* 11.4.2). For what reasons God's unchanging will made a beginning with time and world we do not know. We only know that he did it with reason, not for nothing (*City of God* 11.5). So we know that, even though temporal things are inferior to atemporal ones, this is no good reason to do without them altogether (*City of God* 12.4). To use again an anachronistic expression, there is in this sense reason in history: there is reason for there to be history. Consequently there is reason in history also in the sense that every particular event in history makes sense from God's point of view. Eternal himself, he understands everything temporal, since he gave rise to it. His understanding, however, like his will, does not involve change: "His thinking does not turn from one thing to another, but he sees things altogether invariably. Thus he comprehends what happens in time, things future, present and past, all in a stable and permanent presence" (*City of God* 11.21).[18] All changeable things, then, are willed by a will and understood by an intellect, both of which are changeless. History is owed to what is beyond history.

It may be wondered whether temporal things, having begun at a certain point, will come to an end at another, whether God is going to wipe the slate clean again. According to Augustine he will not. The world will be renewed, changing some of its qualities, and so will our bodies (*City of God* 20.16); but that is not their end, it is a transition (*City of God* 20.17). We will be living forever (*City of God* 19.20, 27) in bodily existence (*City of God* 22.4–21). Thus temporal things will stay. Time will stay.[19] Not that we see why. As little as we know God's reason for creating the world, as little do we know his reason for keeping it in existence. We just know from his word that he will. So it is in fact not the case that the world is just a big accident relative to eternity. Only for us it looks that way, insofar as we do not have a grasp of the reasons for its existence and continuation.

PREHUMAN AND HUMAN HISTORY

History, understood as comprising everything changeable, may be divided in two parts, one involving, the other not involving, humans. Augustine does not doubt that the extrahuman world is older than humanity, though he cannot say by how much (*City of God* 12.17). The prehuman world is a world of nature. Things change, indeed they perish, but in that there is nothing to complain about, given what they are. Eternal being they did not receive, and so in changing, deteriorating, and dying they fulfill "the order of transient things" (*City of God* 12.4, 5). Prehuman history is therefore running on the same spot. Things happen, but these happenings only implement the natural order, which is constant. So in another sense nothing happens in prehuman history. It is just the nature of things that is being realized in time here.

Human history differs in that humans have free will.[20] In human doings it is not just human nature that takes its course. If it were, humans could not have gone wrong: "God, author of natures and by no means of vices, created man right" (*City of God* 13.14; also 14.11). By implication, then, man's wrong act of disobeying God is not the realization of his nature. Speaking anachronistically again, it is "un acte gratuit," something he does not owe to his nature.[21] So with humans entering the scene the concept of nature loses the privilege of covering all that happens. Human history is not the mere display of what it is to be human. In this sense human history admits novelty; the novel being not just what has not been heard of but what does not lie in the order of things. In this respect human doings resemble God's creative act. "Something novel therefore happens in time," Augustine concludes in his attack against those who represent history as running in ever repeated circles (*City of God* 12.14), and he calls God's creation "a new work" (*City of God* 12.18). In the same way humans, making use of their freedom (*City of God* 13.14), bring about what was not there. There is that difference, though: what enables humans to bring about the novel, their will, is itself subject to change, whereas God's will is not (*City of God* 12.18). Some might say that only here, with novelty appearing in the world, the term "history" becomes appropriate. That is, they construe history and nature as opposites. This is only a terminological issue, though. Important is the material difference between human history and, as you prefer, all other history or nature: in human history what happens is no more the mere unfolding of what is.

What happens by nature may be defective, but what happens by will may be wrong: "Cattle and trees and other mutable and mortal things which lack intellect, sense or indeed life have their deficiencies which make their fragile natures perish, but it is ridiculous to consider these deficiencies damnable" (*City of God* 12.4). Damnable is only the voluntary, not the natural (*City of God* 12.3). Natures are better or less good, but no event in nature can be blamed. You may be worse off if your cow breaks a leg, but this is part of cowhood, and cowhood in general, with milk and broken legs and all, is a good thing, even if there are better ones (*City of God* 12.4, 5). That is to say, the goodness of a thing in the nonhuman world does not depend on particular events in its history. Its goodness is fixed once and for all by where its nature ranks in the overall order of entities (*City of God* 12.2). True, its goodness is limited, but it would hardly seem appropriate to complain that this nature is not another, better one instead. This is different with humans. They are good insofar as they have this nature, but they may still be evil insofar as they do evil (*City of God* 12.3). It is possible for them to do evil while being good in nature, because their doings do not merely explicate their nature. So a man is better or worse owing to what happens in his history, and some of these happenings accordingly can be blamed on him. Natural history displays, human history confers or fails to confer, goodness. Human history, unlike natural history, can go awry.

Thus, whereas nothing in nature can be contrary to God, things happening in human history can. Not that the evil deeds of humans could harm God or upset the order of the world as he created it. In fact God knows them and uses them to good purpose (*City of God* 14.26–27). Still, evil human deeds run counter to God's will (*City of God* 22.2); they offend God (*City of God* 22.22). Here it could be asked why it should be important for human history that parts of it offend God. He is in a different realm, beyond all history, so it is not clear why what we are doing *in* history should be any of his business. After all, if my neighbor is offended by my lawn, I do not care either. The answer to this query is that the eternal and the temporal do not stand beside each other; instead, the latter is subordinated to the former: "Reason proclaimed without any doubt that what cannot change is preferable to what can."[22] It is preferable not just in the sense that it serves our needs better but in the sense that in itself it is the higher reality. "That truly is which remains unchangeably" (*Confessions* 8.11.17).

With the phrase (from *De libero arbitrio* 1.3.7) used earlier the unchangeable excels over what is changeable and shows the latter to be falling short of true being. In this way God is the measure of everything, and of human history in particular. In its very being human history is subordinated to God's judgment, whereas my lawn is not subordinated in its being to my neighbor's feelings. For that reason Augustine understands and articulates human history basically in terms of how it is judged by God.

THE THREE STAGES OF HUMAN HISTORY

On this basis human history is divided into three parts. There was a time of faultless humanity, there is the time of sinful humanity, there will be a time of partly redeemed, partly damned humanity. Initially man lived fully in accordance with God's will (*City of God* 12.22; 14.11) and therefore happily as well. The act of disobedience brought a radical corruption of mankind and with it utter misery (*City of God* 13.14). Only helped by God's grace can a human being escape that depravity (*City of God* 19.11). Those who do will, on the day of judgment, begin a life of untempted goodness and undiminished bliss without end. Those who do not will suffer unending punishment (*City of God* 21.12).

History would appear to be rather monotonous in the first and the last of the three stages. It is true that in the first stage, paradise, things do change in time. People eat, for example (*City of God* 13.20), people beget children (*City of God* 14.23–24), people work the fields (*De Genesi ad litteram* 8.9.18); or at any rate they would have done these things if paradise had lasted long enough. Still, while these things involve change, they do not change the basic condition in which humans live; they only realize it again and again in changing time. Nor is there any need to change it: people are happy, since neither death nor pain nor servitude oppresses them (*City of God* 14.10; *De Genesi ad litteram* 8.9.18). And they feel their happiness: they find life "sweet" (*De Genesi ad litteram* 8.16.35). There could have been a narrative of paradise history, but it would have resembled the reports on home news in *Neues Deutschland*, the official party organ of the GDR: this Friday, 29 August, our happy people finished the corn harvest. There is only one event in paradise history that changes things, and that is the end of paradise history, the fall. On the other end of things the third stage of human history is even more uniform than the first. Both the saints and the damned will continue to exist as bodies (*City of God* 13.22; 21.4), so presumably there will be physical movement, hence time. The saints, however, will be free from all bodily needs, and the damned will be unable to do anything about theirs (*City of God* 13.22; 19.28), so neither will, as we do, become active to relieve a need when it arises. The saints will be seeing God, the damned will be suffering: nothing novel will happen. Moreover, the last stage of human history differs from the first in that it cannot end. Like Thomas Hobbes,[23] Augustine thinks that to be insecure about whether one's happiness will last is to that extent to be unhappy (*City of God* 12.14). So the felicity of the saints would not be perfect, as it is supposed to be, if they could not be sure it is inalterable. History, then, does not come to a halt with the last judgment. Change is going to continue. Yet the change will be superficial only. If history is the realm of changing things, then in the literal sense there is no such thing as an end of history. However, history reaches a stable end state in which it runs on forever.

It must be admitted that there is evidence against this interpretation in Augustine's writings. Strikingly, he speaks in the treatise on John of our eventual liberation from time, and in the psalm exegesis he maintains that God's word calls those who are temporal and makes them eternal.[24] On the other hand he insists in *Confessions* on denying the predicate "eternal" to everything besides God.[25] So there is an apparent contradiction here: Augustine seems both to affirm and to deny that we can and will be eternal (i.e., exist without time). The natural solution to the difficulty is this: Augustine uses both "time" and "eternal" in a strict and a loose way. Strictly, we will not and cannot be eternal. We are, and will not cease to be, temporal creatures. However, in a loose sense time can be said to come to an end with the last judgment, since further changes, which do keep occurring, will be insignificant. One could put it this way: formal time does not end, destructive time does.[26] And as this state without significant change is going to continue forever, it can be called, loosely, "eternal."

Both the first and the last stages of human history, then, are similar to natural history: there is change, but it does not fundamentally affect the way in which humans live. "Real" history can only come in the second part of human history, that between fall and judgment, ours, which Augustine sometimes just calls "hoc saeculum" (this time of the world). Here indeed there is change: "Human affairs are so liable to change that no people at any time could be as secure as not to fear a hostile attack on their lives."[27] Security is lacking in this age, precisely that security that renders life in the last age of human history so uniform. Actually, however, our age, for all its instability, is pretty monotonous, too, in Augustine's view. True, human affairs are liable to change, but in another way nothing changes. The human condition was radically debased in the fall, and it cannot be improved by human efforts. It is a miserable condition, and so it will remain, with all historical changes, until the day of judgment. Augustine likes to describe this part of human history between fall and judgment with the traditional image of a river: "in this river, as it were, and torrent of mankind."[28] The image is appropriate. Think of watching a river or especially a torrent: this is enjoyable because there is change at every moment. Still, when you turn away you know that in another way nothing has changed since you came. So it is with the history of fallen humanity: there is much movement, but the basic character of human life, which is misery, does not change.[29] Stressing its pervasive character, Augustine occasionally speaks of these "evil days" (*City of God* 18.49, 51; *Sermo 25* 6): this time itself appears bad, because what is in it is thoroughly bad. Even the good, beautiful, or useful things in our lives that Augustine contemplates in a memorable chapter close to the end of *City of God* are said to be "filled in" into the misery of mankind (*City of God* 22.24): misery remains the fundamental condition. To be sure, human nature is still good and could not be anything else. Yet miserable we are nonetheless: that nature has been ruined by human action.

Thus historical changes that we should normally consider important turn out to be as insignificant as the events of human history before the fall or after judgment, since they change the human predicament as little as these do: "As far as this life of mortals is concerned, a life led and ended in a few days, what does it matter under whose command a man lives who is going to die, provided his rulers do not force him to do what is impious and unjust?" (*City of God* 5.17). This suggests that some historical changes are important, as when a ruler who forces his subjects to commit impiety is replaced by one who does not.[30] Still, this importance only concerns people's moral standing with respect to God. As far as it is a matter of bettering human life in this world, of providing for greater glory, greater comfort, or greater freedom, historical changes count for nothing. First, such attempts are bound to fail. There is in principle no way to improve the way humans live in this world. It is all rotten from the root up (*City of God* 13.14). Second, even if chances of success were better, why bother? The ills of our condition burden us only for these few days until we die, so, given the superiority of the eternal over the temporal, they do not deserve any attention. Thus, when Augustine compares the superhuman deeds of a Brutus who killed his own sons for Rome's sake to the easier tasks of the Christian, like alms-giving (*City of God* 5.18), there is admiration here for what Roman virtue could accomplish but also condescending pity for its having barked up the wrong tree and wasted its efforts on earth rather than on heaven.[31] For people who understand the true value of things there are no final aims of a political nature. They have, literally, better things to do: eternal life is the highest good for which one should be shooting in action (*City of God* 19.4). Augustine's standing image for this attitude toward politics is "peregrinari" (sojourning as a foreigner [e.g., *City of God* preface]). People who are heading for eternal life are not at home in this world of human politics, they are in exile here. Not that they are indifferent to what is around them; after all they do not know how long they will have to stay. They cannot but use the peace that it is the aim of political institutions to provide, since such peace is necessary for the mortal life in which they are dwelling temporarily (*City of God* 19.17). Accordingly they obey the laws of the relevant political community, provided that these do not interfere with their religious commitments (*City of God* 19.17). Even so, their heart is not in it. They are absent-minded citizens of this world: always waiting, though waiting patiently,[32] to reach the unseen but promised (*City of God* 19.14) country they feel to be theirs (*City of God* 5.17).

Augustine, sufficiently close to the classical tradition of political philosophy, insists that their life is still a social life (*City of God* 19.5). Foreigners in human politics, they belong to one another in a different community, God's city, which is in exile in this world for the time being and will come into its own in a renewed world on the day of judgment (*City of God* 20.16). Who is member of this city, however, and who is not cannot be ascertained in this age of human history. The division in question is between "those who live according to man and those who live according to God. These groups we also call, mystically speaking, two cities, i.e. two communities of humans. The one is predestinated to reign with God in eternity, the other to suffer eternal damnation with the devil" (*City of God* 15.1). The first is the city of God, the second is the earthly city. However, nobody knows of anyone, himself included, to what city he belongs, for nobody knows of anyone whether he is one of the elected saints or not. In particular to belong to the city of God it is neither necessary nor sufficient to be a member of the church (*City of God* 1.35). So the city of God is present in human history, but nowhere can it be identified. When Augustine says that "these two cities are interwoven in this world and mixed with each other, until the last judgment will separate them" (*City of God* 1.35), this does not only mean that it is difficult, it means that it is impossible for us to tell them apart. In this world the interwoven threads form one continuous cloth. Only at its end will the threads themselves show. Until the day of judgment God's city is not visible in the historical arena. In this respect the title *The City of God* may mislead. It may give the impression as if it were just another city like those we know. In fact it is a city "mystically speaking": no institution can claim to represent it. As H. Caton puts it, "a Christian state is a contradiction in terms." [33] The saints do enjoy a political existence in the city of God, but it is not a worldly political existence. In the political institutions of this world they remain foreigners.

The monotony of the second part of human history is broken only by the advent of Christ and by everything that points to or derives from it. [34] Here is change. It does not consist in human life ceasing to be miserable and human action ceasing to be sinful. The change is that a future and definitive liberation from this condition becomes possible (*City of God* 22.22; 14.11). Nobody can trust that he will be among those who are saved by God's free grace through Christ. Still, that grace has come. Thus while everything else that happens between fall and judgment only continues our misery, this event opens a door out of it, however many or few will walk through it in the end. This event changes the condition of human life once and for all: redemption has come.

Precisely for this reason it is important that incarnation, crucifixion, and resurrection do not belong to another, special history called sacred history but as historical events are on a par with everything else happening in human history. After all it is ordinary human history in which the misery of fallen humanity endures, and that misery is what needs to be met. Salvation only on the upper floor of history is no use. This is the point of incarnation: that grace arrive right in the middle of misery.

It is true, though, that incarnation, crucifixion, and resurrection are the only really interesting events in this part of human history between fall and judgment (disregarding here and in the following those events that are interesting derivatively, by their relation to that central event). The only interesting event in this age of human history is the appearance of what is beyond history: that "God's only son, remaining in himself unchangeably, puts on the clothes of humanity" (*City of God* 10.29; see also 10.20). It is true for all human history, indeed for all history, that God is its master, ruling and coordinating everything that happens. [35] Yet, as we never, or only very seldom (*City of God* 20.2), see why God directs things the way he does, history does not become transparent. We can only be confident in general that all history is in God's hands, but we cannot watch his hand at work. In incarnation, by contrast, God himself becomes visible, as directly as anything in human history. Bernard Williams not long ago wrote an essay on the tedium of immortality. [36] For Augustine the opposite is true: mortality is boring, boringly miserable, without the epiphany of the immortal. Peter Brown quotes from Augustine's *In Joannis evangelium* 9.6: "The centuries of past history would have rolled by like empty jars, if Christ had not been foretold by means of them."[37] But for Christ's coming all human history after the fall would have rolled by like empty jars.

CONCLUSION

So here is the overall Augustinian picture of history. It is a nested structure, like a Russian doll. First, beyond all history, and indeed beyond time, is God, existing timelessly. What the word "beyond" means in this sentence remains unexplained, given that it does not literally mean "prior to" or "outside of." The idea is, at any rate, that God encompasses everything that is not God. Second, there is the realm of temporal things, the realm of history, as this word has been used here. History has a beginning, creation, and so it has a certain age now, even if we do not know what it is; but it will go on indefinitely. There is a reason there is history, but we do not know that either. Third, within history there is human history. Later than and surrounded by a history that merely unfolds in time the stable nature of things, human history introduces free will and thus novelty: no nature is realized in the workings of free will. Fourth, within human history there is, surrounded by the uniform life in paradise and after judgment, the changing life of fallen humanity, which is unchanging, though, in its basic misery. Fifth, there is within this age of human misery that unique event in which God who is beyond all history enters history. This is the turning point of the whole structure. Thanks to it, a path is opened for humans to leave their misery and to enter a new life that is as much in accordance with the eternal God as is possible for a temporal creature of this kind.

So for Augustine there is not a great deal of important history after all. While history in the present sense of the word comprises everything that happens in the created world since its beginning, only very, very few of these happenings really change the course of things. Under nature, what happens merely unfolds what a thing is. Human history is as uniform in its initial and in its final part, except only for the fall. Even these our bad days, while full of change, are constant in their misery. Christ's coming, the first and the second, are within this age of mutability the only events that have significance. It is not that there are two histories, sacred and secular, or two strands of history. The point is that in the one history of the world there is so little that counts: creation, fall, redemption, judgment, that is all. The rest is waste. Moreover, the central event in all history, the pivot on which the whole structure turns, is the appearance of what is not in history, which promises the elimination of change as far as this is possible for temporal creatures. What Nietzsche's Zarathustra says about man[38] is Augustine's view about history: it is something that must be overcome.

This is reflected in Augustine's conception of peace as the final aim of all our efforts. Perfect peace, peace such that there cannot be any better and greater, is what the city of God expects to find at the end of its travels (*City of God* preface; 19.10). Indeed, "peace is such a great good that even in things of this world, mortal things, nothing more gratifying can be heard, nothing more desirable can be yearned for, simply nothing better can be found" (*City of God* 19.11). Peace in turn is understood in terms of order. True, peace is many different things, depending on the kind of thing whose peace it is. The general formula, though, is "peace is the tranquillity of order" (*City of God* 19.13). The idea is: when things are where they belong and do not move, then there is peace. Peace is to have arrived. Hence, conversely, to be moving is itself a bad thing. To be sure, any peace to which we aspire cannot but involve some change, given that we are temporal creatures. Such changes within peace, however, do not disturb the order. These are changes like that of day and night, changes that do not change anything. In the peace that is, according to Augustine, "devoutly to be wished" any movement has ceased to occur that gives things a new turn. The famous line in the opening chapter of *Confessions*, "you created us toward you and our heart is unquiet until it finds quiet in you," has been taken to express the essence of Augustinian thought. And so it does: it tells of the overwhelming desire to get rid of history, to the extent it is possible for a temporal being.

"Reason proclaimed without any doubt that what cannot change is preferable to what can" (*Confessions* 12.17.23). There are those whose reason does not proclaim any such thing. So what is the interest of Augustine's conception of history, given that it is built on this alleged declaration of reason and tries, in the various ways discussed, to frame history? The interest lies in the fact that with this conception those have been struggling who in more recent times recognized that nothing eternal is in sight and that we have to understand ourselves in terms of history alone. Not that Augustine has been frequently quoted by modern philosophers. His conception has been present all the more just because it had come to represent the traditional understanding rather than being seen as the view of a particular author. So it is largely the picture of history as represented in Augustine against which modern writers in the field implicitly have been arguing. To take just one example, when in his poem "Resignation" Schiller declares, "world history is the world's judgment,"[39] a formula immediately picked up by his contemporaries,[40] then his point is also, implicitly but no less significantly, that nothing other than world history is the world's judgment; that the world will not be judged by anything outside the world—which is what Augustine held. In failing to recognize in Schiller's slogan the challenge to an Augustinian view of history one would be missing a good part of what animates Schiller's thought here and gives it its power. And what holds for Schiller holds, often in more complicated ways than in this example, for a large part of modern philosophy of history. The aim has been, again and again, to cast off what came to be seen as the fetters of the Augustinian framework. The aim has been, against Augustine, to untie history from its transhistorical moorings.

And you do not get your opponents for free. You pay for them in coming to resemble them. So Augustinian ideas have shaped the very conceptions that were meant to replace them. Schiller's line again presents a clear example. Eager to establish that God's son will not come from heaven to judge the world, Schiller turns things around and has world history itself do the judging. However, in rejecting Augustine's doctrine he follows him at the same time, for he accepts the idea that there is such a thing as a judgment of the world. He just puts somebody else on the job rather than scrapping it entirely. Thus Augustine's idea stays in force. Indeed, people say to this day that history will judge what a person did or what a regulation effected. Apparently it is difficult to loosen the grip of the thought that at some point a balance will be struck and a reckoning be made, that the definitive truth about our doings will come out. Similarly for other elements of the Augustinian story: that history is intelligible, that it forms a whole, that it reaches a final stage, and so on—these ideas have dominated our thinking about history from Augustine's time to the present. Modern philosophy of history has been in this sense thoroughly Augustinian. Here lies the interest of Augustine's conception. For all our endeavors we have not yet left it behind.

NOTES

1. Koselleck speaks of "Geschichte überhaupt" and "Geschichte schlechthin." For the history and significance of this use of "history" see his contribution to the article "Geschichte" in O. Brunner, W. Conze, and R. Koselleck, eds., *Geschichtliche Grundbegriffe*, vol. 2 (Stuttgart: E. Klett, 1975).

2. See G. Amari, *Il concetto di storia in Sant' Agostino* (Ph.D. diss., Universitas Gregoriana, Rome, 1951), 17. Amari's view is disputed, though with little argument, by F.-M. Schmölz, "Historia sacra et profana bei Augustin," in H. Rahner, S.J., and E. V. Severus, O.S.B., eds., *Perennitas* (Münster: Aschendorf, 1963), 34. *De Genesi ad litteram* 9.12.22 supports Amari's view with an especially salient opposition between events ("res gestae") and "historia"; see also St. Augustine, *The City of God* 17.1. In fact there is one genuine counterexample to Amari's claim, which C. Meier, Art. "Geschichte," 600, pointed out: in *De doctrina Christiana* 2.28.44 Augustine distinguishes between historical narration, which reports on past human institutions, and history itself, "historia ipsa," which is not a human institution, because things past cannot be made undone and belong into the order of times that is founded and administrated by God. However, this is one of those exceptions that confirm the rule. True, "historia" does refer here to past events, but, given Augustine's standing usage of "historia" as "narrative," the added word "ipsa" here shows only his terminological embarrassment in referring to what "historia" is about; it should not be taken as suggesting that reference to events is the genuine function of "historia." (The division into chapters of *The City of God* is taken from the edition of Bernard Dombart and Alfons Kalb [Stuttgart: Teubner, 1981].) All translations, from Augustine and from other authors, are mine, except where stated otherwise.

3. The point here and some of the expressions are based on St. Augustine, *Confessions* 7.9.13–15; *De Trinitate* 4.16.21; 13.1.2; 8.19.24. Running together these chapters is justified by the evident parallels between them in substance and phrasing.

4. *City of God* 11.3: "things of which we should not be ignorant and which we are not capable of knowing by ourselves."

5. On this topic see the discussion in R. A. Markus, *Saeculum: History and Society in the Theology of St. Augustine* (Cambridge: Cambridge University Press, 1970), 7–9.

6. See *De doctrina Christiana* 2.28.42

7. See the phrase "historiae, quae res veraciter gestas continent" (*City of God* 18.13).

8. Ibid., 18.40. This is also why knowledge about Roman consuls and the like is "childish erudition" (*De doctrina Christiana* 2.28.42).

9. Vico's principle that you can know only what you made seems to be a humanized version of this idea. In sec. 349 of the *New Science* (trans. Thomas G. Bergin and Max H. Fisch [Ithaca: Cornell University Press, 1948]) he writes, "history cannot be more certain than when he who creates the things also narrates them." The telling word here is "creates." See on this topic Karl Löwith, *Vicos Grundsatz: Verum et factum convertuntur* (Heidelberg: C. Winter, 1968).

10. Karl Löwith, *Meaning in History* (Chicago: University of Chicago Press, 1949), chap. 9; Schmölz, "Historia sacra et profana"; Markus, *Saeculum*, chap. 1.

11. See, for instance, *De Genesi ad litteram* 8.1.2.

12. This is Markus's conclusion, too (*Saeculum*, 14f.), though he does not rigorously stick to this line in his text (see 9–11).

13. Markus's phrase (ibid., 9, 11).

14. *City of God* 18.43.46 tells of late Jewish history and of Christ's birth under the reign of Herod in one breath: no shift from profane to sacred history can be felt here.

15. Markus, *Saeculum*, 11.

16. If it is urged that this is, rather, Augustine's theology of history (see Alois Wachtel, *Beiträge zur Geschichtstheologie des Aurelius Augustinus* [Bonn: Röhrscheid, 1960], chap. 1)—fine, let that title be used: there is no real difference here, since theology is philosophy by other means.

17. *City of God* 11.6; 12.26; *Confessions* 12.11.14. The compatibility of this conception of time with that in *Confessions* 11 may be questioned.

18. Kant's distinction between intuitive and discursive understanding (see, for instance, *The Critique of Pure Reason* B 135, 138f., 145) clearly stems from this tradition.

19. Augustine sometimes speaks of a "novum saeculum," a "new world-time" (*City of God* 22.10; 19) that is going to open after judgment.

20. Ibid., 22.1; *De Genesi ad litteram* 8.23.44.

21. In fact God set up man's nature in such a way that "if he offended the Lord, his God, by using his free will proudly and disobediently, then he would live like a beast, tied to death, dominated by lust, destined to eternal damnation after death" (ibid., 12.22). It is not man's nature to be disobedient; it is man's nature to be punished if disobedient.

22. *Confessions* 7.17.23. Metaphors of above and below, of superiority, and rise and ascent abound in Augustine; see especially the second half of *Confessions*.

23. Thomas Hobbes, *De homine*, chap. 10, sect. 3.

24. St. Augustine, *In Joannis evangelium* 31.5; idem, *Enarrationes in Psalmos* 101.2.10. On this topic see the discussion in Wachtel, *Beiträge*, 46f.

25. See *Confessions* 7.15.21; 12.9.9; 12.11.11; 12.11.12.

26. The passage in the treatise on John supports this interpretation by speaking of our arriving "where there is no mutability of time any more." So there may still be time, only no mutability; which is to say, no serious change.

27. *City of God* 17.13; see also 17.9; 19.4; 20.3.

28. Ibid., 22.24; also *De Trinitate* 4.16, 21; *Sermo 25* 6.

29. "Series calamitatis" in *City of God* 13.14 makes the same point with a different image.

30. Peter J. Burnell, "The Status of Politics in St. Augustine's *City of God*," *History of Political Thought* 13 (1992): 20, insists on this point against Markus, *Saeculum*, 70.

31. This alludes to Hegel's statement that "it was left to our days in particular to vindicate as human property, in theory at least, the treasures wasted on heaven" (*Hegels theologische Jugendschriften*, ed. H. Nohl [Tübingen: Mohr, 1907], 225).

32. *City of God* preface; 19.4; but cf. St. Augustine, *Epistulae* 27.1.

33. Hiram Caton, "St. Augustine's Critique of Politics," *New Scholasticism* 47 (1973): 453.

34. On the relevance of prophetic history see Peter Brown, *Augustine of Hippo* (Berkeley: University of California Press, 1967), 317–19.

35. *City of God* 4.33; see also 5.11; 22.2.

36. B. Williams, "The Macropulos Case: Reflections on the Tedium of Immortality," in *Problems of the Self* (Cambridge: Cambridge University Press, 1973).

37. Brown, *Augustine of Hippo*, 318.

38. Friedrich Nietzsche, *Also Sprach Zarathustra* 1.3, in *Sämtliche Werke: Kritische Studienausgabe*, 15 vols., ed. Giorgio Colli and Mazzimo Montimari (Berlin: De Gruyter, 1980).

39. "Die Weltgeschichte ist das Weltgericht."

40. Koselleck, "Geschichte," 667.

TWENTY

Plights of Embodied Soul*

Dramas of Sin and Salvation in Augustine and Updike

Richard Eldridge

No two writers are more continuously concerned with sex and salvation than Augustine and Updike. Augustine describes his own life prior to his conversion as an ongoing and intense struggle between the demands of the spirit and the temptations of the body:

> But when I rose in pride against you and "made onslaught" against my Lord, "proud of my strong sinews [Job 15:26]," even those lower things became my masters and oppressed me, and nowhere could I find respite or time to draw my breath. Everywhere I looked they loomed before my eyes in swarms and clusters, and when I set myself to thinking and tried to escape from them, images of these selfsame things blocked my way, as though they were asking where I meant to go, unclean and undeserving as I was.[1]

Updike has similarly remarked on the allures of the body as a perilous housing for the soul, seeing us as subject to "the power of sex to bind souls to the transient, treacherous world," wherein "sexual appetite . . . calls into activity our most elegant faculties of self-display, of social intercourse and of internal idealization."[2] Updike is aware of his affinities with Augustine in emphasizing the moral perils posed by our embodiment, noting that a "dark Augustinian idea lurked within my tangled position [on the Vietnam War], . . . [a refusal to pretend] that bloody hands didn't go with having hands at all. A plea, in short, for the doctrine of Original Sin."[3] This avowed Augustinianism represents, for Updike, a rejection of "an easy humanism that insists that man is an animal which feeds and sleeps and defecates and makes love and isn't that nice and natural and let's all have more of

*Work on this chapter was supported by a grant from the Swarthmore College Faculty Research Fund and by the Stanford Humanities Center. I am grateful to my research assistant Kurt Leege for his careful and insightful work in compiling a critical bibliography of writing on John Updike. Joan Vandegrift read an earlier draft of the chapter and made useful suggestions for its improvement.

that," a position that omits "intrinsic stresses in the human condition—you foresee things, for example, you foresee your own death. You have really been locked out of the animal paradise of unthinking natural reflex."[4] This Augustinian sense of the allures and perils of embodied consciousness informs all of Updike's fiction. The intimate detail of his observations of the travails of embodiment is the signature of his style, evident, for example, in his tracing of Harry Angstrom's thoughts about how women make love:

> That wonderful way they have of coming forward around you when they want it. Otherwise just fat weight. Funny how the passionate ones are often tight and dry and the slow ones wet. They want you up and hard on their little ledge. The thing is play them until just a touch. You can tell: their skin under the fur gets all loose like a puppy's neck.[5]

For both Augustine and Updike, in a position that has come to be identified as Augustinian, the body is something to be struggled with, a vehicle of both the soul's life and of original sin. Our very ability to know human and divine reality—and hence our politics and morality insofar as they depend on an understanding of these realities—is deeply shaped by how we engage in this inevitable struggle, by whether we succumb to lust or embrace a pious continence.

But something in us—whether it is pride or good sense is unclear—resists this distinctive construal of embodiment as original sin. Both Augustine and Updike are consistently accused of confusion, of promoting dangerously unhealthy views without really having given them much thought. It is difficult to think of two writers who are more often condescended to than these two, praised for minor virtues while being condemned for somehow having gone massively wrong, chiefly through a lack of thought.

Augustine, Copleston tells us, "deals with man in the concrete," producing "an approach, an inspiration, certain basic ideas" that are distinctive for their "suggestiveness." But "he never elaborated a philosophical system as such, nor did he develop, define and substantiate his ideas in the manner to which a Thomist is accustomed. . . . There is often an aura of vagueness, allusion, lack of definition about his ideas which leaves one dissatisfied, perplexed and curious." We never get "a complete system to be accepted, rejected or mutilated."[6] The implication here is that Augustine was so absorbed in his personal struggles that he never stopped to sort things out, never separated epistemology from ethics from aesthetics from theology, so that it's hard to tell what kind of thinker or writer he is. Gareth Matthews, while praising Augustine's concentration on the first-person standpoint and arguing his interest as a philosopher, echoes this reservation in noting that Augustine is "only, so to speak, a major 'minor' philosopher" without "formal training in philosophy" and "without the benefit of an academic environment or the stimulus of astute philosophical colleagues, or students."[7] There is, as Copleston puts it, in Augustine's writings a "mingling of theological and philosophical themes [that] may appear odd and unmethodical to us to-day."[8]

But not only does Augustine fail to sort things out, the picture of human virtues and vices that he abstracts from excessive concentration on his own struggles may very well be a dangerous one. In setting continence as the chief virtue against "that stream of boiling pitch, the hideous flood of lust" (*Confessions* 3.2), the chief vice, Augustine at the very least promotes an unhealthy, unnatural repressiveness. At worst the sort of obsession with the control of the body that he manifests may lead to anorexia or other forms of neurotic self-loathing. As Updike has observed, "How strangely on modern ears falls the notion that lust—sexual desire that wells up in us as involuntarily as saliva—in itself is wicked! . . . Impotence, frigidity, unattractiveness—these are the sins of which we are truly ashamed."[9] Elaine Pagels has noted that Augustine's views about sin "will appear to many readers . . . antinatural and even preposterous,"[10] and she has gone on to suggest that his focus on the control of the body promotes political authoritarianism. "By insisting that humanity, ravaged by sin, now lies helplessly in need of outside intervention, Augustine's theory could not only validate secular power but justify as well the imposition of church authority—by force, if necessary—as essential for human salvation."[11] Piety construed as continence, the control of an essentially unruly body, engenders unhealthy self-loathing and potentially brutal political authoritarianism.

Things are no better when it comes to Updike. A chorus of critics has praised his style while condemning his thought. Thus Harold Bloom characterizes Updike as "a minor novelist with a major style."[12] Though he is "perhaps the most considerable stylist among the writers of fiction in his American generation," Updike is, Bloom argues:

> somewhat victimized aesthetically by . . . conventional religious yearnings. . . . Piety, hardly an imaginative virtue in itself, becomes polemical [in Updike], and testifies unto us with considerable tendentiousness, belatedness, and a kind of supernatural smugness that allows Updike to say "the natural is a pit of horror" and "one has nothing but the ancient assertions of Christianity to give one the will to act."[13]

Bloom's suggestion here is that Updike, too, has not sorted things out: he has let dogma get in the way of the exercises of iconoclastic, creative imagination that are, for Bloom, proper to art. This charge of a failure to sort, to think, is echoed in John W. Aldridge's remark that "as a rule one senses that [Updike] does not, after all, know quite what he means to say and is hoping that sheer style will carry him over the difficulty,"[14] a criticism that is itself a transcription of Norman Mailer's 1963 sneer: "trouble is that young John, like many a good young writer before him, does not know exactly what to do when action lapses, and so he cultivates his private vice, he *writes*."[15] Garry Wills has similarly jibed that Updike's "endless verbal cleverness . . . can run unimpeded by the weights of moral insight or of judgment."[16]

The common thread of these criticisms is that Updike's prose is too comfortable, too easy, too seductive. Behind this complaint lurks the charge that his plot of human experience is either, like Augustine's, tendentious and authoritarian in urging a dogmatic pietism or, failing that, simply absent, so that Updike is taken to be evading serious political realities, offering us instead a narcotic entertainment that encourages bourgeois complacency and thoughtlessness. It just can't be right, seemingly, to spend all that lush prose on patterns of wallpaper in the late afternoon sun or on memories of pulling a young sister on a sled or on the look of leaves on a copper beech tree. Where's the action? And if there's no action, is there then any thought about politics or human life? Isn't it all just too comfortable, too middle class? Or if not that, then too piously repressive?

An enormous certainty lies at the hearts of these judgments: the certainty that reality manifests itself to us (and in us) in distinct kinds that do not muddle one another's natures. Thus God's reality is a distinct kind of thing that is properly treated by theology or philosophy of religion rather than by ethics or psychology. Human interactions in exchanging and competing for goods are the proper subject of politics, not of a theory of salvation. Sexual behavior is the concern of ethics or psychology, or maybe, lately, politics, but not of the philosophy of religion. Aesthetics treats iconoclastic artistic imaginings, according to Bloom, but art has little per se to do with religion (except for the fact that J., the Yahwist, was a great precursor writer). Epistemology, ontology, and logic are best left to philosophers, probably to philosophers who have a healthy understanding of mathematics and the natural sciences; certainly ethicists, philosophers of religion, philosophers of art, and writers of fiction ought not to intrude upon them.

Underneath this certainty about the kinds of realities that we confront lies the further thought that ordinary life is not terribly interesting, that the things most worth knowing are in the province of one or another expert rather than surfacing fitfully in the consciousnesses of gas station attendants, childcare workers, or, say, linotype operators, car dealers, or lawyer-rhetoricians. In seeing reality as divided into kinds, each of which is to be studied by its appropriate experts, it is as though we don't find ordinary human life itself very deep or interesting.

Yet virtually all theologies would contest this certainty about kinds of realities and this thought about the banality of everyday life. The notion that reality is created inevitably refers all kinds and natures to God, seeing kinds on the model of interrelated roles, each intelligible only in terms of the others, in an ordained plot. Within Christian theology each person's life is of full and independent interest, in that each person's soul is a locus for the playing out of the infinitely important drama of salvation or condemnation. In the eyes of God no aspect of reality is self-sustaining, and no person's life is banal.

Both Augustine and Updike write deliberately out of this sort of theological conviction in the existence of created reality in which human beings have an especially dramatic role to play as objects of God's judgment, directed at all their behavings, political, economic, sexual, parental, consumptive, artistic, and so on, as may be. Their writings aim at dramatizing how a human identity is built up, sustained, and articulated in a single, specifically situated person, whether in

fourth-century Thagaste, Carthage, and Milan or in Brewer, Pennsylvania, between 1932 and 1989, in such a way that divine reality is or is not fitfully honored
and realized in it. That divine reality should be honored, realized, in a situated
human life is, for Augustine and Updike, always a dramatic possibility, one that
impinges on politics, sexual behavior, artistic imagining, and consumption without
these behaviors going their own ways one by one.

But while the terms of the dramas are similar the fates of the protagonists are
not. Augustine in a certain way claims salvation, or at least accord with the will of
God, as that accord is manifested in his postconversion continence, for the protagonist of the *Confessions*. Updike's Harry Angstrom dies comparatively young,
following a sense-dominated, present-experience-oriented life that consistently
lacks continence and self-discipline. But, for all their differences, juxtaposing the
plots of Augustine's and Harry Angstrom's developments (as their writers recount
them) helps to bring out two things. First, it shows the pattern of necessities of embodied soul and of possibilities of response to them that are, for a Christian sensibility, built into the fact of our existence as God's creatures. A kind of ground
human plot, a set of temptations, threats, and possibilities necessarily encountered
and variously dealt with, informs each human life on such a view. This ground
human plot emerges through the comparison of Augustine's and Updike's two different ways of playing it out. Second, this juxtaposition shows how finally tentative
is each writer's account of the meaning of the life he treats. Some of Augustine's
uncertainties survive his conversion, and, more deeply, the narrative's sense of its
human protagonist lapses after the conversion is accomplished, as though to suggest that an intelligible human life requires ongoing temptation, struggle, difficulty.
Harry Angstrom is, whatever his failings, interesting. His sense-oriented sensibility
affords him moments of awareness, especially of beauty, but also of nothingness,
in any case of engagement with a divine order, that many of us block or refuse. If
he is unable to integrate these moments of awareness into a way of life, perhaps
because of the fragmentation and antiritualism of his public culture and the
routes of identity formation its economy affords, he nonetheless has them in the
face of his culture's scanting of them. It is not, in the end, so easy for us to say
where or how grace might have manifested itself, where or how salvation might
have been attained. In comparing the narrated developments of Augustine and
Harry Angstrom we can see both the narrative delicacy of Augustine (the writer's)
development of his protagonist and the thoughtful weight of Updike's inheritance
of theological tradition. The comparison helps to illuminate what it is to try to
narrate, to understand, any human life, once grace, and salvation, sin, and condemnation are regarded as possibilities, perhaps inevitabilities.

It will in the end remain unclear whether any such narratives, or comparisons
among them, can or should unseat our temptations to regard reality as finally articulated into kinds, understandings of which are the proper provinces of experts,
and to find ordinary life banal. The comparison will not tell us whether grace is a
genuine present possibility for us. But it will perhaps be no more unclear whether

we should regard a divine intermingling of created natures and a divine interest in ordinary life as actual than it is unclear whether we should regard Augustine or Harry as saved or condemned. If their salvation is an issue for us, perhaps our salvation should be too. It will be some achievement if Augustine and Updike, by recounting their protagonists' developments, can make our often hard certainties about reality as uncertain as the possibilities of grace. What, then, do their plots of the necessary temptations and possible manners of response to embodiment show? The ground plot of human necessities and possibilities that underlies their specific narratives looks something like this.

The starting point for each writer's narrative is an overwhelming sense of the embodiment of consciousness and personality in a sensing, fleshly human body. Consciousness and personality are neither reduced to material facts nor regarded as independent of them. It is impossible either to explain human conceptual consciousness as a bodily process or to regard one's personality as existing unhoused by a body, at least in its present earthly life. Augustine refers naturally to himself as formed by God from the flesh of his parents, "the two from whose bodies you formed me in the limits of time" (*Confessions* 1.6.). The realities of the body are prior to the rational deliverances of God-attuned intellect. In infancy, Augustine tells us, "all I knew was how to suck, and how to lie still when my body sensed comfort or cry when it felt pain" (1.6). These bodily realities are, moreover, on earth inescapable: "soon I was dragged away from you by my own weight and in dismay I plunged again into the things of this world. The weight I carried was the habit of the flesh. . . . For 'ever the soul is weighed down by a mortal body, earth-bound cell that clogs the manifold activity of its thought' [Wisdom 9:15]" (7.17). His opening question—roughly, "How might I praise God?"—modulates quickly into the questions, "What are my possible manners of life as an embodied human consciousness? What way of embodied life would count as God's praise?" While eternal life for the soul is at stake in addressing these questions, the soul's merit is tested by how it comports itself in its present ineluctable embodiment. The turmoils of lust and reverence, concupiscence and charity, are playings out of possibilities that are built into the fact of embodiment.

Harry Angstrom is no less an embodied personality. He notices things not through abstract intellection but by having bodily experience. In picking up a basketball at the age of twenty-six he finds that "That old stretched-leather feeling makes his whole body go taut, gives his arms wings. It feels like he's reaching down through the years to touch this tautness." "That his touch still lives in his hands elates him. He feels liberated from long gloom. But his body is weighty and his breath grows short. It annoys him that he gets winded." Remembering that elation of touch, and seeing it in another player, he thinks, "Naturals know. It's all in how it feels" (*Run*, 10, 11).

Awareness of bodily sensation, including visual sensations of the detritus of culture, is Harry's principal mode of awareness of himself through time. "He recognizes elapsed time in the parched puffiness on his lips." As Ruth thinks to herself about Harry, "That was the thing about him, he just lived in his skin and didn't give a thought to the consequences of anything" (*Run*, 43, 139).

This tendency to be aware of himself and to think through sensory experience does not change much as Harry ages. At forty-seven "a big bland good guy is how he sees himself, six three and around two ten by now, with a forty-two inch waist the suit salesman at Kroll's tried to tell him until he sucked his gut in and the man's thumb grudgingly inched the tape tighter." Bodily coordination remains for him the chief virtue, "uncoördination the root of all evil as he feels it" (*Rich*, 6, 48).

Crucially, it is not that bodily processes are all there are; it is rather that something is experiencing the world through its embodiment. There's something in there, held within the flesh. "Sometimes Rabbit's spirit feels as if it might faint from lugging all this body around. Little squeezy pains tease his ribs, reaching into his upper left arm. He has spells of feeling short of breath and mysteriously full in the chest, full of some pressing essence." (*Rest*, 6–7). Perhaps no one but Updike is as capable of writing a nine-page description of what it feels like to the person to have a heart attack in one's body (*Rest*, 134–42), during which Harry "closes his eyes intermittently in obedience to the animal instinct to crawl into a cave with your pain" (*Rest*, 137). To be a person, as Augustine and Updike know it, is to be subject to pains and pleasures, motions of one's fleshly weight.

It is not simply that we are embodied, it is also that our intelligence enjoys and sustains itself on sensory experience. Not only do we exist as embodied persons, "we know that we exist and we love that fact and our knowledge of it." [17] While Augustine typically represents knowledge of our own existence as inner and as more certain than knowledge of external things, his narrative suggests that love of one's own existence is love of oneself as a locus of experience, sensory experience initially and most powerfully and experience of God perhaps later. "By [the bodily senses] we have learned to know the heaven and the earth." [18] Bodily sensations are both vehicles of our embodied life—without them we would not be as we are—and revelations of God to the inner self:

> it was to the inner part of me that my bodily senses brought their messages. They delivered to their arbiter and judge the replies which they carried back from the sky and the earth and all that they contain, those replies which stated, "We are not God" and "God is he who made us." (*Confessions* 10.6)

God "made . . . beautiful shapes of different sorts and bright and attractive colors . . . all 'very good' [Genesis 1:31]" (10.34), all at once attractions in themselves, vehicles of perceptive and bodily life through our awareness of them and use of them, and evidences of their maker. If sensation is, for Augustine, someday to be transcended as a mode of experience in favor of inward contemplation of God, it is nonetheless a first and central mode, full of its own charms, shaped by and revelatory of God's making of its objects, and never fully transcended by us as long as we live on earth.

Harry Angstrom likewise, and even more desperately, lives his experiences of sensible objects. They are his principal evidences of realities: their own, his, and, fitfully, God's. "He walks downhill. The day is gathering itself in. He now and then touches with his hand the rough bark of a tree or the dry twigs of a hedge, to give himself the small answer of a texture" (*Run*, 20). Harry's continual recoverings of the sensory realities of objects, realities that inform and survive immediate experience, are his principal means of experiencing the goodness of the world: the light on the copper beech trees outside his bedroom window, water from the ice plant running in the gutter, Lotty Bingaman raising her arm, Janice's "inside softly grainy, like a silk slipper" (*Run*, 18). These are Harry's reassurances of visible realities, of his own reality, and of their goodness, hence perhaps of something higher. Janice's "girl friend at work had an apartment in Brewer they used. Pipe-frame bed, silver medallions in the wallpaper; a view westward of the great blue gas tanks by the edge of the river. . . . Lying side by side on this other girl's bed, feeling lost, having done the final thing; the wall's silver and the fading day's gold" (*Run*, 18). As Harry watches people going to church on Sunday morning he thinks, "Their clothes, they put on their best clothes: he clings to the thought giddily; it seems a visual proof of the unseen world" (*Run*, 87). A sense of the goodness of the world, God's work, surfaces within sensory experience, which is sought out and recalled for the evidences and reassurances that it provides.

Sensory experience is also, however, by no means always either innocent or evidently indicative of God's reality. We know the sensible world first, only thereafter knowing ourselves as sensers of it and then yet further, perhaps, knowing God as its creator. The result of this ordering is that the beauties of the world are capable immediately of attracting us on their own. Attraction by the sensible in itself or for its own sake is the primary form of human sinfulness for Augustine, the principal manifestation of pride, of trusting to one's own way and powers rather than God's. "My sin was this, that I looked for pleasure, beauty, and truth not in [God] but in myself and his other creatures, and the search led me instead to pain, confusion, and error" (*Confessions* 1.20). "I could not conceive of the existence of anything else" than a "bodily substance" (5.1); "I could imagine no kind of substance except such as is normally seen by the eye" (7.1).

Sensing nothing else, and seeing bodily substances as things that fill the eye in vision or the body in eating, hence things to be made use of, Augustine represents himself as pursuing the possession of objects, visually, bodily, and sexually. Seeing nothing else, the will "veers towards things of the lowest order, being 'boweled alive' [Ecclesiastes 10:10] and becoming inflated with desire for things outside itself" (*Confessions* 7.16). Desire, not reverence, becomes the fundamental form of relationship to sensible objects, whether other persons, foods, or sights. A wish to be filled up, again and again, predominates. Beginning with being naturally filled with the sight and nourishment of objects, but straying by desiring this filling up on its own, one falls into the habit of repeated consumption of the world, sexual, gustatory, and visual. Augustine treats each modality of experience—sexual, gustatory, visual, and later aural—as involving an effort to be filled up by or centered on an object of experience, an effort that must inevitably, addictively, be repeated once the object has been consumed. The self that seeks to find itself, to center itself and confirm its identity through its sensory experience of objects, therein repeatedly dissipates itself. With regard, notoriously, to sex Augustine writes, "Foolhardy as I was, I ran wild with lust that was manifold and rank. . . . Love and lust together seethed within me. In my tender youth they swept me away over the precipice of my body's appetites and plunged me in the whirlpool of sin. . . . I was tossed and spilled, floundering in the broiling sea of my fornication" (2.1–2). Repetitive consumption of unnourishing food is put forward as a metaphor for, perhaps part of the substance of, concern with material reality for its own sake under the influence of the Manichaeans. "But I gulped down this food, because I thought that it was you. . . . And it did not nourish me, but starved me all the more" (3.6). Visually, Augustine sought the spectacle of plays: "I was much attracted by the theater" (3.2); "I liked . . . to have my ears tickled by the make-believe of the stage, which only made them itch the more. As time went on my eyes shone more and more with the same eager curiosity" (1.10).

Each of these forms of experience is a form of lust, understood as the wish repeatedly to possess material objects regarded not as created beings but as self-subsistent substances of reality in their own right. "Man . . . is able to 'catch sight of God's invisible nature through his creatures' [Rom.: 1:20], but his love of these material things is too great. He becomes their slave, and slaves cannot be judges" (*Confessions* 10.6). The substance of this slavery is lust, the compulsion repeatedly to fill oneself up with material objects through various modalities of experience, a compulsion that becomes an addictive, self-strengthening habit. "For my will was perverse and lust had grown from it, and when I gave in to lust habit was born, and when I did not resist the habit it became a necessity. These were the links in which together formed what I have called my chain, and it held me fast in the duress of servitude" (8.5). Thus out of pride in loving one's own way, "a truant's freedom" (3.3), taking sensible objects as objects of lust to be possessed so as to fill oneself up, "we are carried away by custom to our own undoing and it is hard to struggle against the stream" (1.16).

Harry Angstrom struggles rather less than most. "All I know," he tells Ruth, "is what feels right. You feel right to me. Sometimes Janice used to. Sometimes nothing does" (*Run*, 281). Immediate feeling, or the prospect of it, dominates his motivations. The job of sorting out his relations with Ruth is blocked by the thought of consuming something immediately. As they discuss her pregnancy and its implications for them,

In fact he has hardly listened; it is too complicated and, compared to the vision of a sandwich, unreal. He stands up, he hopes with soldierly effect, and says, "That's fair. I'll work it out. What do you want at the store?" A sandwich and a glass of milk, and then undressing her, getting her out of that cotton dress harried into wrinkles and seeing that thickened waist calm in its pale cool skin. . . . If he can just once more bury himself in her he knows he'll come up with his nerves all combed. (*Run,* 281–82)

When one is concerned most with the feel of a thing as a way of filling oneself up, then desire is notoriously labile. Not the identity and significance but the filling sensation of what one seeks is what matters. "Oh to close your eyes and just flicker out with your tongue for Cindy's nipples as she swung them back and forth, back and forth, teasing" (*Rich,* 176).

Harry's way of relating to the objects of his desire is to wish to possess them. He sees them as instruments for his satisfaction that he might own, not persons to be respected for their own nature. Janice is for him "his stubborn prize" (*Rich,* 455), Ruth in her coat is "like a great green fish, his prize" (*Run,* 70), Cindy is not his, but "What a package" (*Rich,* 237). The sight of Ruth's bottom breaking the surface of a swimming pool "made him harden all over with a chill clench of ownership" (*Run,* 133).

Harry similarly seeks to fill himself up with, to own, visual sensations. In watching television he and Nelson "channel-hop, trying to find something to hold them" (*Redux,* 29). When he reads the comics in the newspaper, he thinks "God-dam 'Apartment 3-G': he feels he's been living with those girls for years now, when is he going to see them with their clothes off? The artist keeps teasing him with bare shoulders in bathrooms, naked legs in the foreground with the crotch coming just at the panel edge, glimpses of bra straps being undone" (*Redux,* 323). Harry wants more, and he wants it to be his, and it matters more for its ability to fill his sensory consciousness than it matters for what it is. Too much definiteness is even a bad thing. "The tops of tits are almost the best part, nipples can be frightening" (*Rich,* 237).

These attitudes of Harry's toward people and objects of sight extend to food as well. "He rattles around in the apartment, turning on all the lights and television, drinking ginger ale and leafing through old *Lifes,* grabbing anything to stuff into the emptiness" (*Run,* 212). The foods he prefers are all surface and sensation, providers of sensory excitement, not nourishment. "[A]s a kid Rabbit loved bland candy like Dots; sitting in the movies he used to plow through three nickel boxes of them, playing with them with his tongue and teeth, playing, playing, before giving himself the ecstasy of the bite" (*Redux,* 103). Some forty-five years or so later, eating a Planter's Peanut Bar, "It is not so much the swallowing and ingesting he loves as the gritty-edgy feeling of the first corner in his mouth, the first right-angled fragment slowly dissolving" (*Rest,* 17–18). Even after his heart attack, he takes a few macademia nuts into his fingers. Nuggets, they are like small lightweight nuggets with a fur of salt. He especially loves the way, when he holds one in his mouth a few seconds and then gently works it between his crowned molars, it breaks into two halves, the surface of the fissure smooth to the tongue as glass, as baby skin. (*Rest*, 196–97)

When one seeks objects for the sake of their ability to surfeit the senses, then they never really fill you up, and you need more and more of them to continue to achieve the sensory effect. "What did his old basketball coach, Marty Tothero, tell him toward the end of his life, about how when you get old you eat and eat and it's never the right food?" (*Rest*, 6).

The main reason it's never the right food, just as it's never the right woman or the right television program, is that there is in Harry's character, as Derek Wright has noted "a general failure to differentiate between distinct orders of experience."[19] Objects are, for Harry, objects of, for, his possessive sensory consciousness—objects, that is, of lust:

It matters very little to his free-floating lust, as it matters little to his animal-namesake's promiscuous, voracious appetite, that the sexual impulse was awakened by another woman [Lucy Eccles, not Janice]. Harry "loves" all women: Janice, Ruth, Lucy Eccles, the waitress in the restaurant, the nurse in the hospital. . . . "Innocent" in the sense of undiscriminating and unchoosing, Harry's appetite effects [an] entropic merging of differences, [a] rubbing out of identities.[20]

"We are carried away by custom to our own undoing and it is hard to struggle against the stream."

One senses the world, and feeds on it, before one either knows its natures or turns within and above toward the nature of God. A longing for the continual suffusion of our senses is a primordial feature of our embodied condition and an ever-present possible mode of human being in the world. It is a mode of being that is encouraged, just as other possible modes of being are blocked, by friends and flatterers who tempt us to continue in this way that is already so easy and alluring. Seeking not to change, "I was pleased," Augustine tells us, "with my own condition and anxious to be pleasing in the eyes of men" (*Confessions* 2.1).

Those among whom his lot fell were usually not chaste lovers of God. They were, at first, children, with whom Augustine "enjoyed playing games" (1.9), "[f]or I liked to score a fine win at sport" (1.10). The sense of winning, of being seen to be a master of experience in the eyes of others, reinforces the tendency to consume experience, to seek spectacle and satiety.

Among older children at school Augustine "kept company with [the 'Wreckers'] and there were times when I found their friendship a pleasure," despite their "outbursts of violence" and their hazings of newcomers (*Confessions* 3.3). Their behavior was able to influence his sense of himself and of his possible manners of life: "I lived amongst them, feeling a perverse sense of shame because I was not like them" (3.3). His resistance to their ways is difficult and far from complete. Among grownups he "fell in with a set of sensualists," the Manichaeans, "men with glib tongues who ranted and raved and had the snares of the devil in their mouths" (3.6). When "the world is drunk with the invisible wine of its own perverted, earthbound will" (2.3), then it is, as Augustine says, difficult to live differently from one's fellows and under their disapprobation.

Harry Angstrom finds this difficulty insuperable. His sense of himself and his own possibilities is massively shaped by what he thinks other people think about him. When he first runs from Janice, he seeks shelter and advice from his old basketball coach, Marty Tothero, who introduces him to his friends as "my finest boy, a wonderful basketball player, Harry Angstrom, you probably remember his name from the papers, he twice set a county record" (*Run*, 53). Tothero legitimates for Harry his flight from Janice and his affair with Ruth, to whom Tothero has introduced him. As he later drifts through the affair Harry is willing to put up with Reverend Eccles because, in talking with him, "[h]e feels flattered; Eccles has this knack" (*Run*, 99). When Janice ten years later runs off with Charlie Stavros, Harry thinks about what the affair means by thinking about what the world thinks of it, imagining it reported in headlines in the *Brewer Vat*: "Linotyper's Wife Lays Local Salesman. Verity Employee Named Cuckold of the Week" (*Redux*, 72, 96). In thinking about that affair yet ten years later, and having regained possession of Janice, Harry thinks, "[a] man fucks your wife, it puts a new value on her, within limits" (*Rich*, 12). Dominated as he is by the pursuit of sensory experience, the world's opinion, no matter how founded, matters more to him, as it is reflected to him in glances or fantasy or tone of voice, than does conscience. He buys his house in Penn Park partly out of envy of Webb Murkett's sunken living room. In his late forties Harry takes his cues largely from the behavior of his golfing companions, and their wives, at the Flying Eagle Country Club, as that behavior itself refracts the ways of the public culture: "now both sexes have watched enough beer commercials on television to know that this is how to act, jolly and loud, on weekends, in the bar, beside the barbecue grill, on beaches and sundecks and mountainsides" (*Rich*, 60). Later his Jewish golf friends in Florida "usually make him feel good about himself. With them he is a big Swede, . . . a comical pet gentile, a big pale uncircumcised hunk of the American dream" (*Rest*, 57). In retirement Harry has become "more clothes-conscious than before," as he dresses explicitly to achieve the look that those around him affect (*Rest*, 245). These experiences of direction by the actions and reactions of others accumulate for a lifetime, until they seem to Harry to be the stuff of human life itself:

Fact is, it has come to Rabbit this late in life, you don't have a way, except what other people tell you. Your mother first, and poor Pop, then the Lutheran minister, that tough old heinie Fritz Kruppenbach, you had to respect him though, he said what he believed, and then all those schoolteachers, Marty Tothero and the rest, trying to give you an angle to work from, and now all these talk-show hosts. Your life derives, and has to give. (*Rest*, 451)

When one's consciousness is dominated by sensory experience, then what one takes from the actions and reactions of others, and from the public, media culture, is "an angle to work from," one that becomes the line of one's life.

Perhaps in reaction to a sense of dependence on sensory experience and on the reactions and judgments of others it is easy to wish to hide oneself as a consumer of sensory experience. Where one doesn't really believe in the value of what one consumes, but simply seeks intensities, shame is likely to ensue. Since one doesn't know how others will react to one's pursuits of sensory experiences, one may well fear their reactions and prefer instead privacy and darkness. This preference helps to account for the attraction to the theater that Augustine notes in his younger self.

The action of the *Confessions* in the moment of its writing is that of unburdening, the overcoming of shame and the wish to hide oneself, from others and ultimately from God. Against this action of unburdening, which requires considerable effort, Augustine sees as the main counterforce a standing wish or temptation of the human mind to hide itself in its consumptions of experience. "In its blind inertia, in its abject shame, [the human mind] loves to lie concealed, yet it wishes that nothing should be concealed from it" (10.23). For dependent, embodied subjectivities concealment has overwhelming charms.

Harry regularly succumbs to them. Spectatorship tending toward voyeurism is a signature of his personality. At twenty-six "Rabbit Angstrom, coming up the alley in a business suit, stops and watches" boys playing basketball (*Run*, 9). He remembers as a child climbing to the tops of telephone poles "where you could hear the wires sing. Their song was a terrifying motionless whisper. . . . Listening to the wires as if you could hear what people were saying, what all that secret adult world was about" (20). As he lies in Marty Tothero's bed above the Sunshine Athletic Association the "clangor of the body shop comes up softly. Its noise comforts him, tells him he is hidden and safe." (48). In conversation with Eccles he is wary of revealing too much of himself. "The more he tells, the more he loses. He's safe inside his own skin, he doesn't want to come out" (118). Though uneasy and too frightened to act himself, he watches Jill suck Skeeter:

> A most delicate slipping slivery sound touches up the silence now; but Rabbit cannot precisely see. He needs to see. The driftwood lamp is beside him. Not turning his head, he gropes and switches it on. Nice. (*Redux*, 261)

Harry "likes . . . domestic peace. Women circling with dutiful footsteps above him and the summer night like a lake lapping at the windows" as he reads *Consumer Reports* alone and fantasizes that the model on the cover is a prostitute or one of "the girls in blue movies" (*Rich*, 81). He "has always loved that feeling, of being inside when it rains. Shingles in the attic, pieces of glass no thicker than cardboard keeping him dry. Things that touch and yet not" (117). Privacy, safety, and concealment enable him to consume sensory experience without fear of discovery. He repeatedly spies on Ruth's farm, hoping for a glimpse of his possible daughter, though when someone calls "Hey," "Rather than face who it is, he runs" (113). He goes through the Murketts' medicine cabinet (285) and bedside table, in astonished rapture at the photos he finds of Webb and Cindy naked and having sex. As Uncle Sam in the Mt. Judge July 4 parade, Harry feels "as if he has been lifted up to survey all human history," above it all, safe (*Rest,* 371).

Harry's wish to hide himself in his consumptions of sensory experience further underlies his passivity in his relations with others. Janice complains that he simply lets her affair with Charlie continue (*Redux,* 193). His father chides him for his inaction: "Your mother always says you let people push you around. . . . I'm beginning to see she may be right" (210). When Janice asks him what they might do as Nelson seeks to come home with Melanie, his best suggestion is, "Ride with the punches?" (*Rich,* 48). Fusing his relations with people with his consumptions of visual experience, Harry finds that Janice is for him "a channel that can't be switched" (*Rest,* 170). When in the hospital after his first heart attack, he finds that he likes being taken care of by anonymous others:

> His collapse twenty-six hours ago did have its blissful aspect: his sense, beginning as he lay helpless and jellyfishlike under a sky of red, of being in the hands of others, of being the blind, pained, focal point of a world of concern and expertise, at some depth was a coming back home, after a life of ill-advised journeying. (162–63)

He finds himself unable to follow his doctor's advice to take an interest in something. "Harry tries to care but has trouble. Ever since Schmidt retired. Get interested is the advice, but in truth you are interested in less and less. It's nature's way" (477).

Consistently, Harry's passivity, wish for concealment, and voyeurism lead him to envision his own death and even to long for it. On top of the telephone pole "it always tempted you to fall, to let the hard spikes in your palms go and feel the space on your back, feel it take your feet and ride up your spine as you fell" (*Run,* 20). On top of Mt. Judge "he used to wonder if you jumped would you die or be cushioned on those green heads [of trees] as on the clouds of a dream" (107). Throughout his last year he courts his own death, as he would rather die, achieving ultimate concealment, the final consumption, and release from the demons of sensory addiction, than take reasonable care for his bodily health. To Nelson, in dying "Rabbit thinks he should maybe say more, the kid looks wildly expectant, but enough. Maybe. Enough" (*Rest,* 512). Better concealment than the demands of human relationship; better death as a final evasion of those demands than life. Thus do men "fall back upon what they are able to do and find contentment in this way" (*Confessions* 10.23).

When addictiveness to sensory experience, susceptibility to the influences of others, voyeurism, and wishes for concealment are inherent possibilities for us as embodied intelligences, then so too is the destruction of our identity or personality. The soul or self is dissipated, broken apart, in its submissions to the temptations of eye and ear and touch. "Truly it is by continence that we are made as one and regain that unity of self which we lost by falling apart in the search for a variety of pleasures" (*Confessions* 10.29). Augustine's image of the risk run in searching for pleasure is one of the fracturing or breaking apart of the soul, to the point that it is unable any longer to play its role in guiding perception and action and is hence no longer even identifiable. The will has in it a tendency toward self-disintegration that is the essence of evil, "that which falls away from essence and tends to non-being, . . . [that which] tends to make that which is cease to be." [21] Rather than being metaphysically fixed in its identity as a substance, embodied soul admits of being undone by perversity of will. What we are is in part a function of what we do.

This is the thought that figures at the heart of Augustine's depiction of his loss of himself in sensuality as a young man. "I ran," he tells us, "wild with lust" (*Confessions* 2.1), therein making himself into something other than himself. "My inner self was a house divided against itself" (8.8). The soul is "wrenched in two" by sensuality and truth "and suffers great trials" (8.11).

The plot of the *Confessions* is then the story of Augustine's progressive simultaneous discovery and realization of himself as a more stably ensouled creature of God manifesting its ensoulment in its continence. Thought, ultimately thought of God, is the characteristic and appropriate activity for embodied intelligence, and Augustine construes the nature of thought as a kind of collection or assembly of the self's contents into a unity that is an achievement, not a metaphysical fact. "This is the derivation of the word *cogitare*, which means *to think* or *to collect one's thoughts*. For in Latin the word *cogo*, meaning *I assemble* or *I collect*, is related to *cogito*, which means *I think*" (10.11). To confess, recalling one's past and revealing it before God and humanity, is to recollect oneself, forging identity and wholeness out of disintegration.

In Harry Angstrom, not surprisingly, disintegration predominates. This disintegration is a function of a failure to think or to recollect himself, a failure that is due to his powerful wish instead to feel, to be natural or part of nature. Harry thinks of leaving high school and becoming an adult not as a process of forging an identity through rational recollection or self-command but as something more like an inevitable loss of self into nature:

> You climb up through the little grades and then get to the top and everybody cheers; with the sweat in your eyebrows you can't see very well and the noise swirls around you and lifts you up, and then you're out, not forgotten at first, just out, and it feels good and cool and free. You're out, and sort of melt, and keep lifting, until you become like to these kids just one more piece of the sky of adults that hangs over them in the town. (*Run*, 11)

George W. Hunt has perceptively noted that "the strong possibility of confusing Nature with Nothingness" lies at the heart of "the thematic debate that arises continually throughout Updike's fiction. There that 'possibility' or temptation becomes actual." [22] Hunt traces Updike's dramatization of this possibility to his interest in Karl Barth's theology of evil, and behind Barth lies Augustine.

Harry's disintegration into the natural and sensual continues throughout his life. His will not to think makes him other and less than he might otherwise be. After turning off the radio, "[i]nto the silence that results he refuses to let thoughts come. He doesn't want to think, he wants to fall asleep and wake up, pillowed by sand" (*Run*, 37). "Why can't you," Ruth asks him, "make up your mind what you want to *do*?" (280). Jill admonishes him that

> your problem is that you've never been given a chance to formulate your views. Because of the competitive American context, you've had to convert everything into action too rapidly. Your life has no reflective content; it's all instinct, and when your instincts let you down, you have nothing to trust. That's what makes you cynical. (*Redux*, 202)

Mim finds that Harry is unable to tend his own garden (321). Harry "loves Nature, though he can name almost nothing in it" (*Rich*, 139). "I never was too good at thinking things through," he admits to Ruth (449). Without reflectiveness, without the sustenances of reciprocal respect, without welding his personality to an occupation, there is not, it seems, much there but a tendency toward nonbeing.

When one is prone to addiction to the sensible, to distraction by flattery, to a wish to hide oneself in one's consumptions of sensible experience, and to the undoing of one's very identity through the refusal of thought, then conversion to integrity of soul, continence, and thoughtfulness will present itself as requiring a transfiguration of one's mode of being. Prescriptions about conduct that are generalized out of a prior mode of being will not be enough. Such prescriptions might sketch the conditions of maximum comfort or intensity or safety in one's consumptions of experience, but they would not point to the inauguration of a new mode of being. Indicators of the possibility and value of such a transfiguration must, it seems, come from outside our own experience and powers. Human identity and integrity cannot be fully achieved by a man, it seems, "by his own strength." [23] This is the thought—that our lives stand in need of transfiguration, radical reversal of orientation, if we are to achieve integrity of soul—that Augustine expresses as our need for grace:

> For, whatever powers [a man] has, "did they not come to him by gift?" [1 Cor. 4:7]. By the gift of grace he is not only shown how to see you, who are always the same, but is also given the strength to hold you. By your grace, too, if he is far from you and cannot see you, he is enabled to walk upon the path that leads him closer to you, so that he may see you and hold you. . . . What is man to do in his plight? "Who is to set him free from a nature thus doomed to death? Nothing else than the grace of God, through Jesus Christ our Lord." (8.21)

Against the background of the ontological account of the soul's tendency to undo itself in habitual sensuality one of the most moving features of the *Confessions* is Augustine's transcription of the ways in which grace presented itself to him so as to enable his conversion. Not only is the person of Jesus as the intercessor and bearer of grace presented in the Bible, there are also the manifold smaller and more immediate motions of grace in the writings, bearings, and actions of other people. Augustine notes in particular Cicero's *Hortensius*, a book that, in its recommendation to study philosophy, "altered my outlook on life . . . and provided me with new hopes and aspirations" (3.4), his mother Monica, "'sent down [as] your help from above' [Ps. 143:7]," who "wept to you for me" (3.2), the influence of Academic Skepticism, which helped to break his attachment to Manicheanism (5.14), the preaching of Ambrose, whose eloquence brought "his meaning, which I tried to ignore, . . . into my mind together with his words, which I admired so much" (5.14), Simplicianus's telling of the story of the conversion of Victorinus (8.1–4), and finally "the sing-song voice of a child in a nearby house" saying, "'Take it and read, take it and read,'" which he receives as a command "to open my book of Scripture and read the first passage on which my eyes should fall" (8.12), therein completing his conversion. The soul here finds its helps in various vehicles of godliness that surround it in ordinary life, if it but attends to them aright.

In Harry Angstrom's experience grace presents itself as a possibility that is sensed or felt—in trees or grass, or in women, or in the look of flowerpot-red Brewer from the top of Mt. Judge—but not as a possibility that is grasped or articulated into his life. He is, as it were, stopped or struck, but never moved, by the possibility of a grace that might lend his life shape and meaning. "His feeling that there is an unseen world is instinctive, and more of his actions than anyone suspects constitute transactions with it" (*Run*, 217). He fitfully perceives but does not really grasp the invisible in the visible. His experiences of grace are more interruptive than accumulative. Jill's breast "had been soft enough in his mouth, quite soft enough, and abundant, as grace is abundant, that we do not measure, but take as a presence, that abounds" (*Redux*, 301). In Voyager Two's "feeble but true transmissions across billions of miles . . . Harry feels a fine excessiveness, . . . a grace of sorts that chimes with the excessive beauty of this crystalline late-summer day" (*Rest*, 412), but he never integrates these intermittent feelings, never quite responds to their dim messages.

Harry's feelings for other persons are similarly rich but obscure as they remain rooted in sensation rather than in the joint development of a way of life. He experiences moments of sensory enchantment by Charlie ("he loves this savvy Greek, dainty of heart beneath his coat of summer checks" [*Rich*, 223]), Nelson ("Nelson's hair makes a whorl in the back that Harry knows so well his throat goes dry, something caught in it" [242]), and Judy as a newborn ("the tiny stitchless seam of the closed eyelid aslant, lips bubbled forward beneath the whorled nose as if in delicate disdain" [467]). He notices how Janice keeps up her shape as she ages. "At least she hasn't let herself go to fat like some of the women her age in the class" (*Rest,* 312). But, as is especially evident in his relations with Janice, these moments of sensory affection soon shade off into either pride of possession or antagonism. Instead of being articulated into mutuality, they amount to grace presented but refused. It's easier for Harry just to feel them and then to let the feeling pass. "Harry has no taste for the dark, tangled, visceral aspect of Christianity, the *going through* quality of it, the passage *into* death and suffering that redeems and inverts these things, like an umbrella blowing inside out" (*Run,* 219). He dimly senses but refuses what Augustine claims, the conversion from sensuality into godliness and integrity of soul.

Throughout comparison with Augustine, Harry Angstrom emerges, it seems, as a passive failure in humanity, overmastered by an addiction to sensory experience, with motivations shaped by flattery and envy rather than independent judgment, cravenly hiding himself as a consumer from judgment, dissipating his very identity in his consumptions, and refusing the possibility of grace. But are things really as simple as all that? And is Augustine's conversion really quite so complete and convincing in contrast with Harry's failure?

Harry does on occasion act, even displaying a kind of concern for others that at least momentarily outweighs his demand for self-satiety. "When you get children growing under you, you try to rise to the occasion" (*Rest,* 139). He reassures Judy that she did not cause his heart attack but instead saved his life, and he promises that "Grandma and I will take good care of your daddy and all of you" (264). He confronts Nelson about hitting Pru, about his cocaine habit, and about his stealing from the business in order to support it. While such moments often stem from anger or passing affection and are not integrated into a way of life, they nonetheless evince a capability of human feeling and action that has not altogether been lost.

Above all, Harry is alive. As a human subject he intensely notices and recalls the looks and feels of objects: the Norway maple outside his window in Florida, the copper beech tree outside his bedroom window in the Springer's house, "a few dead leaves shed by the weeping cherry, and the flower stalks of the violet hosta dying back" (*Rest,* 395). These moments in Harry's mind of lyrical sensory experience recall a kind of archaic, childhood experience of wonder at the world in the dawning of one's own consciousness of objects and of one's awareness of oneself as conscious. The recurrence of such moments throughout his life suggests that it is in or in relation to such sensory moments that human subjectivity exists at all. Without their surprises and lingering intensities we would not be alive or would not be what we are.

Yet Harry, again, does not actively make a human life with others over a period of time. It's too much trouble; its intensities, unlike those of food or sex, require too much of one. Family life "was for him like a bush in some neglected corner of the back yard that gets overgrown, a lilac bush or privet some bindweed has invaded from underneath with leaves so similar and tendrils so tightly entwining it gives the gardener a headache in the sun to try to separate bad growth from good"

(*Rest*, 47). Harry will not readily suffer such headaches. Yet he remains humanly alive, not transfigured into some chaste, disembodied, and unrecognizable intelligence. We find ourselves having the sort of "Yes, but" experience or judgment of Harry's failures that is, Updike suggests, proper to any rich exploration of human reality's secrecies, music, and tension.[24]

Despite its different shape, Augustine's development too is not free from ambiguities that make our, and his, judgment of it uncertain. Is the conversion that Augustine claims for himself quite as complete and convincing as Augustine might wish to suggest but perhaps can't help doubting? Do we, for example, accept his claim that after his conversion "I no longer desired a wife or placed any hope in this world but stood firmly upon the rule of faith" (*Confessions* 8.12)?

Augustine does not always seem quite so sure, as though the text of the *Confessions* betrayed more knowledge of the ambiguities of human life than its official moral theology would allow. Augustine tends to disappear as a character after his conversion (book 8) and a short denouement (book 9) recounting his return to Africa and Monica's life and death. After book 9 the text cycles away into a general philosophical examination of the temptations of the senses (10.30–35) and an interpretation of *Genesis* (book 11–13). Once the conversion that results in the withdrawal of all hope from the world is accomplished, there is, this disappearance suggests, no human life left to narrate, so that the thought hidden in this disappearance is that human life itself requires both attraction to sensory experience and placing hope in the world.

The postconversion catalogue of temptations of the senses further suggests that they may not disappear even after conversion. "What excuse can I make for myself when often, as I sit at home, I cannot turn my eyes from the sight of a lizard catching flies or a spider entangling them as they fly into her web?" (10.35). The eye and ear and hand continue, it seems, to make their demands felt within embodied intelligence, according to their own law, not God's.

Augustine even betrays a certain anxiety about his own claim to know himself as having accomplished his conversion. "I cannot prove to [my readers] that my confessions are true," he notes, though he claims, "I shall be believed by those whose ears are opened to me by charity" (10.3). But who are they? Are they easy to recognize within the ways of the world? And how will they express their belief in his confessions, as they continue to go about the daily businesses of their lives? "Can they really know me?" (10.3). And if there is doubt about this—doubt about how his life and his confession will be received, even by those who approach his book with charity—then perhaps too there is doubt in Augustine about his own claims to conversion: "there are some things in man which even his own spirit within him does not know" (10.5), perhaps even the most important things. If God's law is, as Augustine insists (3.7), flexible, even nearly inscrutable, in how it engages with the changing temporal conditions and experiences of embodied, acculturated creatures, then it is not so easy to know what an accomplished conversion to a life of praise and faithfulness is.

Being haunted by ambiguities that inhibit any final judgment on the meaning of a life emerges then as part of what it is to live as an embodied consciousness, torn between aspirations, even commands, toward elevation, purity, integrity, and faithfulness and sensuous desire that is a necessary feature of embodied conscious life. "Such is the confusion of this fallen world, where sins lie intermixed with the seeds of being." [25] Hence dramatizations of how we live with this enduring tear in our nature—dramatizations such as we find in *Confessions* and the Rabbit tetralogy—may be as much philosophical thought about, as much acknowledgment of, our condition as it is possible for us to have. What fuller mode of thought about our doubleness could there be?

NOTES

1. St. Augustine, *Confessions* 7.7, trans. R. S. Pine-Coffin (Harmondsworth: Penguin, 1961). All English excerpts are from this edition. Pine-Coffin has rendered Augustine's references to an early Latin translation of the Bible in the English text of Knox, slightly modified in accordance with Augustine's departures from Saint Jerome's Vulgate.

2. John Updike, "Even the Bible Is Soft on Sex," *New York Times Book Review,* June 20, 1993, 29.

3. John Updike, "On Not Being a Dove," in *Self-Consciousness: Memoirs* (New York: Fawcett Crest, 1989), 135–36.

4. John Updike, "One Big Interview," in *Picked-Up Pieces* (New York: Alfred A. Knopf, 1975), 509.

5. John Updike, *Rabbit, Run* (New York: Alfred A. Knopf, 1960), 29. The other Rabbit novels are *Rabbit, Redux* (New York: Alfred A. Knopf, 1971); *Rabbit Is Rich* (New York: Alfred A. Knopf, 1981); and *Rabbit at Rest* (New York: Alfred A. Knopf, 1990). References to these works will be given in the text by the R-word in the title, followed by a page number.

6. Frederick Copleston, S.J., *A History of Philosophy,* vol. 2, pt. 1 (Garden City, N.Y.: Doubleday, 1962), 97, 65.

7. Gareth B. Matthews, *Thought's Ego in Augustine and Descartes* (Ithaca: Cornell University Press, 1992), x.

8. Copleston, *History of Philosophy,* vol. 2, pt. 1, p. 63.

9. Updike, "Even the Bible Is Soft on Sex," 3.

10. Elaine Pagels, *Adam, Eve, and the Serpent* (New York: Random House, 1988), xxvii.

11. Ibid., 125.

12. Harold Bloom, "Introduction," in Harold Bloom, ed., *John Updike: Modern Critical Views* (New York: Chelsea House, 1987), 7.

13. Ibid., 1.

14. John W. Aldridge, "The Private Vice of John Updike," in Bloom, ed., *John Updike,* 10.

15. Norman Mailer, "Norman Mailer vs. Nine Writers," in *Cannibals and Christians* (New York: Dell, 1966), 120.

16. Garry Wills, "Long Distance Runner," *New York Review of Books,* October 25, 1990, 14.

17. St. Augustine, *The City of God* 11.26, cited in Copleston, *History of Philosophy,* vol. 2, pt. 1, p. 69.

18. St. Augustine, *De Trinitate* 15.12.21, cited in Copleston, *History of Philosophy*, vol. 2, pt. 1, p. 70.

19. Derek Wright, "Mapless Motion: Form and Space in Updike's *Rabbit, Run*," *Modern Fiction Studies* 37 (1991): 40.

20. Ibid., 38–39.

21. *De Trinitate* 15.7.13, cited in Copleston, *History of Philosophy*, vol. 2, pt. 1, p. 100.

22. George W. Hunt, *John Updike and the Three Great Secret Things: Sex, Religion, and Art* (Grand Rapids, Mich.: Eerdmans, 1980), 37.

23. St. Augustine, *Expositio quarumdam propositionum ex epistola ad Romanos*, cited in Copleston, *History of Philosophy*, vol. 2, pt. 1, p. 99.

24. Cf. Updike's comments on how his work says "Yes, but" to various issues and to the murky itineraries of the characters who explore them: "One Big Interview," 502–3.

25. Updike, "Even the Bible Is Soft on Sex," 29.

CONTRIBUTORS

Marilyn McCord Adams is Professor of Historical Theology at the Divinity School, Yale University. She is author of the two-volume study, *William Ockham* (1987).

Rüdiger Bittner is Professor of Philosophy at the University of Bielefeld, Germany. He has published in the areas of moral and political philosophy and the theory of action and is the author of *What Reason Demands* (1983).

Myles Burnyeat has been Laurence Professor of Ancient Philosophy at Cambridge University. The author of *The Theaetetus of Plato* (1990), he is now Senior Research Fellow at All Souls College, Oxford University.

Frederick J. Crosson is Cavanaugh Professor of Humanities at the University of Notre Dame.

Richard Eldridge is Professor of Philosophy at Swarthmore College. He is the author of *Leading a Human Life: Wittgenstein, Intentionality, and Romanticism* (1987) and *On Moral Personhood: Philosophy, Literature, Criticism, and Self-Understanding* (1989).

Ishtiyaque Haji is Assistant Professor of Philosophy at the University of Minnesota, Morris. He is the author of *Moral Appraisability: Puzzles, Proposals, and Perplexities* (1998).

John E. Hare is Professor of Philosophy at Calvin College. He is the author of *The Moral Gap: Kantian Ethics, Human Limits, and God's Assistance* (1996).

Simon Harrison is Research Fellow of St. John's College, Cambridge University. His translation of St. Anselm's *Monologion* is forthcoming.

Ann Hartle is Professor of Philosophy at Emory University. She is the author of *Self-Knowledge in the Age of Theory* (1997) and is writing a book on the *Essays* of Montaigne.

Robert L. Holmes is Professor of Philosophy at the University of Rochester and editor of *Public Affairs Quarterly.* He is the author of *On War and Morality* (1989).

Christopher Kirwan is a Fellow and Lecturer at Exeter College, Oxford University. He has published on Aristotle and logic and is the author of *Augustine* (1989) in the Arguments of the Philosophers series.

Simo Knuuttila is Academy Professor at the Academy of Finland and Professor of Theological Ethics and the Philosophy of Religion at the University of Helsinki. He is the author of *Modalities in Medieval Philosophy* (1993).

Genevieve Lloyd is Professor of Philosophy at the University of New South Wales in Sydney, Australia. She is the author of *The Man of Reason: "Male" and "Female" in Western Philosophy* (2d. ed., 1993), *Part of Nature: Self-Knowledge in Spinoza's "Ethics"* (1994), and *Spinoza and the "Ethics"* (1996).

Scott MacDonald is Professor of Philosophy and Norma K. Regan Professor in Christian Studies at Cornell University. He edits the journal *Medieval Philosophy and Theology.*

William E. Mann is Professor of Philosophy at the University of Vermont. He has written extensively in philosophical theology and medieval philosophy.

Gareth B. Matthews is Professor of Philosophy at the University of Massachusetts, Amherst. He is the author of *Thought's Ego in Augustine and Descartes* (1992).

Martha Nussbaum is Ernst Freund Professor of Law and Ethics at the University of Chicago. She is perhaps best known for *The Fragility of Goodness: Luck and Ethics in Greek Tragedy and Philosophy* (1986). Her latest book is *Cultivating Humanity: A Classical Defense of Reform in Liberal Education* (1997).

Alvin Plantinga is John A. O'Brien Professor of Philosophy at the University of Notre Dame and Director of the Notre Dame Center for the Philosophy of Religion. He has written, among other works, *God and Other Minds* (2d ed., 1990) and *Warrant: The Current Debate* (1993).

Philip L. Quinn is also John A. O'Brien Professor of Philosophy at the University of Notre Dame. He is the author of *Divine Commands and Moral Requirements* (1978) and co-editor of *A Companion to the Philosophy of Religion* (1997).

Paul J. Weithman is Associate Professor of Philosophy at the University of Notre Dame. He has published widely on contemporary political philosophy, religious ethics, and medieval political thought and is the editor of *Religion and Contemporary Liberalism* (1997).

INDEX

Compositor: Impressions Book and Journal Services, Inc.
Text: 10/12 Baskerville
Display: Baskerville
Printer and Binder: Haddon Craftsmen, Inc.